# The Internet of Things in the Modern Business Environment

In Lee
*Western Illinois University, USA*

A volume in the Advances in E-Business Research (AEBR) Book Series

IGI Global
DISSEMINATOR OF KNOWLEDGE
www.igi-global.com

Published in the United States of America by
IGI Global
Business Science Reference (an imprint of IGI Global)
701 E. Chocolate Avenue
Hershey PA, USA 17033
Tel: 717-533-8845
Fax: 717-533-8661
E-mail: cust@igi-global.com
Web site: http://www.igi-global.com



Library of Congress Cataloging-in-Publication Data

Names: Lee, In, 1958-, editor.
Title: The internet of things in the modern business environment / In Lee, editor.
Description: Hershey : Business Science Reference, [2017]
Identifiers: LCCN 2016054474| ISBN 9781522521044 (hardcover) | ISBN 9781522521051 (ebook)
Subjects: LCSH: Information technology--Management. | Management information systems. | Industrial management--Technological innovations.
Classification: LCC HD30.2 .I5588 2017 | DDC 658/.054678--dc23 LC record available at https://lccn.loc.gov/2016054474

This book is published in the IGI Global book series Advances in E-Business Research (AEBR) (ISSN: 1935-2700; eISSN: 1935-2719)

British Cataloguing in Publication Data
A Cataloguing in Publication record for this book is available from the British Library.

# Advances in E-Business Research (AEBR) Book Series

In Lee
Western Illinois University, USA

ISSN:1935-2700
EISSN:1935-2719

## Mission

Technology has played a vital role in the emergence of e-business and its applications incorporate strategies. These processes have aided in the use of electronic transactions via telecommunications networks for collaborating with business partners, buying and selling of goods and services, and customer service. Research in this field continues to develop into a wide range of topics, including marketing, psychology, information systems, accounting, economics, and computer science.

The **Advances in E-Business Research (AEBR) Book Series** provides multidisciplinary references for researchers and practitioners in this area. Instructors, researchers, and professionals interested in the most up-to-date research on the concepts, issues, applications, and trends in the e-business field will find this collection, or individual books, extremely useful. This collection contains the highest quality academic books that advance understanding of e-business and addresses the challenges faced by researchers and practitioners.

## Coverage

- Collaborative commerce
- Virtual organization
- Online consumer behavior
- Valuing e-business assets
- Electronic communications
- Electronic Supply Chain Management
- E-business systems integration
- B2B e-marketplaces
- Telework and Telecommuting
- Virtual Collaboration

IGI Global is currently accepting manuscripts for publication within this series. To submit a proposal for a volume in this series, please contact our Acquisition Editors at Acquisitions@igi-global.com or visit: http://www.igi-global.com/publish/.

The Advances in E-Business Research (AEBR) Book Series (ISSN 1935-2700) is published by IGI Global, 701 E. Chocolate Avenue, Hershey, PA 17033-1240, USA, www.igi-global.com. This series is composed of titles available for purchase individually; each title is edited to be contextually exclusive from any other title within the series. For pricing and ordering information please visit http://www.igi-global.com/book-series/advances-business-research/37144. Postmaster: Send all address changes to above address. 

## Titles in this Series

*For a list of additional titles in this series, please visit: www.igi-global.com/book-series*

*Driving Innovation and Business Success in the Digital Economy*
Ionica Oncioiu (Titu Maiorescu University, Romania)
Business Science Reference • copyright 2017 • 321pp • H/C (ISBN: 9781522517795) • US $200.00 (our price)

*Social Media Listening and Monitoring for Business Applications*
N. Raghavendra Rao (FINAIT Consultancy Services, India)
Business Science Reference • copyright 2017 • 470pp • H/C (ISBN: 9781522508465) • US $205.00 (our price)

*Analyzing the Strategic Role of Social Networking in Firm Growth and Productivity*
Vladlena Benson (Kingston University, UK) Ronald Tuninga (Kingston Business School, UK) and George Saridakis (Kingston University, UK)
Business Science Reference • copyright 2017 • 525pp • H/C (ISBN: 9781522505594) • US $220.00 (our price)

*Securing Transactions and Payment Systems for M-Commerce*
Sushila Madan (University of Delhi, India) and Jyoti Batra Arora (Banasthali Vidyapeeth University, India)
Business Science Reference • copyright 2016 • 349pp • H/C (ISBN: 9781522502364) • US $205.00 (our price)

*E-Retailing Challenges and Opportunities in the Global Marketplace*
Shailja Dixit (Amity University, India) and Amit Kumar Sinha (Amity University, India)
Business Science Reference • copyright 2016 • 358pp • H/C (ISBN: 9781466699212) • US $215.00 (our price)

*Successful Technological Integration for Competitive Advantage in Retail Settings*
Eleonora Pantano (Middlesex University London, UK)
Business Science Reference • copyright 2015 • 405pp • H/C (ISBN: 9781466682979) • US $200.00 (our price)

*Strategic E-Commerce Systems and Tools for Competing in the Digital Marketplace*
Mehdi Khosrow-Pour (Information Resources Management Association, USA)
Business Science Reference • copyright 2015 • 315pp • H/C (ISBN: 9781466681330) • US $185.00 (our price)

*The Evolution of the Internet in the Business Sector Web 1.0 to Web 3.0*
Pedro Isaías (Universidade Aberta (Portuguese Open University), Portugal) Piet Kommers (University of Twente, The Netherlands) and Tomayess Issa (Curtin University, Australia)
Business Science Reference • copyright 2015 • 407pp • H/C (ISBN: 9781466672628) • US $235.00 (our price)

IGI GLOBAL
DISSEMINATOR OF KNOWLEDGE
www.igi-global.com

701 East Chocolate Avenue, Hershey, PA 17033, USA
Tel: 717-533-8845 x100 • Fax: 717-533-8661
E-Mail: cust@igi-global.com • www.igi-global.com

## Editorial Advisory Board

# Table of Contents

# Detailed Table of Contents

To improve the overall impact of the Internet of Things (IoT), intelligent capabilities must be developed at the edge of the IoT 'Cloud.' 'Smart' IoT objects must not only communicate with their environment, but also use embedded knowledge to interpret signals, and by making inferences augment their knowledge of their own state and that of their environment. Thus, intelligent IoT objects must improve their capabilities to make autonomous decisions without reliance to external computing infrastructure. In this chapter, we illustrate the concept of smart autonomous logistic objects with a proof of concept prototype built using an embedded version of the Prolog language, running on a Raspberry Pi credit-card-sized single-board computer to which an RFID reader is attached. The intelligent object is combining the RFID readings from its environment with embedded knowledge to infer new knowledge about its status. We test the system performance in a simulated environment consisting of logistics objects.



IoT devices offer a cheap and powerful approach to identifying real world states and situations and acting on this real world environment to change these states and the environment. Augmenting real world things with IoT technology enables the capture of real world context to support decision making and actions in the real world via powerful smart objects in a human- IoT ecosystem. Increasingly we will have to understand the Human-IoT or smart device ecosystem interaction in order to optimise and integrate the design of human and IoT systems. This chapter explores the design and categorisation of IoT devices in terms of their functionality and capability to support context to add to human perception. It then proposes how we can model the context information of both IoT devices and humans in a way that may help progress Human-IoT Ecosystem design using situation theory.



The evolution of the big data and new techniques related to the processing and analysis of large databases is revolutionizing the management of companies in the age of the Internet of Things (IoT). In this chapter, we examine the possibilities of big data to improve the services offered by companies and the customer experience and increase the efficiency of these companies. Companies must accept the challenge of self-assessment and measure the barriers that threaten to prevent them from reaching to get the maximum potential derived from big data and analytics. The combination of big data and computational business intelligence will change completely processes, logistics and distribution strategies, the choice of marketing channels and any aspect of the production and marketing of products and services. A case of GE is presented to showcase the use of the IoT and big data. All companies, regardless of size or sector, will improve their business operations due to big data generated from the social media and IoT applications and its use in computational business intelligence.

# Preface

The Internet of Things (IoT), also called the Internet of Everything or the Industrial Internet, is a new technology paradigm envisioned as a global network of machines and devices capable of interacting with each other. The true value of the IoT for firms can be fully realized when connected devices are able to communicate with each other and integrate with enterprise systems, cloud computing, and business analytics. IDC (2014) predicts that the IoT base will grow at a 17.5% compound annual growth rate (CAGR), reaching 28.1 billion installed units by 2020, up from 9.1 billion in 2013 and the value of the market will reach $7.1 trillion by 2020, up from $1.9 trillion in 2013. The adoption of this technology is rapidly gaining momentum as technological, societal, and competitive pressures push firms to innovate and transform themselves. Many firms such as GE, Amazon, and Google are developing numerous IoT applications to capture real-time operational data and offer better services to clients.

Over the last decade, the IoT industry has experienced rapid transformation. Many factors, such as digital convergence, smart phone, wireless network technologies, sensor technologies, and RFID, have contributed to this transformation. Connected cars, smart metering, and smart farming are examples of transforming traditional products and services into digital ones equipped with real-time data captured with IoT devices and sensor networks. However, as with any disruptive innovation, the IoT will present multiple challenges to adopting enterprises. For example, due to the explosion of the data generated by IoT machines, Gartner (2014) identified that data centers will face challenges in security, the enterprise, consumer privacy, data, storage management, server technologies, and data center networking. The IoT developers must build the ability to mitigate these challenges to accelerate the diffusion speed.

Because of the potential yet uncertain benefits and high investment costs of the IoT, firms need to carefully assess every IoT-induced opportunity and challenge to ensure that their resources are spent judiciously. They need to understand the impact of the IoT on business operations, business models, and competitiveness, and address managerial challenges that firms have faced.

However, there is still a paucity of studies on the social, behavioral, economic, and managerial aspects of the IoT. This makes it very challenging for firms to make informed decisions on IoT adoption, development, and management.

*The Internet of Things in the Modern Business Environment* provides a repository for researchers and industry practitioners to exchange their research ideas, industries, technologies, and practical experiences, and discuss challenges and opportunities. This book is composed of fourteen chapters in three sections: Section 1, "IoT Adoption and Implementation," which presents literature review on its use in supply chain management, behavioral models, and privacy issues: (1) A Literature Review of the Emerging Field of IoT Using RFID and Its Applications in Supply Chain Management, (2) User Acceptance of IoT Applications in Retail Industry, (3) Technopsychology of IoT Optimization in the Business World, (4) The

Internet of Things (IoT): Capabilities and Applications for Smart Supply Chain, and (5) Privacy in the Internet of Things; Section 2, "IoT Management," which discusses various enablers, issues, opportunities, guidelines in IoT management: (1) The Internet of Things: Assessing its Potential and Identifying the Enablers Needed to Capture the Opportunity, (2) The Internet of Things: From Things to Valuable Outcomes, (3) Industrial Guidelines for Stimulating Entrepreneurship: the Internet of Things, and (4) The Internet of Things: Opportunities, Issues, and Challenges; Section 3, "IoT Technologies and Applications," which discusses various technologies, techniques, and standards for IoT services and presents state of the art IoT applications: (1) IoT Objects Driven New Product Innovation and Prototyping Using 3D Printers, (2) Towards Autonomous IoT Logistics Objects, (3) The Human-IoT Ecosystem: An Approach to Functional Situation Context Classification, (4) Computational Business Intelligence, Big Data, and Their Role in Business Decisions in the Age of the Internet of Things, and (5) IoT for Hospitality Industry: Paperless Buffet Management. A brief introduction of each chapter follows:

Section 1, "IoT Adoption and Implementation," consists of five articles. "A Literature Review of the Emerging Field of IoT Using RFID and Its Applications in Supply Chain Management" by Suvendu Naskar, Preetam Basu, and Anup K. Sen attempts to understand extant literature studying applications of RFID in implementing IoT in the context of supply chain management.

"User Acceptance of IoT Applications in Retail Industry" by M S Balaji, Sanjit Kumar Roy, Aditi Sengupta, and Alain Chong examines the customer adoption of IoT applications in retail setting. The model drew on the technology acceptance model, trust perspective, task-technology fit, and organizational reputation perspective. "Technopsychology of IoT Optimization in the Business World" by Tommy Prayoga and Juneman Abraham argues that technology, however improved and innovative, will not fulfil its full potential if users do not adopt and accept it as part of their lives. They suggest that acceptance and appropriation are the two of the most important areas to explore in the field of IoT optimization in the business world. "The Internet of Things (IoT): Capabilities and Applications for Smart Supply Chain" by In Lee presents a conceptual framework of the IoT applications essential for smart supply chain. This chapter also discusses technical and managerial challenges faced by supply chain managers in implementing the IoT. "Privacy in the Internet of Things" by Jayashree Kanniappan and Babu Rajendira presents the IoT technology, the various applications, and privacy issues. Various other issues such as security and performance are also addressed.

Section 2, "IoT Management," consists of four articles. "The Internet of Things: Assessing Its Potential and Identifying the Enablers Needed to Capture the Opportunity" by Jacques Bughin and Michael Chui highlights some of the fundamental enablers that will be necessary for economic value to be realized, including industrial adoption, interoperability standards, cybersecurity, and regulatory certainty regarding issues such as data sharing and liability. "The Internet of Things: From Things to Valuable Outcomes" by Thomas Ochs and Ute Riemann outlines the key enabling technologies, drivers and business value as well as benefits and challenges. "Industrial Guidelines for Stimulating Entrepreneurship: the Internet of Things" by Mohammad Zarei, Ahmad Jamalian, and Rohollah Ghasemi ranks the importance of 13 industries for corporate, social, SME IoT-based entrepreneurs, and makes recommendations to promote entrepreneurial activities. "The Internet of Things: Opportunities, Issues, and Challenges" by Edward T. Chen presents a list of IoT devices and application examples as well as descriptions of the benefits and limitations alongside an assessment of each respective technology's potential for success in the future. This chapter addresses potentials, issues, and challenges for managers to be prepared for the new wave brought forth by the IoT.

Section 3, "IoT Technologies and Applications," consists of five articles. "IoT Objects Driven New Product Innovation and Prototyping Using 3D Printers" by Ravi Ramakrishnan and Loveleen Gaur provides an integrated framework for IoT enabled devices to integrate with remote 3D printers capturing customer insights. "Towards Autonomous IoT Logistics Objects" by Bill Karakostas illustrates the concept of smart autonomous logistic objects with a proof of concept prototype built using an embedded version of the Prolog language, running on a Raspberry Pi credit-card-sized single-board computer to which an RFID reader is attached. "The Human-IoT Ecosystem: An Approach to Functional Situation Context Classification" by Vaughan Michell and James Olweny shows how we can model the context information of both IoT devices and humans in a way that may help progress Human-IoT ecosystem design using situation theory. "Computational Business Intelligence, Big Data, and Their Role in Business Decisions in the Age of the Internet of Things" by Javier Vidal-García, Marta Vidal, and Rafael Hernandez Barros examines the possibilities of big data and the IoT to improve the services offered by companies and the customer experience and increase the efficiency of these companies. "IoT for Hospitality Industry: Paperless Buffet Management" by Asim Sinan Yuksel, Ibrahim Arda Cankaya, and Sadi Fuat Cankaya develops a flexible, cost effective, easy-to-use, customer-friendly and staff oriented paperless buffet management system for the restaurants that have all-you-can-eat buffet.

*The Internet of Things in the Modern Business Environment* is an excellent collection of the latest research and practices associated with the IoT economy, evolution, technologies, new applications, and trends. This book is one of the first comprehensive books that present aspects from the economics, engineering, research and development, and management sides of the IoT. As leading experts in the IoT area, the contributors did an outstanding job of providing our readers with extensive coverage of the most important research topics - new applications, economic aspects, business models, privacy, and emerging technologies. The projected audience includes researchers, managers, application developers, services providers, engineers, corporate managers, professors, and undergraduate/graduate students in various academic disciplines.

*In Lee*
*Western Illinois University, USA*
*February 2017*

## REFERENCES

Gartner. (2014). *Gartner says the internet of things will transform the data center*. Retrieved September 23, 2016 from http://www.gartner.com/newsroom/id/2684616

IDC. (2014). *Worldwide and regional internet of things (IoT) 2014–2020 forecast: A virtuous circle of proven value and demand*. Retrieved May 28, 2015, http://www.idc.com/downloads/idc_market_in_a_minute_iot_infographic.pdf

# Acknowledgment

I would like to acknowledge the help of the members of the Editorial Advisory Board and the reviewers without whose support it could not have been satisfactorily completed. I sincerely thank Mehdi Khosrow-Pour and other members of the IGI Global, whose supports throughout the whole process from the inception of the initial idea to the final publication have been invaluable. I also thank my family for their understanding and support for this book project. In closing, I would like to express my gratitude to the all chapter contributors for their invaluable contributions and collaboration.

# Section 1

# IoT Adoption and Implementation

# Chapter 1

# A Literature Review of the Emerging Field of IoT Using RFID and Its Applications in Supply Chain Management

**Suvendu Naskar**
*Indian Institute of Management Calcutta, India*

**Preetam Basu**
*Indian Institute of Management Calcutta, India*

**Anup K. Sen**
*Indian Institute of Management Calcutta, India*

## ABSTRACT

*The Internet of Things (IoT) envisions an ecosystem where smart and interconnected objects can sense surrounding changes, communicate with each other, process information and take active roles in decision making. Optimizing supply chain performance is a primary concern of manufacturing and logistics organizations. Radio Frequency Identification (RFID) is helping organizations to build automated and interconnected smart environment by object identification and tracking, motivating the first step towards an IoT-enabled world. This chapter attempts to understand extant literature studying applications of RFID in implementing the IoT in supply chain management. We categorize extant literature, firstly, based on research methodology and secondly, based on supply chain processes. We find that presently academic activity is around conceptualizing the usability of RFID in the IoT with limited analytical and empirical evidence. Supply chain processes such as demand planning, procurement, retail shelf space management and product returns are prospective areas for interesting future research.*

DOI: 10.4018/978-1-5225-2104-4.ch001

## INTRODUCTION

Today's world consists of smart objects (e.g. smart mobile, smart AC etc.) that have the capability to sense surroundings, capture certain signals about changes and communicate their presence to other smart devices. There has been a revolution in the product design leveraging the power of information technology. Massive computation capability, network flexibility, usage of electromechanical components have provided new dimension in product specification. In this new world, products not only perform what they are supposed to but also perform additional activities like intelligent assessment and self-adjustment based on surrounding changes. This smart-connected object eco-system has brought new challenges and opportunities (Porter & Heppelmann, 2014). In light of the rapid emergence of smart products and possibilities, the term Internet of Things (IoT) was coined by MIT in the late 1990's. IoT means "devices or sensors connected world" where things i.e. the smart objects can communicate, monitor surroundings and take necessary steps to complete certain tasks managed by some external agency or by the connected devices depending on the application context. Thus smart objects are connected and integrated virtually and seamlessly by information technology so that the real world can be more accessible when necessary (Atzori et al., 2010; Uckelmann et al., 2011). Applications of smart objects connected through internet in industry oriented applications e.g. telemedicine (e.g. smart medical devices), utility (e.g. smart meter) has made IoT popular and practitioners are considering the possibilities of applying smart connected devices in other industries (e.g. supply chain, automobiles etc.).

One of the technologies that is driving the vision of IoT is Radio Frequency Identification (RFID). RFID is a technology for automatic identification of any device and capturing data stored in embedded microchips. A RFID tag is a chip attached to any object whose position is to be tracked. RFID system consists of an antenna to communicate with scanning devices that can read the chip information remotely, a reader that emits radio signal and receive information for tags, a middleware that bridges RFID hardware with enterprise applications (McFarlance & Yossi sheffi, 2006). Each RFID tag consists of a unique code which identifies the object it is attached to. Global standard for this code is EPC (Electronic Product Code). EPC codes can be of different length. A real life analogy of EPC code is our mobile number which can identify the consumer, network types, location of a person or service provider details. An EPC of 96 bits can identify more than 268 million manufacturers, more than 16 million types of objects and almost 69 billion articles for each manufacturer (Brock, 2001). This unequivocal ability of contactless communication, surrounding information capture, presence of real time centralised processing and unified view of objects give rise to numerous potential applications across different domains.

In this chapter, our objective is to review different applications of IoT using RFID in the domain of supply chain management. A supply chain is a system consisting of organisations, people, material, information, activities and other resources involved in moving a product or service from supplier to customers. In other words, a supply chain is a complex network of suppliers, manufacturers, warehouses, distribution centres, retail outlets that work collectively to provide products or services to the end customers (Wikipedia, 2016). Supply chain management encompasses the planning and management of all activities involved in sourcing, procurement, manufacturing and distribution. Importantly, it also includes coordination and collaboration with channel partners, which can be suppliers, intermediaries, third party service providers, and customers. In essence, supply chain management integrates supply and demand management within and across companies (CSCMP, 2016). The Supply Chain Operations Reference model (SCOR) is the world's leading supply chain framework, linking business processes, performance metrics, practices and people skills into a unified structure. Level 1 processes include Plan, Source, Make, Deliver and Return (APICS, 2016). A high level schematic view of SCOR model is shown in Figure 1.

In the context of supply chain management, RFID helps in identification and tracking of tools, devices, materials that are key supply chain resources. RFID tagged and networked devices support increasing transparency in supply chain by providing decision makers real time status about the current state of objects, devices and materials. Comprehensive list of possibilities of RFID enabled IOT are yet to be explored however anecdotal evidence shows that there are plenty of opportunities where automated identification and tracking coupled with integrated processing can improve supply chain performance; e.g. helping organisations in better inventory management, product tracking, inventory matching, order management, logistics and distribution management and waste reduction. This new field of IoT enabled by RFID has immense potential in different domains of supply chain management and demands a closer review of contemporary research to motivate future extension. For example, an RFID enabled product, in a smart IoT eco-system, can decide its next destination based on demand situation, and accordingly trigger signal to the logistics department. These innovative applications necessitate RFID not acting as dumb tracking device but as an active decision engine. Some of these applications, based on extant literature are discussed in subsequent sections of this chapter.

The urge to understand the contemporary academic discourse on this emerging field is the key motivation for this chapter. This will help not only in understanding the current research directions but also help identify potential directions for future research. IoT brings integrated capability beyond mere tracking which practitioners are constantly trying to exploit for cost, effort and profit optimization. Academic research not only follows real life applications but can propose possibilities of innovative applications of RFID and IoT, complementing practitioners thought process. This chapter reviews the extant literature on the use of RFID enabled IoT in two broad categories. Firstly, we study the literature based on type of research methodology (e.g. conceptual, analytical, and empirical) and then we map the extant literature on supply chain processes given by the SCOR model (e.g. Plan, Source, Make, Deliver and Return). So, the objective of this chapter is two-fold:

*Figure 1. SCOR model*
*(Supply Chain Council, 2009)*

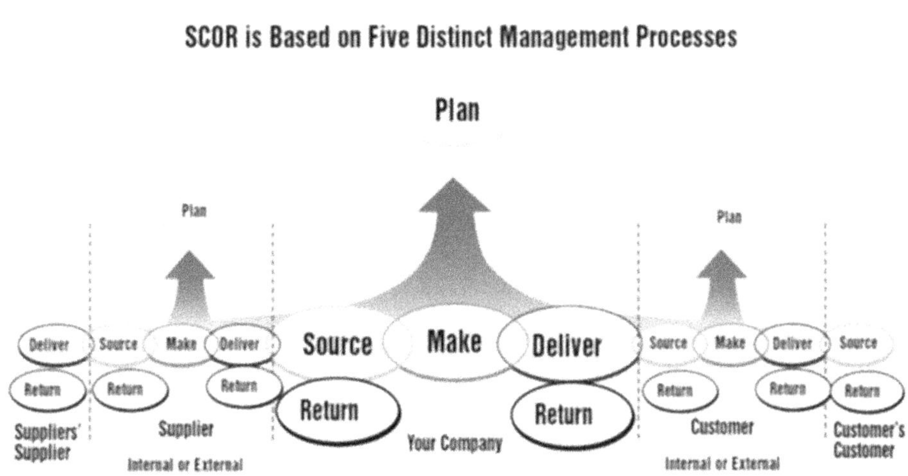

1. To review the extant literature on RFID and its application in IoT in terms of research methodology and supply chain processes.
2. To identify possible research gaps in terms of research methodology and supply chain application areas.

The rest of this chapter is organised as follows: We provide brief description of RFID operating principles and the role of RFID in IoT in Section 2. We discuss noticeable research agenda based on research methodology/approach in Section 3. After providing brief descriptions of key papers in these categories, we highlight potential future research opportunities. Next in Section 4, we review research papers based on supply chain sub-processes given by the SCOR model and present our findings in a two-dimensional heat-map matrix. We then provide a process centric perspective of contemporary research and follow it up with an overall chapter conclusion in Section 5.

## KEY TENETS OF RADIO FREQUENCY IDENTIFICATION AND ITS APPLICATION IN IOT

Radio-frequency identification (RFID) uses electromagnetic fields to automatically identify and track tags attached to objects. The tags contain electronically stored information. Unlike a barcode, the tag need not be within the line of sight of the reader, so it may be embedded within the object. RFID is a method for Automatic Identification and Data Capture (AIDC) (Wikipedia, 2016).

An RFID system consists of a tag or level and a reader. An RFID tag consists of an antenna attached to a microchip. The microchip works for storing and information processing whereas the antenna does the transmission and reception of signal with RFID reader. Passive RFID tags get power through the reader and are activated only in presence of a reader. Whereas an active RFID has an inbuilt battery to power the antenna and the microchip. As evident, active RFID tags have longer reach to communicate with RFID reader. An RFID reader (also known as an interrogator) is a two-way communication device attached to a computer or central server. RFID tags respond to the reader with information stored in the microchip which is stored in the central server. RFID tags attached to any object act as an identity card for the object (using EPC code written on the tags) and are also capable of identifying the position and other details with proper coding. An RFID system consists of one or multiple RFID tags, with each tag attached to an object which requires unique identification. The building blocks of RFID system and high level operational steps are shown in Figure 2:

The importance of RFID in the context of IoT stem from the fact that RFID tags can act not only as object identifiers but can also process information for the surrounding conditions such as temperature, noise, weight etc. They can also seamlessly communicate with the central computation system (through a reader) to establish a unified integrated smart object eco-system. In other words, exploiting the potential of RFID is a stepping stone towards the vision of IoT. The vision of IoT, advocates capability to interconnect objects without manual intervention. Interconnection among objects has to be anywhere, anytime, anything with any path or protocols. In terms of IoT vision, the world seem to be a dynamic, self-adjusting, interconnected integrated gigantic network. IoT envision things or objects to sense the environment and talk to each other. IoT environment consists of functionalities like object identification, tracking and location mapping, sensors, actuators, processing, devices and communication protocols. RFID provides the capability of object identification, tracking and localization in its current form whereas

*Figure 2. RFID basic operating model*

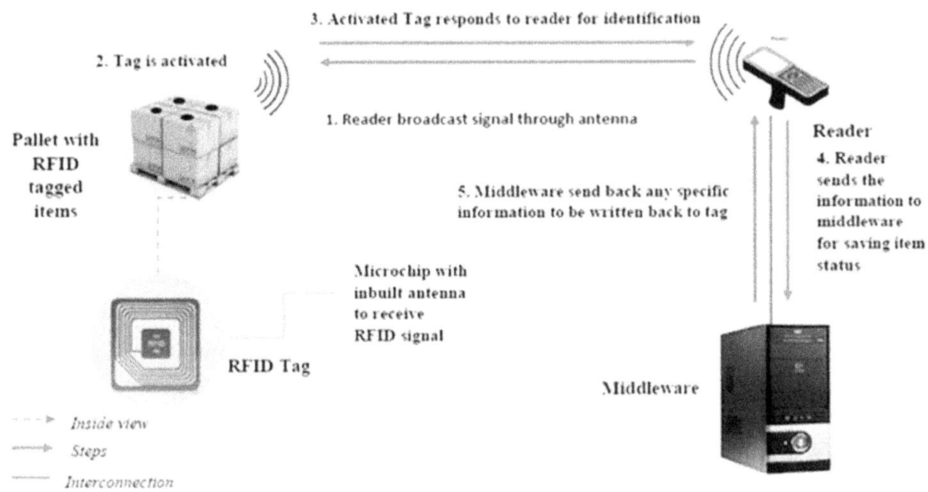


RFID readers bring the capability of sensors. When integrated with capabilities of other devices (e.g. faster processors, actuators) RFID can fulfil the vision towards IoT. For example, a manufacturing shop floor with RFID tagged devices can communicate about object status and position with a central server through RFID readers. Similarly use of RFID with integrated actuators can help automatic tracking of new orders received and updating the inventory position in real time.

Next we study the extant academic literature on IoT and its application in supply chain management from the perspective of different research methodologies.

## LITERATURE REVIEW

This section covers the extant literature and academic discussion around the applications of IoT using RFID in the context of Supply Chain Management. Research papers (publicly available) published after 2009 are considered for this purpose. Research papers published earlier discussing the use of RFID (starting from late 1980's and early 2000) are intentionally kept out of scope since the concepts of ioT and potential usage was not the primary driving force behind adoption of RFID during this period. Motivation for the current literature survey stems from the fact that there is no single place to refer the ongoing research agenda about applications of smart objects and RFID across supply chains in presence of the emerging concept of IoT. To the best of our knowledge, there is no literature review post 2010 that discuss the emerging applications of RFID in light of IoT. The objective of the current review is to identify the current academic discourse and applications of RFID in supply chain in light of the emerging trends of IoT. Close to 50+ papers published in leading journals are studied for this review. Academic research carried on related areas like cloud manufacturing are kept out of scope of this review to reinforce the intended purpose.

Use of RFID in supply chain is not a new concept. Research has been going on even before the concept of IoT was in place. However, the emergence of IoT and phenomenal growth of concomitant technology (e.g. big data, cloud) has opened up plethora of opportunities for organisations to rethink and revamp the conventional operations in supply chains. On one hand, due to advancement of technology, cost of implementation of RFID has reduced significantly and on the other hand, faster information processing capability has opened up opportunities of real time information update. Hence, organisations are able to project better ROI to justify the capital investments. In line with the developments taking place in business sphere, academicians are also constantly exploring the possibilities of RFID applications in light of IoT. However, at this moment wide adoption of RFID and integrated IoT in real world supply chains are at its diffusion phase. The early diffusion is still continuing at piecemeal manner and on a case to case basis.

Here, we categorize the extant literature according to research methodology. We observe that majority of academic discourse on IoT and SCM are around few core ideas where RFID is leveraged for object identification and tracking purposes. Integrated models discussing RFID/IoT and SCM are still at their conceptual stage. Accordingly, we have classified research papers under three broad categories viz. conceptual models, analytical models and empirical research. Majority of papers as of date are conceptual models. These conceptual papers offer a schematic view of component integration (RFID/IoT/Computation) without bringing the technology and associated implementation details. This type of research aids to build understanding of the key components and potential integration requirements for successful adoption of IoT in supply chain, by providing an architectural overview of the future landscape. On the other hand, there are research articles that convey the quantitative elements of IoT-specific business drivers e.g. cost of RFID, benefits due to improved inventory information etc. We categorize such articles under analytical models. Analytical models are contrived based on the assumptions that RFID adoption will bring additional cost components that were not so far considered in a conventional supply chain design. At the same time, RFID (and IoT) will fetch opportunities through improved communication, real time material tracking and reduced information asymmetry among the supply chain players. Research papers dealing with analytical models use mathematical optimization or simulation to identify numerous what-if scenarios during RFID adoption and associated pay-offs. Few papers include conceptual models followed by analytical expressions, however there are not many. Nevertheless, any academic value addition to this emerging trend is crucial for future research. Research articles studying empirical evidence either through survey or field study, that demonstrate supply chain ROI by using RFID enabled IoT are limited in numbers. We discuss such papers under the empirical research category. A schematic view of these three research dimensions is shown in Figure 3. An exhaustive list of papers is provided in the Appendix. More detailed description of research agenda and key findings from selected papers are discussed in subsequent sections.

## CONCEPTUAL MODELS

Developing conceptual models seem to be the predominant research agenda at present, specifically while discussing supply chain performance improvement through smart networked objects. Out of 50 papers studied, 32 papers propose conceptual models and discuss validity of these models. Few papers (4 out of these 32 papers viz. Chen et al., 2013; Dimakopoulou et al., 2014; Ondemir & Gupta, 2014; Reaidy et al., 2015) also provide complementary analytical models aligned with the conceptual architecture. Conceptual models elaborated in these papers can be identified according to certain supply chain functions as the focal agenda of the model. Because of its huge scope, drafting a unified architecture to capture use of RFID and IoT covering all aspects of the supply chain is quite an impossible task. Even if that is tried, the model will be too complex to comprehend for future research extensions. Hence, these research

*Figure 3. Research areas*

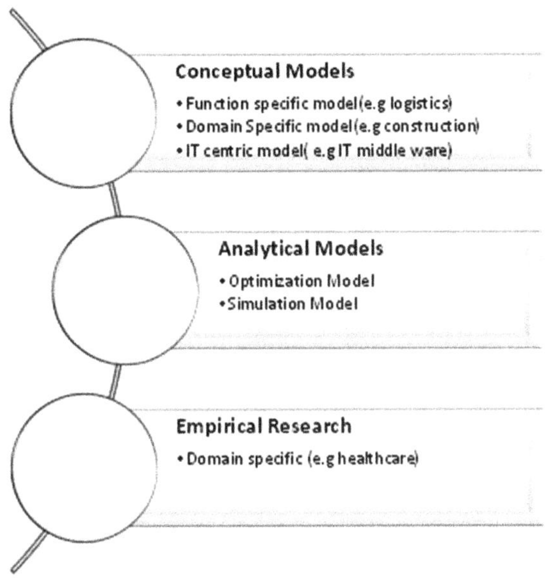


papers zoom out specific functions of the supply chain and propose a model to improve performance. Examples of few predominant functions discussed, are logistics, reverse logistics, procurement, material tracking, warehouse management etc. However, equally large number of academic research focus on particular domain (e.g. construction, FMCG) and propose hierarchical models depicting improved integration and communication in presence of RFID (and IoT) along the supply chains in those domains. Since, real time information collection, processing, automated decision and information dissemination are some of the key attributes of IoT, essentially, some of these models are dealing with the technology aspect of IoT and RFID (e.g. the communication protocols, IT architecture) Although there is no clear demarcation in categorization of conceptual research articles, we strive to do so for better exposition and understanding of the research agendas. We categorize conceptual models predominantly focusing on supply chain functions (e.g. logistics, manufacturing etc.) independent of any industry as function specific models. Models focussing on industry specific supply chain issues (e.g. supply chain of perishable goods) are categorized under domain specific models. Proposed models aiming improvement and integration of information technology/architecture aspects are categorized under IT centric models. Based on the above categorization, key research agendas and extant literature are expounded below:

## Function Specific Models

Improving logistics service is an important handler for optimizing supply chain performance. Real time tracking of goods and supplies while in-transit is critical for future planning. Several papers have discussed possible models that can help improve tracking in-transit materials and products. An integrated model bearing in mind IoT applications with associated impact on the material, information and fund flow is proposed by Liu & Gao (2014). This paper adopted a holistic approach, rather than concentrating only on RFID as a logistics tracking entity. This model is especially helpful for third party logistics providers illustrating the key considerations for them while deciding integration IoT in the entire logistic network. Sun (2012) discussed the impending utility of RFID in detecting fake items (using the RFID tag and user mobile). Based on the proposed model, the consumer and the corporate server can interact to ascertain the genuineness of the product delivered. Mingxiu et al. (2012) presented a conceptual diagram explaining how EPC (Electronic Product Code) can be used in tracking logistics pallets or materials using integrated processing architecture (IoT) built on EPC reader, ONS (Object Name Resolution) server and PML (Physical Mark-up Language) server. This paper presented a simplistic scheme about how RFID/EPC together can improve performance in logistics tracking and control. Many of these models can be extended to other aspects of supply chain apart from logistics. Magruk, 2012, discussed how IoT and the associated technology can help organisations enhance logistics management through real time communication using RFID/GPRS. In order to support the claim, the author used case snippets from multiple past scholarly works. One such example, is the case of Walmart. Walmart used RFID for logistics management across its 15000 stores, integrating real time traffic signal. Such approach helped the retail giant managing one of the world's largest logistics network impeccably by reducing stock-out scenarios, solving the bullwhip problem, improving service levels and reducing administrative cost.

Gu and Qingqi (2014) conceptualised a model on the use of RFID enabled IoT in reverse logistics information management. The authors analysed the key Management Information System (MIS) decision variables and components of reverse logistics and how IoT can help in better decision making. This paper established the model of reverse logistics with the applications of IoT technology. They adopted the viewpoint of building the supply chain by core enterprises and extending producers' responsibilities to the consumer side of the supply chain. The conversation is based on the major impediments of building a Management Information System (MIS) for efficient reverse logistics. Kiritsis (2011) applied the smart product concept while modelling a closed loop PLM (Product Life cycle Management) where he endorsed integrating active product tracking PEID (Product Embedded Information Device) information, PLM agent (e.g. mobile reader) and PLM System (PLM DB). The model is developed based on the premise that assessing quality of recovered product is key to successful closed loop supply chain. The proposed model is focused on tracking the product life-cycle information along the product usage seamlessly by capturing product history.

From our study we conclude that transportation and logistics functions, reverse logistics, product quality management are some of the widely explored areas under the domain of conceptual research. In next section we look at the models that focus on industry specific applications.

## Domain Specific Models

Domain specific models discuss use of RFID/IoT in supply chains of specific industry domains e.g. construction, agriculture etc. In order to address domain specific attributes and complexities, associated supply chain should embed industry specific design principles. Hence, discussions around adoption of IoT/RFID in order to improve supply chain enactment, specific industry individualities require distinct consideration. Wang & Nannan (2014) argued that the three layers of IoT architecture (application layer, network layer and perception layer) can be applied in agriculture supply chain for refining the entire material flow from produce collection, storage and thereby reaching market space. The paper theoretically established that if the product type, category and shelf life are captured and encapsulated through active RFID that will help improve supply chain efficiency.

One challenge facing the construction industry from supply chain point of view is that in construction sites, often the material needed for construction cannot be stored at the sites, yet the project has to be completed under extreme time pressure. As a result any initiative that can help real time monitoring of resource usage and material flow will improve decision making. Dave et al. (2016) proposed a lean production management model in construction industry by means of IoT standards and features like sensors and camera. Through a block diagram of a construction site and IoT tools like camera, sensors and associated monitoring devices, the authors conceptually highlighted improvement in site planning, control, monitoring of work progress, co-ordination, material handling, ordering, and resource sharing. On similar lines, Shin et al. (2011) suggested a RFID/WSN (wireless sensor network) based material tracking scheme for construction sites. According to this model RFID/WSN based reader, mover, trailer and gate can act as smart objects that interact with each other to provide real time construction site status to corporate ERP or any central information system. They proposed a multilayer Service Oriented Architecture (SOA) for seamless service delivery to improve change management. The proposed model is scalable to large site operations as well. Demiralp et al. (2012) conceptualized the use of an active RFID tag in construction scenario for tracking, storing, retrieving, and dispatching prefabricated panels from the firm's warehouse to construction sites. Using a simulation model of the changed process in presence of RFID, authors have established that considerable effort can be saved by the integrated tracking mechanism using RFID and IoT.

Verdouw et al. (2013) deliberated the concept of virtualisation of floricultural supply chain in presence of IoT. The model provided a view of a supply chain scheme that can avoid the need for physical proximity of resources by leveraging the idea of virtual team, technology, reality and things. The conceptual model is then applied to floricultural supply chains in Netherlands as case scenarios by comparing with the existing supply chain processes. This model is aligned with integrated information system enabled by IoT to decouple control and co-ordination in virtual space that can improve quality control, market information co-ordination, logistics and associated activities among geographically distributed supply chain participants.

A rather deviation from earlier papers and yet quite an applicable concept is emphasized by Rosenthal (2011). The paper conceptualised paradigm shift in manufacturing innovation in presence of IoT. Highlighting 3D printing (manufacturing) industry, this paper underlined how different stages of IoT innovation (component level to architectural innovation) takes place in presence of IoT. This multistage innovation can enhance innovation outcome from modular (component level) changes to radical structural shift. In order to establish their claim, authors espoused the concept of "Henderson-Clark model of innovation" as the theoretical foundation (Henderson & Clark, 1990).

Agriculture and food supply chain is characterised by highly fragmented stakeholders such as farmers, brokers, transporters. In addition, diversity and perishability of materials add further complexity. Reducing wastage through improved co-ordination is one of the foremost objective of this industry. Emergence of cost effective RFID tags and integrated supply chain using IoT can act as an enabler for designing an enhanced supply chain. Research on different dimensions and possibilities in this regard is currently on-going. An integrated supply chain model using internet technologies is suggested by Kaloxylos et al. (2013). Starting with key concerns (firming, logistics and selling) in this domain, the author organised a futuristic theoretical scheme of an integrated agri-chain using sensors, actuators, tracking system at firm level to retail stores. Entities such as public registry, trade and logistics partners are included as part of this integrated cloud. This paper also discussed the basic hurdles for achieving vendor independent integrated food supply chain. On similar lines, model of virtual food-chain in presence of IoT has been proposed by Verdouw et al. (2015). Food traceability using RFID tag and IoT can be improved along different stages of food-supply chain starting from firm, transportation, processing, logistics to supermarket and finally to consumer. Karol et al. (2014) discussed the use of RFID applications with help of IoT middleware for improved food traceability (Furdik et al., 2014). This model highlighted the sensors and IT applications that help improved tracking of food materials throughout the entire chain. This model can be extended to other supply chain logistic systems that deal with perishable goods.

Alejandro et al. (2009) applied the concepts of smart objects to active containers in order to optimize material supply for fresh products (Martinez-Sala et al., 2009). They used an example of a Spanish company (ECOMOVISTAND) that developed a patented product MT (a movable plastic container with active tracker). This product can act as a container starting from material loading at producer to retailers at supermarkets and back with returnable/left out perishable products. If such active containers can be made cost effectively, that could possibly open up opportunities for considerable optimization in fresh produce supply chain, provided a robust IT support is backing the enhanced capability to track products.

Domain specific conceptual models highlight solutions that address industry specific issues. As we have highlighted above, models exist to address such issues like perishability of products (e.g. food industry, floriculture) or lack of storage space (e.g. construction industry). These models propose novel applications that would leverage the power of RFID in implementing IoT to overcome specific industry challenges. Next we focus on the models that focus more on the technical aspects of IoT and RFID integration.

## IT Centric Models

The technical details of IoT architecture is another vibrant research area. Globalisation has brought new challenges to supply chain design arising due to cross border movement of raw materials, semi-finished and finished products. One of the key constituent of efficient logistics flow is tracking of pallets for cross border or long distance shipment. Under such arrangement, information about pellet position, any interim changes shifts from one server (geo-location) to another. This raises a challenge in terms of tracking material and containers in real time unless all servers are synchronised in real time and connected with centralised processing and decision making. Karakostas (2013) extended the real world concepts of Domain Name Server (DNS) to IoT architecture in logistics for spontaneous tracking of pallets during trans-shipment. Drawing an analogy of how URL's are tracked in internet (the machines or URL's are tracked by using DNS architecture), this paper proposed efficient container tracking during transhipment. The proposed three tier DNS architecture, resolved object tracking in transhipment analogous to the way internet traffic is resolved. The core idea of the proposed model is: to be scalable in presence of IoT, objects (e.g. products, pallets, containers etc.) should have unique identifier that is globally accepted and can be resolved unequivocally by any server at any part of the universe.

Gnimpieba et al. (2015) proposed a technology architecture using advanced technologies related to IoT, cloud computing, GPS/GPRS and RFID for tracking material using sensors, positioning, planning, data sharing and advance interaction through data sharing. This high level architecture elucidated an integrated supply chain. This paper discussed about increasing supply chain efficiency through improved collaboration using RFID as the data capture and event handler tool and GPRS for interconnection of objects. The paper also proposed a thematic view of cloud storage data structure to handle the 'things identity' using EPC (Electronic Product Code) code. According to this paper, use of cloud storage to store event data captured in an IoT-enabled supply chain will bring scalability, availability and ubiquity. On similar lines, Xu (2011) provided a detailed description of different technologies (e.g. RFID, Service Oriented Architecture, workflow management software and agent software's) involved and corresponding usability in supply chain quality management. This paper taking help of earlier research highlighted numerous dimensions and key concerns in supply chain design. Using supportive architectures e.g. emerging technologies like IoT, Service Oriented Architecture (SOA) etc. a more domain agnostic view of technologies, platforms, existing as well as upcoming protocols that can enable integrated supply chain framework is discussed by Borgia (2014). A major contribution of this paper is to direct readers towards an integrated and collaborative supply chain using emerging technologies. This paper looked at supply chain information processing and real time decision making from the view point of management information systems.

## ANALYTICAL MODELS

While conceptual models are good starting points to understand the high level potential applications of RFID and IoT in supply chains, they provide little insight about measureable traits such as cost, revenue or profitability. It is evident that RFID tags and integrated information framework comes with associated costs. The major cost components are cost of software, hardware cost for initial set up, cost of subsequent servicing and maintenance. Notable intangible cost is the cost of re-engineering business processes. It is crucial for top management to understand the business process re-engineering cost due to adoption of RFID/IoT, if IoT is to be exploited to its full potential. Once organisations decide to leverage these emerging concepts, the existing business processes have to be aligned to tap their full potential. Such costs are difficult to measure during the initial stages of IoT adoption. Analytical research models are crucial from that perspective to identify quantitative (e.g. cost, effort, revenue, profit) triggers for adoption, break even conditions and finally optimising stakeholder objectives. A point of reminder, the potential benefits of cost optimization when RFID is used alone are considerably low as compared to RFID usage in connection with the entire organisation's IT ecosystem. The differences stem from improved temporal and information processing, co-ordination and decision based on automated real time information exchange. Some of the pivotal analytical papers are detailed subsequently

Fan et al. (2015) explored the impact of RFID technology (IoT) in supply chain decision making in presence of inventory shrinkage and misplacement cost. The model considered possible combinations of centralised and decentralised supply chain, with and without RFID. This model considered fixed and variable cost of RFID tags in different set up and obtained the sensitivity of total supply chain profit in diverse conditions. The result showed that in decentralised supply chain and uniform demand scenario, with wholesale price contract, retailer is more sensitive to RFID tag price. In another paper Fan et al. (2014) analytically modelled a retailer profit (newsvendor problem) function in presence of inventory shrinkage. Retailers can use RFID to improve the inventory shrinkage. However, the cost justification for considered problems (similar to Newsvendor problem) is dependent on the wholesale price, price at which retailer is operating at and how efficiently the RFID tag can reduce shrinkage. The result proves retailer's incentive is more when 'RFID read rate' improves. Certainly, fixed cost of RFID plays significant role triggering retailer's consideration which is not explicitly demonstrated in this analysis.

Thiesse & Buckel (2015) assessed the economic benefits of RFID while the technology is used at the component level vis-à-vis at case level in case of shelf replenishment in retail stores. They considered retailer replenishment scenario using periodic review. With help of simulation, the paper established that using RFID will improve replenishment process by self-tracking components and cases, however while only component level tagging is applied it will result in sub-optimal performance. They also briefly discussed about the potential extensions for backroom tracking, shrinkage and misplacement reduction, stock out reduction, fixed shelf space. Future research can take clue from these models and carry on further scientific investigation in order to capture all key tenets of RFID and IoT in supply chain optimisation.

Dimakopoulou et al. (2014) analysed the real options of IT investment for RFID/IoT. Fixed cost and operational costs of using RFID are considered as key model parameters. The authors took the base case from real example of '3E Coco Cola HBC Greece' to simulate the model and came out with a strategy for staggered implementation of RFID tagging in all of its warehouses and distribution centres. The optimisation model elaborates the real options of timing and cost (depending on the pallet volume of a warehouse) of RFID implementation across multiple warehouses.

## EMPIRICAL RESEARCH

In this section we review the extant literature based on empirical research methodology. The adoption of IoT in supply chain and related areas are still at its diffusion phase. This is due to the fact that the infrastructure, supporting architecture and complementary technologies are still evolving. Although companies have adopted RFID to improve material tracking for quite some time but adoption took place in silos rather than in light of IoT as an integrated eco-system. Emerging technologies such as big data, cloud and virtualisation etc. are acting as technology enablers for real-time, automated interaction of smart objects. In the backdrop of these changes, empirical research studying adoption of RFID in implementing IoT is much less in number as compared to conceptual or even analytical models. Out of the 50 papers that we studied, only two have discussed empirical evidence for establishing the research findings. Chong et al. (2015) studied RFID adoption using the framework of technology adoption theory UTAUT (Unified Theory of Acceptance and Use of Technology). They conducted empirical studies on 252 physicians and doctors to identify the key drivers of RFID adoption. They applied artificial neural network to demonstrate the importance of key variables in deciding IoT adoption in service industry supply chain (e.g. healthcare).

Vlachos (2014) conducted online survey of 300 retail companies to study the impact of RFID on supply chain performance. Factor analysis on the data revealed seven primary factors: suppliers, inventory, distribution, ordering, plan, sales and forecasting as key performance indicators of supply chain. By using multiple hierarchical regression models and firm size as a control variable, the author established that RFID adoption has significant impact on first six of the seven performance indicators. Eight RFID applications were considered for this survey which were 'use of RFID at supplier warehouse', 'retailer central warehouse', 'retailer local warehouse', 'retailer owned stores', standards, transportation, pellet level and specialised software.

Bottani & Rizzi (2008) tested the impact of RFID and EPC code on the main process of a fast moving consumer good supply chain. Using questionnaire based survey on three echelon supply chain, they established that RFID adoption does not provide same outcome in different (integrated and not-integrated) supply chain. For example, pellet level adoption seems to deliver positive performance whereas case level usage does not justify the investment cost of RFID. However since cost of RFID is reducing rapidly and integrated technology frameworks are maturing, we need more of empirical study to understand and deliberate over the new developments.

## Research Gap Identification Based on Different Research Methodology

Here, we identify possible gaps for future research based on the review that we presented. IoT is not any single technology but a smart object eco-system interacting with each other enabled by integration of numerous technology components. The adoption of smart devices and components is not an option but obligation for organisations to remain competitive in future. It is only a matter of time, when it is about to happen. Also, due to cost pressure and competitive threats supply chain will constantly seek for optimized, effective yet sustainable solutions. This will eventually push supply chains to adopt smart objects that can reduce manual intervention while providing faster information interchange. Next generation supply chains will be built around these core philosophies giving rise to "smart" supply chain management. Use of Radio Frequency identification is the first stepping stone towards that direction.

Based on extant literature, the trends of current research agenda related to RFID in presence of IOT are:

- Building conceptual models, in the form of black-box supply chain entities form the dominant research agenda. Such models help in understanding the potential usability which subsequently needs to be tested through real life adoption of RFID and IoT.
- There is inclination to carry on analytical work addressing quantitative dimensions such as, cost, revenue and break even analysis of the future investments in RFID and IoT. These models are extension of existing models with additional cost components brought in due to RFID and IoT.
- Retail perishable goods, healthcare and construction industry are major Industry in focus, where better device and material tracking can possibly help in inventory shrinkage to build agile operation or distribution management.
- Current research lacks empirical evidences to support the anticipated potential of RFID/IoT. Although there are few research papers based on empirical data, clearly when compared to the number of conceptual or analytical models, research based on empirical data are significantly less.

Some of the future research agenda worth exploring are:

- Current research interest is around building conceptual models in isolated supply chain aspects like logistics where RFID tag is used as a tracking device. Models highlighting the use of RFID in the shop floor planning in presence of smart interconnected devices (IoT) are less discussed.
- By being smart does not mean only the ability to communicate but also about the ability to self-reconfigure and regulate during time of contingencies. Very few models are able to deliver clear direction in this aspect of smart supply chain.
- Industries like healthcare, construction, retail are some of the domains where conceptual models are visualised but many other industries are yet to be explored. Future research should concentrate on supply chain in domains such as e-commerce, automobiles, pharmaceutical etc.
- Security, privacy and trust are very critical when stakeholders are sharing information in presence of IoT. This is due to the fact that in IoT, information can be shared between any object, using any protocol at any time. This improves transparency of information but brings security and privacy risks. Such concerns in terms of data privacy and security unquestionably are important potential research directions. Big data analytics, multi-node processing and centralised decision making in view of IoT should be studied in much greater detail.

- In complex and large supply chains, having millions of smart objects, the processing capability has to complement the objects' smartness. An important research agenda could be: how much information contained by smart components are optimum for a given supply chain eco-system?
- With wider adoption, possibilities of more empirical research will open up, however given the current adoption rate and current state of empirical research, there are untapped research areas to study the adoption of IoT in different supply chains. One possibility could be to use existing theoretical frameworks like agency theory to study current adoption and performance outcomes.
- There is need for more case-based research, on industry/organisations using RFID/IoT to improve supply chain efficiency. Such cases will not only be helpful to drive academic discourse but also be an opportunity for cross leveraging best practices and possibilities among various industries.

## CATEGORIZATION OF RESEARCH BASED ON THE SCOR MODEL

We discussed, the extant literature in RFID enabled IoT in supply chain management based on research methodology e.g. conceptual models, analytical models and empirical papers. The above approach helped us in understanding the current stage of maturity of the emerging trends and the associated research. The complementary stance is to understand the process centric view of current research coverage. RFID brings certain capability of tracking, communicating and identifying objects. However, in trying to achieve the same, not all business sub-processes will be equally impacted. For example, the impact of RFID in supply chain planning (demand planning, sourcing planning, risk management etc.) are less straight forward as compared to inventory management in retail stores or product tracking in distribution. Hence it is imperative to develop a process centric view of current research agenda which we endeavour to do in this section. We map the extant literature onto the various supply chain processes based on the discussions provided in the respective papers. In doing so we took the help of the Supply Chain Operations Reference model (SCOR) model developed by the Supply Chain Council. The SCOR model is the world's leading supply chain framework, linking business processes, performance metrics, practices and people skills into a unified structure. Level 1 processes include Plan, Source, Make, Deliver and Return (APICS, 2016). Readers may refer the Supply Chain Council website ("http://www.apics.org") for more details on the SCOR model. The motivation for using SCOR model comes from the fact that this is a widely accepted supply chain process model.

Table 1 provides a heat-map matrix of supply chain sub-functions that these papers cover. A heat-map is a graphical representation of data where the individual values contained in a matrix are represented as colours (Wikipedia, 2016). The rows in the matrix correspond to the research articles, whereas the column represent the supply chain sub-processes. To reduce complexity, we used a single color-coding. Single colour coding scheme is suitable when data associated is in binary form (Ilkinson & Riendly, 2009). In this case, our consideration is that a research article either pondered about a supply chain sub process or not. For example, the first row represents the article by Dave et al. (2016) covering the use of RFID in construction site production management. The blue circle represents which supply chain sub-process (2nd row) the paper/model address. The top row indicates 5 high level supply chain functions as per the SCOR model.

There are some models that address more than one supply chain sub-processes. This is predominantly apparent for models addressing the technical aspects (e.g. IT architecture) of RFID in supply chain to enable IoT. In such cases, all possible sub-functions are marked (e.g. Gu & Qingqi, 2014). Another approach, which we have consciously avoided, could have been to use different shades for different sub-functions depending on the coverage and focus. If a model is highly focused on one sub-processes, use dark colour codes, and for less focused sub-processes, use lighter shades. According to our approach of supply chain sub-function mapping, the assumption is either the sub-function is covered or not covered at all. The purpose of our analysis is to identify, which business sub-processes of supply chain functions are highly explored vis-à-vis which are less covered to provide a clue of future research scopes. Hence, we use the same colour code for our analysis.

## Heat-Map Matrix of Supply Chain Sub-Processes

The journal articles and conference papers cover different supply chain functions and sub-functions. Below is heat-map matrix of supply chain functionality that these papers covered in the discussion. A blue dot represent that the concept discussed address the mentioned supply chain sub-function.

*Table 1.*

| *PAPERS* | PLAN | SOURCE | MAKE | | DELIVER | | | | | | RETURN | | |
|---|---|---|---|---|---|---|---|---|---|---|---|---|---|
| | *Demand Planning* | *Distribution Sourcing* | *Production Management* | *Operational Efficiency Improvements* | *Inventory Management (increased accuracy)* | *Distribution/ delivery Management* | *Distribution/ Collaborative order fulfilment* | *Distribution/ Shelf space management* | *Retail shelf replenishment* | *Logistics/ transportation Management* | *Reverse logistics* | *Return Prediction* | *Quality assessment* |
| Dave et al., 2016 | | | ● | | | | | | | | | | |
| Gu & Qingqi, 2014 | | | | | | | | | | | ● | ● | |
| Gnimpieba et al., 2015 | | | | | ● | ● | | | | ● | | | |
| X. Wang & Nannan Liu, 2014 | | | | ● | ● | | | | | ● | | | |
| Liu & Gao, 2014 | | | | | | | | | | ● | | | |
| T. Fan et al., 2015 | | | | | ● | | | | | | | | |
| Sun, 2012 | | | | | | | | | | ● | | | |
| Decker et al., 2008 | | | | | | | | | | ● | | | |
| MrFarlance & Yossi sheffi 2006 | | | | | | | | | | ● | | | |
| Verdouw et al., 2013 | ● | ● | | ● | | ● | | ● | ● | ● | | | |
| Thiesse & Buckel, 2015 | | | | | | | | | ● | | | | |
| Dimakopoulou et al., 2014 | | ● | | | | ● | | | | | | | |
| T. J. Fan et al., 2014 | | | | | ● | | | | | | | | |
| Mingxiu et al., 2012 | | | | | | | | | | ● | | | |
| Magruk, 2012 | | | | | | | | | | ● | | | |
| Dimakopoulou et al., 2014 | | | ● | | | | | | | | | | |
| Ondemir & Gupta, 2014 | | | | | | | | | | | | | ● |
| Furdik et al., 2014 | | | | ● | ● | | | | ● | ● | | | |
| Mingxiu et al., 2012 | | | | | | | | | | ● | | | |
| Kaloxylos et al., 2013 | | | | ● | | | | | | | | | |
| Zhou, Chong, & Ngai, 2015 | | | | | | | | | | | | | |
| Yee-Loong Chong et al., 2015 | | | | ● | | | | | | | | | |
| Kiritsis, 2011 | | | | | | | | | | | ● | ● | |
| Realdy, Gunasekaran, & Spalanzani, 2015 | | | | | ● | | ● | | | | | | |
| Chuu, 2014 | ● | ● | | | ● | | | | | | | | |
| S. Shin & Eksioglu, 2015 | | | | | ● | | | | | | | | |
| Vlachos, 2014 | | | | ● | ● | ● | | | | | | | |
| Chen et al., 2013 | | | | | ● | ● | | | | ● | | | |
| T. H. Shin et al., 2011 | ● | | | ● | ● | ● | | | | ● | | | |
| Nativi & Lee, 2012 | | | | | | | | ● | | | | | |
| Martinez-Sala et al., 2009 | | | | | | | | | | | | ● | ● |
| S. J. Wang, Wang, Huang, & Chen, 2011 | ● | | | | ● | | | | | | | | |
| Ustundag & Tanyas, 2009 | ● | ● | | | ● | ● | | ● | | | | | |
| Leung, Cheung, & Chu, 2014 | | | | | | | | | | | | | |
| Dai & Tseng, 2012 | | | | | ● | | | | | | | | |
| Demiralp et al., 2012 | | | | ● | | | | | | | | | |
| Bottani & Rizzi, 2008 | | | | | | ● | | | | | | | |
| Ngai, Cheung, Lam, & Ng, 2014 | | | | | | | | | | | | | ● |
| Grunow & Piramuthu, 2013 | | | | | ● | | | | ● | | | | |

## Research Gap Identification Based on the SCOR Model

From the above matrix it is evident that use of RFID for managing supply chain delivery is a widely discussed research agenda. Within delivery, managing logistics by using RFID for automated product and pallet tracking are most common research topics. Another common area that is focussed upon is inventory management. Clearly the fundamental capability of RFID is identifying and tracking of products/devices. This traditional application of RFID is explored both by practitioners and academicians extensively.

Next we identify some supply chain processes that are prospective research areas for IoT using RFID:

- With growing importance of green supply chain, product recovery is becoming an important supply chain process. Product recovery process has multiple challenges. Challenges assessing quality and quantity of product returned, evaluating value of remaining product life and establishing parallel efficient reverse logistic network. RFID enabled IoT can help improving product return quality by capturing product life-cycle information during its usage. Product valuation based on life cycle history captured by using an active RFID tag, is certainly an interesting future research agenda.
- RFID and IOT brings enhanced capabilities of automated planning of materials movement, production planning and updating of schedules. Extant literature does not address these aspects adequately. As we can see, not many papers address how RFID enabled IoT can support an efficient supply chain planning (e.g. Demand planning, sourcing decisions etc.). The immediate impact of RFID on supply chain planning is not so straightforward. RFID and IoT can bring in capabilities of automated planning. Use of RFID in retail stores help in providing real-time inventory and demand fluctuations which can be leveraged for demand planning as well as strategized procurement. We see future research scope in these areas.
- Production management is another less researched area. Although RFID provides capability for real time component level availability and tracking of material movement from sourcing to delivery, there is very limited work that address the entire chain either conceptually or empirically. When coupled with demand planning capability, the IoT eco-system can certainly leverage automated production planning across production sites and demand points. There is need for further research consideration to build integrated models that consider the entire flow of material from the sourcing to return. Efficient and real time tracking of materials not only increases supply chain agility, but in presence of IoT and faster processing, this capability provides sea of opportunities to rebuild new business processes. This opens up potential research around - an extension from automated manufacturing to automated self-adjusting supply chain.
- There are plenty of innovative solution possibilities of managing shelf space, retail shelf replenishments. IoT powered by RFID, can be an enabler for building automated shelf space management starting from demand tracking, advertising, object identification, billing and replenishment. There is immense scope of carrying research on building conceptual as well analytical models addressing shelf space management challenges.

## CONCLUSION

In this chapter we provided a basic understanding of RFID, IoT and its application in various supply chain functions. We reviewed extant literature based on research methodology (conceptual models, analytical models and empirical research). We also provided supply chain sub-process level segregation of current literature. Based on our categorisation we identified the current research trends while building an understanding of potential future research agenda. The purpose of this review is to understand the trend in current research related to RFID adoption for implementing IoT in supply chains. We find conceptual papers outnumber analytical models as well as empirical papers - which is expected as RFID in presence of IoT is still emerging. Specially, the emerging applications of IoT is keeping organisations apprehensive about the usability within existing business processes and risk of process redesign. Although research papers are addressing different applications of IoT and RFID in the context of supply chain, but little emphasis is given to leverage the full capability that IoT provides. Currently research is focussed on piecemeal applications ignoring the full capability of IoT using RFID. While applications of RFID as a tracking device for inventory management, transportation and logistics management have been studied, leveraging full potential of IoT eco-system for supply chain performance improvement is still at an early stage of adoption. Supply chain processes such as demand planning, procurement, production management and product returns under reverse supply chain management are prospective areas for interesting novel applications of IoT.

From business process perspective supply chain has its own complexity. Vision of IoT brings in technological and integration challenges. Hence, it is bound to have a long gestation period before the true potential can be realised. From this perspective, the current review is a valuable exercise providing directions of current research agenda and possible gaps for future extensions.

## REFERENCES

APICS. (2016). *SCOR*. Retrieved August 26, 2015, from http://www.apics.org/sites/apics-supply-chain-council/frameworks/scor

Atzori, L., Iera, A., & Morabito, G. (2010). The Internet of Things : A survey. *Computer Networks*, *54*(15), 2787–2805. doi:10.1016/j.comnet.2010.05.010

Borgia, E. (2014). The internet of things vision: Key features, applications and open issues. *Computer Communications*, *54*, 1–31. doi:10.1016/j.comcom.2014.09.008

Bottani, E., & Rizzi, A. (2008). Economical assessment of the impact of RFID technology and EPC system on the fast-moving consumer goods supply chain. *International Journal of Production Economics*, *112*(2), 548–569. doi:10.1016/j.ijpe.2007.05.007

Brock, D. L. (2001). *The Electronic Product Code (EPC) A Naming Scheme for Physical Objects*. Retrieved from http://cocoa.ethz.ch/downloads/2014/06/None_MIT-AUTOID-WH-002.pdf

Chen, J. C., Cheng, C. H., Huang, P. B., Wang, K. J., Huang, C. J., & Ting, T. C. (2013). Warehouse management with lean and RFID application: A case study. *International Journal of Advanced Manufacturing Technology*, *69*(1–4), 531–542. doi:10.1007/s00170-013-5016-8

Chuu, S. J. (2014). An investment evaluation of supply chain RFID technologies: A group decision-making model with multiple information sources. *Knowledge-Based Systems*, *66*, 210–220. doi:10.1016/j.knosys.2014.05.012

CSCMP. (2016). *Supply chain management*. Retrieved August 26, 2016, from https://cscmp.org/supply-chain-management-definitions

Da Xu, L. (2011). Information architecture for supply chain quality management. *International Journal of Production Research*, *49*(1), 183–198. doi:10.1080/00207543.2010.508944

Dai, H., & Tseng, M. M. (2012). The impacts of RFID implementation on reducing inventory inaccuracy in a multi-stage supply chain. *International Journal of Production Economics*, *139*(2), 634–641. doi:10.1016/j.ijpe.2012.06.005

Dave, B., Kubler, S., Främling, K., & Koskela, L. (2016). Opportunities for enhanced lean construction management using Internet of Things standards. *Automation in Construction*, *61*, 86–97. doi:10.1016/j.autcon.2015.10.009

Decker, C., Berchtold, M., Chaves, L. W. F., Beigl, M., Roehr, D., Riedel, T., … Herzig, D. (2008). Cost-benefit model for smart items in the supply chain. Lecture Notes in Computer Science (Including Subseries Lecture Notes in Artificial Intelligence and Lecture Notes in Bioinformatics), 4952, 155–172. doi:<ALIGNMENT.qj></ALIGNMENT>10.1007/978-3-540-78731-0_10

Demiralp, G., Guven, G., & Ergen, E. (2012). Analyzing the benefits of RFID technology for cost sharing in construction supply chains: A case study on prefabricated precast components. *Automation in Construction*, *24*, 120–129. doi:10.1016/j.autcon.2012.02.005

Dimakopoulou, A. G., Pramatari, K. C., & Tsekrekos, A. E. (2014). Applying real options to IT investment evaluation: The case of radio frequency identification (RFID) technology in the supply chain. *International Journal of Production Economics*, *156*, 191–207. doi:10.1016/j.ijpe.2014.06.005

Fan, T., Tao, F., Deng, S., & Li, S. (2015). Impact of RFID technology on supply chain decisions with inventory inaccuracies. *International Journal of Production Economics*, *159*, 117–125. doi:10.1016/j.ijpe.2014.10.004

Fan, T. J., Chang, X. Y., Gu, C. H., Yi, J. J., & Deng, S. (2014). Benefits of RFID technology for reducing inventory shrinkage. *International Journal of Production Economics*, *147*(PART C), 659–665. doi:10.1016/j.ijpe.2013.05.007

Furdik, K., Pramudianto, F., Ahlsén, M., & Rosengren, P. (2014). *Food traceability chain supported by the ebbits IoT middleware*. Academic Press.

Gnimpieba, D. R., Nait-Sidi-Moh, A., Durand, D., & Fortin, J. (2015). ScienceDirect Using Internet of Things technologies for a collaborative supply chain: Application to tracking of pallets and containers. *Procedia - Procedia Computer Science, 56*, 550–557. <ALIGNMENT.qj></ALIGNMENT>10.1016/j.procs.2015.07.251

Grunow, M., & Piramuthu, S. (2013). RFID in highly perishable food supply chains - Remaining shelf life to supplant expiry date? *International Journal of Production Economics*, *146*(2), 717–727. doi:10.1016/j.ijpe.2013.08.028

Gu, Y., & Qingqi, L. (2014). Research on the application of the internet of things in Reverse Logistics Information Management. *Energy Development, 860–863*(4), 3017–3020. http://doi.org/<ALIGNMENT.qj></ALIGNMENT>10.4028/www.scientific.net/AMR.860-863.3017

Henderson, R. M., & Clark, K. B. (1990). Architectural innovation: The reconfiguration of existing product technologies and the failure of established firms. *Administrative Science Quarterly*, *35*(1), 9–30. doi:10.2307/2393549

Ilkinson, L. W., & Riendly, M. F. (2009). *History Corner: The History of the Cluster Heat-Map*, *60622*. doi:10.1198/tas.2009.0033

Kaloxylos, A., Wolfert, J., Verwaart, T., Terol, C. M., Brewster, C., Robbemond, R., & Sundmaker, H. (2013). The Use of Future Internet Technologies in the Agriculture and Food Sectors: Integrating the Supply Chain. *Procedia Technology, 8*, 51–60. <ALIGNMENT.qj></ALIGNMENT>10.1016/j.protcy.2013.11.009

Karakostas, B. (2013). A DNS architecture for the internet of things: A case study in transport logistics. *Procedia Computer Science, 19*, 594–601. <ALIGNMENT.qj></ALIGNMENT>10.1016/j.procs.2013.06.079

Kiritsis, D. (2011). Closed-loop PLM for intelligent products in the era of the Internet of things. *CAD Computer Aided Design*, *43*(5), 479–501. doi:10.1016/j.cad.2010.03.002

Leung, J., Cheung, W., & Chu, S. C. (2014). Aligning RFID applications with supply chain strategies. *Information & Management*, *51*(2), 260–269. doi:10.1016/j.im.2013.11.010

Liu, W., & Gao, Z. (2014). Study on IOT based Architecture of Logistics Service Supply Chain. *International Journal of Grid and Distributed Computing*, *7*(1), 169–178. doi:10.14257/ijgdc.2014.7.1.15

Magruk, A. (2012). *The internet of things as the future technological trend of the innovative development of logistics*. Academic Press.

Martinez-Sala, A. S., Egea-Lopez, E., Garcia-Sanchez, F., & Garcia-Haro, J. (2009). Tracking of Returnable Packaging and Transport Units with active RFID in the grocery supply chain. *Computers in Industry*, *60*(3), 161–171. doi:10.1016/j.compind.2008.12.003

McFarlance, D., & Sheffi, Y. (2006). The impact of automatic identification on Supply Chain Operations. *International Journal of Retail & Distribution Management*, *34*(1), 6–24. doi:10.1108/02656710210415703

Mingxiu, Z., Chunchang, F., & Minggen, Y. (2012). The Application used RFID in Third Party Logistics. *Physics Procedia*, *25*, 2045–2049. doi:10.1016/j.phpro.2012.03.348

Nativi, J. J., & Lee, S. (2012). Impact of RFID information-sharing strategies on a decentralized supply chain with reverse logistics operations. *International Journal of Production Economics*, *136*(2), 366–377. doi:10.1016/j.ijpe.2011.12.024

Ngai, E. W. T., Cheung, B. K. S., Lam, S. S., & Ng, C. T. (2014). RFID value in aircraft parts supply chains: A case study. *International Journal of Production Economics, 147*(Part B), 330–339. 10.1016/j.ijpe.2012.09.017

Ondemir, O., & Gupta, S. M. (2014). Quality management in product recovery using the Internet of Things: An optimization approach. *Computers in Industry*, *65*(3), 491–504. doi:10.1016/j.compind.2013.11.006

Porter, M. E., & Heppelmann, J. E. (2014). *How Smart, Connected Products Are Transforming Companies.* Retrieved August 24, 2016, from https://hbr.org/2014/11/how-smart-connected-products-are-transforming-competition

Reaidy, P. J., Gunasekaran, A., & Spalanzani, A. (2015). Bottom-up approach based on Internet of Things for order fulfillment in a collaborative warehousing environment. *International Journal of Production Economics*, *159*, 29–40. doi:10.1016/j.ijpe.2014.02.017

Rosenthal, D. M. (2011, July). Forthcoming in. *New York*, 1–22.

Shin, S., & Eksioglu, B. (2015). An empirical study of RFID productivity in the U.S. retail supply chain. *International Journal of Production Economics*, *163*, 89–96. doi:10.1016/j.ijpe.2015.02.016

Shin, T. H., Chin, S., Yoon, S. W., & Kwon, S. W. (2011). A service-oriented integrated information framework for RFID/WSN-based intelligent construction supply chain management. *Automation in Construction*, *20*(6), 706–715. doi:10.1016/j.autcon.2010.12.002

Sun, C. (2012). Application of RFID Technology for Logistics on Internet of Things. *AASRI Procedia*, *1*, 106–111. doi:10.1016/j.aasri.2012.06.019

Thiesse, F., & Buckel, T. (2015). A comparison of RFID-based shelf replenishment policies in retail stores under suboptimal read rates. *International Journal of Production Economics*, *159*, 126–136. doi:10.1016/j.ijpe.2014.09.002

Uckelmann, D., Harrison, M., & Michahelles, F. (2011). *An Architectural Approach Towards the Future Internet of Things*. <ALIGNMENT.qj></ALIGNMENT>10.1007/978-3-642-19157-2

Ustundag, A., & Tanyas, M. (2009). The impacts of Radio Frequency Identification (RFID) technology on supply chain costs. *Transportation Research Part E, Logistics and Transportation Review*, *45*(1), 29–38. doi:10.1016/j.tre.2008.09.001

Verdouw, C. N., Beulens, A. J. M., & van der Vorst, J. G. A. J. (2013). Virtualisation of floricultural supply chains: A review from an internet of things perspective. *Computers and Electronics in Agriculture*, *99*, 160–175. doi:10.1016/j.compag.2013.09.006

Verdouw, C. N., Wolfert, J., Beulens, A. J. M., & Rialland, A. (2015). Virtualization of food supply chains with the internet of things. *Journal of Food Engineering*, *176*, 128–136. doi:10.1016/j.jfoodeng.2015.11.009

Vlachos, I. P. (2014). A hierarchical model of the impact of RFID practices on retail supply chain performance. *Expert Systems with Applications*, *41*(1), 5–15. doi:10.1016/j.eswa.2013.07.006

Wang, S. J., Wang, W. L., Huang, C. T., & Chen, S. C. (2011). Improving inventory effectiveness in RFID-enabled global supply chain with Grey forecasting model. *The Journal of Strategic Information Systems*, *20*(3), 307–322. doi:10.1016/j.jsis.2011.03.003

Wang, X., & Liu, N. (2014). The application of internet of things in agricultural means of production supply chain management. *Advanced Materials Research, 926–930*(7), 4118–4121. http://doi.org/<ALIGNMENT.qj></ALIGNMENT>10.4028/www.scientific.net/AMR.926-930.4118

Wikipedia. (2016). *Radio Frequency Identification*. Retrieved August 19, 2016, from https://en.wikipedia.org/wiki/Radio-frequency_identification

Yee-Loong Chong, A., Liu, M. J., Luo, J., & Keng-Boon, O. (2015). Predicting RFID adoption in healthcare supply chain from the perspectives of users. *International Journal of Production Economics*, *159*, 66–75. doi:10.1016/j.ijpe.2014.09.034

Zhou, L., Chong, A. Y. L., & Ngai, E. W. T. (2015). Supply chain management in the era of the internet of things. *International Journal of Production Economics*, *159*, 1–3. doi:10.1016/j.ijpe.2014.11.014

## KEY TERMS AND DEFINITIONS

**Distribution Management:** Overseeing the movement of goods from supplier or manufacturer to point of sale. Distribution management is an overarching term that refers to numerous activities and processes such as packaging, inventory, warehousing, supply chain and logistics.

**Inventory Management:** Inventory management is primarily about specifying the size and placement of stocked goods. Inventory management is required at different locations within a facility or within multiple locations of a supply network to protect the regular and planned course of production against the random disturbance of running out of materials or goods. The scope of inventory management concerns the fine lines between replenishment lead time, carrying costs of inventory, asset management, inventory forecasting, inventory valuation, inventory visibility, physical inventory, available physical space for inventory, quality management, replenishment and returns.

**Internet of Things(IOT):** IoT means “devices or sensors connected world” where things i.e. the smart objects can communicate, monitor surroundings and take necessary steps to complete certain tasks managed by some external agency or by the connected devices depending on the application context. IoT envisions an eco-system where smart and interconnected objects can sense surrounding changes, communicate with each other, process information and take active roles in decision making.

**Logistics Management:** Logistics management is the part of supply chain management that plans, implements, and controls the efficient, effective forward, and reverse flow and storage of goods, services, and related information between the point of origin and the point of consumption in order to meet customer’s requirements.

**Procurement:** The act of obtaining or buying goods and services. The process includes preparation and processing of a demand as well as the end receipt and approval of payment.

**Radio Frequency Identification (RFID):** Radio Frequency Identification (RFID)is a technology for automatic identification of any device/objects and capturing data stored in embedded microchips.It uses electromagnetic fields to automatically identify and track tags attached to objects. The tags contain electronically stored information.

**Supply Chain Management (SCM):** Supply chain management encompasses the planning and management of all activities involved in sourcing, procurement, manufacturing and distribution. Importantly, it also includes coordination and collaboration with channel partners, which can be suppliers, intermediaries, third party service providers, and customers. In essence, supply chain management integrates supply and demand management within and across companies.

**The Supply Chain Operations Reference (SCOR) Model:** SCOR model is the world's leading supply chain framework, linking business processes, performance metrics, practices and people skills into a unified structure.

# APPENDIX

*Table 2. List of papers – Summary view*

| Sl No | Author | Paper Name | Publication | Year of Publication | Conceptual Model | Analytical Model | Empirical |
|---|---|---|---|---|---|---|---|
| 1 | Bhargav Dave, Sylven Kubler, Kary Framling, Lauri Koskela | Opportunities for enhanced lean construction management using Internet of Things standards | Automation in Construction | 2015 | Y | N | N |
| 2 | Yuexia gu, Qingqi liu | Research on the application of the internet of things in reverse logistics information management | Journal of Industrial Engineering and management | 2013 | Y | N | N |
| 3 | Animesh Tiwari, Megha Jain | Analysis of supply chain management in cloud computing | International Journal Innovative Technology and Exploring Engineering | 2013 | Y | N | N |
| 4 | Prashant Satpute, Omprakash Tembhurne | A review of cloud centric IoT based framework for Supply Chain Management in precision Agriculture | International Journal of Advanced Research in Computer Science and Management Studies | 2014 | N | N | N |
| 5 | Aline Senart | Towards Self organising global supply chains in the internet of Things | Trinity college Dublin | 2009 | N | N | N |
| 6 | David R gnimpieba Z, Ahmed net-sidi moh, David Durand, Jerome Fortin | Using Internet of Things Technologies for collaborative supply chain: Application to tracking of pallets and containers | International workshop on Mobile Spatial Information Systems | 2015 | Y | N | N |
| 7 | Xiaohui Wang, Nannan Liu | Applications of Internet of Things in agricultural means of production supply chain management | Journal of Chemical and Pharmaceutical research | 2014 | Y | N | N |
| 8 | Wei Liu, Zhijun Jao | Study of IoT based architecture of logistics service supply chain | International Journal of Grid and Distributed computing | 2014 | Y | N | N |
| 9 | Tijun fan, Feng Tao, Sheng Deng, Shuxia Li | Impact of RFID Technology on supply chain decisions with inventory inaccuracies | International Journal of Production economics | 2014 | N | Y | N |
| 10 | Li Da Xu | Information Architecture for Supply Chain Management | International Journal of Production research | 2011 | Y | N | N |

| Sl No | Author | Paper Name | Publication | Year of Publication | Conceptual Model | Analytical Model | Empirical |
|---|---|---|---|---|---|---|---|
| 11 | Rolf H weber | Internet of Things -Need for new legal environments | Computer Law and Security Review | 2009 | Y | N | N |
| 12 | Chunling Sun | Application of RFID Technology for Logistics on internet of Things | AASRI Conference on Computational Intelligence and Bioinformatics | 2012 | Y | N | N |
| 13 | Christian Decker, Martin Berchtold, Leonardo | Cost benefit model for smart items in the supply chain | IOT'08 Proceedings of the 1st international conference on The internet of things | 2008 | N | Y | N |
| 14 | Duncan McFralane | The Impact of Automatic identification on Supply Chain operation | International Journal of Logistics Management | 2003 | Y | N | N |
| 15 | Eleonora Borgia | The internet of Things Vision: Key features, applications and open issues | Computer Communications | 2014 | Y | N | N |
| 16 | C.N.Verdouw, A.J.M Beulens, J.G.A.J Van der dorst | Virtualisation of floricultural supply chain: a review from an internet of things perspective | Computers and Electronics in Agriculture | 2013 | Y | N | N |
| 17 | Frederic Thiesse, Thomas Buckel' | A comparison of RFID-based shelf replenishment policies in retail stores under sub-optimal read rates | Int. journal of Production economics | 2015 | N | Y | N |
| 18 | Andriana G Dimakopoulou, Katerina C Pramatari, Andrianos E Tsekrekos | Applying Real Options to IT Investment evaluation: The case of radio frequency identification(RFID) technology in the supply chain | Int. journal of Production economics | 2014 | Y | Y | N |
| 19 | Ti-Jun Fan, Xiang-Yun Chang, Chun-Hua Gu, Jian-Jun Yi, Sheng Deng | Benefits of RFID technology for reducing inventory shrinkage | Int. journal of Production economics | 2014 | N | Y | N |
| 20 | Xian Yi Chen, Zhi-Gang Jin | Research on key technology and applications for Internet of Things | International Conference on Medical Physics and Biomedical Engineering | 2012 | Y | N | N |

| Sl No | Author | Paper Name | Publication | Year of Publication | Conceptual Model | Analytical Model | Empirical |
|---|---|---|---|---|---|---|---|
| 21 | Zheng Mingxiu, Fu Chunchan | The application used RFID in third party logistics | International Conference on Solid State Devices and Materials Science | 2012 | Y | N | N |
| 22 | Andrzej Magruk | The Internet of Things as the future technological trend of the innovative development of logistics | Research in logistics and Production | 2016 | Y | N | N |
| 23 | Andrea Caputo, Giacomo Marzi, Massimilano M pellegrini | The Internet of things in Manufacturing innovation process: Development and application of a conceptual framework | Business Process Management Journal | 2016 | Y | N | N |
| 24 | Onder Ondemir, Surendra M. Gupta | quality management in product recovery using Internet of Things: an optimization approach | Computers in Industry | 2014 | Y | Y | N |
| 25 | Karol Furdik, Ferry Parmudianto, Matts Ahlsen,Peter rosengren, Peeter Kool et all | Food Traceability chain supported by ebbits IoT middleware | Springer Book chapter: "Dynamic in Logistics" | 2014 | Y | N | N |
| 26 | Zheng Mingxiu, Fu Chunchang, Yang Minggen | The Application used RFID in Third Party Logistics | International Conference on Solid State Devices and Materials Science | 2012 | Y | N | N |
| 27 | Alexandros Kalokxylos, J Wolfert, Tim Verwaart, Carlos Maestre Terol, Christofer Brewster, Harald Sundmaker | The use of future internet technologies in the agriculture and food sectors: Integrating the supply chain | 6th International Conference on Information and Communication Technologies in Agriculture, Food and Environment | 2013 | Y | N | N |
| 28 | Li Zhou, Alaing Y.L Choong, Eric W.T.Ngai | Supply Chain Management in the era of internet of things | International Journal of Production Economics | 2015 | N | N | N |
| 29 | C.N.Verdouw, A.J.M Beulens, J.Wolfert, A.Rialland | Virtualization of Food Supply Chain with internet of Things | Journal of Food Engineering | 2016 | Y | N | N |
| 30 | Alain Yee-Loong Chong, Martin. J. Liu, Jun Luo, Ooi Keng-Boon | Predicting RFID adoption in healthcare supply chain from the perspectives of users | International Journal of Production Economics | 2015 | N | N | Y |

| Sl No | Author | Paper Name | Publication | Year of Publication | Conceptual Model | Analytical Model | Empirical |
|---|---|---|---|---|---|---|---|
| 31 | Guido L.Geerts, Daniel E.O'Lerry | A supply chain of things The EAGLET ontology for highly visible supply chains | Decision Support Systems | 2014 | Y | N | N |
| 32 | Bill Karakostas | A DNS Architecture for the Internet of Things A Case Study in Transport Logistics | The 4th International Conference on Ambient Systems, Networks and Technologies | 2013 | Y | N | N |
| 33 | Dimitris Kiritsis | Closed loop PLM for intelligent products in the era of the Internet of things | Computer Aided Design | 2011 | Y | N | N |
| 34 | Paul J.Reaidy, Anagappa Gunasekaran, Alain Spalanjani | Bottom up approach based on Internet of Things for order fulfilment in a collaborative warehousing environment | International Journal of Production Economics | 2015 | Y | Y | N |
| 35 | Shiang Jong Chuu | An investment evaluation of supply chain RFID technologies: A group decision making model with multiple information sources | Knowledge Based System | 2014 | N | Y | N |
| 36 | Seungjae Shin, Burak Eksiglu | An empirical study of RFID productivity in the US retail supply chain | International Journal of Production Economics | 2015 | N | Y | N |
| 37 | Ilias P. Vlachos | A hierarchical model of the impact of RFID practices on retail supply chain performance | Expert Systems with Applications | 2014 | N | N | Y |
| 38 | James C.Chen, Chen-Huan Cheng, PoTsang B Huang | Supply chain management with lean production and RFID application A case study | Expert Systems with Applications | 2013 | Y | Y | N |
| 39 | Tae Hong Shin, Sangyoun Chin, Su-Won Yoon, Soon-Wook Kwon | A service oriented integrated information framework for RFID/ WSN based intelligent construction supply chain management | Automation in Construction | 2011 | Y | N | N |
| 40 | Juan Jose Nativi, Seokcheon Lee | Analytical model of adoption of item level RFID in a two echelon supply chain with shelf space and price dependent demand | Decision Support System | 2011 | N | Y | N |

| Sl No | Author | Paper Name | Publication | Year of Publication | Conceptual Model | Analytical Model | Empirical |
|---|---|---|---|---|---|---|---|
| 41 | Alesandro S. martinez Sala, Esteban Egea Lopez, Felip Garcia-sanchez, Joan-Garcia Haro | Tracking of Returnable Packaging and Transport Units with active RFID in the grocery supply chain | Computers in Industry | 2009 | Y | N | N |
| 42 | S-J Wang, W-L Wang, C.-T. Huang, S.-C. Chen | Improving inventory effectiveness in RFID enabled global supply chain with Grey forecasting model | The Journal of Strategic Information Systems | 2011 | N | Y | N |
| 43 | Alp Ustundag, Mehmat Tanyas | The impacts of Radio Frequency Identification RFID technology on supply chain costs | Transportation Research Part E | 2009 | N | Y | N |
| 44 | Jerrel Leung, Waiman Cheung, Sung Chi Chu | Aligning RFID applications with supply chain strategies | Information and Management | 2014 | Y | N | N |
| 45 | Hongyan Dai, Mitchell M. Tseng | The impacts of RFID implementation on reducing inventory inaccuracy in a multi stage supply chain | International Journal of Production Economics | 2012 | N | Y | N |
| 46 | G Demiralp, G. Guven, E. Ergen | Analyzing the benefits of RFID technology for cost sharing in-construction supply chains: A case study on prefabricated precast components | Automation in Construction | 2012 | Y | N | N |
| 47 | Elenora Bottani,Antonio Rizzi | Economical assessment of the impact of RFID technology and EPC system on the fast moving consumer goods supply chain | International Journal of Production Economics | 2008 | N | N | Y |
| 48 | Eric W.T Ngai, Bernard K.S.Cheung, S.S.Lam, C.T Sg | RFID value in aircraft parts supply chains A case study | International Journal of Production Economics | 2014 | N | Y | N |
| 49 | Damianos Chatziantoniou, Katerina Pramatari, Yannis Sotiropoulos | Supporting real time supply chain decisions based on RFID data streams | Journal of Systems and Software | 2011 | Y | N | N |
| 50 | Martin Grunowa, Selwyn Piramuthu | RFID in highly perishable food supply chains Remaining shelf life to supplant expiry date | International Journal of Production Economics | 2013 | N | Y | N |

# Chapter 2
# User Acceptance of IoT Applications in Retail Industry

**M. S. Balaji**
*University of Nottingham – Ningbo, China*

**Aditi Sengupta**
*IBS Hyderabad, India*

**Sanjit Kumar Roy**
*University of Western Australia, Australia*

**Alain Chong**
*University of Nottingham – Ningbo, China*

## ABSTRACT

*With the rapid advancements in the internet technology, many retailers are embracing internet of things technology to enhance customer experience and improve efficiency. Specifically, many customer-facing IoT technologies such as augmented reality, smart shopping carts, smart displays, and RFID tags are expected to change the way customers experience retailing shopping. Drawing on the technology acceptance model, trust perspective, task-technology fit, and organizational reputation perspective, this study examines the customer adoption of IoT applications in retail setting. Responses collected from 289 actual retail shoppers were analyzed using structural equation modeling. Results reveal that perceived usefulness, perceived ease of use, task-technology fit, retailer reputation, and initial trust are significant predictors of customer attitude and intentions to use IoT in retail stores. The study findings have key implications for academicians and retailers in improving customer acceptance and in delivering superior customer experience.*

## INTRODUCTION

The advancements in information technology is rapidly transforming the retail industry. Especially, the emergence of internet of things (IoT) is providing strategic opportunities for retailers to engage customers and transform their shopping experience. IoT is a novel technology that involves delivery of retail services to users through smart or intelligent objects or devices. IoT is considered as a distinct step in the evolution of the retail industry as it combines the physical and virtual dimensions of retail environment to create a seamless and personalized shopping experience tailored to the customer's need (CBR, 2016). It is argued that the implementation of IoT in the retail industry is expected to bring out substantial increase in efficiencies for retailers and customers in terms of cost reduction, time savings,

DOI: 10.4018/978-1-5225-2104-4.ch002

and increased accessibilities. Moreover, IoT enhances value through interconnectedness and networking, augmented intelligence, and augmented behavior (Kambies et al., 2016). According to Gartner (2015), IoT is identified as one of the top strategic technology trends that is expected to reshape retail opportunities through 2020. Some of the notable applications of IoT in retail industry are Radio Frequency Identification (RFID) tagged products, smart shopping carts, near field communication systems, smart shopping carts, and virtual mirrors etc. Given the rapid growth of IoT in the retail industry, it is critical for academicians and retailers to understand the adoption process.

The technology acceptance model (TAM; Davis, 1989) provides one means by which customer acceptance of new technology can be investigated. TAM is a robust yet parsimonious model which is widely used to understand the role of technology beliefs in customer attitude and intentions to use new technology. Although TAM is a useful model for explaining user acceptance, it is argued that there is a need to integrate it with other constructs that are related to the contextual factors and factors from other theories (King & He, 2006). As IoT is still in its early stages of implementation, this study considers initial trust (individual characteristic), retailer reputation (organizational characteristic), and task-technology fit (task characteristic) along with TAM technology beliefs to investigate customer adoption of IoT in a retail context. Since customers have limited experience and information with IoT technology, this study considers initial trust as the expectations of the user with the IoT technology (Li, Hess, & Valacich, 2008). Similarly, retailer reputation can act as a cue or signal for consumers to evaluate the quality of services offered by the retailer (Morgan-Thomas & Veloutsou, 2013). Finally, task-technology fit suggests that a fit between the technology features and task requirements might motivate customers to adopt new technology (Goodhue & Thompson, 1995). As there is limited research in regards to customer acceptance of IoT technology in the retail industry, this study proposes and examines an integrated model of customer acceptance of IoT products in retail stores based on technology acceptance model (Davis, 1989), task-technology perspective (Goodhue & Thompson, 1995), initial trust perspective (Li, Hess, & Valacich, 2008), and retailer reputation (Morgan-Thomas & Veloutsou, 2013). Specifically, this study centered on the following research questions:

- What are the predictors of adoption intentions of IoT technology in retail stores? Specifically, which factors (perceived usefulness, perceived ease of use, task-technology fit, initial trust, and retailer reputation) explain the adoption intentions of IoT technology in retail stores?

The rest of the article is structured as follows. The next section presents the background on internet of things, retail IoT, technology acceptance model, initial trust perspective, task-technology fit, and retailer reputation. The research framework and hypothesis development are presented in section 3. The methodology, results, and discussion of results follow, and finally conclusion and limitations of the study are presented in the last section.

## THEORETICAL BACKGROUND

### Internet of Things

The expression 'internet of things' first coined by Kevin Ashton in 1999 refers to uniquely identifiable objects that are connected with radio-frequency identification (RFID) technology. The European Centre of Excellence for AIDC (Clark, 2008) defines internet of things as "a global network infrastructure, linking physical and virtual objects through exploitation of data capture and communications capabilities." According to Ferber (2013) internet of things is a "dramatic development in the internet's function: the fact that, even more than among people, it now enables communication among physical objects." While the many definitions of IoT that have been proposed differ somewhat, they all imply that the concept of IoT involves a dynamic and global network of interconnected objects with sensing, communicating, networking, and processing capabilities that links physical and virtual worlds (Hoffman & Novak, 2015; Li et al., 2015; Yang, Yang, & Plotnick, 2013).

According to the extant literature, IoT is a complex system that can be realized from the convergence of three perspectives namely internet-oriented, semantic-oriented, and objects-oriented (Atzori, Iera & Morabito, 2010; Gubbi et al., 2013). The internet-oriented perspective refers to the connectivity and infrastructure aspects resulting from the internet and web of things. The objects-oriented perspective consists of embedded devices or things such as sensors and actuators which respond to stimuli from the environment (Aggarwal, Ashish, & Sheth, 2013). These include RFID, near fields communication (NFC), unique identifiers, and wireless identification and sensing platforms. The semantic-oriented perspective involves the processing, analytics, and management of massive data generated by smart objects. Thus, IoT represents an integrated system of systems with technology, communication and networking, and intelligence level capabilities that facilitate smart interactions between people and objects to exchange information and knowledge for new value creation to customers, firms, and citizens (Zorzi et al., 2010).

Want, Schilit, and Jenson (2015) state that IoT provides interconnectedness among objects anytime and anywhere thereby allowing people to take advantage of the Internet in all aspects of daily life. Thus, IoT involves networking of everyday objects such that internet extends into the real world. In fact, many consider IoT as the next generation of information and communication technology (Uckelmann, Harrison, & Michahelles, 2011; Zorzi et al., 2010). The European Commission states that IoT is an integrated part of the future internet (Clark, 2008). Given the enormous opportunities of IoT, there has been a strong momentum for its implementation across the world in numerous applications such as in the areas of supply chain and logistics, healthcare, retail, environment and energy, transportation, building management, and public services (Hernández-Muñoz et al., 2011; Xu, 2011; Zhou, Liu, & Wang, 2012; Amendola et al., 2014; Li et al., 2015; Evanschitzky et al., 2015).

According to Iansiti and Lakhani (2014) adopting IoT in the modern economy will allow firms to achieve competitive advantage. Specifically, by connecting and integrating with other devices and networks, IoT can provide a more seamless and personalized experience for its users. It can help firms gain better insights into the value creation processes. This allows the firms to form new and sustainable relationship with the customers as well as adopt new marketing strategies and competencies (Wang, Li, & Li, 2013). The data generated by IoT can be used by firms to create a favorable brand image and engage in effective communication strategies (Porter & Heppelmann, 2014). Thus, IoT can have a profound impact on firms' marketing strategy and business performance.

## IoT in the Retail Industry

The retail industry is under increasing pressure from globalization and competition to achieve better performance (Reinartz et al., 2011). In order to sustain competitive advantage and to improve the operational and marketing efficiency, the retail industry is pushing and being pushed to implement new technologies (Pantano & Timmermans, 2014). With the rapid advancements in internet technology, many retailers view IoT as a potential basis for achieving sustainable competitive advantage and long-term profitability. According to a recent report, investments in IoT in the retail industry is estimated to grow 20 percent annually to US$36 billion by 2020 (Research and Markets, 2015). McKinsey predicts that the economic impact of IoT in the retail industry to be between US$0.4 - 1.2 trillion a year by 2025 (Manyika & Chui, 2015). Another report by Juniper Research predicts that much of the IoT investments in the retail sector are directed towards catering to the needs and preferences of individual customers (Girish, 2016). These reports indicate a rapid diffusion of IoT in the retail industry.

The concept of IoT in the retail setting involves smart networked objects or devices that are tagged with unique object identifiers such as RFID that can identify and provide information through smart devices such as mobile phones or tablets. The applications of IoT in the retail industry are enormous ranging from supply chain and logistics, pricing, inventory management, product display and packaging, product information and advertising, shopping aisles and shelf management, customer assistance and checkout, and virtual shopping stores (Bardaki, Kourouthanassis, & Pramatari, 2012; Papagiannidis et al., 2013; Choi, Yang, Yang, & Cheung, 2015). Implementation of IoT can help retailers manage their stocks more efficiently, get more accurate and relevant information about customers and products, and assist in determining an appropriate retail strategy (Xie and Allen, 2013). In other words, IoT can provide a vastly improved retail ecosystem that can enhance the retailers' ability to create value, competitiveness, and business performance.

IoT offers retailers opportunities in three critical areas, namely supply chain and logistics, new channels and revenue management, and customer experience (Gregory, 2015). Much of the prior research have centered on the first two areas in improving efficiencies that result in lower costs (Thiesse, Al-Kassab, & Fleisch, 2009; Ng, 2010). However, IoT can also have a tremendous impact on the way in which customers shop at retail stores. Unlike the traditional retail technologies that provide static information, IoT can expand the opportunities for multiple interactions between the retailer and the customer. Also, it can offer real-time and bidirectional interaction with customers. IoT can provide information about the products/services, ingredients, process, and embedded intelligence about the customer needs. It can anticipate customer needs, operate autonomously, proactively approach customers, and provide comprehensive services tailored to the customer needs. By connecting and networking with other devices, IoT allows convergence and connectedness which leads to a more seamless and personalized retail shopping experience for customers (Pantano & Timmermans, 2014). Thus, IoT allows retailers to provide their customers with innovative, interactive, and intelligent retail shopping experience.

Many retailers are keen to utilise the significant opportunities offered by IoT. For example, Carrefour is using iBeacons to track customers' retail journey. Tesco is using virtual stores to improve the customer experience. Ikea uses augmented reality to help customers visualize how furniture could look inside their houses. McDonalds in Australia uses smart interactive self-service kiosks to aid customers build their burgers and meals. The jewellery retailer, BaubleBar, uses interactive displays with sensors and unique identifiers to provide additional information about its products. In addition, retailers such as Walmart are trialling the use of smart carts for customers in retail stores (Ryan, 2016). Because of the potential benefits it offers, IoT is considered as a novel innovation and rapidly gaining significant ground in the retail industry.

## Customer-Facing IoT Technology in the Retail Industry

Many customer-facing IoT technologies have being introduced in the retail industry. These include in-store technology, systems based on smart phones such as apps, and hybrids that consists of both in-store and smart phone systems. Some of the examples of customer-facing IoT retail technologies include smart shopping carts, augmented reality, interactive displays and mirrors, RFID tags, NFC-based systems, smart kiosks, and others. Smart shopping carts are shopping carts or trolleys attached with a tablet. The smart shopping carts are connected to the wireless technology which can provide customers information related to the products and services available in the retail store (Ryan, 2016). It can retrieve and store information in real-time, answer queries, and enable check-out without waiting in the line. Further, the smart shopping cart can be synced to the consumers' smart phone through which it can provide real-time updates and information on the promotion of products, price, coupon availability, in-store location of the product, and information on complementary products. One example of this is the Shanghai retailer Lotus supermarket whose smart shopping carts provide easy access to product information and a personalized shopping experience (Volpe, 2011).

Augmented reality is an emerging type of customer-facing IoT technology in the retail industry. With augmented reality, the view of the real world can be superimposed with virtual objects (Danado et al., 2003). Augmented reality integrates digital content in the real environment thereby providing realistic and immersive experience for users. It offers natural and real-time interactions through its seamless integration of real and digital worlds (Akçayır et al., 2016). For example, Ikea augmented reality smart phone application allows users to visualize what certain furniture could look inside their homes. Another example is De Beers augmented tool which lets users to virtually try on jewelry. By augmenting the real environment, augmented reality can enhance the customers' external surroundings and improve their shopping experience (Brandpipe, 2015).

Smart mirrors are life-sized interactive mirrors with touch-based interface or gestures. It overlays the shopper's image with virtual cloths or accessories that are available with the retailer (Kim et al., 2016). The smart mirror creates avatars of the shoppers wearing the various clothes and accessories which can be shared with friends on social media, ask feedback for, and make in-store purchase. Further, it can store previous outfit avatars of the shopper to compare with other outfits and accessories (Woollaston, 2015). For example, Ray-Ban uses virtual mirror to allow customers try-on different models of sunglasses. Another example is Uniqlo's magic mirror which allows customers to try-out different outfits, colors, and projects.

Smart displays are in-store based virtual walls that display the various products and services available in the retail store. Customers can access the product information, customer reviews, and can order the product. For example, Adidas virtual footwear wall enable 3D view of the footwear products along with customer reviews (Tischler, 2011). While IoT technology is being rapidly introduced by the retailers around the world, there have been reports about customer frustration and difficulties with understanding, comprehending and coping with them (Lee & Yang, 2013; Bhattacharya, 2015). Since successful implementation of IoT depends on customer adoption and continued use, there is a need to better understand the factors that determine customer adoption of IoT in retail industry.

## Technology Acceptance Model

The technology acceptance model (TAM) is used in this study to understand the customer adoption of IoT technology in the retail industry. The TAM is developed by Davis (1989) based on the theory of reasoned action (Ajzen & Fishbein, 1980) and the theory of planned behavior (Ajzen, 1985) to understand user adoption of new information system in the workplace. Later, this was extended to understand the adoption of new technologies in various contexts such as online shopping, internet banking, mobile banking, self-service technology, smart-card payment system, online education, mobile computing and others (Beldona, Morrison, & O'Leary, 2005; Chong et al., 2010; Upadhyay & Jahanyan, 2016).

According to TAM, customer adoption of new technology is driven by two beliefs namely perceived ease of use and perceived usefulness (Davis, 1989). Perceived usefulness refers to the degree to which a user believes that using the new technology would enhance his or her performance. Perceived ease of use is defined as the extent to which a user believes that using new technology would involve little effort. According to the technology acceptance model, perceived ease of use and perceived usefulness would influence the user' attitude and intentions towards the new technology which would lead to its actual use (Davis, 1989). In addition to perceived ease of use and perceived usefulness, various external variables are considered to influence user beliefs about adoption of new technology (Davis, 1989).

## Initial Trust Perspective

Trust refers to an individual's expectation about other party's behavior. Due to greater uncertainty associated with new technology (Pavlou, 2003), trust has received considerable attention in technology adoption context. Trust can be divided into initial trust and continuance trust. Initial trust refers to trust in a new situation where the user does not yet have significant information or experience with the new technology (Li, Hess, & Valacich, 2008). Continuance trust, on the other hand, is the expectations of the new technology following the user's direct experience (Carter & Weerakkody, 2008).

As initial trust reflects the willingness of an individual to take risk and trial the technology, it is considered to play a significant role in customer acceptance of IoT technology in a retail context. Prior research studies suggest that initial trust has an influential role in adoption of new technology. For example, Kim and Prabhakar (2004) show that initial trust in the electronic channel positively influences adoption of internet banking. Johnson, Bardhi, and Dunn (2008) find that trust in the technology leads to greater satisfaction with self-service technology. Zhou (2014) demonstrate that initial trust significantly impacts the performance expectancy and usage intentions of mobile payment. In another study, Gao and Waechter (2015) show that initial trust influences customer adoption of mobile payment system. As lack of trust is considered to be a deterrent to user's technology acceptance, this study considers the role of initial trust along with TAM in examining the customer adoption of IoT technology in a retail setting.

## Task-Technology Fit

Task-technology fit (TTF) refers to the fit between the task and technology. Goodhue and Thompson (1995) propose that an information technology will have a positive impact on individual performance if "the technology must be utilized, and the technology must be a good fit with the tasks it supports" (p. 213). Prior research measured TTF as the extent to which the technology meets the requirements of the user's task and supports them in effectively performing the tasks. According to TTF, customer acceptance depends on how well the new technology fits with the task requirements (Dishaw & Strong, 1999). In other words, the extent to which IoT technology fits with the retail shopping tasks would determine its successful adoption. Greater fit is obtained when IoT technology provides features and supports the requirements of retail shopping tasks. Thus, TTF represents the correspondence between functionality of the IoT technology and retail shopping task requests.

Extant literature reveals that TTF determines customers' expectations of the task performance using the new technology. For example, Lu and Yang (2014) show that task characteristics and technology characteristics jointly determine users' perception of TTF and intentions to use social networking site. Yang, Kang, Oh, and Kim (2013) demonstrate that TTF results in information system use and task performance. In another study, Chen and Huang (2016) show that perceived performance risk and privacy risk moderate the effect of TTF on purchase intentions. In the context of IoT technology, Kim, Park, Ahn, and Rho (2015) find that fit between RFID technology and users' tasks results in greater individual performance. This study extends TAM model to include TTF in examining the adoption of IoT technology. While TAM is based on the user's beliefs towards the new technology, TTF is based on the rational expectations that using the new technology provides benefits such as improved task performance. Since both beliefs and expected consequences influence adoption of new technology (Klopping & McKinney, 2004), it is argued that combining TTF and TAM would provide a better understanding of the customer adoption and use of IoT in retail setting.

## Retailer Reputation

Retailer reputation refers to the overall evaluation of the customers of the retailer's capabilities, intentions, and desirability (Morgan-Thomas & Veloutsou, 2013). According to Chang et al. (2015) organizational reputation is defined as "how an organization is perceived by customers who receive informational signals from companies, the media and other people that form their beliefs, attitudes, and impressions about the company" (p. 50). Thus, retailer reputation is the customers' overall assessment of the retailers' expertise in offering products, services and experiences. This assessment is based on the customers' direct experience with the retailers, as well as, indirect experiences based on communication or information about the retailers' actions (Yang, 2007). In this study, retailer reputation is considered as an organizational characteristic facilitating customer adoption of IoT technology. Prior studies propose that firms with a higher level of reputation enhances customer trustworthiness which leads to a more favorable attitude and behavior towards the retailer (Ou, Abratt, & Dion, 2006). Further, retailer reputation can act as a signal or cue for customers regarding the quality of retail services offered by IoT technology. Since, reputation of the retailers assists in establishing a favorable store image and perception of better customer retail services (Deb & Chaudhuri, 2014), this study examines the role of retailers' reputation in customer adoption of IoT technology.

# HYPOTHESES DEVELOPMENT

The research model presented in Figure 1 proposes that technological beliefs of perceived usefulness, perceived ease of use, initial trust, retailer reputation, and task-technology fit to influence customer attitude, which in turn, affects the intentions to use IoT technology in retail stores.

*Figure 1. Conceptual framework of this study*

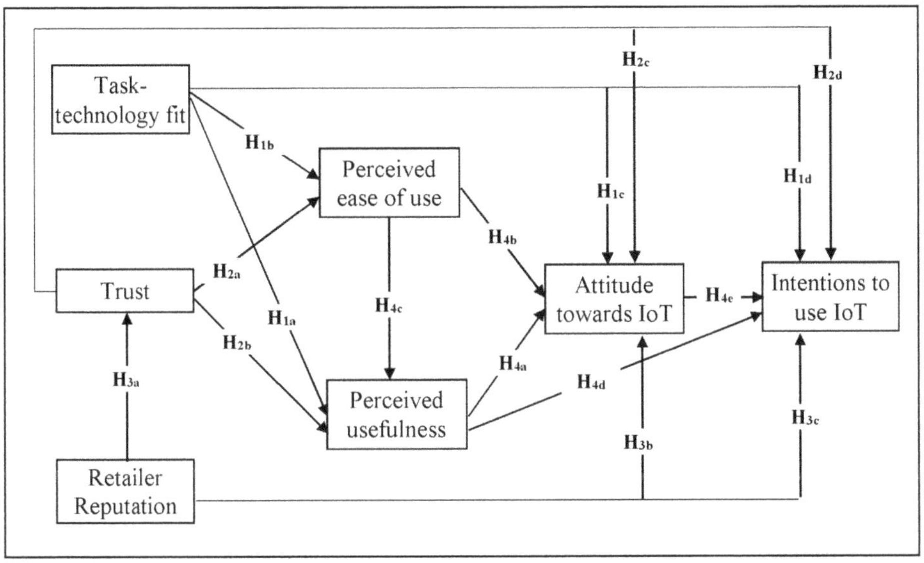


This research model integrates the theory of technology acceptance model (Davis, 1989), initial trust perspective (Carter & Weerakkody, 2008), task-technology fit (Goodhue & Thompson, 1995), and retailer reputation (organizational characteristic; Morgan-Thomas & Veloutsou, 2013) in developing an integrated model of customer acceptance of IoT technology in retail setting. Although TAM is a useful model to understand customer acceptance of IoT there has been call to integrate it by including human, organizational, technology, and social variables (Legris, Ingham, & Collerette, 2003; King & He, 2006). Thus, this study develops an integrated customer IoT acceptance model based on the technology beliefs (perceived usefulness and perceived ease of use), task characteristics (task-technology fit), individual characteristics (initial trust), and organizational characteristics (retailer reputation).

Prior research studies have found that TTF to be significant determinant of new technology adoption. For example, Dishaw and Strong (1999) show that task-technology fit to have a strong effect on perceived ease of use and actual tool use. Zhou, Lu and Wang (2010) demonstrate that TTF positively influences both user intentions and performance expectancy of mobile banking. In the context of online auction, Chang (2010) show that fit between online auction task and agent technology positively impacts perceived ease of use and usefulness of the website. Similarly, Yen et al. (2010) show TTF to significantly influence behavioral intentions. In the context of revolutionary technology-driven products, Park et al. (2015) find that customers' initial perception of TTF to positively influence their perception of ease of using the technology and usefulness of technology with task performance. These studies suggest that when consumers perceive greater fit between the IoT technology and shopping task, they are more likely to perceive as usefulness and ease to use. This leads to positive attitude and intentions to use IoT in retail stores. Thus, the following hypothesis are proposed:

**$H_{1a}$:** TTF has a direct effect on perceived usefulness of IoT in retail stores.
**$H_{1b}$:** TTF has a direct effect on perceived ease of use of IoT in retail stores.
**$H_{1c}$:** TTF has a direct effect on attitude towards IoT in retail stores.

**$H_{1d}$:** TTF has a direct effect on intentions to use IoT in retail stores.

Various studies have integrated TAM with initial trust perspective in examining technology adoption. For example, Gefen, Karahanna, and Straub (2003) show that trust resulting from calculative, knowledge, and institutional factors significant influences perceived usefulness and intended use of online shopping. Similarly, Chen and Barnes (2007) demonstrate that initial trust is positively related to online purchase intentions. Pavlou (2003) use initial trust and TAM to understand customer acceptance of electronic commerce. The author argue that trust reduces the need for customers to understand and control the electronic transaction process and this facilitates its use. In their study, initial trust was found to positively affect perceived ease of use, perceived usefulness, and intentions to transact. In the context of retail mobile payments, Slade et al. (2015) show that trust reduces perceived risk which in turn affects customers' intentions to use. Based on the above discussion, the following hypothesis are proposed:

**$H_{2a}$:** Initial trust has a direct effect on perceived usefulness of IoT in retail stores.
**$H_{2b}$:** Initial trust has a direct effect on perceived ease of use of IoT in retail stores.
**$H_{2c}$:** Initial trust has a direct effect on attitude towards IoT in retail stores.
**$H_{2d}$:** Initial trust has a direct effect on intentions to use IoT in retail stores.

In the present study, the retailer reputation, an organizational characteristic is considered to play a significant role in the customer adoption of IoT technology in retail stores. Recent studies show that organizational factors influence new technology acceptance. For example, Wang and Li (2012) show that brand equity positively influences customer acceptance of mobile services. Also retailer reputation can reduce perceived risk and enhance trust, and this increases the intentions to adoption new technology (De Ruyter, Wetzels, & Kleijnen, 2001). Beck and Kenning (2015) find that retail store image enhances customer perception of trustworthiness and purchase intentions of new FMCG products. Beldad et al. (2012) propose that organizational reputation cultivates trust and this increases the online transaction. Moreover, retailer reputation acts as trust cue and this leads to favorable attitude and use of IoT in retail stores. Based on the above discussion, the following hypothesis are proposed:

**$H_{3a}$:** Retailer reputation has a direct effect on initial trust towards IoT.
**$H_{3b}$:** Retailer reputation has a direct effect on attitude towards IoT in retail stores.
**$H_{3c}$:** Retailer reputation has a direct effect on intentions to use IoT in retail stores.

The technology acceptance model (Davis, 1989) has been widely used to determine the motivations or willingness of customers to adopt new technology. The TAM is a parsimonious and robust model which suggests that customers' attitude and behavioral intentions of a new technology is significantly driven by two determinants namely perceived usefulness and perceived ease of use of the new technology (Davis, 1989). Specifically, Davis (1989) propose that perceived usefulness and perceived ease of use indirectly influences behavioral intentions through attitude, perceived ease of use indirectly affects attitude through perceived usefulness, and perceived usefulness to directly influence behavioral intentions.

Ha and Stoel (2009) find that perceived ease of use and perceived useful are key determinants of successful adoption of online shopping. More recently, Dutot (2015) found that both perceived usefulness and ease of use directly influence intentions to use NFC. In the context of fashion retailing, Kim et al. (2016) found that perceived usefulness and perceived enjoyment are significant factors determining the adoption of smart in-store technology such as RFID music tags, virtual mirror, and interactive dressing rooms. The findings show that both perceived usefulness and perceived ease of use directly influence attitude which affects behavioral intentions. Additionally, perceived ease of use indirectly affects attitude through perceived usefulness of SRT and perceived usefulness directly impacts behavioral intentions. For consistency and comparison with other studies on new technology acceptance, the following hypotheses are presented for testing:

**$H_{4a}$:** Perceived usefulness has a direct effect on attitude towards IoT in retail stores.
**$H_{4b}$:** Perceived usefulness has a direct effect on intentions to use IoT in retail stores.
**$H_{4c}$:** Perceived ease of use has a direct effect on attitude towards IoT in retail stores.
**$H_{4d}$:** Perceived ease of use has a direct effect on perceived usefulness of IoT in retail stores.
**$H_{4e}$:** Attitude has a direct effect on intentions to use IoT in retail stores.

## METHOD

### Sample and Procedure

A pilot test was carried out with a sample of thirty-five students who provided feedback on readability and clarity as well as ease of completion of the questionnaire. Based on suggestions, the survey instrument was revised to capture accurately the context of IoT technology in the retail setting. Upon the pilot testing, a web-based survey using the data collection software Qualtrics was used to collect responses from actual retail shoppers in Australia. The survey questionnaire introduced the concept of IoT in retail stores and the participants were instructed to rate the questionnaire based on their evaluation of IoT technologies in retail setting. Eventually, the sample consists of 289 usable responses of which 48 percent were male and 52 percent were female. 57.4 percent were in the age group of 21 - 35 years of age and 52 percent had bachelors' degree or higher level of education. Based on Soper (2014) sample size calculator, the total number of responses required for model structure was found to be sufficient. The t-tests did not reveal significant difference in the study constructs for the early and late response groups, suggesting that non-response bias is not a problem in this study.

### Measurement

Task-technology fit was measured using three-item scale from Klopping and McKinney (2004). Retailer reputation was operationalized using six-item scale from Bao, Bao, and Sheng (2011). Perceived initial Trust was measured using four-item scale from Li, Jiang and Wu (2014). Perceived usefulness and ease of use were measured using four-item scales adapted from Venkatesh and Davis (2000). Attitude towards IoT was measured using a three-item scale adapted from Weijters et al. (2007) and intentions to use was measured using three-item scale from Gao and Bai (2014). Responses to each of these perceptual items were elicited on seven-point scales ranging from = strongly disagree to7 = strongly agree.

## RESULTS

### Measurement Model

The set of 26 items comprising measures of study constructs were initially subjected to exploratory factor analysis (principal component) with varimax rotation. This analysis yielded an eight-factor solution based on the eigenvalue criterion. The factors collectively accounted for 76.66 percent of the variance in item scores. The first factor explained 36.66 percent variance, which suggests that common method bias may not be a problem.

After eliminating one item each of usefulness and trust, and two items of retailer reputation construct due to higher cross-loading, the remaining 22 items were re-analyzed and a seven-factor solution emerged with item loading on respective factors consistent with this study's theoretical expectation. Total variance explained by the seven-factor solution was 82 percent. The first factor explained 40 percent of the variance, which suggests that common method bias may not be a problem (Podsakoff et al., 2003). The measures were also subjected to confirmatory factor analysis using AMOS 20. The measurement model fit well to the data with $\chi^2(186) = 347.3$; GFI = 0.90; CFI = 0.96; NFI = 0.93; RMSEA = 0.05. Table1 presents scale items and the internal consistency reliabilities (Cronbach's Alpha) of the measures. The reliabilities ranged from .80 to .94. Table 1 also shows that the overwhelming majority of the standardized item loadings are well above 0.70 suggesting strong reliability at the item level as well.

The measures were further examined for potential common method variance. Since common method variance is one of the most cited concerns in the self-reported surveys, common method factor approach was used to control for the method bias (Podsakoff *et al.* 2003). In this study Facebook use intensity, an unrelated factor is used as a method factor. As shown in Table 1, the fit statistics indicated reasonable fit to the data in both the models (with method factor and without method factor). However, the factor loadings and average variance extracted decreased considerably in the model with method factor, the chi-square statistic did not show any significant improvement in the model with method factor. This suggests that common method variance is not a potential source of error in the measurement model.

Table 2 provides correlations, means and standard deviations of the study constructs. Table 2 also provides average variance extracted and shared variance values for each underlying construct. All average variances extracted are above the desirable cut-off value of 0.50 (Fornell and Larcker, 1981) and are consistently larger than the shared variance between the corresponding pair of constructs. The results collectively provide evidence of convergent and discriminant validity.

### Structural Model

To test the theoretical linkages in Figure 1, composite scale scores for each construct were used as input to AMOS 20. The model, including all the proposed direct relationships was estimated via path analysis. Table 3 shows that the model fits the data well (Model fit: $\chi^2_{34} = 118.5$; GFI = 0.93; CFI = 0.91; NFI = 0.87; RMSEA = 0.08).

$H_1$ states that task technology fit has direct positive impact on (a) perceived usefulness, (b) perceived ease of use, (c) attitude and (d) intentions to use. As presented in Table 3, task-technology fit has positive and significant effect on perceived usefulness ($\beta = 0.63$, $p < 0.01$), ease of use ($\beta = 0.14$, $p < 0.05$), attitude ($\beta = 0.17$, $p < 0.01$), and intentions to use ($\beta = 0.58$, $p < 0.01$) providing support for $H_{1a}$ through $H_{1d}$.

*Table 1. Measurement and psychometric properties of the scale*

| | Without MF | With MF |
|---|---|---|
| **Constructs and Items** | **Λ** | **Λ** |
| **Task-Technology Fit (TTF) (α= 0.86;** $AVE^{a}=0.69$; $AVE^{b}=0.32$) | | |
| TTF1. The IoT is accurate enough for shopping purpose | 0.77 | 0.42 |
| TTF1. The IoT is accurate enough for shopping purpose | 0.90 | 0.62 |
| TTF1. The IoT is accurate enough for shopping purpose | 0.82 | 0.65 |
| **Retailer Reputation (REP) (α= 0.86;** $AVE^{a}=0.61$; $AVE^{b}=0.55$) | | |
| IMA1. Overall, I have a favorable view of [retail store] | 0.78 | 0.71 |
| IMA2. [Retail store] is a high performing retailer | 0.74 | 0.73 |
| IMA3. [Retail store] is close to my 'ideal' store | 0.82 | 0.77 |
| IMA4. [Retail store] provides good overall service | 0.80 | 0.76 |
| **Initial Trust (TRU) (α= 0.84;** $AVE^{a}=0.72$; $AVE^{b}=0.37$ ) | | |
| TRU1. This retailer appears to be one who would keep promises and commitments | 0.82 | 0.54 |
| TRU2. I believe in the information that this retailer provides me. | 0.88 | 0.68 |
| **Perceived Usefulness (USE) (α= 0.91;** $AVE^{a}=0.76$; $AVE^{b}=0.54$) | | |
| USE1. I do my shopping faster when I use IoT | 0.88 | 0.74 |
| USE2. I spend less time at the store if I use IoT | 0.86 | 0.74 |
| USE3. Shopping is more efficient using IoT) | 0.88 | 0.73 |
| **Ease of Use (EOU) (α= 0.90;** $AVE^{a}=0.71$; $AVE^{b}=0.56$) | | |
| EOU1. Using IoT does not require a lot of my mental effort | 0.76 | 0.66 |
| EOU2. I find IoT to be easy to use | 0.88 | 0.82 |
| EOU3. Using IoT is clear and understandable | 0.86 | 0.79 |
| EOU4. I find it easy to get the IoT to do what I want it to do | 0.88 | 0.71 |
| **Attitude (ATT) (α= 0.94;** $AVE^{a}=0.84$; $AVE^{b}=0.67$) | | |
| How would you describe your attitude towards using IoT in retail stores? | | |
| ATT1. Unfavourable – Favourable | 0.91 | 0.82 |
| ATT2. I dislike it – I like it | 0.93 | 0.84 |
| ATT3. Bad – Good | 0.91 | 0.80 |
| **Intentions to Use (INT) (α= 0.91;** $AVE^{a}=0.71$; $AVE^{b}=0.38$) | | |
| INT1. Given the chance, I intent to use IoT in the future for shopping | 0.82 | 0.61 |
| INT2. I am willing to use IoT for shopping in the near future | 0.82 | 0.56 |
| INT3. I will frequently use IoT in retail stores in the future | 0.90 | 0.67 |

Notes: Model fit (without MF): $\chi^2(186) = 347.3$; GFI = 0.90; CFI = 0.96; NFI = 0.93; RMSEA = 0.05.
Model fit (With MF): $\chi^2(254) = 445.9$; GFI = 0.90; CFI = 0.96; NFI = 0.92; RMSEA = 0.05.
a – without MF; b –with MF
All Λ –values are significant at $p < 0.01$

*Table 2. Correlations, descriptive statistics and convergent and discriminant validity of the measures*

| | TTF | REP | TRU | USE | EOU | ATT | INT |
|---|---|---|---|---|---|---|---|
| **TTF** | ***0.69*** | 0.06 | 0.42 | 0.18 | 0.17 | 0.18 | 0.47 |
| **REP** | 0.24** | ***0.62*** | 0.07 | 0.04 | 0.04 | 0.08 | 0.12 |
| **TRU** | 0.65** | 0.26** | ***0.72*** | 0.14 | 0.11 | 0.16 | 0.41 |
| **USE** | 0.43** | 0.20** | 0.37** | ***0.76*** | 0.39 | 0.32 | 0.20 |
| **EOU** | 0.41** | 0.20** | 0.33** | 0.62** | ***0.72*** | 0.26 | 0.09 |
| **ATT** | 0.42** | 0.28** | 0.40** | 0.57** | 0.51** | ***0.84*** | 0.23 |
| **INT** | 0.69** | 0.35** | 0.64** | 0.45** | 0.31** | 0.48* | ***0.72*** |
| **Mean** | 5.58 | 5.16 | 4.91 | 5.09 | 5.46 | 5.30 | 5.10 |
| **S.D.** | 1.02 | 0.92 | 1.13 | 1.28 | 1.01 | 1.14 | 1.13 |

Notes: The diagonal elements are the average variance extracted (AVE) by the corresponding constructs; the triangle above the diagonal is the shared variance between two corresponding constructs. **Correlation between two constructs (triangle below the diagonal) is significant at the 0.01 level

*Table 3. Model hypotheses and structural paths*

| Hypothesis | Path Relationships | Significance | Inference |
|---|---|---|---|
| $H_{1a}$ | TTF → USE | 0.63** | Supported |
| $H_{1b}$ | TTF → EOU | 0.14* | Supported |
| $H_{1c}$ | TTF → ATT | 0.17 ** | Supported |
| $H_{1d}$ | TTF → INT | 0.58** | Supported |
| $H_{2a}$ | TRU → USE | 0.10 | Not Supported |
| $H_{2b}$ | TRU → EOU | 0.30** | Supported |
| $H_{2c}$ | TRU → ATT | 0.16** | Supported |
| $H_{2d}$ | TRU → INT | 0.39** | Supported |
| $H_{3a}$ | REP → TRU | 0.11* | Supported |
| $H_{3b}$ | REP → ATT | 0.13** | Supported |
| $H_{3c}$ | REP → INT | 0.11* | Supported |
| $H_{4a}$ | USE → ATT | 0.35** | Supported |
| $H_{4b}$ | EOU → ATT | 0.20** | Supported |
| $H_{4c}$ | EOU → USE | 0.54** | Supported |
| $H_{4d}$ | USE → INT | 0.11* | Supported |
| $H_{4e}$ | ATT → INT | 0.16** | |
| ***Controls*** | Age → INT | 0.03 | |
| | Gender → INT | 0.03 | |
| | Occupation → INT | 0.01 | |
| | Education → INT | 0.09* | |

Notes: Model fit: $\chi 234 = 118.5$; GFI = 0.93; CFI = 0.91; NFI = 0.87; RMSEA = 0.08.

** β estimate is significant at the 0.01 level

* β estimate is significant at the 0.05 level

$H_2$ posits that initial trust is positively related to (a) perceived usefulness, (b) ease of use, (c) attitude, and (d) intentions to use. Table 3 provides support for the positive influence initial trust on perceived ease of use ($\beta = 0.30$, $p < 0.01$), attitude ($\beta = 0.16$, $p < 0.01$) and intentions to use ($\beta = 0.39$, $p < 0.01$). The results are consistent with the hypothesized relationships in $H_{2b-2d}$. Hypothesis $H_{2a}$ was not supported as initial trust does not influence perceived usefulness of IoT ($\beta = 0.16$, $p > 0.05$).

Hypotheses $H_{3a}$ and $H_{3b}$ predict retailer reputation to have direct positive impact on trust, attitudes and intentions to use IoT respectively. Results demonstrate that retailer reputation has a positive and significant effect on trust ($\beta = 0.11$, $p < 0.05$), attitude ($\beta = 0.13$, $p < 0.01$), and intentions to use ($\beta = 0.11$, $p < 0.05$). Thus, $H_{3a-3c}$ are supported by the data.

$H_{4a}$ and $H_{4b}$ state that perceived usefulness and perceived ease of use have positive relationship with attitude towards retail technology. Corroborating previous findings, this study results reveal that both perceived usefulness ($\beta = 0.35$, $p < 0.01$) and perceived ease of use ($\beta = 0.20$, $p < 0.01$) have significant positive impact on attitude, supporting $H_{4a}$ and $H_{4b}$. Hypothesis $H_{4c}$ prediction that perceived ease of use has a significant positive impact on perceived usefulness was supported by the data ($\beta = 0.54$, $p < 0.01$). Further, perceived usefulness ($\beta = 0.11$, $p < 0.05$) and attitude ($\beta = 0.16$, $p = 0.01$) were found to have a significant positive impact on intentions to use, thereby supporting hypotheses $H_{4d}$ and $H_{4e}$.

Of the four control variables, only education was found to have significant positive impact on intentions to use ($\beta = 0.10$, $p < 0.05$). Age, gender and occupation did not have any impact on intentions to use.

## DISCUSSION

This study proposed and tested an integrated model of IoT acceptance. Specifically, based on the technology acceptance model, task-technology fit theory, initial trust theory, and organizational theory, this study investigates the factors that determine adoption of customer-facing IoT technology in a retail setting. The study results show that technological beliefs (perceived ease of use and perceived usefulness), individual characteristic (initial trust), task characteristic (task-technology fit) and organizational factor (retailer reputation) determine the customer acceptance of IoT retail technology. These factors explain 65 percent variance in intentions to use IoT. This value was much higher than value achieved by Venkatesh et al. (2003) user acceptance model. Moreover, all research hypotheses (except for the effect of trust on perceived usefulness) are empirically supported which provides further support for the strength of the integrated model in predicting customer adoption of IoT in retail stores in the Australian context.

As shown in Table 3, task-technology fit has the strongest effect on intentions to use IoT technology. This means that when customers see fit between the task requirements and IoT they are more likely to evaluate it as useful and this motivates them to adopt it. Such results regarding the important role of TTF in technology adoption has been supported by prior literature (Lin, 2012).

Initial trust is found to be the second strongest factor predicting intention to use IoT in retail stores. This suggests, that customers are more likely to be motivated to adopt IoT when they perceive trust in the IoT technology. This finding is in line with what has been established in the previous literature that initial trust reduces risk and diminishes complexity (Siau et al., 2004) thereby leading to greater intentions to adopt IoT.

As anticipated, organizational reputation was found to have a significant influence on intentions to use. This relationship suggests that IoT adoption will increase among customers who evaluate the retailer as highly reputed and regarded. Previous research studies suggest that organizational reputation can reduce risk perceptions and strengthen customers' confidence (Keh & Xie, 2009). Existing literature related to technology acceptance model has largely acknowledged the role of perceived usefulness and attitude in predicting intentions to use (Kim et al., 2016). The findings in this regard provide further support regarding the role of technology beliefs in customer adoption of IoT retail technology.

## CONCLUSION AND IMPLICATIONS

This study adds to the existing literature through creation of an integrated model to identify the factors affecting retail consumers' intentions to adopt IoT technology that has received limited attention so far. By gaining a better understanding of the factors determining customers' intentions to adopt IoT, retailers can both introduce and market the technology so that there is a continued acceptance of IoT in retail stores. A conceptual model comprising four factors namely technology beliefs, individual characteristic, initial trust perspective, and organizational characteristic was proposed. Empirical data was obtained from 289 Australian retail consumers. The data analyzed using SEM largely supported the hypotheses proposed. Further, the model fitness as well as the predictive power suggests that perceived usefulness, perceived ease of use, initial trust, task-technology fit, and retailer reputation positively influences attitude and intentions to use IoT in retail stores.

This study contributes to the existing knowledge by providing an understanding of the factors that determine customer adoption of IoT. Specifically, this study extends technology acceptance model by considering new factors and proposing new casual paths in consumer adoption of IoT technology in retail context. Further, this study provides retailers with guidelines to help them promote acceptance of IoT technology among the customers. First, given the significance of TTF, it is recommended that retailers should focus their attention on the fit between shopping tasks and IoT technology features. Second, initial trust was found to be important in customer adoption of IoT. Trust can be developed through direct experience or through communication strategies. Third, retailers should continue to improve in usefulness and ease of use for successful adoption of IoT.

## LIMITATIONS AND FUTURE RESEARCH DIRECTIONS

Despite the contributions, this study is not without limitations. First, this study takes a cross-sectional approach and thus future research should take a longitudinal approach. Second, this study considered sample from one country and future studies can examine the cross-cultural comparisons in customer acceptance of IoT retail technology. Finally, future studies should consider demographic differences such as age, gender, and technology experience in understanding their impact of independent factors on attitude and intentions to use IoT.

## REFERENCES

Aggarwal, C. C., Ashish, N., & Sheth, A. (2013). The internet of things: A survey from the data-centric perspective. In Managing and mining sensor data (pp. 383-428). Springer US. doi:10.1007/978-1-4614-6309-2_12

Ajzen, I. (1985). From intention to actions: a theory of planned behavior. In J. Kuhl & J. Beckmann (Eds.), *Action-control: From cognition to behavior*. Heidelberg, Germany: Springer. doi:10.1007/978-3-642-69746-3_2

Ajzen, I., & Fishbein, M. (1980). *Understanding and predicting social behavior*. Englewood Cliffs, NJ: Prentice Hall.

Akçayır, M., Akçayır, G., Pektaş, H. M., & Ocak, M. A. (2016). Augmented reality in science laboratories: The effects of augmented reality on university students laboratory skills and attitudes toward science laboratories. *Computers in Human Behavior*, *57*, 334–342. doi:10.1016/j.chb.2015.12.054

Amendola, S., Lodato, R., Manzari, S., Occhiuzzi, C., & Marrocco, G. (2014). RFID technology for IoT-based personal healthcare in smart spaces. *IEEE Internet of Things Journal, 1*(2), 144-152.

Atzori, L., Iera, A., & Morabito, G. (2010). The internet of things: A survey. *Computer Networks*, *54*(15), 2787–2805. doi:10.1016/j.comnet.2010.05.010

Bao, Y., Bao, Y., & Sheng, S. (2011). Motivating purchase of private brands: Effects of store image, product signatureness, and quality variation. *Journal of Business Research*, *64*(2), 220–226. doi:10.1016/j.jbusres.2010.02.007

Bardaki, C., Kourouthanassis, P., & Pramatari, K. (2012). Deploying RFID-enabled services in the retail supply chain: Lessons learned toward the internet of things. *Information Systems Management*, *29*(3), 233–245. doi:10.1080/10580530.2012.687317

Beck, S., & Kenning, P. (2015). The influence of retailers family firm image on new product acceptance: An empirical investigation in the German FMCG market. *International Journal of Retail & Distribution Management*, *43*(12), 1126–1143. doi:10.1108/IJRDM-06-2014-0079

Beldad, A., van der Geest, T., de Jong, M., & Steehouder, M. (2012). A cue or two and Ill trust you: Determinants of trust in government organizations in terms of their processing and usage of citizens personal information disclosed online. *Government Information Quarterly*, *29*(1), 41–49. doi:10.1016/j.giq.2011.05.003

Beldona, S., Morrison, A. M., & OLeary, J. (2005). Online shopping motivations and pleasure travel products: A correspondence analysis. *Tourism Management*, *26*(4), 561–570. doi:10.1016/j.tourman.2004.03.008

Bhattacharya, M. (2015). A conceptual framework of RFID adoption in retail using Rogers stage model. *Business Process Management Journal*, *21*(3), 517–540. doi:10.1108/BPMJ-06-2014-0047

Brandpipe. (2015). *How augmented reality is shaping the retail industry*. Retrieved from http://www.brandpipe.co.uk/how-augmented-reality-is-shaping-the-retail-industry/

Carter, L., & Weerakkody, V. (2008). E-government adoption: A cultural comparison. *Information Systems Frontiers*, *10*(4), 473–482. doi:10.1007/s10796-008-9103-6

CBR. (2016). *Re-inventing retail with Internet of Things: Engaging with connected consumers to earn their loyalty*. Retrieved from http://www.cbronline.com/blogs/cbr-rolling-blog/re--inventing-retail-with-internet-of-things-engaging-with-connected-consumers-to-earn-their-loyalty

Chang, H. H. (2010). Task-technology fit and user acceptance of online auction. *International Journal of Human-Computer Studies*, *68*(1), 69–89. doi:10.1016/j.ijhcs.2009.09.010

Chang, H. H., Tsai, Y. C., Wong, K. H., Wang, J. W., & Cho, F. J. (2015). The effects of response strategies and severity of failure on consumer attribution with regard to negative word-of-mouth. *Decision Support Systems*, *71*, 48–61. doi:10.1016/j.dss.2015.01.007

Chen, Y. H., & Barnes, S. (2007). Initial trust and online buyer behaviour. *Industrial Management & Data Systems*, *107*(1), 21–36. doi:10.1108/02635570710719034

Chen, Y. S., & Huang, S. Y. (2016). The effect of task-technology fit on purchase intention: The moderating role of perceived risks. *Journal of Risk Research*, 1–21. doi:10.1080/13669877.2016.1165281

Choi, S. H., Yang, Y. X., Yang, B., & Cheung, H. H. (2015). Item-level RFID for enhancement of customer shopping experience in apparel retail. *Computers in Industry*, *71*, 10–23. doi:10.1016/j.compind.2015.03.003

Chong, A. Y.-L., Ooi, K. B., Lin, B., & Tan, B. I. (2010). Online banking adoption: An empirical analysis. *International Journal of Bank Marketing*, *28*(4), 267–287. doi:10.1108/02652321011054963

Chong, A. Y.-L., Ooi, K. B., Lin, B., & Tan, B. I. (2010). Online banking adoption: An empirical analysis. *International Journal of Bank Marketing*, *28*(4), 267–287. doi:10.1108/02652321011054963

Clark, S. (2008). *Casagras takes a step towards defining the 'Internet of Things'*. Retrieved from http://www.nfcworld.com/2008/12/12/3387/casagras-takes-a-step-towards-defining-the-internet-of-things/

Danado, J., Dias, E., Romão, T., Correia, N., Trabuco, A., Santos, C., . . . Serpa, J. (2003, January). *Mobile augmented reality for environmental management (MARE)*. In Eurographics 2003 Conference, Granada, Spain.

Davis, F. D. (1989). Perceived usefulness, perceived ease of use, and user acceptance of information technology. *Management Information Systems Quarterly*, *13*(3), 319–340. doi:10.2307/249008

De Ruyter, K., Wetzels, M., & Kleijnen, M. (2001). Customer adoption of e-service: An experimental study. *International Journal of Service Industry Management*, *12*(2), 184–207. doi:10.1108/09564230110387542

Deb, M., & Chaudhuri, H. R. (2014). Impact of firms reputation and ethnocentrism on attitude towards foreign products. *Marketing Intelligence & Planning*, *32*(5), 646–664. doi:10.1108/MIP-04-2013-0070

Dishaw, M. T., & Strong, D. M. (1999). Extending the technology acceptance model with task–technology fit constructs. *Information & Management*, *36*(1), 9–21. doi:10.1016/S0378-7206(98)00101-3

Dutot, V. (2015). Factors influencing Near Field Communication (NFC) adoption: An extended TAM approach. *The Journal of High Technology Management Research*, *26*(1), 45–57. doi:10.1016/j.hitech.2015.04.005

Evanschitzky, H., Iyer, G. R., Pillai, K. G., Kenning, P., & Schütte, R. (2015). Consumer trial, continuous use, and economic benefits of a retail service innovation: The case of the personal shopping assistant. *Journal of Product Innovation Management*, *32*(3), 459–475. doi:10.1111/jpim.12241

Ferber, S. (2013). How the internet of things changes everything? *Harvard Business Review*. Retrieved from https://hbr.org/2013/05/how-the-internet-of-things-cha/

Fornell, C., & Larcker, D. F. (1981). Structural equation models with unobservable variables and measurement error: Algebra and statistics. *JMR, Journal of Marketing Research*, *18*(3), 382–388. doi:10.2307/3150980

Gao, L., & Bai, X. (2014). A unified perspective on the factors influencing consumer acceptance of internet of things technology. *Asia Pacific Journal of Marketing and Logistics*, *26*(2), 211–231. doi:10.1108/APJML-06-2013-0061

Gao, L., & Waechter, K. A. (2015). Examining the role of initial trust in user adoption of mobile payment services: An empirical investigation. *Information Systems Frontiers*, 1–24.

Gartner. (2015). *Gartner says the Internet of things installed base will grow to 26 billion units by 2010.* Retrieved from http://www.gartner.com/newsroom/id/2636073

Gefen, D., Karahanna, E., & Straub, D. W. (2003). Trust and TAM in online shopping: An integrated model. *Management Information Systems Quarterly*, *27*(1), 51–90.

Girish, D. (2016). *4 Innovative Internet of things examples in retail.* Retrieved from http://blog.beaconstac.com/2015/10/4-innovative-internet-of-things-examples-in-retail/

Goodhue, D. L., & Thompson, R. L. (1995). Task-technology fit and individual performance. *Management Information Systems Quarterly*, *19*(2), 213–236. doi:10.2307/249689

Gregory, J. (2015). The Internet of things: Revolutionizing the retail industry. *Accenture Strategy*. Retrieved from https://www.accenture.com/_acnmedia/Accenture/Conversion-Assets/DotCom/Documents/Global/PDF/Dualpub_14/Accenture-The-Internet-Of-Things.pdf

Gubbi, J., Buyya, R., Marusic, S., & Palaniswami, M. (2013). Internet of Things (IoT): A vision, architectural elements, and future directions. *Future Generation Computer Systems*, *29*(7), 1645–1660. doi:10.1016/j.future.2013.01.010

Ha, S., & Stoel, L. (2009). Consumer e-shopping acceptance: Antecedents in a technology acceptance model. *Journal of Business Research*, *62*(5), 565–571. doi:10.1016/j.jbusres.2008.06.016

Hernández-Muñoz, J. M., Vercher, J. B., Muñoz, L., Galache, J. A., Presser, M., Gómez, L. A. H., & Pettersson, J. (2011, May). Smart cities at the forefront of the future internet. In The Future Internet Assembly (pp. 447-462). Springer Berlin Heidelberg. doi:10.1007/978-3-642-20898-0_32

Hoffman, D. L., & Novak, T. P. (2015). *Emergent experience and the connected consumer in the smart home assemblage and the Internet of things.* Available at SSRN 2648786

Iansiti, M., & Lakhani, K. R. (2014). Digital Ubiquity: How Connections, Sensors, and Data Are Revolutionizing Business (Digest Summary). *Harvard Business Review*, *92*(11), 91–99.

Johnson, D. S., Bardhi, F., & Dunn, D. T. (2008). Understanding how technology paradoxes affect customer satisfaction with self-service technology: The role of performance ambiguity and trust in technology. *Psychology and Marketing*, *25*(5), 416–443. doi:10.1002/mar.20218

Kambies, T., Raynor, M. E., Pankratz, D. M., & Wadekar, G. (2016). *Closing the digital divide: IoT in retail's transformative potential*. Retrieved from http://dupress.com/articles/internet-of-things-iot-retail-strategies/

Keh, H. T., & Xie, Y. (2009). Corporate reputation and customer behavioral intentions: The roles of trust, identification and commitment. *Industrial Marketing Management*, *38*(7), 732–742. doi:10.1016/j.indmarman.2008.02.005

Kim, H. Y., Lee, J. Y., Mun, J. M., & Johnson, K. K. (2016). Consumer adoption of smart in-store technology: assessing the predictive value of attitude versus beliefs in the technology acceptance model. *International Journal of Fashion Design, Technology and Education*, 1-11.

Kim, K. K., & Prabhakar, B. (2004). Initial trust and the adoption of B2C e-commerce: The case of internet banking. *ACM SIGMIS Database, 35*(2), 50-64.

Kim, S. K., Park, M. J., Ahn, E. J., & Rho, J. J. (2015). Investigating the role of task-technology fit along with attractiveness of alternative technology to utilize RFID system in the organization. *Information Development*, *31*(5), 405–420. doi:10.1177/0266666913513277

King, W. R., & He, J. (2006). A meta-analysis of the technology acceptance model. *Information & Management*, *43*(6), 740–755. doi:10.1016/j.im.2006.05.003

Klopping, I. M., & McKinney, E. (2004). Extending the technology acceptance model and the task-technology fit model to consumer e-commerce. *Information Technology, Learning and Performance Journal*, *22*(1), 35.

Lee, H. J., & Yang, K. (2013). Interpersonal service quality, self-service technology (SST) service quality, and retail patronage. *Journal of Retailing and Consumer Services*, *20*(1), 51–57. doi:10.1016/j.jretconser.2012.10.005

Legris, P., Ingham, J., & Collerette, P. (2003). Why do people use information technology? A critical review of the technology acceptance model. *Information & Management*, *40*(3), 191–204. doi:10.1016/S0378-7206(01)00143-4

Li, H., Jiang, J., & Wu, M. (2014). The effects of trust assurances on consumers initial online trust: A two-stage decision-making process perspective. *International Journal of Information Management*, *34*(3), 395–405. doi:10.1016/j.ijinfomgt.2014.02.004

Li, S., Da Xu, L., & Zhao, S. (2015). The internet of things: A survey. *Information Systems Frontiers*, *17*(2), 243–259. doi:10.1007/s10796-014-9492-7

Li, X., Hess, T. J., & Valacich, J. S. (2008). Why do we trust new technology? A study of initial trust formation with organizational information systems. *The Journal of Strategic Information Systems*, *17*(1), 39–71. doi:10.1016/j.jsis.2008.01.001

Lin, W. S. (2012). Perceived fit and satisfaction on web learning performance: IS continuance intention and task-technology fit perspectives. *International Journal of Human-Computer Studies*, *70*(7), 498–507. doi:10.1016/j.ijhcs.2012.01.006

Lu, H. P., & Yang, Y. W. (2014). Toward an understanding of the behavioral intention to use a social networking site: An extension of task-technology fit to social-technology fit. *Computers in Human Behavior*, *34*, 323–332. doi:10.1016/j.chb.2013.10.020

Manyika, J., & Chui, M. (2015). *By 2025, Internet of things applications could have $11trillion impact.* Retrieved from http://www.mckinsey.com/insights/mgi/in_the_news/by_2025_Internet_of_things_applications_could_have_11_trillion_impact

Morgan-Thomas, A., & Veloutsou, C. (2013). Beyond technology acceptance: Brand relationships and online brand experience. *Journal of Business Research*, *66*(1), 21–27. doi:10.1016/j.jbusres.2011.07.019

Ng, I. C. (2010). The future of pricing and revenue models. *Journal of Revenue and Pricing Management*, *9*(3), 276–281. doi:10.1057/rpm.2010.11

Ou, W. M., Abratt, R., & Dion, P. (2006). The influence of retailer reputation on store patronage. *Journal of Retailing and Consumer Services*, *13*(3), 221–230. doi:10.1016/j.jretconser.2005.08.014

Pantano, E., & Timmermans, H. (2014). What is smart for retailing? *Procedia Environmental Sciences*, *22*, 101–107. doi:10.1016/j.proenv.2014.11.010

Papagiannidis, S., Pantano, E., See-To, E. W., & Bourlakis, M. (2013). Modelling the determinants of a simulated experience in a virtual retail store and users product purchasing intentions. *Journal of Marketing Management*, *29*(13-14), 1462–1492. doi:10.1080/0267257X.2013.821150

Park, J., Gunn, F., Lee, Y., & Shim, S. (2015). Consumer acceptance of a revolutionary technology-driven product: The role of adoption in the industrial design development. *Journal of Retailing and Consumer Services*, *26*, 115–124. doi:10.1016/j.jretconser.2015.05.003

Pavlou, P. A. (2003). Consumer acceptance of electronic commerce: Integrating trust and risk with the technology acceptance model. *International Journal of Electronic Commerce*, *7*(3), 101–134.

Podsakoff, P. M., MacKenzie, S. B., Lee, J. Y., & Podsakoff, N. P. (2003). Common method biases in behavioral research: A critical review of the literature and recommended remedies. *The Journal of Applied Psychology*, *88*(5), 879–903. doi:10.1037/0021-9010.88.5.879 PMID:14516251

Porter, M. E., & Heppelmann, J. E. (2014). How smart, connected products are transforming competition. *Harvard Business Review*, *92*(11), 64–88.

Reinartz, W., Dellaert, B., Krafft, M., Kumar, V., & Varadarajan, R. (2011). Retailing innovations in a globalizing retail market environment. *Journal of Retailing*, *87*, S53–S66. doi:10.1016/j.jretai.2011.04.009

Research and Markets. (2015). *Retail IoT Market Growth & Forecast 2015 to 2020*. Retrieved from http://www.marketsandmarketsblog.com/retail-iot-market.html

Ryan, T. (2016). *Would 'driveless' carts enhance shopping in stores?* Retrieved from http://www.retailwire.com/discussion/would-driverless-carts-enhance-shopping-in-stores/

Siau, K., Sheng, H., Nah, F., & Davis, S. (2004). A qualitative investigation on consumer trust in mobile commerce. *International Journal of Electronic Business*, *2*(3), 283–300. doi:10.1504/IJEB.2004.005143

Slade, E. L., Dwivedi, Y. K., Piercy, N. C., & Williams, M. D. (2015). Modeling consumers adoption intentions of remote mobile payments in the United Kingdom: Extending UTAUT with innovativeness, risk, and trust. *Psychology and Marketing*, *32*(8), 860–873. doi:10.1002/mar.20823

Soper, D. S. (2014). *A-priori sample size calculator for structural equation models* [software]. Available from http://www.danielsoper.com/statcalc

Thiesse, F., Al-Kassab, J., & Fleisch, E. (2009). Understanding the value of integrated RFID systems: A case study from apparel retail. *European Journal of Information Systems*, *18*(6), 592–614. doi:10.1057/ejis.2009.33

Tischler, L. (2011). *Intel's virtual footwear wall for Adidas turns boutiques into shoe-topias*. Retrieved from http://www.fastcompany.com/1715933/intels-virtual-footwear-wall-adidas-turns-boutiques-shoe-topias-video

Uckelmann, D., Harrison, M., & Michahelles, F. (2011). An architectural approach towards the future internet of things. In *Architecting the internet of things* (pp. 1–24). Springer Berlin Heidelberg. doi:10.1007/978-3-642-19157-2_1

Upadhyay, P., & Jahanyan, S. (2016). Analyzing user perspective on the factors affecting use intention of mobile based transfer payment. *Internet Research*, *26*(1), 38–56. doi:10.1108/IntR-05-2014-0143

Venkatesh, V., & Davis, F. D. (2000). A theoretical extension of the technology acceptance model: Four longitudinal field studies. *Management Science*, *46*(2), 186–204. doi:10.1287/mnsc.46.2.186.11926

Venkatesh, V., Morris, M. G., Davis, G. B., & Davis, F. D. (2003). User acceptance of information technology: Toward a unified view. *Management Information Systems Quarterly*, *27*(3), 425–478.

Volpe, J. (2011). *SK Telecom's Smart Cart syncs to phones, reminds you to buy milk*. Retrieved from https://www.engadget.com/2011/07/27/sk-telecoms-smart-cart-syncs-to-phones-reminds-you-to-buy-milk/

Wang, D., Li, X. R., & Li, Y. (2013). Chinas smart tourism destination initiative: A taste of the service-dominant logic. *Journal of Destination Marketing & Management*, *2*(2), 59–61. doi:10.1016/j.jdmm.2013.05.004

Wang, W. T., & Li, H. M. (2012). Factors influencing mobile services adoption: A brand-equity perspective. *Internet Research*, *22*(2), 142–179. doi:10.1108/10662241211214548

Want, R., Schilit, B. N., & Jenson, S. (2015). Enabling the Internet of things. *Computer*, *48*(1), 28–35. doi:10.1109/MC.2015.12

Weijters, B., Rangarajan, D., Falk, T., & Schillewaert, N. (2007). Determinants and outcomes of customers use of self-service technology in a retail setting. *Journal of Service Research*, *10*(1), 3–21. doi:10.1177/1094670507302990

Woollaston, V. (2015). *The end of fitting room queues? Smart mirrors lets you virtually try on clothes and order drinks*. Retrieved from http://www.dailymail.co.uk/sciencetech/article-2906563/The-end-fitting-room-queues-Smart-mirrors-lets-virtually-try-clothes-order-drinks.html#ixzz4D2FoDyhs

Xie, Y., & Allen, C. (2013). Information technologies in retail supply chains: A comparison of Tesco and Asda. *International Journal of Business Performance and Supply Chain Modelling*, *5*(1), 46–62. doi:10.1504/IJBPSCM.2013.051648

Xu, L. D. (2011). Information architecture for supply chain quality management. *International Journal of Production Research*, *49*(1), 183–198. doi:10.1080/00207543.2010.508944

Yang, H. D., Kang, S., Oh, W., & Kim, M. S. (2013). Are all fits created equal? A nonlinear perspective on task-technology fit. *Journal of the Association for Information Systems*, *14*(12), 694.

Yang, L., Yang, S. H., & Plotnick, L. (2013). How the internet of things technology enhances emergency response operations? *Technological Forecasting and Social Change*, *80*(9), 1854–1867. doi:10.1016/j.techfore.2012.07.011

Yang, S. U. (2007). An integrated model for organization—public relational outcomes, organizational reputation, and their antecedents. *Journal of Public Relations Research*, *19*(2), 91–121. doi:10.1080/10627260701290612

Yen, D. C., Wu, C. S., Cheng, F. F., & Huang, Y. W. (2010). Determinants of users intention to adopt wireless technology: An empirical study by integrating TTF with TAM. *Computers in Human Behavior*, *26*(5), 906–915. doi:10.1016/j.chb.2010.02.005

Zhou, H., Liu, B., & Wang, D. (2012). Design and research of urban intelligent transportation system based on the internet of things. In *Internet of Things* (pp. 572–580). Springer Berlin Heidelberg. doi:10.1007/978-3-642-32427-7_82

Zhou, T. (2014). An empirical examination of initial trust in mobile payment. *Wireless Personal Communications*, *77*(2), 1519–1531. doi:10.1007/s11277-013-1596-8

Zhou, T., Lu, Y., & Wang, B. (2010). Integrating TTF and UTAUT to explain mobile banking user adoption. *Computers in Human Behavior*, *26*(4), 760–767. doi:10.1016/j.chb.2010.01.013

Zorzi, M., Gluhak, A., Lange, S., & Bassi, A. (2010). From todays intranet of things to a future internet of things: A wireless-and mobility-related view. *IEEE Wireless Communications*, *17*(6), 44–51. doi:10.1109/MWC.2010.5675777

# Chapter 3
# Technopsychology of IoT Optimization in the Business World

**Tommy Prayoga**
*Bina Nusantara University, Indonesia*

**Juneman Abraham**
*Bina Nusantara University, Indonesia*

## ABSTRACT

*There are at least two complementary levels in the Internet of Things. The first (back) end comes from the big data companies that mine and analyze every log of activities through every device that are attached to the second (front) end, i.e., the many aspects of our lives. However, what keeps this wheel of innovation going forward is actually the front end user. Technology, however improved and innovative, will not fulfill its full potential if users do not adopt and accept it as part of their lives. They must be willing to work with the technology - sold as way to ease and improve lives - for the machine to work and be meaningful. By then the big data companies can gather information about what users want and how they behave to grasp a better understanding and make better decisions about next technology improvement. Users' acceptance and decisions to appropriate shape how big data companies work and innovate. Acceptance and appropriation are the two of the most important areas to explore in the field of IoT optimization in the business world.*

## INTRODUCTION

Right before I[1] started writing this chapter, a video suggestion popped-up in my YouTube homepage. The title says "*A New History for Humanity – The Human Era*" uploaded by Kurzgesagt – In a Nutshell (2016). The video explained about how the Gregorian calendar underplays the 12,000 years of human progress, from building the first temple to travel beyond the sky. What humans had begun then, set the motion for something bigger and bigger that is happening right now.

DOI: 10.4018/978-1-5225-2104-4.ch003

Progression is the key to survival. But, what is the key to progression? Knowledge seems to be a vague and subjective answer. To answer this, we have to think beyond that. We have to think like a statistician. We have to think what big business and tech media like *Forbes, TechCrunch, Business Insider*, and *Tech in Asia* feed their readers everyday. We have to think of data. That's the key of progression, the key to survival and beyond.

Ten thousand years ago, humans gathered data based on vague observations toward each other. We see other tools being forged, we see cities and settlements being built, and we see society being developed. Now, that technique is long overdue. Human minds and written papers are just not proficient enough to process and store information. We live in an era where we give machines intelligence and communications capabilities (Sousa Nunes, Zhang, & Sa Silva, 2015) that do most of the work of calculating and processing incomprehensible amount of data in a blink of an eye; imagine the time it will take for 10 Ph.D. to give you one search result on *Google* (Larson, 2016)!

There are many kinds of data. Not that you have to care about all of them, but some of them are pretty hard to ignore, considering the fact that the data some of the supercomputers and great minds out there are analyzing and processing about is you.

Humans are always in dire need to move forward. We get bored easily, and we always think about improvement and innovation. We do not stay the same. We explore and understand. Sometimes that means challenging our ways of life, questioning why we behave and what we really need and want. To do that, we cannot simply observe each other and pitch ideas. We realize that we have to include everybody to really do that. How do we get this information and analyze it?

This is where our creation enters—the machines. We rely on the capability to think and communicate bestowed upon them, by us, to help us understand ourselves better. Having them asking us questions would be as silly. But if we are giving them the information (sometimes unknowingly) they needed by just living, then we have ourselves a great start.

We begin to tag ourselves and things around us that every action and every word is recorded and analyzed. From social media interaction to health trackers utilization, millions of pattern habits emerges. Then data scientists can use the information to make decisions for our next milestone in human era, whether in the health, business, tech, or education sector. This is what's happening in the era of Internet of Things.

Internet of Things (IoT) is an essentially interconnected network of things. It is a fast developing field that represents the idea of everything that is connected together via an information network (Pfeiffer & Stevens, 2015). The idea of 'connected' means that every object involved in the network has an identity, abilities to receive and collect information from the real world and communicate about the information within the virtual world. The IoT faces and produces what we call the *Big Data*.

How big is Big Data? Statistically, you have a high chance of being a social media user. When you are using social media, you are feeding the company behind it an enormous amount of data from your activity logs. The company will have access to where you are, when do you log in, who or what do you follow, who do you connect with, what do you like, what you don't like, what are you browsing, and how often you are doing all that. Imagine this data mining is done 24/7. Also imagine that this being done with a couple billions people in the world.

If you are running an online fashion store, what would you do if you have the knowledge about the demographics that like what you sell, bought what you have sold, and in need with what you are selling? You'd be most likely to approach and persuade them to make purchases because they are the exact target customer you are looking for.

What about offline store goers, you ask? Although it is not yet widespread, smart stores like *Amazon Go* is on its way to sweeping away all the traditional stores that employ clerks and managers. *Amazon Go* is a new self-checkout store that allows any customers to take anything they need from the store that will be charged with their *Amazon* account (Balakrishnan, 2016) when they leave. So there is no need for people to stay in line for check-out, not even self-checkout counters. It saves money and certainly saves times. Would any giant e-commerce launch this ground-breaking ideas without knowing the habits (what they want and what they purchase) of its paying customers?

Also, think about how your news feed on most social media seems tailored to your interests and previous experiences. Pages you have liked, videos you have watched, and account you follows will generate similar suggestions for you to like, watch, and follow more—on different platforms. Where ever you go, you will be 'followed' by the Artificial Intelligence running these systems.

On the bright side, we do receive many positive implications from the application of IoT. Traffic cameras, smart kitchen, self-driving cars, and health trackers possess many beneficial features that in no doubt the bottom line is to improve human life. They are all the product of years of researches in economy, medical biology, urban architecture, psychology, and cognitive science.

However, there are clearly two sides of IoT. It is one of the biggest milestone human has ever achieved. There is no telling of whether it will become the biggest threat towards humanity or not. It arguably possesses a potential threat to privacy and the essence of a human at its core. But, the end result of a product of IoT is always largely determined by the users themselves. Users, in a very significant way, shapes the idea of IoT, from the design, usability, features, and ultimately the success. Because at the end of the day, users are the utmost reason that the technologies are created. This comes down to Acceptance of IoT.

In this chapter, we are going to talk about the Acceptance of IoT. We will first go through the definition of IoT and Big Data, and discuss in-depth about how acceptance plays important key-role in their development. We will then cover the definition of Acceptance, and how is it different with Adoption. Finally, we will map out they key elements of IoT acceptance based on techno-psychological points of view. In other words, explaining the acceptance of IoT in terms of its affective, cognitive, behavioral, and technological elements.

## THE FUNDAMENTALS

### Big Data and Privacy

In order to understand the concept of Internet of Things, we may begin with the understanding of Big Data, and how it relates to our privacy.

According to the Director of Emerging Technologies for *SAS Best Practices*, Tamara Dull (2014), Big Data is all about plain old data—that we can use any adjective to describe. It is one of the subsets (but not exclusive to) in the discussion of Internet of Things. Big Data simply means massive amounts of information, sometimes more than what we can imagine. A Big Data report (VoucherCloud News, 2015) claimed that we create 2.5 quintillion bytes or roughly 2.5 billion GB. By 2018, the number will increase almost twice as large, to around 4.32 billion GB or 50,000 GB a second.

Big Data consist of anything that is recorded that can be structured or unstructured (Kushmaro, 2016). Big Data comes from many sources, like web interaction and hardware sensors. For example, company like *UPS* that delivers more than 16 millions packages a day need to maintain and improve efficiency and lessen environmental impact, thus they are installing sensors that gather information about seat belt status, engine status, and bulkhead door operation to produce and array of information in a day (Garrett, 2016).

Expertise and understanding of Big Data allow company like *Dattabot* knows that Indonesian housewives watch a lot of porn on a mobile phone and Chinese Horoscope tend to be a great predictor of farmer's productivity (McIntyre, 2016a). They even partnered with *General Electric Digital* to amplify Jakarta's smart city idea by bringing the capability of gathering round-the-clock data for power plants (to give employees warning days before the machines are about to break) to Indonesia (McIntyre, 2016b). This might signal as the first step to a better, power-efficient Indonesia.

When we are talking about Big Data, we cannot exclude the definition of the *V*s. Big Data is all about *V*olume, *V*elocity, *V*ariety, *V*eracity (McLellan, 2015), *V*alue, and *V*ariability and Complexity (Gandomi & Haider, 2014). Volume refers to the amount of data that exist in every area or storage that accounts for how huge data set in the world of Big Data is. Velocity is the speed or rate which information are being processed. This means how many data points are analyzed, numbers are crunched, and the pattern is analyzed in a period of time. Variety is the amount of types or the mixture of information that is both structured and unstructured (McLellan, 2015). Veracity describes the nature of unreliability inherent in sources of data (Gandomi & Haider, 2015). These are often important information but is very fluctuating, somewhat predictable, constantly changing, with many factors that influence it. Until the Veracity is decoded and processed, it will be hard to include it in a structured part of Big Data. Variability and Complexity mean that data comes from many complex sources that flow through networks at different rates (Gandomi & Haider, 2014). They are what makes the process of analysis, extracting and gain insight challenging. Value (Pfeiffer & Stevens, 2015) means the potential benefit that the processing data possess. It refers to how insightful the data is and the impact it may bring to the real world application. No doubt that all these characteristics, especially veracity play important parts that will explain how acceptance is integral in IoT.

Examples of the use of Big Data mentioned previously are only some of the most prominent use of Big Data (mainly through IoT devices). On a more personal level, Big Data can be considered as your identity. Within the cloud-based storage of data, there is information about who you are, literally. Think about it–your name, your ID, biodata, your location, your activity log. Your every comment on a forum, your ticket purchase, your visit to that restaurant, and even the time you're sleeping. Try sending an e-mail, post a comment, or watch a video about burgers. Before you know it, your social media will be filled by a particular burger retail chain that invites you to dine at their place. The company has bought your information that you agreed to share online, and use that information to monetize you. You cannot do anything about it because you agreed to share your data online before engaging with the Internet.

What many people have not realized yet is that often the data that is obtained from us is real-time. Your moments, your stories, your live streams that reveal not only what you do, but who you with, where you are, and what the things that are around you. This is due to the portability of communication and entertainment devices. You are always in sync with the cloud and the net. Some company even plans to extend their reach of your personal experience by encouraging you to use their *Google* glasses and spectacles so that they know what you see.

This brings up the issue of privacy, in which we will explain why acceptance matters. If you are a fan of movies that involves elements like cyber security, data crunching, and fraud related technological films like *Mr. Robot, The Fifth Estate, Snowden, Moneyball*, and *The Circle*, you know what we mean. No ones want to end up being targeted by ads personally like what happened in the movie *Minority Report*. CEO of *Apple*, Tim Cook, said almost two years ago that we all have the right to our privacy.

But in 2015, he was criticized for patenting the system that serves to target users with ads based on their account balance (Estes, 2015). Where is your privacy now?

Don't worry, however, because the privacy is not dead yet. While many people seem to think so, Tamara Dull (2015a) sums up Big Data privacy well:

*... in today's data economy, we're sharing a ton of personal information about ourselves online. And this privacy discussion is only going to get bigger, especially as companies and government agencies get better at collecting, analyzing, and sometimes selling the data we're freely sharing with them. Trust is at the heart of the privacy issue and is the glue that will keep the data ecosystem together. [...] I firmly believe that as more consumers and everyday citizens continue to understand what's at stake with their personal data, we will see changes—in government and in businesses. It's already happening.*

## The Internet of Things

The Internet of Things (IoT) is the hot trends in the tech and business world. We are sure that many of you have heard of and have at least the basic understanding of what is it about. McLellan (2015) puts it in a simple way:

*... IoT is a fast-growing constellation of Internet-connected sensors attached to a wide variety of 'things'. Sensors can take a multitude of possible measurements; Internet connections can be wired or wireless, while 'things' can literally be any object (living or inanimate) to which you can attach or embed a sensor. If you carry a smartphone, for example, you become a multi-sensor IoT 'thing', and many of your day-to-day activities can be tracked, analyzed and acted upon.*

What matter most in IoT at the end is how the data that is collected from these sensors are interpreted and used. This makes understanding the CPS or cyber-physical space within important to solve physical problems through intuitive manipulation and awareness of the context of how the system operates (Sousa Nunes, Zhang, & Sa Silva, 2015).

There is a lot of gray areas when we are talking about IoT, especially in relation to Big Data. Is social media a part of IoT, or vice-versa? We think that it is safe to say that social media is a part of IoT, and this is mainly caused by the breakthrough of portable communication and entertainment devices. You carry social apps with you everywhere, which connects you to the Internet in real-time. Is your key tag that is only capable of communicating through radio frequency transmission to your phone a 'thing' of the IoT? Technically, it is. Anything that is given an identity and capability to connect is a part of IoT. Why is it so popular?

The driving force behind IoT is efficiency and innovation. To improve and survive, we, as humans must always improve. We can make a long process short, expensive procedure cheap, and turn long progress into a blink of an eye. We had, we will, and we are not stopping anytime soon. Along with that, humans also create completely new things to improve life areas that were thought to be unimprovable.

Perhaps, a number of things connected and the speed which IoT grows can show how big a deal IoT is. A report by Gartner (2015) predicted that in 2016 there will be 6.4 billion things that are connected to the Internet (compare to the population of the Earth that is roughly 7.5 billion people). The number is expected to rise to 20.8 billion things that are connected in the year 2020. How many data will be generated by IoT alone then? Around 600 trillion GB (McKendrick, 2016)!

You can expect to live with more (subtle) sensor-equipped devices by then. Although now, we already can enjoy many unique and groundbreaking services and products because of the development of IoT. Indonesia-based *eFishery* offers fish farmers a system that sense fish's appetite then feed them automatically, and you can monitor the process all in real-time from a smartphone (Cosseboom, 2014). Singapore/India-based *OCEO* helps rural communities purify water based on their need for quality & quantity monitoring system via smartphones (Yon, 2016). *Sigfox* from France is building a global network to connect, monitor, and control devices like smart-home alarms, machinery, refrigerator, and even streetlights (Lunden, 2016). *IoT.nxt* from South Africa aims to connect all the apps, sensors, devices, and machines in an operating system to 'breed' the best technology in all industries (Jackson, 2016). South Korea's *Nare* system can distinguish between harmless and dangerous electrical arcs that cause fire (Mu-Hyun, 2016). Yang, Qiu, and Zhang (2011) introduced a smart solution to make ease and secure the bike-renting system in China with a smart system that provides real-time location and conditions of the bikes. In addition to all this, smart-home, self-driving cars, biological/health trackers, and smart wearable devices, and even cities are taking on the world's every industry at once (Kashyap, 2016).

Notice that these are all the technologies built by human for human. However, most researches and phenomenon of IoT has focused on the big technical pictures that the human element is often forgotten or left out from the discussion of the system. Human is the one who gains insight, able to manipulate, and generate more ideas from the cyber-physical system of IoT. We have to keep in mind the nature of the data harnessed, who will access it, and from where when designing an IoT and Big Data strategy (Townsend, 2016).

There are both good and bad players out there taking advantage of our digital trails; we could almost do nothing about how they manipulate or even misuse the data, but we certainly have the control over what and how much data we are sharing online (Dull, 2015b). Take a step back; we even have the control as much as accepting the technology in the first place. What all of us accept and use will eventually take off, and what we do not accept will eventually fall off. We are the one that rose Facebook to the top, and we are the same people that bring down *Google Glass*.

The fact that all tech companies are struggling to scours for users and consumers shows that user acceptance is not something easy to understand, let alone mastering it. The immense complexity of acceptance across industries makes studying the phenomenon seems almost impossible. However, we can at least connect the dots and provide scientific assumptions of how acceptance happens in a bigger picture. Hopefully, by doing this, we will be more aware of what influences our thoughts, feelings, behaviors, beliefs, when we come face to face with a technology that contains ourselves in it. To do that, we must first understand what acceptance is and how complex it is.

## Meaning of Acceptance

In this section, we are going to talk about the concept of Acceptance. There are a lot of reason that IoT enthusiasts (or any technology for that matter) from the business and science communities are taking an interest in acceptance of the technology. It's the gateway information to know the UX component of the tech. They want to see how technology is perceived by consumers, how satisfied they are, and in what way they can increase their satisfaction (Dominici, Roblek, Abbate, & Tani, 2016). In return, they will make changes based on users' responses. What they are looking for is the occurrence of tentative acceptance or the trial period that will allow individual to accept the use of the technology and ultimately determine whether to continue using it or not (Brown et al., 2013). In other words, we know that acceptance is not an instant action that has a clear absolute line that differentiates between accepting and not accepting. Rather, it is a process that involves time and incorporating many factors that lead a novel technology to be used. It's the cycle that will begin the next revolution in industry. It can be illustrated below:

A technology is created based on needs → Test user's acceptance → Obtain feedbacks on why people accept/do not → Make tweaks based on feedbacks → Test again until all factors that influences the acceptance of a particular tech are discovered → Test new novel factors/shift towards other industry/area of life.

In a sustainable energy technology context, Huijts, Molin, and Steg (2012, p. 526) provide better insights on why we should understand acceptance:

*It is important to understand how people form an opinion on more sustainable energy technologies and why people take action in favor or against such technologies, as this yields important insights in how the design of the technology or the way the technology is implemented should be adapted, and how the technology should be communicated, such that the acceptance of the technology increases and its implementation is more successful.*

Due to many variations of IoT technology, needs, and method of delivery, defining acceptance is not a straightforward task. Coming up with a one-size-fits-all definition is almost impossible. One way we can do it is by breaking down all of the elements one by one, and then try to apply it in a different context. First, let's start from the two paradigms that are often used to explain the concept of acceptance in the technological context. The first one focuses on individual's propensity, while the second one, taking from the other side, focus on how technology's attributes affect an individual's perceptions and, ultimately, use of that technology (Porter & Donthu, 2006). Often in studies, researchers try to find the relationships between the components of the two to determine the best way to describe user's acceptance. These are usually two models or more that is used to explain both paradigms.

For example, it is not rare that we can find studies that try to link personality traits with components of acceptance models. Each personality traits are used to predict the affect, beliefs, and cognitive factors that are present in the mode. At the end of the study, researchers usually provide a conclusion that explains what they have found, in hoping to shed light on the understanding of acceptance. However sometimes, certain conditions of the acceptance require extra variables to be incorporated to explain it.

In the early days, researches rely on determining the factors that affect user's attitude and resistance towards a technology that stems from the famous Theory of Reasoned Action (Lee, Kozar, & Larsen, 2003). Theory of Reasoned Action explains that individual's subjective norms and attitude towards the behavior and behavior intention predict whether the action is actually carried out. Acceptance here is a form of behavior. That means that the fundamental two factors that affect it, according to the model, is attitude and subjective norm.

Attitude towards the behavior is the degree of favorability of behavior to an individual, while Subjective Norm is the social pressure to carry out (or not) the behavior in mind (Sheldon, 2016). Attitude shows how much we like to perform a behavior, with all considerations that we have. How we feel, positively or negatively that accepting will do and make of us is our attitude towards accepting. Subjective norms show how much the behavior is valued among the social standard around the individual engaging in said behavior. In other words, how our social environment views the behavior of accepting an object influences our decision in accepting it. This has to do with the culture, virality, the consequences, situational factors, and the meaning of the acceptance itself.

To understand more about technology acceptance, let's take a look at the theoretical model that is often used to explain it.

## THEORETICAL MODEL FOR IOT ACCEPTANCE

### The Variables

In the context of technology acceptance, many refer to *Technology Acceptance Model* (TAM). This model is integral in our discussion of technology acceptance. This model have been doing great in predicting and explaining technology acceptance in a wide range of area not only in IoT, but from Cloud Computing (Eltayeb & Dawson, 2016), to mobile technology (Kim, Gajos, Muller, & Grosz, 2016) and e-learning platform (Al-Azawei, Parslow, & Lundqvist, 2016), and even health trackers (Prayoga & Abraham, 2016). In this chapter, we are going to talk about what the model has to offer, and all possible frequently used factors to compliment TAM for a better understanding of IoT Acceptance. We will be talking about Behavioral Intention, Attitude towards the Behavior, Beliefs, Cognitive Factors, Individual Differences, Affect, and Other factors that are often inseparable to the model across contexts.

### Attitude and Behavioral Intention to Adopt/Accept

Conscious, purposive action begins with intention. Without intention, behaviors are accidental. Acceptance as a complex behavioral process is by no means accidental. Thus, there must be the intention that precedes it. In the realm of TAM, Intention or Behavioral Intention (BI), is the main indicator of acceptance—higher the BI, the higher the likeliness to accept the technology (Prayoga & Abraham, 2016). It can be defined as a measure of users' responsiveness for liking/disliking to use a particular system in the future which is often validated by the actual use (Qaji et al., 2015). The intention to use a new technology in response to a request to use it is then referred to as the acceptance (Broman Toft, Schuitema, & Thøgersen, 2014). However, without influencing variables, this intention cannot be formed.

Behavioral Intention is often influenced directly by a person's Attitude, defined as the degree of interest one has towards the technology (Armenteros, Liaw, Fernández, Díaz, & Sánchez, 2013). In most researches, the output measurement of Attitude is often the extent to which we value something as positive or negative. Positive attitude indicates a higher likelihood of acceptance, while negative attitudes indicate the lower possibility of acceptance. It is rooted in perceived costs, risks, benefits, and affect, that we can see it as an evaluative integration of cognitions and affects experienced in relation to an object (Huijts et al., 2013). This explanation means that Attitude is not a mere fluctuation of the positive-negative dichotomy of evaluation towards a certain behavior or object. It is a product of many interplaying variables that is dynamic and constantly influencing it, which eventually affect the decision whether to use or not to use.

From the definition, we can interpret that Attitude is a result of weighing the all of the influencing variables. We can see this in the context of IoT devices and systems. For example, perceived cost refers to how much effort a person have to exert in order to accept the IoT device. Energy to learn and operate, mental preparation, and money spent fall into this category. Risks are the virtual, psychological, and physical potential disadvantage that you may encounter using the technology. For example, in the context of the use of e-learning, perceived risk include socio-psychological perceived risk, perceived performance risk, and perceived source and time-demand risk, and this perception is influenced by email phishing literacy and anomia (feeling of lack of moral standards) (Abraham & Sharron, 2015). Your biodata and personal real-time information is another examples of virtual risks (Kennedy, 2016). Greater demand due to the reason of non-stop interconnected device may lead to morale and psychological exhaustion (Lumb, 2015), and not to mention more impersonal workplace (Starner, 2015), and addiction. The physical disadvantage may be a result of mishandling the device, or the side-effect from the technology that affect our health directly. The benefit is a vague concept to describe here. At large, the benefit can be described as anything positive, helpful, and desirable that is happened due to the usage of the IoT device. From better health to safer navigation, there is no limit to this as almost all IoT systems and devices are tailored to a specific industry. Finally, affect, is your personal feeling when using the technology, it is the extent of how happy overall you are with the IoT device you are using. For the next part, we are going to go through all the variables above one by one, starting from the belief.

## Belief

### Perceived Usefulness and Perceived Ease of Use

The general idea about Technology Acceptance Model states Behavioral Intention to use technology is influenced by mainly two factors: the Perceived Usefulness (PU) and Perceived Ease of Use (PEOU) (Schepers & Wetzels, 2007). This means that for a person to use technology, he or she has to perceive that the technology has a significant use that is relevant to his activities and discourse. In addition, the technology must be relatively easy enough for the person to use. These are the two main beliefs that often influence the Attitude and Behavioral Intention directly in cases of technology acceptance. Depending on how useful and how easy to use an individual perceive a technology to be, his or her attitude will differ. The idea is that the easier the useful technology to use, the more likely individual will develop a positive attitude and intention to adopt it.

Let's take an example of a salaryman named Kyle. Let say that Kyle is having trouble with his clothes cleaned because his old washing machine would break down if it is loaded too much. Kyle has to wash his clothes in three to four cycles, with the same amount of water, electricity, and time spent each cycle. He used to only have to wait for one cycle for the same amount of clothes to be washed. A friend suggested that he get one of that foot paddle-powered washing machines to have a cost effective laundry experience. He did and decided that he wanted to try it out. If Kyle does not perceive that a new foot paddle-powered washing machine is a great solution to his laundry problem, Kyle will not use the machine. For example, Kyle might find that he has to wash in more cycles now because the new non-electric laundry machine has even less space. Kyle does not find this useful at all. He also has to paddle the machine many times before all the clothes he wants to clean is finished washing. He does not find the machine to be easily used. As a result, he does not intend to use the machine at all.

### Perceived Enjoyment

One of the most notable affective element that is frequently included in the model of technology acceptance is the element of enjoyment. Questions asked for this variables would be "how much fun could we have when using a particular technology?" or "how much enjoyment can be perceived/felt when engaging with a brand new technology?". Note that this variable might be more important in some technology over the others (educational games versus new accounting software), but the relevancy of Perceived Enjoyment (Suki & Suki, 2011) in the model of technology acceptance is certainly undeniable. The reason that Perceived Enjoyment is heavily considered as an influencing variable is that organizations or society can be incentivized to spread the technology by the element of fun and leisure that prompts the acceptance of it (Brown et al., 2013).

IoT device that will be likely to be perceived enjoyable is *Snap Inc.*'s spectacle (Carson, 2016). The purpose of this device is already for leisure/entertainment purposes (capturing everyday moments through glasses and share them on the Snapchat platform). With fun design and social sharing feature, it is not hard to enjoy this device. One other example of IoT device acceptance that is based on enjoyment is the drone technology. The air-bone remote-control vehicles are considered as a toy by many people, using it to race each other, taking pictures from the sky, and even dropping things! Its usefulness that somewhat overlaps with high enjoyability is one of the main factors that leads to the acceptance of the technology.

### Perceived Behavioral Control

Some studies also incorporated the belief element of Perceived Behavioral Control. Although a person has a positive attitude (that make him seems likely to accept a technology), when he or she has a feeling of no control over the activities acted upon it, likelihood to accept the technology will be lowered (Cheung & Vogel, 2013). Often derived from the model of Theory of Planned Behavior by Ajzen (1991), Perceived Behavioral Control is the belief that an individual has control over the behavior he or she is engaging (Aboelmaged & Gebba, 2013). It reflects a person's perception of the ease or difficulty of implementing the behavior in question (Yaghoubi & Bahmani, 2010). The difference this concept has from the Perceived Ease of Use is the end to which we view the difficulty of using the technology comes from while Perceived Ease of Use explains about how the technology is easy enough to pick up, mastered, and used on-demand, Perceived Behavioral Control reflects individual's perception of the extent that he or she have control over accepting or using the technology. As for easiness to use is relative, however, easy a technology might be, when an individual perceived that he or she has no control over the technology, the chance of it being picked up and used is less likely.

## Social Influence

You might argue that although the logic of the premises seems true, in a complex world full of possibilities and influencing factors the model seems to be oversimplifying the concept of acceptance. This is somewhat true. For example, the model did not incorporate the element of social influence. For a more advanced context of technology acceptance, Venkatesh and Davis (2000) offered a new extended Technology Acceptance Model, commonly known as TAM2. There are some extension to what is usually included in the original model. One of the main extension is the element of Social Influence (Wu, Chou, Weng, & Huang, 2011), which consists of Subjective Norm, Image, and Voluntarity. In the story above, the element of subjective norm can be represented by Kyle's friend. Subjective norm is the variable of human and social changes that makes individual comply and internalize, voluntarily or mandatory (Schepers & Wetzels, 2007).

## Subjective Norm, Image, and Voluntariness

Kyle's intention to use is influenced by his friend's suggestion, therefore shows a significant role of social influence. Nowadays, smartphones are usually bought after some hefty considerations. Specs, features, camera quality, and physical aesthetics are all important aspects to consider about. Tech blogs and online forums that users refer to for the latest or the best are great examples of the subjective norm in play.

Now let's move to your social circles. Possession are one of the many ways to showcase or maintain social status in one's social circle. A feature phone that is very limited in online social media participation will leave the users out of many social activities. In order to maintain and keep up a basic communication ability within our current social environment, we need to have a smartphone. This is what TAM2 refers to as Image, or the attempt to maintain or enhance one's social status by engaging the technology in context (Venkatesh & Davis, 2000).

In addition, you do not want to feel forced when using technology. Too much and heavy of social influence will render your inner intention to use the minimum. When your boss at work tells you to switch from Apple to an Android phone even though you might not like it, you will be less likely to accept it. Sure, you may use it, but the chance of you to perceive it positively will be very little because it is mandatory. That is why, when accepting a technology, like Kyle with his washing machines, Voluntariness, defined as the degree that user perceives the use of technology to be not mandatory or personal willingness to use (Wu, Chou, Weng, & Huang, 2011), is pivotal.

Health trackers are examples of IoT devices that went popular due to the hype that it brings. Since the last couple years, health has been the new trend. Exercise and workout regimens are rising in popularity. However, as the term 'quantified self' is gaining popularity, there comes a need to quantify and track the progress in real-time things like blood and oxygen level, calories burned, body fat percentage, and physical performance (Holmes, 2014). With this craze, people quickly jumps into the bandwagon and begin popularizing health trackers that have become more and more advanced. As companies are making them more and more sophisticated, wearable, social, and versatile, discourse to level up (because it is easier with the quantification machines) along with the others. This is not only shown in discussion over the Internet and social circle, but companies are investing a lot of money in marketing these products, selling them as not only as health, but also social devices. Breaking a personal record, sharing them online, or even compare with others' progress becomes some of the important purposes of exercising. With the social aspect and effective marketing strategy on the rise, health trackers become widely accepted, especially among health-enthusiasts.

Around three years ago, there was a meme going around about how wearing *Google Glass* makes a person looks like a dork (Wohlsen, 2013). It is arguably one of the reasons that made the spectacle infamous. The Glass were not ready yet for the public; it has a lot of problems to fix like battery life and privacy issues. Aside from that, the Internet had undeniably created a negative image of the product that associates it with stereotypes that are definitely not encouraging people to wear the product. Wearing them at that time will not help you maintain your image around your peer, due to the negativity it has brought to your privacy and image.

## Cognitive Instrumentals

The extended model of TAM also posit the cognitive instrumental factors. These are the factors describe the considered applicable function of the technology. There are three variables that are in the category (Venkatesh & Davis, 2000), i.e. Job Relevance, Output Quality, and Result Demonstrability. Job relevance refers to the relevancy of the technology in the job (or most any task that the technology supposes to ease out) that is carried out by the user. Output Quality generally refers to the desirability of the performance result of the technology. In short, it is how well a system do what it does (Venkatesh & Davis, 2000).

Finally, we also need to know if the well-done relevant technology really has an impact on the actual task or job we want to accomplish. This concept is heavily related to Perceived Usefulness as the logic dictates that if a certain technology is highly relevant and essential to the job or task being carried out, it has the higher chance to be perceived as useful as the relevancy has to increase the productivity (Banderker, & Van Belle, 2009). If said relevant technology is able to produce the desired result that increases productivity, we would be able to conclude that the technology is useful to the user, as a result, is able to be demonstrated.

These three factors will be crucial in determining the Perceived Usefulness of the technology. Usually, devices that are aligned with company role are quicker to be perceived useful by man. For example, drones and delivery services. Even more flexible, remote-access technologies that enable remote management over and across devices like PC, tablets, and smartphones boxes allow an opportunity to establish a stronger collaboration practices among employee due to the ability of the devices to communicate (Myler, 2015).

*MARS*, the customized-massage robot from *AiTreat*, is claimed to be able to serve multiple customers at the same time after programming (Quek, 2016), which reduces the need to train and certifies employee that is costly. If the manager and massage parlor operators find client satisfaction and visit increases while client turnover, waiting line, and serving time decreases over a period of time after utilizing the massage-bots, they can conclude that they have a good case study of result demonstrability from the technology.

## Trust

If we take a step back and see the bigger picture, we realize that often technology acceptance is not just about the individual and the technology, but rather the individual, their social circle, the technology, the company that created and benefit from it from time to time. Accepting also does not mean that we accept and use. The fact that IoT devices require your data constantly indicates that more amount of effort and thought should be put in. As mentioned in the previous section regarding privacy and control over acceptance, one particular variable is integral with the acceptance of IoT. That is the element of Trust.

Trust is a defining feature of most economic and social interactions in which uncertainty is present (Pavlou, 2003). It is highly related to security since ensuring system security, and user safety is a necessity to gain trust (Yan, Zhang, & Vasilakos, 2014). It can be described as individual's belief that the other party will behave in a responsible manner, fulfilling his/her expectations without taking advantage of the vulnerability that is willingly given after taking the characteristic of what the other party has to offer (Pavlou, 2003; Gefen, Karahanna, & Straub, 2003).

Trust is not something simple to be conceptualized. It has a lot to do not just with our belief, but also what the technology has to offer, how is it represented, and the aftermath of the acceptance. It depends on the trustee's objective properties, such as security and dependability, and subjective properties, like honesty, benevolence, and goodness (Yan et al., 2014). It has been found to be a good predictor for usefulness, ease of use, behavioral intention, and attitude (Ha & Stoel, 2009). It can even be said that Trust is the gateway to technology acceptance, especially in IoT where any information of you are at potential risk.

Trust is by far the heaviest challenge companies and developers have to take on. It is a common thing that people have nowadays, considering many of their trusted application and devices are rumored to sell their data or was breached. Montgomery (2016), CEO of *Connect in Private*, listed out 10 of the most terrifying IoT security breach that has not been widely known. The list included much major organization, such as the computer system in the US Department of Energy, breached steel plant in Germany that caused major damage, and even UCLA's hospital network that keep private information of 4.5 million people. One of the biggest recent breaches in 2016 has to be *Mirai*, a malware that attacks vulnerable devices that use telnet protocol to have full control over the hacked device and launch DDoS attacks (Franceschi-Bicchierai, 2016).

## Facilitated Appropriation

At times, technology will serve another purpose than it was intended to. The same with IoT devices, as it can be appropriated in many ways. Appropriation refers to the flexibility of technologies to be adopted, adapted, and incorporated into working practice and mapped onto user's needs (Riemer, Overfeld, Scifleet, & Richter, 2012). This definition tells us that the process does not stop after the initial acceptance, but rather is adapted to be used as the user intended to, no matter how deviated from the intended purpose. Although this might be a threat to the rational objectives of management captured in the notion of 'unfaithful use', appropriation also explains the variance in the outcomes that can be produced by the technology (Riemer & Johnston, 2012).

How is appropriation related to technology acceptance; is it is a product of the acceptance itself? Prayoga and Abraham (2016) discussed the term Facilitated Appropriation in their study about IoT Acceptance. The term "*Facilitated Appropriation*" is used to describe the appropriation process that is influenced by facilitating factors such as information available, guidelines, and other examples derived from another form of appropriation, that results in much more variety, versatility, and creativity in meeting user's end goal (Prayoga & Abraham, 2016). A user who is facilitated to appropriate better will expect and find a better use of the technology. Thus, will find the technology even more useful, increasing his or her belief of Perceived Usefulness (Prayoga & Abraham, 2016) and Enjoyment that will drive his or her intention to accept the technology further.

How someone appropriates may depend on the flexibility of the IoT object. Wearing IoT glasses for fashion can be considered as appropriation, but it is not the kind that has anything to do with the technology. One example of a very flexible IoT object is the *AWS* IoT button that is programmable to do many tasks, from starting cars to automating postmasters. Most of the function is work and daily activity related. But for leisure purposes, one can use it to program the button to turn on a specific *Netflix* series on TV when pressed. This requires not only one or two simple actions, but rather an extended knowledge of programming complemented by personal enjoyment. This is what we meant by Facilitated Appropriation.

## THE INDIVIDUAL DIFFERENCES

This section discusses other factors beyond individual differences are discussed in TAM, namely past experience, personality, cultural values, and cyber-resilience.

### Past Experience

Past Experience is the extent to which a user has been exposed to the technology or similar technology usage prior to current innovation. Abraham and Falah (2016) found that the previous illusory experience in the online dating affects the tendency to have positive attitude toward virtual marriage. In the context of the hospitality industry, Ozturk and Hancer (2015) found that users who had experience in using RFID technology will be more likely to use the technology than their counterpart who had never used them. This indicates that people who accepted similar technology in the past will be more likely to accept and use the technology again in the future. This result makes prior exposure crucial to new technology's acceptance. Satisfactory prior experience may create 'fans' that are loyal to the particular brands. Take *Apple* for example. In IoT context, this phenomenon might be observable in a more personalized IoT tech, like camera spectacles (Carson, 2016) or health trackers (Maslakovic, 2016). Repeated account of performance also can result in a better-established attitude and intention (Venkatesh, Thong, & Xu 2012). Thus, accounting experience as a moderating factor when using attitude and belief to explain acceptance is very important.

### Personality and Cultural Values

The centrality of personality and cultural factor in relation to technology acceptance is reflected upon research by Schumacher, Erol, and Sihn (2016) titled "*Industry 4.0 Readiness and Maturity Model*". According to their research report, there are at least 9 dimensions that a manufacturing company needs in facing the challenge of the overgrowing tech world that integrates the element and the interaction of people, machine, business processes, and organization more and more. Two of the most relevant factors that we will talk about are People and Culture Dimension. The former holds the key of Openness and Autonomy. These are the two personality traits variables that determine how well a system that comprises of the four elements work.

Personality traits can be seen as unique individual characteristics that govern behavior. (Mennicken et al., 2016). It is relatively stable across behavior and any situations of life (Montag, Duke, & Markowetz, 2016). Its relevancy in the context of technology acceptance lies on the idea of compatibility between the system and how the users (human) behave that will allow better and easier engagement (da Silva Junior, de Souza, & Maciel, 2016). It is technology built by human for the humans, after all.

That's not all. Personality is not just about human. Artificial Intelligence (AI) also possesses personality. Take smart home device like *Apple HomeKit, Samsung SmartThings, Amazon Echo*, and *Google Homes*. The devices are humanized to encourage and promote trust and perceived enjoyment/usability from the users (Mennicken et al., 2016). Machines that could not only talk, but also communicate and understand what the user's are talking about. Soon enough, AI that mimics human expressions and feelings might be a common phenomenon.

In the context of technology adoption/acceptance (especially in IoT/RFID related device), The Big Five Model is often used to represent and explain the role personality traits in influencing the adoption, e.g. among health workers (Yee-Loong Chong, Liu, Luo, & Keng-Boon, 2015). Four out of five personality traits, namely conscientiousness, openness, extraversion, and agreeableness correlate positively with technology acceptance. However, the train neuroticism correlates negatively. Different research context might offer a different explanation on this finding. One might argue that the more extraverted and open we are, the more we are susceptible to new ideas and technologies. This is because people who are open often are more curious and love them. People who want to maintain their social status (mostly the extraverts) will be influenced socially to accept. The more disciplined, organized, and cooperative a person is, the more likely he or she will perceive new opportunities that is designed to help (such as IoT technologies) as useful. Motivation to achieve productivity in accordance with their goal (conscientiousness) promote acceptance. On the other hand, neurotic tendency tends to drift user away from potential benefits. He or she will be likely to focus on what will go wrong and experience technology anxiety.

In one study that involves same variables but in the context of students, we hypothesized that personality traits (the Big Five) are indirect predictors of behavioral intention to use IoT health device through perceived usefulness (Prayoga & Abraham, 2016). However, the result showed otherwise. We found out that none of the five trait factors actually predict perceived usefulness, thus rejecting the hypothesis. This finding can be seen as a "blessing in disguise", as we do not have to put so much weight and consideration on personality trait differences in the training or learning process to adopt and accept the technology. The concern comes from research such as the one by Montag et al. (2016) stating that personality traits' data may be used to eliminate personnel with different personality requirement in the IoT industry. We might be able to conclude that this suggestion might not be viable from our perspective.

In addition, Zhong, Jin, and Chen (2012) stated that decision style plays a huge role in influencing the IoT business. In their study, they explained that five types of decision styles (e.g. autocratic, decision by experience) essentially influence one or more of the twelve aspects of decision types (e.g. conformity, rapid decisions, trust the analytical tool). This, in turn, will determine how an individual will form an attitude towards creative opportunity towards utilizing the IoT technology. Acknowledging its importance, one way to train and develop the decision style is through empowering mental models by matching it with appropriate and relevant case or problem.

On the other hand, Criel, Vanderhulst, Kawsar, and Trappeniers (2011) reminded us of one fundamental aspect: freedom. What they meant by freedom is the liberty to involve, delve, participate, create, and share the concepts and visualization of data, in which the manipulation process is customizable according to preferences of the users. This brings up the question, must we also include Perceived Freedom as one of the influencing belief? Or rather something that is more closely related and relevant with personality.

Mellis, Buechley, Resnick, and Hartmann (2016) emphasized the role of self-efficacy that according to them plays a huge role in the fabrication of the IoT. The similarity between fabrication and acceptance lies on the element of challenge. Efficacy in facing challenges is the one that eventually differentiates personnel with the same skill, competition, and other psychological fundamentality in the acceptance of IoT. Therefore it is also important to investigate predictors of online self-efficacy (e.g. Abraham & Pane, 2014).

From a cultural standpoint, ICT value and knowledge sharing are the central point of focus. One of the most interesting cultural model perhaps is the one proposed by Ning and Liu (2015). In a model they called "cyber-physical-social-thinking (CPST) space", they proposed that the Chinese culture of Five Elements of Wood, Fire, Water, Earth, and Metal are key determinants whether a system of IoT actually works well. They all represent a certain aspect of the system. Wood represents structure and strength. Earth represents stability. Fire represents dynamism. Water represents flexibility, and Metal represents persistence and determination. IoT itself, without human, is not sufficient to be called an industry, mainly because it is only "a phase of intelligentization and informatization development" (Ning & Liu, 2015, p. 3). To increase participation, Barricelli et al. (2015) recommended a focus on emphasizing the factors that determine the "culture of participation", i.e. reciprocity, empathy, altruism, and trust. These are the elements that enable co-creation, which can be seen as the creative process in the collaboration of IoT participation.

As far as this chapter is being written, there has not been researches that specifically correlate cultural value orientations with IoT acceptance except for Prayoga and Abraham (2016). However, we can still find a few that predict acceptance. Most of the studies that we have now position cultural value orientations as direct predictors (Erumban & de Jong, 2006; Nistor, Gögüs, & Lerche, 2013) or moderating variables (e.g. Baptista & Oliveira, 2015; Yoon, 2009) that confirm their relationship within the framework of acceptance models. In their study regarding social network and online shopping behavior, Pookulangara and Koesler (2011) argued that (1) Technology is constructed by the culture, making it one of the cultural phenomenon. (2) Social network is a "melting pot" of cultural interactions, where all of the aspects and parties share wisdom, knowledge, and trust with each other. These interactions bridge the cultural differences between people of the Eastern and Western culture towards technology. Here, cultural orientations can be seen as a factor that contribute to the promotion of acceptance and understanding of technology within the interactions in the social networks (physically and virtually) (Pookulangara & Koesler, 2011). Sole reliance on developers, investors, marketers, and even natural occurrence in seeing IoT acceptance is like looking into a two-dimensional painting; we cannot really see what's behind the central object of the art. To Steers, Meyer, and Sanchez-Runde (2008), culture is an axiological dimension that combines with demographical factors (such as education level, well-being and prosperity, and resources availability) that is able to facilitate human capacity to reflect upon today, and envision the progressive future to innovate, make a change, and evolve.

A meta-analysis done by Cardon and Marshall (2008) studied 95 peer-reviewed TAM articles from 29 countries found out that Uncertainty Avoidance (UA)–one of Hofstede's (2001) cultural value orientations–is able to moderate the correlation between Perceived Ease of Use and Perceived Usefulness, Perceived Ease of use and Behavioral Intentions, and Perceived Usefulness and Behavioral Intention. This finding is based on the thought that ICT adoption is almost never culture-free, and often it is something found in the thin air that is almost impossible to grasp and measure. Uncertainty Avoidance is the tendency for people to avoid ambiguous, unstructured, and novel situations that make them uncomfortable. It is seen as one of the positive predictors of technology acceptance, as technologies are often the solutions to ease anxiety and ambiguity. Although it is often associated with the rejection of new ideas, according to Cardon and Marshall (2008), it does not directly imply technology rejection. When UA is integrated into rules and procedures in the interplay between TAM dimensions, its role becomes more significant, important, and complex.

Haghighy (2009) further argued that acceptance models like TAM need to be "reconfigured" or modified to address the cultural problem so it can work well when implemented in the certain cultural setting. In his research involving 243 participants from 20 countries, Haghighy found that Uncertainty Avoidance, Individualism/Collectivism, and Power Distanc–all Hofstede's (2001) cultural dimensions–are able to moderate the relationship between the dimensions of TAM (namely Perceived Usefulness, Perceived Ease of Use, Social Norm, and Perceived Behavioral Control) in various directions and significance. On the same line, Fernández Robin, McCoy, Yáñez Sandivari, and Yáñez Martínez (2014) and also Prayoga and Abraham (2016) found out that in Chile (country level) and Indonesia (individual level), surprisingly cultural factors are not very relevant in explaining the relation between the TAM's dimension. Fernández Robin et al. (2014) stated that in Chile, intention to use technology is influenced more by familiarity (experience) and social reference (social norm). While Prayoga and Abraham (2016) found out that only Long Term Orientation (LTO) needs to be considered to promote behavioral intention to accept and use, in which the relationship is moderated by Facilitated Appropriation. They found that Power Distance, Uncertainty Avoidance, Masculinity/Femininity, and Collectivism/Individualism dichotomies have the potential correlation that could be positive or negative towards facilitated appropriation. However, Long-term Orientation is compatible with the purpose of IoT health-device that is the persistence of health.

If we would generalize the findings above, one thing that we can conclude from the role that cultural value orientations plays in IoT Acceptance is the context specificity that depends on the type of technology (sensor, interpreter, etc.), its purpose (education, health, etc.), level of analysis (individual, country), and tangibility (value, practice). However, the implication is obvious, findings from these studies ought to be considered by the business organizations to increase acceptance rate of its employee and consumers.

## Cyber-Resilience

One construct that is often overlooked when the discussion of IoT optimization is brought up is cyber-resilience. Cyber-resilience is the "ability to continuously deliver the intended outcome despite adverse cyber events" (Björck, Henkel, Stirna, & Zdravkovic, 2015, p. 311). This definition uses the organizational perspective that is embodied in the ICT system. Organizations that are strong in cyber-resilience will be loyal to serve its purpose (whether service or product), tough in terms of facing crisis and challenges, and is systematically able to recover from setbacks and disadvantageous situations that threaten its integrity, availability, and confidentiality from outside or within. This definition is often ameliorated to the extent that it is applicable to the individual level, which translates to the concept of "online resilience" that serves as the opposition towards "online vulnerability" (Vandoninck, d'Haenens, & Roe, 2013).

People with high level of cyber-resilience do not easily feel negative emotions or revert back to the offline world, such as in a situation where they are challenged or demotivated in using an IoT device. Vandoninck et al. (2013) in their research studying online sexual temptation among children and young teenagers found that there are a few determinant factors of online resilience, namely age, self-efficacy, pro-active coping response, digital literacy, and previous experiences in facing cyber-risks. What is interesting about this finding is that socio-economic status and parental mediation and monitoring do not correlate with cyber-resilience.

Moreover, Butler, Bateman, Gray, and Diamant (2014) studied cyber-resilience in community level that they define as "the extent to which a community's membership is willing to remain involved in the face of variability and change in topics (online) discussed" (p. 2). As for the factors, the "cyber-community-resilience" is very dynamic and is a Gestalt of hope, choice, and communication behavior-dependent between all of the members. Cyber-community-resilience is very important to be considered if one set to optimize the acceptance and use of IoT device. This is mainly because the resilience is the factors that sustain behaviors, invest knowledge and even effort when using IoT device when things are going south. Thus, we feel that there is a need for intervention in situations where IoT system works or introduced. Intervention can take form of message modification or delivery within the IoT-human interaction framework. These messages are expected to be curated to close the gap between perceived cost/harm and perceived benefit from the usage of IoT.

## CONCLUSION

IOT usage optimization can be improved by identifying the theoretical models that involve simultaneously human ecosystem–with its individual, organizational, social, and cultural dimensions–and technology ecosystem. Studies on IoT optimization in the business world is necessary to continuously clarify the interplays between the components discussed above in relation to the technology acceptance, adoption, and appropriation in daily life. The entire discussion has raised the urgency of the birth of a new field, "*Technopsychology*", which melts the boundaries between humans and technology (especially information and communication technology). Gosling and Mason (2015) were true when they stated that the opportunities to do technopsychological researches have undergone multiplication and we are able to benefit from novel paradigms to face the exponential growth of technology and to give positive impact to the society.

## REFERENCES

Aboelmaged, M., & Gebba, T. R. (2013). Mobile banking adoption: An examination of Technology Acceptance Model and Theory of Planned Behavior. *International Journal of Business Research and Development*, *2*(1), 35–50. doi:10.24102/ijbrd.v2i1.263

Abraham, J., & Sharron. (2015). Perceived risk of anti-corruption e-learning, email phishing literacy, and anomia. In J. J. J. H. Park, Y. Pan, H.-C. Chao, & G. Yi (Eds.), *Lecture notes in electrical engineering: Vol. 331. Ubiquitous computing application and wireless sensor* (pp. 577-584). Springer. 10.1007/978-94-017-9618-7_59

Abraham, J., & Falah, A. (2016). Is virtual marriage acceptable? A psychological study investigating the role of ambiguity tolerance and intimacy illusion in online dating among adolescents and early adults. *Journal of Psychological and Educational Research*, *24*(2), 117–143.

Abraham, J., & Pane, M. M. (2014). The mediating role of social competition identity management strategy in the predictive relationship between susceptibility to social influence, Internet privacy concern, and online political efficacy. In Lecture notes in computer science: Vol. 8407. Information and communication technology (pp. 492-499). Berlin: Springer. doi:10.1007/978-3-642-55032-4_50

Ajzen, I. (1991). The Theory of Planned Behavior. *Organizational Behavior and Human Decision Processes*, *50*(2), 179–211. doi:10.1016/0749-5978(91)90020-T

Al-Azawei, A., Parslow, P., & Lundqvist, K. (2016). Investigating the effect of learning styles in a blended e-learning system: An extension of the Technology Acceptance Model (TAM). *Australasian Journal of Educational Technology*, *33*(2), 1–23. doi:10.14742/ajet.2741

Armenteros, M., Liaw, S.-S., Fernández, M., Díaz, R. F., & Sánchez, R. A. (2013). Surveying FIFA instructors behavioral intention toward the multimedia teaching materials. *Computers & Education*, *61*, 91–104. doi:10.1016/j.compedu.2012.09.010

Balakrishnan, A. (2016, December 5). *There's no need to check out at the Amazon Go store.* Retrieved January 4, 2017, from NBC News: http://www.nbcnews.com/tech/tech-news/there-s-no-need-check-out-amazon-go-store-n692201

Banderker, N., & Van Belle, J.-P. (2009). Adoption of mobile technology by public healthcare doctors. *International Journal of Healthcare Delivery Reform Initiatives*, *1*(3), 38–54. doi:10.4018/jhdri.2009070103

Baptista, G., & Oliveira, T. (2015). Understanding mobile banking: The unified theory of acceptance and use of technology combined with cultural moderators. *Computers in Human Behavior*, *50*, 418–430. doi:10.1016/j.chb.2015.04.024

Barricelli, B. R., Fischer, G., Mørch, A., Piccinno, A., & Valtolina, S. (2015). Cultures of participation in the digital age: Coping with information, participation, and collaboration overload. In P. Díaz, V. Pipek, C. Ardito, C. Jensen, I. Aedo, & A. Boden (Eds.), Lecture notes in computer science: Vol. 9083. *End-user development* (pp. 271–275). Springer International Publishing. doi:10.1007/978-3-319-18425-8_28

Björck, F., Henkel, M., Stirna, J., & Zdravkovic, J. (2015). Cyber resilience – fundamentals for a definition. In A. Rocha, A. M. Correia, S. Costanzo, & L. P. Reis (Eds.), *Advances in intelligent systems and computing: New contributions in information systems and technologies* (Vol. 353, pp. 311–316). doi:10.1007/978-3-319-16486-1_31

Broman Toft, M., Schuitema, G., & Thøgersen, J. (2014). Responsible technology acceptance: Model development and application to consumer acceptance of smart grid technology. *Applied Energy*, *134*, 392–400. doi:10.1016/j.apenergy.2014.08.048

Brown, M., Coughlan, T., Lawson, G., Goulden, M., Houghton, R. J., & Mortier, R. (2013). Exploring interpretations of data from the Internet of Things in the home. *Interacting with Computers*, *25*(3), 204–217. doi:10.1093/iwc/iws024

Butler, B. S., Bateman, P. J., Gray, P. H., & Diamant, E. I. (2014). An attraction-selection-attrition theory of online community size and resilience. *Management Information Systems Quarterly*, *38*(3), 699–728.

Cardon, P., & Marshall, B. A. (2008). National culture and technology acceptance: The impact of uncertainty avoidance. *Issues in Information Systems*, *9*(2), 103–110.

Carson, B. (2016, September 24). *REVEALED: Secret video shows Snapchat's new glasses.* Retrieved January 4, 2017, from Business Insider: http://www.businessinsider.com/snapchat-glasses-2016-9

Cheung, R., & Vogel, D. (2013). Predicting user acceptance of collaborative technologies: An extension of the Technology Acceptance Model for e-learning. *Computers & Education*, *63*, 160–175. doi:10.1016/j.compedu.2012.12.003

Cosseboom, L. (2014, September 26). *This startup is building smartphone-powered "fishtech" for Indonesia's commercial aqualife.* Retrieved January 4, 2017, from *Tech in Asia*, https://www.techinasia.com/this-startup-is-building-smartphone-powered-fishtech-for-indonesias-commercial-aqualife

Criel, J., Vanderhulst, G., Kawsar, F., & Trappeniers, L. (2011). *A co-creation platform for creative engagement of end-users in a connected object space. In Proceedings of the 2011 International Workshop on Networking and Object Memories for the Internet of Things - NoME-IoT'11* (pp. 9–14). New York, NY: Association for Computing Machinery. doi:10.1145/2029932.2029936

da Silva Junior, D. P., de Souza, P. C., & Maciel, C. (2016). Establishing guidelines for user quality of experience in ubiquitous systems. In N. Streitz & P. Markopoulos (Eds.), Lecture notes in computer science: Vol. 9749. *Distributed, ambient and pervasive interactions* (pp. 46–57). Springer International Publishing. doi:10.1007/978-3-319-39862-4_5

Dominici, G., Roblek, V., Abbate, T., & Tani, M. (2016). Click and drive: Consumer attitude to product development: Towards future transformations of the driving experience. *Business Process Management Journal*, *22*(2), 420–434. doi:10.1108/BPMJ-05-2015-0076

Dull, T. (2014, December 10). *Big data and the Internet of things: Two sides of the same coin?* Retrieved January 4, 2017, from http://www.smartdatacollective.com/tamaradull/286381/big-data-and-internet-things-two-sides-same-coin

Dull, T. (2015a). *Is privacy dead? And the survey says …* Retrieved January 4, 2017, from http://www.sas.com/en_id/insights/articles/marketing/is-privacy-dead.html

Dull, T. (2015b, July 27). *It's your life, starring your data.* Retrieved January 4, 2017, from http://www.socialmediatoday.com/technology-data/tamaradull/2015-07-24/its-your-life-starring-your-data

Eltayeb, M., & Dawson, M. (2016). Understanding user's acceptance of personal cloud computing: Using the Technology Acceptance Model. In S. Latifi (Ed.), *Information technology: New generations* (Vol. 448, pp. 3–12). Springer International Publishing. doi:10.1007/978-3-319-32467-8_1

Erumban, A. A., & de Jong, S. B. (2006). Cross-country differences in ICT adoption: A consequence of culture? *Journal of World Business*, *41*(4), 302–314. doi:10.1016/j.jwb.2006.08.005

Estes, A. C. (2015, July 16). *Apple might start showing people ads based on their bank balances.* Retrieved January 4, 2017, from http://gizmodo.com/apples-thinking-about-showing-people-ads-based-on-their-1718218638

Fernández Robin, C., McCoy, S., Yáñez Sandivari, L., & Yáñez Martínez, D. (2014). Technology acceptance model: Worried about the cultural influence? In F. F.-H. Nah (Ed.), Lecture notes in computer science: Vol. 8527. *HCI in business* (pp. 609–619). Springer International Publishing. doi:10.1007/978-3-319-07293-7_59

Franceschi-Bicchierai, L. (2016, October 21). *Blame the Internet of Things for destroying the Internet today.* Retrieved December 11, 2016, from http://motherboard.vice.com/read/blame-the-internet-of-things-for-destroying-the-internet-today

Gandomi, A., & Haider, M. (2015). Beyond the hype: Big data concepts, methods, and analytics. *International Journal of Information Management*, *35*(2), 137–144. doi:10.1016/j.ijinfomgt.2014.10.007

Garrett, R. (2016, December 5). *Taming big data in the IoT | supply & demand chain executive.* Retrieved January 4, 2017, from http://www.sdcexec.com/article/12271216/taming-big-data-in-the-iot

Gartner. (2015, November 10). *Gartner says 6.4 Billion connected "things" will be in use in 2016, up 30 percent from 2015*. Retrieved January 4, 2017, from http://www.gartner.com/newsroom/id/3165317

Gefen, D., Karahanna, E., & Straub, D. W. (2003). Trust and TAM in online shopping: An integrated model. *Management Information Systems Quarterly*, *27*(1), 51–90.

Gosling, S. D., & Mason, W. (2015). Internet research in psychology. *Annual Review of Psychology*, *66*(1), 877–902. doi:10.1146/annurev-psych-010814-015321 PMID:25251483

Ha, S., & Stoel, L. (2009). Consumer e-shopping acceptance: Antecedents in a technology acceptance model. *Journal of Business Research*, *62*(5), 565–571. doi:10.1016/j.jbusres.2008.06.016

Haghighy, T. K. (2009). *Internet banking Technology Acceptance Model: A focus on Hofstede cultural dimensions* (Unpublished doctoral dissertation.). Graduate School of Business Faculty of Business and Accountancy, University of Malaya, Malaysia.

Hofstede, G. (2001). *Culture's consequences: Comparing values, behaviors, institutions, and organizations across nations* (2nd ed.). Thousand Oaks, CA: Sage Publications.

Holmes, R. (2014, June 5). *Fitness trackers: A narcissist's dream, but what else is behind the boom?* Retrieved January 4, 2017, from http://fortune.com/2014/06/03/fitness-trackers-a-narcissists-dream-but-what-else-is-behind-the-boom/

Huijts, N. M. A., Molin, E. J. E., & Steg, L. (2012). Psychological factors influencing sustainable energy technology acceptance: A review-based comprehensive framework. *Renewable & Sustainable Energy Reviews*, *16*(1), 525–531. doi:10.1016/j.rser.2011.08.018

Jackson, T. (2016, June 15). *IoT.Nxt plots Internet of things "revolution" from SA*. Retrieved January 4, 2017, from Features: http://disrupt-africa.com/2016/06/iot-nxt-plots-onternet-of-things-revolution-from-sa/

Kashyap, S. (2016, August 26). *10 real world applications of Internet of things (IoT) – explained in videos*. Retrieved January 4, 2017, from https://www.analyticsvidhya.com/blog/2016/08/10-youtube-videos-explaining-the-real-world-applications-of-internet-of-things-iot/

Kennedy, J. (2016, February 1). *Internet of Things to raise stakes in cyber security*. Retrieved January 4, 2017, from https://www.siliconrepublic.com/machines/internet-of-things-cyber-attacks-pwc

Kim, S., Gajos, K. Z., Muller, M., & Grosz, B. J. (2016). *Acceptance of mobile technology by older adults: A preliminary study. In Proceedings of the 18th International Conference on Human-Computer Interaction with Mobile Devices and Services - MobileHCI '16* (pp. 147–157). New York, NY: Association for Computing Machinery. doi:10.1145/2935334.2935380

Kurzgesagt – In a Nutshell. (2016, December 7). *A new history for humanity – the human era*. Retrieved January 4, 2017, from https://www.youtube.com/watch?v=czgOWmtGVGs

Kushmaro, P. (2016, September 23). The IoT and big data: Making the connection. *Huffington Post*. Retrieved from http://www.huffingtonpost.com/philip-kushmaro/the-iot-and-big-data-maki_b_12116608.html

Larson, Q. (2016, December 5). *Connecting Asia's startup ecosystem*. Retrieved January 4, 2017, from Tech in Asia: https://www.techinasia.com/talk/learn-code

Lee, Y., Kozar, K. A., & Larsen, K. R. T. (2003). The technology acceptance model: Past, present, and future. *Communications of the Association for Information Systems*, *12*, 752–780.

Lumb, D. (2015, March 11). How the Internet of Things is changing work. *The Future of Work*. Retrieved January 4, 2017, from https://www.fastcompany.com/3052936/the-future-of-work/how-the-internet-of-things-is-changing-work

Lunden, I. (2016, November 18). *French IoT startup Sigfox nabs €150M series E, reportedly at €600M valuation*. Retrieved January 4, 2017, from https://techcrunch.com/2016/11/18/french-iot-startup-sigfox-confirms-e150m-series-e-at-a-valuation-of-around-e600m/

Maslakovic, M. (2016, November 22). *Top fitness trackers and health gadgets you can buy right now - health & fitness gadgets & wearables*. Retrieved January 4, 2017, from http://gadgetsandwearables.com/2016/11/22/best-fitness-trackers/

McIntyre, K. (2016a, December 2). *What does housewives' porn consumption have to do with your startup? It's in the data*. Retrieved January 4, 2017, from https://www.techinasia.com/how-to-big-data-insights-tiajkt2016

McIntyre, K. (2016b, November 23). *GE partners with Indonesian big data startup to make unforeseen blackouts history*. Retrieved January 4, 2017, from https://www.techinasia.com/dattabot-ge-digital-partnership-iot-tiajkt2016

McKendrick, J. (2016, November 13). With Internet of Things and big data, 92% of everything we do will be in the cloud. *Forbes*. Retrieved from http://www.forbes.com/sites/joemckendrick/2016/11/13/with-internet-of-things-and-big-data-92-of-everything-we-do-will-be-in-the-cloud/#66823f49593f

McLellan, C. (2015, March 2). *The Internet of Things and big data: Unlocking the power*. Retrieved January 4, 2017, from http://www.zdnet.com/article/the-internet-of-things-and-big-data-unlocking-the-power/

Mellis, D. A., Buechley, L., Resnick, M., & Hartmann, B. (2016). *Engaging amateurs in the design, fabrication, and assembly of electronic devices. In Proceedings of the 2016 ACM Conference on Designing Interactive Systems - DIS'16* (pp. 1270–1281). New York, NY: Association for Computing Machinery. https://doi.org/10.1145/2901790.2901833

Mennicken, S., Zihler, O., Juldaschewa, F., Molnar, V., Aggeler, D., & Huang, E. M. (2016). "It's like living with a friendly stranger": Perceptions of personality traits in a smart home. *Proceedings of the 2016 ACM International Joint Conference on Pervasive and Ubiquitous Computing - UbiComp '16* (pp. 120-131). New York, NY: Association for Computing Machinery. doi:10.1145/2971648.2971757

Montag, C., Duke, É., & Markowetz, A. (2016). Toward Psychoinformatics: Computer science meets psychology. *Computational and Mathematical Methods in Medicine*, *2016*, 1–10. doi:10.1155/2016/2983685 PMID:27403204

Montgomery, B. (2016). *The 10 most terrifying IoT security breaches you aren't aware of (so far)*. Retrieved January 4, 2017, from http://www.iotone.com/guide/the-10-most-terrifying-iot-security-breaches-you-aren-t-aware-of-so-far/g456

Mu-Hyun, C. (2016, December 11). *Korean startup prevents fire with the power of IoT*. Retrieved January 4, 2017, from http://www.zdnet.com/article/korean-startup-prevents-fire-with-the-power-of-iot/

Myler, T. (2015, October 22). *How the Internet of Things will impact our productivity*. Retrieved January 4, 2017, from https://www.infoq.com/articles/iot-impact-productivity

Ning, H., & Liu, H. (2015). Cyber-physical-social-thinking space based science and technology framework for the Internet of Things. *Science China Information Sciences*, *58*(3), 1–19. doi:10.1007/s11432-014-5209-2

Nistor, N., Gögüs, A., & Lerche, T. (2013). Educational technology acceptance across national and professional cultures: A European study. *Educational Technology Research and Development*, *61*(4), 733–749. doi:10.1007/s11423-013-9292-7

Ozturk, A. B., & Hancer, M. (2015). The effects of demographics and past experience on RFID technology acceptance in the hospitality industry. *International Journal of Hospitality & Tourism Administration*, *16*(3), 275–289. doi:10.1080/15256480.2015.1054756

Pavlou, P. A. (2003). Consumer acceptance of electronic commerce: Integrating trust and risk with the Technology Acceptance Model. *International Journal of Electronic Commerce*, *7*(3), 101–134.

Pfeiffer, D. U., & Stevens, K. B. (2015). Spatial and temporal epidemiological analysis in the big data era. *Preventive Veterinary Medicine*, *122*(1-2), 213–220. doi:10.1016/j.prevetmed.2015.05.012 PMID:26092722

Pookulangara, S., & Koesler, K. (2011). Cultural influence on consumers usage of social networks and its impact on online purchase intentions. *Journal of Retailing and Consumer Services*, *18*(4), 348–354. doi:10.1016/j.jretconser.2011.03.003

Porter, C. E., & Donthu, N. (2006). Using the Technology Acceptance Model to explain how attitudes determine Internet usage: The role of perceived access barriers and demographics. *Journal of Business Research*, *59*(9), 999–1007. doi:10.1016/j.jbusres.2006.06.003

Prayoga, T., & Abraham, J. (2016). Behavioral intention to use IoT health device: The role of perceived usefulness, facilitated appropriation, Big Five personality traits, and cultural value orientations. [IJECE]. *Iranian Journal of Electrical and Computer Engineering*, *6*(4), 1751–1765. doi:10.11591/ijece.v6i4.10546

Qazi, A., Raj, R. G., Tahir, M., Waheed, M., Khan, S. U. R., & Abraham, A. (2015). Corrigendum to "A preliminary investigation of user perception and behavioral intention for different review types: Customers and designers Perspective". *The Scientific World Journal*, *1–2*. doi:10.1155/2015/258150 PMID:25945359

Quek, C. (2016, May 16). *5 innovative made-in-Singapore IoT solutions to improve labour productivity*. Retrieved January 4, 2017, from https://www.techinasia.com/talk/madeinsingapore-iot-solutions-improve-labour-productivity

Riemer, K., & Johnston, R. B. (2012). Place-making: A phenomenological theory of technology appropriation. *Proceedings of the 33rd International Conference on Information Systems - ICIS 2012* (pp. 1-19). Orlando, FL: Association for Information Systems. Retrieved January 4, 2017, from http://aisel.aisnet.org/icis2012/proceedings/SocialImpacts/5/

Riemer, K., Overfeld, P., Scifleet, P., & Richter, A. (2012). Eliciting the anatomy of technology appropriation processes: A case study in enterprise social media. *Proceedings of the 20th European Conference on Information Systems – ECIS 2012*. Barcelona, Spain: Association for Information Systems. Retrieved January 4, 2017, from http://aisel.aisnet.org/ecis2012/134/

Schepers, J., & Wetzels, M. (2007). A meta-analysis of the technology acceptance model: Investigating subjective norm and moderation effects. *Information & Management*, *44*(1), 90–103. doi:10.1016/j.im.2006.10.007

Schumacher, A., Erol, S., & Sihn, W. (2016). A maturity model for assessing industry 4.0 readiness and maturity of manufacturing enterprises. *Procedia CIRP*, *52*, 161–166. doi:10.1016/j.procir.2016.07.040

Sheldon, P. (2016). Facebook friend request: Applying the theory of reasoned action to student-teacher relationships on Facebook. *Journal of Broadcasting & Electronic Media*, *60*(2), 269–285. doi:10.1080/08838151.2016.1164167

Sousa Nunes, D. S., Zhang, P., & Sa Silva, J. (2015). A survey on human-in-the-loop applications towards an Internet of all. *IEEE Communications Surveys and Tutorials*, *17*(2), 944–965. doi:10.1109/COMST.2015.2398816

Starner, T. (2015, November 4). *How the Internet of Things will affect the workplace*. Retrieved January 4, 2017, from http://www.hrdive.com/news/how-the-internet-of-things-will-affect-the-workplace/408593/

Steers, R. M., Meyer, A. D., & Sanchez-Runde, C. J. (2008). National culture and the adoption of new technologies. *Journal of World Business*, *43*(3), 255–260. doi:10.1016/j.jwb.2008.03.007

Suki, N. M., & Suki, N. M. (2011). Exploring the relationship between perceived usefulness, perceived ease of use, perceived enjoyment, attitude and subscribers' intention towards using 3G mobile services. *Journal of Information Technology Management*, *22*(1), 1–7. Retrieved from http://jitm.ubalt.edu/XXII-1/article1.pdf

Townsend, K. (2016, December 6). *Examine data collection problems with big data, IoT in mind*. Retrieved January 4, 2017, from http://searchdatacenter.techtarget.com/feature/Examine-data-collection-problems-with-big-data-IoT-in-mind

Vandoninck, S., dHaenens, L., & Roe, K. (2013). Online risks. *Journal of Children and Media*, *7*(1), 60–78. doi:10.1080/17482798.2012.739780

Venkatesh, V., & Davis, F. D. (2000). A theoretical extension of the Technology Acceptance Model: Four longitudinal field studies. *Management Science*, *46*(2), 186–204. doi:10.1287/mnsc.46.2.186.11926

Venkatesh, V., Thong, J. Y. L., & Xu, X. (2012). Consumer acceptance and use of information technology: Extending the unified theory of acceptance and use of technology. *Management Information Systems Quarterly*, *36*(1), 157–178.

VoucherCloud News. (2015, April 5). *Every day big data statistics – 2.5 quintillion bytes of data created daily*. Retrieved January 4, 2017, from http://www.vcloudnews.com/every-day-big-data-statistics-2-5-quintillion-bytes-of-data-created-daily/

Wohlsen, M. (2013, May 2). *Guys like this could kill Google Glass before it ever gets off the ground*. Retrieved January 4, 2017, from Business: https://www.wired.com/2013/05/inherent-dorkiness-of-google-glass/

Wu, M.-Y., Chou, H.-P., Weng, Y.-C., & Huang, Y.-H. (2011). TAM-2 based study of website user behavior-using web 2.0 websites as an example. *WSEAS Transactions on Business and Economics, 4*(8), 133-151. Retrieved January 4, 2017, from http://www.wseas.us/e-library/transactions/economics/2011/53-665.pdf

Yaghoubi, N.-M., & Bahmani, E. (2010). Factors affecting the adoption of online banking: An integration of Technology Acceptance Model and Theory of Planned Behavior. *Pakistan Journal of Social Sciences*, *7*(3), 231–236. doi:10.3923/pjssci.2010.231.236

Yan, Z., Zhang, P., & Vasilakos, A. V. (2014). A survey on trust management for Internet of Things. *Journal of Network and Computer Applications*, *42*, 120–134. doi:10.1016/j.jnca.2014.01.014

Yang, L., Qiu, X., & Zhang, L. (2011). Design of urban public rental bicycle system based on the Internet of Things. *Proceedings of the Third International Conference on Transportation Engineering - ICTE 2011* (pp. 2784-2789). Reston, VA: American Society of Civil Engineers. doi:10.1061/41184(419)460

Yee-Loong Chong, A., Liu, M. J., Luo, J., & Keng-Boon, O. (2015). Predicting RFID adoption in healthcare supply chain from the perspectives of users. *International Journal of Production Economics*, *159*, 66–75. doi:10.1016/j.ijpe.2014.09.034

Yon, H. T. (2016, December 2). *AIRmaker unveils 5 new IoT startups that will tackle critical problems, from maternal care to clean water*. Retrieved January 4, 2017, from https://e27.co/airmaker-unveils-5-new-iot-startups-that-will-tackle-critical-problems-20161202/

Yoon, C. (2009). The effects of national culture values on consumer acceptance of e-commerce: Online shoppers in China. *Information & Management*, *46*(5), 294–301. doi:10.1016/j.im.2009.06.001

Zhong, Y., Jin, L., & Chen, X. (2012). Relationship between decision styles and decision types for innovative opportunities: Empirical study on Chinese Internet of Things industry and the cognitive decision support approach. *Journal of Computers*, *7*(7), 1574–1582. doi:10.4304/jcp.7.7.1574-1582

## KEY TERMS AND DEFINITIONS

**Appropriation:** The use of a technology that is not as intended by the developers or the designers – does not necessarily mean positive or negative.

**Artificial Intelligence (AI):** High performing, extensive and versatile cognitive system made by human to automate and let machines learn.

**Cyber-Resilience:** The ability of a person or organization to withstand the pressure of cyber-related adversaries.

**Data Economy:** An emerging economy trend that is data-driven. Data, especially IoT-generated, is seen as the driving force behind the dynamic interaction between consumers and companies.

**Personality:** The cognitive, affective, and behavior patterns, characteristics that is unique, can be influenced and dynamic that define an individual.

**Psychology:** The scientific study of the mind and behavior.

**Technopsychology:** The branch of Psychology that covers the convergence of and interaction between human and technology.

## ENDNOTE

1 The word 'I' refers to the authors.

# Chapter 4
# The Internet of Things (IoT): Capabilities and Applications for Smart Supply Chain

**In Lee**
*Western Illinois University, USA*

## ABSTRACT

*As the Internet of Things (IoT) opens up new business opportunities, firms are trying to understand the impacts of the IoT revolution on their supply chain. Despite the tremendous interest by supply chain managers to leverage the IoT, there are still a paucity of studies that integrate the management side of supply chain with the technical side of the IoT. This chapter attempts to fill the current gap in research. This chapter discusses capabilities of the IoT-based supply chain applications. Then, it presents a conceptual framework of the IoT applications essential for smart supply chain. Finally, this chapter discusses technical and managerial challenges faced by supply chain managers in implementing the IoT.*

## INTRODUCTION

In today's hypercompetitive environments in which competition is among supply chain networks rather than individual firms, firms need to effectively manage increasingly extending supply chain activities. The supply chain has become the central organizing unit in today's global industries (Miles & Snow, 2007). As the Internet of Things (IoT) is opens up new business opportunities, firms are trying to understand the impacts of the IoT revolution on their supply chain. IDC (2014) predicts that the IoT base will grow at a 17.5% compound annual growth rate (CAGR), reaching 28.1 billion installed units by 2020, up from 9.1 billion in 2013 and the value of the market will reach $7.1 trillion by 2020, up from $1.9 trillion in 2013.

The IoT has significant impact on several aspects of everyday life and behavior of potential users (Bandyopadhyay & Sen, 2011). Assisted living, smart homes, e-health, and enhanced learning are a few examples of possible application scenarios in which the IoT will play a leading role in the near future (Atzori, Iera, & Morabito, 2010). The IoT will provide new opportunities for services and applications able to leverage the interconnection of physical and virtual realms (Miorandi, Sicari, De Pellegrini, &

DOI: 10.4018/978-1-5225-2104-4.ch004

Chlamtac, 2012) and firms in most industries will rapidly adopt IoT-enabled applications in order to stay competitive. Many firms such as GE, Amazon, and Google are developing numerous IoT applications to capture real-time operational data and offer better services to clients. Connected cars, smart metering, and smart farming are examples of transforming traditional products and services into digital ones equipped with real-time data captured with IoT devices and sensor networks.

Recently, the IoT was recognized as a disruptive technology for supply chain. The use of the IoT for supply chain management is rapidly rising. For example, a large European cargo rail consortium, Deutsche Bahn installed a network-wide monitoring system to manage its entire rail network which comprises over 1 billion supply chain "nodes", collecting data on each segment of track, rail car, station, engine, and switch, and monitoring the condition of all of these things in real time. The collected data are fed into a control tower that aggregates them every five seconds to provide near-real-time information across the entire fleet. Deutsche Bahn has used these data to improve risk management practices such as real-time rerouting and optimization, considering all existing network traffic through nodes (Mariani, Quasney, & Raynor, 2015). Whirlpool is another example of using the IoT for internal supply chain optimization in routing work and locating misplaced inventory. Instead of using bar codes or a similar solution, Whirlpool used radio frequency identification (RFID) tags and readers across a manufacturing plant to give managers and operators real-time access to information for inbound logistics to the paint line (Mariani, Quasney, & Raynor, 2015).

The IoT helps supply chain partners monitor the process of a supply chain execution in real time and improve the efficiency and effectiveness of supply chain (Ping, Liu, Zhou, & Wang, 2011). Recent developments in the IoT have generated the capabilities of a highly visible supply chain where the location of arbitrary individual things can be determined at any point in time by all appropriate supply chain partners (Geerts & O'Leary, 2014). For example, the IoT benefits the food and agricultural product supply chain by improving the visualization and traceability of agriculture products and ensuring people's food safety (Zhou & Zhou, 2012). Industrial deployment of the IoT provides development of an ideal platform for decentralized management of warehouses and collaborative warehouse order fulfillment with RFID, ambient intelligence and multi-agent system (Reaidy, Gunasekaran, & Spalanzani 2015).

Despite the tremendous interest by supply chain managers to leverage the IoT, there are still a paucity of studies that integrate the management side of supply chain with the technical side of the IoT. This chapter attempts to fill the current gap in research. This chapter discusses capabilities of the IoT-based supply chain applications. Then, it presents a conceptual framework of the IoT applications essential for smart supply chain. Finally, this chapter discusses technical and managerial challenges faced by supply chain managers in implementing the IoT.

## CAPABILITIES OF IOT-BASED SUPPY CHAIN APPLICATIONS

Based on the technology trends and literature review, this section discusses three capabilities of IoT-based supply chain applications: (1) monitoring and control, (2) information sharing and collaboration, and (3) big data and IoT data analytics.

## Monitoring and Control

According to the Digital Agenda for Europe (European Union, 2015), monitoring and control refers to the control of any system, device or network through automated procedures managed by a control unit with or without the capability to display information. IoT-enabled monitoring and control systems are gaining popularity in the environmental and manufacturing sectors, where companies have operated basic applications such as real time observation with sensors and alerting about machines and devices (Bi, Xu, & Wang, 2014; Lazarescu, 2013; Tao, Zuo, Xu, & Zhang, 2014). The IoT-enabled monitoring and controlling technologies are essential in many business processes related to supply chain activities such as manufacturing, logistics, and transportation. Monitoring and control systems collect and send key data on asset condition, equipment performance, testing, energy usage, and environmental conditions and allow managers and automated controllers to respond to changes in real time anywhere, anytime. These capabilities are key to smart supply chain activities where visibility and traceability of objects are required.

Radio frequency identification system (RFID) is part of the IoT systems related to supply chain activities. RFID allows automatic identification and data capture using radio waves, a tag, and a reader. The tag can store more data than traditional barcodes. The tag contains data in the form of the Electronic Product Code (EPC), a global RFID-based item identification system developed by the Auto-ID Center. RFID readers can identify, track and monitor the objects attached with tags globally, automatically, and in real time, if needed.

In addition to the RFID, wireless technologies have played a key role in industrial monitoring and control systems. In a typical supply chain, monitoring and control applications use sensors, GPS, RFID tags, and sensor networks to minimize misplacement, theft, loss, and spoilage in warehouse, transportation, and store shelves (Ha, Song, Chung, Lee, & Park, 2014). Sensors are used to maintain goods at the correct temperature and protect them from chemical spills to spoilage (Grunow & Piramuthu, 2013). Sensor networks monitor traffic conditions, and navigation devices track the location of transportation vehicles to make routing more efficient. Wireless sensor network (WSN) consists of spatially distributed autonomous sensor equipped devices to monitor physical or environmental conditions and can cooperate with RFID systems to better track the status of things such as their location, temperature, and movements (Atzori et al., 2010).

WSN has been primarily used in cold chain logistics which involves the transportation of temperature sensitive products along a supply chain through thermal and refrigerated packaging methods (Hsueh & Chang, 2010; White III & Cheong, 2012). WSN is also used for maintenance and tracking systems. General Electric deploys sensors in its jet engines, turbines, and wind farms. By analyzing data in real time, GE saves time and costs due to timely preventive maintenance. American Airline also uses sensors capable of capturing 30 terabytes of data per flight for services such as preventative maintenance.

## Information Sharing and Collaboration

Resources invested in supply chain relationships enable information sharing and collaboration between supply chain partners (Patnayakuni, Rai, & Seth, 2006; Pramatari, 2007). To achieve SCM objectives successfully, firms need to conduct a series of SCM activities. Supply chain partners must perceive accurate, current, and reliable information from other firms in order to facilitate information sharing and collaboration (Petersen, Ragatz, & Monczka, 2005). To maximize SCM's full potential, supply chain partners need information sharing and collaboration. Information sharing and collaboration refers to the electronic movement of information and purpose-driven collaboration between people, between people and things, and between things.

Information sharing and collaboration applications enhance the decision-making of the channel partners through better visibility of materials flow in the supply chain. Inter-organizational data sharing becomes real-time via wireless communications. As supply chain partners increase information sharing and collaboration activities, they reduce inter-firm uncertainty and strengthen strategic relationship (Krause, Handfield, & Tyler, 2007; Lee & Kim, 1999).

Wireless sensors are widely used for information sharing and collaboration among objects and human decision makers. Enterprises can improve their capabilities by leveraging the IoT-related information sharing mechanisms within and across industries (Li, Hou, Liu, & Liu, 2012). Inter-device information sharing and collaboration benefit from the standardization of communication protocols and devices. Monitoring and control components are often embedded into the information sharing and collaboration devices and detect a predefined event which triggers information sharing and collaboration among people and things. Recent research shows that there exist more potential applications of IoT in information intensive sectors such as healthcare services due to information sharing capability of the IoT (Xu et al., 2014). Information sharing allows devices and people to collaborate at the same time, with the same information collected or retrieved from multiple sources. Supply chain partners can share information generated by IoT devices to track inter-organizational logistic flows of materials and products and collaborate their delivery activities based on the level of inventory and the rate of sales. The information sharing and collaboration will be more beneficial for global supply chain partners where the uncertainty of lead time is greater than for the domestic supply chain partners.

One key technology of the IoT for information sharing and collaboration is high-speed network technology (Wang, Zhang, Quan, & Dong, 2013). The potential of the IoT for supply chain will be realized via IoT standardization with which devices from different manufacturers share information seamlessly among supply chain partners. Standards are required for bidirectional communication and information exchange among things, their environment, their digital counterparts that have an interest in monitoring, controlling or assisting the things (Bandyopadhyay & Sen 2011).

## Big Data and Data Analytics

Big data and data analytics refers to the process of collecting, organizing and analyzing massive amount of data to discover useful patterns and knowledge (Lee & Lee, 2015). Big data presents both big opportunities and big challenges to our society. The opportunities include better-informed business decisions, more efficient supply-chain management and resource allocation, more effective targeting of products and advertisements, and faster turnaround of scientific discoveries (Kumar, Niu, & Ré, 2013). IoT devices and machines with embedded sensors and actuators generate enormous amount of data to be processed by business intelligence and analytics tools for decision making. A number of studies focus on using or developing effective methods to convert the data generated or captured by the IoT into knowledge useful for decision making and problem solving (Bin, Yuan, & Xiaoyi, 2010; Tsai, Lai, Chiang, & Yang., 2014). Innovative IoT applications are using seamless large scale sensing, data analytics, and information representation, and cloud computing (Gubbi, Buyya, Marusic, & Palaniswami, 2013).

Data generated from the multiple partners' machines and devices are fed into a cloud datacenter and merged into a supply chain-wide database for simulation, data analytics, and optimization. Big data and data analytics applications enhance the predictive maintenance of the fleet, demand forecast, delivery lead time, and customer services. The big data generated by IoT has different characteristics compared with general big data because of the different types of data collected, of which the most classical characteristics include heterogeneity, variety, unstructured feature noise, and high redundancy (Chen, Mao, & Liu, 2014).

Big data and data analytics helps supply chain managers to make more informed decisions. While IoT-enabled monitoring and control applications may perform minimum level of intelligent activities, they are mostly reactive to predefined events. Since the IoT applications for supply chain activities generate a huge amount of real-time or near real-time data, it is critical to exploit data analytics to achieve data-driven supply chain innovations. For example, supply chain key performance indicators can be expanded and analyzed in real time to have deeper and timely understanding of supply chain efficiency and effectiveness. Various data mining techniques (Arora & Ravi, 2013; Priya, Vadivel, &. Thakur, 2012) and knowledge management support systems (Zeleny, 2013) can be applied to data analytics to discover hidden relationships among data. Once monitoring and information sharing IoT applications acquire data, big data and business analytics uses machine learning, advanced statistical techniques, and other predictive analytics to resolve any business issues such as changes in customer demand and market conditions, to discover ways to meet customer demands, and to develop value added services for customers.

Data analytics can be done at a cloud center in a batch mode once data are stored (Fisher, DeLine, Czerwinski, & Drucker, 2012). Alternatively, in a more time-sensitive environment, streaming analytics can be used to analyze data in real time while devices transmit data to the cloud center (Lee & Lee, 2015). Cloud computing is a model for on-demand access to a shared pool of configurable resources (e.g. compute, networks, servers, storage, applications, services, and software) that can be easily provisioned as infrastructure as service (IaaS) or software as service (SaaS). Many IoT applications require massive data storage, huge processing speed to enable the real-time decision making, and high speed broadband networks to stream data, audio, or video. Cloud computing provides an ideal solution for handling huge data streams from the supply chain activities and processing them in real time for multiple supply chain partners.

## IOT APPLICATIONS FOR SMART SUPPLY CHAIN

Supply chain innovation is critical to sustainable competitive advantages for firms. The introduction of new products and services, or entry into new markets, is likely to be more successful if innovative supply chain management practices, innovative supply chain designs, and enabling technology are accompanied (Arlbjørn, de Haas, & Munksgaard, 2011). Supply chain data will increasingly be generated by a network of sensors, RFID tags, meters, actuators, GPSs, and other devices and systems (Butner, 2010). IBM (2010) suggests the Smarter Supply Chain of the Future has the instrumentation, interconnectedness and intelligence to predict, if not prevented, disruptions before they occur. From production floor and warehousing to the distribution and store shelving, the IoT enables supply chain partners to create smart supply chain by providing real-time data and business intelligence for all partners in the supply chain. Firms will invest in the IoT to increase visibility of materials flow, reduce loss of materials, and lower distribution costs.

As the IoT penetrates into core business processes and an increasing number of firms invest in green supply chain, leveraging the IoT for smart supply chain will become a subject of great interest for the managers (Lee, 2015). The IoT for smart supply chain will generate value in inventory management, preventive maintenance, and transportation, and allow multi-way communications with the partners and customers, rich data analysis, and timely responses to unexpected events. However, the value of the IoT can be realized only when managers fully understand what data the IoT devices collect, how the data should be processed, and when they should make the decisions on supply chain problems. It is also very important to analyze technical and managerial security risks of the IoT (Kim, Cho, Kim, & Lim, 2015).

Overall architecture will have a significant bearing on the field itself and needs to be investigated (Gubbi et al., 2013). For successful IoT-based supply chain management, basic IoT architecture needs to be established and updated continuously to commission and decommission various IoT assets. Reaidy, Gunasekaran, and Spalanzani (2015) propose an IOT infrastructure for collaborative warehouse order fulfillment based on RFID, ambient intelligence and multi-agent system. It consists of a physical devices layer, a middleware ambient platform, a multi-agent system and an enterprise resource planning. It integrates a bottom-up approach with decision support mechanisms such as self-organization and negotiation protocols.

For smart supply chain, the basic architecture includes four layers (Lee, 2015): (1) object layer, (2) communication layer, (3) application layer, and (4) data service layer. Each layer has core components and essential functionalities described below: *Object layer* consists of physical objects such as devices, machines, sensors, RFID tags, and readers. The object layer is responsible for sensing the environment, identifying and tracking objects, and collecting data. The physical objects get miniaturized to be more energy-efficient, location-independent, and cost-effective (Sundmaeker, Guillemin, & Friess, & Woelfflé, 2010). RFID tags and sensors are often embedded in the machines and devices. *Application layer* consists of a set of problem-specific software tools that interact with users, solve problems, process data, and share solutions with other applications. The application layer is responsible for presenting data and information to the users in a user-friendly format. While device-to-device applications do not necessarily require data visualization, more and more human centered IoT applications provide visualization to present information to end users in an intuitive and easy-to-understand way and to allow interaction with the environment. It is important for IoT applications to be built with intelligence so devices can monitor the environment, identify problems, communicate with each other, and potentially resolve problems without the need for human intervention. *Communication layer* consists of a network of wired/wireless networks, the Internet, and protocols. Its main function is to handle transmission of data obtained from the object layer to other devices or datacenters. The wireless network is preferred to the wired network due to its flexibility and low implementation cost. *Data service layer* consists of private/public cloud and related data management systems. Its main function is to store data generated by sensors, devices, and machines, conduct data analytics, and provide users, devices, and machines with access to the data. One of the most important outcomes of the IoT is an enormous amount of data generated from devices connected to the Internet (Gubbi et al., 2013). At the request of the users, a real-time analysis of supply chain data is conducted for decision making. The cloud data service system should be able to dynamically prioritize requests and provision resources such that critical requests are served in real time (Gubbi et al., 2013). Data mining technologies are used to discover knowledge hidden in the sea of data (Bose, 2008). Unlike the other three layers which are typically owned by an individual firm, the data service layer is often owned and managed by public cloud service providers.

The IoT facilitates the development of myriads of industry-oriented and user-specific IoT applications (Lee, 2015). Whereas devices and networks provide the physical connectivity, IoT applications enable the device-to-device and human-to-device interactions in a reliable and robust manner. IoT applications on devices need to ensure that data/messages have been received and acted upon properly in a timely manner. For example, transportation and logistics applications monitor the status of the transported goods such as fruits, fresh-cut produce, meat, and dairy products. During the transportation the conservation status (e.g., temperature, humidity, and shock) are monitored constantly and appropriate actions are taken automatically to avoid spoilage when the status is out of range. For example, Fedex uses SenseAware to keep tabs on the temperature, location and other vital signs of a package, including when it is opened and whether it was tampered with along the way.

Table 1 shows the conceptual framework of IoT applications for smart supply chain. The applications row represent the specific applications and the specific IoT category developed/adopted by the Fortune 200 companies. The last column shows the benefits/values derived from the IoT applications. The last three rows show core technologies, emerging technologies, and current technology platforms, respectively. The mapping of the IoT applications to the industries in the supply chain will help firms understand the nature and effects of the IoT on their unique supply chain, reduce the trials and errors in the implementation process, and maximize the value of the investment in the IoT (Lee, 2015).

The bottom three rows of Table 1 show the core and emerging IoT technologies and current technology platforms for smart supply chain. *The core technology* is the current backbone of the IoT infrastructure. The core technology refers to relatively mature and established technologies which have a low degree of uncertainty in functionality and performance. These technologies include: sensors and actuators, sensor networks, RFID, sensors built in to mobile devices, and storage networks and power networks *for monitoring and control applications*; the Internet, mobile apps, NFC in mobile phones, IoT-based social software, and IoT-based enterprise applications *for information sharing and collaborations*; cloud computing, data mining, serial data processing, parallel data processing, and IoT-oriented RDBMS *for big data and data analytics*.

As the technology advances, communication and processing capabilities of the IoT are becoming more and more accessible and versatile, and advances in interconnectivity will drive the desire to make use of the IoT's potentials (Sundmaeker et al., 2010). *Emerging technology* refers to technology under development or at the stage of the proof-of-concept (POC), which has a high risk of technical failure but has potentially significant market value. For example, monitoring and controlling technology is moving to unobtrusive tiny and energy-efficient wireless sensor technology which allows applications to be deployed more flexibly and location-independently. Mobile crowdsensing is a promising development where individuals with sensing and computing devices collectively share data and extract information to measure and map phenomena of common interest (Ganti, Ye, & Lei, 2011). The sensor network is evolving towards a context aware self-organizing, self-repairing autonomous network. Technology for information sharing and collaboration is moving to user-oriented, distributed intelligence system, things-to-things collaboration environments, and things-to-humans collaboration. For more secure information sharing and collaboration between devices, the emerging technology will strengthen interoperability, connectivity, privacy, and intelligence features of the IoT. The future of big data and data analytics includes context aware data processing, cognitive processing, and optimization (Lee & Lee, 2015).

Supply chain IoT devices generate enormous amount of data that needs to be collected and processed in real time to provide information on status, location, functionality, and environment of products and services. Since a large amount of sensor data in real time will increase workloads of devices at an

*Table 1. A conceptual framework of IoT investment for smart supply chain and the IoT adoption by the industries in the supply chain*

| Category | Monitoring and Control | Information Sharing and Collaboration | Big Data and Data Analytics | Value Created |
|---|---|---|---|---|
| **Applications** | Connected Car Dashboards to analyze data collected from vehicles and to improve vehicle performance<br>Fleet monitoring: an entire fleet of vehicles are at any time<br>IoT home electronics (washers, refrigerators and other household appliances)<br>Consumer products with Smartphone Application<br>Fleet tracking devices to cut costs and improve driver efficiency<br>Sensors to keeps tabs on the temperature, location and other vital signs of a package<br>Smart homes applications such as a smart garage door controller, a window blind controller, and a hose faucet water timer that help the home owner manage this home anytime, anywhere<br>Retailer intelligence for store security and surveillance | Interactive Electric Consumer Products links with a smartphone such as smart brush<br><br>Inventory system to optimize its warehouse and supply chain operations with vendors<br>Smart technology that sends special offers and recommendations to the customers' smartphones based on vicinity | Trip Optimizer that allows the driver to steer the locomotive to maintain the most efficient speed at all times and reduce fuel burn.<br>Analytics Solutions that help customers around the world better understand the health of their equipment and optimize machine availability<br>Smart machines collecting real-time data about customer behavior and equipment<br>Smart shelves located in the checkout aisle and near snacks, employing sensors and to get basic demographic information about the shopper and analytics to analyze their purchase patterns<br>A new Industrial Internet of Things platform to improve mining operations and react to near real-time situations in the mine.<br>Smart coffee brewers which can connect to the cloud, track customer preferences, update recipes digitally, and self-monitor performance so problems can be flagged up. | Improved information quality,<br>Decreased cost,<br>Increased productivity,<br>Enhanced knowledge management<br>Lower inventory,<br>Partner relationship management,<br>Enhanced business intelligence,<br>Consumer loyalty,<br>Open innovation,<br>Increased consumer satisfaction,<br>Increase revenue,<br>Targeted marketing,<br>Custom-tailored experiences,<br>Enhanced brand image |
| **Core Technologies for Smart Supply Chain** | Sensors and actuators;<br>Sensor networks;<br>RFID Tags;<br>Sensors built in to mobile devices;<br>Storage networks and power networks | Mobile apps;<br>NFC in mobile phones;<br>IoT-based social software;<br>IoT-based enterprise applications | Cloud computing; Serial data processing,<br>Parallel data processing,<br>IoT-oriented RDBMS | |
| **Emerging Technologies for Smart Supply Chain** | Mobile crowdsensing; Smart sensors;<br>Tiny sensors;<br>Nanotechnology and new materials;<br>Self-repairing networks;<br>Self-organizing networks;<br>Hybrid networking technologies;<br>Context aware network | Distributed intelligence system;<br>Things-to-things collaboration;<br>Things-to-humans collaboration | Context aware data processing;<br>Cognitive processing and optimization | |
| **Current Technology Platforms for Smart Supply Chain** | Proprietary;<br>Open innovation | Open innovation;<br>Industrial alliance | Industrial alliance;<br>Cloud computing (Things as a service) | |

(Adapted from Lee (2015))

exponential rate, it is not feasible to process all the streaming data available to those devices. Context-aware data processing enables sensors and devices to use context specific information such as location, temperature, and the availability of a certain device to decide what types of data to collect and interpret to provide relevant information for decision-making. For example, context-aware data processing can deliver relevant information to a truck driver by knowing the truck's current location (e.g., on a highway, a congested inner city area, or at a hazardous manufacturing plant). By integrating the human cognition process into IoT applications, a cognitive data processing application learns to sense things, predict future events, and form opinions based on evidence in different environments. For example, cognitive data processing uses artificial intelligence techniques to understand the warehousing environment, processes environmental data such as chemicals and pollution for a manager, and utilizes a feedback from the manager to learn further. The optimization of data processing is critical to a timely process of the continuous stream of massive amounts of data. Technological advances in optimized data processing help make timely decisions in big data applications in the smart supply chain.

*IoT technology platform* is a technological foundation and development strategy with which each company develops their IoT applications for new value generation and competitive advantage. These platforms are developed mostly by IT firms and used by non-IT firms. IT firms set IoT standards and develop a variety of foundational technologies for industrial machines, environmental sensors, home appliances, and healthcare equipment. The choice of the IoT technology platforms by non-IT firms should be made in consideration of the overall business and technology strategy. Currently, there are four widely adopted technology platforms: proprietary IoT technology, open innovation IoT technology, industry alliance IoT technology, and IoT as a Service (TaaS).

*Proprietary IoT technology* has been developed by many firms to reap early-mover advantage, to become a technology leader, and to be branded as an innovator in their industry. For example, Apple has its own patented proprietary IoT technology for in-home device communication, HomeKit. Proprietary IoT technology is widely developed for monitoring and control applications.

*Open innovation IoT technology* is often used by a firm whose technologies are limited in creating value added IoT applications. Open Innovation has been regarded as relevant primarily to 'high-technology' industries and has received greater attention in light of the debate about globalization and the potential for the R&D function to be outsourced (Chesbrough & Crowther, 2006). A number of open-source platforms are considered more promising compared with the proprietary ones due to the following reasons. First, the use of the open source is expected to enable the faster integration of new IoT solutions across the application domains (Mineraud, Mazhelis, Su, & Tarkoma, 2016). Second, the use of the open source has been reported to speed up the adoption of a software technology in a bottom-up fashion. Finally, when seen from the social surplus perspective, the industry based on the open-source platforms has been found to provide larger total welfare, compared with the industry structures based on proprietary platforms (Economides & Katsamakas, 2006).

Open innovation is known to accelerate innovation process and create synergy between enterprises of different technology capabilities. A leading company initiates the open innovation and creates an open innovation network with other smaller companies which contribute their technological know-how to a specific problem. For example, the Kimberly-Clark Digital Innovation Lab (D'Lab) brought open-source innovation to the consumer package goods category with the second annual KChallenge startup competition at the 2015 Consumer Electronics Show (CES) in Las Vegas (Kimberly-Clark, 2014). The winning startups will receive the opportunity to pilot a project with one of Kimberly-Clark's global brands such as Depends, Scott, and Kotex to find new ways to connect with their consumers. Kimberly-Clark serves as an orchestrator and a facilitator of innovation and participating startups play a critical role in advancing innovation for various brands of Kimberly-Clark.

*Industry alliance IoT technology* has been created by leading IT firms to establish industry standards and multi-device interoperability and to provide customers value-added services such as controlling multiple home networking devices. Leading IT firms create a consortium, joint venture, or partnership.

Google, through its in-home device unit Nest Labs, has launched an industry alliance in concert with several other firms to set a standard called Thread for Internet-connected home device communications. Participants of the industry alliance called the Thread Group include Google, Samsung Electronics, and ARM Holdings (Thread Group http://www.threadgroup.org). AllSeen Alliance, another group of more than 100 companies including Microsoft and Qualcomm, was established for the development and evolution of an interoperable peer connectivity and communications framework (AllSeen, https://allseenalliance.org). The use of the industry alliance and open innovation is a good development strategy for information sharing and collaboration applications.

*(Internet of) Things as a Service (TaaS)* is provided as services similar to the public cloud services. The emergence of TaaS lies in the monetization of excessive IoT capacity, economies of scale and scope of shared IoT assets, ubiquitous connectivity via the Internet and wireless networks, commoditization of IoT devices and applications, and industry standardization and interconnectivity. While TaaS shares common characteristics with public cloud services, unique value propositions may come from combining IoT architectural components such as physical objects, network, data storage, and applications and providing customized services to firms on a pay-as-you-go basis. For big data and data analytics, the industry alliance and TaaS are suitable technology platforms.

## CHALLENGES IN IOT DEVELOPMENT FOR SMART SUPPLY CHAIN

As with any disruptive innovation, the IoT present multiple challenges to firms. This section identifies and discusses challenges in IoT application development for smart supply chain. For example, Gubbi et al. (2013) suggests that due to the explosion of the data generated by IoT machines, data centers will face challenges in security, quality of service, data analytics, storage management, server technologies, and data center networking. Khan, Khan, Zaheer, and Khan (2012) identify challenges from technical perspectives: naming and identity management, interoperability and standardization, information privacy, objects safety and security, data confidentiality and encryption, network security, spectrum, and greening of IoT. Many studies predominantly point out the security challenge of the IoT (Farooq, Waseem, Khairi, & Mazhar, 2015; Jing, Vasilakos, Wan, Lu, & Qiu, 2014; Roman, Zhou, & Lopez, 2013). This section discusses five technical and managerial challenges: data quality, data security, velocity of technological change, supply chain process redesign, and investment justification (Lee, 2015). The discussion focuses on how these challenges may have impacts on the development and adoption of supply chain IoT applications.

### Data Quality

Data quality is defined as the value of data generated and collected by IoT objects. Data quality is crucial to gain user engagement and acceptance of the IoT paradigm and services (Karkouch, Mousannif, Al Moatassime, Noel, 2016). If data are of poor quality, trust in the decision based on the data will be low and the adoption of IoT technologies can be hindered. When data collection cost is high and the quality of the data is low, the value of the IoT decreases rapidly. Other times, the data required for decision making is not available or not timely. If partners do not provide timely data on the amount and timing of a purchase, suppliers will not be able to develop an effective production plan (Chapman & Carter, 1990). For the monitoring and control IoT applications, data quality is critical to the value of and confidence in the IoT. For firms adopting the IoT applications for their supply chain, machines may not function properly, data collected may not be reliable, and critical decisions may be made by users or machines based on inaccurate data. Supply chain partners must perceive data from other firms to be accurate, current, and reliable in order to facilitate information sharing and collaboration (Petersen et al., 2005). Managers will not use big data and data analytics IoT applications if they do not have a confidence in the data quality, and may not want to share their data with their partners.

## Data Security

As IoT is built on the basis of the Internet, security issues of the Internet will also occur in IoT (Jing et al., 2014). Once the IoT data is leaked or interrupted in any part of the IoT system, the security of the entire IoT systems will be in danger. As the number of connected devices increases, the number of the end-to-end connection points increases exponentially and the number of potential security holes increases in proportion. Protecting the IoT is a complex and difficult task. The number of attack vectors available to malicious attackers might become staggering, as global connectivity ("access anyone") and accessibility ("access anyhow, anytime") are key tenets of the IoT (Roman et al., 2013). These security holes to individual monitoring and control IoT applications open the doors for security breaches such as denial-of-service (DOS) attacks and Trojan horse attacks from hackers and other cyber-criminals. For supply chain collaboration, the data collected from the IoT applications needs to be securely protected to keep the confidentiality of supply chain partners' data. A recent study by HP reveals that 70 percent of the most commonly used IoT devices contain serious vulnerabilities in password security, encryption, and user access permissions (HP, 2014). Scanning of 10 most popular IoT devices reveals on average, each device contained 25 vulnerable holes or risks of compromising the IoT security. The IoT devices typically do not use data encryption techniques. Weak security will create the user resistance to the adoption of big data and data analytics IoT applications for smart supply chain. Security challenge may be alleviated by training application developers to incorporate security solutions such as intrusion prevention systems, encryptions, and firewalls into products and encouraging users to utilize the IoT security features that are incorporated into their devices.

## Velocity of Technological Change

Velocity of technological change refers to the rate of technological change in the IoT. Innovation is accelerating at a stupendous speed in many IoT technology frontiers. The convergence of technologies in objects, networks, data storage, and applications is furthering the velocity of the IoT innovation. The increase in the velocity of the technological change leads to a greater degree of environmental uncertainty (Bensaou, 1997; Guimaraes, Cook, & Natarajan, 2002). The rapid technological development in the IoT is tied to the value of the market of $7.1 trillion by 2020, up from $1.9 trillion in 2013 as the growth of market demand drives the technological advances in the IoT. Wireless sensor networks (WSNs) have been recognized as a promising technology for the IoT, and technological advances in hardware have made robust and cost effective devices in sensing applications (Singh, Tripathi, & Jara, 2014). Smart supply chain is being developed with advances in sensor technologies and miniaturized embedded computational devices. Because technological changes cannot be dealt with by an individual firm, firms need to build a close business relationship to jointly develop new technologies and products (Mentzer, Min, & Zacharia, 2000). Mendelson and Pillai (1998) show that as the business environment becomes more uncertain, firms need to update and revise existing supply chain collaboration strategy more frequently. While various collaboration IoT applications increase the overall supply chain productivity, it will be more difficult to predict which IoT technology will become a disruptive innovation in supply chain management. The question of what firms should do to minimize the threat of displacement brought on by the IoT's disruptive innovation remains to be answered.

## Supply Chain Process Redesign

The IoT is an enabler of supply chain process redesign as well as a disruptive innovation. At bthe same time, this new innovation brought out new challenges for the design of increasingly more complex supply chains. Changing consumer behaviours and the emergence of transformative technologies such as industry 4.0, artificial intelligence, big data analytics, the Internet of Things are driving a series of innovations with major implications for the enterprises in their design of supply chains (Harrington & Srai, 2016). While the use of the IoT in supply chain is expected to improve accountability in organizations, it is unclear how such expectations will actually be met because new technologies not only address, but also produce new accountability demands and managers might experience difficulties in satisfying these accountabilities (Boos, Guenter, Grote, & Kinder, 2013). Supply chain process redesign efforts aim to improve order fulfillment, inventory management, warehousing, distribution management, and customer relationship management. Supply chain IoT's potential values discussed in the conceptual framework can be fully realized by integrating it with supply chain process redesign. Devaraj and Kohli (2000) find that IT capital investment combined with business process reengineering improved profitability in the health care industry. While monitoring and control IoT applications may successfully meet operational efficiency, they may still be poorly integrated with collaboration-intensive supply chain processes such as forecasting and order fulfillment. As a result, firms may create silos of monitoring and control IoT applications without fully realizing the benefits of collaborative IoT applications. New supply process redesign may require job analysis, job eliminations, job creation, and job training due to elimination of existing process activities and creation of new process activities. A change management program for affected supply chain professionals needs to be established before the adoption of the IoT.

## Investment Justification

While the IoT is relatively new, investment opportunities abound along with the advances of various IoT technologies. Innovative firms are expected to leverage various capabilities of the IoT technologies. While implementing an IoT environment requires massive investment, the investment decision where things are not open and interoperable in terms of hardware and software makes it difficult for companies to adopt this technology (Ahmed et al., 2016). To realize the potential benefits, firms need an appropriate measure in order to properly assess the risks and rewards of the technology (Lee & Lee, 2015). Many IoT projects have unclear problem definitions and are using emerging technologies, thus causing a higher risk of project failure and higher irreversibility of investments than traditional technology projects. In general, investments in big data and data analytics IoT applications are more complex and riskier than investments in the other two IoT application categories. The standard measures firms typically use to value projects, Net Present Value (NPV) and Return on Investment (ROI), often may not capture true value of the IoT projects due to the fact that these standard measures ignore flexibility in investment such as reversibility and scalability in the evaluation period. NPV tends to reject a project's worth when there is high uncertainty of project success, and is not suitable for high risk projects such as projects for big data and data analytics. In order to value high risk IoT projects, real option approach may be more appropriate (Lee & Lee, 2015).

## CONCLUSION

Because the IoT is such a recent development, there remains a paucity of studies on the supply chain aspects of the IoT. This makes it very challenging for enterprises to make informed decisions in regard to IoT adoption/implementation. Many enterprises invest in a variety of IoT applications for their supply chain innovation. The IoT became a reality beyond hype. However, converting the IoT investment into real performance and profit improvement is challenging. Our chapter contributes to the literature in this emerging field by presenting a foundational knowledge for building smart supply chain.

This chapter presented a conceptual framework of the Internet of Things (IoT) for smart supply chain management and identified three capabilities of the IoT: monitoring and control, information sharing and collaboration, and big data and data analytics. This chapter also examined how the IoT applications support the supply chain management of Fortune 200 companies. This chapter presents core and emerging IoT technologies and technology platforms for smart supply chain. Finally, this chapter discussed five technical and managerial challenges in implementing IoT applications for smart supply chain: data quality, data security, velocity of technological change, supply chain process redesign, and investment justification.

## REFERENCES

Ahmed, E., Yaqoob, I., Gani, A., Imran, M., & Guizani, M. (2016). Internet-of-things-based smart environments: State of the art, taxonomy, and open research challenges. *IEEE Wireless Communications*, *23*(5), 10–16. doi:10.1109/MWC.2016.7721736

Arlbjørn, J. S., de Haas, H., & Munksgaard, K. B. (2011). Exploring supply chain innovation. *Logistics Research*, *3*(1), 3–18. doi:10.1007/s12159-010-0044-3

Arora, V., & Ravi, V. (2013). Data mining using advanced ant colony optimization algorithm and application to bankruptcy prediction. *International Journal of Information Systems and Social Change*, *4*(3), 33–56. doi:10.4018/jissc.2013070103

Atzori, L., Iera, A., & Morabito, G. (2010). The Internet of Things: A survey. *Computer Networks*, *54*(15), 2787–2805. doi:10.1016/j.comnet.2010.05.010

Bandyopadhyay, D., & Sen, J. (2011). Internet of Things: Applications and challenges in technology and standardization. *Wireless Personal Communications*, *58*(1), 49–69. doi:10.1007/s11277-011-0288-5

Bensaou, M. (1997). Interorganizational cooperation and the use IT: An empirical comparison of U.S. and Japanese supplier relations. *Information Systems Research*, *8*(2), 107–124. doi:10.1287/isre.8.2.107

Bi, Z., Xu, L. D., & Wang, C. (2014). Internet of things for enterprise systems of modern manufacturing. *IEEE Transactions on Industrial Informatics*, *10*(2), 1537–1546. doi:10.1109/TII.2014.2300338

Bin, S., Yuan, L., & Xiaoyi, W. (2010). Research on data mining models for the internet of things. *Proc. International Conference on Image Analysis and Signal Processing*, 127-132.

Boos, D., Guenter, H., Grote, G., & Kinder, K. (2013). Controllable accountabilities: The Internet of Things and its challenges for organisations. *Behaviour & Information Technology*, *32*(5), 449–467. doi :10.1080/0144929X.2012.674157

Bose, R. (2008). Competitive intelligence process and tools for intelligence analysis. *Industrial Management & Data Systems*, *108*(4), 510–528. doi:10.1108/02635570810868362

Butner, K. (2010). The smarter supply chain of the future. *Strategy and Leadership*, *38*(1), 22–31. doi:10.1108/10878571011009859

Chapman, S., & Carter, P. (1990). Supplier/customer inventory relationships under just-in-time. *Decision Sciences*, *21*(1), 35–51. doi:10.1111/j.1540-5915.1990.tb00315.x

Chen, M., Mao, S., & Liu, Y. (2014). Big data: A survey. *Mobile Networks and Applications*, *19*(2), 171–209. doi:10.1007/s11036-013-0489-0

Chesbrough, H., & Crowther, A. K. (2006). Beyond high tech: Early adopters of open innovation in other industries. *R & D Management*, *36*(3), 229–236. doi:10.1111/j.1467-9310.2006.00428.x

Devaraj, S., & Kohli, R. (2000). Information technology payoff in the health-care industry: A longitudinal study. *Journal of Management Information Systems*, *16*(4), 41–67. doi:10.1080/07421222.2000.11518265

Economides, N., & Katsamakas, E. (2006). Two-sided competition of proprietary vs. open source technology platforms and the implications for the software industry. *Management Science*, *52*(7), 1057–1071. doi:10.1287/mnsc.1060.0549

European Union. (2015). *Digital agenda for Europe: Monitoring and control.* Retrieved from http://ec.europa.eu/digital-agenda/en/monitoring-and-control

Farooq, M. U., Waseem, M., Khairi, A., & Mazhar, S. (2015). A Critical Analysis on the Security Concerns of Internet of Things (IoT). *International Journal of Computers and Applications*, *111*(7), 1–5. doi:10.5120/19547-1280

Fisher, D., DeLine, R., Czerwinski, M., & Drucker, S. (2012). Interactions with big data analytics. *Interaction*, *19*(3), 50–59. doi:10.1145/2168931.2168943

Ganti, R. K., Ye, F., & Lei, H. (2011). Mobile Crowdsensing: Current State and Future Challenges. *IEEE Communications Magazine*, *49*(11), 32–39. doi:10.1109/MCOM.2011.6069707

Gartner Press Release. (2014). *Gartner's 2014 Hype Cycle for Emerging Technologies Maps the Journey to Digital Business.* Retrieved May 22, 2015 http://www.gartner.com/newsroom/id/2819918

Geerts, G. L., & OLeary, D. E. (2014). A supply chain of things: The EAGLET ontology for highly visible supply chains. *Decision Support Systems*, *63*(1), 3–22. doi:10.1016/j.dss.2013.09.007

Grunow, M., & Piramuthu, S. (2013). RFID in highly perishable food supply chains - Remaining shelf life to supplant expiry date? *International Journal of Production Economics*, *146*(2), 717–727. doi:10.1016/j.ijpe.2013.08.028

Gubbi, J., Buyya, R., Marusic, S., & Palaniswami, M. (2013). Internet of Things (IoT): A vision, architectural elements, and future directions. *Future Generation Computer Systems*, *29*(7), 1645–1660. doi:10.1016/j.future.2013.01.010

Guimaraes, T., Cook, D., & Natarajan, N. (2002). Exploring the importance of business clockspeed as a moderator for determinants of supplier network performance. *Decision Sciences*, *33*(4), 629–644. doi:10.1111/j.1540-5915.2002.tb01659.x

Ha, O. K., Song, Y. S., Chung, K. Y., Lee, K. D., & Park, D. (2014). Relation model describing the effects of introducing RFID in the supply chain: Evidence from the food and beverage industry in South Korea. *Personal and Ubiquitous Computing*, *18*(3), 553–561. doi:10.1007/s00779-013-0675-x

Harrington, T. S., & Srai, J. S. (2016). Designing a 'concept of operations' architecture for next-generation multi-organisational service networks. *AI & Society*, 1–13. doi:10.1007/s00146-016-0664-5

HP. (2014). *HP Study Reveals 70 Percent of Internet of Things Devices Vulnerable to Attack*. Retrieved January 12, 2015 from http://www8.hp.com/us/en/hp-news/press-release.html?id=1744676#.VNKPaRE5A2w

Hsueh, C.-F., & Chang, M.-S. (2010). A model for intelligent transportation of perishable products. *International Journal of Intelligent Transportation Systems Research*, *8*(1), 36–41. doi:10.1007/s13177-009-0004-y

IBM. (2010). *The Smarter Supply Chain of the Future*. Retrieved January 21, 2015 from http://www-935.ibm.com/services/us/gbs/bus/html/gbs-csco-study.html

IDC. (2014). *Worldwide and Regional Internet of Things (IoT) 2014–2020 Forecast: A Virtuous Circle of Proven Value and Demand*. Retrieved May 28, 2015, http://www.idc.com/downloads/idc_market_in_a_minute_iot_infographic.pdf

Jing, Q., Vasilakos, A. V., Wan, J., Lu, J., & Qiu, D. (2014). Security of the Internet of Things: Perspectives and challenges. *Wireless Networks*, *20*(8), 2481–2501. doi:10.1007/s11276-014-0761-7

Karkouch, A., Mousannif, H., Al Moatassime, H., & Noel, T. (2016). Data quality in internet of things: A state-of-the-art survey. *Journal of Network and Computer Applications*, *73*, 57–81. doi:10.1016/j.jnca.2016.08.002

Khan, R., Khan, S. U., Zaheer, R., & Khan, S. (2012). Future Internet: The Internet of Things Architecture, Possible Applications and Key Challenges. In *2012 10th International Conference on Frontiers of Information Technology (FIT): Proceedings* (pp. 257-260). Institute of Electrical and Electronics Engineers Inc.

Kim, D. H., Cho, J. Y., Kim, S., & Lim, J. (2015). *A Study of Developing Security Requirements for Internet of Things (IoT). In Advanced Science and Technology Letters* (Vol. 87, pp. 94–99). Art, Culture, Game, Graphics, Broadcasting and Digital Contents.

Kimberly-Clark. (2014). *Kimberly-Clark Connecting With Startup Innovation at CES 2015*. Retrieved January 22, 2015 from http://investor.kimberly-clark.com/releasedetail.cfm?ReleaseID=886180

Krause, D. R., Handfield, R. B., & Tyler, B. B. (2007). The relationships between supplier development, commitment, social capital accumulation and performance improvement. *Journal of Operations Management*, *25*(2), 528–545. doi:10.1016/j.jom.2006.05.007

Kumar, A., Niu, F., & Ré, C. (2013). Hazy: Making it easier to build and maintain big-data analytics. *Communications of the ACM*, *56*(3), 40–49. doi:10.1145/2428556.2428570

Lazarescu, M. T. (2013). Design of a WSN platform for long-term environmental monitoring for IoT applications. *IEEE Journal on Emerging and Selected Topics in Circuits and Systems*, *3*(1), 45–54. doi:10.1109/JETCAS.2013.2243032

Lee, I. (2015). The Internet of Things (IoT) for Supply Chain Innovation: A Conceptual Framework and Analysis of Fortune 200 Companies. *Asia Pacific Journal of Innovation and Entrepreneurship*, *9*(1), 81-103. Accessible at http://apjie.org/wp/?page_id=4808&uid=32&mod=document

Lee, I., & Lee, K. (2015). The Internet of things (IoT): Applications, investments and challenges for enterprises. *Business Horizons*, *58*(4), 431–440. doi:10.1016/j.bushor.2015.03.008

Lee, J., & Kim, Y. (1999). Effect of partnership quality on IS outsourcing success: Conceptual framework and empirical validation. *Journal of Management Information Systems*, *15*(4), 29–61. doi:10.1080/07421222.1999.11518221

Li, Y., Hou, M., Liu, H., & Liu, Y. (2012). Towards a theoretical framework of strategic decision, supporting capability and information sharing under the context of Internet of Things. *Information Technology Management*, *13*(4), 205–216. doi:10.1007/s10799-012-0121-1

Mainetti, L., Patrono, L., & Vilei, A. (2011). Evolution of wireless sensor networks towards the Internet of Things: A survey. *2011 19th International Conference on Software, Telecommunications and Computer Networks (SoftCOM)*, 1-6.

Mariani, J., Quasney, E., & Raynor, M. E. (2015). Forging links into loops: The Internet of Things' potential to recast supply chain management. *Deloitte Review*, (17). Retrieved from https://dupress.deloitte.com/content/dam/dup-us-en/articles/internet-of-things-supply-chain-management/DUP1159_DR17_ForgingLinksIntoLoops.pdf

Mendelson, H., & Pillai, R. (1998). Clockspeed and information response: Evidence from the information technology sector. *Information Systems Research*, *9*(4), 415–433. doi:10.1287/isre.9.4.415

Mentzer, J. T., Min, S., & Zacharia, Z. G. (2000). The nature of interfirm partnering in supply chain management. *Journal of Retailing*, *76*(4), 549–568. doi:10.1016/S0022-4359(00)00040-3

Miles, R. E., & Snow, C. C. (2007). Organization theory and supply chain management: An evolving research perspective. *Journal of Operations Management*, *25*(2), 459–463. doi:10.1016/j.jom.2006.05.002

Mineraud, J., Mazhelis, O., Su, X., & Tarkoma, S. (2016). A gap analysis of Internet-of-Things platforms. *Computer Communications*, *89-90*, 5–16. doi:10.1016/j.comcom.2016.03.015

Miorandi, D., Sicari, S., De Pellegrini, F., & Chlamtac, I. (2012). Internet of things: Vision, applications and research challenges. *Ad Hoc Networks*, *10*(7), 1497–1516. doi:10.1016/j.adhoc.2012.02.016

Patnayakuni, R., Rai, A., & Seth, N. (2006). Relational antecedents of information flow integration for supply chain coordination. *Journal of Management Information Systems*, *23*(1), 13–49. doi:10.2753/MIS0742-1222230101

Petersen, K. J., Ragatz, G. L., & Monczka, R. M. (2005). An examination of collaborative planning effectiveness and supply chain performance. *Journal of Supply Chain Management*, *41*(2), 14–25. doi:10.1111/j.1055-6001.2005.04102002.x

Ping, L., Liu, Q., Zhou, Z., & Wang, H. (2011). Agile supply chain management over the Internet of Things. *2011 International Conference on Management and Service Science (MASS)*, 1-4. doi:10.1109/ICMSS.2011.5998440

Pramatari, K. (2007). Collaborative supply chain practices and evolving technological approaches. *Supply Chain Management: An International Journal*, *12*(3), 210–220. doi:10.1108/13598540710742527

Priya, R. V., Vadivel, A., & Thakur, S. (2012). Maximal pattern mining using fast CP-Tree for knowledge discovery. *International Journal of Information Systems and Social Change*, *3*(1), 56–74. doi:10.4018/jissc.2012010106

Reaidy, P. J., Gunasekaran, A., & Spalanzani, A. (2015). Bottom-up approach based on Internet of Things for order fulfillment in a collaborative warehousing environment. *International Journal of Production Economics*, *159*, 29–40. doi:10.1016/j.ijpe.2014.02.017

Roman, R., Zhou, J., & Lopez, J. (2013). On the features and challenges of security and privacy in distributed internet of things. *Computer Networks*, *57*(10), 2266–2279. doi:10.1016/j.comnet.2012.12.018

Singh, D., Tripathi, G., & Jara, A. J. (2014). A survey of Internet-of-Things: Future vision, architecture, challenges and services. *2014 IEEE World Forum on Internet of Things (WF-IoT).*

Sundmaeker, H., Guillemin, P., Friess, P., & Woelfflé, S. (2010). *Vision and challenges for realising the Internet of Things, CERP-IoT – Cluster of European Research Projects on the Internet of Things.* Retrieved August 16, 2014 from http://www.researchgate.net/publication/228664767_Vision_and_challenges_for_realising_the_Internet_of_Things

Tao, F., Zuo, Y., Xu, L. D., & Zhang, L. (2014). IoT based intelligent perception and access of manufacturing resource towards cloud manufacturing. *IEEE Transactions on Industrial Informatics*, *10*(2), 1547–1557. doi:10.1109/TII.2014.2306397

Tsai, C.-W., Lai, C.-F., Chiang, M.-C., & Yang, L. T. (2014). Data mining for Internet of Things: A survey. *IEEE Communications Surveys and Tutorials*, *16*(1), 77–97. doi:10.1109/SURV.2013.103013.00206

Wang, H., Zhang, T., Quan, Y., & Dong, R. (2013). Research on the framework of the Environmental Internet of Things. *International Journal of Sustainable Development and World Ecology*, *20*(3), 199–204. doi:10.1080/13504509.2013.783517

White, C. C. III, & Cheong, T. (2012). In-transit perishable product inspection. *Transportation Research Part E, Logistics and Transportation Review*, *48*(1), 310–330. doi:10.1016/j.tre.2011.08.006

Xu, B., Xu, L. D., Cai, H., Xie, C., Hu, J., & Bu, F. (2014). Ubiquitous data accessing method in IoT-based information system for emergency medical services. *IEEE Transactions on Industrial Informatics*, *10*(2), 1578–1586. doi:10.1109/TII.2014.2306382

Zeleny, M. (2013). Integrated knowledge management. *International Journal of Information Systems and Social Change*, *4*(4), 62–78. doi:10.4018/jissc.2013100104

Zhou, Z., & Zhou, Z. (2012). Application of Internet of things in agriculture products supply chain management. *International Conference on Control Engineering and Communication Technology (ICCECT)*. doi:10.1109/ICCECT.2012.262

## KEY TERMS AND DEFINITIONS

**Application Layer:** A layer which consists of a set of problem-specific software tools that interact with users, solve problems, process data, and share solutions with other applications.

**Communication Layer:** A layer which consists of a network of wired/wireless networks, the Internet, and protocols.

**Data Service Layer:** A layer which consists of private/public cloud and related data management systems.

**Internet of Things (IoT):** A global network of interacting machines and devices over the Internet.

**Object Layer:** A layer which consists of physical objects such as devices, machines, sensors, RFID tags, and readers.

**Supply Chain Management:** The management of the flow of goods and services in the supply network.

# Chapter 5
# Privacy in the Internet of Things

**Jayashree Kanniappan**
*Rajalakshmi Engineering College, India*

**Babu Rajendiran**
*Rajalakshmi Engineering College, India*

## ABSTRACT

*Internet of Things technology is rapidly gaining popularity, not only in industrial and commercial environments, but also in personal life by means of smart devices at home. The Internet of Things (IoT) spawn new businesses and make buildings, cities and transport smarter. The IoT allows for ubiquitous data collection or tracking, but these useful features are also examples of privacy threats that are already limiting the success of the IoT vision when not implemented correctly. Privacy should be protected in the device, in storage, during communication, and at processing. The privacy of users and their data protection have been identified as one of the important challenges that need to be addressed in the IoT. The chapter presents the IoT technology, the various applications, and privacy issues. Various other issues such as security and performance are also addressed.*

## INTRODUCTION

The Internet of Things (IoT) paradigm envisions the pervasive interconnection and cooperation of smart things over the Internet infrastructure. Realization of IoT paradigm depends on integration of Radio Frequency Identification (RFID) systems for tracing and addressing items non-contact and automatically, Wireless Sensor Networks (WSN) for integrating distributed information collection, transmission and processing, Machine to Machine systems and intelligent signal processing and nanometer technologies (Dey et al., 2015). The IoT encompasses a set of technologies that enable a wide range of appliances, devices, and objects to interact and communicate among themselves using networking technologies (Tarouco et al., 2012).

The IoT enables many new services for people's everyday lives, spawns new businesses and makes buildings, cities and transportation systems smarter. It is based on intelligent and self-configuring nodes interconnected in a dynamic and global network infrastructure that relies on sensory, communication, networking, and information processing technologies (Ziegeldorf et al., 2014). The IoT is generally char-

DOI: 10.4018/978-1-5225-2104-4.ch005

acterized by small things with limited storage and processing capacity, and issues regarding reliability, performance, security, and privacy have been a challenge.

Examples of IoT systems includes healthcare, emergency, advanced building management systems, smart home, smart grids for energy distribution, intelligent transport systems, public surveillance and data acquisition, smart factory and smart retail stores (Zanella et al., 2014). By employing the IoT technologies in the activities of healthcare servicing, doctors are able to access different kinds of data resources online quickly and easily, make emergency medical decisions, and reduce costs in the process (Xu et al., 2014). Health-related IoT applications are used to monitor the conditions of patients inside hospitals and old people at home (Khanna & Misra, 2014). For example, a tiny, wearable device can detect a person's vital signs and send an alert to a healthcare professional if a certain threshold is reached or if a person has fallen down. Also, when an accident occurs, the victim's medical journals are automatically made available to the ambulances to ensure that optimal treatment can be provided (Virkki & Chen, 2013).

The vision for the IoT is to make our everyday lives easier and boost the efficiency and productivity of businesses and employees. The data collected will help us to make smarter decisions. The ubiquity and interactions involved in the IoT provides many conveniences and useful services for individuals and organizations, but it is vulnerable to privacy. One of the most significant challenges in convincing users to adopt emerging technologies is the protection of data and privacy (Badkas et al., 2015). To solve the privacy problems created by IoT applications of the future, the privacy policies for each system domain must be specified. Once specified, either the individual IoT application or the IoT infrastructure must enforce privacy. The IoT system must be able to elicit users' requests for data access and the policies, and evaluate the requests against the policies in order to decide if they should be granted or denied.

In this chapter various issues related to IoT will be discussed. IoT privacy challenges and open problems will be elaborated. Finally, possible solutions and recommendations will be discussed.

## BACKGROUND

The Internet security glossary (RFC) defines privacy as "the right of an entity, acting in its own behalf, to determine the degree to which it will interact with its environment, including the degree to which the entity is willing to share information about itself with others. A Request for Comments (RFC) is a formal document from the Internet Engineering Task Force (IETF) that is the result of committee drafting and subsequent review by interested parties.

Information privacy was defined as "the right to select what personal information about me is known to what people" by Westin (1968). Westin's surveys measure attitudes and concerns about privacy and provide data on how these attitudes and concerns change over time. Westin has surveyed the general level of privacy concern of the public and has also studied the attitudes about specific privacy-related topics, for example, confidence in organizations that handle personal information, acceptance of a national identification system, and use of medical records for research. Westin classified the public into three categories. Westin has interchangeably used the following categories to refer to the groups of people that he created: (1) High and Fundamentalist, (2) Medium and Pragmatist, (3) Low and Unconcerned.

Lu et al. (2015) have defined privacy as "privacy information" refers to personal data or transactions that can be stored in IoT/CPS systems, not the personal thought or feeling that will not be stored usually. The personal privacy is usually a very subjective concept, so the understanding of the privacy of different individuals is different. The private information that some people regard as private may be insignificant to others. In addition, the privacy is closely associated with the situation and environment. People would like to share their privacy with their friends in a private environment. The privacy may not be an entirely objective existence, but a cognitive process, and everyone has his or her own privacy boundary and threshold. However, the privacy is a kind of the general public psychology of the human society; hence it still needs to be studied in accordance with the standards of the general public. Thus it is necessary to research the privacy and privacy attributes with greater pertinence.

Privacy in RFID systems has been defined as "The ability of the RFID system to keep the meaning of the information transmitted between the tag and the reader secure from non-intended recipients" (Banks, 2008). Traceability and inventorying relate to the ability of an unauthorized entity to read the identifiers sent by RFID tags without necessarily being concerned as to what the tag is affixed to or who/what is carrying it. In other words, just by capturing the signals emitted by an RFID tag, a third party could trace where the tag is or has been as well as to what tags have been detected.

Medaglia and Serbanati (2010) have discussed that networks of constrained devices and data-collection systems, generally characterized by very limited resources, aim to collect and transport sensible and sometimes critical data. Hence privacy is considered to be one of the most dominant challenges in the IoT due to the involvement of citizens and increasingly ubiquitous data collection. The IoT technologies such as RFID, WSN, etc., could provide many benefits in the healthcare domain. For example, a person's health status could be inferred from the RFID tags on clothes or from discovering a wearable medical device. And the applications in hospital could be categorized into: tracking of hospital staff and patients, identification and authentication of people, automatic data collection and sensing, and remote healthcare. In the remote healthcare system in, everyday a human's blood oxygen concentration, blood glucose level and blood pressure are collected automatically by sensor nodes, transmitted wirelessly to base-station, and displayed against time on the LCD screen. Furthermore, by connecting the base-station with a networked home PC, the data can be transferred to the remote server. Doctors may check the data to see if the result is normal or not. The data can also be transmitted to doctor's mobile device through the GSM short messages from the home base station. This system is able to bring benefits to remote healthcare at home or in the hospitals.

## Privacy Categories

Personally Identifiable Information (PII) can be gathered from gateway devices without consent, and can be used to conduct unscrupulous activities. PII is any information that can be used to uniquely identify, contact or locate an individual, or can be used with other sources to uniquely identify a person. It consists of a broad range of information that can identify individuals, including dates of birth, addresses, driver's license numbers, credit card numbers, bank account numbers, health and insurance records, and much more (Stringer, 2011).

Chaudhuri (2015) has described that privacy can be broadly classified into the following four categories based on how to establish truly smart cities with a host of smart services:

1. **Identity:** As IoT devices are owned by individuals and organizations, the identity of these devices helps identify their owners. Therefore, these devices and the data they generate should be marked as private.
2. **Location:** Data that can be used to identify a user's or device's location is also measured secretive. An IoT device's location can be used to gather information about the owner's location, which may be leveraged for deceitful activities and hence, such information should be concealed.
3. **Search Query:** Search queries can disclose information about the person who initiated it by tracking the IP address of the source. This data can then be used for target advertising without the individual's consent.
4. **Digital Footprint:** IoT-enabled devices are always online, and therefore they leave behind traceable data on the internet. The devices should therefore be secured through effective security protocols to prevent increase of digital footprints related to devices and their owners. Cookie invasion of IoT devices should also be prevented to ensure operational privacy.

## Privacy Requirement for the IoT

Vasilomanolakis et al. (2015) have elaborated on data privacy, anonymity, pseudonymity, and unlinkability as the privacy requirement for the IoT. Some IoT applications are tightly linked to sensitive infrastructures and strategic services such as the distribution of water and electricity and the surveillance of assets. Other applications handle sensitive information about people, such as their location and movements, or their health and purchasing preferences. Confidence in and acceptance of IoT will depend on the protection it provides to people's privacy and the levels of security it guarantees to systems and processes.

### Data Privacy

Data privacy complements confidential data transmission in the sense that a stored data record must not expose undesired properties, such as the identity of a person. This requirement is an enormous challenge in the IoT, as so many sensing devices collect personal information. Large amount of such data becomes PII when combined together. (Daubert et al., 2015).

### Anonymity

Pfitzmann and kohntopp (2000) described the property of a single person not being identifiable as the source of data or an action. Achieving anonymity is a tough challenge as wearable and mobile devices may leak PII such as IP addresses and location unknowingly. Technologies such as anonymous credentials and onion routing exist, but may not scale well with the IoT.

### Pseudonymity

Pseudonymity trades off anonymity with accountability. With pseudonymity, actions of a person are linked with a pseudonym, a random identifier, rather than an identity. While pseudonyms may resolve privacy and accountability concerns in the IoT, standardized solutions that accompany multiple domains are required.

### Unlinkability

Unlinkability qualifies pseudonymity in the sense that specific actions of the same person must not be linked together. Unlinkability protects from profiling in the IoT. While pseudonyms may solve unlinkability, i.e., a different pseudonym is used for every action, cross-implications with anonymity, in particular unknown meta-data, remain a challenge. Furthermore, some entity can always link every pseudonym to a person, and can thus also link all actions of that person.

The IoT paradigm finds application in many fields, such as health-care, home automation, smart cities, and environmental monitoring. All the IoT applications must protect user's movements, habits, interactions and private life. Hence it is more important to develop privacy solutions so that the sensitive information of the user will be protected.

## IoT Issue Areas

Rose et al. (2014) explain the five key IoT issue areas that are examined to explore some of the most pressing challenges and questions related to the technology. These areas include security; privacy; interoperability and standards; legal, regulatory, and rights; and emerging economies and development.

### Security

Since the loT technology has been more integrated with our daily lives, priority should be given to ensure the security in loT products and services. Because the loT implementations are capable of upbringing new and unique security challenges, we have to ensure the security for the loT devices and related data services are safe and secure from vulnerabilities. IoT presents a variety of potential security risks that could be exploited to harm consumers by: enabling unauthorized access and misuse of personal information; facilitating attacks on other systems; and creating risks to personal safety.

### Privacy

IoT data collection and use becomes a privacy consideration when the individuals who are observed by IoT devices have different privacy expectations regarding the scope and use of that data than those of the data collector. Seemingly benign combinations of IoT data streams also can jeopardize privacy. When individual data streams are combined or correlated, often a more invasive digital portrait is painted of the individual than can be realized from an individual IoT data stream. For example, a user's Internet-enabled toothbrush might capture and transmit innocuous data about a person's tooth-brushing habits. But if the user's refrigerator reports the inventory of the foods he eats and his fitness-tracking device reports his activity data, the combination of these data streams paint a much more detailed and private description of the person's overall health. This data-aggregation effect can be particularly potent with respect to IoT devices because many produce additional metadata like time stamps and geo location information, which adds even more specificity about the user. In other situations, the user might not be aware that an IoT device is collecting data about the individual and potentially sharing it with third parties. This type of data collection is becoming more prevalent in consumer devices like smart televisions and video game devices. These kinds of products have voice recognition or vision features that continuously listen to conversations or watch for activity in a room and selectively transmit that data to a cloud service for processing, which sometimes includes a third party. A person might be in the presence of these kinds of devices without knowing their conversation or activities are being monitored and their data captured. These kinds of features may provide a benefit to an informed user, but can pose a privacy problem for those who are unaware of the presence of the devices and have no meaningful influence over how that collected information is used. Independent of whether the user is aware of and consents to having their IoT data collected and analyzed, these situations highlight the value of these personalized data streams to companies and organizations seeking to collect and capitalize on IoT information. The demand for this information exposes the legal and regulatory challenges facing data protection and privacy laws. (Sartori, 2016)

### Interoperability and Standards

Full interoperability across products and services is not always feasible or necessary. Purchasers may be hesitant to buy IoT products and services if there is integration inflexibility, high ownership complexity, and concern over vendor lock-in.

In addition, poorly designed and configured IoT devices may have negative consequences for the networking resources they connect to and the broader Internet. Appropriate standards, reference models, and best practices also will help curb the proliferation of devices that may act in disrupted ways to the Internet.

### Legal, Regulatory, and Rights

The use of IoT devices raises many new regulatory and legal questions as well as amplifies existing legal issues since the new development over the devices frequently outpaces the policies and regulatory structures already available.

### Emerging Economics and Development

Areas such as sustainable agriculture, water quality and use, healthcare, industrialization, and environmental management, etc. are much benefited from the IoT implementations by social and economic benefits to emerging and developing economies. The broad scope of IoT challenges will not be unique to industrialized countries. Developing regions also will need to respond to realize the potential benefits of IoT. In addition, the unique needs and challenges of implementation in less-developed regions will need to be addressed, including infrastructure readiness, market and investment incentives, technical skill requirements, and policy resources.

## IoT PRIVACY CHALLENGES AND OPEN PROBLEMS

Bertino (2016) has described that privacy is predominantly significant in the context of IoT. As medical and well-being devices are increasingly being adopted by users and personalized medicine and health care applications are being designed and deployed that rely on continuous fine-grained data acquisition from these devices, the human body is becoming a rich source of information. Such information is typically collected from devices and then uploaded to some cloud and/or transmitted to other devices, such as mobile phones, which in turn may forward the information to other parties. The collected information is typically very rich and often includes meta-data such as location, time, and context, thus making possible to easily infer personal habits, behaviors, and preferences of individuals. It is thus clear that on one side such information has to be carefully protected by all parties involved in its acquisition, management, and use, but also users should be provided with suitable, easy to use tools to protect their privacy and support anonymity depending on specific contexts.

The Article 29 Working Party (WP29) on the IoT, which highlights the privacy and Data Protection (DP) challenges posed by the IoT, puts forward recommendations to help stakeholders comply with current European Union data protection legislation for the development of a sustainable IoT. WP29 is an independent European advisory body on data protection and privacy. The privacy and data protection challenges related to IoT that WP29 identifies are:

1. Lack of control and information asymmetry: interaction between objects that communicate automatically and by default, between objects and individual devices, between individuals and other objects, and between objects and back-end systems, which will result in the generation of data flows that can hardly be managed with the traditional tools used to ensure the adequate protection of the data subject's interests and rights.
2. Quality of the user´s consent: the possibility of rejecting certain services is not a real alternative in IoT and classic mechanisms used to obtain consent may be difficult to apply. Therefore, new ways of obtaining the user´s valid consent should be considered, including implementing consent mechanisms through the devices themselves as privacy proxies.
3. Inferences derived from data and repurposing of original processing: The IoT stakeholders will make sure the raw information is used for purposes that are compatible with original purposes which the users know already.
4. Intrusive identification of behaviour patterns and profiling: Proliferation of sensors is used to generate knowledge even from anonymous data source which in turn helps to get the detailed behavior patterns.
5. Limitations on the possibility of remaining anonymous when using services; and
6. Security risks - weak points can occur not only at device level but also in the communication links, storage infrastructure and other inputs of this ecosystem.

## Privacy Issues in IoT Applications

Al-mawee (2012) has discussed that IoT applications for the people with disabilities that collect and analyze massive amounts of health data. The most common privacy issues in IoT applications for the people with disabilities along with IoT-based solutions have been conferred.

A Personal Health Record (PHR) is "an individual electronic record of health-related information that conforms to the nationally recognized interoperability standards. PHR can be drawn from multiple sources while being managed, shared and controlled by the individual" (Khan et al., 2009). PHRs are reported to the e-health center directly, and the primary privacy and security goal is to keep the patients' PHRs confidential. Li et al. (2012) proposed a method to encrypt each PHR with one-to-many encryption methods, such as the Attribute Based Encryption (ABE) technique. Encryption algorithms such as Advanced Encryption Standard and Message-Digest algorithm5, together with efficient key management, have been used to encrypt each PHR file. A health system can be divided into two security domains, namely PUblic Domains (PUDs) and PerSonal Domains (PSDs), according to the different users' data access requirements. PUDs consist of users who need access based on their professional roles, such as doctors, nurses and medical researchers. In practice, a PUD can be mapped to an independent economic sector, such as healthcare, government or insurance sectors. For each PSD, its users are personally associated with a data owner, and they make accesses to PHRs based on access rights assigned by the owner.

## Threats of Cyber-Attacks on Privacy

Cyber-attacks can inject false data into a system, causing critical damage in IoT applications. It is fundamental to provide the adequate level of protection against cyber-attacks in smart home applications for the disabled. However, the resource-constrained natures of many of IoT devices present in a smart home environment do not allow implementing the standard security solutions. Tajer et al. (2011) recommended a framework that guarantees detection of the cyber-attacks and recovering from them. Different controlling agents, distributed across the network, constitute the attack detection subsystem. System recovery involves iterative local processing and message passing.

## Data Eavesdropping and Data Confidentiality

The health data of patients are held under the legal obligations of confidentiality, and made available only to the authorized caregivers. It is important to prevent stealing data from storage or eavesdropping on them while they flow over the wireless links. For example, a popular IoT-based glucose monitoring and insulin delivery system utilizes wireless communication links, which are frequently used to launch privacy attacks. Li et al. (2011) proposed rolling-code cryptographic protocols and body-coupled communication to mitigate the eavesdropping. Miaou et al. (2000) suggested a bi-polar multiple-base data hiding technique for images, where a pixel value difference between an original image and its default Joint Photographic Experts Grouplossy decompressed image is taken as the number conversion base. The algorithm allows to hide doctors' digital seals and PHR within a still image. The still image could be a logo of a hospital identifying where the PHR comes from. A diagnostic report and a biomedical signal, such as an electrocardiogram, can also be hidden in an image. The proposed approach allows hiding multiple data types in the same image. All these data can be separated and restored perfectly by the intended users. Data confidentiality can be further improved by using Public Key Infrastructure (PKI). PKI creates an effective approach to data encryption as it can provide high level of confidence for exchanging information in an insecure environment (Tanwar & Prema, 2012).

## Location Privacy

Location privacy is concerned with privacy threats and eavesdropping on a user's location. Location privacy in WSNs, specifically hiding the message sender's location, can be achieved through routing to a randomly selected intermediate node (RRIN) (Ran et al., 2007). Eavesdropping and tracing of packets can be prevented by the Location Privacy Routing (LPR) protocol, which uniformly distributes the directions of incoming and outgoing traffic at sensor nodes (Jian et al., 2007).

## Privacy in Device

The sensitive information may be leaked out in case of unauthorized manipulation or handling of hardware and software in these devices (Borgohain et al., 2015). For example, an intruder can "reprogramme" a surveillance camera, such that it sends data not only to the legitimate server, but also to the intruder. Thus, for devices that gather sensitive data, robustness and tamper resistance are especially important. To ensure IoTs security, trusted computing technologies including device integrity validations, tamper-resistant modules and trusted execution environments are useful. In order to provide the privacy in the devices, one need to address location privacy of the device holder, non-identifiability and resilience to side channel attacks. Non-identifiability means protecting the identification of the exact nature of the device, protecting the personal information in case of the device theft or loss.

## Privacy During Communication

To assure data confidentiality during the transmission of the data, the most common approach is encryption. Encryption on certain occasions adds data to packets which provides a way for tracing, e.g., sequence number, IPsec-SecurityParameterIndex, etc. These data may be victimized for linking packets to the analysis of same flow traffic. Secure Communication Protocol could be the suitable approach. A secure communications protocol ensures the authenticity of both parties and protects the confidentiality, integrity and freshness of the information that is transmitted (Mavrogiannopoulos, 2013). During the communication Pseudonyms can be replaced for encryption in case it is not feasible to the device's identity or user's in order to decrease the vulnerability. One of the examples is Temporary Mobile Subscriber Identity (TMSI) (Polonetsky & Wolf, 2014). Devices should communicate if and only if when there is a need, to derogate privacy disclosure induced by communication. In 3rd Generation Partnership Project (3GPP) machine type communications, in order to avoid unnecessary collection of location information by the network after a certain period of inactivity the devices will detach from the network.

## Privacy in Storage

For protecting privacy of information storage, the following principles should be considered (Kumar & Dhiren, 2014).

- Only the least possible amount of information should be stored that is needed.
- Personal information is retained at mandatory cases only.
- Information is brought out on the basis of "need-to-know".

## Privacy at Processing

It is mainly of two folds. Firstly, personal data must be treated in a way that it should be simpatico with the intended purpose. Secondly, without explicit acceptance and the knowledge of the data owner, their personal data should not be disclosed or retained to third parties (Madhura et al., 2014). By considering the above two points, Digital Rights Management (DRM) systems is most suitable which controls the consumption of commercial media and defends against re-distribution (Liu et al., 2014). One can define privacy policies for personal data in a rights object or license instead of exercising principles for commercial media which must be obeyed during the data processing. DRM requires trusted devices, secure devices to work efficiently and effectively. User's permission and their awareness are requirements for distribution of personal data.

Evans and Eyers (2012) proposed a data tagging for managing privacy in IoT. Data representing physical phenomena or related to individuals are tagged with their privacy properties. Tagging within resource-constrained sensors raises several issues due to the expensive tags computation. A well investigated solution is based on the k-anonymity. Definition of k-anonymity (Ciriani et al., 2007). Let T (A1, . . ., Am) be a table, and QI be a quasi-identifier associated with it. T is said to satisfy k-anonymity with respect to QI iff each sequence of values in T[QI] appears at least with k occurrences in T[QI]. Wang and Wen (2011) analyze the privacy risk that occurs when a Static Domain Name is assigned to a specified IoT terminal smart device. In this work the authors propose a privacy protection enhanced Domain Name System (DNS) scheme for smart devices, which can authenticate the original user's identity and reject illegal accesses. Alcaide et al. (2013) suggested that privacy and access control mechanisms are considered together. They presented a fully decentralized anonymous authentication protocol aimed at implementing privacy-preserving IoT applications. Such a proposal is based on a credential system, which defines two roles for the participant nodes: Users, which are the nodes originating the data and Data Collectors, which are the entities responsible for the collection of data only from authorized Users. Users can anonymously authenticate themselves in front of Data Collectors proving the ownership of a valid Anonymous Access Credential (AAC) encoding a particular set of attributes. Such a system relies on no central organization. The parameters required by the system are generated in a cooperative way.

### Privacy Preservation

Rehiman and Veni (2015) discussed that increasing amount of data, users and communication in IoT lead to the need of privacy preservation. Huang et al. (2012) suggested a user interactive privacy preserved access control mechanism and designed a content aware k-anonymity privacy policy and filter. By this a user can control his personal data from being collected. The major issue associated with the design is that a user needs to pay attention to ensure privacy, but it is not practical, because the majority of users in IoT environment are from business fields.

## SOLUTIONS AND RECOMMENDATIONS

Stankovic (2014) discussed that the ubiquity and interactions involved in IoT will provide many conveniences and useful services for individuals, but also create many opportunities to violate privacy. To solve the privacy problem created by IoT applications of the future, the privacy policies for each domain must be specified. Once specified, either the individual IoT application or the IoT infra-structure must enforce privacy. The IoT system must be able to elicit users' requests for data access and the policies, such that the requests can be evaluated against the policies in order to decide if they should be granted or denied. A new language is required to express privacy policies because the following requirements are not easily expressed in current privacy languages.

1. The need to express different types of context in the environment such as time, space, physiological sensing, environmental sensing, and stream-based noisy data. Most of the context needs to be

collected and evaluated in real time. But what will collect policies and data and support privacy? Is it the utility infrastructure, an individual application, both, or some new approach?

2. The need to represent different types of data owners and subjects in the system as well as external users and their rights when domains interact. Unlike other privacy enforcing systems where the subjects and data owners are human individuals or groups, an IoT privacy language might also support physical entities such as "refrigerator," "room," "floor," and other system entities (things) as request issuers and data owners.
3. The need to represent high-level aggregating requests such as querying the average, maximum, or minimum reading of specified sensing data. This capability must be supported by anonymizing aggregation functions. This capability needs to exist for real-time streams and across the big data repositories. Inference is very powerful, and by having access to vast amounts of data and inference techniques, it is often easy to violate privacy in spite of anonymization.
4. The need to support not only adherence to privacy for queries of data, but also privacy on requests to set a system's parameters, e.g., a private use of an actuator.
5. The need to allow dynamic changes to the policies, and perform a myriad of analyses some of which are context dependent. One of the more difficult privacy problems is that systems interact with other systems, each having their own privacy policies. Consequently, inconsistencies may arise across systems in the IoT world. Online consistency checking and notification and resolution schemes are required.

Finally, privacy introduces new challenges, including how to prevent personal devices from acquiring and/or transmitting information depending on the user location and other context information, and how to allow users to understand risks and advantages in sharing their personal data. Strategies need to be developed to respect individual privacy choices across a broad spectrum of expectations, while still fostering innovation in new IoT technology.

WP29 made the following recommendations (Escribano, 2014):

The recommendations common to all stakeholders are: the performance of Privacy Impact Assessments prior to the launch of any new IoT application; stakeholders must delete raw data as soon as data required for data processing is extracted; privacy by design and privacy by default principles should be applied; the user should be in control of the data at any time and for that purpose, offering a right to refuse/request consent should be made as user-friendly as possible (understandable and not hidden in a general privacy policy); and devices and applications should be designed so as to inform users and non-user data subjects.

For the specific stakeholders, most of the recommendations have been mentioned above, but those addressed specifically to Operating System (OS) and device manufacturers are such that OS and device manufacturers should: inform users about type of data collected and processed and they should inform other stakeholders in the value chain as soon as the data subject withdraws its consent or opposes data processing; offer granular choices when granting access to applications as for instance, a "do not collect option" to schedule or quickly disable sensors; data including aggregated data should be stored and exported in a structured/commonly used/standardized format allowing data portability; security by design should be followed; ensure that devices are capable of distinguishing between different users using the same device, and enable local control of data through personal privacy proxies; and work together with standardisation bodies and data platforms to support common protocols for preferences with regard to data collection/processing.

## CONCLUSION

The IoT has brought about huge changes in people's daily life and the tangible benefits of the billions of interconnected devices are materialized to society and organizations. However, security and privacy concerns are major obstructions in the successful deployment of IoT enabled smart services. The need for privacy in the IoT and the various issues that pose challenges to the IoT have been discussed in the chapter. This chapter also elaborates the literature review on the privacy issues and the measures to prevent them.

The IoT presents abundant benefits to consumers, and has the potential to change the ways that consumers interact with technology in fundamental ways. The pervasiveness and communications included in IoT can give numerous accommodations and helpful administrations for people, but additionally make numerous chances to abuse security- i.e., it creates many opportunities to violate privacy (Vyas et al., 2015). In the future, the IoT is likely to meld the virtual and physical worlds together in ways that are currently difficult to comprehend. From a security and privacy perspective, the predicted pervasive introduction of sensors and devices into currently intimate spaces such as the home, the car, and even the body poses particular challenges. As physical objects in our everyday lives increasingly detect and share observations about us, consumers will likely continue to want privacy. Various regulatory agencies will continue to enforce laws, educate consumers and businesses, and engage with consumer advocates, industry, academics, and other stakeholders involved in the IoT to promote appropriate security and privacy protections.

The research and practice communities should work together towards privacy from the social, legal, and culture viewpoints; protection of privacy of communication and user data such that personal data collected should be used only in the aim of supporting authorized services by authorized service providers; and the above data should be stored only until it is strictly needed. The dangers to personal information privacy within IoT should also be addressed by vendors, manufacturers and service providers. Privacy-preserving machine learning algorithms can also be implemented for privacy issues.

## REFERENCES

Al-Mawee, W. (2012). *Privacy and Security Issues in IoT Healthcare Applications for the Disabled Users* (Master Thesis). Computer Science., Western Michigan University.

Alcaide, A., Palomar, E., Montero-Castillo, J., & Ribagorda, A. (2013). Anonymous authentication for privacy-preserving IoT target driven applications. *Computers & Security*, *37*, 111–123. doi:10.1016/j.cose.2013.05.007

Badkas, C.K., Shahade, M.R., & Ramteke, U.S. (2015). Review of Internet of Things (IoT): A vision and future directions. *International Journal of Research in Science & Engineering, 1*(1), 129-134.

Banks, J. (2008). *Understanding RFID Part 9: RFID Privacy and Security*. Retrieved May 5, 2016 from http://www.secureidnews.com/news-item/understanding-rfid-part-9-rfid-privacy-and-security

Bertino, E. (2016). Data Security and Privacy in the IoT Paper. *9th International Conference on Extending Database Technology (EDBT)*, 1-3.

Borgohain, T., Kumar, U., & Sanyal, S. (2015). Survey of Security and Privacy Issues of Internet of Things. *Int. J. Advanced Networking and Applications*, *6*(4), 2372–2378.

Chaudhuri, A. (2015). *Address Security and Privacy Concerns to Fully Tap into IoT's Potential*. White paper. Retrieved May 5, 2016 from http://www.tcs.com/resources/white_papers/Pages/Security-Privacy-IoT-Potential.aspx

Ciriani, V., Vimercati, C.D., Foresti, S., & Samarati, P. (2007). k-Anonymity. In *Secure Data Management in Decentralized Systems* (pp. 323-353). Springer US.

Daubert, J., Wiesmaier, A., & Kikiras, P. (2015). A view on privacy & trust in IoT. IoT/CPS-Security Workshop. *IEEE International Conference on Communications, ICC*. doi:10.1109/ICCW.2015.7247581

Dey, S., Joshi, S. D., Patil, S., Kumar, K., & Kagi, V. K. (2016). A Survey of the Internet of Things. *IOSR Journal of Computer Engineering*, *18*(1), 80–85. doi:10.9790/0661-18138085

Escribano, B. (2013). *Privacy and security in the Internet of Things: challenge or opportunity*. Retrieved May 10, 2016 from http://www.olswang.com/media/48315339/privacy_and_security_in_the_iot.pdf

Evans, D., & Eyers, D. (2012). Efficient data tagging for managing privacy in the Internet of Things. *GREENCOM '12 Proceedings of the 2012 IEEE International Conference on Green Computing and Communications*, 244-248. doi:10.1109/GreenCom.2012.45

Huang, X., Fu, R., Chen, B., Zhang, T., & Roscoe, A. (2012). User interactive Internet of Things Privacy Preserved access control. *Seventh International conference for Internet Technology and secured transaction ICITST United Kingdom*, 597-602.

Internet of Things Privacy & Security in a Connected World. (2015). FTC Staff Report January. Retrieved March 25, 2016 from https://www.ftc.gov/news-events/press-releases/2015/01

Jian, Y., Chen, S., Zhang, Z., & Zhang, L. (2007). Protecting Recevier-Location Privacy in Wireless Sensor Networks. *IEEE 26th International Conference on Computer Communications,* 955-1963. doi:10.1109/INFCOM.2007.227

Khan, J. S., Aulakh, V., & Bosworth, A. (2009). What It Takes. *Characteristics of the Ideal Personal Health Record Health Aff (Millwood)*, *28*(2), 369–376. doi:10.1377/hlthaff.28.2.369 PMID:19275992

Khanna, A., & Misra, P. (2014). *The Internet of Things for Medical Devices - Prospects, Challenges and the Way Forward*. Retrieved May 10, 2016 from http://www.tcs.com/resources/white_papers/Pages/Internet-of-Things-Medical-Devices.aspx

Kumar, J., & Patel, D. (2014). A Survey on Internet of Things: Security and Privacy Issues. *International Journal of Computer Applications*, *90*. doi: 10.5120/15764-4454

Li, C., Raghunathan, A., & Jha, N. K. (2011). Hijacking an Insulin Pump: Security Attacks and Defenses for a Diabetes Therapy System. *IEEE 13th International Conference on e-health Networking, Applications and Services.* doi:10.1109/HEALTH.2011.6026732

Li, M., Yu, S., Zhen, Y., Ren, K., & Lou, W. (2012). Scalable and Secure Sharing of Personal Health Records in Cloud Computing using Attribute-based Encryption. *IEEE Transactions on Parallel and Distributed Systems*, *24*(1), 131–143. doi:10.1109/TPDS.2012.97

Liu, E., Liu, Z., & Shao, F. (2014). Digital Rights Management and Access Control in Multimedia Social Networks. *Genetic and Evolutionary Computing*, *238*, 257–266. doi:10.1007/978-3-319-01796-9_27

Lu, X., Qu, Z., Li, Q., & Hui, P. (2015). Privacy Information Security Classification for Internet of Things Based on Internet Data. *International Journal of Distributed Sensor Networks*, *11*(8), 932941. doi:10.1155/2015/932941

Madhura, P.M., Bilurkar, N., Jain, P., & Ranjith, J. (2015). A Survey on Internet of Things: Security and Privacy Issues. *International Journal of Innovative Technology and Research*, *3*(3), 2069 – 2074.

Mavrogiannopoulos, N. (2013). *Secure communications protocols and the protection of cryptographic keys* (Dissertation). Arenberg Doctoral School of Science, Engineering & Technology. Available at: https://securewww.esat.kuleuven.be/cosic/publications/thesis-225.pdf

Medaglia, C., & Serbanati, A. (2010). Internet of things: An overview of privacy and security issues in the Internet of things. *20th Tyrrhenian Workshop on Digital Communications Springer*, 389-395. doi:10.1007/978-1-4419-1674-7_38

Miaou, S. G., Hsu, C. M., Tsai, Y. S., & Chao, H. M. (2000). A Secure Data Hiding Technique with Heterogeneous Data-Combining Capability or Electronic Patient Records. *22nd Annual EMBS International Conference*, 280-283. doi:10.1109/IEMBS.2000.900730

Pfitzmann, A., & Kohntopp, M. (2000). Anonymity, unobservability, and pseudonymity - A proposal for terminology. *International Workshop on Design Issues in Anonymity and Unobservability*, 1-9. doi:10.1007/3-540-44702-4_1

Polonetsky, J., & Wolf, C. (2014). *RE – Spring Privacy Series: Mobile Device Tracking, PROJECT NO. P145401*. Retrieved from https://fpf.org/wp-content/uploads/Comments-of-the-Future-of-Privacy-Forum-on-Mobile-Device-Tracking.pdf

Rehiman, R. K., & Veni, S. (2015). Security, Privacy and Trust for Smart Mobile devices in Internet of Things. *International Journal of Advanced Research in Computer Engineering & Technology*, *4*(5), 1775-1779.

Ren, J., Li, Y., & Li, T. (2009). Routing-Based Source-Location Privacy in Wireless Sensor Networks. *IEEE International Conference on Communications*, 1-5. Doi:10.1109/ICC.2009.5199430

Rose, K., Eldridge, S., & Chapin, L. (2015). *The Internet of Things: An Overview Understanding the Issues and Challenges of a More Connected World*. ISOC.

Sartori, M., (2016). *Integration of an IEEE802.15.4g compliant transceiver into the Linux-based AMBER platform*. Universit`a degli studi di Padova.

Shirey, R. (2000). *RFC 2828 Internet Security Glossary*. Retrieved May10, 2016 from https:// www. ietf. Org /rfc/rfc2828.txt

Stankovic, J.A., (2008). When Sensor and Actuator Networks Cover the World. *ETRI Journal, 30*(5), 627-633.

Stringer, J. (2011). *Protecting personally identifiable information: What data is at risk and what you can do about it.* A Sophos White Paper.

Tajer, S., Poor, H. V., & Cui, S. (2011). Distributed Joint Cyber Attack Detection and State Recovery in Smart Grids. *IEEE International Conference on Smart Grid Communications*, 202-207. doi:10.1109/SmartGridComm.2011.6102319

Tanwar, S., & Prema, K.V. (2012). Solution to PKI Inter- Domain Interoperability Issue. *International Journal of Scientific and Engineering Research.*

Vasilomanolakis, E., Daubert, J., Luthra, M., Gazis, V., Wiesmaier, A., & Kikiras, P. (2015). On the Security and Privacy of Internet of Things: Architectures and Systems. *International Workshop on Secure Internet of Things (SLOT),* 49-57. doi:10.1109/SIOT.2015.9

Virkki, J., & Chen, L. (2013). Personal Perspectives: Individual Privacy in the IOT. *Advances in Internet of Things*. doi: 10.4236/ait.2013.32003

Vyas, D. A., Bhatt, D., & Jha, D. (2016). IoT: Trends, Challenges and Future Scope. *International Journal of Computer Science & Communication*, *7*(1), 186–197. doi:10.090592/IJCSC.2016.028

Wang, Y., & Wen, Q. (2011). A privacy enhanced dns scheme for the internet of things. *International Conference on Communication Technology and Application, ICCTA 2011*, 699-702. doi:10.1049/cp.2011.0758

Westin, A. F. (1968). Privacy and freedom. *Washington and Lee Law Review*. Retrieved May 10, 2016 from http://scholarlycommons.law.wlu.edu/wlulr/vol25/iss1/20

Xu, B., Xu, L., Cai, H., Xie, C., Hu, J., & Bu, F. (2014). Ubiquitous Data Accessing Method in IoT-Based Information System for Emergency Medical Services. *IEEE Transactions on Industrial Informatics.*, *10*, 2233–2243. doi:10.1109/TII.2014.2300753

Xu, L. D., He, W., & Li, S. (2014). Internet of things in industries: A survey. *IEEE Transactions on Industrial Informatics*, *10*(4), 2233–2243. doi:10.1109/TII.2014.2300753

Zanella, A., Bui, N., Castellani, A. P., Vangelista, L., & Zorzi, M. (2014). Internet of things for smart cities. *IEEE Internet of Things*, *1*(1), 22–32. doi:10.1109/JIOT.2014.2306328

Ziegeldorf, J. H., Morchon, O. G., & Wehrle, K. (2014). Privacy in the Internet of Things: Threats and Challenges. *Security and Communication Networks*, *7*(12), 2728–2742. doi:10.1002/sec.795

## KEY TERMS AND DEFINITIONS

**Anonymization:** Data anonymization is the process of either encrypting or eliminating personally identifiable information from data sets, so that the people whom the data describe remain anonymous.

**Attack:** An action taken against a target with the intention of doing harm.

**Confidentiality:** Confidentiality is a metric to analyze the ability of the system to protect its data from unknown access.

**Eavesdropping:** Eavesdropping is the act of interrupting communications between two points.

**IoT:** The Internet of Things (IoT) is an integration of interdependent computing devices, mechanical and digital machines, objects, animals or people that are provided with uncommon identifiers and the power to transmitting data across networks without requiring human-to-human or human-to-computer interaction.

**Privacy:** Data privacy is the capability of an individual or organization to decide on what data in a computer system can be shared with third parties.

**Pseudoanonymization:** Pseudonymization is a procedure by which the most identifying fields within a data record are replaced by one or more artificial identifiers, or pseudonyms.

**Security:** Security is the process of protecting data from unauthorized (accidental or intentional) modification, destruction, or disclosure.

**Threat:** The expressed potential for the occurrence of a harmful event such as an attack.

# Section 2
# IoT Management

# Chapter 6
# The Internet of Things:
## Assessing Its Potential and Identifying the Enablers Needed to Capture the Opportunity

**Jacques Bughin**
*McKinsey Global Institute, Belgium*

**Michael Chui**
*McKinsey Global Institute, USA*

## ABSTRACT

*The Internet of Things ("IoT"), networks of connected machines and sensors with the ability to monitor and manage objects in the physical world electronically, has substantial economic potential. IoT technology has a wide range of applications, such as optimizing the performance of industrial operations and infrastructure systems, coordinating self-driving cars; managing the energy efficiency and security of homes and offices; and monitoring patients remotely. Drawing on a body of research by the McKinsey Global Institute (most notably, The Internet of Things: Mapping the value beyond the hype, June 2015), this chapter finds that the IoT could generate anywhere from $3.9 trillion to $11.1 trillion in annual economic impact by 2025. We arrive at these figures through a bottom-up quantification of economic surplus that examines multiple use cases clustered in nine types of settings where IoT technology has relevance. We also highlight some of the fundamental enablers that will be necessary for this value to be realized, including industrial adoption, interoperability standards, cybersecurity, and regulatory certainty regarding issues such as data sharing and liability. While these factors are not yet certain, we conclude that the current hype of IoT is somewhat justified. Indeed, if these issues are resolved quickly and fully, the eventual economic value may exceed current expectations.*

DOI: 10.4018/978-1-5225-2104-4.ch006

## INTRODUCTION

The physical world is increasingly becoming an information network, populated by sensors and intelligent devices that capture continual streams of real-time information. These devices transit enormous volumes of data that can be processed with advanced analytics to choreograph the way complex systems operate. This web of connected devices, commonly referred to as the Internet of Things (IoT), represents the convergence of ubiquitous connectivity, the cloud, big data, and advanced analytics.

The purpose of the IoT is to help companies and consumers get far more out of their physical assets. These systems are already being applied in myriad ways: minimizing downtime on factory floors, tracking the progress of ships at sea, helping energy grids respond to spikes in demand, or controlling smart home appliances and security systems. The applications extend to the most personal of uses: patients with chronic diseases, for instance, can be outfitted with wearable devices and portable monitors to signal the need for preventive care before a crisis occurs, reducing both health-care costs and the enormous human toll of conditions such as diabetes. New IoT developments such as the rollout of connected and even self-driving cars continue to make headlines and capture the public's imagination.

Many business leaders have expressed a bullish outlook about the IoT's potential; Cisco chairman John Chambers, for example, has referred to it as "the biggest transition for the internet since [its] birth."[1] Some have dubbed this wave of technology the "Fourth Industrial Revolution." This degree of enthusiasm is backed up by investment dollars. CB Insights reports that nearly US$4 billion had flowed into IoT projects by 2016, including startups backed both by major venture capital firms such as Andreessen-Horowitz or Sequoia Capital as well as by companies including GE, Qualcomm, and Cisco Systems.[2]

As when any new technology arrives on the scene, there is a risk that the hype will exceed the reality. In this chapter, we aim to step back and present a fact-based analysis of the IoT's potential to generate economic value, based on an analysis of multiple use cases. Instead of estimating the total market for IoT technologies or taking an industry-by-industry approach, we look at the full range of industrial or user settings in which the IoT could be deployed. We also consider the enablers that would be required to realize this potential.

Using this approach, we highlight three crucial figures in this chapter:

1. **More Than 10 Trillion of Annual Value:** *The economic value linked to the IoT is necessarily uncertain at this stage of its development and deployment, but in all likelihood, it is substantial.* Considering a wide range of applications and assuming all consumer surplus linked to the IoT is fully reinjected into the economy, we estimate that the IoT could generate economic impact of $3.9 trillion to $11.1 trillion annually by 2025. This is equivalent to 11 percent of estimated world GDP in that year.
2. **40% of Value Driven by Inter-Operability:** *The development of open interfaces between the multiple devices and environments in which IoT systems are deployed will be a critically important '"external" factor* determining how much of this potential value is actually realized. We estimate that up to 40 percent of the potential value hinges on the ability to achieve interoperability.
3. **70% of Value Linked to Industrial Internet:** *A significant part of the IoT's value potential is specifically linked to the so-called "industrial internet"*—that is, the deployment of these systems in the world's vast industrial machinery, processes, and operations. Like any new technology diffusion, it will take time for companies to invest in the IoT and then to create systems and new business

models to take full advantage of it. There will also likely be large variations in their adoption and success in extracting value from this technology.

This chapter is organized as follows. Section 1 defines the IoT and sets out the scope of the use cases we examined to arrive at our estimates of the economic potential. Section 2 highlights the findings case by cases. Section 3 synthesizes and describes avenue for research. As this chapter relies on work completed by the authors in a recent report by the McKinsey Global Institute (Manyika et al., 2015), we suggest that interested readers refer to this report for a more comprehensive discussion.

## DEFINING THE INTERNET OF THINGS AND DESCRIBING THE SCOPE OF OUR ANALYSIS

### Definition

In 2005, the International Telecommunications Union issued research on the Internet of Things, defining it as "embedding short-range mobile transceivers into a wide array of additional gadgets and everyday items, enabling new forms of communication between people and thing, and between things themselves." It further predicted that "[c]onnections will multiply and create an entirely new dynamic network of networks."[3]

This chapter similarly defines the Internet of Things as sensors and actuators connected by networks to computing systems. These systems can monitor or manage the health and action of connected objected and machine; they can also monitor the natural world. We explicitly exclude systems in which the sensors' primary purpose is to receive intentional human input, such as smartphone apps where data input comes primarily through a touchscreen, or other networked computer software where the sensors consist of the standard keyboard and mouse.

### Scope

We analyze the economic potential of the IoT through a taxonomy of use cases. This way of scoping the market has become standard for new technologies, - see Moura and Hutchison (2016). This chapter's analysis rests on an examination of more than 150 IoT use cases across the global economy, with the full detail being available in Manyika et al. (2015) and Bughin et al. (2015).

These use cases fall into broad categories: managing inventory, conducting maintenance precisely when needed, boosting human productivity, optimizing operations through other means, enabling sales, managing health, managing energy consumption, managing the environment, ensuring safety and security, developing products, and operating autonomous vehicles. Using economic modeling for each use case, we then estimated the economic impact of these applications by the potential benefits they can generate, including productivity improvements, time savings, and improved asset utilization.

Importantly, we analyze each use case *in the context of settings.* This gives a more comprehensive view of the potential benefits of IoT applications and how interoperability among systems could amplify those benefits. Looking through the lens of particular industries—for example, the automotive industry—would enable computation of how companies might capture manufacturing efficiencies and reduce costs through applications such as predictive maintenance (that is, using sensors to monitor machinery continuously to avoid breakdowns rather than relying on scheduled maintenance). However, by viewing IoT applications through the lens of larger settings, we capture a broader set of effects, particularly those that require the interaction of IoT systems and often produce the greatest impact.

The urban setting is a prime example that illustrates the interaction of multiple IoT systems. The IoT offers a rich variety of potential applications for so-called "smart cities," with interlocking and cascading benefits. Because they can be more fully utilized, autonomous vehicles, for instance, reduce fuel use, demand for parking, and congestion. They can work in concert with systems designed to optimize traffic flow, including synchronized signals, real-time signage and re-rerouting, and notifications of parking availability. Furthermore, these can be coordinated with tighter management of bus and train schedules and real-time passenger notifications. While any one of these systems can yield benefits, their interaction can dramatically improve mobility for urban residents, creating a more livable city while saving time, saving energy, and reducing pollution.

We consider the potential uses of IoT systems across nine diverse settings, from homes, offices, factories, to worksites (such as mines, oil and gas fields, and construction sites), retail environments, cities, vehicles, and the outdoors. We also include a "human" setting, analyzing the potential benefits of wearable devices that attach to the human body. Some of these enable health and wellness applications such as monitoring the vital signs of patients with chronic disease or tracking exercise; others offer productivity-enhancing applications (by, for example, using augmented reality to guide workers performing complex physical tasks).

The following section on findings discusses both the uses of IoT systems and the estimated economic potential associated with them.

## THREE CRUCIAL FINDINGS

### Between $3.9 to $11.1 Trillion in Full Economic Surplus by 2025

As described above, we set out to measure the potential impact of the Internet of Things using a bottom-up approach that considers how applications could be deployed across nine settings. Our estimates refers to full *potential* impact of IoT applications, that is including both user surplus as well as increased profit for companies.

We believe that IOT potential could be as large as between $3.9 trillion to $11.1 trillion annually by 2025. Below we briefly describe the uses of IoT systems in each of these settings along with how much of the potential economic impact each of these settings contributes to the total. We begin with factories and cities, where we find that IoT use has the greatest economic potential. The other settings following in descending order of potential impact (based on the high end of our estimates).

#### Factories

The importance of the industrial internet is discussed among others by DaXu et al. (2014). It is recognized that The Internet of Things seamlessly fuses devices and process management—and that capability can yield tremendous value when applied to any standardized production environment. Resources and inputs can be used at maximum efficiency, while defects, downtime, and waste can be held to a minimum. Real-time production dashboards bring together the vast streams of data generated by sensors throughout the operation, providing a comprehensive view of where individual units are at any given time. This visibility, combined with advanced algorithms, can improve responsiveness, decision-making, quality control, and safety. As networks connect, the IoT can go beyond systems within individual plants to connect multiple plants in different regions; this could transform the way companies coordinating complex supply chains.

The factory setting is therefore the largest source of potential value.[4] We estimate that IoT systems could yield a substantial productivity boost, potentially generating an economic impact of $1.2 trillion to $3.7 trillion per year by 2025. This would include a 10 to 20 percent energy savings and a 10 to 25 percent potential improvement in labor efficiency.

The most valuable application in the factory setting is the use of IoT systems to optimize operations—by, for example, using sensor data to adjust workflows and the performance of machinery, thereby eliminating room for human error and addressing bottlenecks in real time. General Motors, for example, uses sensors to monitor humidity when vehicles are ready for painting; if conditions are unfavorable, process is routed to another part of the plant,

thereby reducing the need for repainting.[5] This capability is closely related to the growing use of autonomous robots in production facilities, shifting human labor away from assembly and into the oversight of these complex systems. Predictive maintenance is another key sources of productivity gains; the use of sensors to monitor machinery continuously can signal when corrective action is needed, avoiding breakdowns and the resulting downtime. Another critical application of IoT systems in the factory setting is for tighter inventory management; systems can automatically track and replenish individual components and supplies.

## Cities

Cities are the engines of economic growth; in fact, the world's 600 largest cities generate two-thirds of global GDP growth.[6] But as cities grow, the demands on infrastructure, resources, space, and services intensify. Given their outsize economic footprint, it is not surprising that urban environments are among the most promising settings for a technology that promises to make physical assets more efficient. Indeed, "smart cities" are at the forefront of innovation with the Internet of Things, experimenting with systems to improve services, relieve congestion, conserve water and energy, and improve the quality of life for residents (Zanella, et al. 2014).

Overall, we estimate that deploying IoT applications in urban environments worldwide could have an annual economic impact of $930 billion to $1.6 trillion by 2025.

Municipal governments face the daunting task of running complex systems, allocating resources, and responding to the ever-changing demands that arise when millions of people live, work, and interact in a concentrated area. Cities as diverse as Singapore, Barcelona, Hamburg, and Houston are now using IoT applications to manage systems such as parking, traffic flow, transit, street lighting, utilities, and crime prevention and monitoring. They can enable local agencies to allocate resources, respond to emergencies, improve revenue collection, and prevent disruptions in backbone infrastructure systems.

Various applications focused on transportation combine to produce the greatest contribution to our estimate of the potential economic value of IoT systems in the urban setting, since mobility is directly related to productivity. IoT-based systems can adaptively manage traffic flow, and these capabilities are likely to improve over time as autonomous vehicles are introduced. Beyond managing the flow of cars, IoT technologies are also used to manage complex transit systems; this could involve adjusting train and bus schedules based on actual tracking of usage data or applying more predictive maintenance to systems to reduce disruptions. Up to 70 percent of commuting time today is "buffer time," or the extra time between when the rider arrives at a stop or station and when the bus or train actually leaves; reducing this would produce time savings that can increase a city's overall productivity.

The next-biggest impact would be in public health, mainly from air and water quality improvements that would reduce pollution, saving lives and health-care costs. Using IoT smart meters to reduce loss of electricity in distribution and sensors to detect water leaks is another major source of value.

## Personal

IoT systems even have applicability for the human body, as wearable devices and monitors provide information that people can use to guide their actions and decisions. The economic potential derives from two main sets of applications: health and fitness as well as human productivity.

In the realm of health, the IoT encompasses wearable devices and sensors that can monitor patients remotely. This has tremendous potential to change the way the way we treat chronic diseases such as diabetes, kidney disease, COPD, and heart disease. Patients with these conditions can be provided with a range of intelligent devices such as scales, blood glucometers, blood pressure cuffs, pulse oximeters, and spirometers that can transmit readings automatically to a health-care provider for real-time feedback. In addition to improving patient adherence to prescribed therapies, these systems can provide early signals when intervention is needed so that patients can avoid hospitalizations. This could have an economic impact of $170 billion to $1.6 trillion per year by 2025. Furthermore, we conservatively estimate that remote monitoring can reduce spending on clinical trials by 10 to 15 percent.

In addition, wearable devices are making inroads with consumers as a means of tracking and encouraging exercise and wellness and physical activity. Improved fitness levels have an economic impact by saving on health-care costs and adding to life expectancy, while better sleep can have real productivity impacts. We estimate that the economic impact of IoT systems on wellness could be around $600 billion per year by 2025, with most of the benefit realized in advanced economies.

Beyond the IoT applications related to health, there are new types of systems that can enhance human productivity in the workplace. These include the use of augmented-reality devices such as goggles through which data can be displayed to guide the performance of factory workers. The goggles can present information such as instructions for physical tasks, which would appear to float in in the worker's field of vision, allowing the worker to refer to the correct procedures without having to find a computer terminal. Companies can harness IoT data to redesign jobs and processes; they can also monitor mobile workers in the field more effectively. Together these applications could have an impact of $150 billion to $350 billion globally in 2025.

## Retail

Retailers have been toying for a while with internet of things. A well-known case is Mark and Spencer, the UK clothing and merchandise retailer, which has rolled out a full RFID tag for all its merchandises at more than 750 of its UK stores and inside 200 factories spread across its footprint of 20 countries [7]. In our scoping, we define retail environments as physical spaces where consumers consider or purchase goods or services. This includes traditional stores as well as showrooms, bank branches, theaters, and sports arenas. It does not include online retailing, which has significantly disrupted physical retail--but IoT systems may enable traditional retailers to compete more effectively or to coexist with e-commerce, creating new "omni-channel" shopping experiences. IoT systems are highly relevant to retail environments. With beacons that connect to mobile phones to track customers within the store, retailers can launch custom promotions in real time, texting personalized coupons to encourage in-store purchases. They can also capture data that can be analyzed to optimize store layouts and fine-tune inventory management. These and other innovations could enable new business models and help retailers boost sales, reduce costs, and improve productivity.

Self-checkout systems are a key part of the economic potential. Some have been introduced in retail environments, but most offer only limited improvement over the traditional cashier system. But IoT technology has the potential to completely automate checkout by scanning the contents of shopping carts and automatically charging the sale to the customer's mobile payment account. Amazon, for instance, recently announced that it was developing a brick-and-mortar retail store with a seamless system designed to allow customers to simply walk out of the store with goods in hand, without any pause to pay.

We estimate that deploying IoT technologies in retail environments could have an economic impact of $410 billion to $1.2 trillion annually by 2025.

## Worksites

These environments include oil and gas exploration and production sites, mining operations, and construction sites. In all of these settings, work is done outside, in changing and sometimes dangerous conditions. Moreover, no two sites or projects are the same, which makes it all the more challenging to coordinate heavy machinery, supplies, and labor. Downtime can keep machinery idle 40 percent of the time. IoT systems have the potential to address many of the issues that make projects challenging in these industries, including equipment reliability, harsh weather and environmental conditions, and complex supply chains (Wei et al., 2011).

Leading resource companies have been early adopters of IoT technology. A typical oil drilling platform today might use 30,000 sensors, watching over the performance of dozens of systems. Many offshore rigs have exceptionally advanced instruments and robotics on board; they may be connected to a command center thousands of miles away. Mining companies such as Rio Tinto are deploying fleets of self-driving vehicles, including giant ore trucks that follow predefined routes and load and unload material without an operator.[8]

The most significant economic impact of wider adoption would come from improvements in operating efficiency. The second major source of value would be improved equipment maintenance, which can reduce breakdowns, improve utilization rates, and extend the useful life of machinery. Another economic benefit would involve using IoT technology to improve worker safety, which is a critical concern on dangerous worksites.

In total, we estimate that IoT applications in the worksites setting can have an economic impact of $160 billion to $930 billion per year by 2025.

## Outside

This setting captures uses of IoT technology that take place outdoors (exclusive of urban environments and worksites, which are discussed above). This category encompasses the use of IoT applications to improve the routing of ships, airplanes, trucks, and other vehicles between cities using advanced navigation informed by various sensors. It also includes condition-based maintenance of rail lines and other transportation infrastructure.

IoT capabilities are particularly relevant for the logistics industry (Karakostas, 2013). The global trucking industry carries goods from one link in the supply chain to another—from ports to warehouses, from warehouses to distribution centers, and from distribution centers to retail outlets and consumers. Freight and parcel delivery services can use real-time IoT data to send vehicles on the least congested routes and track individual orders with greater accuracy. We estimate that these applications could have an economic impact of $560 billion to $850 billion per year in 2025.

## Cars and Vehicles

This setting assesses the potential value of IoT applications within vehicles themselves. This includes uses of IoT systems to monitor and improve how planes, trains, cars, and trucks are serviced, maintained, and designed.

Air China, for instance, is installing a system that will download performance data from aircraft to ground-based systems in real time to improve maintenance, reduce downtime, and extend the useful life of each plane. We estimate that shifting from rules-based maintenance to a condition-based and predictive approach informed by real-time data in aircraft could help air carriers reduce maintenance spending by 10 to 40 percent and reduce delays due to mechanical issues by 25 percent.

Condition-based maintenance has similar potential for cars and trucks. In addition, IoT technology in passenger vehicles can detect obstacles and trigger automatic braking to avoid collision. This capability, combined with applications to deter auto theft, can minimize personal injuries and property damage, all of which would enable lower insurance premiums. We estimate that IoT systems in vehicles could potentially generate $210 billion to $740 billion in annual economic value by 2025.

## Homes

A wide range of IoT devices and applications are emerging for use in the home, including connected thermostats, smart appliances, and self-guided vacuum cleaners. Most of them are focused on achieving greater energy efficiency, ensuring security, and automating some domestic chores.

As these devices evolve, we expect that the IoT's greatest economic impact in the home will be automating chores, which we estimate can cut 100 hours of labor per year for the typical household. The possibilities include self-propelled vacuum cleaners and lawn mowers, smart fridges that can signal when to restock certain items, and eventually robots that can perform more intricate household tasks such as laundry or food preparation.

Other applications include smart thermostats and appliances to improve energy efficiency. IoT systems that combining sensors, cameras, and analytics can protect residents from break-ins, fire, water damage, and injuries in the home by detecting when inhabitants are at risk and either alerting them or calling for emergency response. As in other settings, there is an opportunity for the makers of appliances and other equipment to use monitoring data to improve the performance and design of their products and to identify when a household is in the market for a replacement model.

In total, we estimate that IoT applications in the home could have an economic impact of $200 billion to $350 billion per year by 2025.

## Offices

We define offices as commercial spaces in which knowledge work is the primary activity. As in homes, IoT systems in office settings are principally designed to enhance security and energy management. Commercial spaces consume a significant share of energy, but much of it is wasted by heating, cooling, and lighting unoccupied offices. Intelligent systems can automatically sense when a room is unoccupied and adjust temperature and lighting accordingly. We estimate that intelligent energy management systems can reduce energy use in offices by 20 percent. In terms of security, IoT systems relying on pattern-recognition software can be more effective than traditional security cameras. Altogether office IoT applications could have an economic impact of $70 billion to $150 billion per year in 2025.

# Key Internal Sensitivities to Achieve Potential

For the Internet of Things to deliver its full potential economic impact, certain conditions would need to be in place and several obstacles would need to be overcome. Some are technical, while some others are structural and behavioral. Consumers, for example, need to trust IoT-based systems, and companies need to embrace the data-driven approaches to decision making that the IoT enables. This section highlights the three most important internal sensitivity drivers of our estimates as well as external constraints that will be need to be resolved.

## IoT Component Costs

Affordable, low-power sensors are essential to the Internet of Things, and the first critical driver is a decreasing cost curve of the basic technology components. Capturing the full estimated economic potential of the IoT depends on whether these components undergo the same kind of steep price declines that have occurred with the introduction of many other digital technologies. The price of sensors for micro-electromechanical systems used in smartphones, for example, has dropped by 30 to 70 percent over the past five years. A similar trajectory is needed for radio-frequency identification (RFID) tags and other hardware to make IoT tracking practical for low value, high-volume items in package delivery and retailing. Progress in inexpensive, low-cost battery power is also needed to keep distributed sensors and active tags operating. Low-cost data communication links (both short- and long-distance) are essential for almost all IoT applications to deliver on their potential. For IoT users to get the most out of their data—and to use more data—the cost of computing and storage must also continue to drop, and further development will be needed in analytical and visualization software.

## Pace of Adoption

The second-most important driver is the *speed* at which IoT will be adopted and deployed. The typical S-curve of adoption has been well-established in academic literature since Rogers (1995). Rogers classifies consumers using four key categories: "early adopters," "early majority," "late majority," and "laggards." The tipping point occurs when the late majority adopts a new innovation; this is the point at which a mass market takes shape. The speed at which this unfolds depends on the dynamics of the imitation effect among users. The internet itself, for example, spread rather quickly. Turk and Trkman (2012) computed that the inflection point at which diffusion started to accelerate for internet access was slightly more than seven years for developed countries. Regarding the adoption of internet *applications*, Wong et al. (2011) conclude that the inflection point was reached in just below 5 years, while Franses (2015) found that adoption rates for most consumer social networks peak between two and four years.

Putting this dynamic into the context of companies introduces another factor: competition. This is particularly critical for cases in which a certain technology is disruptive and adoption creates lasting competitive advantage.

In general, however, companies must integrate technologies into their workflow to generate return on investment, and this process takes time. In the case of the IoT, which combines the physical and digital worlds, conventional notions of organizational responsibilities may be challenged. Traditionally, companies kept their IT operations separate and distinct from the parts of the organization charged with managing most physical assets. In a retail store, the IT function managed the point-of-sale machine but little else. But in an IoT world, IT is embedded into all physical assets and inventory, directly affecting the business metrics against which all operations are measured. These functions will have to be much more closely aligned. Furthermore, companies need more than simply knowledge about how IoT systems work with the context of their operations. They also need the capacity and mindset to use the IoT systems to guide data-driven decision making as well as the ability to adapt their organizations to new processes and business models.

While we expect slower enterprise than user adoption, the calibration is unknown for IoT systems. Daim and Suntharasaj (2009) use a Bass model of adoption to assess the diffusion of RFID technology in retail. Their results are that it would take seven or eight years for companies to adopt it at scale. Regarding other types of technologies, Bughin (2010) estimates the peak diffusion rate at 10 years for a sample of enterprise 2.0 technologies, and about 6 years for big data (Bughin, 2016). Our estimates of the IoT's economic potential are based on such a pace of adoption.

## Data Analytics Capabilities

Last but not least, IoT sensors are meant to capture data in real time—but that flood of data yields value only if it can be translated into actionable insights. This means that IoT diffusion is likely to be complementary to (and bounded by) the adoption of advanced analytics. This kind of complementarity is often seen in technology systems (see, for example, Dewan et al., 2010). At its current stage, however, big data diffusion is still patchy at best among companies, and the returns from these investments are not yet well distributed (Bughin, 2016).

Recent research on the state of data and analytics measures the progress various industries have made toward capturing revenue and efficiency gains identified five years earlier (MGI, 2016). It finds that the retail sector, spurred on by digital-native competitors, has captured about 30 to 40 percent of the margin improvements and productivity growth identified in 2011. Manufacturing has captured some 20 to 30 percent of the potential, while the public sector and health care make the worst showings, realizing only 10 to 20 percent of the value. However, these benchmarks for overall sector progress mask large disparities in performance between a few firms at the cutting edge and the average company in any given industry.

In a recent survey, 86 percent of executives reported that their organizations were only somewhat effective at meeting the goals they set out for their data and analytics initiatives.[9] Some of this may reflect a time lag; deeper organizational changes may be needed when a traditional company shifts to more data-driven decision-making processes. Legacy firms may also need to add new skills and capabilities as well as developing algorithms that are fully customized for their specific business needs. Companies will need to work through these issues in order to use IoT systems and data to their full potential.

## Key External Sensitivities to Achieve Potential

In addition to the internal parameters above, external factors will determine how much of the economic potential associated with the Internet of Things can be generated and captured. These include the interoperability of systems; the approach to privacy and cybersecurity; and the development of regulatory framework to cover many of the new issues posed by IoT systems.

### Interoperability

Different digital systems can communicate and work together on a data network if they adhere to widely accepted interface standards that provide a "common language"; alternatively, they can work together through the use of "middleware" translation or aggregation systems. At present, while traditional Internet protocols have been widely adopted, the development and adoption of IoT standards is still in its early stages.

However, our sizing exercise underscores the importance of interoperability in generating maximum value from IoT applications. Consulting with industry experts as we conducted our bottom-up analysis, we estimate that situations in which two or more IoT systems must work together account for at least 40 percent of the IoT's economic potential. In other words, our high-end estimate of the IoT's potential would be reduced from $11.1 trillion annually in 2025 to only about $7 trillion without widespread interoperability.

Interoperability is particularly critical for the complex array of machinery and processes involved in the worksites setting, affecting almost 60 percent of the economic potential. Today much of the data collected by IoT sensors is used for monitoring discrete machines or systems, but fully integrating these data streams could provide decision makers with a more integrated view of an entire operation. Oil and gas experts interviewed for this research, for example, estimate that interoperability could boost the effectiveness of equipment maintenance in their industry by 100 to 200 percent. The economic potential of the IoT in the cities setting is similarly dependent on interoperability. A centralized traffic-control system, for instance, becomes much more effective when it can combine data from thousands of sensors and traffic cameras with data streams from individual vehicles, parking meters, and transit systems.

Ensuring interoperability will require collaboration among supplier companies and among suppliers, users, and policy makers to set standards and protocols. It is primarily a technical challenge, but it also requires a good deal of non-technical work, which might include government assistance in supporting standards.

### Security

The Internet of Things introduces new types of risks to personal privacy and the confidentiality and integrity of organizational data. Consumers may have no idea what kind of information is being acquired about them; this can include data regarding their whereabouts at any given time (collected, for example, in retail or urban settings) as well as personal data about their health and wellness and their purchasing behavior. In some cases, this information can affect employment, access to credit, and insurance rates, and if misused, it can be used for discriminatory purposes. A common understanding of who has what rights to data produced by various connected devices will be required to unlock the full potential of IoT systems. Handling this issue thoughtfully will be critical to helping build consumer trust in IoT-based systems.

For companies, the IoT multiplies cybersecurity risks. Each device added to the system increases the "surface area" available for breaches. Additionally, the consequences of compromised IoT systems that control the physical world could be extremely dangerous, particularly when those systems control vital infrastructure or vehicles.

## Public Policy

Governments will need to provide enabling action and regulatory certainty for IoT applications to achieve their full economic and societal potential. Governments and other policy-making organizations, such as industry groups, can encourage and support the development of interoperability standards that will enable interoperability of IoT devices and systems. A common understanding of ownership rights to data produced by various connected devices will be required to unlock the full potential of IoT. Policy makers also often have a role to play in shaping market rules that affect IoT adoption, such as creating appropriate incentives in health care.

In the realm of cybersecurity, for example, governments can invest in research, convene and fund multi-stakeholder centers to set standards and share information, model good security practices, and craft thoughtful rules to encourage security management and punish bad actors. In addition, IoT applications for infrastructure systems and public spaces could create national security risks that have to be managed, given the nature of the data, the risks of IoT-controlled physical assets, and the proliferation of access points for hackers to target.

Certain IoT applications will not be able to proceed without regulatory approval. The most obvious is self-driving cars. Even if many auto and technology companies are investing in this area, it remains unclear where and when self-driving cars will be allowed to operate. Also, new regulatory frameworks will be needed to enable autonomous vehicles to coexist with other cars and trucks. For example, it will need to be determined if the owner or manufacturer of a self-driving vehicle (or another party) is liable if the vehicle injures a person or causes property damage. In the United States, for example, the federal government unveiled preliminary guidelines in late 2016, including some safety standards, but they were intentionally made in broad terms with the intention of encouraging innovation as the technology evolves. US states are issuing their own guidelines, and it remains to be seen if this will result in a patchwork of regulatory approaches.

The deployment of self-driving cars also depends on governments releasing the necessary spectrum. Given density of traffic in cities, for instance, current spectrum would be insufficient to ensure real-time, always-on connections to traditional mobile networks. Even newer 5G networks may not be adequate, and network upgrades take time. In Europe, for example, government bids for 5G networks are still a few years away, and networks would need to be synchronized across the European market.

## CONCLUSION

The range of applications leveraging the Internet of things (IoT) is expanding rapidly, as is the number of users and companies adopting those technologies for their own benefits. This chapter has provided a synthesis of the most promising domains, making the case that IoT can rapidly build game-changing opportunities, when it relates to the industrial domain. In fact, our own bottom-up quantification suggests that business-to-business applications will account for nearly 70 percent of the value that will flow from IoT in the next ten years.

If IoT offers large potential, the later may be at risk of showing only a portion of its value, however. Among others, we have emphasized the fact that inter-firm diffusion of technologies may take years, and that there is typically a large variance in adoption propensity by firms, even within the same sector. This is due to the prevalence of organizational capabilities to really make beneficial use of those technologies. Also, two major structural problems loom with IoT. The first is the security issue linked to the proliferation of devices; the second is the ability to make all systems fully inter-operable. We estimate that the absence of standardization among IoT building blocks may reduce the benefits to be generated by IoT, by up to 40%.

## REFERENCES

Battisti, G., Canepa, A., & Stoneman, P. (2009). E-Business usage across and within firms the UK: Profitability, externalities and policy. *Research Policy*, *38*(1), 133–143. doi:10.1016/j.respol.2008.10.021

Brown, I. (2015). *Regulation and the Internet of Things. GSR discussion paper*. ITU.

Bughin, J. (2010). The power laws of enterprise 2.0. In Encyclopedia of e-business development and management in the global economy. IGI Global. doi:10.4018/978-1-61520-611-7.ch003

Bughin, J. (2016). Reaping the benefits of big data in telecom. *Journal of Big Data*, *3*(2), 3–14.

Bughin, J., Chui, M., & Manyika, J. (2015). An executive guide to the Internet of Things. *The McKinsey Quarterly*, *3*.

Da Xu, L., He, W., & Li, S. (2014). Internet of things in industries: A survey. *IEEE Transactions on Industrial Informatics, 10*(4), 2233-2243.

Daim, T., & Suntharasaj, P. (2009). Technology diffusion: Forecasting with bibliometric analysis and Bass model. *Foresight*, *11*(3), 45–55. doi:10.1108/14636680910963936

Dewan, S., Ganley, D., & Kraemer, K. (2010). Complementarities in the diffusion of personal computers and the Internet: Implications for the global digital divide. *Information Systems Research*, *21*(5), 924–940.

Franses, P. H. (2015). The life cycle of social media. *Applied Economics Letters*, *22*(10), 796–800. doi:10.1080/13504851.2014.978069

Henke, N. (2016). *The age of analytics: Competing in a data-driven world.* McKinsey Global Institute.

Karakostas, B. (2013). A DNS architecture for the internet of things: A case study in transport logistics. *Procedia of Computational Science*, *19*, 594–601. doi:10.1016/j.procs.2013.06.079

Karshenas, M., & Stoneman, P. L. (1993). Rank, stock, order, and epidemic effects in the diffusion of new process technologies: An empirical model. *The Rand Journal of Economics*, *24*(4), 503–528. doi:10.2307/2555742

Manyika, J. (2015). *Unlocking the potential of the Internet of Things.* McKinsey Global Institute.

Moura, J., & Hutchison, D. (2016). Review and analysis of networking challenges in cloud computing. *Journal of Network and Computer Applications*, *60*, 113–129. doi:10.1016/j.jnca.2015.11.015

Pal, A. (2015). Internet of Things: Making the hype a reality. *IT Professional*, *17*(3), 2–4. doi:10.1109/MITP.2015.36

Rogers, E. M. (1995). *Diffusion of innovations* (4th ed.). New York: The Free Press.

Turk, T., & Trkman, P. (2012). Bass model estimates for broadband diffusion in European countries. *Technological Forecasting and Social Change*, *79*(1), 85–96. doi:10.1016/j.techfore.2011.06.010

Wei, Q., Zhu, S., & Du, C. (2011). Study onkey technologies of internet of things perceiving mine. *Procedia Eng.*, *26*, 2326–2333. doi:10.1016/j.proeng.2011.11.2442

Wong, D.H., & all. (2011). Predicting the diffusion pattern of Internet-based communication applications using Bass model parameter estimates for e-mail. *Journal of Internet Business*, *9*, 26–50.

Zanella, A., Bui, N., Castellani, A., Vangelista, L., & Zorzi, M. (2014). Internet of things for smart cities. *IEEE Internet of Things Journal, 1*(1), 22-32.

## KEY TERMS AND DEFINITIONS

**Adoption:** The purchase, deployment, use, and acceptance of a new technology tool or innovation.

**Big Data:** Datasets of a size that is beyond the ability of typical database software tools to capture, store, manage, and analyze large pools of data that can be captured, communicated, aggregated, stored, and analyzed.

**Fourth Industrial Revolution:** The fourth major era of the industrial revolution. The previous three phases introduced new technologies for mass production (the steam engine, electricity, and eventually information technology). The technologies being introduced in the phase now beginning include the Internet of Things, big data and advanced analytics, robotics, artificial intelligence, autonomous vehicles, and 3D printing.

**Industrial Internet:** The application of the Internet of Things, analytics, and advanced computing to industrial machinery, facilities, and fleets, thereby digitizing production systems.

**Internet of Things:** Sensors and actuators connected by networks to computing systems. These systems can monitor or manage the health and actions of connected objects and machines, thereby digitizing the physical environment. Connected sensors can also monitor people and the natural world. We exclude systems in which sensors receive intentional human input (as through touchscreens or keyboards).

**Interoperability:** The ability of discrete IoT devices and systems to work together. This can be facilitated through the use of common standards or the use of systems or platforms that enable discrete IoT systems to communicate with one another.

## ENDNOTES

1 Olga Kharif, "Cisco CEO pegs Internet of Things as $19 trillion market," Bloomberg, January 8, 2014.

2 "The most active VCs in the Internet of Things and their investments in one infographic," CB Insights blog, October 23, 2016, available at www.cbinsights.com/blog/iot-most-active-investor-infographic/.

3 *ITU internet reports 2005: The Internet of Things,* International Telecommunications Union, November 2005.

4 Note that we define this setting in the broadest sense to include all dedicated, standardized production environments. This category therefore includes setting such as farms and hospitals in addition to manufacturing plants.

5 Building smarter manufacturing with the Internet of Things (IoT), part two, Lopez Research, January 2014.

6 McKinsey Global Institute, Urban world: Mapping the economic power of cities, March 2011.

7 See https://www.rfidjournal.com/retail/case-studies.

8 Disruptive technologies: Advances that will transform life, business and the global economy, McKinsey Global Institute, May 2013.

9 "The need to lead in data and analytics," McKinsey & Company survey, April 2016, available at http://www.mckinsey.com/business-functions/digital-mckinsey/our-insights/the-need-to-lead-in-data-and-analytics. The survey was conducted in late 2015, and its respondents included more than 500 executives representing companies across the spectrum of industries, regions, and sizes.

# Chapter 7
# The Internet of Things: From Things to Valuable Outcomes

**Thomas Ochs**
*Villeroy & Boch, Germany*

**Ute Anna Riemann**
*SAP SE, Germany*

## ABSTRACT

*Objects become embedded and gain the ability to communicate. The resulting information networks promise to create new business models, improve business processes, and reduce costs and risks. The massive numbers of connected things and the explosion of data generated by these things will change the way we do business forever. Connected devices are proliferating in a communicating and actuating network named "Internet of Things" (IoT) wherein sensors and actuators blend seamlessly with the environment around us, and the information is shared across platforms in order to develop a common operating picture (Gubi et al., 2013). The IoT digitizes the physical world and is a basis for new business models whose main objective is to integrate or connect things. This chapter outlines the key enabling technologies, drivers and business value as well as benefits and challenges.*

## INTRODUCTION

The IoT describes a system where items in the physical world, and sensors within or attached to these items are connected via wireless and wired Internet connections (Lopez Research, 2013; Meadon, 2013), this system is a key part of the so called future internet (Gavras et al., 2010; Haller, Karnouskos, & Schroth, 2008).

The IERC has formulated the following definition (International Telecommunication Union, 2012) on the IoT: "A global infrastructure for the information society, enabling advanced services by interconnecting (physical and virtual) things based on existing and evolving interoperable information and communication technologies". NOTE 1 — Through the exploitation of identification, data capture, processing and communication capabilities, the IoT makes full use of things to offer services to all kinds

DOI: 10.4018/978-1-5225-2104-4.ch007

of applications, whilst ensuring that security and privacy requirements are fulfilled. NOTE 2—from a broader perspective, the IoT can be perceived as a vision with technological and societal implications.

The IERC definition (Vermesan, et al., 2013) states that the IoT is "a dynamic global network infrastructure with self-configuring capabilities" based on standard and interoperable communication protocols (van Kranenburg, 2007) where physical and virtual "things" have identities, physical attributes, and virtual personalities using intelligent interfaces, and are seamlessly integrated into the information network. The IoT integrates a large number of technologies and envisions that the things connected to the internet are clearly distinguished from the things participating within the Internet around us (Bleecker, 2006) – through unique addressing schemes and standard communication protocols. These things are able to interact with each other and cooperate with their neighbors to reach common goals (Atzori, Iera, & Morabito, 2010; Sarma, Brock, & Ashton, 1999). The combination of the internet and emerging technologies such as near field communications, real-time localization, and embedded sensors (Miorandi, 2012) allow the transformation of everyday objects into smart objects that can understand and react to their environment and transform this environment to a smart environment. The IoT infrastructure components and services of a city administration, education, healthcare (Domingo, 2012), public safety (Andrews, El-Attrash, Jarvis, Johnson, & Moss), real estate, transportation (Atzori, Iera, & Morabito, 2010) and utilities (SAP, 2014) lead to a more aware, interactive and efficient environment (Belissent, 2010). The IoT addresses the following topics:

- *Connect* core business operations to intelligence at the edge of the network generated by newly connected things connecting anytime, anyplace for anyone, for anything" (Dunkels & Vasseur, 2008). Cyber-physical integration occurs at the edge of a network and connection with intelligence on the edge.
- *Transform* existing business processes to gain efficiencies and provide competitive advantages in terms of process optimization (Spiess & Karnouskos, 2007). The IoT acts as a catalyst for the networked economy and transforms the business operations. A core element of IoT in the context of a "connections economy" is that value will accrue to those who best foster, embody, and exploit network effects. (The Networked Economy, 2014)
- *Reimagine* products, services and business models and as a result reimagine the customer experience. By reimagining the business models the operational technology (OT) and the information technology (IT) will merge towards new business models. These new business models heavily rely on the decomposition and decentralization of existing business processes, increase scalability and performance, allows better decision making, and lead to new revenue streams (Odenwald, 2007).

These IoT roles guide the development of novel computing applications (Kortuem et al, 2010). The following give a brief view on what have been discussed in the IoT community:

- The IoT refers to the use of sensors, actuators, and data communication infrastructure built into physical objects (Toma, Simperl, & Hench, 2009) that enable those objects to be tracked, coordinated, or controlled across a data network or the Internet (McKinsey, 2013).
- The IoT and the world of smart systems are ushering in an era where people, machines, devices, sensors, and businesses are all connected and able to interact with one another. As these previously disaggregated parties come together, new modes of collaboration and intelligence will abound fostering a trend called "Smart Business" (Harbor-Research, 2013).

- The IoT change the types of items over a network (van Kranenburg et al., 2011) - enabled objects share information about their condition and the surrounding environment with people, software systems and other machines (Lopez Research, 2015).

The development of the IoT and the evolution toward smart business practices enable a truly connected world. Inputs from machines, people, cars, household equipment, home interiors, and sensors will be digitized and placed onto networks (Tan & Wang, 2010).

## THE INTERNET OF THINGS: DIGITALIZE THE PHYSICAL WORLD

### How Did the Internet of Things Emerge?

The "IoT idea" is not new (e.g. The Guardian, 2003, Sun Microsystems, 2003, Boston Globe, 2004). However, the IoT only recently became relevant to the practical world, mainly because of the progress made in hardware development in the last decade (Fleisch, 2010). In 1999 Kevin Ashton had the idea of the IoT at MITs AutoID lab (Ashton, 2009) – "If we had computers that knew everything there was to know about things—using data they gathered without any help from us -- we would be able to track and count everything, and greatly reduce waste, loss, and cost. We would know when things needed replacing, repairing or recalling, and whether they were fresh or past their best. We need to empower computers with their own means of gathering information, so they can see, hear, and smell the world for themselves, in all its random glory. RFID and sensor technology enable computers to observe, identify and understand the world—without the limitations of human-entered data" (Lopez Research, 2013a). In 2000 the idea was that P&G connect all their products to RFID tags (Bonsor & Keener, 2010). Starting from this idea the concept of IoT has emerged and times are now mature enough.

### Core Elements of the IoT

The IoT is a global network infrastructure (Li, Xu, Wang, & Wang, 2012; Li et al., 2013; Ren et al., 2014; Tao, Laili, Xu, & Zhang, 2013; Uckelmann, Harrison, & Michahelles, 2011; Wang, Xu, Bi, & Xu, 2014), linking physical and virtual objects through the exploitation of data capture and communication capabilities. This infrastructure includes existing and emerging internet and network developments offering specific object-identification, sensors and connection capability as the basis for the development of independent cooperative services and applications (Atzori, Iera, & Morabito, 2010; Guinard, Trifa, Karnouskos, Spiess, & Savio, 2010; Miorandi, Sicari, De Pellegrini, & Chlamtac, 2012). These capabilities are characterized by a high degree of autonomous data capture, event transfer, network connectivity, and interoperability. According to Cisco the IoT can be characterized by six core elements (Cisco, 2012):

- **Data:** With IoT, the capability to gather, analyze and stream data while being connected to the internet will emerge (Uckelmann, Harrison, & Michahelles, 2011). Rather than just reporting raw data, the connected things will send higher-level information back to machines, computers, and people for further evaluation and decision making (Gubbi, Buyya, Marusic, & Palaniswamia, 2013). This (de-central) transformation from data to information due to IoT will enable us to make faster, more intelligent decisions, as well as control our environment more effectively.

- **Things:** The IoT links the physical world of things to the virtual world of the internet. By linking together computer networks, sensors, actuators, machines and devices, the IoT offers a multitude of new opportunities for the businesses to develop new products and services. In IoT these things will sense more data of higher relevance, become context-aware, and provide more experiential information to help people and machines make more relevant and valuable decisions (Kortuem et al, 2010).
- **Processes:** Processes play an important role in how each of the entities — people, data, and things — work with the others to deliver value in the connected world of IoT. With the correct processes, connections become relevant and add value because the right information is delivered to the right person at the right time in the appropriate way (Coetzee & Eksteen, 2011).
- **Users:** The focus of the IoT is the generation of benefits for the various users. As the internet evolves toward IoT, we will be connected in more relevant and valuable ways. To encourage users to take advantage of these connections, products and services need to capture the users' interest in their own personal environment, enhance their quality of life, and be easy to use (Kortuem et al, 2010).
- **Companies:** Process optimization, device management, end-to-end processes, real-time decisions, and data integration are just some of the critical topics that are increasingly demanding the attention of businesses worldwide. The IoT will help companies to optimize their existing products and services or develop new ones (Chui, Loeffler, & Roberts, 2010).
- **Partners:** In the connected world, partnerships between businesses are becoming more important than ever. This is because no single company can successfully tackle all the increasingly complex challenges on its own. These partnerships can be anything from technology partnerships and service partnerships to groups of companies that have decided to market their products on a joint, collaborative basis. If companies can model and implement these partnerships using software, they can cooperate more quickly and efficiently, benefiting all involved (Spiess, Karnouskos, & Guinard, 2009).

## How Does the Internet of Things Differ From Traditional Computing?

The IoT is the next wave in the era of computing and will be outside the realm of the traditional desktop (Gubi et al, 2013) as there are many differences between traditional computing and the IoT which allows for more connectivity & data transmissions, these are the core differences as stated in Table 1.

## Technical and Commercial Integration

From an economic perspective, the IoT is the basis for a web-based service economy (ISTAG Working Group Report, 2008). According to the analyst firm Machina Research, five markets will generate almost 80 percent of IoT-based revenues by 2022. These are: manufacturing, connected cities, utilities, automotive, and intelligent buildings. The most common IoT outcomes to realize are: lower cost, optimized productivity, improved turnarounds and increased uptime. We can define three steps to achieve the full degree of benefit:

*Table 1. Differences between traditional computing and IoT*

| Criteria | Traditional Computing | Internet of Things |
|---|---|---|
| Data size | Larger data size & less frequently transmitted to other devices. | Small data size & more frequent in transmission. |
| Data collection | Narrower range of data types are collected or available. | Broad range of data becomes collectable & processed. |
| Connectivity | Less devices connected to a network either fixed or mobile and via single media. | More devices connected to a network either hybrid or SDN enabled and multi-modal. |
| Dependencies | Tasks dependent on a central cloud or on premise application. | Tasks become more independent, not relying on a central application for processing. |
| Security | Non-connected devices have lower security risks (European Union 2010). | Data networking & security are more challenging with higher risks. |
| Apps & Analytics | • Single entity usage.<br>• Single application per device. | • Vertical supply chain usage.<br>• Multiple applications per device. |
| Platforms | • Stand-alone platforms.<br>• Reliance on standalone analytics tool. | Orchestrate rich platforms and; database federation; rich platform-based analytics. |
| Hardware / Devices | • Device variability.<br>• Point Security Solutions. | Intelligent edge devices; end-to-end security packages. |

(adapted from Lopez Research, 2013, CMI 2015)

- **Things to Insight:** This step is about having a clear understanding of where risks and opportunities exist inside the business network utilizing the data from connected things. All data in the world becomes increasingly valuable when the insight can be derived from it. The IoT provides these insights with real-time data and its processing. This allows businesses to act in the moment with data driven decisions and furthermore to transform data into meaningful insights and strategy.
- **Insight to Action:** This step is about developing the business processes and the business model towards the IoT. An IoT-ready IT platform simplifies, streamlines, and informs processes to make the business more efficient and effective at the core, the edge and in the business network (Janssen, 2015). The established business process infrastructure is the key to turning insight into actionable outcomes. The business will become more agile by connecting all devices, people and partners.
- **Action to Outcomes:** The final step aims to create new business value and ecosystem advantages. Having set the basis for new business opportunities, sources of value and ecosystem advantage can be achieved. The IoT allows businesses to be agile and create new business models, drives innovation, generate new revenue streams and new sources of value across the entire business ecosystem.

In general, there is already a high value when knowing where the opportunities are. By transforming data into valuable insight, it becomes possible to pre-empt the risks and to know where new business opportunities and revenue streams are. The ultimate value of IoT can be realized by allowing the combination of historical data with current data, acting in the moment with data driven decisions and innovating new business models and revenue streams across the entire business ecosystem.

## Interoperability as the Way From Silos to Ecosystems

Simply connecting devices is not a target in itself. Connecting and integrating devices is intended to unlock new potentials such as predictive maintenance (Bandyopadhyay & Sen, 2011). In order to realize a sustainable value, the IoT connects the world of things and the world of IT. This IT world consists primarily of the IoT platform and the services built on it. Specifically, devices need to be integrated in IoT platforms that provide flexible ways to integrate any IP-enabled device into enterprise and partner backend systems. Such a software platform acts as middleware between the physical and the IT world, facilitating development of IoT applications and solutions via platform as a Service (PaaS) / Software as a Service (SaaS) environments (Zhou, Leppänen, & Harjula, 2013). Integrating devices on this platform also aids application development. It fulfills these requirements with an agile composition of devices, processes, and rules management and enables linking things, users, and enterprise and partner systems on one platform and provides a basis for building IoT application. These applications can be classified in various ways according to Fleisch or Chui (Coezee & Eksteen, 2011). The "as-a-service" approach give a more intimate tie between actors of the value chain (Fleisch, 2010) with the target to build adjacent businesses, such as e-commerce on the web.

## Interoperability Between Existing and New Business Models

The IoT offers value to businesses, consumers, as well as it impacts every business as it completely revolutionizes the logistics & supply chain (Bechtel & Jayaram, 1997). The IoT allows the tracking of the location and the state of an object throughout the full product life-cycle and throughout the supply chain. Nowadays this is already used to detect diversions into illicit or grey markets as well as the introduction of counterfeit products (Lehtonen, Oertel, & Vogt, 2007). It will help a business gain efficiency, harness intelligence from a wide range of equipment, improve operations, and increase customer satisfaction. It will have a profound impact on people's lives, as it will improve public life, individual degree of satisfaction, etc. with better information and faster communications of this information. The phases of transformation can be structured as follows:

- **Optimization:** Improve the status quo to be ready for the IoT. Integrate the data for reactive, ex post monitoring (Atzori, Iera, & Morabito, 2010).
- **Acceleration:** Create new revenue by adding services to connected products. Open up business by connecting things. This phase focused on proactive monitoring, service cost optimization, predictive maintenance and data analytics (Johnson).
- **Innovation:** Breakup value chains by connecting things. This phase considers end-to-end process integration, new revenue-generating capabilities, and remote management of products. Through software and services the company is creating new lines of business and recurring revenue streams from security, maintenance monitoring, heating, entertainment, and gardening. That is not a disruptive technology it is a disruptive business model and it is transformational (Uckelmann, Harrison, & Michahelles, 2011).

Having outlined the phases of transformation it becomes obvious that there are many possible business models that the IoT can support. As summarized in Table 2, Harbor Research identified the core business models driven by IoT.

*Table 2. Business models driven by IoT*

| Business Model | Key Elements |
|---|---|
| • Business Model Transformation<br>• New Value-Added Services<br>• Product Design and Engineering Insights<br>• Sales, Fulfilment & Supply Chain Services<br>• Ecosystem Orchestration<br>• New User Experience Design<br>• Installed Base Support Services | • Selling results, outcomes or performance.<br>• Optimization based on analytics and modelling.<br>• Collect machine-operating history to determine priorities for future designs.<br>• Predictive modelling of demand for channel partners and ecosystem participants.<br>• Orchestrate services around machines and systems.<br>• Intimate understanding of machine behaviours and how users interact with the system.<br>• Help customers maintain installed systems and equipment. |

Due to the novelty of the entire IoT the truly innovative business models are still to come and conclusively not appraisable at this moment in time.

- **Using IoT to Improve Current Business Models:** First, companies need to identify and prioritize opportunities for IoT. This is the initial step to enable the performance improvement in their current operations and lines of business. These opportunities are extensions of the opportunities that have been identified with the use of big data and advanced analytics. IoT data will allow companies to personalize services based on consumer behavior, usage, and context. However, the majority of potential benefits will be in B2B applications, such as manufacturing and supply chain (Sullivan & Thomson, 2013). It is also important to keep the substantial potential of benefits in mind when deploying the IoT in businesses in developing markets as well as in advanced economies. Depending on the conditions in the specific developing economy, IoT applications can be used to create large amounts of value, often from different sources than those in advanced economies. Companies should bear in mind that interoperability is here key to obtaining much of the value from the IoT. As sophisticated and powerful customers, companies can demand interoperability when they write specifications and procure IoT systems. As companies identify and prioritize opportunities to use IoT applications, they should inventory all potential sources of data, particularly those they might already own but have not yet fully exploited. IoT is an incredible source of data generated in the course of operations that can be used for other purposes. The largest source of potential impact is operations optimization, such as inventory management and condition-based maintenance, which requires optimization and prediction.
- **Using IoT for New Business Models:** In addition of gaining operating efficiencies and the other benefits that companies can derive from using IoT in their existing businesses, companies can create new business models based on IoT (Kortuem, Kawsar, & Sundramoorthy, 2010):
    - **New Pricing Models:** The IoT creates a continuous, fine-grained stream of real-time data. These data enable insights into consumer willingness to pay. Customized, dynamic pricing models based on specific customer preferences, as well as the usage context, can provide benefits for both companies and consumers (Bucherer & Uckelmann, 2011).
    - **Service-Based Business Models:** The internet has enabled the "as a service" business model for IT infrastructure and software. The IoT enables "anything as a service" business models for all kinds of other products, potentially letting many kinds of companies shift from selling products to selling services based on those products (Guinard, Trifa, & Karnouskos, 2010).

IoT technology enables companies to better maintain and upgrade the equipment that is used in these services, removing the maintenance burden from customers and creating the basis of long-term relationships. IoT-based service businesses can also use consolidated customer usage data and data about individual customers for cross-selling, guiding product development, and other purposes. Furthermore, IoT can allow products to become better while provided as a service.

## Organizational Implications of IoT

Companies build strategies around the IoT, need to develop new organizational capabilities and - in many cases - adopt different behaviors (Kortuem, Kawsar, Sundramoorthy, & Fitton, 2009). To make the most out of IoT technology, the companies must embrace data-driven decision making, specific capabilities and create environments in which relevant information are made available to the right decision makers (which could be people or algorithms) in a timely manner. This requires change management, training in new skills and investing in new software systems to capture and analyze IoT data. All of the implications of big data and analytics apply to IoT data (Ashton, 2009). Whatever the application is about, the value of IoT data always depends on its effective use (Marti, Ganesan, & Garcia-Molina, 2004; Yu, Kaminsky, Gibbons, & Flaxman, 2006). Organizations need to become adept at data-driven decision making, which requires an analytical rigor. As companies build up their data analytics capabilities (both technologies and talent) to handle the flood of IoT data, the analytics experts must be connected with decision makers as well as employees; both groups need to learn how to apply insights from large, real-time data streams in a timely manner. And when real-time action needs to be taken on a large scale (Bandyopadhyay & Sen, 2011) —such as optimizing machine control across an entire factory or providing real-time marketing offers to shoppers—organizations will have to develop processes that enable algorithms to make decisions automatically, while allowing decision makers to monitor metrics and set policy. (Bughin & Manyika, 2013; McKinsey Global Institute, 2011; Varian, 2007).

Consequently, the role of the IT function within organizations need to be transformed: the scope of responsibilities of IT departments will no longer be primarily in data centers and managing desktop and mobile devices. IoT applications will extend IT systems into physical assets, facilities, and inventory. Thus, more than ever, the IT organization will have to be closely aligned and even integrated with the operating parts of the business. Additionally, the metrics of success for IT will have to measure more than technology, extending to the performance of the business itself. Synthesizing data from different sources will take more than interoperable systems; it will also require collaboration among leaders and teams in different parts of the organization. Owners of various IT systems must be receptive to linking up their systems and providing data access across the organization. Many IoT applications will also require collaboration – or, even further they depend on competitors working together. To get insights from data on the characteristics of an ore body in one mine and make effective predictions requires a large comparative data set, which small operators may not be able to get unless they pool their data.

If we take a look at the value that the IoT add for both businesses and consumers every business process in essentially every industry on this globe is affected (Fleisch, 2010). The change triggered by the IoT is inevitable and according to Lopez Research, there are four characteristics to understand when dealing with the IoT (Lopez Research, 2013b):

- Includes living, as well as inanimate things;
- Uses sensors for data collection;
- Changes what is communicating;
- Requires a robust IP network.

Overall market forces support the expansion of the IoT. There are core value drivers affecting the IoT as outlined in Table 3.

## ENABLERS, BENEFITS, AND CHALLENGES

The IoT links information to one another, processes the information collaboratively, and takes action automatically. This is a new paradigm that offers both challenges and opportunities (Chen, 2012). To gain the maximum of impact from the IoT a large-scale adoption is necessary that depends on having certain technologies, organizational capabilities, and policies in place – they may called enabler and the types of enablers are listed in Table 4. It will also require collaboration within the companies and across companies to get benefits of the interoperability of IoT systems to maximize value.

With built-in sensors and connectivity, the smart products and services enable manufacturers to provide anomaly detection and sometimes even predictive maintenance. However, some failure modes can be predicted only when data are combined from multiple systems. Furthermore, being able to analyze data from multiple pieces of equipment could enable optimization of total processes. But these systems are often not interoperable. There are many barriers to interoperability, including lack of common software interfaces, and standard data formats.

### Enablers

In addition to advances in low-cost hardware, connectivity, and software, achieving the potential of the IoT requires improvements in security and methods for ensuring privacy, protection of intellectual prop-

*Table 3. Business drivers behind the IoT*

| Business Driver | Effect |
|---|---|
| • The cost of devices (silicon, packaging, etc.) is continuously dropping.<br>• Ubiquitous broadband infrastructure is spreading all over (Gubbi et al, 2013).<br>• Telephone carriers' monthly fees for consumers and businesses are dropping.<br>• Storage capacity & processing power of computers are growing.<br>• Miniaturization of components and the integration of a broad range of sensing capabilities are on the rise.<br>• IT systems, the internet and next generation telecommunication network architecture are being further developed.<br>• Simplified design & better interactions are on the rise continuously. | • More affordable for businesses and consumers.<br>• More people in developed countries are becoming connected to one another to processing technology and storage infrastructure.<br>• More people are connected, fostering a stronger market adoption of the IoT.<br>• Faster management of data to support new managed services.<br>• Broaden the range of possible applications available.<br>• More accurate data - movement and analysis of very large amounts of information, extending the value of managed services.<br>• Drives adoption of new business models & acceptance by younger generations. |

*Table 4. Types of enablers are needed for maximum IoT impact*

| Enabler | Impact |
|---|---|
| • Software and hardware technology<br>(Kortuem, Kawsar, Sundramoorthy, & Fitton, (2010). | • Low power, inexpensive sensors and computers.<br>One of the basic requirements of IoT is to have the devices to talk each other. For this, two types of base technology are needed: cheap, low-power hardware and ubiquitous connectivity (ITU Internet Reports, 2005) The cost of components and computing power must continue to drop to make IoT applications cost-effective. IoT applications will require both low-cost processing power and cost-effective data storage methods.<br>• Ubiquitous connectivity/low-cost mesh connectivity.<br>Complex analytic computing of data from diverse sources will need ubiquitous connectivity.<br>• Additional capacity and bandwidth in the cloud, as cloud (Buyya, Yeo, Venugopal, Broberg, & Brandic, 2009) is the most recent paradigm to emerge which promises reliable services delivered through next generation data centres that are based on virtualised storage technologies. (Atzori, Iera, & Morabito, 2010).<br>• Confidence in security across entire IoT ecosystem. |
| • Interoperability<br>The Internet of Things heightens risks to personal privacy and the confidentiality and integrity of organizational data (Uckelmann, Harrison, & Michahelles, (2011). | • Standardization in the technology stack and ability to integrate across technology vendors.<br>• Standard protocols for sharing between IoT systems<br>• Standard access to external data sources. |
| • Security, privacy, and confidentiality.<br>The IoT heightens existing concerns about cybersecurity and introduces new risks. It multiplies the normal risks associated with any data communication (Hargreaves, 2011).<br>• Every node is a potential entry point, and interconnection can spread the damage (Wan & Jones, 2013). | • Establishing trust for sharing data.<br>• Collaboration across companies and industry verticals. (Karnouskos, 2010).<br>• Horizontal data aggregators.<br>• Data commerce platforms. |
| • Business organization and culture (Castells, 2002; Sundmaeker et al, 2010). Implementing IoT-based systems will require major organizational and behavioural shifts<br>o for businesses. The nature and degree of adaptation required will vary by settings.<br>o for applications. For example, health care remains a high-touch culture—patients expect to interact with a physician.<br>• The Internet of Things could enable a shift toward payment for patient wellness, rather than for treatments. Such a shift may require considerable adjustments by both patients and physicians.<br>• More tasks could shift from doctors to physician assistants and technicians. IoT raises different organizational challenges. Industries that have unionized workforces (many forms of transportation, for example) may need to negotiate changes in labour practices to enable IoT applications. | • Industry structure, e.g., organized labour cooperation, third-party servicing.<br>• Hardware-focused companies developing core competency in software.<br>• Companies committing to up-front investment based on clear business cases. |
| • Public policy (Weber, 2009). | • Regulation for autonomous control of vehicles and other machinery.<br>• Government and payer subsidy of health-care IoT.<br>• Agreements on fair practices for data sharing and use. |

(McKinsey, 2016)

erty, and assignment of data ownership. Companies and other organizations that want to maximize the benefits of IoT applications and perhaps build business models around them will need the proper attitude to manage successful IoT initiatives and make data-driven decisions. Because IoT applications touch on so many areas of regulatory and government responsibility (managing roads and regulating other forms of transportation, for example), policy makers will play a key role in enabling the IoT. Policy makers can also help by addressing concerns about security and privacy and encouraging the development of standards to promote interoperability (McKinsey Global Institute, 2014).

- **Privacy and Confidentiality:** With IoT applications, consumers may have no idea what kind of information is being acquired about them. To make the right in-store offers in the retail environments, a retailer need data about a shopper's previous purchases at that store, the items the shopper viewed at the retailer's website, data about the shopper, and location data about the shopper's path through the store. Consumers have a possible embarrassment to worry about from the misuse of private data. Personal data about health and wellness and purchasing behaviour can affect employment, access to credit, and insurance rates. For example, underwriting programs that use personal information in addition to credit scores to evaluate applicants for credit could be used in ways that enable companies to discriminate against certain types of consumers. Many consumers are becoming more wary of sharing personal information with businesses and other institutions. Privacy and security risks to both consumers and organizations will have to be addressed to derive the full benefits from the IoT. Creating compelling value propositions for those whose data are collected and used is critical to adoption.
- **Security:** An IoT-based home security system could pose serious risks: a hacker attack on a smart grid system (Celenec, online) could potentially turn off businesses, creating massive economic harm and threats to safety. Mission-critical IoT applications should therefore have high levels of security before they are adopted on a large scale. Additionally, consumers will not accept applications such as touchless payment systems in retail unless they believe that their payment data are secure. It may be a hard sell, according to the Identity (Identity Theft Resource Centre, 2015).
- **Intellectual Property and Data Ownership:** A common understanding of who has what rights to data produced by various connected devices will be required to unlock the full potential of IoT. With the exploding growth of IoT data from consumers and enterprises, questions arise about who owns the data. To capture maximum value and avoid misuse of data, this issue needs to be addressed early in the contract phase of an IoT implementation. In consumer applications, the rights to use data generated in the course of doing business and for what purpose should be clearly spelled out in the agreement that consumers must accept.
- **Organizational Shift:** Across industries, the most fundamental cultural and organizational shift required for implementing the IoT in corporations is to develop the skills and mind-sets to embrace data-driven decision making. Despite the enormous investments that companies have made in data and analytics, many still fail to use data effectively in decision making. Also, because IoT combines the physical and digital world (Yoo et al., 2010), it challenges conventional notions of organizational responsibilities. Traditionally, the IT organization was separate and distinct from the operating organization that manages the physical environment. In an IoT world, IT is embedded throughout store operations, from merchandise tagging to automated checkout. These applications more directly affect the business metrics on which store operations are measured.
- **Public Policy:** The digitization of physical systems will require a range of actions from policy makers. Not only will they be called upon to update and strengthen policies to protect the privacy and property rights of businesses and consumers, but they will also need to regulate entirely new forms of activity in the public sphere. Autonomous vehicles are the most obvious example of this challenge. In privacy, security, data ownership, and data sharing, existing regulations will have to be reviewed and updated. Finally, policy makers can do a great deal to advance the IoT and gener-

ate the economic and social benefits that will play a critical role in setting the pace of adoption of the IoT applications (Brynjolfsson, Hitt & Kim, 2011).

## Benefits

The IoT offers value to businesses, consumers, and impacts every business as it completely revolutionizes the logistics & supply chain. It will have a profound impact on people's lives, as it will improve public life, individual degree of satisfaction, etc. with better information and faster communications of this information. While there are many ways that the IoT could affect society and business, there are at least three major benefits that will influence every business and these are: (Harbor Research, 2013)

- **Communication:** The IoT communicates information to people and systems, such as state and health of equipment (e.g., it's on or off, charged, full or empty). In most cases, we didn't have access to this information before or it was collected manually and infrequently. The key benefit is the ability to continuously and seamlessly communicate.
- **Control / Automation:** In a connected world, a business will have visibility into a device's condition. In many cases, a business or consumer will also be able to remotely control a device. Once a performance baseline has been established, a process can send alerts for anomalies and possibly deliver an automated response. For example, if the brake pads on a truck are about to fail, it can prompt the company to take the vehicle out of service and automatically schedule maintenance.
- **Cost Savings / Increase Revenue:** Companies will adopt the IoT to save money or – even better – increase revenue. Measurement provides actual performance data and equipment health, instead of just estimates. Businesses, particularly industrial companies, lose money when equipment fails. With new sensor information, the IoT can help a company save money by minimizing equipment failure and allowing the business to perform planned maintenance (Wilson & Rosenbaum, 2005). Sensors can also measure items, such as driving behaviour and speed, to reduce fuel expense and wear and tear on consumables (Swan, 2012). With the ability to understand or generate the customers demand at a very early stage by connecting its demand and behaviour, the companies are able to provide products and services and thus generate the new revenue streams earlier.

## Challenges

The IoT promises many opportunities and benefits. However, there are a number of issues that need to be solved in order to realize the vision (Cha, Shah, Schmidt, & Leicher, 2009). The IoT enables physical assets to become elements of an information system, creating the ability to capture, compute, communicate, and collaborate in novel ways. In the following, we look at the challenges of IoT for different stakeholders as there are technical and non-technical challenges (Meister, Pias, Töpfer, & Coulouris, 2008) —companies and consumers that use IoT technology, policy makers, and the companies that supply IoT technology. We begin with implications for users of IoT technology and policy makers. Then we examine implications for the companies that will supply IoT technologies.

- **Implications for Users and Policy Makers:** The introduction of IoT systems has the potential to create value in new ways and to alter how people live and work. IoT applications will affect the full range of stakeholders, from individuals, whose home and work routines will change, to corporations that will have new ways to compete (as well as new competitors) (Porter, & Heppelmann, 2014). The IoT can enable new business models, including those that monetize the data generated by IoT technology.

- **Consumers:** The IoT applications offer the potential to drive down the costs and enhance the quality of goods and services, as manufacturers, retailers, and other suppliers employ IoT systems to improve product design and operations. Additionally, as our sizing analysis makes clear, another source of value for consumers will be greater consumer convenience and time savings. IoT benefits come along with a new range of risks. The internet has already raised concerns about consumer privacy, and the mobile Internet (smartphones) has heightened those concerns by collecting passive tracking data. IoT devices will go beyond that. In the workplace, IoT systems can be used to monitor and manage employee performance. Consumers will need to be diligent about monitoring the data that are being gathered about them. Consumers will have to manage information overload. They need to think about which IoT systems to adopt and how to integrate the use of those systems into their lives.
- **Employees:** The IoT will affect employees in different ways. Some types of workers are likely to benefit as the IoT creates new needs for specific skills. Workers who have skills in developing and deploying IoT systems will find themselves in greater demand. During the period of rapid growth in IoT deployments, developers and data scientists are likely to benefit the most. Over time, applications enabled by IoT are likely to enable the automation of an increasing number of tasks currently performed by service workers. In general, manual work will come under increasing pressure from IoT and smart machines, but IoT will open up some new employment opportunities, too. Workers who can install and maintain sensor networks, autonomous vehicles, and other IoT systems will be needed.
- **Organizations That Use the IoT:** The businesses and other organizations that use IoT systems are faced with a multitude of opportunities—and maybe just as many challenges. Depending on the industry, IoT applications can have far-reaching effects on how companies operate and may even force changes in business models. Some businesses (automobile manufacturers, for example) need to master use of IoT in their operations and in their products. We look at implications for businesses in three ways: using IoT to improve current business models, new business models enabled by IoT, and organizational issues related to IoT implementation.

In Table 5, we highlight some of what we believe to be major issues in the years ahead (Haller et al, 2008).

One key challenge is accentuated by connectivity and storage. Issues of data ownership within and across organizations can even further complicate aggregation. Owners of data from one system might not find it in their own interest to have their data combined with data from other systems. In addition, once data are aggregated, the analysis of these data to derive actionable information is a challenge in itself. Making IoT data actionable human judgment is required. The technical challenge is to build visualizations and user interfaces that synthesize large amounts of data into formats that can be easily understood by human decision makers. To harness the potential power of such a system, organizations will need to adapt. Teams performing analysis must be linked with teams making operational decisions and with those on the ground that are responsible for implementation.

*Table 5. Challenges*

| Challenge | Description |
|---|---|
| • IoT Reference Architecture. | • Develop an effective cross-industry technology reference architecture that will allow for true interoperability and ease of deployment. |
| • Delivery Ecosystem. | • Complex services and solution delivery eco-systems that require supply-side players to relate in new and different ways. |
| • Vendors' landscapes. | • Vendors offering smart systems still have fragmented "smart" landscapes which poorly aligned with the larger IT infrastructure and network services players (Toma, Simperl, & Hench, 2009). |
| • High demand for vertical solutions. | • Requirement for vertically focused solutions from a supply-side world that historically has been far more horizontally driven. |
| • Security. | • Communication between the various systems become essential as the data are the core value and therefore any risk needs to be mitigated (Floerkemeier, Roduner, & Lampe, 2007), |

## CONCLUSION

The IoT is a framework, where physical objects, augmented with computing and networking capabilities, will become active participants within business processes. It goes beyond operational monitoring and control. Rich operational context from connected devices can be used to optimize existing business processes and enable innovations and business models.

In such an environment, augmented physical objects connected to the Internet will rearrange the rules of occupancy and patterns of mobility within the physical world and thus has the potential to fundamentally shift the way we interact, we drive our business and we generate value within a company.

The IoT brings concepts and technical components together — pervasive networks, mobile communication, optimization, and decomposition of business processes, as well as innovative new business process models. By bringing all the chain links together – the physical world, the internet connection, and the IT world – forms an IoT value chain.

The concepts of the IoT go beyond utilizing enabling technologies like RFID tags (Madlmayr, Ecker & Langer, 2008), sensor/actuator networks, and embedded systems. The ability to monitor and manage objects in the physical world electronically makes it possible to bring data-driven decision making to new realms of human activity—to optimize the performance of systems and processes, save time for people and businesses, and improve quality of life. The main technical pillars of the IoT are as follows:

- *Applications* (e.g. enterprise applications, composite applications, desktop applications, …),
- *Services* (e.g. system integration, support, smart services),
- *Enabling software components and technologies* (e.g. sensors, actuators, passive/active RFID, embedded system) to put real world data into business context (e.g. management and execution components),
- *Networks* (e.g. fixed, wireless, proprietary, open connectivity) (Pering, Agarwal, Gupta, & Want, 2006).

The IoT builds and extends value and benefits via collaboration with customers, suppliers, channels, and providers. These business benefits are:

- Improved *performance, visibility and scalability* of business process automation; providing better, more cost effective service through real-time high-resolution visibility /capture and analysis of real-time product performance information (Atzori et al. 2010; Mattern, 2013; Vermesan et al. 2014).
- Better *transparency* of physical flows and detailed status information.
- Creation/transformation of new and existing *business processes* hereby potentially increasing the efficiency (Karnouskos, Baecker, Moreira, & Spiess, 2007).

The IoT expands the reach and impact of IT and networking. The myriad possibilities that arise from the ability to monitor and control things in the physical world electronically have inspired a surge of innovation and enthusiasm.

We-summarize it with a quote: Internet + Internet of Things = Wisdom of the Earth (MacManus, 2010).

## REFERENCES

Andrews, C., El-Attrash, F., Jarvis, E., Johnson, N., & Moss, H. (n.d.). *The Internet of Things: What IoT means for the public sector*. Retrieved from GovLoop: http://www.isaca.org/Groups/Professional-English/cybersecurity/GroupDocuments/IoT%20in%20the%20Public%20Sector.pdf

Ashton, K. (2009). That 'internet of things' thing. *RFiD Journal*, *22*(7), 97–114.

Atzori, L., Iera, A., & Morabito, G. (2010). The internet of things: A survey. *Computer Networks*, *54*(15), 2787–2805. doi:10.1016/j.comnet.2010.05.010

Bandyopadhyay, D., & Sen, J. (2011). Internet of things: Applications and challenges in technology and standardization. *Wireless Personal Communications*, *58*(1), 49–69. doi:10.1007/s11277-011-0288-5

Bechtel, C., & Jayaram, J. (1997). Supply chain management: a strategic perspective. *The International Journal of Logistics Management*, *8*(1), 15-34.

Bélissent, J. (2010). *Getting clever about smart cities: new opportunities require new business models.* Academic Press.

Bleecker, J. (2006). A Manifesto for Networked Objects - Cohabiting with Pigeons, Arphids and Aibos in the Internet of Things - Why Things Matter What' s a Blogject? What about Spimes? *Proc. of the 13th International Conference on Human-Computer Interaction with Mobile Devices and Services, MobileHCI.*

Bonsor, K., & Keener, C. (2010). *How Stuff Works "How RFID Works"*. Retrieved from http://electronics.howstuffworks.com/gadgets/high-tech-gadgets/rfid.htm

Brynjolfsson, E., Hitt, L. M., & Kim, H. H. (2011). *Strength in numbers: How does data-driven decisionmaking affect firm performance?* Available at SSRN 1819486

Bucherer, E., & Uckelmann, D. (2011). Business models for the internet of things. In *Architecting the internet of things* (pp. 253–277). Springer Berlin Heidelberg. doi:10.1007/978-3-642-19157-2_10

Bughin, J., Chui, M., & Manyika, J. (2013). Ten IT-enabled business trends for the decade ahead. *The McKinsey Quarterly*, *13*(May).

Buyya, R., Yeo, C. S., Venugopal, S., Broberg, J., & Brandic, I. (2009). Cloud computing and emerging IT platforms: Vision, hype, and reality for delivering computing as the 5th utility. *Future Generation Computer Systems*, *25*(6), 599–616. doi:10.1016/j.future.2008.12.001

Castells, M. (2002). *The Internet galaxy: Reflections on the Internet, business, and society*. Oxford University Press.

CENELEC. Smart Grids. (n.d.). Online at http://www.cenelec.eu/aboutcenelec/whatwedo/technology-sectors/smartgrids.html

Cha, I., Shah, Y., Schmidt, A. U., Leicher, A., & Meyerstein, M. V. (2009). Trust in M2M communication. *IEEE Vehicular Technology Magazine*, *4*(3), 69–75. doi:10.1109/MVT.2009.933478

Chen, Y. K. (2012, January). Challenges and opportunities of internet of things. In *17th Asia and South Pacific Design Automation Conference* (pp. 383-388). IEEE. doi:10.1109/ASPDAC.2012.6164978

Cisco. (2012). *The Internet of Everything How More Relevant and Valuable Connections Will Change the World*. Retrieved February 1, 2016 from http://www.cisco.com/c/dam/en_us/about/ac79/docs/innov/IoE.pdf

CMI. (2015, January). Things on the Internet to 'The Internet of Things - Market Overview. *Competitive Market Intelligence*.

Coetzee, L., & Eksteen, J. (2011, May). The Internet of Things-promise for the future? An introduction. In *IST-Africa Conference Proceedings, 2011* (pp. 1-9). IEEE.

Domingo, M. C. (2012). An overview of the Internet of Things for people with disabilities. *Journal of Network and Computer Applications*, *35*(2), 584–596. doi:10.1016/j.jnca.2011.10.015

Fleisch, E. (2010). What is the internet of things? An economic perspective. *Economics, Management, and Financial Markets,* (2), 125-157.

Floerkemeier, C., Roduner, C., & Lampe, M. (2007). RFID application development with the Accada middleware platform. *IEEE Systems Journal*, *1*(2), 82–94. doi:10.1109/JSYST.2007.909778

Gartner. (2014). *Gartner says 4.9 billion connected 'things' will be in use in 2015*. Press release, November 11, 2014.

Gavras, A., Karila, A., Fdida, S., May, M., & Potts, M. (2007). Future internet research and experimentation: The FIRE initiative. *Computer Communication Review*, *37*(3), 89–92. doi:10.1145/1273445.1273460

Gubbi, J., Buyya, R., Marusic, S., & Palaniswami, M. (2013). Internet of Things (IoT): A vision, architectural elements, and future directions. *Future Generation Computer Systems*, *29*(7), 1645–1660. doi:10.1016/j.future.2013.01.010

Guinard, D., Trifa, V., Karnouskos, S., Spiess, P., & Savio, D. (2010). Interacting with the soa-based internet of things: Discovery, query, selection, and on-demand provisioning of web services. *IEEE Transactions on Services Computing, 3*(3), 223-235.

Haller, S., Karnouskos, S., & Schroth, C. (2008, September). The internet of things in an enterprise context. In *Future Internet Symposium* (pp. 14-28). Springer Berlin Heidelberg.

Harbor Research. (2013). *IoT Market Opps*. Paper 2013.

Hargreaves, I. (2011). *Digital opportunity: a review of intellectual property and growth: an independent report*. Academic Press.

Identity Theft Resource Center (2015). *Identity Theft, Resource Center breach report hits record high in 2014*. Author.

International Telecommunication Union. (2012). *ITU-T Y.2060 — (06/2012) — Next Generation Networks — Frameworks and functional architecture models — Overview of the Internet of things*. ITU.

ISTAG. (2008). *Working Group Report on "Web-based Service Industry"*. Retrieved from ftp://ftp.cordis.europa.eu/pub/ist/docs/web-based-service-industry-istag_en.pdf

ITU. (2012). *New ITU standards define the internet of things and provide the blueprints for its development.* Retrieved from http://www.itu.int/ITU-T/newslog/New_ITU_Standards_Define_The_Internet_Of_Things_And_Provide_The_Blueprints_For_Its_Development.aspx

ITU Internet Reports. (2005). *The Internet of Things, November 2005*. ITU.

Janssen, C. (2015). *Platform*. Retrieved from http://www.techopedia.com/ definition/3411/platform

Johnson, K. D. (2015). *Machine-to-Machine: Reinventing Embedded Devices for Smart Services*. Academic Press.

Karimi, K., & Atkinson, G. (2013). *What the Internet of Things (IoT) needs to become a reality*. White Paper, FreeScale and ARM.

Karnouskos, S. (2011, July). Cyber-physical systems in the smartgrid. In *2011 9th IEEE International Conference on Industrial Informatics* (pp. 20-23). IEEE. doi:10.1109/INDIN.2011.6034829

Karnouskos, S., Baecker, O., De Souza, L. M. S., & Spiess, P. (2007, September). Integration of soa-ready networked embedded devices in enterprise systems via a cross-layered web service infrastructure. In *2007 IEEE Conference on Emerging Technologies and Factory Automation (EFTA 2007)* (pp. 293-300). IEEE. doi:10.1109/EFTA.2007.4416781

Kortuem, G., Kawsar, F., Sundramoorthy, V., & Fitton, D. (2010). Smart objects as building blocks for the internet of things. *IEEE Internet Computing*, *14*(1), 44–51. doi:10.1109/MIC.2009.143

Lehtonen, M., Oertel, N., & Vogt, H. (2007, June). Features, identity, tracing, and cryptography in product authentication. In *2007 IEEE International Technology Management Conference (ICE)* (pp. 1-8). IEEE.

Li, Q., Wang, Z. Y., Li, W. H., Li, J., Wang, C., & Du, R. Y. (2013). Applications integration in a hybrid cloud computing environment: Modelling and platform. *Enterprise Information Systems*, *7*(3), 237–271. doi:10.1080/17517575.2012.677479

Li, S., Xu, L., Wang, X., & Wang, J. (2012). Integration of hybrid wireless networks in cloud services oriented enterprise information systems. *Enterprise Information Systems*, *6*(2), 165–187. doi:10.1080/17517575.2011.654266

Lopez Research. (2013a). *An Introduction to the Internet of Things*. White Paper published by Cisco.

Lopez Research. (2013b). *Things Your Business Should Know About Internet of Things*. Retrieved February 15, 2016, from: http://www.lopezresearch.com/2013/12/10/4-things-your-business-should-know-about-internet-of-things/

MacManus. (2010). Chinese Premier Talks Up Internet of Things. Journal of Democracy, 22(2), 32-46.

Madlmayr, G., Ecker, J., Langer, J., & Scharinger, J. (2008). Near field communication: State of standardization. *Internet of Things*, *177*, 10.

Marti, S., Ganesan, P., & Garcia-Molina, H. (2004, March). SPROUT: P2P routing with social networks. In *International Conference on Extending Database Technology* (pp. 425-435). Springer Berlin Heidelberg.

Mattern, F. (2013). Die technische Basis für M2M und das Internet der Dinge. M2M und das Internet der Dinge. *Münchner Kreis*, 46-69.

McKinsey. (2013). *The Internet of Things and the Future of Manufacturing*. McKinsey & Company. Retrieved February 15, 2016, from: http://www.mckinsey.com/insights/business_technology/the_internet_of_things_and_the_future_of_manufacturing

McKinsey Global Institute (2011). *Big data: The next frontier for innovation, competition, and productivity*. Author.

Meister, M., Pias, M., Töpfer, E., & Coulouris, G. (2008). Application Scenarios for Cooperating Objects and their Social. *Legal and Ethical Challenges. In Adjunct Proceedings First International Conference on The Internet of Things*.

Miorandi, D., Sicari, S., De Pellegrini, F., & Chlamtac, I. (2012). Internet of things: Vision, applications and research challenges. *Ad Hoc Networks*, *10*(7), 1497–1516. doi:10.1016/j.adhoc.2012.02.016

Odenwald, T. (2007). Putting M2M into Business Context. *M2M Pioneer Magazine, 5*(2).

Pering, T., Agarwal, Y., Gupta, R., & Want, R. (2006, June). Coolspots: reducing the power consumption of wireless mobile devices with multiple radio interfaces. In *Proceedings of the 4th international conference on Mobile systems, applications and services* (pp. 220-232). ACM. doi:10.1145/1134680.1134704

Porter, M. E., & Heppelmann, J. E. (2014). How smart, connected products are transforming competition. *Harvard Business Review*, *92*(11), 64–88.

Ren, L., Zhang, L., Tao, F., Zhang, X., Luo, Y., & Zhang, Y. (2012). A methodology towards virtualisation-based high performance simulation platform supporting multidisciplinary design of complex products. *Enterprise Information Systems*, *6*(3), 267–290. doi:10.1080/17517575.2011.592598

SAP SE. (2014). *CEO Perspective: The Internet of Things for Utilities, Top Priorities to Build a Successful Strategy*. Retrieved from https://www.sap.com/bin/sapcom/ko_kr/downloadasset.2014-10-oct-28-03.ceo-perspective-the-internet-of-things-for-utilities-pdf.html

SAP SE. (2014). *SAP Solutions for the Internet of Things – Built for Your Business*. Author.

Sarma, S., Brock, D. L., & Ashton, K. (2000). *The networked physical world.* Auto-ID Center White Paper MIT-AUTOID-WH-001.

Spiess, P., & Karnouskos, S. (2007, July). Maximizing the business value of networked embedded systems through process-level integration into enterprise software. In *Pervasive Computing and Applications, 2007. ICPCA 2007. 2nd International Conference on* (pp. 536-541). IEEE.

Sullivan, B., & Thompson, H. (2013). Brain, interrupted. *New York Times, 3.*

Sundmaeker, H., Guillemin, P., Friess, P., & Woelfflé, S. (2010). *Vision and challenges for realizing the Internet of Things. Cluster of European Research Projects on the Internet of Things*. European Commision.

Swan, M. (2012). Sensor mania! the internet of things, wearable computing, objective metrics, and the quantified self 2.0. *Journal of Sensor and Actuator Networks*, *1*(3), 217–253. doi:10.3390/jsan1030217

Tan, L., & Wang, N. (2010, August). Future internet: The internet of things. In *2010 3rd International Conference on Advanced Computer Theory and Engineering (ICACTE)* (Vol. 5, pp. V5-376). IEEE.

Tao, F., LaiLi, Y., Xu, L., & Zhang, L. (2013). FC-PACO-RM: a parallel method for service composition optimal-selection in cloud manufacturing system. *IEEE Transactions on Industrial Informatics, 9*(4), 2023-2033.

The Networked Economy. (2014). *Revolution in Progress: in MIT Technology Review*. Retrieved February 1, 2016, from: https://s3.amazonaws.com/files.technologyreview.com/p/pub/campaign/sap/2014/SAP_Networked_Economy.pdf

Toma, I., Simperl, E., & Hench, G. (2009, June). A joint roadmap for semantic technologies and the internet of things. *Proceedings of the Third STI Roadmapping Workshop*, 1.

Uckelmann, D., Harrison, M., & Michahelles, F. (2011). An architectural approach towards the future internet of things. In *Architecting the internet of things* (pp. 1–24). Springer Berlin Heidelberg. doi:10.1007/978-3-642-19157-2_1

van Kranenburg, R. (2007). *The Internet of Things: A Critique of Ambient Technology and the All-Seeing Network of RFID*. Amsterdam, The Netherlands: Institute of Network Cultures.

van Kranenburg, R., Anzelmo, E., Bassi, A., Caprio, D., Dodson, S., & Ratto, M. (2011). The internet of things. A critique of ambient technology and the all-seeing network of RFID. *Network Notebooks, 2*.

Varian, H. (2007, February 8). Kaizen, that continuous improvement strategy, finds its ideal environment. *New York Times*.

Vasseur, J. P., & Dunkels, A. (2008). *Ip for smart objects.* IPSO Alliance, White paper, 1.

Vermesan, O., Friess, P., Guillemin, P., Gusmeroli, S., Sundmaeker, H., Bassi, A., & Doody, P. (2011). Internet of things strategic research roadmap. Internet of Things: *Global Technological and Societal Trends, 1*, 9-52.

*Vision and Challenges for Realising the Internet of Things.* (2010). European Union.

Wan, J., & Jones, J. (2013). Managing IT service management implementation complexity: From the perspective of the Warfield version of systems science. *Enterprise Information Systems, 7*(4), 490–522. doi:10.1080/17517575.2011.625572

Wang, L., Da Xu, L., Bi, Z., & Xu, Y. (2014). Data cleaning for RFID and WSN integration. *IEEE Transactions on Industrial Informatics, 10*(1), 408–418. doi:10.1109/TII.2013.2250510

Weber, R. H. (2009). Internet of things–Need for a new legal environment?. *Computer Law & Security Review, 25*(6), 522-527.

Wilson, C. E., & Rosenbaum, S. (2005). Categories of return on investment and their practical implications. Cost-Justifying Usability. *An Update for the Internet Age, 2*, 215–263.

Yoo, Y., Henfridsson, O., & Lyytinen, K. (2010). Research commentary-The new organizing logic of digital innovation: An agenda for information systems research. *Information Systems Research, 21*(4), 724–735. doi:10.1287/isre.1100.0322

Yu, H., Kaminsky, M., Gibbons, P. B., & Flaxman, A. (2006, September). Sybilguard: Defending against sybil attacks via social networks. *Computer Communication Review, 36*(4), 267–278. doi:10.1145/1151659.1159945

Zhou, J., Leppänen, T., Harjula, E., Ylianttila, M., Ojala, T., Yu, C., & Jin, H. (2013, June). Cloudthings: A common architecture for integrating the internet of things with cloud computing. In *Computer Supported Cooperative Work in Design (CSCWD), 2013 IEEE 17th International Conference on* (pp. 651-657). IEEE. doi:10.1109/CSCWD.2013.6581037

## KEY TERMS AND DEFINITIONS

**B2B:** A type of transaction that exists between businesses, such as one involving a manufacturer and wholesaler, or a wholesaler and a retailer. Business to business refers to business that is conducted between companies, rather than between a company and individual consumers. Business to business stands in contrast to business to consumer (B2C) and business to government (B2G) transactions.

**Business Driver:** A business driver is a resource, process or condition that is vital for the continued success and growth of a business. A company must identify its business drivers and attempt to maximize any that are under their control. There are always outside business drivers that a company cannot influence, such as economic conditions or trade relations with other nations.

**Business Model:** A business model is the way in which a company generates revenue and makes a profit from company operations. Analysts use the metric gross profit as a way to compare the efficiency and effectiveness of a firm's business model. Gross profit is calculated by subtracting the cost of goods sold from revenues.

**Digitalization:** The use of digital technologies to change a business model and provide new revenue and value-producing opportunities; it is the process of moving to a digital business.

**Internet of Things:** The Internet of Things (IoT) is a computing concept that describes a future where everyday physical objects will be connected to the Internet and be able to identify themselves to other devices. The term is closely identified with RFID as the method of communication, although it also may include other sensor technologies, wireless technologies or QR codes.

**RFID:** RFID (radio frequency identification) is a technology that incorporates the use of electromagnetic or electrostatic coupling in the radio frequency (RF) portion of the electromagnetic spectrum to uniquely identify an object, animal, or person. RFID is coming into increasing use in industry as an alternative to the bar code. The advantage of RFID is that it does not require direct contact or line-of-sight scanning. An RFID system consists of three components: an antenna and transceiver (often combined into one reader) and a transponder (the tag). The antenna uses radio frequency waves to transmit a signal that activates the transponder. When activated, the tag transmits data back to the antenna. The data is used to notify a programmable logic controller that an action should occur.

# Chapter 8
# Industrial Guidelines for Stimulating Entrepreneurship with the Internet of Things

**Mohammad Zarei**
*University of Tehran, Iran*

**Ahmad Jamalian**
*University of Mazandaran, Iran*

**Rohollah Ghasemi**
*University of Tehran, Iran*

## ABSTRACT

*Entrepreneurs are known as the engine of economic growth and prosperity. Entrepreneurs have relocated resources for the aim of introducing new economic, social, or socio-economic values. Revolutionary technologies such as the Internet of Things (IoT) have provided opportunities for entrepreneurs. The IoT is globally known as a new paradigm that rose from the world of ICT and changed dynamics of businesses and communities. However, there has been a lack of guidelines for promoting entrepreneurial initiatives by using of the IoT in industries. By conducting a comprehensive investigation of more than 120 commercialised IoT-based cases, this chapter identified 80 opportunity areas, and categorised them into the 13 main industries/sectors. Analysing 29 Iranian corporate, social, and SME entrepreneurs with the use of Analytic Hierarchy Process (AHP) technique, this chapter measured the importance of each industry. Based on the results, this chapter presents recommendations to promote entrepreneurial activities.*

## INTRODUCTION

The IoT is a paradigm that aims at enhancing our awareness of the environment. The IoT is not in infancy anymore and it has been adopted rapidly by many industries. For example, the IoT has played a significant role in the transportation sector with several capabilities such as navigation, vehicle to vehicle connections, fleet management, vehicle controls, and infrastructure monitoring. The IoT has

DOI: 10.4018/978-1-5225-2104-4.ch008

also been a great source of improvement for the supply chain partners. Real-time monitoring and tracking has improved visibility of material flows and facilitated collaborative activities of the supply chain partners. In addition to the positive impact on the established businesses, the IoT can be a great source of innovation for entrepreneurs.

Entrepreneurs aim to create new values by identifying unexploited opportunities and relocating the resources to achieve a higher level of productivity. One of the bottlenecks for having a successful entrepreneurial process is opportunity recognition (Jones & Butler, 1992; Kirzner, 1985). Recognising the valuable opportunities with a high ability or potential of commercialisation is crucial for all kinds of entrepreneurship. In spite of the significant implications of the IoT on the entrepreneurship, there have been few guidelines for entrepreneurs to exploit the IoT. The purpose of our study is to provide evidence-based guidelines to stimulate entrepreneurship with the IoT. To achieve our purpose, entrepreneurial opportunities of the IoT were identified by conducting a survey and analysing a number of industrial IoT adoption cases.

The remaining parts of this chapter are as follows: first the literature review of the definition, challenges and economics of the IoT is presented. Next, corporate entrepreneurship, social entrepreneurship, and small and medium-sized (SME) entrepreneurship are discussed. Then, the research methodology and the Analytic Hierarchy Process (AHP) model are elaborated. Finally, the research findings and various challenges are discussed.

## LITERATURE REVIEW

### Definition of the IoT

Atzori et al. (2010) discuss the very first definition of the IoT as a things oriented concept which includes Radio-Frequency IDentifications (RFIDs) tags and smart devices. Jara et al. (2011) suggest the IoT has an ability to provide a global connectivity and a management architecture of several devices. Vermesan et al. (2011) describe the IoT as an integrated part of the Future Internet with the capability of self-configuration. Xu et al. (2014) refer to the IoT as a dynamic global network infrastructure based on the protocols where virtual and physical things such as sensors and RFIDs have identities, and can be integrated in the information network. Gubbi et al. (2013) depict the IoT as an infrastructure for enabling the innovative applications by connecting devices from different platforms through a unified framework. Some components are large scale ubiquitous sensing, data analytics, and cloud computing. Wu et al. (2014) refer to the IoT as a new network paradigm and interconnected physical/virtual things with the minimum intervention of humans that pursue two main goals: 1) bridging the physical and the social world together to form an intelligent physical-cyber-social system, and 2) enabling smartness – from resource allocation to automatic network operations. Vermesan (2013) believes that, the full use of things will be attained by offering several distinguished services.

### The IoT in Industries and Its Applications

Several industries/sectors which adopted the IoT have been mentioned by various IoT studies: Healthcare and life science (Al-Turjman et al., 2013; Atzori et al., 2014; Gubbi et al., 2013; Perera et al., 2014; Zheng et al., 2011); Transportation (Xu et al., 2014; He et al., 2014; Kortuem et al., 2010; Vermesan et al., 2013; Zheng et al., 2011); Environment (Chui et al., 2010; Da Xu et al., 2014; Miorandi et al., 2012; Tsai et al., 2014; Zheng et al., 2011), Accommodation (Akyildiz et al., 2002; Atzori et al., 2010; Xu et al., 2014; Kortuem et al., 2010; Perera et al., 2014); Retail (Chui et al., 2010; Konomi & Roussos, 2007; Thiesse & Köhler, 2008), Industrial production (Xu et al., 2014; Gluhak et al., 2011; Vermesan et al., 2013); Energy (Gubbi et al., 2013; Miorandi et al., 2012; Perera et al., 2014; Vermesan et al., 2013); Government (Miorandi et al., 2012; Tsai et al., 2014); ICT (Chui et al., 2010; Vermesan et al., 2011); Military (Akyildiz et al., 2002; Vermesan et al., 2013; Xu, 2002). Zarei et al. (2016) based on the Iranian "1404 economic outlook" prioritised five industries/sectors: Healthcare, Transportation, Smart home, Energy, and Retailing for the aim of achieving sustainable development by the country. They argue that the IoT brings continuous social, environmental, and economic progress, and introduced the term of "sustainable IoT".

Except a few studies such as Vermesan et al. (2013), most previous studies have two main issues: firstly, they have generally mentioned IoT applications based on their imaginations not commercialised samples. Secondly, most studies discussed the IoT from a technical perspective. Our study tries to address these issues.

In the past few years various IoT products and services from several industries have been successfully launched and introduced to the market. For developing an industrial guideline for entrepreneurs and classifying the most active industries in the field of the IoT, we applied a bottom-up approach; we reviewed the commercialised/launched IoT products and services from various industries around the globe by surveying almost 147 cases. At the same time, we categorised the commercialised samples into 80 main groups, as is shown in Table 1, that are called "recognised opportunity areas". For categorising "recognised/ commercialised samples" into "recognised opportunity areas" as is shown in Table 2, we applied a grounded theory methodology (GTM). In our study, only the first round of coding has been used. The GTM method was developed by Glaser and Strauss (1967).

## Limiting Factors to the IoT

In spite of the growing interest in the application of the IoT in industries, the IoT industry struggles with some challenges. IoT challenges are far greater to be tackled by individual companies. As a result, various international associations, societies, strategic alliances and jointly research projects, and research clusters around the world have collaborate to address the IoT challenges. Some of these groups are: European Research Cluster on the Internet of Things (IERC), Global System for Mobile communication (GSM) Association, Organisation for Economic Co-operation and Development (OECD), and METIS consortium that has collected more than 29 global partners including manufacturers, telecommunication operators, and academic institutions.

Some of the IoT challenges discussed by Weber (2009) include: control, data protection, identity management, interoperability, naming, privacy, security, and standardisation. Privacy, security, and trust are among important challenges for context-aware computing (Perera et al., 2014). The European Consumer Voice in Standardisation (ANEC) and BEUC have supported the commission for improving the current situation in term of security (Weber, 2009). Governance is another challenge for implementing of an international network infrastructures. On top of the above-mentioned challenges, there have been several other technical complications (e.g., the heterogeneity of devices or the IoT).

Another challenge in the IoT is related to the market size of the IoT, because still the market size and even revenue for the IoT products and services are vague at best. Without having a clear prediction of

*Table 1. Recognised, industry/sector and opportunity areas based on IoT*

| Industry and/or Sector | Recognised Opportunity Areas | Recognised/Commercialised Samples |
|---|---|---|
| Accommodation and Residence | 7 | 15 |
| Agriculture and Animal Husbandry | 3 | 4 |
| Energy | 6 | 14 |
| Enterprise, Manufacture, Production | 8 | 17 |
| Entertainment, Media, Recreation and Sports | 7 | 10 |
| Environment | 9 | 11 |
| Finance and Insurance | 2 | 2 |
| Healthcare and Life Science | 9 | 14 |
| Information and Communications Technology (ICT) | 10 | 27 |
| Military and Defence | 2 | 3 |
| Public Administration, Governmental and Public Safety | 5 | 7 |
| Research and Education | 3 | 4 |
| Transportation and Retail | 9 | 19 |
| Total | 80 | 147 |

*Table 2. Application of the IoT*

| Industry and/or Sector | Samples of the Opportunity Areas | References |
|---|---|---|
| Accommodation and Residence | Smart Home | Twine (B)<br>Alarm (C)<br>Econais (C)<br>AT&T Digital Life (B)<br>G4S (C) |
| | Smart Furniture | Smart Refrigerator of Samsung (B) |
| | Smart Beds | Ohea (C) |
| | Smart Lighting Systems | Econais (C) |
| | Hot Water Heaters | Nest (C)<br>Honeywell (C) |
| | Smart Parking and Parking Management | Parkifi (C)<br>SpotHero (C)<br>Spaceek (C)<br>ADLINK Technology Inc. (C) |
| | Heating, Ventilation and Air Conditioning (HVAC) | Emerson (C) |
| Agriculture and Animal Husbandry | Smart Farming | Observant (C)<br>Link Labs (A) |
| | Smart Irrigation | ThingWorx (PTC) (B) |
| | Smart Herds | Litams (C) |

*continued on next page*

*Table 2. Continued*

| Industry and/or Sector | Samples of the Opportunity Areas | References |
|---|---|---|
| Energy | Smart Lighting | Echelon (C)<br>Microsens (C) |
| | Smart Grids | Tendril Networks Inc. (C)<br>Itron (C)<br>Silver Spring Networks (C)<br>Siemens (C)<br>ABB (C)<br>Industrial Internet Consortium (A) |
| | Smart Meters | AMI (C)<br>Itron (C)<br>Peterborough Utilities (C) |
| | Monitoring Oil Pipelines | Orbcomm (C) |
| | Station Finder | ChargePoint, Inc. (C) |
| | Monitoring Oil Wells | Osprey Informatics (C) |
| Enterprise, Manufacture, Production | Smart Industrial Robots | IoTSP (ABB), (B) |
| | Structural Health | Libelium (C) |
| | Industrial Processes and Operations | Air Liquide (C)<br>Osprey Informatics (C)<br>ABB (C) |
| | Beverage Production | Heineken (C) |
| | Assets Management | IBM® Maximo® Asset Management (B)<br>Logitrac Inc. (C)<br>Masternaut (C) |
| | Enterprise Resource Planning (ERP) and Supply Chain Management (SCM) | Heineken (C)<br>E2open network (C)<br>MEMS & Sensors Industry Group® (C)<br>First Sensor (C) |
| | Industrial IoT Platforms | Itron Riva platform (B)<br>Jasper (C) |
| | Producing IoT Hardware | Bosch (C)<br>Infineon (C) |
| Entertainment, Media, Recreation and Sports | Wearables | Garmin Ltd (C)<br>AAC Technologies Holding Inc. (C)<br>Acton (C)<br>Allianz (C) |
| | Sports Tracker | Flaik (C) |
| | Museums and Theme Parks | QRator (B) |
| | Connected Entertainment | Microsoft (C) |
| | Health Platforms | KAA IoT Platform (A) |
| | Connected Athlete | Cisco (C) |
| | Bicycling | Glasgow, Scotland (D) |

*continued on next page*

*Table 2. Continued*

| Industry and/or Sector | Samples of the Opportunity Areas | References |
|---|---|---|
| Environment | Snow Level Monitoring | Sommer (C) |
| | Smart Waste Management | Smart Waste Management Solutions (B)<br>Enevo (C) |
| | Forest Fire Detection | Libelium (C) |
| | Air Pollution | Aeroqual (C), New Zealand (D) |
| | Earthquake Early Warning System (EEW) | Cascadia, Vancouver Island (D) |
| | Water Monitoring | Stevens (C)<br>Censar Technologies, Inc. (C) |
| | Soil Pollution | Smart Storm Ltd (C) |
| | Ozone Analyser | Ozone Analyzer Module (B) |
| | Animal Tracking Solution & Wildlife Researches | Cats (C) |
| Finance and Insurance | Smart Insurance | (Pay-As-You-Drive of) Baseline Telematic (C) |
| | Smart Shopping | Groceries (Samsung) (B) |
| Healthcare and Life Science | Treating Depression | Boston Scientific (C) |
| | IoT Medicating | Philips (C)<br>Boston Scientific (C) |
| | Dementia Monitoring | Acetek (C) |
| | Eldercare | Tacera Tag (B/P)/Austco (C) |
| | Special Care Patients | (Parkinson) Great Lakes NeuroTechnologies (C) |
| | Hospital and Healthcare Center | Masimo Radical (B)<br>IP Nurse Call (B)/Acetek (C) |
| | Monitoring Core Body Temperature (CBT) and Heart Attacks and Etc. | UroSense (B)<br>Boston Scientific (C) |
| | Respiratory Disorder | Niox Mino (B) |
| | Fall Detection | Medical Guardian (C)<br>ResponseNow (C)<br>Philips Lifeline (C), Philips |
| Information and Communication Technology (ICT) | IoT Search Engines | Shodan (B)<br>Thingful (B)<br>Censys (C)<br>SPITFIRE (C) |
| | IoT Test Beds | NetEye (B)<br>Ear-IT project (A)<br>TutorNet (B)<br>MIRAGE Intel (B)<br>FIT IoT-Lab (B) / The FIT consortium (A)<br>DES-Testbed (B) |
| | IoT Platforms | Arkessa Platform (C)<br>Axeda Platform (C)<br>EVRYTHNG Platform (C)<br>Thingworx Platform (C)<br>SensorCloud Platform (B)<br>Thingspeak Platform (B) |
| | IoT Operating Systems | Windows 10 IoT Core (B)<br>RIOT (B) |
| | Analysing IoT Data | CSL DualCom Group Ltd (C)<br>Jasper (C) |
| | IoT/M2M SIM Cards | GSMA Embedded SIM (P) / GSM Association (A)<br>Globalm2msim (B)<br>Neo (B) |
| | IoT Application Software | Bluemix™ applications (B) |
| | Securely Protection | Symantec (C) |
| | Critical Connectivity | CSL DualCom Group Ltd (C) |
| | IoT CCTV Cameras | Foscam (B) |

*continued on next page*

*Table 2. Continued*

| Industry and/or Sector | Samples of the Opportunity Areas | References |
|---|---|---|
| Military and Defence | Combat Systems | C4ISR (The U.S. Department of Defense (DoD)) (A) |
| | Monitoring Military Shipments | DSG groups (C) |
| Public Administration, Government and Public Safety | Controlling Gun Violence | SST (C) |
| | Surveillance | Eurotech (C)<br>National Security Agency, USA (A) |
| | Public Safety | Cisco surveillance technology (B)<br>Hitachi Data Systems Federal (HDS Federal) (A) |
| | Crisis Management | Hitachi Data Systems Federal (HDS Federal) (A) |
| | Wildfire Management | Wildland Fire Decision Support System (NASA) (A) |
| Research and Education | Smart Classrooms | Office of Education Technology (A)<br>Beijing Middle School 105 (A) |
| | Pupils Safety | Cisco Physical Access Control technology (B) |
| | Fauna Researches | Cats (C) |
| Transportation and Retail | Collision Monitoring | eCall (European Union) (A) |
| | V2V Ice Warning | Volvo (C) |
| | Human-Vehicle Interface | Nismo Watch (Nissan) (P) |
| | Connected Car | Tesla Motors (C)<br>BMW AG (C)<br>Daimler AG (C)<br>Fiat Chrysler Automobiles (C) |
| | Smart Roads | Oss, Netherland (D)<br>LED Variable Message Signs (B)<br>Automatic Incident Detection (B) |
| | Traffic Congestion and Mapping | São Paulo, Brazil (D) |
| | Integrates Wearables | Nismo Watch (B) /Nissan (C)<br>Ford (C) |
| | Truck/Assets Tracking | Certified Tracking Solutions (C)<br>Sendum (C) |
| | Retailing | Store of the Future (B)<br>Wal-Mart Stores (C)<br>Best Buy (C)<br>Target Corporation (C) |

*Table 3. Place and/or location*

| Abbreviation | Extended Meaning |
|---|---|
| A | Association, project and/or official department |
| B | Brand, product or service |
| C | Company, corporate, and/or SME |
| D | Place and/or location |

the market size no company is able to invest in the IoT with confidence. A number of companies and market research institutes such as Cisco, Gartner, Markets and Markets, IDG Enterprise, and TCS have predicted revenues of the IoT. For instance, Blanter and Holman (2014) announced the $3.5 trillion revenue by 2020; TCS (2016) predicted $7.1 trillion by 2020; Statista (2016) announces $1.7 trillion by 2019; Grand View Research (2016) declares $1.88 trillion until 2022. However, the measurements have not been standardised (e.g., smart phones and the other time microprocessors have been included in some predictions, but not included in other predictions).

## ENTREPRENEURSHIP

Entrepreneurship is an old concept with more than 250 years of history (Austin et al., 2006). The term has rooted in the fields of economics, sociology, psychology, and management. Entrepreneurialism is a school, an approach, a concept, and a collection of thoughts that has at any time or shape sought to bring novel values – economic, social, or both. Based on the targeted market which an entrepreneur has decided to create value for, entrepreneurs can be divided into three main categories: corporate entrepreneurs, social entrepreneurs and SME entrepreneurs. Attributes of entrepreneurship include opportunity recognition, innovation, commercialisation, and risk taking.

Entrepreneurialism literature can be divided into two dominant group of investigations. First, cognitivism or ontology studies that aim to draw a comprehensive view of the field by discussing its components and branches. These kinds of studies are rare but valuable (Jones et al. (2011). The second group can be known as exploratory studies which a researcher by conducting a qualitative, quantitative or mixed methods aims to investigate the relationships between two or more dimensions or aims to explore an unseen effect; such as the relationship between corporate entrepreneurship and firm performance, or the effect of pure social capitals on entrepreneurial networks and launching a business. In the following sections, several types of entrepreneurship will be briefly discussed.

### Corporate Entrepreneurship

Corporate entrepreneurship is studied in the context of an established business (Antoncic & Hisrich, 2004; Biniari, 2012; Ferreira, 2001; Kuratko et al., 1993; Shepherd et al., 2009; Zahra, 1991). During a corporate entrepreneurship process a corporate entrepreneur aims to bring innovation into the organisation by renewing strategies, increasing the competitiveness, introducing, or opening-up a new market, product, and service. in this regard, Lumpkin and Dess (1996) refer to corporate entrepreneurship as an organisational process that contributes to the firms' survival and performance.

Castrogiovanni et al. (2011) express corporate entrepreneurship as a set of activities which an organisation undertakes to enhance its product and process innovations, risk-taking and pro-active responses to the environmental forces. Miles et al. (2003) clarify the corporate entrepreneurship as activities that are designed [within an established organisation] to capture a unique business opportunity. Antoncic and Zorn (2004) by examining sample of 477 Slovenian established firms and investigating process innovativeness, new venture formation, organisational support and etc. show that corporate entrepreneurs have had a significant role on organisational performance. Furthermore, the authors argue that corporate entrepreneurs have had an important influence on organisational performance, economic development, wealth creation, developing of new products, services, technologies, administrative techniques, strategies and competitive, process innovation. One of the main features of corporate entrepreneurs is opportunity recognition (Jones & Butler, 1992).

## Social Entrepreneurship

The number of non-profit organisations in the recent years has been increasing steadily. Some of these non-profit organisations are social entrepreneurs. The main driver for social entrepreneurs is to solve social problem (Austin et al., 2006), and simultaneously generating wealth for their stakeholders. However social entrepreneurship has not been adequately explored (Austin et al., 2006). Social entrepreneurship is a nascent but important subject for societies because of its contribution to societies, so there has been an increasing interest in the domain during the recent years (Rey-Martí et al. 2016). The apparent form of social entrepreneurship can be discussed in the context of society. Austin et al. (2006) discuss that the term has been used in different backgrounds such as society, corporate, non-profit sector, governmental or even across sectors.

## SME Entrepreneurship

The ability of governments to recruit individuals and establishing businesses for the citizens are extremely limited by global phenomena such as decentralisation and privatisation. As a result, individuals have to find out solutions to create job by and for themselves, and nascent businesses have been launched by individual/business/SME entrepreneurs around the world. Haltiwanger et al. (2013) argue that young firms and start-ups are known as the important sources of job creations. SME entrepreneurs have been known as a great source of economic development. Mazanai and Fatoki (2012) discuss the SMEs as the spine of economic welfare, and Lin (1998) labels the SMEs as one of the main economic progress engines. SME entrepreneurship is frequently discussed as the act of starting a new business and to some extent such entrepreneurs can be recognised by their start-ups (e.g., see Liñán, 2008; Liñán and Chen, 2009).

## Other Kinds of Entrepreneurship

Entrepreneurship in the broad point of view has not been limited to the corporate, social, and SME entrepreneurship and there have been several other kinds of entrepreneurship.

### International Entrepreneurship

McDougall (1989) refers to International entrepreneurship as the expansion of new international ventures or start-up in a new international market. Some businesses have been born as international, and others been launched in a domestic market and after a while export their products/services into the international market. The contributor to such international businesses can be known as international entrepreneurs. These kinds of entrepreneurial activities are commonly discussed in the context of Internationalisation. For the aim of investigating and fostering the internationalisations, several models have been developed including Foreign direct investment (FDI)-expansion model, Innovation-related models, Internalisation model, Product cycle model, Structural model, and Uppsala internationalisation models (Cuervo-Cazurra & Ramos, 2005, p.111).

### Government Entrepreneurship

The function of government entrepreneurship is somehow distinguished from other types of entrepreneurship, since, this type of entrepreneurship aims to develop a supportive business ecosystem for the aim of supporting entrepreneurs, and this aim can be achieved by tools such as legislations and implementation of supportive policies. Yu (2001) discuses when the private sector fails to respond properly, the government entrepreneurship can be important – e.g., in the times of recession. Government entrepreneurship is not limited to the governments and is used for the individuals as well. For instance, Purwaningsih (2015) alludes to the Prime Minister of Singapore as a government entrepreneur, and the author argues a government entrepreneur as a leader who has the skills and spirit of entrepreneurship.

### High-Tech Entrepreneurship

Lin et al. (2006) describe a high-tech entrepreneurship as a complex phenomenon with a variety of factors such as entrepreneurial strategies and societal contexts. Some of these factors interrelated with each other. Due to the state of the art technologies used by high-tech entrepreneurs, this type of entrepreneurship is limited to those who have fairly good academic background in high-tech fields (e.g., nanotechnology or the IoT). Because of the high rate of technological changes these entrepreneurs have been faced with the high rate of failure (Lasch, 2011). However, entrepreneurial failure rate is generally high (Jing et al., 2016). In addition, high-tech entrepreneurs should keep themselves up with what is the most recent in their field. It is worth mentioning that developing high-tech entrepreneurship relies on the research and development capabilities (Zhou & Peng, 2008).

## RESEARCH METHODOLOGY

The aim of this study is to provide guidelines for entrepreneurs to create value from the IoT. The preferences of entrepreneurs toward each of 13 industries/sectors industry/sector are assessed and ranked. We identified the corporate entrepreneurs based on the Castrogiovanni et al. (2011) and Miles et al. (2003); Social entrepreneurs were chosen from the Austin et al. (2006) definition of the term; and finally, SME entrepreneurs were selected from those who successfully launched their businesses during the past three years.

Determining samples for the three types of entrepreneurs was a challenging and time-consuming job. In this study, snowball sampling was used. As Heckathorn (2002) discusses, snowball sampling or chain sampling is a non-probability sampling that is appropriate for identifying the hidden populations. By deploying Snowball sampling 35 entrepreneurs were identified - 11 of them were corporate entrepreneurs, 12 social entrepreneurs; and 12 SME entrepreneurs. To prioritise industries/sectors, Analytic Hierarchy Process (AHP) was used.

### Analytic Hierarchy Process (AHP)

The AHP is coined by Saaty and widely known as a method for multi-criteria decision support (Durbach et al., 2014). AHP is a technique for decision-making that is widely manipulated for assessing typically multiple conflicting criteria. The technique also has been used for determining the performance of each alternative (Abdullah & Najib, 2014). AHP as a multiple criteria decision-making tool is an Eigen value method for the pair-wise comparisons. The range of the scale could be from 1 to 9; that 1 is used for equal, and 9 for absolutely more central ones (Vaidya & Kumar, 2006). Cay and Uyan (2013) describe the main steps of AHP as follows:

- A (n × n) pairwise comparison matrix should be created. The sample of such matrix is drawn below:

$$A = \begin{bmatrix} a_{11} & a_{12} & \cdots & a_{1n} \\ a_{21} & a_{22} & \cdots & a_{2n} \\ \vdots & \vdots & \vdots & \vdots \\ a_{n1} & a_{n2} & \cdots & a_{nn} \end{bmatrix} \quad (1)$$

The $a_{ij}$ specifies to what extent important the $i^{th}$ objective is with regards to the $j^{th}$ objective. It is necessary for all $i$ as well as $j$, that $a_{ii}$ equals to 1 and $a_{ij}$ equals $1/a_{ji}$. As Table 4 shows, for evaluating the value of $a_{ij}$ the pairwise comparison matrix can be used.

## Intermediate Values

- Then, each value in column $j$ should be divided by the total values of the column j. As a result, a new $A_w$ matrix will be generated, so the normalised pairwise comparison matrix is found, as shown below:

$$A_w = \begin{bmatrix} \frac{a_{11}}{\sum a_{i1}} & \frac{a_{12}}{\sum a_{i2}} & \cdots & \frac{a_{in}}{\sum a_{in}} \\ \cdots & \cdots & \cdots & \cdots \\ \cdots & \cdots & \cdots & \cdots \\ \frac{a_{n1}}{\sum a_{i1}} & \frac{a_{n2}}{\sum a_{i2}} & \cdots & \frac{a_{nn}}{\sum a_{in}} \end{bmatrix} \quad (2)$$

- Then we calculated $c_i$ as the mean of the values in the row of $i$ of $A_w$ matrix to generate the column vector $C$. Furthermore, $c_i$ value displays the relative degree of weight of the $i^{th}$ objectives.

*Table 4. AHP evaluation scale*

| **Numerical Value of aij** | **1** | **3** | **5** | **7** | **9** | **2, 4, 6, 8** |
|---|---|---|---|---|---|---|
| Definition | Equal importance of i over j | Moderate importance of i over j | Strong importance of i over j | Very strong importance of i over j | Extreme importance of i over j | Intermediate values |

Cay & Uyan, 2013.

$$C = \begin{bmatrix} c_1 \\ c_2 \\ \vdots \\ c_n \end{bmatrix} = \begin{bmatrix} \frac{\frac{a_{11}}{\sum a_{i1}} + \frac{a_{12}}{\sum a_{i2}} + \cdots + \frac{a_{in}}{\sum a_{in}}}{n} \\ \cdots \quad \cdots \quad \cdots \quad \cdots \\ \cdots \quad \cdots \quad \cdots \quad \cdots \\ \frac{\frac{a_{n1}}{\sum a_{i1}} + \frac{a_{n2}}{\sum a_{i2}} + \cdots + \frac{a_{nn}}{\sum a_{in}}}{n} \end{bmatrix} \tag{3}$$

- For the aim of assessing the consistency of the weight values ($c_i$), first the A×C matrix should be calculated. The sample of A×C matrix is drawn below. for calculating the $x_i$, the A matrix should be multiplied at C matrix.

$$A \times C = \begin{bmatrix} a_{11} & a_{12} & \cdots & a_{1n} \\ a_{21} & a_{22} & \cdots & a_{2n} \\ \vdots & \vdots & \vdots & \vdots \\ a_{n1} & a_{n2} & \cdots & a_{nn} \end{bmatrix} \times \begin{bmatrix} c_1 \\ c_2 \\ \vdots \\ c_n \end{bmatrix} = \begin{bmatrix} x_1 \\ x_2 \\ \vdots \\ x_n \end{bmatrix} \tag{4}$$

After achieving the A×C matrix the $\lambda_{max}$ by using of the following formula is calculated:

$$\lambda_{max} = \frac{1}{n} \sum_{i=1}^{n} \frac{x_i}{c_i} \tag{5}$$

By calculating the $\lambda_{max}$, the Consistency Index (CI) can be considered according to the following formula:

$$CI = \frac{\lambda_{max} - n}{n - 1} \tag{6}$$

- In the final step, to make sure about consistency of the pairwise comparison matrix the consistency has to be checked. For this, CR can be calculated based on the following formula. CR is known as Consistency Rate.

$$CR = \frac{CI}{RI} \tag{7}$$

Because of the number of the criteria – 13 industries/sectors – that have been used in this research we had to follow the RI table values of Yavuz et al. (2008), that is drawn in Table 5, and also it is noted that all of the RI values are developed based on the Saaty (1990) consumptions of AHP.

*Table 5. RI table values*

| n | 1 | 2 | 3 | 4 | 5 | 6 | 7 | 8 | 9 | 10 | 11 | 12 | 13 |
|---|---|---|---|---|---|---|---|---|---|---|---|---|---|
| RI | 0.00 | 0.00 | 0.58 | 0.90 | 1.12 | 1.24 | 1.32 | 1.41 | 1.45 | 1.49 | 1.51 | 1.48 | 1.56 |

Yavuz et al., 2008.

## Data Collection and Analysis

By snowball sampling a total of 35 entrepreneurs were identified. For corporate entrepreneurship, the total of 7 questionnaires were collected, for social entrepreneurship the total of 8 questionnaires collected, and for the SME entrepreneurship 9 questionnaires were gathered for analysis (the total of 24 collected questionnaires). The other 11 entrepreneurs' questionnaires were discarded because of the unfilled and inappropriate co-operation with the researchers. Also based on the group aggregation procedures a geometric mean has been used. As mentioned, the Consistency Rate for the pair-wise comparison matrixes should be lower than 0.1. These rates for corporate entrepreneurship, social entrepreneurship, and SME entrepreneurship were 0.0767; 0.0305; 0.0952, respectively. Table 6 shows the achieved weights and ranks by industries/sectors for each entrepreneurship.

The cylinder chart of the achieved ranks and weights for each industry/sector based on the three types of entrepreneurship are presented in Figure 1.

*Table 6. The achieved weights and ranks by industries/sectors*

| **Industries/Sectors** | **Corporate Entrepreneurship** | | **Social Entrepreneurship** | | **SME Entrepreneurship** | |
|---|---|---|---|---|---|---|
| | **Weights** | **Ranks** | **Weights** | **Ranks** | **Weights** | **Ranks** |
| Accommodation and Residence | 0.031 | 12 | 0.042 | 9 | 0.181 | **1** |
| Agriculture and Animal Husbandry | 0.029 | 10 | 0.088 | 5 | 0.047 | 9 |
| Energy | 0.145 | **3** | 0.031 | 11 | 0.045 | 10 |
| Enterprise, Manufacture, Production | 0.171 | **1** | 0.033 | 10 | 0.065 | 8 |
| Entertainment, Media, Recreation and Sports | 0.041 | 8 | 0.055 | 6 | 0.120 | **2** |
| Environment | 0.018 | 13 | 0.228 | **1** | 0.040 | 12 |
| Finance and Insurance | 0.066 | 6 | 0.028 | 12 | 0.074 | 6 |
| Healthcare and Life Science | 0.051 | 7 | 0.137 | **3** | 0.091 | 4 |
| Information and Communication Technology (ICT) | 0.128 | 4 | 0.043 | 8 | 0.105 | **3** |
| Military and Defence | 0.088 | 5 | 0.027 | 13 | 0.040 | 11 |
| Public Administration, Governmental and Public Safety | 0.029 | 11 | 0.150 | **2** | 0.035 | 13 |
| Research and Education | 0.037 | 9 | 0.089 | 4 | 0.087 | 5 |
| Transportation and Retail | 0.165 | **2** | 0.050 | 7 | 0.070 | 7 |

*Figure 1.*

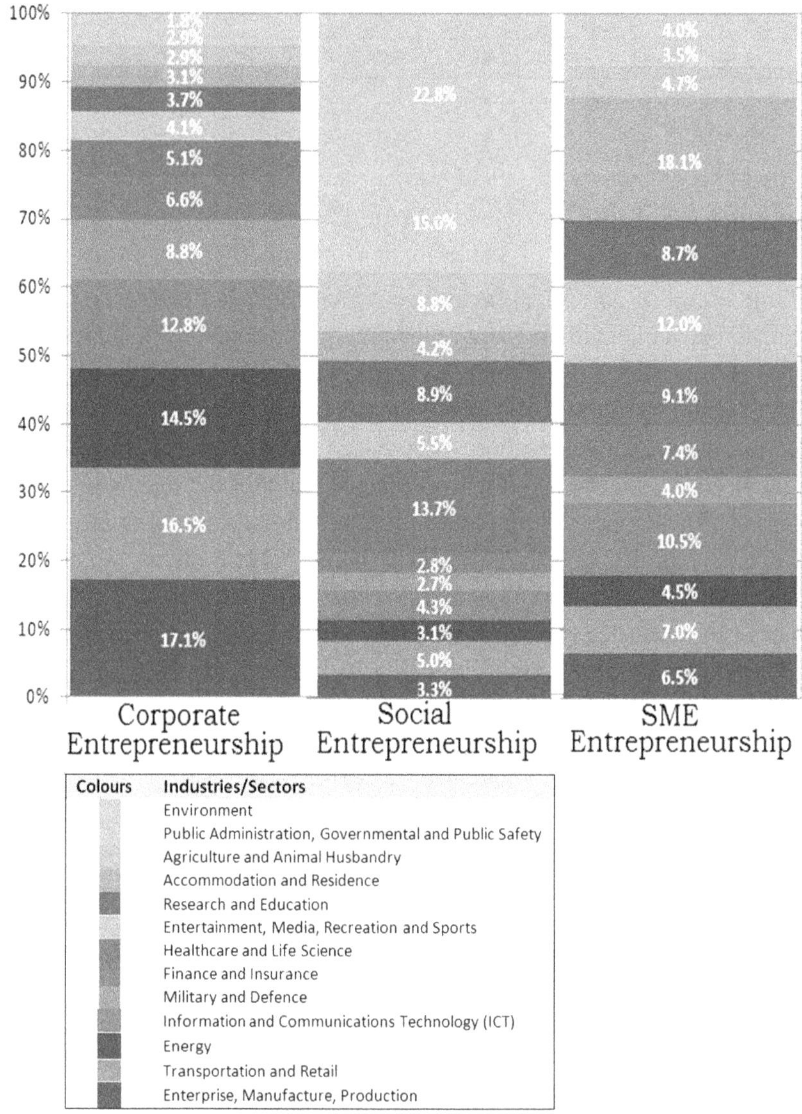


## DISCUSSION AND CONCLUSION

### Corporate Entrepreneurs

Our results show that corporate entrepreneurs have ranked the industries/sectors as follows: 1) Enterprise, Manufacture, Production, 2) Transportation and Retail, 3) Energy, and 4) Information and Communication Technology (ICT). These industries/sectors need a heavy financial investment and strong R&D units, which are completely congruent with the nature of corporate entrepreneurship.

On the one hand, corporate entrepreneurs are among the real assets of organisations. On the other hand, they have simply been affected from the organisational culture and social capital of organisations. As a result, those organisations which try to be the pioneer of a IoT market have to promote entrepreneurial culture through various ways (e.g., encouraging employees to be aware about the abilities and applications of the IoT). In this regard, developing an appropriate rewarding system is important as well.

Resource availability has been known to positively influence a firm's entrepreneurial activities within the R&D units. Thus, corporate entrepreneurs should be given an opportunity to act entrepreneurially by experimenting and launching IoT prototypes in the market.

## Social Entrepreneurs

Social entrepreneurs have ranked the industries/sectors as follows: 1) Environment, 2) Public Administration, Governmental and Public Safety, and 3) Healthcare and Life Science. These industries/sectors need high level of social capitals and really make sense with the nature of social entrepreneurship, since they have been among the best sources of social ventures. Social capital has had an important role for all kinds of entrepreneurship, especially for social entrepreneurs, due to the fact that their social missions are deeply rooted in their social and cultural background. To gain these capitals, broadening the entrepreneurial networks can be proposed as a strategy. These networks can even be a great source of crowdfunding.

## SME Entrepreneurs

SME entrepreneurs have ranked the industries/sectors as follows: 1) Accommodation and Residence, 2) Entertainment, Media, Recreation and Sports, and 3) Information and Communications Technology (ICT). Smartness is one of the main features of the IoT in accommodation and residence sector. Developing smart home applications can be a good investment for an SME.

In this study, we examined Iranian entrepreneurs and Iran is known as a transition economy. The entrepreneurial reactions toward new technologies can vary from one economy to another. Global Entrepreneurship Monitor (GEM) declares that it is not applicable to deliver one specific prescriptive policy to all regions in term of promoting entrepreneurship (Kelley et al., 2011). Etemad (1999) argues in developing countries such as Iran low protections have been received by SMEs from governments. Our study needs to be extended to the other countries such as the innovation-driven ones to generalise our findings.

In spite of the relative maturity of the IoT in the developed world, the Iranian IoT is still in infancy. According to the Moore's (1993) evolutionary stages of business ecosystems, it can be argued that the Iranian IoT-business ecosystem is in the stages between birth and expansion. The Iranian entrepreneurs who have wanted to generate value from the IoT should take the following challenges into account.

In the birth and expansion stages of the IoT-business ecosystem they have two main challenges, which are cooperative and competitive challenges.

- In the birth stage of the IoT-business ecosystem entrepreneurs have to "Work with customers and suppliers to define the new value proposition around a seed innovation." To overcome cooperative challenges, entrepreneurs have to "Protect your [their] ideas from others who might be working toward defining similar offers. Tie up critical lead customers, key suppliers, and important channels." (Moore, 1993).
- In the expansion stage of the IoT-business ecosystem entrepreneurs have to "Bring the new offer to a large market by working with suppliers and partners to scale up supply and to achieve maximum market coverage." To overcome competitive challenges, entrepreneurs have to "Defeat alternative implementations of similar ideas. Ensure that your approach is the market standard in its class through dominating key market segments." (Moore, 1993).

## REFERENCES

Abdullah, L., & Najib, L. (2014). A new type-2 fuzzy set of linguistic variables for the fuzzy analytic hierarchy process. *Expert Systems with Applications*, *41*(7), 3297–3305. doi:10.1016/j.eswa.2013.11.028

Akyildiz, I. F., Su, W., Sankarasubramaniam, Y., & Cayirci, E. (2002). A survey on sensor networks. *IEEE Communications Magazine*, *40*(8), 102–114. doi:10.1109/MCOM.2002.1024422

Al-Turjman, F. M., Al-Fagih, A. E., Alsalih, W. M., & Hassanein, H. S. (2013). A delay-tolerant framework for integrated RSNs in IoT. *Computer Communications*, *36*(9), 998–1010. doi:10.1016/j.comcom.2012.07.001

Antoncic, B., & Hisrich, R. D. (2004). Corporate entrepreneurship contingencies and organizational wealth creation. *Journal of Management Development*, *23*(6), 518–550. doi:10.1108/02621710410541114

Atzori, L., Iera, A., & Morabito, G. (2010). The internet of things: A survey. *Computer Networks*, *54*(15), 2787–2805. doi:10.1016/j.comnet.2010.05.010

Atzori, L., Iera, A., & Morabito, G. (2014). From" smart objects" to" social objects": The next evolutionary step of the internet of things. *IEEE Communications Magazine*, *52*(1), 97–105. doi:10.1109/MCOM.2014.6710070

Austin, J., Stevenson, H., & Wei-Skillern, J. (2006). Social and commercial entrepreneurship: Same, different, or both? *Entrepreneurship Theory and Practice*, *30*(1), 1–22. doi:10.1111/j.1540-6520.2006.00107.x

Biniari, M. G. (2012). The emotional embeddedness of corporate entrepreneurship: The case of envy. *Entrepreneurship Theory and Practice*, *36*(1), 141–170. doi:10.1111/j.1540-6520.2010.00437.x

Blanter, A., & Holman, M. (2014). Internet of Things 2020: A Glimpse into the Future. Last Access at https://www.atkearney.com/documents/4634214/6398631/A.T.+Kearney_Internet+of+Things+2020+Presentation_Online.pdf/af7e6a55-cde2-4490-8066-a95664efd35a

Castrogiovanni, G. J., Urbano, D., & Loras, J. (2011). Linking corporate entrepreneurship and human resource management in SMEs. *International Journal of Manpower*, *32*(1), 34–47. doi:10.1108/01437721111121215

Cay, T., & Uyan, M. (2013). Evaluation of reallocation criteria in land consolidation studies using the Analytic Hierarchy Process (AHP). *Land Use Policy*, *30*(1), 541–548. doi:10.1016/j.landusepol.2012.04.023

Chui, M., Löffler, M., & Roberts, R. (2010). The internet of things. *The McKinsey Quarterly*, *2*, 1–9.

Cuervo-Cazurra, A., & Ramos, M. (2005). Explaining the process of internationalization by building bridges among existing models. In S. W. Floyd, J. Roos, C. D. Jacobs, & F. W. Kellermanns (Eds.), *Innovating strategy processes*. Wiley & Sons.

Durbach, I., Lahdelma, R., & Salminen, P. (2014). The analytic hierarchy process with stochastic judgements. *European Journal of Operational Research*, *238*(2), 552–559. doi:10.1016/j.ejor.2014.03.045

Etemad, H. (1999). Globalization and the small and medium-sized enterprises: Search for potent strategies. *Global Focus*, *11*(3), 85–104.

Ferreira, J. (2001). Corporate entrepreneurship: A strategic and structural perspective. *New England Journal of Entrepreneurship*, *4*(2), 59.

Glaser, B. G., & Strauss, A. L. (1967). *The discovery of grounded theory*. London: Weidenfeld and Nicholson.

Gluhak, A., Krco, S., Nati, M., Pfisterer, D., Mitton, N., & Razafindralambo, T. (2011). A survey on facilities for experimental internet of things research. *IEEE Communications Magazine*, *49*(11), 58–67. doi:10.1109/MCOM.2011.6069710

Grand View Research. (2016). IoT Market Analysis By Component (Devices, Connectivity, IT Services, Platforms), By Application (Consumer Electronics, Retail, Manufacturing, Transportation, Healthcare) And Segment Forecasts To 2022. Last access at http://www.grandviewresearch.com/industry-analysis/iot-market

Gubbi, J., Buyya, R., Marusic, S., & Palaniswami, M. (2013). Internet of Things (IoT): A vision, architectural elements, and future directions. *Future Generation Computer Systems*, *29*(7), 1645–1660. doi:10.1016/j.future.2013.01.010

He, W., Yan, G., & Xu, L. D. (2014). Developing vehicular data cloud services in the IoT environment. *IEEE Transactions on Industrial Informatics*, *10*(2), 1587–1595. doi:10.1109/TII.2014.2299233

Heckathorn, D. D. (2002). Respondent-driven sampling II: Deriving valid population estimates from chain-referral samples of hidden populations. *Social Problems*, *49*(1), 11–34. doi:10.1525/sp.2002.49.1.11

Jara, A. J., Zamora, M. A., & Skarmeta, A. F. (2011). An internet of things–based personal device for diabetes therapy management in ambient assisted living (AAL). *Personal and Ubiquitous Computing*, *15*(4), 431–440. doi:10.1007/s00779-010-0353-1

Jing, T., Dancheng, L., & Ye, Z. (2016). Study of Impact on Undergraduates Entrepreneurial Failure based on the Model of Psychological Resilience-Knowledge Acquisition. *English Language Teaching*, *9*(8), 224. doi:10.5539/elt.v9n8p224

Jones, G. R., & Butler, J. E. (1992). Managing internal corporate entrepreneurship: An agency theory perspective. *Journal of Management*, *18*(4), 733–749. doi:10.1177/014920639201800408

Jones, M. V., Coviello, N., & Tang, Y. K. (2011). International entrepreneurship research (1989–2009): A domain ontology and thematic analysis. *Journal of Business Venturing*, *26*(6), 632–659. doi:10.1016/j.jbusvent.2011.04.001

Kelley, D., Bosma, N. S., & Amorós, J. E. (2011). Global Entrepreneurship Monitor 2010 Executive Report. Last access at http:// www.gemconsortium.org

Kirzner, I. M. (1985). *Discovery and the capitalist process*. University of Chicago Press.

Konomi, S. I., & Roussos, G. (2007). Ubiquitous computing in the real world: Lessons learnt from large scale RFID deployments. *Personal and Ubiquitous Computing*, *11*(7), 507–521. doi:10.1007/s00779-006-0116-1

Kortuem, G., Kawsar, F., Sundramoorthy, V., & Fitton, D. (2010). Smart objects as building blocks for the internet of things. *IEEE Internet Computing*, *14*(1), 44–51. doi:10.1109/MIC.2009.143

Kuratko, D. F., Hornsby, J. S., Naffziger, D. W., & Montagno, R. V. (1993). Implementing entrepreneurial thinking in established organizations. *SAM Advanced Management Journal*, *58*(1), 28.

Lasch, F. (2011). Beyond the concept of human and social capital: The impact of the regional environment on high-tech venturing. *International Journal of Entrepreneurship and Small Business*, *14*(1), 56–76. doi:10.1504/IJESB.2011.042163

Lin, B. W., Li, P. C., & Chen, J. S. (2006). Social capital, capabilities, and entrepreneurial strategies: A study of Taiwanese high-tech new ventures. *Technological Forecasting and Social Change*, *73*(2), 168–181. doi:10.1016/j.techfore.2004.12.001

Lin, C. (1998). Success factors of small-and medium-sized enterprises in Taiwan: An analysis of cases. *Journal of Small Business Management*, *36*(4), 43–56.

Liñán, F. (2008). Skill and value perceptions: How do they affect entrepreneurial intentions? *The International Entrepreneurship and Management Journal*, *4*(3), 257–272. doi:10.1007/s11365-008-0093-0

Liñán, F., & Chen, Y. W. (2009). Development and Cross-Cultural application of a specific instrument to measure entrepreneurial intentions. *Entrepreneurship Theory and Practice*, *33*(3), 593–617. doi:10.1111/j.1540-6520.2009.00318.x

Lumpkin, G. T., & Dess, G. G. (1996). Clarifying the entrepreneurial orientation construct and linking it to performance. *Academy of Management Review*, *21*(1), 135–172.

Mazanai, M., & Fatoki, O. (2012). Access to finance in the SME sector: A South African perspective. *Asian Journal of Business Management*, *4*(1), 58–67.

McDougall, P. P. (1989). International versus domestic entrepreneurship: New venture strategic behavior and industry structure. *Journal of Business Venturing*, *4*(6), 387–400. doi:10.1016/0883-9026(89)90009-8

Miles, M. P., Paul, C. W., & Wilhite, A. (2003). Modeling corporate entrepreneurship as rent-seeking competition. *Technovation*, *23*(5), 393–400. doi:10.1016/S0166-4972(02)00156-6

Miorandi, D., Sicari, S., De Pellegrini, F., & Chlamtac, I. (2012). Internet of things: Vision, applications and research challenges. *Ad Hoc Networks*, *10*(7), 1497–1516. doi:10.1016/j.adhoc.2012.02.016

Moore, J. F. (1993). Predators and prey: A new ecology of competition. [PubMed]. *Harvard Business Review*, *71*(3), 75–83.

Perera, C., Zaslavsky, A., Christen, P., & Georgakopoulos, D. (2014). Context aware computing for the internet of things: A survey. *IEEE Communications Surveys and Tutorials*, *16*(1), 414–454. doi:10.1109/SURV.2013.042313.00197

Purwaningsih, A. (2015). Analysis of customer mindset change and accounting practice of garbage bank as medium of edupreneurship. *International Journal of Monetary Economics and Finance*, *8*(4), 332–344. doi:10.1504/IJMEF.2015.073228

Rey-Martí, A., Ribeiro-Soriano, D., & Sánchez-García, J. L. (2016). Giving back to society: Job creation through social entrepreneurship. *Journal of Business Research*, *69*(6), 2067–2072. doi:10.1016/j.jbusres.2015.12.010

Saaty, T. L. (1990). How to make a decision: The analytic hierarchy process. *European Journal of Operational Research*, *48*(1), 9–26. doi:10.1016/0377-2217(90)90057-I

Shepherd, D. A., Covin, J. G., & Kuratko, D. F. (2009). Project failure from corporate entrepreneurship: Managing the grief process. *Journal of Business Venturing*, *24*(6), 588–600. doi:10.1016/j.jbusvent.2008.01.009

Statista. (2016). Revenue of the Internet of Things in Japan from 2013 to 2020 (in billion U.S. dollars). Last access at http://www.statista.com/statistics/512254/iot-revenue-japan

TCS. (2016). Enterprise Insights. Last access at http://sites.tcs.com/blogs/enterpriseinsights/establishing-iot-strategy

Thiesse, F., & Köhler, M. (2008). An Analysis of Usage-Based Pricing Policies for Smart Products. *Electronic Markets*, *18*(3), 232–241. doi:10.1080/10196780802265751

Tsai, C. W., Lai, C. F., Chiang, M. C., & Yang, L. T. (2014). Data mining for internet of things: A survey. *IEEE Communications Surveys and Tutorials*, *16*(1), 77–97. doi:10.1109/SURV.2013.103013.00206

Vaidya, O. S., & Kumar, S. (2006). Analytic hierarchy process: An overview of applications. *European Journal of Operational Research*, *169*(1), 1–29. doi:10.1016/j.ejor.2004.04.028

Vermesan, O., & Friess, P. (2013). *Internet of Things: From Research and Innovation to Market Deployment*. River Publishers.

Vermesan, O., Friess, P., Guillemin, P., Gusmeroli, S., Sundmaeker, H., Bassi, A., & Doody, P. (2011). Internet of Things Strategic Research Roadmap. In O. Vermesan & P. Friess (Eds.), *Internet of Things - Global Technological and Societal Trends*. River Publishers.

Weber, R. H. (2009). Internet of things–Need for a new legal environment? *Computer Law & Security Report*, *25*(6), 522–527. doi:10.1016/j.clsr.2009.09.002

Wu, Q., Ding, G., Xu, Y., Feng, S., Du, Z., Wang, J., & Long, K. (2014). Cognitive internet of things: A new paradigm beyond connection. *IEEE Internet of Things Journal*, *1*(2), 129–143. doi:10.1109/JIOT.2014.2311513

Xu, L. D., He, W., & Li, S. (2014). Internet of things in industries: A survey. *IEEE Transactions on Industrial Informatics*, *10*(4), 2233–2243. doi:10.1109/TII.2014.2300753

Xu, N. (2002). A survey of sensor network applications. *IEEE Communications Magazine*, *40*(8), 102–114. doi:10.1109/MCOM.2002.1024422

Yavuz, M., Iphar, M., & Once, G. (2008). The optimum support design selection by using AHP method for the main haulage road in WLC Tuncbilek colliery. *Tunnelling and Underground Space Technology*, *23*(2), 111–119. doi:10.1016/j.tust.2007.02.001

Yu, T. F.-L. (2001). Towards a theory of the entrepreneurial state. *International Journal of Social Economics*, *28*(9), 752–766. doi:10.1108/EUM0000000005692

Zahra, S. A. (1991). Predictors and financial outcomes of corporate entrepreneurship: An exploratory study. *Journal of Business Venturing*, *6*(4), 259–285. doi:10.1016/0883-9026(91)90019-A

Zarei, M., Mohammadian, A., & Ghasemi, R. (2016). Internet of Things in Industries: A Survey for Sustainable Development. *International Journal of Innovation and Sustainable Development*, *10*(4), 419–442. doi:10.1504/IJISD.2016.079586

Zheng, J., Simplot-Ryl, D., Bisdikian, C., & Mouftah, H. T. (2011). The internet of. *IEEE Communications Magazine*, *49*(11), 30–31. doi:10.1109/MCOM.2011.6069706

Zhou, C., & Peng, X. M. (2008). The entrepreneurial university in China: Nonlinear paths. *Science & Public Policy*, *35*(9), 637–646. doi:10.3152/030234208X363187

## KEY TERMS AND DEFINITIONS

**Analytic Hierarchy Process (AHP):** A method for multi-criteria decision support and a technique for decision-making that is widely applied for assessing typically multiple conflicting criteria and determining the performance of each alternative.

**Corporate Entrepreneurship:** A corporate process that aims to increase innovation and performance of an established organisation through various ways and techniques such as: renewing strategies, increasing the competitiveness; finding new raw materials, improving the processes, exploring a new market, starting-up a spin-off, etc.

**Internet of Things (IoT):** A technological paradigm that aims to grow our knowledge from our business environments, by gathering and computing data through heterogeneous and unique embedded devices on various networks.

**IoT-Business Ecosystem:** An advanced cross-industry interactions, exchanges, and networks among all the actors of IoT value chain consist of suppliers, producers, and competitors.

**SME Entrepreneurship:** SME entrepreneurship is known as a kind of entrepreneurship that is frequently discussed as the act of starting a new business. All entrepreneurial start-ups to some extent have developed under uncertainty and some other limitations.

**Social Entrepreneurship:** A kind of entrepreneurship that concentrates on solving social problems and generating economic values simultaneously.

# Chapter 9
# The Internet of Things: Opportunities, Issues, and Challenges

**Edward T. Chen**
*University of Massachusetts – Lowell, USA*

## ABSTRACT

*The Internet of Things (IoT) has the potential to increase quality of life, heighten performance of systems and processes, and save valuable time for businesses and people. Common objects and devices are being linked with Internet connectivity and have capabilities for data analytics that affect day-to-day experiences of both individuals and businesses. The notions of Smart Health, Smart Cities, and Smart Living come into play as the Internet of Things plays a role in today's world. This chapter presents IoT devices and application examples as well as descriptions of the benefits and limitations alongside an assessment of each respective technology's potential for success in the future. Security and privacy are important factors that need to be addressed within the different domains. This chapter addresses these potentials, issues, and challenges for managers to be prepared for the new wave brought forth by the IoT.*

## INTRODUCTION

The phrase "Internet of Things" (IoT) was first introduced by Kevin Ashton in 1999 (Ashton, 2009). Ashton was a product manager at Oil of Olay where a popular lipstick was often out of stock. After investigating the reasons why, he found a problem within the supply chain that led him to drive the development of the RFID label. He used the term "Internet of Things" to describe how the RFID labels would connect an "object" to the Internet. At that time, there were more questions than answers to the IoT concept including how would everything be connected? What could be built into devices to enable it to communicate wireless? How would the infrastructure need to change in order to support the communication of billions of devices? What would power them? How would this be done cost effectively?

Today many of these problems have been addressed (Umar, 2005; Xu, He, & Li, 2014). Wireless technology has gotten smaller and less expensive. Wi-Fi and cellular wireless connectivity is being built into many devices (Li & Xiong, 2013; Jo, Paik, & Lee, 2014). Networks are offering broadband speeds and mobile data coverage is widespread. What exactly is the IoT? It is described as a network of "things"

DOI: 10.4018/978-1-5225-2104-4.ch009

including people-people, people-things, and things-things connected to the Internet either through wireless or wired Internet connections (Dorsemaine, Gaulier, Wary, Kheir, & Urien, 2016).

The IoT is intended to do the following:

- Connect both inanimate and living things. Any device with an on and off switch can be connected to the Internet and/or to each other. Examples include cell phones, coffee makers, washing machines, headphones, lamps, wearable devices (e.g., fitbit), etc. They can also include living objects. Your refrigerator may know what you want to eat based on your weight loss plan or the time of day you arrive home (Xiao, Guo, Xu, & Gong, 2014).
- Use sensors for data collection. The objects will contain sensors that will collect data such as motion, location, vibration, and temperature (Ding, Cooper, Pasquina, Fici-Pasquina, 2011). Further, these sensors will connect with each other and to systems to make sense of the data or at least present the data from the sensors (Albrecht & Michael, 2013). As a result, people or companies will have a lot of new information (Li & Xiong, 2013).
- Allow equipment to communicate. Now objects can communicate with each other (Ding et al., 2011; Albrecht & Michael, 2013). Imagine your alarm clock goes off at 5:00 a.m. than notifies your coffee pot to start brewing coffee. Or in the office, they automatically re-order when supplies run low.
- The Internet of Things (IoT) is a prominent topic in today's world of technology that is constantly growing and evolving. This is a concept in which everyday objects are connected to the Internet, allowing them to send and receive data. In order for the IoT framework to be successful, wireless networks are essential because sensors need to be able to link without the limitations of physical wiring. The benefits are almost infinite as IoT devices and applications are altering the ways that people live and work on a day-to-day basis by saving time, making resources more efficient, and opening new doors to development and innovation. The far-reaching use of IoT products and devices shows the high capacities of automated home and work appliances, energy management, health monitoring gadgets, enhanced traffic systems, and countless more improvements within institutions and cities.
- The ultimate goal of IoT is to enable things to be connected at any time or place, by anything or any person who is using the network. Moreover, CEO of Cisco, Chuck Robbins, predicts that 50 billion devices will be connected to the Internet by 2020 (Vanian, 2015). The success of certain IoT devices will really be contingent on the ways that security and privacy matters are approached in the development stages as well as how those types of issues will be addressed if the concern becomes a reality. This paper will discuss and give examples of specific devices or applications used within the spectrum of Smart Health, Smart Cities, and Smart Living. Each section will give an overview of the industry, description of specific examples, and any further limitations or implications that it may have.
- As with the majority of information systems (IS), the Internet of Things depends on a variation of different hardware, software, and architectures. According to Whitmore, Agarwal, and Xu (2015), technology can be classified into three sub-categories. However, these are not exclusively separate from each other because architecture is developed and forms alongside software and hardware.
- In regards to hardware, the bulk of its foundation has already been around for some time now so this allows IoT to build upon its present framework. As Whitmore et al. (2015) illustrates, within the sub-sub-category of hardware, there are some important infrastructures to distinguish, such as

RFID (Radio-Frequency Identification), NFC (Near Field Communication) and Sensor Networks. Furthermore, software must continue to evolve by using middleware to sustain interoperability between various unrelated devices and examining the data produced by them. The domain for what application topics IoT can influence is virtually endless but all come with the trials of security and privacy that need to be addressed to safeguard IoT acceptance and dissemination. As previously noted, this research will focus primarily on matters of IoT in healthcare, within cities or municipalities, and the overall way of life in the midst of technology with an emphasis on the benefits and challenges of each.

## HOW DOES THE IoT WORK?

It all starts with "smart objects" which are objects that can communicate with people and other smart objects. It includes both physical interaction and virtual computing interaction. Smart objects are created when RFID tags or sensors are embedded into non-smart physical objects (Ashton, 2009). The IoT is not a technology within itself but a conglomerate of complementary technologies and capabilities that work together to bring together the virtual and physical world (Martin, 2015). These capabilities include:

- **Communication and Cooperation:** Wireless technologies including Wi-Fi and Bluetooth give objects the ability to network with the Internet.
- **Addressability:** Objects need to be located and addressed via discovery, look-up, or name services. Therefore, they can be interrogated or configured remotely.
- **Identification:** RFID, NFC (Near Field Communication), and optically readable bar codes uniquely identify objects so that data can be retrieved from a server related to the particular object. Assumes the object is connected to a network.
- **Sensing:** Information is recorded from objects with sensors; the object may forward the information or react directly to it.
- **Actuation:** Objects can manipulate their environment by converting energy into motion and control processes via the Internet.
- **Embedded Information Processing:** Processers and storage capacity can be used to process and interpret sensor information or give products a "memory" of how they are used.
- **Localization:** GPS, mobile phone networks, Ultra-Wide band or radio beacons allow objects to know their physical location or be located.
- **User Interfaces:** Allow objects to communicate with people i.e. smart phone.

## BUSINESS PROBLEMS THAT IoT IS INTENDED TO SOLVE

The IoT creates huge opportunities for the economy and individuals. The IoT has no boundaries and will impact every business and person. With new devices connecting into company's systems, new types of data will be accessible. At least three of the major benefits are communication, control, and cost savings which lead to transformed business processes, improved customer retention, new business models, and an increase in the quality of life. A study done by McKinsey Global Institute (2015) predicts that the IoT has potential economic impact of $3.9 trillion to $11.1 trillion per year in 2025 – the value of this impact would be equivalent to approximately 11% of the world economy in 2025. The study goes on to describe how the IoT will impact nine settings:

- **Human:** IoT impacts humans in two ways, health and fitness. Using connected devices patients with chronic conditions can be continuously monitored. Monitoring conditions can lead to increased adherence to prescribed therapies, and avoidance of hospitalizations. Remote services such as emergency detection and first aid can be used. Secondly, human productivity can be increased with technologies such as augmented-reality devices, job redesign or processes efficiencies, and allow mobile workers to be more connected.
- **Home:** There is a growing trend for IoT devices in the home including thermostats, appliances, and self-guided vacuum cleaners. Your refrigerator and cabinets may be able to talk to your phone and let you know what you need to buy at the grocery store. A thermostat could be linked to a garage door opener and adjust the temperature to that persons liking. Leading to chore automation, life-style improvement, energy management, and increased security.
- **Retail Environments:** Retailers can gain efficiencies in checkout automation, layout optimization, smart customer relationship management (CRM), in-store personalized promotions, and the prevention of inventory shrinkage. Resulting in increased customer satisfaction, revenue, profit, and working capital optimization.
- **Offices:** The main benefits are increased security, utility management, and improved productivity.
- **Factories**: Predicted to gain the largest value from productivity improvements including labor and energy, improvements in maintenance, working capital optimization, and employee health and safety.
- **Worksites:** Can benefit from operational improvements, improved equipment maintenance, and overall improvement in human health and safety.
- **Vehicles:** Monitor and improve the performance of planes, trains, and other vehicles. Your car can become a mobile hotspot allowing passengers to surf the web or watch a movie. Over the air updates can be downloaded to avoid visits to the dealership. Safety and security features can automatically alert emergency services when an accident occurs.
- **Cities:** Can benefit from the IoT in four main areas, transportation to manage traffic flow, public safety and health from increased air and water quality, resource management, and service delivery.
- **Outside:** Improve routing and tracking of ships, airplanes, and other vehicles.

## SMART HEALTH

### Overview

The old industry for health monitoring tools and machines were distinguished to be composed of various architectures that were commonly non-interoperable. Although some specific products nowadays are intended to be cost cognizant, the long-standing objective of reducing the current and future technology expenses within the medical field will inescapably be quite difficult to achieve unless a different approach can be implemented. The concept of IoT can be applied in medical care where patients that are hospitalized, whose physiological conditions involve frequent examinations and trips to the doctor's office, can be regularly observed by using unobtrusive IoT devices and applications. In order for this to occur, sensors must be able to gather comprehensive physiological data and utilize the cloud to evaluate and house the information to then transmit it wirelessly to a physician for further analysis and review.

According to Vermesan and Friess (2014), the commonalities among various applications in health monitoring contain the following features:

- The capacity to collect and record data by utilizing sensors.
- The ability to corroborate and maintain user interfaces and displays.
- Access to the Internet to connect infrastructural services.
- The overall competence of the application to be reliable, dependable, and accurate.

These functionalities enhance the quality of care of those that need it because monitoring can now occur around the clock at a reduced cost since the prior obligation of having caregivers collect and evaluate the data in person is no longer a requirement. Furthermore, another great benefit of using these IoT devices is that it can acquire the health information of a patient in a secure manner and evaluate the data based on the algorithms that have been set up. Lastly, after the devices' procedures are complete, there is the ability to share the information with the patient's doctor or physician, who can subsequently communicate the proper recommendations after reviewing the facts and figures.

## Examples of IoT Devices and Applications

The items described below are examples of IoT devices and applications in different domains that are all within the industry of Smart Health (Laplante & Laplante, 2016; Pang, 2013; Vermesan & Friess, 2014).

- **Devices That Detect When an Individual Has Fallen or Collapsed:** This can assist seniors or people with disabilities that are living autonomously.
- **Devices That Monitor Physical Activity:** there are many reasons for the need to collect and track vital signs, weight, blood pressure, and movement, or lack thereof. This could be done by using sensors on the body that will discreetly log the activity and transmit the data to be evaluated.
- **Devices That Control Medical Fridges:** Regulating the temperature and other settings inside freezers are very important, especially when those fridges are repositories for vaccines and other medications that are sensitive to their external conditions.
- **Devices That Are Used for Surveillance:** There can be a need to observe patients and their surroundings in hospitals, sanatoriums, nursing homes, or hospices.
- **Devices That Assist With Managing Chronic Diseases:** Patients who are living with chronic diseases can reduce their medical costs and their trips to the hospital by remotely transmitting their data for their medical professional to analyze.
- **Devices That Gauge UV Rays:** Computing ultraviolet radiation can permit individuals sensitive to that exposure a notice of caution during specific times of the day.
- **Devices That Regulate Hygiene:** In order to reduce the spreading of germs in hospital settings, RFID wristbands coupled with Bluetooth LE tags can assist with managing patient's hand hygiene. The tags on the doorway communicate with the wristbands by sending a vibration that alerts the individual wearing it that it's time for a hand wash. It also gathers data that could possibly track infections that spread from patients to specific healthcare employees.

- **Devices That Monitor Sleep:** In order to track breathing, heart rate, tossing, and other small or large motions, wireless sensors are positioned on the bed and deliver data that can be viewed on a smartphone.
- **Devices That Track Dental Routines:** A smart toothbrush that is connected via Bluetooth can track brushing habits and provide that information for the individual on the next dentist visit or simply to monitor for personal use.

## Chronic Disease Management

IoT devices have greatly assisted with patient-monitoring systems that allow patients suffering from chronic ailments, such as lung or heart diseases, to be evaluated from the comfort of their own homes. This improves their quality of life by reducing the unfavorable trips to the hospital or doctor's office that would have otherwise been mandatory. According to Pal (2015), in the United States, approximately 75 percent of healthcare dollars are expended towards chronic disease treatment and 2 out of every 3 people who are on Medicare suffer from at least 2 chronic diseases. The rising cost of healthcare and the pervasiveness of chronic diseases in this day and age demand the need for change that can only be accomplished with the help of technology. One specific IoT example is the AliveCor Heart Monitor which was cultivated by a cardiologist in Nebraska named Dr. David Albert. In 2008, he devised the concept of using the computing power of a smartphone to offer inexpensive medical care by making this compatible electrocardiogram (ECG) heart monitor, which is also FDA-approved, for over-the-counter use. The device is small, lightweight, and very easy to setup by downloading the app following the instructions to register and connect.

## Benefits of AliveCor Heart Monitor

It has been projected that in the subsequent decades to come there will be a transformation from the current "hospital-centered" practice to a different approach. First, it will come to be a "hospital-home-balanced" tactic in the 2020's and then ultimately to become a "home-centered" patient monitoring routine in 2030's (Moosavi et al., 2016). This important change obliges the fact that the merging and overlay of the IoT technologies and architectures for healthcare domains and "smart spaces" should become more keenly reflected. Moreover, the CEO of AliveCor, Euan Thomson, believes that as healthcare continues to develop, the rise of mobile health will shift into the typical method of care within the next 10 years. Mobile health has the capacity to facilitate data-driven healthcare which will, in turn, be able to assist with predicting as well as preventing adverse health circumstances and conditions. Thomson has confidence that it will undeniably influence the practice of medicine, but even more so the manner in which medical research is carried out (Fowler, 2014).

In conjunction with AliveCor's actual heart monitor comes the free app called Kardia (which means 'heart' in Greek) that records and houses single channel ECGs and is accessible for both Android and iOS. The patient is able to add detailed notes about their circumstance or symptoms and can then share those details with their doctor at no charge by simply printing or sending an email with the PDF attached. There is also another piece of functionality within AliveCor where a doctor can establish a "provider dashboard" to evaluate the ECG recordings from their patients even if they are overseas because it is a free web-based application.

## Limitations, Caveats, and Future Implications of Smart Heath

Even with all the benefits, the AliveCor Heart Monitor does have some limitations to consider. According to Mirsa (2015), one major caveat is that a single channel ECG does not specify all of the essential information needed for the evaluation of ischemia. Ischemia is a short supply of blood to a portion of the body caused by the blockage of an artery. Thus, it has technical limits in identifying many conditions. Another limitation is that the monitor cannot be used as an event recorder for all disorders of rhythm. Despite the fact that the AliveCor Heart Monitor can be used as a substitute for the standard 12 lead ECG or the Holter Monitor, there will still be instances when a patient will have no other choice but to take those respective tests because of these limitations.

For the technology industry overall, as more and more devices become perceptible due to IoT, the increase of risk to individual privacy becomes a more acute reality. Not only do people and organizations need to consider the risks and repercussions if their confidential information became exposed, but they also need to consider the balance of data ownership in order to encourage people to feel at ease while utilizing IoT. Additionally, the ownership of data accumulated from these devices must be manifestly determined and confirmed by ensuring that the personal information will not be used without consent. Whitmore, et al. (2015) describe that one method to safeguarding personal info could be implementing the use of privacy policies. IoT devices can be furnished to include private policies where the object and the reader can assess the other's privacy policy to make sure they are consistent and permitted to communicate.

Overall, the AliveCor Heart Monitor and associated Kardia app grant individuals who have heart conditions and require this type of technology with the capability to track heart health at an affordable price at any given time or place. Though there are known limitations in regards to the single lead ECG not being able to detect several conditions, the overall practicality and simplicity of the device will unlock new boundaries for data collection in cardiology. It is currently being used by numerous cardiologists to track and evaluate their patients who have atrial fibrillation, and in some situations, the expenses have even been covered by Medicare. It will be interesting to see how the AliveCor Heart Monitor alters the management of cardiac patients and what new IoT enhancements the company will bring in the future.

## SMART CITIES

### Overview

A smart city can be described as a developed urban area that is connected and monitors a wide variety of essential infrastructures to optimize resources, plan maintenance projects for preventative purposes, and create a balanced economic development while maximizing services to its residents (Vermesan & Friess, 2014). The infrastructure within the city can range from the roadways, train stations, tunnels, bridges, underground subways, and airports to even the power lines, water pipes, sewers, and overall means of communication. According to Hajduk (2016), the concept of a smart city was first brought up in 1994, but since 2011 it has been described more prevalently in journals and publications because of the endorsement from the European Union and the creation of projects within municipalities to promote a smart city model. This model would have three main components: people, organizations, and of course technology.

It is projected that by 2050, 70 percent of the people on this planet will reside in cities, and this indicates that more and more businesses will rely on the efficient inner workings of a city to gauge the means for their success or failure (Sundmaeker, Guillemin, Friess, & Woelffle, 2010).

In the case of a crisis within a city, whether it be an environmental or manufactured issue, emergency response management must be able to adhere to protocol. By having intricate monitoring systems and sensors that have been assembled around the city, facts and figures can be gathered and analyzed instantly, improving the decision-making process for the municipality. Picture the sensors on a bridge sending out a signal that the climate conditions are such that workers need to come spread salt at that particular time and section. Or maybe the need for inspectors can be reduced because sensors on buildings and other infrastructure can automatically determine if the structure is sound or has any vulnerability. The future goals and ambitions of a smart city could take it a step further and not only have the infrastructure evaluate its own conditions, but also self-renovate and restore as needed.

## Examples of IoT Devices and Applications

The items described below are examples of IoT devices and applications in different domains that are all within the industry of Smart Cities (Vermesan & Friess, 2014).

- **Devices That Assist With Parking:** The option to promptly check where there are currently available parking spaces in the area can help residents pinpoint and reserve the most convenient spot. Some benefits are a decrease of traffic blockages due to parking as well as a potential boost in revenue because parking prices can be computed to compete with the demand.
- **Devices That Help Determine the Structural Health of Infrastructure:** Automating the calculations of natural tremors or vibrations and the physical state of buildings and bridges is a proactive way to detect minor issues before they become hazardous.
- **Devices That Aid the Flow of Traffic:** An improvement in driving or walking conditions can be initiated by monitoring the concentrations of cars on the road and pedestrians on the sidewalks.
- **Smart Lighting:** Allowing the ability to conserve power by having street lights turn on only when there is movement or having lights that adapt to certain weather conditions.
- **Devices the Deal With the Handling of Waste:** Identifying if a trash bin needs to be emptied can increase efficiency for trash collecting workers. RFID tags permit sanitation teams the ability to monitor recycle bins and disposal. The implementation of "pay as you throw" initiatives within the city could potentially improve recycling endeavors.
- **Devices That Facilitate Transportation:** Creating infrastructure on roads and highways that can automatically detect and send out cautionary signals or detours can be crucial in emergency situations such as accidents or weather circumstances.
- **Devices That Contribute to the Safety of the City:** Some examples could be digital recording, fire control and public broadcast systems. According to Ryu (2015), organizing a fire emergency response system that uses IoT can decrease injuries and fatalities by pinpointing where the emergency is within in a building, effectively reducing the uncertainty of which direction to exit the building by triggering the appropriate lights and signals.
- **Devices That Improve Irrigation of Community Areas:** Wireless sensors can be concealed in the ground to monitor irrigation and assist with the maintenance of city commons and parks.

- **Devices That Promote Tourism:** Utilizing QR codes can provide appealing ways to explore the city, visit museums and attractions, and gather beneficial tourist information directly through a smartphone.

## Waste Management

Choosing just one of the above examples to elaborate on, waste management is one of the most difficult processes that cities in today's day and age have found ways to overcome and make more efficient. The United States alone produces about 230 million tons of garbage per day, averaging to approximately 4.6 pounds per individual living in this country (Rowley, 2016). Unfortunately, the majority of it is buried in landfills or burned and only less than one-fourth of the trash is actually recycled. Waste management entails several distinct procedures, starting from collecting and transporting the trash to discarding and monitoring the end result. Inclusively, this is an expensive and systematic practice in regards to time, labor, and cost. The money saved from making waste management more efficient can be allocated toward one of the many other issues a city needs to undertake.

There are several different groups who are concerned with waste in a smart city, including the recycling and manufacturing companies along with the city boards and committees that are associated with health and welfare. According to Perera, Zaslavsky, Christen, and Georgakopoulos (2014), utilizing the "Sensing-as-a-Service" framework, those organizations that are interested in monitoring waste can share the cost of implementing sensors and gathering the information together instead of individually. The most popular and key characteristic of such an alliance is the huge mitigation of cost that those groups would have had to otherwise pay for by themselves. All those who decide to collaborate can simultaneously obtain the information from the sensors to review and complete their own tasks.

## Challenges and Security Issues

In a smart city, the playing field is huge for any sort of security hack or privacy breach because there are countless of devices and cyber-physical things that are connected to each other and gather sensitive data, often without individual's explicit consent. An infringement of one piece of data security could incite a small portion to contaminate other systems and ultimately lead to the collapse of the entire system if not confined and dealt with appropriately. Overall, the citizens of a smart city need to be aware of the associated risk involved and should become well-informed of its components instead obliviously trusting the system without due diligence.

Another challenge is recognizing that the group efforts and partnerships with many public organizations to link infrastructure with IoT has, in a way, made them autonomous and that could lead to future security issues that will need to be addressed. According to Popescul and Radu (2016), the city government officials and authority need to be aware and conversant with all the issues that fall within the spectrum of IoT, including the connected devices and infrastructure and the privacy and security of the city's residents. There should be protocol in place from vetted security providers that have been reviewed and selected with perspicacity. There are many other tangents in respect to security and privacy. Therefore, future direction could lead to researching vulnerabilities and analyzing the current security measures in place as well as potential loopholes.

# SMART LIVING

## Overview

Home automation has always been an interesting element in science fiction literature for decades. However, since the progression and diffusion of technology, it has become a pragmatic reality across the world. In the simplest of descriptions, it is the automation of housework, appliances, or the overall activities within the home to provide convenience, security, and efficiency. According to Bhide (2014), home automation could consist of an integrated means of monitoring and regulating the use of power for AC, heat, lights and many other appliances. It could also aid people with disabilities or the elderly by providing an easier means of performing day to day tasks that otherwise would have to be completed by a caregiver. A smart home and the potential devices and appliances are connected to the Internet alongside the different service provider domains. Wi-Fi plays one of the most prevalent roles in home automation and smart living overall as the majority devices and appliances have become assimilated with smartphones and the home IP network.

## Examples of IoT Devices and Applications

The items described below are examples of IoT devices and applications in different domains that are all within the industry of Smart Living (Vermesan & Friess, 2014).

- **Applications That Simplify Shopping:** Whether it be buying items online or in person, the checkout or point of sale can enable recommendations based the consumer's previous preferences or behaviors. The applications could also alert the shopper if their purchase has any ingredients that they are allergic to as well as check the dates of expiration.
- **Devices That Monitor Energy, Gas, and Water Consumption:** The applications could also provide guidance on methods to reduce cost and conserve resources. Furthermore, replacing certain products such as light bulbs and thermostats to incorporate IoT could boost energy efficiency.
- **Smart Home Appliances:** Fridges and freezers that have the ability to transmit what food items are getting close to their expiration date, what foods the household is running low on and need to be replenished, and overall what food and ingredients are left to be cooked or consumed. Another example is washing machines that run automatically when energy rates are the lowest and having the ability to monitor this from afar. Furthermore, appliances in the kitchen that can interface to a phone-based app which can control self-cleaning settings or temperature.
- **Devices Used for Safety Monitoring:** Installing security alarm systems and cameras in and around the home. Baby monitoring could also be included in this category for when parents are in a different room and can still hear or see if their child cries out.
- **Wearable Sensors:** Carrying or wearing a type of Bluetooth enabled jewelry can assist children, elderly or anyone who needs help and activates the jewelry. This will send an alert and location to specific contacts within a smartphone.

## Home Automation: Belkin WeMo Light Switch

The entire home automation industry has a clear and concise IoT vision to make things, including the home, communicate each other. The WeMo Light Switch is replacing the traditional light switch by giving direct control of any one-way connection light from a smartphone, wherever people are positioned in the world (Geller, 2014). The WeMo device, which has a built-in energy usage meter, connects to the home network via Wi-Fi and is available with several options, such as the dimmable LED light bulb. In addition, Belkin's webcam has been improved with WeMo technology, plus a separate motion sensor. These devices can be used to trigger other WeMo devices. For example, if noise is detected from people in the back yard, the floodlight will instantly turn on.

The WeMo light switch is interesting in that is has some "If this then that" (IFTTT) recipes allow the lights to change based on the choice of events or arrangements made. Once the IFTTT feature from the menu is selected, users are able to create their own recipe using a PIN (Delaney, 2014). For example, a homeowner can set up the light to blink whenever their favorite team starts a game or, using the location from their smart phone, the porch lights will turn on when they get close to the house. A user can imagine nearly any recipe they want. The Belkin WeMo Light Switch facilitates control from the outside by homeowners and even works with "Amazon Alexa", in the way that the lights can respond to voice commands.

## Challenges and Security Issues

There is an overall technical issue that IoT devices are intrinsically inclined to have security weaknesses. On occasion, the Internet of Things has enticed negative publicity due to growing apprehensions over privacy and data security. According to Peppet (2014), small IoT devices such as routers, security cameras and smart TVs in the home were targeted by Internet hackers and the whole ordeal was uncovered by a security software company called Symantec Corporation. It was considered one of the first wide-ranging security breaches within the smart home industry that involved over one hundred thousand devices that were manipulated by hackers to distribute unsolicited and fraudulent emails.

Security in the cloud is an additional aspect of research that is critical and has been creating more awareness. Not only does it store indispensable information, it also manages the economics of the IoT to a certain degree, which makes this a broader security risk. As Gubbi, Buyya, Marusic, and Palaniswami (2013) stipulate, privacy and identity protection are even more important in hybrid clouds because that is where both private and public clouds are utilized by people and businesses. The concept of "remembering forever" within the framework of the Internet of Things is a challenge that induces privacy concerns because the stored data could be accessed and used for either constructive or destructive purposes. One course of direction for individuals and organizations concerned with this could be the notion of "digital forgetting," which is developing as one of the strategic fields of research to cope with the interest and improvement of different methods to safeguard personal information.

## LIMITATIONS OF IoT TECHNOLOGY

Though many enterprises are testing or implementing IoT services, they are experiencing challenges regarding connectivity and interoperability.

### Compatibility Issues

As almost a trillion of objects connected to the Internet, it will be important to have a solid architecture that allows accurate connectivity, communications, and control by use of applications (Akhbar, Chang, Yao, & Muñoz, 2016). It is questionable how all these different objects interact with each other correctly through applications. To provide this option, there should be an International standard of compatibility for monitoring objects and tagging. The manufacturing companies of devices/equipment need to be in compliance with an international standard, as devices from different manufacturers will be interconnected (Bandyopadhyay & Sen, 2011; Li, Xu, & Zhao, 2015; Pace, Aloi, Caliciuri, & Fortino, 2016).

Even after a common International standard adoption, technical issues could still exist due to complexity of IoT. All usage of complex systems brings more potential of failure and challenges. An adoption of Internet of Things on a large scale will require a large amount of data to be collected, stored, and processed (Martin, 2015).

### Complexity Issues

With vast amount of sensors in the marketplace, all of these connected devices will mean that data traffic will reach a level where there could be systems interference problems. Even though each application should solve its own errors, sensor sharing across simultaneously running applications might end up in some degree of disruptions (Thramboulidis, 2015).

As an example, let us think that a consumer receives a message stating that an item is expired in the fridge. All household each get the message and buy the item. This will result in extra spending. Or simply there may be an error in software that ends up ordering new item erroneously when it is not needed. After a simple power reset, a device might send the message again. The IoT is a diverse and complex network which any failure in the software or hardware might result in serious consequences.

### Sensor Energy

In order for IoT to reach to a high potential usage, sensors will need to be self-sustaining. It will be time consuming and very hard to charge all devices settled across the planet (Mishra, Gunasekaran, Childe, Papadopoulos, Dubey, & Wamba, 2016). What could be useful are sensors using electricity generated from environmental sources such as light, airflow, or vibrations (Tao, Zuo, Xu, & Lv, 2014).

## DOES IoT CREATE ANY NEW PROBLEMS?

Keeping vast amounts of data can also increase the risk of harm regarding to privacy and security of information collected (Mayer, 2009; Ning, Liu, & Yang, 2013). To answer if IoT is a complete solution or not, we should carefully examine its purpose and advantages and discuss if any disadvantages arise from it. While IoT brings these advantages and create vast amount of solutions for people and businesses, it is still at an early stage of development and also raise concerns about data privacy and safety (Roman, Najera, & Lopez, 2011).

### Increase of Privacy Concerns

With all of this IoT data being transmitted, the risk of violation of privacy increases. Data traveling across will carry sensitive information and should be encrypted. How will the well-encrypted data be kept and transmitted with? Consumers will most likely want to know, what information companies are collecting and if this information is shared with other parties. Just to name a few, from health information to financial information of individuals will be available to companies and an uncertainty on which information should be used and kept, and if it is beneficial or harmful to consumer privacy will have severe consequences (Mayer, 2009; Oppliger, 2011; Perera, Ranjan, Wang, Khan, & Zomaya, 2015).

### Increased Concerns on Safety of Data

On IoT devices a lack of security could provide intruders with access to use sensitive information collected, kept, and transmitted (Martin, 2015). What would be the result of information hacking? A hacker can reach extended level of information through connected devices and gather full scoop of knowledge about personal lives. An intruder can hack into a car's network could cause a car to crash. Security failure in a device can promote attacks on user's network and furthermore lead attacks on other systems. When household appliances or critical services such as water supply, gas, and electricity, and other devices connected to the Internet, very sensitive information is available. It would be very harmful if sensitive information is accessed by intruders (Perera, Zaslavsky, Christen, & Georgakopoulos, 2014).

### Potential Increase of Job Loss Due to Automation

With daily activities getting automated in consumer's life and changing businesses process models, there will be less need for unskilled workers. The unskilled workers might lose their jobs due to automation caused by IoT. This might increase unemployment in society. Even though this is inevitable with invention of any new technology that leads to automation, it will still be an issue from a social and economic perspective to be concerned (Ambasna-Jones, 2015; Spanjol, Tam, & Tam, 2015).

### Increased Dependency for Technology in Life

With all these new automation options and devices connecting/communicating to each other to perform functions we manually do, our lives will be increasingly controlled and will be dependent on IoT (Albrecht & Michael, 2013; Fuchs, 2014; Rainie & Wellman, 2012). How much of our lives we are willing to let technology to control and what it will bring to consumers in the future is an uncertainty that we will have to experience (Atzori, Iera, Morabito, & Nitti, 2012; Hillman, Withers, & Collins, 2009).

## Ethics, Rules, and Regulations

With the increase of IoT technologies and devises, businesses will have to create and operate within a new legal and regulatory landscape. IoT requires consumer information to be stored and be retrieved by relevant parties. Data traveling across businesses and consumers will be more sensitive. Thus, companies should identify carefully what information companies is collecting and to whom is shared with. Organizations should get prepared for new and changing rules, policies, and regulations that IoT will bring forth (Dutton, 2014).

## Managerial Implications

Enterprise applications of IoT will likely to become very important and will provide organizations with opportunity to increase efficiency and effectiveness of their operations. Managers focus on strategical and tactical issues to develop most effective and efficient approaches to achieve goals and manage challenges. IoT will create new markets for businesses and provide opportunities to gain competitive advantage. To minimize challenges and use IoT effectively, managers should understand how IoT works, analyze their institutions current situation and risk levels carefully. Some of the challenges that managers will face include leadership, staffing, ethics and regulations, interoperability, and cybersecurity.

## Managers Need to Know IoT

Handling huge amount of data is complex. When data is received from many different streaming devices, it is imperative for managers to know how to get data securely to the right place at the right time. When customer demands and requirements changes rapidly, managers should correctly analyze the reliability of data, how and when it is received to make correct decisions (Kaur & Sood, 2015; Li, Oikonomou, Tryfonas, Chen, & Xu, 2014). The value of streaming data creating new data and changing into valuable information to make decisions is a complicated task that managers should need to master to succeed (Atzori, Iera, & Morabito, 2010; Dutton, 2014).

## Managing Complexity: Developing Risk Tolerances

Developing solutions for the IoT requires good coordination, collaboration, and connectivity of each piece in the system. Before implementing IoT, managers should examine the current infrastructure of their organizations and examine risk and cost levels. IoT will be successfully implemented only if a platform can acquire and manage data on a standard-based scalable and secure platform (Pace et al., 2016). Creating business value will require an architecture that can deploy applications faster, process and analyze at high speeds since many components involved in the process. Interoperability and cybersecurity of systems and data is crucial since decisions, planning and actions might rely on data received and analyzed (Gerpott & May, 2016).

## Leadership

IoT is a new technology and ever-changing. Organizations will have advantage of gaining more ways to collect data and perform analysis to find solutions. The advancement of IoT enables new ways for businesses to increase performance and deliver new services (Brody & Pureswaran, 2015). This capability of firms will increase knowledge management (KM) systems to analyze and use information from many different aspects. Developing a better capacity of KM will provide companies with competitive advantage against competitors (Yu, Chen, & Nguyen, 2014).

## Staffing and Employment Preferences

As IoT emerges the business models and operations process will shift towards a level that aligns with IoT technology. This change will require companies to realign their workforce planning to match the demands of competition. Businesses will be requiring employees to understand, analyze, and operate under IoT model. Managers should consider focus on people and human systems finding the best way to maximize advantage what the IoT will offer (Westerlund, Leminen, & Rajahonka, 2014).

# OBSERVATIONS AND FUTURE DIRECTION

Throughout all the readings and research, one recurring notion that seemed to always come up and be acclaimed is that the Internet of Things has the potential to dramatically improve the lives of people and organizations through a wide variety of domains and aspects. The proficiencies accessible by the IoT not only can save individuals and businesses resources, but can also assist with making difficult assessments and decisions about a particular issue on hand. It is well known that IoT progresses on foundations that have already been built and enhances the way present technologies, like RFID and sensor networks, work and communicate with other devices. According to Whitmore et al. (2015), one future direction for IoT is the "Web of Things," which is a concept of using the World Wide Web to completely assimilate smart objects. This could enhance the interoperability of different devices in such a way that it would support developers to create applications in a much simpler way. Furthermore, some researchers suggest applying the Web 2.0 concept of a mashup, where an application taps into an assortment of web resources for information, but instead, harnessing it to physical devices rather than applications.

These discoveries initiate a few more personal observations and inquiries. For instance, it will be interesting to see if the Internet of Things will persevere in a world of ever-changing philosophies to become a permanent technology, or if it will evolve into a different paradigm. A couple different future avenues of research could be examining how IoT measures up into the "Big Data" movement or maybe looking into some uncommon domains that IoT has yet to encounter. Perhaps diving into the IoT business models that assist and promote global commerce could be an inquisitive direction as well. Nevertheless, only time has the capacity to show the potential and reality of IoT to reshape our world of technology.

## CONCLUSION

The IoT creates huge opportunities for the economy and individuals. The IoT has no boundaries and will impact every business and person. With new devices connecting into a company's systems, new types of data will be accessible. It will become a tool with advanced technology in sensing, controlling, communications, and in delivering solutions from huge amounts of gathered data. This will change lifestyles and business models from today. We cannot predict the exact outcomes. IoT's potential success in the market place is inevitable as the world requiring for greater connectivity and benefits of IoT is limitless to vast majority. Hospitals and patients are seeking for earlier detection of chronic diseases through IoT indicators. People are looking for ways to ease their lives. It is certain that IoT will have enormous impact on consumers and businesses. IoT is still at an early stage of development. Even though IoT problems of privacy and security arise, with the help of research communities and companies investing in R&D, new solutions will be developed to help build trust in consumers for new IoT technologies. A common understanding of IoT benefits will help fasten the advancement of the IoT market for both enterprises and consumers.

Explaining the functions of one device or method with the field of Smart Health, Smart Cities, and Smart Living in this paper is only a minuscule scratch on the surface in regards to the wide range of products and services that are available with IoT capabilities. As with all things, there are benefits and limitations that naturally come with every device. As IoT devices serve as solutions to a variety of countless things, there is always a risk of a security breach. IoT applications must be able to detect and prevent system compromises and should have multiple layers of protection to ensure that hackers are kept out. Monitoring should be a constant and continuous process because even the most safeguarded systems will always have some vulnerability for a motivated hacker. However, the most vital processes are the damage control procedures set in place for if a breach does in fact transpire. The organization behind the IoT device or application must be able to mitigate the losses and recover as fast as possible (Gantait, Patra, & Mukherjee, 2016). The AliveCor Heart Monitor, the sensors used for waste management, and the Belkin WeMo Light Switch are three devices from completely different industries with very little in common other than the fact that they are connected to the Internet wirelessly and assist people in their own ways. The Internet of Things will remain a notion that will allow innovators to continue to grow and exceed the boundaries of technology.

The convergence of sensors, hardware and connectivity are what power the IoT. It is obvious that IoT is becoming a permanent part of our technological landscape. Subsequent connections and almost-unlimited amount of data have moved devices beyond a simple reporting function to smart tool of enabling better and quicker decision-making. IoT drives business both in consumer and enterprise applications, representing trillions of dollars in potential economic impact. While taking advantage of the multitude of opportunities IoT represents, we must also keep an eye on the potential problems and limitations. Security, privacy, incompatibles, and problems in data movement and storage are primary concerns. Managers today and in the future will need to address these issues.

## REFERENCES

Akhbar, F., Chang, V., Yao, Y., & Muñoz, V. M. (2016). Outlook on moving of computing services towards the data sources. *International Journal of Information Management*, *36*(4), 645–652. doi:10.1016/j.ijinfomgt.2016.03.014

Albrecht, K., & Michael, K. (2013). Connected: To everyone and everything [Guest Editorial: Special Section on Sensors]. *IEEE Technology and Society Magazine*, *32*(4), 31–34. doi:10.1109/MTS.2013.2291170

Ambasna-Jones, M. (2015). *Will automation and the internet of things lead to mass unemployment?* Retrieved March 5, 2016 from https://www.theguardian.com/media-network/2015/may/27/internet-of-things-automation-unemployment

Ashton, K. (2009). That internet of things' thing. *RFID Journal*, *22*(7), 97–114.

Atzori, L., Iera, A., & Morabito, G. (2010). The Internet of Things: A survey. *Computer Networks*, *54*(15), 2787–2805. doi:10.1016/j.comnet.2010.05.010

Atzori, L., Iera, A., Morabito, G., & Nitti, M. (2012). The social Internet of Things (SIoT) - when social networks meet the Internet of Things: Concept, architecture and network characterization. *Computer Networks*, *56*(16), 3594–3608. doi:10.1016/j.comnet.2012.07.010

Bandyopadhyay, D., & Sen, J. (2011). Internet of Things: Applications and challenges in technology and standardization. *Wireless Personal Communications*, *58*(1), 49–69. doi:10.1007/s11277-011-0288-5

Bhide, V. (2014). A Survey on the Smart Homes using Internet of Things (IoT). *International Journal of Advance Research in Computer Science and Management Studies*, *2*(12), 243–246.

Brody, P., & Pureswaran, V. (2015). The next digital gold rush: How the internet of things will create liquid, transparent markets. *Strategy and Leadership*, *43*(1), 41–36. doi:10.1108/SL-11-2014-0094

Delaney, J. (2013). Belkin WeMo Light Switch. *PC Magazine*. Retrieved September 10, 2016 from http://www.pcmag.com/article2/0,2817,2426758,00.asp

Ding, D., Cooper, R. A., Pasquina, P. F., & Fici-Pasquina, L. (2011). Sensor technology for smart homes. *Maturitas*, *69*(2), 131–136. doi:10.1016/j.maturitas.2011.03.016 PMID:21531517

Dorsemaine, B., Gaulier, J., Wary, J., Kheir, N., & Urien, P. (2016). Internet of Things: A definition and taxonomy. *Proceedings of The 9th International Conference on Next Generation Mobile Applications, Services and Technologies*, 72-77. doi:10.1109/NGMAST.2015.71

Dutton, W. H. (2014). Putting things to work: Social and policy challenges for the Internet of things. *Info*, *16*(3), 1–21. doi:10.1108/info-09-2013-0047

Fowler, T. (2014). AliveCor Heart Monitor Now Available Over the Counter: Interview with CEO Euan Thomson. *medGadget*. Retrieved September 10, 2016 from http://www.medgadget.com/2014/02/ fda-over-the-counter-approval-for-alivecor-heart-monitor-interview-with-ceo-euan-thomson.html

Fuchs, C. (2014). *Social media: A critical introduction*. London: Sage Publications. doi:10.4135/9781446270066.n2

Gantait, A., Patra, J., & Mukherjee, A. (2016). Securing IoT devices and gateways: From authentication, including certificate-based authentication, to authorization, to application ID validation. *IBM DeveloperWorks*. Retrieved September 12, 2016 from http://www.ibm.com/developerworks/library/iot-trs-secure-iot-solutions1/index.html

Geller, J. (2014). Why home automation is being disrupted? *SmartThings*. Retrieved 29 Sept 2016 from https://blog.smartthings.com/editorial/why-home-automation-is-being-disrupted/

Gerpott, T. J., & May, S. (2016). Integration of Internet of Things components into a firms offering portfolio - a business development framework. *Info*, *18*(2), 53–63. doi:10.1108/info-11-2015-0051

Gubbi, J., Buyya, R., Marusic, S., & Palaniswami, M. (2013). Internet of Things (IoT): A vision, architectural elements, and future directions. *Future Generation Computer Systems*, *29*(7), 1645–1660. doi:10.1016/j.future.2013.01.010

Hajduk, S. (2016). The concept of a smart city in urban management. *Business. Management in Education*, *14*(1), 34–49.

Hillman, A. J., Withers, M. C., & Collins, B. J. (2009). Resource dependence theory: A review. *Journal of Management*, *35*(6), 1404–1427. doi:10.1177/0149206309343469

Jo, H. J., Paik, J. H., & Lee, D. H. (2014). Efficient privacy-preserving authentication in wireless mobile networks. *IEEE Transactions on Mobile Computing*, *13*(7), 1469–1481. doi:10.1109/TMC.2013.134

Kaur, N., & Sood, S. K. (2015). Cognitive decision making in smart industry. *Computers in Industry*, *74*, 151–161. doi:10.1016/j.compind.2015.06.006

Laplante, P. A., & Laplante, N. (2016). The Internet of Things in healthcare: Potential applications and challenges. *IT Professional Magazine*, *18*(3), 2–4. doi:10.1109/MITP.2016.42

Li, F., & Xiong, P. (2013). Practical secure communication for integrating wireless sensor networks into the Internet of Things. *IEEE Sensors Journal*, *13*(10), 3677–3684. doi:10.1109/JSEN.2013.2262271

Li, S., Oikonomou, G., Tryfonas, T., Chen, T. M., & Xu, L. (2014). A Distributed Consensus Algorithm for Decision Making in Service-Oriented Internet of Things. *IEEE Transactions on Industrial Informatics*, *10*(2), 1461–1468. doi:10.1109/TII.2014.2306331

Li, S., Xu, L. D., & Zhao, S. (2015). The internet of things: A survey. *Information Systems Frontiers*, *17*(2), 243–259. doi:10.1007/s10796-014-9492-7

Martin, J. (2015). Data, data, everywhere. *Mechanical Engineering (New York, N.Y.)*, *137*(7), 46–51.

Mayer, C. P. (2009). Security and privacy challenges in the internet of things. *Electronic Communications of the EASST*, *17*, 1–12.

McKinsey Global Institute. (2015). *The internet of things: Mapping the value beyond the hype*. Retrieved September 18, 2016 from https://www.mckinsey.de/sites/mck_files/files/unlocking_the_potential_of_the_internet_of_things_full_report.pdf

Mirsa, S. (2013). Physician review of the iPhone AliveCor ECG heart monitor, the clinical reality of the device. *iMedicalApps + MedPage Today*. Retrieved October 2, 2016 from http://www.imedicalapps.com/2013/03/physician-review-iphone-alivecor-ecg-heart-monitor/

Mishra, D., Gunasekaran, A., Childe, S. J., Papadopoulos, T., Dubey, R., & Wamba, S. (2016). Vision, applications and future challenges of Internet of Things: A bibliometric study of the recent literature. *Industrial Management & Data Systems*, *116*(7), 1331–1355. doi:10.1108/IMDS-11-2015-0478

Moosavi, R., Gia, N., Nigussie, E., Rahmani, M., Virtanen, S., Tenhunen, H., & Isoaho, J. (2016). End-to-end security scheme for mobility enabled healthcare Internet of Things. *Future Generation Computer Systems*, *64*(C), 108–124. doi:10.1016/j.future.2016.02.020

Ning, H., Liu, H., & Yang, L. T. (2013). Cyberentity security in the Internet of Things. *Computer*, *46*(4), 46–53. doi:10.1109/MC.2013.74

Oppliger, R. (2011). Security and privacy in an online world. *Computer*, *44*(9), 21–22. doi:10.1109/MC.2011.292

Pace, P., Aloi, G., Caliciuri, G., & Fortino, G. (2016). A Mission-oriented coordination framework for teams of mobile aerial and terrestrial smart objects. *Mobile Networks and Applications*, *21*(4), 708–725. doi:10.1007/s11036-016-0726-4

Pal, S. (2015). How IoT is helping to address chronic disease management. *Electronic Health Reporter*. Retrieved September 20, 2016 from http://electronichealthreporter.com/iot-helping-address-chronic-disease management/#more-11473

Pang, Z. (2013). *Technologies and architectures of the Internet-of-things (IoT) for health and well-being*. Royal Institute of Technology Stockholm.

Peppet, S. (2014). Regulating the Internet of things: First steps toward managing discrimination, privacy, security, and consent. *Texas Law Review*, *93*(1), 85–176.

Perera, C., Ranjan, R., Wang, L., Khan, S. U., & Zomaya, A. Y. (2015). Big data privacy in the Internet of Things era. *IEEE IT Professional Magazine*, *17*(3), 32–39. doi:10.1109/MITP.2015.34

Perera, C., Zaslavsky, A., Christen, P., & Georgakopoulos, D. (2014). Sensing as a Service Model for Smart Cities Supported by Internet of Things. *Transactions on Emerging Telecommunications Technologies*, *25*(1), 81–93. doi:10.1002/ett.2704

Perera, C., Zaslavsky, A., Christen, P., & Georgakopoulos, D. (2014). Context aware computing for the Internet of Things: A survey. *IEEE Communications Surveys and Tutorials*, *16*(1), 414–454. doi:10.1109/SURV.2013.042313.00197

Popescul, D., & Radu, D. (2016). Data security in smart cities: challenges and solutions. *Informatica Economica, 20*(1). Retrieved September 15, 2016 http://dx.doi.org.libproxy.uml.edu/10.12948/issn14531305/20.1.2016.03

Rainie, L., & Wellman, B. (2012). *Networked: the new social operating system*. Cambridge, MA: The MIT Press.

Roman, R., Najera, P., & Lopez, J. (2011). Securing the Internet of Things. *Computer*, *44*(9), 51–58. doi:10.1109/MC.2011.291

Rowley, M. J. (2016). How the Internet of Things is aiding the garbage crisis. *The network Cisco's Technology News Site*. Retrieved October 5, 2016 from https://newsroom.cisco.com/feature-content?articleId=1757267

Ryu, C. (2015). IoT-based intelligent for fire emergency response systems. *International Journal of Smart Home*, *9*(3), 161–168. doi:10.14257/ijsh.2015.9.3.15

Spanjol, J., Tam, L., & Tam, V. (2015). Employer-employee congruence in environmental values: An exploration of effects on job satisfaction and creativity. *Journal of Business Ethics*, *130*(1), 117–130. doi:10.1007/s10551-014-2208-6

Sundmaeker, H., Guillemin, P., Friess, P., & Woelffle, S. (Eds.). (2010). *Vision and challenges for realizing the Internet of things*. European Commission Information Society and Media.

Tao, F., Zuo, Y., Xu, L., & Lv, L. (2014). Internet of Things and BOM based life cycle assessment of energy-saving and emission-reduction of product. *IEEE Transactions on Industrial Informatics*, *10*(2), 1252–1261. doi:10.1109/TII.2014.2306771

Thramboulidis, K. (2015). A cyber-physical system-based approach for industrial automation systems. *Computers in Industry*, *72*(C), 92–102. doi:10.1016/j.compind.2015.04.006

Umar, A. (2005). IT infrastructure to enable next generation enterprises. *Information Systems Frontiers*, *7*(3), 217–256. doi:10.1007/s10796-005-2768-1

Vanian, J. (2015). Cisco's CEO: The Internet of things is real (and confusing). *Fortune*. Retrieved September 15, 2016 from http://fortune.com/2015/10/05/cisco-chuck-robbins-Internet/

Vermesan, O., & Friess, P. (Eds.). (2014). *Internet of Things- from research and innovation to market deployment*. River Publishers.

Westerlund, M., Leminen, S., & Rajahonka, M. (2014). Designing Business Models for the Internet of Things. *Technology Innovation Management Review*, *4*(7), 5–14.

Whitmore, A., Agarwal, A., & Xu, L. (2015). The Internet of things—A survey of topics and trends. *Information Systems Frontiers*, *17*(2), 261–274. doi:10.1007/s10796-014-9489-2

Xiao, G., Guo, J., Xu, L., & Gong, Z. (2014). User interoperability with heterogeneous IoT devices through transformation. *IEEE Transactions on Industrial Informatics*, *10*(2), 1486–1496. doi:10.1109/TII.2014.2306772

Xu, L., He, W., & Li, S. (2014). Internet of Things in industries: A survey. *IEEE Transactions on Industrial Informatics*, *10*(4), 2233–2248. doi:10.1109/TII.2014.2300753

Yu, X. Y., Chen, Y., & Nguyen, B. (2014). Knowledge management, learning behavior from failure and new product development of new technology ventures. *Systems Research and Behavioral Science*, *31*(3), 405–423. doi:10.1002/sres.2273

## KEY TERMS AND DEFINITIONS

**Home Automation:** It consists of an integrated means of monitoring and regulating the use of power for AC, heat, lights and many other home appliances that use WiFi for remote monitoring.

**Internet of Things (IoT):** The Internet of Things (IoT) is a system of interrelated physical objects such as computing devices, mechanical machines, and digital components, animals or people that are provided with unique identifiers and the ability to transfer data over the Internet.

**Privacy:** Area of information control involved with the right to be left alone; involved with the protections from intrusion and information gathering by others; an individuals' ability to personally control information about themselves.

**Radio Frequency Identification (RFID):** Radio frequency identification, denoting technologies that use radio waves to identify people or objects carrying encoded microchips.

**RFID Tagging:** An ID system that uses small radio frequency identification devices for identification and tracking purposes. An RFID tagging system includes the tag itself, a read/write device, and a host system application for data collection, processing, and transmission.

**Smart City:** A smart city can be described as a developed urban area that is connected and monitors a wide variety of essential infrastructures to optimize resources, plan maintenance projects for preventative purposes, and create a balanced economic development while maximizing services to its residents.

**Smart Health:** Smart health uses unobtrusive IoT sensors, devices and applications to collect patient's comprehensive physiological data and utilize the cloud to evaluate and house the electronic health record (EHR) system or data warehouse that supports the SMART standards. Patients, doctors, and healthcare practitioners can draw on this library of apps to improve clinical care, research, and public health.

**Smart Living:** It is the automation of housework, appliances, or the overall activities within the home to provide convenience, security, and efficiency. Majority devices and appliances have become assimilated with smartphones and the home IP network.

# Section 3

# IoT Technologies and Applications

# Chapter 10

# Innovation in Product Design: IoT Objects Driven New Product Innovation and Prototyping Using 3D Printers

**Ravi Ramakrishnan**
*Amity University, India*

**Loveleen Gaur**
*Amity University, India*

## ABSTRACT

*The IoT and 3D printing can become a potent combination when it comes to launching new business initiatives driven by hard-core data and analytics and not really based on human perceptions or limited survey data. Previous empirical research has shown that drivers of new product performance are a mix of strategic, development process, organizational, and market environmental factors. This chapter attempts (1) to understand how introduction of IoT sensors embedded in customer appliances or wearable's sending real time customer information coupled with rapid prototyping using remotely located 3D printers can help address design considerations for new products, and (2) to provide an overview of how using IoT data and 3D printers for new product development and prototyping as an early stage activity can be done without using human imagination of restricted market survey data.*

## INTRODUCTION

Entering new markets and predicting customer behaviour and analysing his purchase pattern for a market driven product design and development is a risky proposition. The primary advantage of the Internet of Tings (IoT) in such business cases is their ability to create situational awareness and enable applications, human beings and machines to better understand surrounding for timely informed decisions in a dynamic daily changing environment. Sensor generated data related to our physical world can help us understand better and create newer products and services. 3D printing will help convert such data into visible prototypes (Nashiya, 2015).

DOI: 10.4018/978-1-5225-2104-4.ch010

"The worldwide 3D printing industry in expected to grow from $3.07B in revenue in 2013 to $12.8B by 2018 and 3D printing technology is destined to transform almost every major industry (Allied Market Research, 2015). 3D printing also called additive manufacturing is a process of making three dimensional solid objects from a digital file using specific raw materials which can vary from plastic to metal. 3D printing starts with providing a virtual design of the object to be printed in a Computer Aided Design (CAD) file format. Also of relevance are 3D scanners which use different technologies to generate a 3D model such as time-of-flight (uses laser light to probe the subject), structured / modulated light (project a pattern of light on the subject and look at the deformation of the pattern on the subject) or volumetric scanning (industrial computed tomography) (David, 2014).

The next step is to convert the 3D model using specialised software by a process called "Slicing" which is dividing a 3D model into hundreds or thousands of horizontal layers.3D printing has several ways of printing and all are additive with differences in the way layers are built to create the final object. These methods range from melting, selective laser sintering (SLS) and fused deposition modelling (FDM) or curing a photo-reactive resin with a UV laser or another similar power source one layer at a time (known as stereo lithography SLA).

The American Society for Testing and Materials (ASTM) developed a set of standards that classify the Additive Manufacturing processes into 7 categories as below (ASTM52900, 2015):

- **Vat Photo Polymerisation:** This uses a container filled with photopolymer resin which is then hardened with UV light source.
- **Material Jetting:** In this material is applied in droplets and overlapped layer by layer to build an object by using a small diameter nozzle.
- **Binder Jetting:** In this two materials are used: powder base material and a liquid binder, powder is spread in equal layers and binder is applied through jet nozzles that "glue" the powder particles in the shape of a programmed 3D object.
- **Material Extrusion:** This uses a technology called fused deposition modelling (FDM) in which the plastic or metal filament is heated and sprayed from a nozzle, which can move bi-directionally, into layers which gets hardened immediately.
- **Powder Bed Fusion:** The technology involves high power laser to fuse small particles of plastic, metal, ceramic or glass powders into a mass of desired 3D shape.
- **Sheet Lamination:** This involves sheets of metal, paper or polymer welded together by ultrasonic waves or adhesive glue.
- **Directed Energy Deposition:** This consists of a multi axis Robotic arm and a nozzle depositing metal powder with an energy source which can be laser, electron beam or plasma arc.

IoT and 3D printing can become a potent combination when it comes to launching new business initiatives driven by hard-core data and analytics and not really based on human perceptions or limited survey data which are generally bound to fail and may not be fully exhaustive or indicative. Previous empirical research has shown that drivers of new product performance are a mix of strategic, development process, organisational and market environmental factors (Geroski, Machin and Van Reenen 1993, Soni, Lilien and Wilson 1993, Capon, Farley and Hoenig 1990). Entering new markets and predicting customer behaviour and analysing consumers' purchase pattern for a market driven product design and development is a risky proposition.

New product development (NPD) in business or engineering refers to the steps required to bring a product from concept or ideation stage to the market. Krishnan (2001) describes new product development as the transformation of a market opportunity into a product available for sale which can be a tangible product or a service. Reducing time for NPD has led to concepts such as concurrent engineering and traditionally has eight stages namely idea generation, idea screening, idea development and testing, business analysis, beta testing, technical implementation, commercialisation and new product pricing.

In the traditional model, design feedback came from only sales figures and consumer complaints—and generally after design and production have already been completed which is too late for any meaningful corrective action or repairs. The IoT can play a major role in idea screening, beta testing, continuous product improvement and provide inputs for pricing by capturing key data elements in the background relating to the usage and efficiency of the product. Similarly, 3D printing can help in idea development and technical implementation. In this chapter we are explaining how 3D printing and IoT can change the traditional model of NPD to an agile iterative model which will involve a launch – data gather – product evolution cycle thereby reducing time.

## BACKGROUND

Three-dimensional (3D) printing is a manufacturing method in which objects are made by fusing or depositing materials—such as plastic, metal, ceramics, powders, liquids, or even living cells—in layers to produce a 3D object. 3D printing or additive manufacturing starts with a 3D model which is then recreated into a solid form by superimposing layer by layer keeping in consideration all the complexity and detail without additional processing required by traditional manufacturing which involves injecting material into pre-fabricated moulds. Recent technology advancements have made 3D printers more affordable leading to an explosion in the commercial use of this technology (Kalani & Richard, 2014).

NPD teams are continuously dependant on data for product improvement and not hearing the voice of the consumer cause products to fail. Transforming data to actionable insights is the key to success in NPD scenarios. Embedded sensors in products are generating statistical dumps of data generated by actual consumer usage in a real world scenario and are much more realistic than laboratory experiments in controlled environment. These data will provide all departments of a business such as manufacturing, quality, and logistics a tool to make critical decisions.

Elisha et al. (2016) explained the data delivery and gathering in IoT which is of very high significance for this proposed model of 3D printing and introduced literature-backed solutions for topology, reducing costs and measuring network failure. Their work also covers avoiding inaccuracy due to RFID tag collision and ability to revive from node failures based on research from using heuristic approaches, to implementing localization techniques that contributes to finding the optimal network topology.

Mitzi et al. (1994) suggested that new product success is driven by a mix of strategic, development process, organisational and market environmental factors. Previous empirical research on new product performance has proved that a wide variety of factors can influence the outcomes of new product development activity. Mitzi Montoya-Weiss and Roger Calantone (1994) conducted a comprehensive review of this literature and observed a wide variety of study designs and methodological approaches. They developed quantitative comparisons of the results, which provide a look at the persistent exploratory nature of this research. They report a wide variation in results that are surprisingly nonconvergent.

Sue (2016) showed a future vision where it may be possible to even develop a fully functioning organ or rapidly produce made to order fixtures in the operation theatre or even create custom surgical equipment immediately customized for each patient based on human body anatomy 3D bio-printing offers additional important advantages such as highly precise cell placement and high digital control of speed, resolution, cell concentration, drop volume, and diameter of printed cells. Organ printing takes advantage of 3D printing technology to produce cells, biomaterials, and cell-laden biomaterials individually or in tandem, layer by layer, directly creating 3D tissue-like structures.

Ventola (2014) illustrates that medical applications for 3D printing are rapidly expanding with revolutionary consequences for medical industry. These are broadly in seven categories such as tissue and organ fabrication, creation of prosthetics, implants and anatomical models and pharmaceutical research regarding drug dosage forms, delivery and discovery. Companies that use 3D printing for commercial medical applications have also emerged. These include: Helisys, Ultimateker, and Organovo, a company that uses 3D printing to fabricate living human tissue (Klein, 2013).

Angewandte (2016) showed the positive 3D printing developments in the field of microfluidic devices which are still made with extensive manual labour and which can reduce labour and cost by a large extent along with better safety. As part of this 3D model is developed and the design can be assembled in modules by remote teams, and it's mechanical and fluidic behavior can be simulated using finite-element modeling. The processing is environmentally friendly and economically efficient and is predicted to replace most plastic molding techniques.

Bailey (2012) showed some techniques, methodologies and toll sets where challenges of performance, quality and reliability in electronic industry manufacturing can be achieved by reducing downtime in component malfunction for critical appliances. Inkjet printing can be used in electronics packaging as interconnections between electronic components. Conductive inks and dielectric inks substitute traditional printed circuit board (PCB) with inkjet-printed interconnections. Inorganic inks offer better conductivity as they consist of metal nanoparticles and organic solvent which make the ink printable. This will help reduce breakdown of traditional PCB or electronic components while ensuring higher quality aesthetics.

Ramakrishnan (2016) explained how IoT devices can help track location of the source of origin of information using BLE beacons. This might be relevant for NPD driven by IoT-3D printing as it may be necessary to identify the source of request for changes to the product and such changes may be again subject to a specific customer location, situation or context.

Existing research exists in the areas of new product development focuses on managing subjects and sources of ambiguity or, using IoT based configurable platforms for product life cycle management. However, the role of sensor based inputs in prototyping new products using 3D printers dynamically is still a greenfield area with not much research. The authors have tried to present concepts which are empirically tested in order to show the relation and benefits of combining IoT sensors with 3D printers for dynamic prototyping including new product developments and enhancements or corrections to design.

Figueroa (2013) suggested models for 3D printing of objects without manual intervention in the processing pipeline using 3D sensing devices like the Kinect sensor which can monitor and map gestures and movements thereby working in an augmented reality scenario. In this experimental prototype used for validating the model 3D Kinect camera tracks different poses of a human subject and generates a 3D model using a remote 3D printing of the entire subject similar to teleportation. The study presents initial successful results while also addressing the limitations of 3D printer and the speed of printing complex poses.

MacDonald (2014), emphasized how time to market can be reduced leading to better opportunity realisation for next generation products using 3D printing techniques like stereo lithography and fused deposition modelling in electronic products. The main focus of the study is to show the time saved when prototyping or manufacturing using 3D printing to a few hours as compared to designing on traditional technologies like pre printed circuit boards which may take days.

Hakima (2010) listed the architecture and networking technologies that are required to support the internet of things since traditional data requirements are far different from the IoT data networks which transport massive amount of data and hence need a robust and cost effective network. The difference being in terms of interval of data transfer which is much higher than the traditional networks and second is the volume of data. IoT will have to allow connectivity of a large number of objects of different type thereby presenting challenges of heterogeneity and scalability of communication networks with new functionality requirements of identifying, locating and sensing leading to high level of task automation.

Past research has shown that a product launch represents a major investment in revenue and profit for a company (Bhuiyan, 2011). A successful product launch can yield new markets, provide access to new customers, as well as increase business with existing customers. A product launch which is not based on proper market research or customer feedback may result in huge commercial losses and eroding of brand value.

Huang et al. (2014) proposed a unified framework of targeted marketing using customer preferences where the authors investigated two marketing strategies - the customer oriented and product oriented, introduced marketing models to test the relation between customers and products, and explained that the required parameters of a market value function depends on three information: customer profile, product profile, and transaction data.

Horvath (2001) proposed a method to extract knowledge background during definition of product objects in the form of initiated effect on product and also add the human thought process which is the starting point for initiation of a change in product feature. They conclude with an extended and integrated product definition model. Strategic supply chain management demands collaboration from all participants and understanding of customer and supplier constraints and the method will provide benefits such as radically improved customer responsiveness, enhanced customer service and satisfaction, increased flexibility for changing market conditions, improved customer retention and more effective marketing.

Han et al. (2015) conducted an interesting study on modelling customer preferences, proposed a concept selection method to evaluate future market performance of concepts and to choose the best one of them, and validated the method using field study. IoT introduction can further add on to this model by giving real time insight on customer preferences thereby getting the best model to market in a very fast time.

Ramakrishnan et al. (2016) has made an interesting point wherein machines can communicate with each other and follow a human world like hierarchy of superior subordinate relations taking the case of a smart electricity distribution in residential areas. This will help reduce unbilled energy and prevent wastage of energy. The same concept can be applied in IoT driven innovation wherein even the inputs send by IoT sensors can be validated by other IoT machines before being sent for 3d printing.

3D printed world has the potential to bring localised production of consumer goods or industrial goods from the current manufacturing location to right up-to customer door steps. For example, a broken door handle can be just printed and send to a customer immediately from a remote location by the manufacturer. Medical facilities will 3D print ankle replacements and even tissues while manufacturers can use Nano printing to print paper thin batteries. Add to this the IoT capabilities of detecting the requirement continuously and beforehand (without waiting for a break down) and we have a fully automated world with auto replenishment and detection systems across.

The authors are of the opinion that with an integration of 3D printing and IoT we have a technology that will transform the way business is conducted and the speed of responsiveness to customers will increase manifold. The time of fulfillment across extended supply chain will decrease considerably as manufacturing becomes highly customized and real time. Product development will be driven by objects (customer experience managers) communicating with other objects (3D design printers) and product versions will roll out more faster with a very high level of transformation and value addition as compared to the previous versions. This will be in deep contrast to the current slowly evolving product life cycle where each major upgrade is predominantly incremental and not radical different from the previous release. The above literature review shows that the author's views are very much in line with industry trends and have potential to replace human decision making on design and prototyping with intelligent captured data using IoT devices.

## MAIN FOCUS OF THE CHAPTER

### Intelligent Objects Observers: New Product Development

The tasks relating to new product development are as follows (Figure 1).

1. **Generating and Screening Ideas:** This involves a systematic search for new ideas; the sources can be internal customers, employees, competitors, distributors or suppliers. Customers can be a major source of ideas specifically of the company which already has products in the market. The resultant ideas need to be screened for commercial and technical viability and companies do this using formal review committees or market research.
2. **Testing Concepts:** The screened ideas are now converted into detailed concepts and then tested with customers either physically or symbolically to understand the customers perception of the product. The company can then project these findings to get an idea of the sales market volume.
3. **Analysing Market and Business Strategy:** This stage involves describing and identifying the target market, product positioning and sales and the market share and profit goals for the immediate year. It also covers pricing, distribution and marketing strategies. Finally it involves listing down long term sales, profit goals and marketing mix.
4. **Market Testing:** Post development of the concept to a product and test marketing to a restricted target segment are done prior to a full launch but this stage has risks of sabotage or competitors copying the concept.

*Figure 1.*

5. **Commercializing:** The final step is commercialisation which involves manufacturing, advertising and promotion.

Manufacturing systems will become more accurate, environmental friendly and customer focussed with modern information systems. Sensors embedded inside applications or as standalone machines can be used as mobile or fixed robot to monitor an environment such as office building or factory. Craig et al. (1995) described the concept, design and initial implementation of systems called intelligent observers. The Intelligent Observer (IO) is a mobile robot which moves through an environment (such as an office building or a factory) while independently observing moving targets selected by a human operator. The robot carries cameras which allow it to track objects while keeping track of its own location. It interacts with humans who issues task-level commands, such as indicating a target to track by clicking in a camera image. The user could be located far away from the observer itself, communicating with the robot over a network. As the IO performs its tasks, the system provides real-time visual feedback to the user. These intelligent observers can fuse information from various sensors and using geometric information about the environment reconstructs a 2D or 3D view of the observed scene. Sensors today can measure anything from noise vibrations, electricity consumption at appliance level, proximity, timed usage, heat and pressure, frequency and strength of transmitted and received signals from Bluetooth or Infrared or Wireless access and many more as sensors and actuators are emerging as powerhouses of the IoT wave. The observers can be used for shop floor monitoring, security, or landmark detection.

## Existing Reference Cases Worldwide

Since not many organisations have done this kind of dynamic prototyping of products based on inputs from IoT objects on customer preferences and manufacturing bottlenecks, the secondary sources of data including white-papers, scientific journals and feasibility study reports will be referred to on what all types of objects can be readily produced using 3D printing - e.g., Lithium Ion cells or even medical tissues being printed have been possible. We will also research the materials which can be used for 3D printing such as polyester, metals and fibres. Finally using secondary research survey, we will discuss on the kind of information that IoT devices and sensors are able to track in manufacturing products with reference to end consumer behaviour.

This paper will also focus on studies relating to the limitations while keeping a positive view of future trends to suggest solutions which can be implemented either today or maybe over a period of time as more advances are registered in 3D printing and IoT technology.

There are many cases of organisations having implemented IoT to help improve their products or develop new products. The IoT implementation may involve turning products into sensors or integrating them to provide data-based evidence for product engineers and also for better customer service. Data collection with the IoT devices is better than asking a customer to respond to questions relating to service or failures and move towards a proactive approach at a much reduced cost.

Earlier the organization had limited interaction with its customer's up to the point of sale. Organizations relied largely on reporting from field engineers post factor, random survey and product returns to gauge device durability and customer satisfaction. But through new capabilities to analyse the real-time IoT data provided by connected devices, companies can now gain key insights into product performance, consumer trends, and purchasing behaviour.

The first case is of Bosch, a leading healthcare product company. Bosch runs "Health Buddy" an early human response dependant IoT device that monitors the vital signs of patients and records patient inputs. This is targeted at patients with chronic health conditions who can be monitored on a continuous basis from their own homes and data is transmitted to remote medical practitioners. Health Buddy, acquired in 2007 from Health Hero, was a home management platform for CHF, depression, diabetes, hypertension, COPD, or weight management. It consisted of a small box with a screen and four buttons. Health Buddy would ask a patient survey questions daily, as well as prompt them to take their weight or blood pressure via connected devices, and send the data to a care provider. However, Bosch has officially closed its US subsidiary Robert Bosch Healthcare, reducing the scope its healthcare operations to a 50-person team based in Germany. This showed that the attempt was not very successful and also was prone to having human inputs proactively rather than a human independent monitoring. The data from this equipment was planned to be used by remote healthcare providers to develop custom made appliances for weight control which was planned to be done using 3D printers. It also allowed health care providers to track the efficiency of existing medications and thereby provide information to develop new more potent and effective variants of the medicine (Neil, 2011).

Trane, a division of Ingersoll Rand that focuses on industrial air conditioning, has changed both its product development practices and the products delivered based on IoT data and its insights. Trane makes HVAC products for a wide variety of uses, from homes to offices to manufacturing facilities. This segment has seen a major change as per available literature wherein manufacturers like Trane tended to own and control less of the Intellectual Property that went into producing equipment. Suppliers were inventing and controlling innovations. On other hand the purchasing process for HVAC equipment had become highly intermediated. Owners of facilities increasingly relied on consultants for advice about which systems to buy. Trane now addresses a whole new set of questions:

- What is this product's relationship to other building systems? What impact will it have on or from the smart grid?
- What new levels of efficiency and reliability can be achieved, both mechanically and from operational optimizations?
- How will connected products and services change Trane's relationship with customers?

The solutions and insights provided to the above facets by the IoT data shows that Trane is now able to find and defend new sources of value and show value add based on their real-time operating environment versus their initial design. Trane's devices are now not restricted to a turn on and off function during start and end of office hours but can do a lot more things such as matching its operation to the building's actual occupancy load, or a more complicated optimization like switching energy sources. The data allow an intelligent decision to be made at another level and that affects the capabilities needed from the device. Trane is able to address the needs of key influencers in the buying process by creating applications and services that help optimize HVAC systems (IoT World Show, 2016). This shows that IoT has indeed influenced product design using real time data flow and hence added value to the buyer. While as of now Trane is not using 3D printing but Haier in China has already developed the first 3D printed air conditioner (Whiteney, 2015). The authors see a future potential for Trane to integrate the IoT data with the 3D printer in line with what Haier has done in China to design the next generation of HVAC systems.

Coca-Cola uses data from its Freestyle and other vending machines to gain insights on their customers purchasing pattern including where, when, and how they are consuming their products. A rich insight thrown from the connected smart vending machines is spikes in its beverage consumption on college campuses before certain television shows air; this has helped up move towards targeted marketing. Testing of these devices started in around 60 locations in 2009 in US and another 200 locations in 2010 followed by Great Britain 16 locations in London in 2012. The project is a pioneering example of organizations harnessing the power of business mobility to fundamentally transform processes and experiences for consumers. Customers can select a base product and supplement it with additional flavours which provide insights for Coca-Cola to launch new products of the most popular flavours in other locations as a derivate of the customer insight (Wikipedia). Coca-Cola has also pioneered into the use of 3D printing (Ricardo, 2013) in advertisements and for recycling plastic bottles to help protect the environment. As per the authors while currently the two developments i.e. IoT and 3D printing is not being used on combination in future Coca-Cola can integrate the two by adaptations of the Freestyle machine to provide consumers small 3D printed souvenirs and fashionable items (Journey Staff, 2014).

IRhythm, a company that manufactures a patch that can detect heart problems, uses the data flowing from devices to ensure that its products operate as intended and better understand usage patterns. The ZIO Service integrates a discreet patch that continuously monitors and records up to 20,000 minutes worth of patient heartbeats over 14 days, with delivery of a concise, high quality report. With over 400,000+ Patients and 100+ Million Hours of Annotated ECG this product has been very successful and also the data is being used to further fine tune the product for better effectiveness. This data can be used by medical practitioners to understand the efficiency of machines thereby providing more insights than field trials of medicines on real time basis thereby helping with new formulation releases. As per the authors with new developments in the field of medical tissue printing it is now possible to recreate 3D bio printed heart valves (Robert, 2015) and the IRhythm data can be used in conjugation with a 3D printer in the future.

Optomec helps make consumer and industrial devices smart and connected with 3D Printed sensors and antennas for Internet of Things applications. Optomec Aerosol Jet technology is a high volume printing solution for the production of 3D antennas and 3D sensors that are tightly integrated with an underlying product ranging from Smartphones to Industrial Components. With Aerosol Jet systems, customers can print high-precision integrated electronics onto 3D plastic, ceramic and metallic structures at extremely fine resolutions. Aerosol Jet is used to make consumer and industrial products smart and connected so that they can provide feedback to engineers to improve future designs and to service technicians to proactively maintain products based on their condition. This data on product performance, customer behaviors and environmental factors gives manufacturers unprecedented levels of insight, fundamentally changing the way products are developed, maintained and supported. Since life cycle costs of industrial products can be 10 to 15 times higher than the original equipment purchase cost, smart connected devices offer customers and manufacturers significant potential for cost savings and improved product performance. These printers are being used worldwide by companies like Bosch, Air Force Research Laboratory, and Neotech.

Audi's Smart Factory attempts to optimize car production efficiency, with the help of highly specialized equipment that uses the IoT to communicate seamlessly. The factory uses 3D printers to create custom parts as needed, while using 3D projections to match the customized parts to the car chassis. This process also uses drones and other cross-functional electronics, communicating with one another to increase production speed while maintaining a high-quality product. Humans and robots work hand in hand, producing car-body parts from a 3D printer and resulting in cars driving in piloted mode from the assembly line. Employees in the pre-series center combine the virtual and the physical worlds of automobile development extremely precisely. The system allows the projection of virtual 3D components onto the car. In Audi's tooling division, a 3D printer produces complex metal parts, and intelligent tools are able to exactly distribute the high pressure forces to stamp sheet-metal parts that are accurate to one hundredth of a millimeter. And in the assembly process at the Ingolstadt plant, a robot works with the employees on the production line without a protective fence, passing them components at exactly the right speed and in an ergonomically pleasant position (Research and Markets Report, 2015).

Streetline is another example of how a company is using IoT analytics to build new products. The company recently launched Streetline IoT Gateway-to create smart cities and smart campuses. Analysing the data streaming into the Gateway, Streetline realized they could build a successful business by harnessing smart data and advanced analytics to help cities, universities and campuses provide guidance on available parking and parking enforcement. This case illustrates that IoT can help build new data based business models which can be readily 3D prototyped. The Gateway allows Streetline customers to effectively capture data from in-ground sensors and video cameras, for effective decisions. The product has derived value added features such as better parking and ability to decrease congestion, and thereby build a revenue stream for Streetline at the same time which is reflecting positively in the company's top line.

## Potential for Innovation

The above study has thrown up the following areas of business relevance for IoT and 3D Printing with respect to new product development as shown in Figure 2.

### Deliver High Performance Products and Services

The IoT in combination to 3D Printing can vastly speed up product R&D. By using sensor, diagnostic, and user interaction data from devices, companies get full product transparency. By observing how customers are using their products, businesses can quickly update features or adjust future release models to closely align with customer preferences and needs. They can also forecast where consumer preferences are going in the future. This insight about customer future preferences can eliminate tedious trial and error, and companies can know real time what is successful and what has low acceptance, leading to

*Figure 2.*

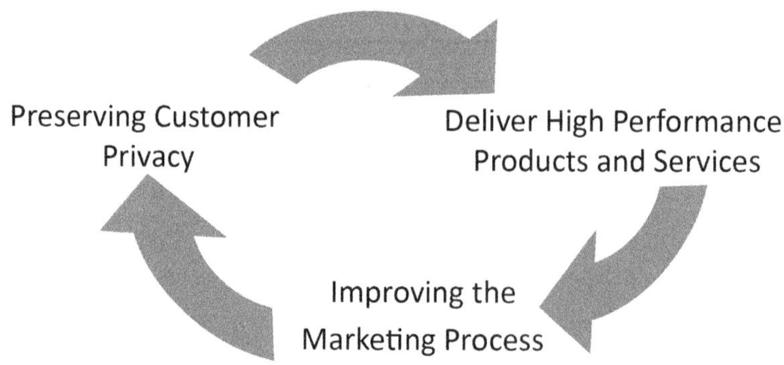

better product usage. With this data, it will be possible to generate a 3D print design of a new prototype. In future it will be possible that IoT devices directly interact with remote 3D printers to print an evolving and progressive prototype for new products with a reduced role for human product engineers.

Customer service improves with access to this level of detail on product usage, product performance and customer preferences. Proactive notification to customers affected by an outage or affected device can achieve very high levels of customer service. Companies can also then better position their customer support centres to allow more immediate service, reducing costs and appeasing customers simultaneously. This is the driving force behind IoT captured customer usage and preference data and 3D printers generating immediate services and parts replacement without the traditional waiting time for procuring or sourcing spares against faulty components as is the norm now.

## Improving the Marketing Process Using IoT Data and 3D Printed Prototypes

One of the ways IoT focussed new product development companies can move away from a general strategy to a tailor made product for customers is by using 3D printers to create models specific to data generated by a customer and his usage pattern. Advertisers and marketers can reach individual segments of their customer base. So instead of flooding all customers with the same offer, marketing teams can create personalized offers that keep the customer engaged and satisfied with the product. Reduced marketing costs result from core targeted, successful marketing efforts. With data-driven insights from connected devices, companies can know from the start of a campaign how and where to position their new product lines on social media and elsewhere to get the best response from the market of customers and prospects. Philips (Gary, 2016) has launched a connected healthcare devices campaign to monitor lifestyle and use that data for positioning their health care services and products which again can be 3D printed.

## Preserving Customer Privacy

Using IoT for product development by capturing buyer's preferences through his actions also raises concerns of protecting customer privacy. These concerns can be reduced by omitting personally identifiable information to limit the identification of individuals Weber (2010), defined privacy in more detail. Privacy includes the concealment of personal information as well as the ability to control what happens with this information, the right to privacy can be considered as either a basic and inalienable human right, or as a personal right or possession. With IoT it may be possible to violate privacy without the knowledge or approval of the subject matter. Privacy data may become the interest of the state as well as private marketers which is a cause of concern.

Traditional product development involved a sequential phase of requirement definition, design or prototyping, building and testing unlike operational performance feedback which is a mainstay of product development in the IoT era. IoT suggests a proactive approach which is very much needed to allow engineers to apply analytics to operational and performance data, deriving meaningful insights. As a result, engineering teams can learn continuously with data and usage, thereby enhancing product performance much more quickly than they can use traditional models.

Figure 3 shows the authors illustration of the three most important aspects to be kept in mind while designing an IoT-3D solution.

*Figure 3.*

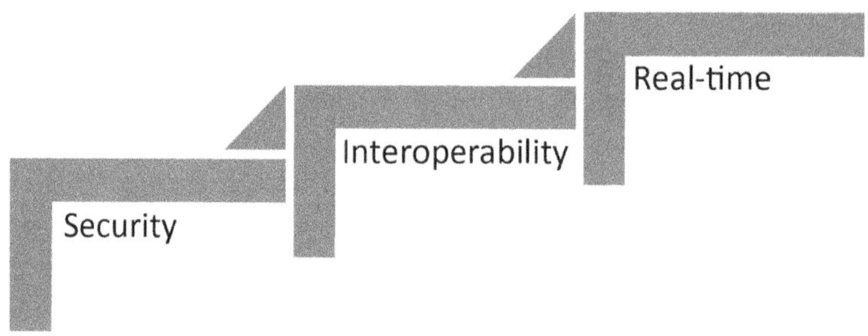


A simple case in reference which can be used by an electronics equipment company is to optimize the positioning of its remote control sensor. Traditionally if a sensor was not fitted properly it would often result in a customer attempting many times in pressing the remote control and ultimately getting through, some customers may complaint or giving a feedback (some may ultimately adjust and change their operating habit) and ultimately result a product recall or design change. However, this would result in a significant loss of goodwill and also it may take a lot of time for such feedback to be consolidated to convince the need for a product change. With an integrated IoT-3D printing technology in place the object - in this case the electronic equipment - would transmit data about this design flaw to a remote 3D printer which will print a revised model to address this design flaw thereby leading to a near real time design change keeping in mind the customer preferences and feedback on existing design limitations.

## RESULTS AND ANALYSIS

Taking the case of automobile industry a car with IoT sensors can transmit and monitor information about car usage per day in kilometers and the speed of travel to suggest a lower model or a higher cost effective laced, all this information can be machine generated without needing human discretion or judgment. Add to this the ability to monitor the wear and tear of tyres or engine which can help in passing data related to these thereby allowing remote 3D printers to come up with different designs which can be more economical to both the customer and the manufacturer. This process of additive intelligence powered by data captured by IoT devices and modeled by 3D printers to arrive at near perfect models of accessories or automobiles will add immense value.

Yet another use case can be of consumer electronics wherein an air conditioner can suggest to the owner or the manufacturer what the optimum capacity should be based on sensors monitoring the running of compressor and give a cost benefit analysis of a replacement viz a viz the running cost. Going to a subcomponent part level it may be easier to predict faults and rectify them in design considerations by combining the data of failures and faults generated by IoT embedded chips inside consumer appliances and remote 3D printers which can actually work intelligently on the point of failure data.

The authors have done research on a very common place problem of the apparel industry and the fashion clothes segments in India. India's population specially the millennial is addicted to buying clothes and their buying trends and frequencies have been driven even more by the proliferation of high street shops and malls and many international and home grown brands in the apparels section for men, women and children riding on the back of an improving economic ecosystem where surplus disposable incomes have increased multi folds with cheap circulation of plastic money. However, for merchants and for garment manufacturers getting insights on what really attracts the customers is more a culmination of traditional thought process, ad hoc market research and sales figures. As a retailer it would be worthwhile to stock goods which are more in demand and can convert to sale quicker to avoid having slow moving apparels with limited commercial viability in stocks. Add to it the crowd generated in trying out different outfits and then repackaging the tried garments leading to investment of human resources. The net result could be a very low ratio of garment trials and actual sales. When the garments are repackaged along with it goes the valuable data insight on how many people actually tried but did not like it thereby losing opportunity to get direct customer insight and review. A Bloomberg report of this year (James, 2016) clearly shows that 3D printing of garments is now a near possibility and will trickle down to masses. However, there are limitations of rigidness and material may not be similar to clothes or as comfortable as normal clothes with the current infrastructure. A rich use case which may develop is the ability of IoT driven SmartMirrors equipped with cameras which can analyze and predict customer preferences for garments and at the instant get a 3D printed garment more attuned to his style thereby making an immediate sale.

In another use case for retailers, IoT technology can in instance of accessories such as hardware, jewelry, footwear, eyewear which can be detected using SmartMirrors or intelligent cameras provide real time data to nearby 3D printers and manufacturing designs on demand.

The concept can also be very relevant in the automobile industry where each consumer has a unique driving habit as a result of which the same vehicle driven by multiple people gives different results and efficiencies. Today it will be impossible to imagine a world where we have tailor made and finely attuned models for a group of customers driven by their behavioral and usage patterns along with tailor made pricing but the situation is possible using IoT sensors sending usage information to remote 3D printers which in turn can design and produce custom made offerings. This is being observed now with Connected Cars project. By 2018, one in five cars on the road will be self-aware and able to discern and share information on their mechanical health, global position, and status of their surroundings (Gartner, 2015).

## SOLUTIONS AND RECOMMENDATIONS

The authors have done a research on the customer behavior on garment shops to further substantiate our findings and assumptions above. As part of the research over 100 prospective buyers of ready-made garments were observed and the summary of findings is listed below.

- 94 of the respondents did not convert to sale or did not buy the clothes from the retail shop. Of these around 68 tried different clothes while the remaining 26 did not like the clothes design hanging and did not feel it worthwhile to go for trials.
- Of the 68 people who tried around 31 did not find color to their liking and 23 did not find the right size while the others felt the cost and the feature were not in sync in other words overpriced.

- The prospects spend on an average around 45 minutes in the retail shop.
- The average sales person took three minutes to bring the clothes back from the trial room and place it in the correct position and rack.

The authors suggest below how the situation could improve using the IoT and 3D printing (assuming technical feasibility with improving technology).

- IoT devices could capture using embedded tags inside the garments on how many times a particular garment reached the trail room (which implies an interest level). The same tags can also see garments which were never picked up and did not evoke any interest and hence may be categorized as ones whose design was not as per customer preferences. This data could provide insights to the garment manufacturer on what has a higher potential to sell so that similar designs can be launched more.
- IoT devices could also tag using SmartMirrors or interactive kiosks customer preferences for a specific color and size. If the color is not available this data can again signal the manufacturer or the retailer on the color preferences being most sought after or size of garments in demand.
- A faster response would mean lesser time spent in the shop thereby making space for new customers or prospects.

The same approach can be used for other areas including customer electronics, automobile manufacturing, and lighting or air conditioning products. Table 1 compares the current methods for design and the IoT and 3D printing-driven design.

*Table 1. Comparison of the current methods for design and the IoT and 3D printing-driven design*

| | Current Methods for Design | IoT and 3D Printing-Driven Design |
|---|---|---|
| When it is initiated | • Before Product Launch<br>• Based on market feedback<br>• Based on technology evolution | • Real time customer behavior analysis<br>• Real time based on complaints, failures and usage patterns |
| How it works | • Usually prototyping happens by design engineers and then a pilot launch happens which helps assess market response.<br>• Next design change is more technology driven rather than customer driven and happens less frequently | • Real time design changes possible based on continuous usage data transmitted across networks and with rich analytical engines supporting and suggesting findings.<br>• Human intervention in design is more of commercial and technical validation. |
| Benefits | • Leverages on human experience which further learns from past mistakes. | • Design is rich interpretation of customer desire and preferences and may lead to perfect design |
| Limitation | • More reactive than proactive.<br>• Based on majority views<br>• Suffers from customer accepting a feature since no credible alternative possible<br>• Feedback mechanism seldom reaches design team and customers settle for the best of the worst approach | • Each customer may have his own perception and style of operating leading to tailor made recommendations at even individual level.<br>• Less standardization<br>• Commercial feasibility, safety or other unstated customer low priorities may be ignored<br>• Product may have hundreds of evolution cycle. |
| Application Areas | Across industries:<br>• More real time in case of food items.<br>• Rarely used for automobiles this goes with expert opinions. | Across industries:<br>• Consumer electronics TV/Fridge/White goods.<br>• Automobiles and transportation.<br>• Apparels and clothing. |

## FUTURE TRENDS AND RESEARCH DIRECTIONS

Future trends in IoT devices will be in the direction of device originated monetary transactions, social objects and devices with limited form factors. This will increase the potential to help further in new product development aligned to customer expectations and preferences based on the data gathered on behavior patterns which will be generated by the above IoT devices.

According to Kubler (2015) in traditional product companies, value creation was identified with customer needs and manufacturing engineered devices while today IoT with analytics, subscription, apps, contextual information and cognitive capabilities has become the future. While information and knowledge is the core of the IoT era, it nonetheless remains challenging to perceive and extract the real value of those assets, as information is not as tangible and concrete as physical assets.

The IoT and the data from connected devices are revolutionizing the interaction between companies and customers and adding value. Product managers with the huge data visibility from IoT devices, sensors can create higher performing superior efficiency products directly based on customer stated and unstated needs. Marketers can build better and sustained relationships with their customers powered from insights of data on customer's behavior and also provide more personalized service and products, while keeping data confidential.

There are numerous use cases in different verticals of product engineering where IoT gathered data will be an input for new product design and adoption while also continuously generating newer prototypes using remote 3D printers at Original Equipment Manufacturers premises for product refinement.

Some use cases of future trends in IoT would involve Intelligent Objects monitoring production lines, conveyor belts, automobile engines/tyres/fuel consumption, energy consumption and distribution, medical treatment and efficacy, logistics movement and many other areas sending data and also receiving instructions based on analysis to act and prevent damage. A transformer or an electric meter shutting down to prevent a blackout when a home appliance draws excess current is one such case. These will further contribute to feature enhancements in new product launches.

Figure 4 shows a schematic of the futuristic models where connected cars (with IoT sensors embedded in all components be it tires, engines, clutch plates) will transmit information of an existing customer to a remote 3D printer which will 3D print a metal and rubber or plastic components of the vehicle tailor-made to the customer to provide him more economy and savings. For example, this might be a custom-made clutch plate which activates with the desired force or even a customized seat with flexible height or fabric based on the height of the driver.

In the above futuristic model which seems very much probable it is suggested that all appliances such as vehicles will be fitted with sensors which will send information on driver specific usage such as gear changes or acceleration patterns, this can be transferred to a 3D printer connected to a computer which will create a new design (based on data being processed) and send to the design department for human approval. Figure 5 shows an iterative prototyping improvement model based on the IoT and 3D printing.

*Figure 4.*

*Figure 5.*

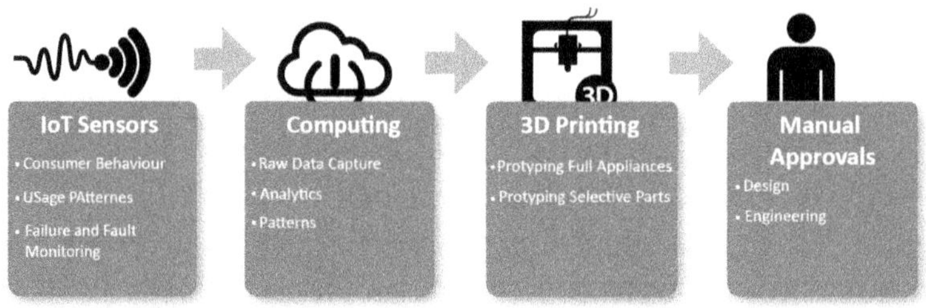


Industrial IoT technologies will open up a host of new capabilities to machine designers. They will add significant value and competitive advantage to their OEM products. But designers will have to anticipate how their machines fit into the new object-driven world. That will require the specification of robust hardware, ample processing power, and sufficient memory to fulfill the enhanced software requirements that lie ahead. In addition, machines must work with the latest standards to transport data to higher-level networks for asset-management applications.

End-user customers will benefit from simpler equipment commissioning at lower cost which is designed and derived from their usage data and their subconscious feedback provided to servers based on their day-to-day usage actions of an appliance, readily prototyped by a remote printer sitting thousands of miles away near the design lab of an equipment manufacturer, and validated at the last stage by human beings primarily from commercial and security viewpoint.

Innovative product development teams are beginning to look at enormous streams of real time machine data into actionable information to improve the product development process by understanding where product innovation is necessary, which features are most used or least user or more desirable, and how to lower their overall cost of ownership.

The area opens up a wide opportunity for engineers and researchers to work on current limitations and disadvantages being faced by consumers due to design faults or short-sightedness of design engineers thereby quantifying the benefits of this technology from the consumer point of view and the manufacturer stand point. The authors see significant benefits in terms of costs and customer conveniences for all stakeholders as faults come down, usage picks up and people more readily adapt to new devices and appliances or newer service offerings.

The inclusion of IoT in devices also increases opportunities and challenges for targeted marketing which focuses on identifying specific group of products with respect to certain customers or vice versa while also developing appropriate solutions for those targeted groups.

## CONCLUSION

In this paper, a collection of current papers on data collection and delivery has been reviewed. Although there are many researches in independent areas of IoT and 3D printing with different solutions but there is no research on merging both these latest technologies to touch upon a hereto human resource dominated area of new product design and enhancements. The chapter objectives of understanding how IoT enabled devices could potentially work as messengers of customer feedback to design team and further how the objects can themselves substitute to some extent the human design team using this information has been discussed by the authors giving real life examples along with technology limitations. Further the benefits of such a fusion of IoT with 3D printing in terms of cost, reduce MTBF and constant upgrade and evolution were highlighted. Current New Product developments practices are still a major disconnect from the field situation in terms of customer observation and feedback and are more laboratory based and confined to the product design team. Numerous cases some of which are futuristic have also been discussed and a small study with a limited sample size on how actual benefits can be realized has also been discussed.

While both IoT and 3D printing are still evolving technologies and hence suffer from nascent issues like network congestion, reliability of sensors, capability limitations of 3D printers, limitations of material and human reluctance to handover control to machines, it is more or less evident from early adopters that both concepts of IoT and 3D printing are going to change the way NPD teams handle design evolution in the coming future. Whether we can combine both of these and handover control to SmartObjects and relegate ourself to secondary citizens of the WWW while making objects the "FirstCitizens" in terms of compute power, data transmission volumes and productivity workloads is something that will become clear in days to come.

Finally, the major drivers which will ensure that this technology combination proves successful from new product design aspect will be three folds: Firstly, manufacturer's willingness to compromise on standardization vis-à-vis meeting customer desires, secondly technology evolution pace in both 3D printing and IoT and finally human behavior to accept data-driven object-suggested design over traditional knowledge and insights.

## REFERENCES

Allied Market Research. (2015). *3D Printing Market by Technology and Material-Global Opportunity Analysis and Industry Forecast 2014-2020*. Electronic Systems and Devices.

ASTM International. (2015). *Standard Terminology for Additive Manufacturing*. Retrieved Sep 09.2013 from http://web.mit.edu/2.810/www/files/readings/AdditiveManufacturingTerminology.pdf

Au, A. U., Huynh, W., Horowitz, L. F., Folch, A., & Angew. (2016). 3D-Printed Microfluidics. Angewandte Chemie International Edition, 55(12), 3862-3881. doi:10.1016/j.wneu.2013.07.009

Bailey, C. (2012). Design, simulation and modelling for nanopackaging applications: current capabilities and future requirements. *12th IEEE Conference on Nanotechnology*. doi:10.1109/NANO.2012.6322238

Barnaghi, P., Wang, W., Henson, C., & Taylor, K. (2012). Semantics for the Internet of Things: Early Progress and Back to the Future. *International Journal on Semantic Web and Information Systems*, *8*(1), 1–21. doi:10.4018/jswis.2012010101

Becker, C., Gonzalez-Ba, H. H., Latombe, J. C., & Tomasi, C. (1995). An Intelligent Observer. *Fourth International Symposium on Experimental Robotics, ISER'95.*

Bhasin, H. (2016). *New Product Development*. Retrieved July 3, 2016 from http://www.marketing91.com/new-product-development/

Bhuiyan, N. (2011). A framework for successful new product development. *Journal of Industrial Engineering and Management*, *4*(4), 746–770. doi:10.3926/jiem.334

Brun, E. & Steinar, A. (2009), Managing ambiguity in New Product Developments. *Creativity and Innovation Management, 18*(1), 24-34. 10.1111/j.1467-8691.2009.00509.x

Capon, N., John, U. F., & Scott, H. (1990). Determinants of Financial Performance: A Meta-Analysis. *Management Science*, *36*(10), 1143–1159. doi:10.1287/mnsc.36.10.1143

Chan, S. L., & Ip, W. H. (2011). A dynamic decision support system to predict the value of customer for new product development. *Elsevier Science Direct*, *52*(1), 178–188.

Colmenar, E., Al-Turjman, F., & Biglarbegian, M. (2014). Data delivery and gathering in IoT applications: An overview. *Local Computer Networks Workshops (LCN Workshops), IEEE 39th Conference*, 790-795.

Craig, B., González-Baños, H., Latombe, J. C., & Tomasi, C. (2005). An Intelligent Observer Human Augmentation. *Lecture Notes in Control and Information Sciences*, *223*(4), 151–160.

Figueroa, N., Dong, H., & Saddik, A. H. (2013, Nov 24). *From Sense to Print: Towards Automatic 3D Printing from 3D Sensing Devices*. Paper presented at IEEE International Conference on Systems, Man, and Cybernetics(SMC). doi:10.1109/SMC.2013.833

Geroski, P., Steve, M., & Reenen, J. C. (1993). The Profitability of Innovating Firms. *The Rand Journal of Economics*, *24*(2), 198–211. doi:10.2307/2555757

Guo, B., Zhang, D., Wang, Z., Zhiwen, Y., & Xingshe, Z. (2013). Opportunistic IoT: Exploring The Harmonious Interaction between Human and the Internet of Things. *Journal of Network and Computer Applications*. 10.1016/j.jnca.2012.12.028

Hakima, C. (2010). *The Internet of Things – Connecting Objects to the Web*. London, UK: Wiley.

Hakima, C. (2013). *The Internet of Things – Connecting Objects*. London, UK: Wiley.

Hausman, K. K., & Horne, R. (2014). *3D Printing for dummies*. Hoboken, NJ: John Wiley & Sons, Incorporation.

Hermans, P. (2014). *How could the Electronics Industry use 3D Printing?* Retrieved Jan 17,2014 from http://www.3dprintingelectronicsconference.com/3d-printing-electronics-conference/how-could-the-electronics-industry-use-3d-printing/

Hongming, C., & Xu, L. D. (2014). IoT based Configurable Information Service Platform for Product Life cycle management. *IEEE Transactions on Industrial Informatics, 10*(2), 1558-1567. doi: 10.1109/TII.2014.2306391

Horvath, L. (2001). Collaboration: The key to value creation in supply chain management. *Supply Chain Management: An International Journal*, *6*(5), 205–207. doi:10.1108/EUM0000000006039

IoT Case Studies. (2016). *Heidelberg Pioneers the Smart, Connected Printing Press*. Retrieved Jan 1,2016 from http://www.ptc.com/internet-of-things/use-cases

iRythm Technologies. (2016). Retrieved on Aug 10,2016 from http://www.irhythmtech.com/patients-heart-arrhythmias-afib.php

James, T. (2016). *The Future of Fashion Is 3D Printing Clothes at Home*. Retrieved April 15, 2016 from http://www.bloomberg.com/news/articles/2016-04-15/3D-printing-is-poised-to-bring-haute-couture-into-the-home

Kime, M. B. (2016). *Trane At IoT World*. Retrieved May 4,2016 from http://www.trane.com/commercial/north-america/us/en/about-us/newsroom/press-releases/trane-at-iot-world.html

Klein, G. T., Lu, Y., & Wang, M. Y. (2013). *3D printing and neurosurgery--ready for prime time?* Retrieved Jul 16, 2013 from https://www.ncbi.nlm.nih.gov/pubmed/23871811

Krishnan, V., & Karl, T. U. (2001). Product Development Decisions: A Review of the Literature. *Journal of Management Science*, *47*(1), 1–21. doi:10.1287/mnsc.47.1.1.10668

Kubler, S., Min-Jung, Y., Cassagnes, C., Främling, K. D., & Skilton, M. (2015). *Opportunity to Leverage Information-as-an-Asset in the IoT -- The Road Ahead*. Paper published in Future Internet of Things and Cloud (FiCloud), 3rd International Conference. doi:10.1109/FiCloud.2015.63

Macdonald, E., Salas, R., Espalin, D., Perez, M., Aguilera, E., Muse, D. & Wicker. (2014). 3D Printing for the Rapid Prototyping of Structural Electronics. *IEEE Access, 2*, 234-242. doi: 10.1109/ACCESS.2014.2311810

McCaskill, S. (2015). *Coca-Cola Is Using The IoT To Create New Coke Flavors*. Retrieved from http://www.techweekeurope.co.uk/networks/m2m/coca-cola-using-iot-create-new-coke-flavours-180916#wBezSPZAQXStZszf.99

Montoya-Weiss, M. M., & Calantone, R. (1994). Determinants of New Product Performance: A Review and Meta-Analysis. *Journal of Product Innovation Management*, *11*(5), 397–417. doi:10.1016/0737-6782(94)90029-9

Moses, A. (2012). *LG smart fridge tells you what to buy*. Retrieved January 10, 2012 from http://www.smh.com.au/digital-life/hometech/lg-smart-fridge-tells-youwhat-to-buy-cook-and-eat-20120110-1ps9z.html

Nashiya, S. (2015). *3D Printing + IoT= Future*. Retrieved Sep 01, 2015 from https://www.fingent.com/blog/3d-printing-iot-the-future

OPTOMEC. (2016). *Technology*. Retrieved August 03, 2016, from Optomec.com: http://www.optomec.com/Additive-ManufacturingTechnology/Overview

Osweiler, K. (2013). *IRhythm drives innovation with the internet of things*. Retrieved Dec 4,2013 from https://gigaom.com/2013/12/04/irhythm-drives-innovation-with-the-internet-of-things-2/

Ramakrishnan, R., & Gaur, L. (2016, Jan 21). Smart electricity distribution in residential areas: Internet of Things (IoT) based advanced metering infrastructure and cloud analytics. *International Conference on Internet of Things and Applications (IOTA)*. doi:10.1109/IOTA.2016.7562693

Ramakrishnan, R., Gaur, L., & Singh, G. (2016). Feasibility and Efficacy of BLE Beacon IoT Devices in Inventory Management at the Shop Floor. *International Journal of Electrical and Computer Engineering, 6*(6). Retrieved from http://iaesjournal.com/online/index.php/IJECE/article/view/10807

Research and Markets. (2016). *Business Report 2016-2022: Intelligent, Digitized & Automated Smart Factories to Transform the Manufacturing Industry - Research and Markets*. Retrieved September 15, 2016 from http://www.researchandmarkets.com/research/s2dt9h/smart_factory

Rex, D., & Stoli, S. (2014). *Application of 3D laser scanning in a Production Environment*. Retrieved Jan 21, 2014 from http://publications.lib.chalmers.se/records/fulltext/202372/202372.pdf

Ricardo, B. (2013). *Coca-Cola shows off the untapped potential for 3D printing in advertising*. Retrieved August 20,2013 from http://venturebeat.com/2013/08/20/coca-cola-3d-printing/

Rishikesha, T. K., & Ganesh, N. P. (1999). *Creating Successful New Products: Challenges for Indian Industry*. Retrieved July 31, 1999 from http://www.iimb.ernet.in/~rishi/epwcsnp.pdf

Soni, P. K., Gary, L. L., & David, T. W. (1993). Industrial Innovation and Firm Performance: A Reconceptualization and Exploratory Structural Equation Analysis. *International Journal of Research in Marketing, 10*(1), 365–380. doi:10.1016/0167-8116(93)90019-U

Staff, J. (2014). *Transforming 3D Printing Using Recycled Plastic Bottles*. Retrieved Jun 17, 2014 from http://www.coca-colacompany.com/stories/ekocycle-transforming-3d-printing-using-recycled-plastic-bottles

Streetline Inc. (2013). Retrieved Jan 10, 2013 from http://www.prnewswire.com/news-releases/streetline-closes-25m-financing-to-enable-internet-of-things-for-smart-cities-186319301.html

Sue, P. (2016). The Atj Report. *American Journal of Transplantation*. Retrieved Sep 10, 2016 from http://onlinelibrary.wiley.com/doi/10.1111/ajt.2016.16.issue-5/issuetoc

Swedberg, C. (2013). Trane Restocks Supplies at Assembly Plant Via RFID. *RFID Journal*. Retrieved online Jul 23, 2013 from http://www.rfidjournal.com/articles/view?10851

Szczerba, R. J. (2015). *No Donor Required: 5 Body Parts You Can Make With 3-D Printers*. Retrieved Jun 17, 2015 from http://www.forbes.com/sites/robertszczerba/2015/06/17/no-donor-required-5-body-parts-you-can-make-with-3-d-printers-2/#7f2b96094a3b

Ventola, C. L. (2014). *Medical Applications for 3D Printing: Current and Projected Uses*. Retrieved Oct 2014 from https://www.ncbi.nlm.nih.gov/pmc/articles/PMC4189697/

Vermesan, O., Friess, P., Guillemin, P., Gusmeroli, S., Sundmaker, H., Bassi, A., & Doody, P. et al. (2011). *Internet of Things Strategic Research Roadmap*. Aalborg, Denmark: River Publishers.

Versel, N. (2011). *Bosch Healthcare chief is bullish on Telehealth-enabled care management*. Retrieved September 15, 2011 from http://www.mobihealthnews.com/13245/bosch-healthcare-chief-is-bullish-on-telehealth-enabled-care-management

Weber, J. (2016). *3D Printing is poised to bring haute couture into the home*. Retrieved April 15, 2016 from http://www.bloomberg.com/news/articles/2016-04-15/3d-printing-is-poised-to-bring-haute-couture-into-the-home

Weber, R. H. (2010). Internet of Things – New security and privacy Challenges. *Computer Law & Security Report, 2010*(January). Retrieved from https://www.researchgate.net/profile/Rolf_Weber3/publication/222708179_Internet_of_Things_-_New_security_and_privacy_challenges/links/0c96053cab03fee371000000.pdf

Whitney, H. (2015). *The 'World's First' 3D Printed Air Conditioner Sells in China for $6395*. Retrieved Mar 13, 2015 from https://3dprint.com/50805/3d-printed-air-conditioner

## KEY TERMS AND DEFINITIONS

**3D Printer:** 3D printing or additive manufacturing is a process of making three dimensional solid objects from a digital file. 3D printers are devices which implement this 3D printing model.

**IoT:** Internet of things is a connected network of smart objects each of which has a capability of uniquely identifying each other, communicating across digital network and intent to broadcast information about itself and surroundings usually aided by sensor technologies.

**MTBF:** Mean time between failures of a machine is a statistical calculation of the time gap between two successive failures

**Smart Mirror:** Traditional mirrors which function more than just showing reflective image to showing data, capturing photographs or displaying other content with capability to accept inputs form the user in written and verbal formats.

# Chapter 11
# Towards Autonomous IoT Logistics Objects

**Bill Karakostas**
*VLTN, Belgium*

## ABSTRACT

*To improve the overall impact of the Internet of Things (IoT), intelligent capabilities must be developed at the edge of the IoT 'Cloud.' 'Smart' IoT objects must not only communicate with their environment, but also use embedded knowledge to interpret signals, and by making inferences augment their knowledge of their own state and that of their environment. Thus, intelligent IoT objects must improve their capabilities to make autonomous decisions without reliance to external computing infrastructure. In this chapter, we illustrate the concept of smart autonomous logistic objects with a proof of concept prototype built using an embedded version of the Prolog language, running on a Raspberry Pi credit-card-sized single-board computer to which an RFID reader is attached. The intelligent object is combining the RFID readings from its environment with embedded knowledge to infer new knowledge about its status. We test the system performance in a simulated environment consisting of logistics objects.*

## INTRODUCTION

The importance of the Internet of Thing (IoT) concept has risen dramatically in recent years. This was in part fuelled by improvements in communications and identification technologies, as constructing the IoT requires amongst others. automatic identification technology, RFID, near field communications (NFC), WiFi, ZiGbee, Bluetooth, and so on. However, as the numbers of IoT objects were projected to rise to over 25 billion by 2015 (Evans, 2011), the management of all the data generated by such large numbers of objects will become a challenge. It is doubtful whether even with large scale data processing technologies such as cloud computing can cope with the magnitude of IoT generated data. Data processing needs therefore to move to the edges of the IoT network, i.e., to the actual objects that comprise it. Objects in IoT environments therefore need to exhibit more autonomous intelligent behaviour by processing locally generated data and making autonomous decisions.

DOI: 10.4018/978-1-5225-2104-4.ch011

In the field of logistics, most of the IoT data processing is currently carried out in the back-office systems, to which IoT data (such as data from sensors such as RFID, attached to physical logistics objects) is transmitted, cross referenced and processed. In many situations, however, the IoT object is better placed to process data locally, and make decisions autonomously, rather than being passively configured by remote systems.

The true benefit of IoT will be experienced when intelligence becomes located both at the server end as well as at devices. Machine learning coupled with AI can be used in order for the IoT object to learn from the data to decipher trends and predict future events in advance.

The concept of IoT object autonomy is fairly recent in the literature. In (Liu & Zhou, 2012) for example, it is proposed to automate many of the IoT object tasks, and to allow objects to make judgments based on their reasoning ability. In their approach, objects can negotiate, understand and adapt their environment, and learn from other objects. In the context of logistics, research projects such as iCargo (Hofman et al, 2016) propose that objects acquire intelligence through cooperative behaviour. One of the most important pieces of such information is their location. The reason for this is that the majority of the objects will be mobile so that the objects themselves need to know about it (e.g., if the logistical object has reached its destination). Aside from the absolute position, the relative position might also be of interest (Uckelmann-et al, 2011). For example, an intelligent parcel object can infer its current position from its relationship with a truck that carries it, assuming that the truck object has location sensors and can transmit location information to other cooperating objects.

Therefore, instead of simply collecting data to send to back-office applications, or to carry out simple calculations such as threshold checks, intelligent IoT objects need to self-monitor their state in the environment. However, the potential and limits of such localised intelligent behaviour is an open research issue. The chapter therefore aims to explore such limits, by proposing an architecture for a 'smart object', prototyping it and testing its behaviour in a simulated logistics context.

This chapter is structured as follows. It surveys IoT enabling technologies such as communication protocols for IoT such as CoAP and object identification technologies of RFID and EPCIS. It next discusses current approaches to intelligent IoT objects. Then, it describes an architecture for a smart object designed around a single board computer with a connected RFID reader and presents the software architecture of the smart object's software that is developed in embedded Prolog. Through examples taken from a logistics scenario, it shows how such an object can exhibit some types of autonomic behaviour by inferring new facts about its environment using combined existing stored facts and received RFID readings, and by applying backward and forward reasoning rules. The software performance of the prototype is tested in a simulated logistics IoT environment to assess the feasibility of the smart object concept in real life environments. Finally, a summary of the findings and proposals for further research are discussed.

## IoT INTELLIGENCE ENABLING TECHNOLOGIES AND STANDARDS

Various networking, service management and operating system technologies exist today that can be utilised in the Internet of Things. In the networking area, protocols include WSAN, RFID, NFC, BLE, ZigBee, IEEE 802.11ah, and 6LoWPAN. Operating systems suitable for the low capability hardware typical of IoT devices include TinyOS, Contiki, and FreeRTOS. IoT service management middleware include platforms such as FIWARE and CityPulse, among others.

Of particular importance are technologies that link the IoT with the wider Internet such as CoAP (Ruta et al, 2012). CoAP, an Internet protocol of IoT devices, adopts a loosely coupled client/server model-based on stateless operations on resource representations, with every resource unambiguously identified by a URI (Uniform Resource Identifier). Clients access (IoT) resources via synchronous request/response interactions, using HTTP-derived methods GET, PUT, POST, and DELETE.

### Technologies for IoT Object Identification

RFID is a wireless identification and tracking technology with many industrial applications including in the field of logistics (Yan et al, 2008). RFID tags used in the supply chain are encoded with an Electronic Product Code (EPC) (GS1, 2010) which is a globally unique identifier for the object being tagged. There are several different encoding formats, and the particular tag to use depends on the tagged object. These formats can be specific to groups of goods-such as shipping containers, or can be specific to each individual asset type. To ensure uniqueness of EPC tags, EPCglobal, the organization driving standards for EPC, assigns each use company a unique master number. Each company is then responsible for assigning the other fields required by the encoding format being used.

RFID readers, handheld devices, and other sensor technologies create low-level events that represent real-world activity. These sensor events however cannot be interpreted without context. RFID has the potential to generate a massive amount of data in a typical production environment. Therefore, in an environment with tens or hundreds of readers the amount of generated data a business application would have to process can become unwieldy. Due to the passive and simple structure of RFID therefore, it is difficult to implement high level intelligence on IoT devices without additional software technologies.

## INTELLIGENT IoT ARCHITECTURES AND AUTONOMIC BEHAVIOUR

### IoT Architectures

Architectures for intelligent IoT have recently appeared in the literature. They typically employ a layered approach, with each layer dedicated to communication/sensing, data processing and knowledge processing/reasoning. For example, the architecture for IoT proposed by (Chen et al., 2010) is divided into three layers:

1. Perception layer where information is collected by using RFID tags, identification code, sensors, etc.
2. Network layer: through which information is transmitted over existing wireless network, mobile network, hardlink, Internet, radio network, etc.
3. Application layer that recognises and perceives objects and their relations with other objects, people etc.

In (Zhang et al, 2012) they propose a 4-layer architecture for intelligent IoT, comprising a data acquisition, data integration, knowledge management and visualisation layers. They have applied it to improve the efficiency of waste management by applying expert systems rules to act upon data received by the sensors. In (Maranda & Kaczmarek, 2015) they introduce a 5-layer architecture of IoT. Starting from the lowest layer, this architecture comprises of perception, access to gateway, network, middleware and application layers.

Data architectures for IoT objects have been proposed in (Koster, 2013) as a 'Smart Object API Toolkit' (Koster, 2013). It distinguishes between autonomic feedback that involves only software making decisions such as a motion sensor turning on a light, and cybernetic feedback loops where a person is participating in the loop making decisions.

## Autonomy in IoT

It has been suggested that in order for the IoT to become widespread, machines and devices must be capable of making decisions autonomously. However, this will depend on their ability to derive context through machine learning. Autonomy has been proposed in IoT as a means to enhance the capabilities, configurability and versatility of IoT architectures. In (Isenberg et al., 2011) for example, autonomous objects that render contextual decisions in collaborative production environments are proposed. Autonomous cooperating logistics processes (Hulsmann & Grapp, 2006) are a prominent example of such research, where "autonomous control" is understood as processes of decentralised decision-making in "heterarchical" structures. In the context of IoT, we propose autonomy in terms of some characteristic behavior that objects should exhibit:

**HG1:** Report to/communicate with other nearby 'parent' and 'friendly' objects, according to preconfigured schedule by broadcasting information that might be useful to the, but without revealing confidential information to unauthorised parties, and by receiving useful information from them

**HG2:** Always attempt to communicate in the most efficient and reliable manner to the extent permitted by its own resources (e.g., state of its battery), the network conditions (e.g., congestion) and other environmental factors.

**HG3:** Always attempt to maintain an internally self-consistent model of its environment.

**HC4:** Try to maintain consistency between internal world model and external world, while understanding that at times there will be inconsistency. Compensate for incomplete or erroneous information received from the environment by applying reasoning techniques that take into account missing inconsistent or incomplete data, such as probability, abductive and other suitable reasoning mechanisms.

**HG5:** When it makes decisions based on facts, or when it reports facts to third parties, inspect the completeness/validity status of internal knowledge base and report the facts in a suitable way, e.g., by attaching a confidence rating to them.

The above autonomic behaviours can only be realised by suitable hardware/software/network architectures. As discussed in the next section, several IoT architectures have been proposed but not many of those focus on the 'edge' objects alone.

## Use of Analytics for Intelligent and Autonomous Behaviour in IoT

To become autonomous, IoT objects need to analyse the data they collect from their environment immediately to identify previously known but also previously unseen patterns and to be able to distinguish between 'normal' and 'exceptional' state, i.e., flag anything that is outside the norm (Jaffe, 2016). This in turn can enable 'behavioural analytics' in the IoT object, i.e., to take appropriate action when certain situations occur. This will often require the ability to process real-time updates to streams of data in milliseconds in order to detect abnormal patterns. As a typical IoT object will have limited self-storage capabilities, the ability to process streams of data that are not stored locally and to compare them against patterns of profiles stored in local memory will be very important.

Each pattern or feature maintained by the IoT object will have a definition of normal range of data values, expected variation and similar statistical parameters to assist the IoT object deciding which sensor data is interesting or relatively uninteresting. The distributions of such interesting and uninteresting features, computed in real-time, will allow the IoT object to determine which ones would be in an outlier state, and how extreme. The outlier features could then be combined to produce a score that can be operationalized as actions the device has authority to perform.

Efficient sensing of the environment has implications on areas such as network traffic, data storage and energy utilization.

### IoT Intelligence in Logistics Environments

The IoT potential to improve logistics has been suggested by many researchers, (e.g., (Chen et al, 2010; Lydan et al, 2011). According to iCargo project (Hofman et al, 2016), "An automated cooperative service is required to link and deduct information from related business objects to enable more use of already existing data." The ability to derive information from other objects-requires awareness of the different relations. First, abstract relations must be defined by the semantic model such as the relations between cargo, means of transportation, a shipment and a transport order. Secondly, operational information about specific instances (entities) needs to be available. For example, a transport order is required to relate cargo with identification code X to a specific truck with identification code Y. Here, rules can also be used to define relations and to link objects to each other.

## PROOF OF CONCEPT PROTOTYPE

### Hardware Architecture

The physical (hardware) architecture of the prototype smart (logistics) object is shown in Figure 1. It comprises of a Raspberry PI single board computer with an RFID reader attached to it. A smart logistics object comes with preconfigured data ('facts') about other objects that it is going to encounter on its journey from the factory to its final destination (e.g. the customer). Such objects include 'container' types of objects (palettes, containers), vehicular objects (e.g. trucks), and locations such as warehouses. The smart object also gets preloaded with approximate times it can expect to encounter such objects. Using the RFID receiver, the system scans for RFID transmissions in its proximity. We assume that such transmissions contain EPCIS data, explained in the last section. However, in a typical logistics RFID environment, there will be large numbers of such RFID signals. Thus, the smart object will need to filters the RFID readings to find objects who have 'interesting' EPC codes. For example, if the goal is to sense whether it is in proximity with a specific pallet, (so that it can infer that it is currently loaded or about to be loaded onto it), the object has to filter through the scanned EPCIS data for the one that corresponds to the pallet's id. The object uses this technique to monitor the presence of the last object it was associated with it. Thus, if it cannot sense such object after a specified time period, it infers a disas-

*Figure 1. Physical architecture of the smart IoT object*

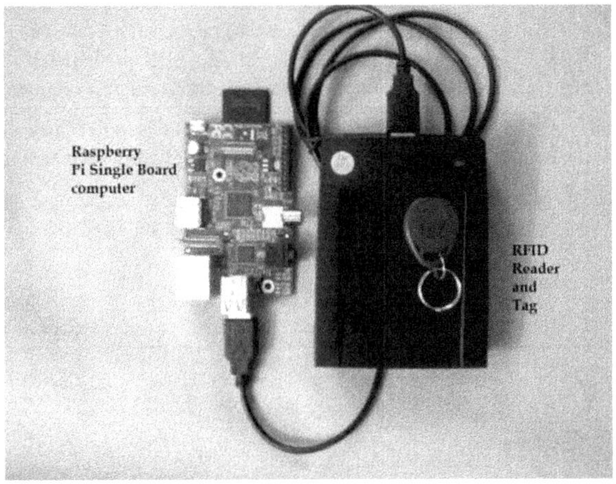


sociation event. Based on the presence of such event and the time it was established, the object infers that it should be looking for another object to associate with. If neither object is found then the object records an exceptional state which means that one or more exceptional events have occurred (sensor malfunction, incorrect or corrupted preconfigured data, etc.).

## Software Architecture

The software architecture of the smart object prototype is illustrated in Figure 2. The prototype was implemented in SWI Prolog running in the Raspbian version of Linux. Prolog embedded in small factor devices has been proposed before for rule-based control systems (Nalepa & Zi, 2006) and has advantages over procedural and object oriented languages, due to its declarative nature and abstract description of objects and logical relationships between them. The main components of the architecture are shown in Table 1.

*Figure 2. Software architecture of the smart IoT object*

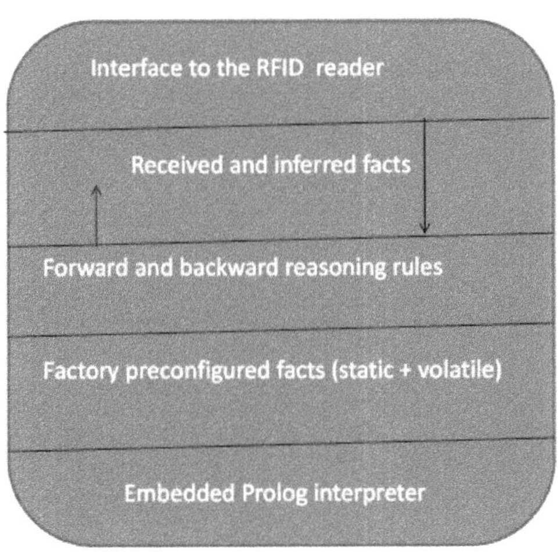

*Table 1. Components of the smart IoT software architecture*

| | |
|---|---|
| Factory preconfigured facts | These are stored in file as Prolog facts (factory settings) and loaded into the main Prolog program, and include the object's EPC id, the initial location EPC id (EPC id of factory or initial warehouse where the object originates), initial association with id pallet, etc. |
| Forward and backward chaining rules | They are stored in a file and loaded when the reasoned starts. Rules can be modified independently from facts. They might differ depending on the type of object and the autonomy degree required |
| Received and inferred facts | They are stored in the main memory and backed up to file when execution stops. |
| RFID data pre-processor | This module connects to the physical RFID device and reads RFID signals over the USB connection. This serves to clean and pre-process data and to feed to the main program only relevant RFID data (that involve the object or its associations). |

## Processing RFID EPC Data

RFID readers typically return the raw hex or binary representation of an EPC, values which must then be decoded to derive a useful representation of the information that a tag holds. RFID EPC values in hexadecimal format must be converted to binary, then decoded programmatically according to the EPC specification to extract the field values. EPC standard uses the Uniform Resource Identifier (URI) representation. An EPC URI looks as follows: urn:epc:tag:sgtin-96:3.0037000.06542.773346595

In the above URI example, the tag is an SGTIN-96 tag that has a Filter value of 3 (meaning that it is tracking a shipping unit), a Company Prefix of 0037000, an Item Reference of 06542, and a Serial Number of 773346595. Depending on the level and type of intelligence, one or more of the above values can be preconfigured in the smart object's database. The way new knowledge is inferred from existing facts and sensed facts is discussed below. Figure 3 shows the algorithm for filtering through RFID EPC data. Sample preconfigured Prolog facts are shown below:

```
Sample Facts:  [[last_known_location  urn:epc:id:sgln:0614141.54321.2528"]] /
* the factory where object was manufactured
[[event_history] [[associated_with "urn:epc:id:grai:0614141.54321.2528"]]] */
```

*Figure 3. Processing of received RFID signals*

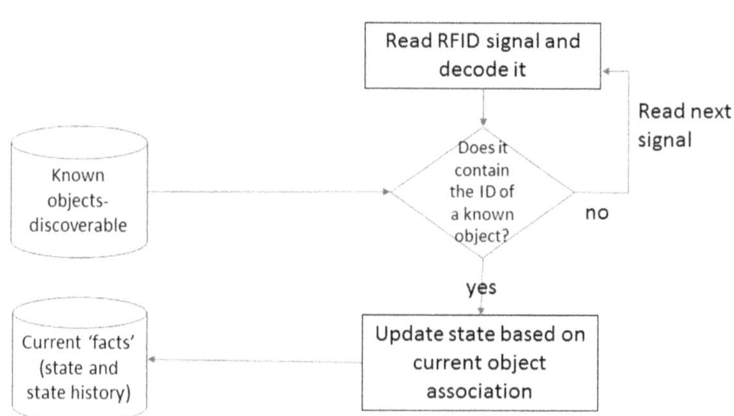

```
loaded on a palette
 [[event_history] [[associated_with  urn:epc:id:sscc:0614141.1234567890"]]] */
loaded on a palette
```

## Reasoning Rules

As argued in Section 3, one of the main required abilities of IoT objects is to filter through the received data and determining outliers in order to decide appropriate actions.

Forward chaining rules are used for inferring new facts to update state of the object. We use logical relationships such as containment between the object and other objects to infer new facts and to remove previously stored facts.-For example, if there is a current contained-in relationship between an object and a pallet, then the location of the object must be the same as the location of the pallet. When the object receives an association event with a pallet, it will store it as an association relationship in its facts knowledge base. When there is a new containment event, the object must de-associate with the previous containment. Because of the new containment relationship, the object might need to update its location. The Prolog forward reasoning rule below states that when a new containment association is added, the system should delete the previous association and should try to infer its new state based on when the association happened, and to which object.

```
process_fact (containment, Pallette,  Time):-  deleteallassociations,  add_
association(containment, Pallete,, start_forward_reasoner (associated_with,
Pallete, Time).
```

Backward chaining rules are used to deduce new facts from existing facts. Backward chaining rules are used to answer external queries to support queries such as: 'has object been in location L1 between time T1 to T2?' Other query types include: 'where are you currently?' 'what was your last known location', and 'the last *n* recorded events.'

## EXPERIMENTATION

As there are no known RFID benchmarks for smart IoT objects in logistics environments, we used a simulated approach where varying numbers of synthetic RFID EPC readings are transmitted to the prototype device, where they are stored in file and subsequently processed by the system. The purpose of this experiment is to test the smart object's ability to handle realistic size event sets and perform reasoning in reasonable time using the limited computing resources expected from IoT object embedded computers.

Figure 4 shows a screenshot of the testing environment where the performance of the system was profiled, using SWI Prolog's *profile* function, for varying numbers of simulated RFID readings. Amongst other things measured was the CPU time and total number of inferences made by the Prolog interpreter. We ran the tests with three sets of RFID data (100, 1000 and 10,000) and with two frequencies of 'interesting' facts amongst the data: 'low', i.e., approximately only 5% of the received data are relevant, and 'high' (approximately 90% of received data are relevant). Each time a useful piece of data is received, there is the firing of one inference rule and the addition or removal of 1-2 Prolog facts from the database.

*Figure 4. Performance test environment*

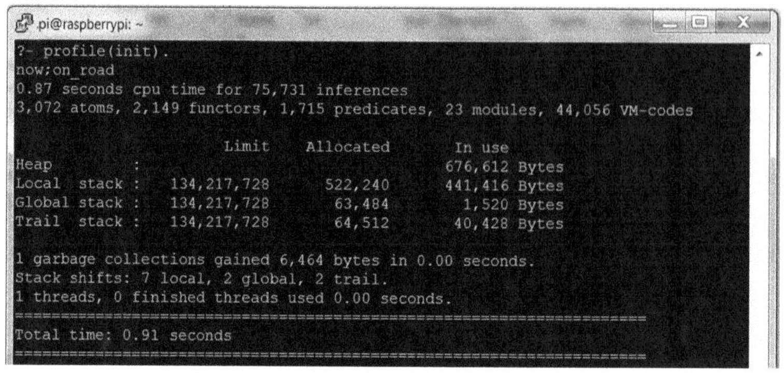


Table 2 shows the performance of the system as the number of RFID signals increases. Such performances (under 1 second time to respond to events) would be acceptable for 'passive' IoT applications in logistics, however, in applications such as real-time process control, where the timing of responses is more critical, the suitability of such response times would have to be re-evaluated. Figure 5 shows performance as a function of the RFID dataset size-in a visual manner.

*Table 2. System performance with low frequencies of 'interesting' data*

| Number of RFID Signals Read | CPU Time (*secs*) | Number of Logical Inferences |
|---|---|---|
| 100 | 0.33 | 12754 |
| 1000 | 0.39 | 17512 |
| 10000 | 0.87 | 75731 |

*Figure 5. RFID handling performance*

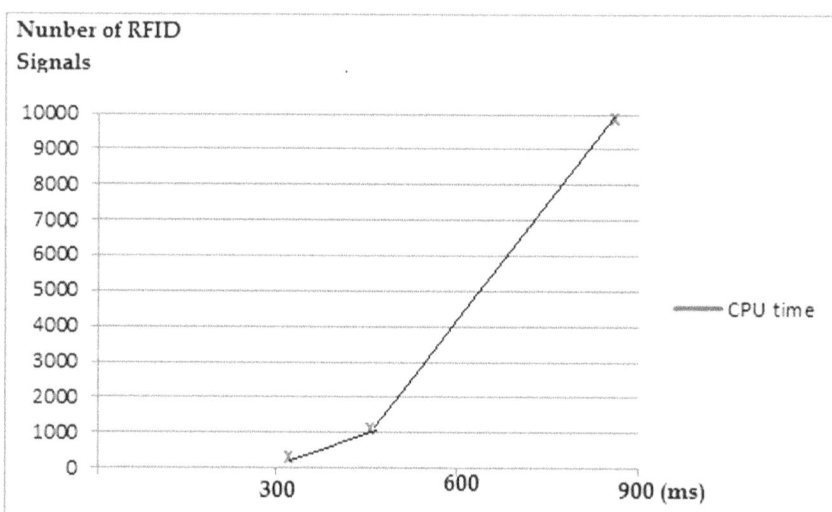

As it can be seen from Table 3, the impact on performance of the additional number of inferences is small (around 1% of additional CPU time).

## DISCUSSIONS AND CONCLUSION

In this chapter, we introduced the concept of intelligent Internet of Things (IoT) objects and their application to logistics. We identified the types of autonomous intelligent behaviour required for a 'smart' object such-as the ability to sense its location and association with other objects.

Finally, we demonstrated how a smart IoT logistics object can be implemented with a hardware/software prototype. In order for the smart IoT object to become a feasible proposition for the industry, a number of research issues must be resolved. These are discussed in the remaining of this section.

### Processing Efficiency and Hardware Advances

Recently, several electronics companies have been trying to put artificial intelligence into chips.

Neuromorphic chips are built with huge numbers of programmable points that act like the neurons and synapses within the brain. In turn, these chips can run applications that solve pattern recognition problems for text and data analytics, vision, audio, and multi-sensory fusion using much less power than existing microprocessors (Morra, 2016).

The prototype system described in this chapter was implemented using commodity hardware. For example, the RFID reader employed is an NFC smart card reader and detects only in very short range (under 10cm). For industrial purposes the type of RFID reader and its capabilities in terms of detection would have to be determined based on the requirements of the environment and its implications for the hardware and software architecture of the system analysed.

### IoT Data Quality and Trust

In order for an IoT object to act intelligently, it will require trusted-quality data from its environment. Trust in IoT is particularly challenging because it often has to be ascertained without reliance to a central authority such as a certification service. Thus, novel trust mechanisms for IoT objects will need to be developed (Kotis & Vouros, 2016). One of the general issues facing smart objects depending only on wireless technologies such as RFID for sensing is the unreliability of the readings (i.e., false negatives and false positives, RFID tags not reading at all, and so on). Relying only on such readings can lead to incorrect beliefs,-for example, that nearby objects are not present, or that the object is associated with

*Table 3. System performance with high frequencies of 'interesting' data*

| Number of RFID Signals Read | CPU Time (*secs*) | Number of Logical Inferences |
|---|---|---|
| 1000 | 0.33 | 13520 |
| 1000 | 0.39 | 18010 |
| 10000 | 0.88 | 77230 |

some other object. Thus, in addition to the forward and backward reasoning techniques used above, additional reasoning that deals with incompleteness, uncertainty (Brusey et al, 2003) and probability of known facts would need to be deployed, for example, by encoding explicit degrees of confidence in facts and using them in reasoning. The implications of implementing such types of reasoning in resource constrained environments would have to be investigated.

Finally, the ability to cope with heterogeneous data formats and identification technologies (i.e., not only on EPC data) would need to be researched. For example, in closed-loop RFID systems, companies can use whatever tag type and whatever data format they want. To cope with such heterogeneity, semantic techniques like the semantic proxy proposed by (Koster, 2013) could be introduced.

## REFERENCES


Böse, F., & Windt, K. (2007). Catalogue of Criteria for Autonomous Control in Logistics. In M. Hülsmann & K. Windt (Eds.), *Understanding Autonomous Cooperation and Control in Logistics - The Impact on Management, Information and Communication and Material Flow*. Berlin: Springer. doi:10.1007/978-3-540-47450-0_5

Brusey, J., Floerkemeier, C., Harrison, M., & Fletcher, M. (2003). Reasoning about Uncertainty in Location Identification with RFID. *Workshop on Reasoning with Uncertainty in Robotics at IJCAI-2003*, Acapulco Mexico.

Chen, Y., Guo, J., & Hu, X. (2010). The research of Internet of things' supporting technologies which face the logistics industry. *International Conference on Computational Intelligence and Security (CIS)*, 59-63.

Evans, D. (2011). *The Internet of Things How the Next Evolution of the Internet Is Changing Everything*. Cisco White Paper.

GS1. (2010). *EPC Tag Data Standard 3 Version 1.5*. Available from http://www.gs1.org/gsmp/kc/epcglobal/tds/tds_1_5-standard20100818.pdf

Gubbi, J., Buyya, R., Marusic, S., & Palaniswami, M. (2013). Internet of Things (IoT): A vision, architectural elements, and future directions. *Future Generation Computer Systems*, *29*(7), 1645–1660. doi:10.1016/j.future.2013.01.010

Hofman, W., Punter, M., Bastiaansen, H., Cornelisse, E., Dalmolen, S., Palaskas, Z., & Gonzalez-Rodriguez, M. et al. (2016). An interorganizational IT infrastructure for self-organization in logistics: Situation awareness and real-time chain composition. *International Journal of Advanced Logistics*, *5*(2), 101–115.

Hülsmann, M., & Grapp, J. (2006). Monitoring of Autonomous Cooperating Logistic Processes in International Supply Networks. *Proceedings of 11th International Symposium on Logistics (11th ISL)*, 113-120.

Isenberg, M. A., Werthmann, D., Morales-Kluge, E., & Scholz-Reiter, B. (2011). The Role of the Internet of Things for Increased Autonomy and Agility in Collaborative Production Environments. In D. Uckelmann, M. Harrison, & F. Michahelles (Eds.), *Architecting the Internet of Things*. Springer-Verlag Berlin Heidelberg. doi:10.1007/978-3-642-19157-2_8

Jaffe, M. (2014). IoT Won't Work without Artificial Intelligence. *Wired*. Retrieved from https://www.wired.com/insights/2014/11/iot-wont-work-without-artificial-intelligence/

Koster, M. (2013). *Data models for the Internet of Things*. Available from iot-datamodels.blogspot.co.uk

Kotis, K., & Vouros, G. (2016). Trust Semantics in IoT Entities' Deployment. *Workshop on Artificial Intelligence and Internet of Things(AI-IoT)*, Athens, Greece.

Lidan, T., Chunxiao, F., Zou, J., & Zhang, X. (2011). Analysis and Research for Fourth Party Logistics Based on Internet of Things. *International Conference Instrumentation, Measurement, Computer, Communication and Control*, Beijing, China.

Lonergan, K. (2016). The autonomous Internet of Things: how the IoT will become context-aware and self-sufficient. *Information Age*. Retrieved from http://www.information-age.com/autonomous-internet-things-how-iot-will-become-context-aware-and-self-sufficient-123460740/

Morra, J. (2016). Artificial Intelligence Gets its Head out of the Cloud. *Electronic Design*. Available from http://electronicsofthings.com/expert-opinion/internet-of-artificial-intelligence

Nalepa, G., & Zi, P. (2006). Integrated embedded Prolog platform for rule-based control systems. *Proceedings of the International Conference Mixed Design of Integrated Circuits and System. MIXDES 2006*. doi:10.1109/MIXDES.2006.1706678

Poniszewska-Maranda, A., & Kaczmare, D. (2015). Selected methods of artificial intelligence for Internet of Things conception. *Proceedings of the Federated Conference on Computer Science and Information Systems*, 1343–1348. doi:10.15439/2015F161

Ruta, M., Scioscia, F., Loseto, G., Gramegna, F., Pinto, A., Ieva, S., & Di Sciascio, E. (2012). A logic-based CoAP extension for resource discovery in semantic sensor networks. *SSN'12 Proceedings of the 5th International Conference on Semantic Sensor Networks, 904,* 17-32.

Uckelmann, D., Harrison, M., & Michahelles, F. (Eds.). (2011). *Architecting the Internet of Things*. Springer-Verlag Berlin Heidelberg. doi:10.1007/978-3-642-19157-2

Yan, L., Zhang, Y., Yang, L. T., & Ning, H. (2008). *The Internet of Things: From RFID to the Next-Generation Pervasive Networked Systems (Wireless Networks and Mobile Communications)*. Auerbach Publications. doi:10.1201/9781420052824

Yuxi, L., & Zhou, G. (2012). Key Technologies and Applications of Internet of Things. *Fifth International Conference on Intelligent Computation Technology and Automation Key Technologies and Applications of Internet of Things*, Zhangjiajie, Hunan, China.

Zhang, L., Atkins, A., & Hongnian, Y. U. (2012). Knowledge Management Application of Internet of Things in Construction Waste Logistics with RFID Technology. *International Journal of Computing Science and Communication Technologies*, *5*(1), 760–767.

Zhou, Z., Tsang, K. F., Zhao, Z., & Gaaloul, W. (2016). Data intelligence on the Internet of Things. *Personal and Ubiquitous Computing*, *20*(3), 277–281. doi:10.1007/s00779-016-0912-1

## KEY TERMS AND DEFINITIONS

**Autonomous Object:** An object that exhibits behaviour that is determined by its internal control system, i.e. without external control.

**Backward Chaining:** A reasoning strategy that starts from a goal and uses available facts and inference rules to create a plan for reaching the goal.

**Embedded Software:** Software used for controlling machinery that is not a computer system, e.g. a sensor.

**Forward Chaining:** A reasoning strategy that starts with available facts and uses inference rules to create more facts until a goal is reached.

**Logistics:** The business area concerned with the planning and execution of the movement of goods, usually from a supplier to a customer.

**Logistics Object:** An object that represents a real world entity from the domain of logistics such as cargo.

**RFID:** A technology for nearfield wireless communications, used mainly for tracking and tracing.

# Chapter 12
# The Human-IoT Ecosystem:
## An Approach to Functional Situation Context Classification

**Vaughan Michell**
*University of Reading, UK*

**James Olweny**
*University of Reading, UK*

## ABSTRACT

*IoT devices offer a cheap and powerful approach to identifying real world states and situations and acting on this real world environment to change these states and the environment. Augmenting real world things with IoT technology enables the capture of real world context to support decision making and actions in the real world via powerful smart objects in a human- IoT ecosystem. Increasingly we will have to understand the Human-IoT or smart device ecosystem interaction in order to optimise and integrate the design of human and IoT systems. This chapter explores the design and categorisation of IoT devices in terms of their functionality and capability to support context to add to human perception. It then proposes how we can model the context information of both IoT devices and humans in a way that may help progress Human-IoT Ecosystem design using situation theory.*

## INTRODUCTION

### Layout of the Chapter

This chapter focuses on IoT sensor functionality and an approach to context modelling that is applicable to both IoT sensors and humans, both of which have to make decisions based on 'context'

We firstly introduce the key IoT context issues to be addressed and describe what constitutes an IoT thing and a model of the basic IoT components. Section 2 develops a functional model to classify IoT devices based on descriptive ontology and explores categorisations of IOT devices in terms of these functions, Section 3 explores smart IOT and context aware objects. Section 4 then applies the basic

DOI: 10.4018/978-1-5225-2104-4.ch012

premises of situation theory to defining the parameters that relate to context to further define the specific capabilities of IoT devices and model specific examples from the literature. Section 4 discusses an integrated approach to analysing Human-IoT task situations using the model to identify IoT design possibilities. Section 5 then discusses the benefits and summarises the work.

## What Is IoT?

IoT objects are everyday objects augmented with sensors and processers and a set of rules to gather data and in some cases interpret and make intelligent decisions (Santos et al., 2014). IoT devices have a digital identity and are ubiquitously interconnected on a network and to the global Internet. This capability enables everyday objects to be augmented with the ability to sense and act on the environment. Rule based processing in the device or information from the device processed in networked applications or middleware enables a range of 'intelligence', the ability to make rule based changes and the ability to interpret and react to their environment (Michell, 2014) These devices can communicate over short 'near field' distances e.g., between sensors and the device using radio frequency links. But a key enabler if IoT objects is their ability to communicate to the web and hence an almost infinite number of other devices and humans and hence application uses (Sundmaeker, 2010). As Miorandi et al. (2012) assert, IoT is a generic term for systems that have embedded identification, sensing and actuation i.e., movement ability distributed spatially and their links to the web with a massive range of user applications. Adding IoT functionality to everyday objects endows that object with 'intelligence' via application logic to make sense of environmental data and global communications options via the web (Kortuem et al., 2010). Things refers to both 'real and virtual entities that are capable of being identified' (de Saint-Exupery, 2009) and used in the human environment. Miorandi et al. (2012) describes "things" as information entities that have:

- Physical existence,
- Communication ability,
- A unique identifier with a systems address,
- Basic computing abilities,
- A means of sensing physical phenomena.

The object or 'Thing' has a physical presence in the real world, it can receive inputs from our world through sensors and communicate with other 'Things' through the internet and if equipped with actuators it can make physical changes to its environment. In summary, the internet of things refers to any system of physical devices that can measure the state of, or make a physical change in, the real world based on its application logic and its own captured data to communicate via the internet real time state information, alone and/or in concert with similar devices.

## IoT Devices and the Human-IoT Ecosystem

### Instrument

Vygotsky's activity theory identified that human agents use artefacts as mediating entities that enable an action on an 'object of attention'– the focus of the action (Béguin, 2007). An IoT device is one such artefact (see Figure 1). The activity involves a transformation in state e.g., a physical movement or increase in knowledge (Michell, 2014). The act of using an artefact in a specific way allocates a specific function to the artefact, i.e., the artefact is a resource to achieve a specific goal i.e., a linkage between the artefact and subject of the action. Instruments are simply artefacts used in a certain way e.g., a shell used to listen to a patient's heart or they may be designed by humans with specific features to perform a function as in a stethoscope (see Figure 2). However, an IoT artefact is both a mediator in providing data or information to support a human goal or objective as well as acting as an autonomous agent in its own right and using its components e.g., sensors, actuators etc. to act on the environment.

*Figure 1. Artefacts as a mediating 'thing'*
*Adapted from Béguin, 2007.*

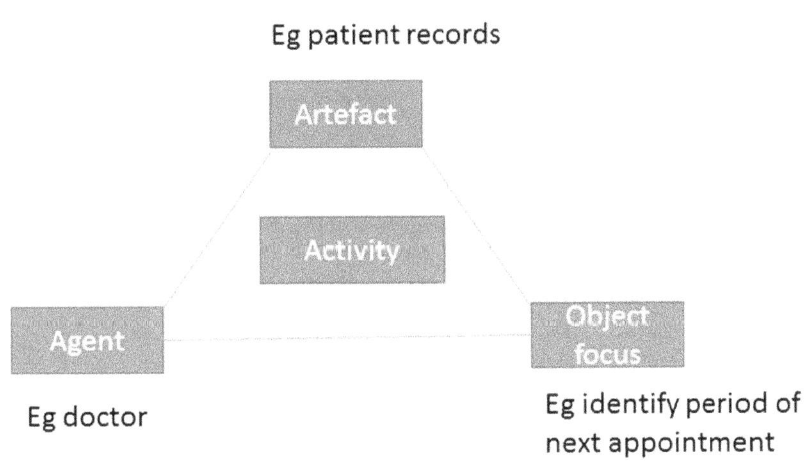


*Figure 2. Instrument definition*
*Adapted from Beguin, 2007.*

## The Human-IoT Ecosystem

Increasingly humans are using IoT devices as part of an 'artefact ecology' of different digital and physical artefacts (Vyas & Dix, 2007). The IoT artefact is 'as a bridge between heterogeneous actors' (Béguin, 2007) Artefact ecologies comprise similar artefacts built for similar purposes (B⊘dker & Klokmose, 2011). The human and IOT composition of such systems obey the five ecological laws explained by Vyas & Dix, as seen in Table 1. We suggest that a corollary of ecology thinking is that a) IoT devices capable of learning adapt to the environment and human agents adapt to a human- IoT environment and b) Human design of IoT systems need to develop to consider both human and IoT interaction.

## Key Components of IoT Devices

We now investigate specific components of IoT instruments and their resources/functions to understand their capability in the human-IoT ecosystem.

*Table 1. Properties of the human-IoT ecosystem*

| Biological Ecology Properties | Details | Human-IOT Ecology |
|---|---|---|
| **Heterogeneity** | An ecology comprises different living organisms and the environment | A human-IoT ecology comprises human and Iot agents in an object environment |
| **Mutual Interaction** | The organisms interact with each other and change each other and the environment | Humans and IoT devices mutually interact |
| **Emergence** | Observed phenomenon arise naturally as emergent properties | New behaviours arise from Human and IoT device interaction |
| **Adaptivity** | The organisms will change in response to changes imposed on them from natural phenomenon and from organised human intervention | IoT devices capable of learning adapt to the environment and human agents adapt to a human-IoT environment |
| **Co-adaptivity (Adaptivity to mutual interaction)** | Organisms change as a result of changes in the behaviour of other organisms and mutual interaction | Human design of IoT systems need to develop to consider both human and IoT interaction |

## Device

IoT artefacts include sensors, communication ability and a unique identity i.e., a human designed artefact with a specific function based on an integrated set of instruments. An IoT device can thus be said to be an 'entity that provides sensor and or actuator resources and is able to communicate to other entities' (Patel et al., 2011). We use Patel's notation where a device hosts a series of resources i.e., physical components and software services each with specific functions that define the specific IoT device capability as a set of 'instruments' each with a specific purpose.

## Sensors and Phenomena

A sensor is a component instrument with a function to detect physical states and changes in the environment (Michell, 2014). Sensors measure phenomena or 'an observable property of the environment or a physical entity' (Patel et al., 2011). This involves measuring some change in the phenomena - relative to a datum value (the measurand) that can be converted to electrical signals (see Figure 3). For example, piezo electric sensors convert pressure or force into an electrical signal hence measuring the 'observable property' pressure by relating it to an electrical output. The mechanism of measurement i.e., the conversion of the signal or change in the observable property will vary with the phenomena that are being captured, e.g. measurement of the presence of a human / animal can be detected by heat via a thermal sensor, location by the relative location of a GPS signal. The sensor is controlled by driver and data processing software to ensure the measurand is converted into appropriate digital values to be passed on to other devices or the web and converted to human understandable data, or as input to decision making applications in middleware or web applications.

## Identity Tag

To enable decision making, many different sensor inputs may be required and hence a unique identifier is used for every IoT object. A standard electronic object identity tag enables automatic scanning and identification of an object and recovery of any information held in its memory (Michell, 2014). The identity tag also links the physical world of objects to the web virtual world of information and hence

*Figure 3. Relationship between device, instrument, and function*

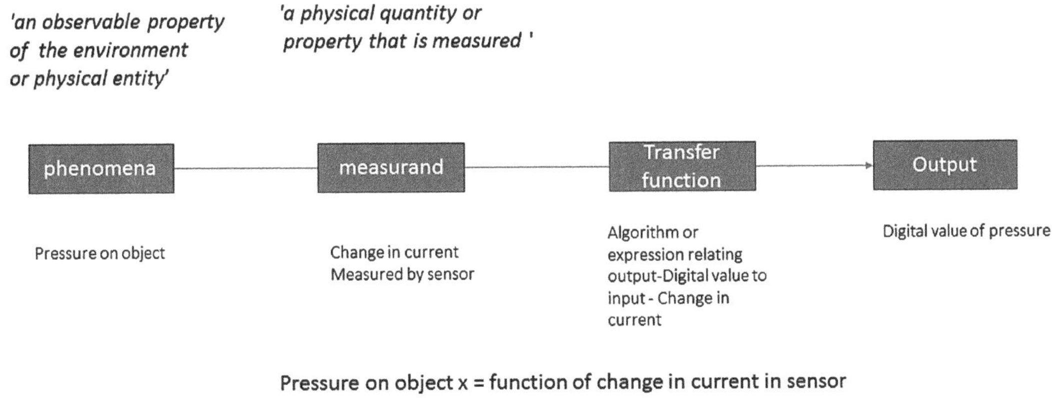

making the real world visible as virtual objects with a unique identifier on the web (Nitti et al., 2016). All IoT devices have a unique virtual identity. Any IoT system has two key components: a radio frequency identity tag that stores the details of the IoT device and the object it is attached to and a wireless RFID reader that can read the tag at short range via wireless (Borgia, 2014). The identity tag enables automatic scanning and identification of an object and recovery of any information held in its memory. This enables tags to be used as either manual or automatic proximity triggers to recognise objects and when linked to actuators open doors or gate to enable access to areas (Fleisch, 2010).

### Actuator

An actuator is a device that can make a physical change on the environment or an artefact in it and hence also changes a phenomena or observable property of the environment (Patel et al., 2011). Actuators are also controlled by driver and control software to ensure the correct force/pressure or movement commanded is achieved and measurand data about the position/force etc. is captured for this purpose (Hachem et al., 2011). Examples of actuators include motors, electromagnetic, hydraulic or pneumatics rams, to open and close doors e.g., in an automatics entry system.

### Application Logic Processing and Storage Software

IOT devices have integrated application logic or are linked to computational processing services to process data and information into an output (Kortuem et al., 2010). Data/information storage services are then needed to read and write data from both a sensor and/or actuator and the processor.

### Communications

A key feature of an IoT device is the ability to communicate information from the device to other devices, sensors and actuators via the universal communication highway – the web. This is usually achieved by using radio frequency communication for 'near field' or short distances between the device and links to the world wide web (Patel et al., 2011) This enables linking the web based digital world to the human three-dimensional world, by linking to analogue devices and analogue states (see Figure 4). A knowledge of complex state information then enables more automated human type decision making (Privat, 2012).

## IOT FUNCTIONS AND CAPABILITIES

Compton et al.'s model of a sensor provides a generic functional model of any sensor as part of an IoT device (Compton et al., 2009).

### Sensor Response and Operational Model

Any sensor has (onboard or distributed) logic, to provide a meaningful response to stimuli from environmental phenomena. The sensor measures a physical effect relative to a datum at a specific real world

*Figure 4. Generic information model of an IoT device*
*Adapted from Patel et al., 2011.*

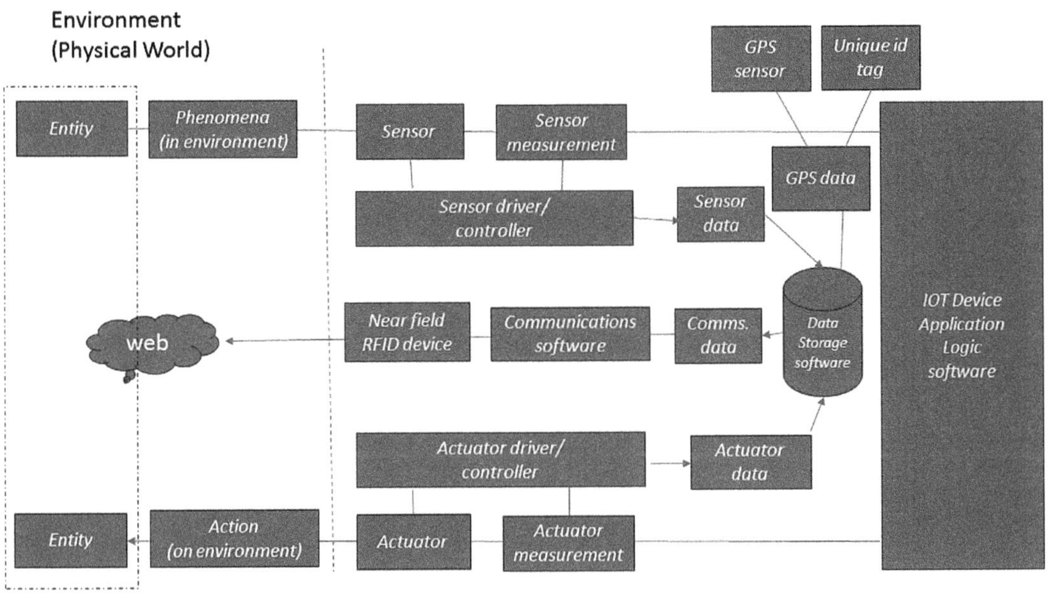


location (LOC). Every sensor has a response model to interpret the sensor readings that includes one or more operational functional models that processes and makes sense of the sensor data (Compton et al., 2009). The sensor operational model(s) will take input data in the form of process variables and process them according to the parameters (or characteristics) of the algorithm to provide a meaningful output. The final sensor output variable(s) e.g., a temperature will be some function of the sensor input data (measurand). The human meaning of the output depends on the way the differences in data measured at a time and location are interpreted by the expression or algorithm. The data process can be divided into a physical process and an abstract process that effectively uses mathematical and also logical expressions to give meaning to the effect measured in the environment. The expression is typically built in the form of production rules for interpreting the measurand data and converting the input parameters to a meaningful information output (see Figure 5). e.g., If condition: a, then process 1, else process 2. (Compton et al., 2009). Complex combinations of rules applied to input data enable a model of how the changes in the environmental phenomena will alter the output data of the sensor. Ultimately the complexity of the operational model can be summarised in a response model or transfer function that relates digital output to input measurand.

## Functionality

A function is the property of a human designed artefact that explains what it is used for and the way in which input to the artefact is converted to output (Crilly, 2010). As Warell suggests a function is 'what an element or a component/part of a product or human actively or passively does in order to contribute to a certain purpose' (Warell, 1999). A functional artefact converts a given input to an output, e.g., a hammer transfers human energy into an impact force on an object of focus to deform it or push it into something.

*Figure 5. Sensor functional model*
*Adapted from Compton et al., 2009.*

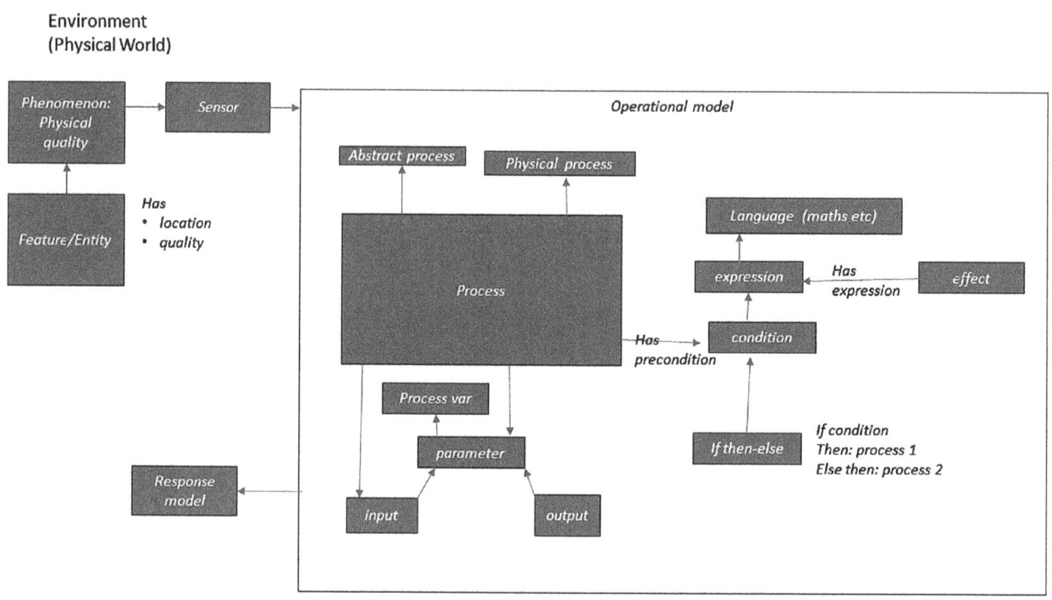


## Sensor Functionality

We can analyse IoT functionality by using basic first order predicate logic to describe intuitively what variables and functionality (i.e., the process between input and output that uses a set of numbers to represent a real world) of different. IoT devices and systems (Van Harmelen, 2008). First order logic is an intuitive formal mathematical system of predicates (confirming the existence or absence of something and propositions or features) and reasoning about the properties of objects through variables and quantifiers (numbers of things) that is also used in situation theory later in the chapter e.g.,

TIM(x) stands for x is a temporal or time measurement e.g., second, day etc.

The expression TIM(x) = f(p1…pn) then summarises the n number and type of input parameters p1, …, pn that determine the output time e.g., TIM(x) = f(time parameters) which is the general expression, but the capability may vary with the specific sensor or source used e.g., it may be atomic clock time, or system clock time etc.

## Device Identity and Location Identification

The IoT device tag enables a unique virtual identifier for the device to be established

ID(x)= f(RFID tag reference)

Most IoT devices are GPS enabled i.e., their id is reported with a specific location to the web as a virtual real world object (Nitti et al., 2016). This enables the location of the device and hence phenomenon which we define as a location (LOC) with a unique reference.

LOC(x) = f(location phenomena, ID)

The exact form of the location phenomena may be simple i.e., the GPS coordinates or it might be more complex such as a digital map or coordinates or an image.

## Sensors for State Assessment

Sensors enable identification of the state of the real world in terms of the measurement of a physical phenomenon hence sensing is a function of real world phenomena. (Michell, 2014).

The state of some aspect of the environment that a sensor senses, i.e., a general sensor measurement MEAS(x) is a function of the specific phenomenon sensed e.g., temperature, pressure, location etc at a unique identifier in time we can label as TIM. i.e., a temperature is a function of the temperature phenomena data captured at a specific location LOC and time TIM by a specific sensor (ID)

TempMEAS(x) = f(tempPhen, LOC,ID, TIM)

## Types of Sensor

Sensors are designed to detect a change in phenomena in the real world either passively from emitted radiation from the object or actively by sending a signal to the object and receiving and processing a reflected signal. Sensors range from those able to detect a specific phenomenon such as temperature or pressure to those equipped to detect specific materials and the presence of objects and animals over time. Sensors can be a single source of employ logic algorithms to integrate multiple sensor parameters into compound sense information.

## DOLCE and IoT Based Sensor Measurement

To model what phenomena IoT sensors and humans can detect in the human-IoT ecosystem we adapt the 'Descriptive Ontology for Linguistic and Cognitive Engineering (DOLCE) (Bottazzi & Ferrario, 2009) (see Table 2, Figure 6 and Figure 7). DOLCE divides the world into two: (a) 'endurant' entities that last in time, such as physical objects, people i.e. entities capable of acting on the environment and driving a change in state (Michell, 2011) and (b) things that are not constant with time are 'perdurant' entities such as the state of an object, its physical, temporal, event based and abstract properties and abstract human concepts (Gangemi et al., 2003) as per examples given in the figures.

*Table 2. Human-IoT environment entities and IoT examples*

| DOLCE Acronym | Metric | Sensor Type | Application | General Function |
|---|---|---|---|---|
| | **ENDURANTS** | | | |
| TQ | Temporal quality | | | TIM= f(TIM relations) |
| PQ | Physical Quality | | | |
| | | infrared detector | temperature | TEMP = f(infrared response) |
| | | inductive | detects types of metals MET | MET(x) = f(induced current values) |
| | | capacitance | detects type of material MAT - liquids, glass | MAT(x)= f(capacitance at distance x) |
| | | PHYSIOLOGICAL MEASURES | | |
| | | electrocardiograph sensor | HR heart activity /rate | HR = f(electrocardial response) |
| NPQ | Non Physical quality | | | |
| | | integrated sensor data | sensitivity of patient to heart disease SHD | SHD(x) = f(age, chest pain, blood pressure...) |
| POB | **PHYSICAL OBJECT** | | | |
| APO | agentive | Infrared | detects animal presence | PRES = f(infrared response) |
| | | RFID tag | detects agent id | ID(x)= f(tag) |
| NAPO | non agentive | | detects inert presence | |
| | | photoelectric | detects presence of opaque object OBJ | OBJ(x) =f(light obstruction level) |
| | | ultrasonic | detects presence of non opaque object NOO | NOO=f(time of sound wave reflection) |
| | **FEATURE** | | | |
| RP | Relevant part | cell part, membrane | detects wavelength from entity volume | Cell boundary RP(x) = f(wavelength of light emitted from a specific region) |
| PL | Place | location | tracking of clinicians | Absolute location = f(REF, LOC, TIM) |
| | **AGGREGATE** | | | |
| M | Amount of matter | Chemical, mass, fluid | disease mass | M = f(volume sensor response) |
| AC | Arbitrary collection | | drugs for patient x | AC = f(grouping characteristics) |
| | | camera/vision algorithms | | |
| | **PERDURANTS** | | | |
| | **STATIVE** | | | |
| ST | State | electro-mechanical sensor | false leg state | |
| PRO | Process (activity) | | Injecting a patient, | process=f(abstract action/activity) |
| | | camera/vision algorithms | diagnosing a patient | |
| EV | **EVENT** | | | |
| ACH | Achievement (atomic events) | smart medical cabinet | removal of a drug d | event = f(sensor variation) |
| ACC | Accomplishment | n/a | A clinical conference | event= f(human input) |
| | **ABSTRACTS** | | | |
| R | **REGION** | | | |
| TR | Temporal region | system clock | measures human time intervals eg seconds, hours | TIM= f(temporal function) |
| PR | Physical region | Galvanic sensors | SR skin responsiveness | SR=f(galvanic response) |
| | | electromyography | MR muscle responsiveness | MR=f(electromyographic response) |
| NPR | Non Physical region | AI/reasoning algorithm | % extent of injury | NPR= f(reasoning algorithm, sensor inputs) |

Based on DOLCE framework.

*Figure 6. Endurant entities in the human environment (adapted from DOLCE)*

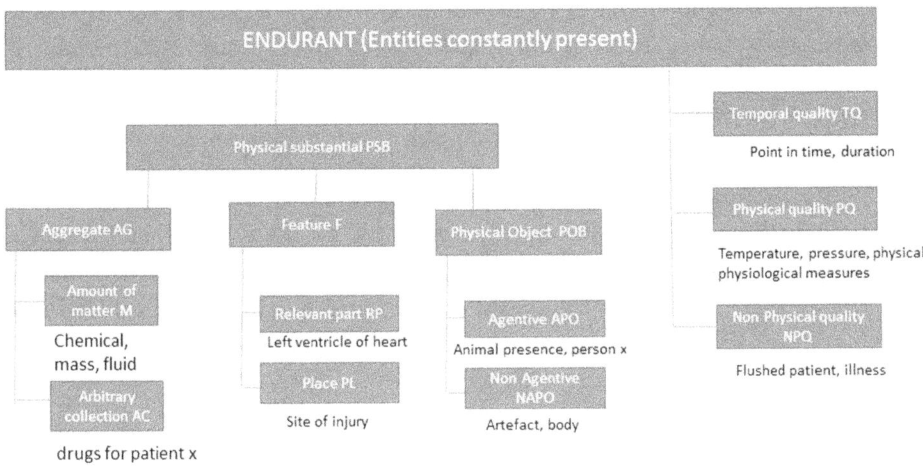


*Figure 7. Perdurant and abstract entities in the human environment (adapted from DOLCE)*

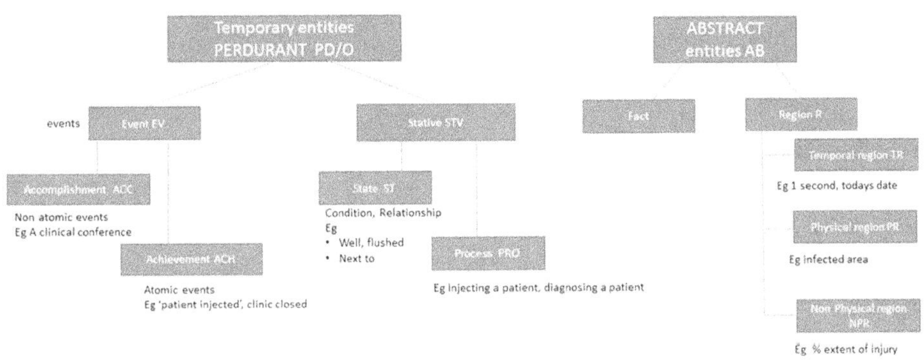


## Physical Quality Measurement (PQ)

There are an enormous range of sensors measuring physical attributes of entities such as temperature, pressure and force sensors. Inductive sensors detect types of metals and capacitance sensors can detect more general material types.

## Location Tracking and Management: PL

A very obvious and widely used advantage of an IoT sensor with rudimentary location and tag information is the ability to track location changes as a function of a location with time, corresponding to a place entity in the DOLCE notation:

Absolute location = f(ID, LOC, TIM), where LOC (x)= f(location function).

Retrofitting sensors to people and objects has enabled the tracking of doctors and patients, resources such as tools and equipment and animals (Tsiatsis et al., 2010). This enables by extension to identify where and when resources change location and hence resource management (Carmichael, 2013).

## Proximity Management

The ability to identify location enables validity and violations of resources in specific locations to be identified. For example, the use of specific bandages and surgical instruments in terms of their location (Lampe & Flörkemeier, 2004). By comparing the distance of relative locations with other facts we can then define entity x is 'near' entity y or entity x is inside entity y. This enables useful environmental context 'facts' for human and/or IoT decision making.

## Agentive Measurement (APO)

The presence and type of an animal or specific agent can be detected by infrared sensors where the size and type of animal is a function of the size and characteristics of their infrared signature. Identification of specific human agents can be detected by their id tag in terms of their role e.g., surgeon, access rights or specific individual identity. Alternatively, an image or video with appropriate algorithms can detect specific individual's. Video information processed with specific image processing software to detect and match specific movement traits e.g., human walking gait can also detect the presence of a specific agent

## Inert (Non-Agentive) Entities (NAPO)

The presence of passive objects that cannot operate on the environment by themselves (Michell, 2011), e.g., an opaque object can be detected by photoelectric sensors and non-opaque objects by ultrasonic detectors (NIBIB, 2017)

## Access Control

The checking of movement of resources into prohibited locations has long been used in simple card readers where card or tag scanning can confirm whether or not an id REF is valid for a specific access location and or time of access. For example, a system that uses infrared detectors to detect the presence of humans in a stock room and match this to the id tag signals. If it detected no staff id tag it set off an alarm) (Codegate, 2017).

This is likely to use a set of rules of the form: If Presence(x) and REF(x) =valid, then denote the intruder as valid and take no action else set off alarm.

When the access control logic is connected to simple door actuators and IoT communication capabilities then powerful access and containment strategies are possible as is seen in simple office swipe card access to banks.

## Resource Use Management (ACH)

This logic can be extended by making assumptions that the resource has been used if missing from a known location in the example of a smart medicine cabinet or smart tool box (Lampe & Flörkemeier,

2004). In this case the smart box identifies the presence of all medicines, missing medicines or incorrect medicines by matching the medicine or object id to a list of what is intended for the location. By extension simple achievement (ACH) events can be defined e.g., 'drug has been removed' – implying use.

## Process Management (PRO)

Knowing the location of a resource at a particular time and the ability to record the value of a phenomenon or input enables a process to be managed. This can be achieved by the addition of information about context or state depending on the data sensed or input to the device at the specific process location. Process and abstract states can be sensed by update from a reader that triggers a signal on the completion of a process or event (Michell, 2014). Arbitrary and conceptual states can be added by simply enabling a coded input from a user to confirm that state as in the case of clinicians completing.

## Equipment Management: State (ST)

By adding sensors to equipment and defining a specific combination of sensor parameters an arbitrary state of the equipment can be determined. For example, smart sensors embedded in orthopaedic implants enable remote monitoring of their use, which can reduce the need for hospital visits (Carmichael, 2013). This information either in the form of qualitative measure or a quantitative value can then be matched to the designed parameter values with action via other devices to inform the user, stop the device etc. The sensor may sense failure states in the device itself for example by recording device or tool parameters and combing specific state values in rule based algorithms when their values over time exceed limits

## Detecting Physical Regions (PR)

Galvanic sensors to detect skin response and electromyography based devices to identify muscle response enable measurement of a quality of the patient within a physical region (Swan, 2012).

## Non-Physical Region Detection (NPR)

This relates to conceptual regions frequently used by humans (Gangemi et al., 2003). These require the development of more sophisticated middleware for sensor information from perhaps multiple devices and human inputs to enable abstract concepts such as business domain regions etc. to be defined (Barnaghi et al., 2012).

## Relevant Part Assessment (RP)

This relates to parts of physical regions. Image processing algorithms combined with cameras of various wavelengths enable analysis and identification of specific regions. For example, wavelength based biosensors are being developed that can measure the presence of biological entities and biological relevant regions such as cells, viruses, membranes (Fan et al., 2008). For more complex parts AI and computer vision algorithms for edge detection can enable abstract regions to be defined.

## Aggregate Amounts (M)

This relates to quantities of material e.g., 'some x'. As seen earlier, many sensors can detect traces of elements which could indicate the presence of 'some', but middleware and rules based logic are required to identify human concepts and aggregate amounts.

## Arbitrary Collections (AC)

For example, parts of a human body or owned items (Gangemi et al., 2003). Detecting the ownership of basic collections can already be achieved by sensor/tag tracking the drugs or equipment for patient x. The ability to conceptualise and categorise more diverse groups of disparate objects is a human facility, but with machine vision algorithms is also becoming an IoT capability.

## Non-Physical Qualities - NPQ

Nonphysical qualities e.g., human concepts such as 'mental state, ill, wellbeing' often measured by combinations of scoresheets relating to physical metrics and human judgements. For example, mental health can be calculated by scores from human tests or qualities can be detected by aggregating sensor readings via an algorithm, emulating the human practice (Roubtsova & Michell, 2013).

## Complex State Assessment and Deduced States

By combining sensors into one device and analysing this information in operational models much more context information is possible. For example, 'fitbit' type devices include a GPS sensor for location (LOC) and accelerometer (ACC) to measure how upright a person is and also the direction of their motion, body temperature sensors (TEMP), and heart rate sensor (Swan, 2012). Algorithms operating on combinations of the measured parameters and basic assumptions then enable an abstract 'fitness' measure to be defined – which will often vary between manufacturers!

Alternatively, if sufficient sensor information is captured and available then the IoT system may be able to deduce the state through logic applied to the state information. For example, a sensor specifically designed to collect heart disease data and cross reference it against data mined patient data can deduce the potential for heart disease (Jambhulkar & Baporikar, 2015). The output – sensitivity to heart disease SHD is a function of a number of parameters including age, chest pain, resting blood pressure etc. Similarly, measurement of a temporal quality (TQ) e.g., duration of an activity can be derived from system clock measurements.

## Real World Decision Making in Context

A key element of IoT capability is that we can relate the state recorded by an IoT device to the state of the environment and hence provide real world information to users and the web. Knowledge obtained from the IoT device can be used to make decisions and act on them – particularly if the IoT device is linked to an actuator (Nitti et al., 2016). This enables the conversion of information systems from simply advice systems in the abstract 2d world of information to systems that can make decisions on and in the real three-dimensional world.

## Smart Objects and Rule Based Reasoning (see p. 402 Michell, 2014)

The ability of a device to perceive and independently act on the environment is often termed 'smart' (Kortuem et al., 2010). Lopez et al. (2012) defined smart objects as having a unique identifier, an ability to sense and store environmental measurements and make independent decisions and communicate those decisions to other smart objects and systems. IoT enables objects with processors equipped with rules to make decisions and send information or operate actuators to move and transform objects.

## Decision Making and Control

A sequence of data points regarding IoT sensor data provides a time-based view of the environment and clues to formal and informal processes taking place as conditions in the IoT environment change. For a smart IoT device to have an effect on the environment a decision must be made about what the data points mean and then an action to produce new information and send it on and/or to make a change in the environment through an actuator. For example; a card reader door entry system. Even a simple process will involve decision points as a choice between options. Typically, decisions have an implicit or explicit goal or objective that the optimum decision should meet, for example, in the case of clinical decisions (Michell et al., 2012). Control involves a decision that evaluates a state achieved by an action vs. a specific goal state.

## Control

Control involves a decision algorithm d, comparing the actual value of the output state of a system or process y to its desired value and adjusting the input control signal to account for the error (as an error signal) based on the difference between the actual and desired value. This feedback error signal is then used to adjust the input by increasing or decrease the control signal.

In open loop control there is no error signal feedback, i.e., the decision rule d adjusts the state if a single specific condition is met. For example, entry control where the access code on a card matches an authorised list then the access door is opened. In linear closed loop control the controller decision d of what new input to make is dependent on the error signal, where the error signal measures the output y vs the input signal x: If state = x-y, then new input x' is a proportion of the error signal or x-y. To avoid systems overshooting or oscillating different control algorithms d can be applied to create an adjusted input signal x'. A simple example is a variant of the smart medical box where drug viability control is possible by ensuring the temperature of the drugs are maintained within the limits indicated by the drug data and a link to a thermostat (Lampe & Flörkemeier, 2004). For example, if temp > critical drug temperature then reduce thermostat setting, else do nothing.

## Cooperative IoT Devices and context

IoT systems become very powerful when devices become collaborative by sharing data and decision making (BØdker & Klokmose, 2011). Real world decision making involves more than simple decisions on sensor states. There is a need to develop knowledge about the environment i.e., information in context to support effective and appropriate decisions. Context awareness is *the capability to acquire, analyse and interpret information about the environment* (Nitti et al., 2016). More complex states and conditions can be assessed by processing a range of sensor information to establish context. This requires additional sensor information and an ability to process it to conclude a reasonably comprehensive state of the environment necessary for decision making. As IoT sensors become more ubiquitous there is a need to integrate them with human behaviour and shared decision making in context. So how can we model context in relation to IoT devices?

## CONTEXT

### Context Aware IoT Supports Human Activity

Kortuem et al. (2010) identified three smart device design dimension a) awareness – the device ability to interpret and react to real world/human events, b) the capability of the device to represent the environment, and c) its ability to converse with the human user by input/output control and feedback. These relate to three levels of smart IoT object awareness: activity awareness, policy awareness, and process awareness.

However, the usefulness of IoT depends on the availability and quality of contextual information provided by the IoT devices and used by them to make their own action decisions. A context aware system can be defined as 'a system that provides relevant information and services to the user that supports the users' tasks or activities' (Perera et al., 2014). Context aware sensors add value to a human activity by adding information about that activity (see Figure 8). Hence, we need to consider the activity and goal of the user with respect to the sensors supporting the user in order to qualify their contextual abilities. Context aware IoT sensors add a set of contextual information that can often be more reliable than the human context data (dependent on human perception) which enables human processing to achieve a task goal. The 'perception process identifies a set of entities that explain the environmental observations' (Barnaghi et al., 2012). Hence IoT context data can check human perception by providing a separate perception of the environment. Linked with actuators IoT sense information can be configured to prevent adverse human activity and decision making, by providing additional facts and reasoning to improve safety decision making (see Michell, 2014 for more details).

*Figure 8. Context information flow with IoT device as an intelligent artefact*

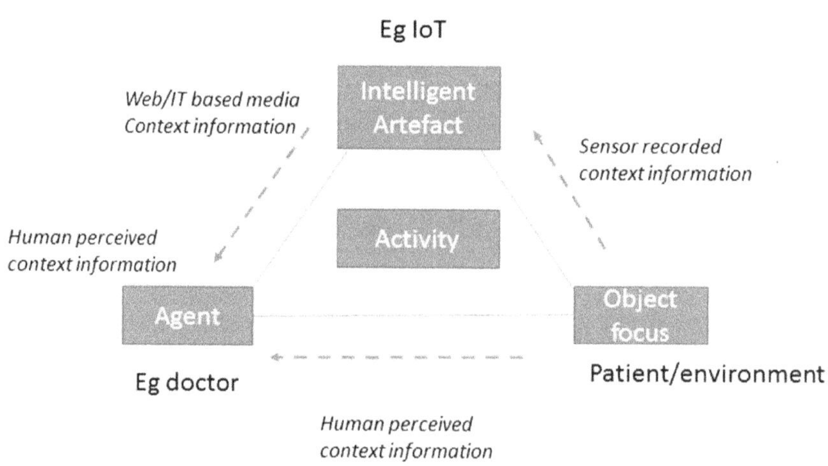

Context aware sensors vary in capability from no context model; i.e., simply gathering and storing information, through internal context models; the processing ability to reason with the information, to those devices and integrated IoT systems with an explicit model of the context or environment they operate in (Perera et al., 2014). The context model produces a subset of information about the task that is useful to it. The function examples given in the tables earlier are examples of context based models for single feature information. Perera et al. (2014) identified key context types (identity), where (location), when (time), and activity (what). This becomes a useful context classification applicable to IoT devices when set against whether the device has a simple primary sensor and algorithm or the device derives secondary data using an algorithm, onboard knowledge and primary sensor information. For example, a simple ID sensor may only identify the RFID tag but a more advanced device might use a range of facial features and a complex algorithm to recognise a unique facial identity (Perera et al., 2014).

## Example Case: Heartlands Hospital

A good example of smart IoT devices is the work at Heartlands Hospital to reduce incorrect operations on patients (see Figure 9). In-patients were given RFID wristbands with photographs attached and these were scanned by clinicians using personal digital assistant devices that linked the patient id to an electronic patient medical record (Heartlands). Clinicians also had a wristband and scanned their ID to

*Figure 9. Heartlands Hospital example*
*Based on (Heartlands).*

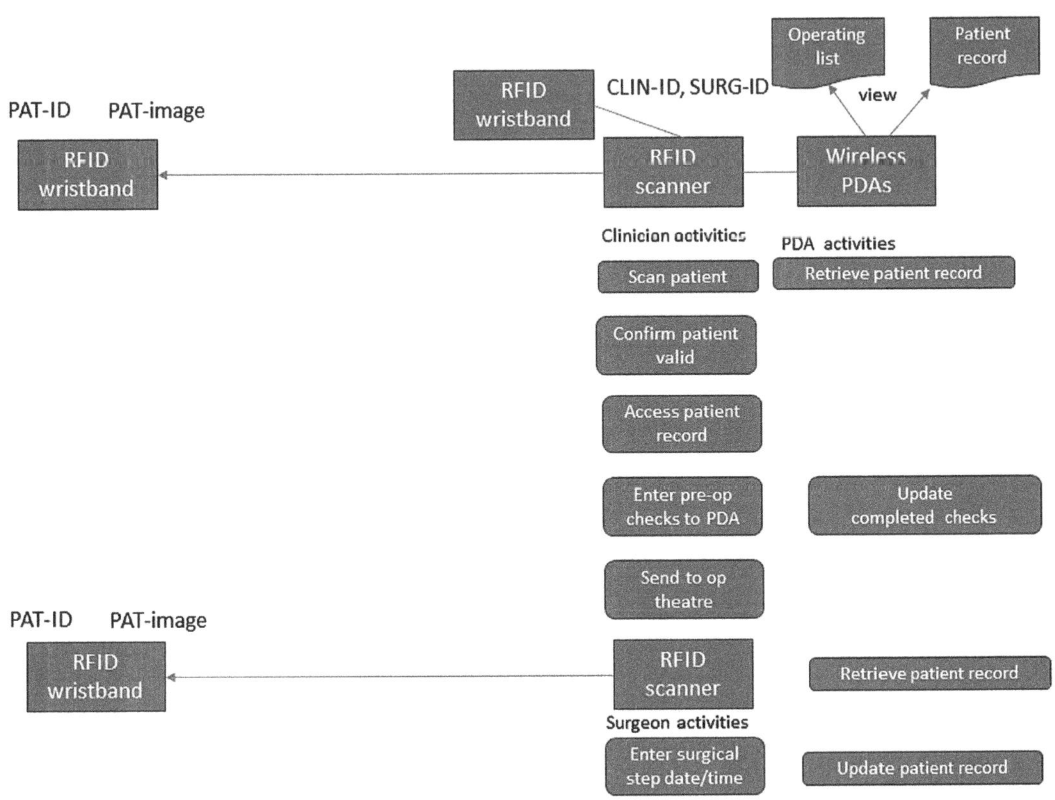

ensure an audit trail of activities. The clinician then performed the pre-operative checks and updated the results on the EPR which ensures completeness and accuracy vs patient needs. The patient was then handed on to surgery where the patient id was again scanned and the operative tasks and notes were updated on the EPR via the PDA.

### Context Level

- The IoT devices provide very basic accurate identification as contextual facts regarding patient and clinician ID(x) at time TIM(x) and location LOC(x) as a fact via an agent RFID tag,
- The bulk of the activity context data and decision making is left to the clinician's perception and their honesty and accuracy in completing the checklist of state and process entities
- An accurate record of pre-op checks and operational procedures is subject to clinician and hence further risk

It is clear that further work is need to break down the activity context information into more detailed information elements. We aim to extend Perera et al.'s approach by using the sensor parameters discussed earlier with the more detailed model of context from situation theory

## SITUATION THEORY AND CONTEXT

We have seen that individual IoT devices can capture parameters about the current state of real world variables and actions, but we need an approach to context modelling that is applicable to both IoT sensors and humans in their work situations. A situation relates to an environment location involving individuals and the relationships between them (Lenarcic, 2011). Barwise and Perry (1980) developed situation theory based on predicate logic. Situation Theory mathematically describes the meaning of a situation, or the information conveyed by humans using statements (predicates) and whether true or false. Whilst the theory is typically used to describe human situation descriptions i.e., sentences (Greeno, 1994), we use/adapt its basic premises to represent smart IoT devices which are recording and acting on facts/truths and interacting with humans as a necessary step for modelling their ecosystem relationships.

Situation theory represents sets of information as infons. An infon is written in the form

<< relationship between elements, elements a1, …, an, a true/false value of 1 or 0)>>

An infon is a truth statement that some entity has a relationship to another entity in the environment.

### Simplified Situation Theory

We use a simplified 'toy' version of situation theory to minimise modelling complexity comprising sets of elemental terms or atoms, sets, states and situations at a specific time (TIM) and location (LOC) (Lenarcic &Winter, 2013).

Atoms refer to separate components of the model from specific sets (i.e., a member of the set of individual participating (IND), relationship terms (REL) time terms (TIM) and location terms (LOC) or pure atoms (ATOM) refer to individual items or component parts e.g., a card or arm etc.

Relations (REL) between individuals are in the form of a set of n parameters or tuple comprising {relation name, number of parts}. For example: 'in' is a binary relation e.g., as someone may say x is in y, 'valid' is a unary relation e.g., a swipe card is 'valid' etc.

States are facts or infons describing the relationships between the model elements or atoms of the form w = <<REL, a1, …, an, 1>> where a1…an are the necessary terms in the relationship e.g., w1 << in, card, cardreader,1) understood as card is in the cardreader, 1 denoting true, 0 false

Situations are effectively sets of states w existing at time TIM and location LOC.

## Example

Situation theory enables us to model and capture the context experienced by sensors that represent 'facts' – or truths in situation theory as well as the context information of human activities that depend on human perception (see Table 3).

We can model examples of the context situations from the hospital example. Limited space permits a comprehensive model, but as we have seen, the situations below are dependent on sensors and hence likely to be more reliable. Examples of factual sensor data are:

*Table 3. Situation theory elements*

| **ATOMS** | **CONTENT** | **FORMAT** |
|---|---|---|
| patient identity | PAT-ID | ATOM (0ary) |
| medical record | MREC | ATOM (0ary) |
| operating theatre | OP-LOC | ATOM (0ary) |
| drug | DRG-ID | ATOM (0ary) |
| **RELATIONSHIPS** | | |
| in (location) - ie a is in b | << a, in, b, 1>> | REL (2 ary) |
| matched - ie a matches b | << a, matched, b,1>> | REL (2ary) |
| in (location) - ie a is in b | << akin, b,1>> | REL (2ary) |
| valid - ie a is valid | << valid, a,1>> | REL ( 1ary) |
| updated - ie medical record is updated | << updated, a,1>> | REL (1ary) |
| **STATES** | | |
| patient is valid | w1 <<valid, PAT-ID, 1>> | ie IoT sensor validation |
| record matched with patient ID | w2 <<matched, MREC, PAT-ID, 1>> | ie IoT sensor validation |
| record is not matched to patient | w3 <<matched, MREC, PAT-ID, 0>> | ie IoT sensor validation |
| patient is in operating theatre | w4 << OP-LOC,in,PAT-ID 1>> | ie IoT sensor validation |
| drug matches patient record | w5 <<matched, DRG-ID, PAT-ID, 0>> | ie IoT sensor validation |
| medical record is updated | w6<<updated, MREC,1>> | human validation |
| **SITUATIONS** | | |
| s1 patient valid and records matched | {w1, w2} | |
| s2 patient records don't match | {w3} | |
| s3 patient is in operating theatre with matched drug | {w1,w2, w4, w5} | |
| S4 patient record is updated | {w1,w2, w4, w5, w6} | |
| s2 semantically entails {w1,w2,w3,w6} | ie it descibes the card reading and validation situaton | |

- Patient id is matched to correct medical records (s1).
- Patient location e.g., in operating theatre (w4).

We can see that situation theory enables us to capture truths (value 1) or falsehoods (value 0) and various situations as combinations of states. In the case of the example given w3 represents a 'safe' situation i.e., there is a reliable test for incorrect patient id match –that could trigger an alarm and prevent iatrogenic injury. For more information see (Michell, 2014).

But the example includes situations that could be modelled that are dependent on human factors:

- Patient notes updated correctly, i.e., s4 – is entirely dependent on clinician perception/action and being recorded as true by the human, which may be a deliberate or accidental error.
- Patient being given the correct drug – may be guided by patient notes – but ultimately is dependent on clinician perception/action.
    - For example, syringes are often muddled and incorrect drugs and/or dosages are given to patients despite accurate guidelines (Frederix, 2009).

The above cases indicate that some situations such as s4 could be high risk and therefore are appropriate for more IoT application to replace human decisions or to check them and hence reduce the risk.

## FUTURE DESIGNED STATE IMPLICATIONS

From the above we can identify risks that may be able to be reduced by further application of IoT sensors that could add more contextual facts at the policy and process awareness levels. Applying Fuhrer and Guinard's smart hospital proposals for IoT capabilities (Fuhrer & Guinard, 2006), and relating these to the DOLCE environmental entities discussed earlier we can propose the following sensors and capabilities:

- All agentive objects to have RFID based badges i.e., patients and clinicians with unique Patient IDs PAT-ID and clinician IDs CLIN-ID.
- Non-agentive devices to have RFID tags enabling location to be ascertained:
    - All medical equipment,
    - Medical records,
    - Drugs.
- Non-agentive devices such as anaesthetic machines and key equipment to have on board diagnostics and process workflow state reporting (e.g., operational, being cleaned, repaired).
- Quantities of drugs are identified by sensors (see mass example in functionality table).
- Collections of drugs for specific patients are identified and grouped.
- Improved temporal control as patient activities and statistics for time of operation activities, waiting time etc. are captured and analysed for relationships and hidden trends offline.

## Context Level

With application of additional sensors and logic, much more detailed context information is available. Nanmbi et al (2014) defined three detailed sub-components for location context as children e.g., sub locations e.g., contained in, neighboring terms such as next to and nearby terms such as 'ciose to'. With more capable sensors we can identify the validity of drugs and drug dose vs patient needs. Knowledge based approaches enable the detection and confirmation of subtle context aspects such as proximity contexts to improve safety e.g., prohibited drug x is near drug y, drug quantity a is in patient b

This addresses aspects of critical high risk iatrogenic examples of drug errors (Michell et al., 2012).

# SOLUTION APPROACH: SITUATION THEORY APPLICATION

## Implications

Situation theory enables modelling of the sensor and human perception information:

- More detailed statements of policy and knowledge based context to be derived as facts.
- Context statements can model both human and IoT situations and hence are ideal to model human-IoT ecologies.
- As IoT sensors measure real world phenomena and facts then the inputs to the situation model can come directly from known device and IoT sensor functionality discussed earlier.
- Corollaries and implication can be logically derived from the situation statements that a) may not be immediately obvious and b) are useful to the design process.

## Situation Theory as Human-IoT Ecosystem Design Tool

To identify how and what IoT sensors can add proximity value to human medical activities we propose the following approach (see Figure 10): A situation study can be made from an analysis of a specific human task where there is an opportunity to reduce risk or improve the activity through the use of IoT type devices e.g., a medical task.

- The task is described and the object/goals defined.
- Areas of high risk involving specific context variables can be identified for the most critical risk activities defined by using failure modes and effects analysis (FMEA), For example see the risk model approach proposed (Michell & Tehrani, 2017).
- The context variables are defined using situation theory.
- These variables can then be evaluated in terms of IoT and sensor device requirements to determine which sensors, in what configuration, could provide a cost-effective solution to reduce the risk.
- Then predictive and IoT sensor controls could be developed for these variables to add context facts and reduce the risk.

*Figure 10. Situation modelling of high risk activities to identify potential IOoT variables*

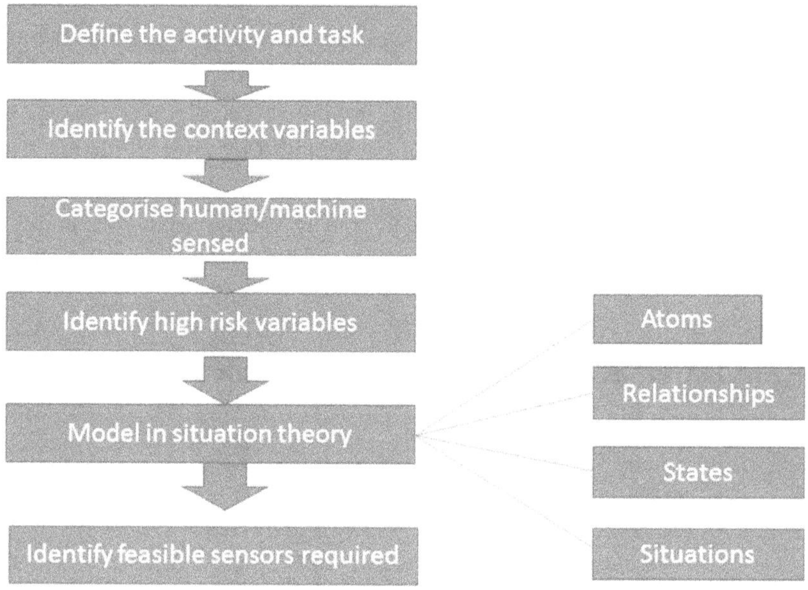


## FUTURE RESEARCH, DISCUSSION, AND CONCLUSION

We have seen how IoT devices can provide real factual information about work environments dependent on the type of sensor and the operational models used. Further we have seen that new information and knowledge can be developed by integrating information from multiple sensors. Thus, IoT technology can provide reliable factual information in support of human-IoT actions in an ecological situation where humans adapt to the IoT information and the IoT sensors and application are developed/evolved ecologically to better support the task. We have suggested a way to help to move forward with the challenge of understanding context by using situation theory to model both human and IoT aspects of a specific work situation and areas where specific IoT sensors could add context information to reduce risk or improve the task decision making.

Incorporation of situation theory enables the extent of a real world situation that an IoT device can capture, to be identified as parameters. Further work using actual medical cases and specific interventions where IoT can add value and reduce risk is in progress. This work is subject to available sensors and limitations of the current control systems and middleware which is not well developed. Both current and future work involves the development of a working example from a local hospital intended to prove the concept from a design perspective in a real world context.

## REFERENCES

Barnaghi, P., Wang, W., Henson, C., & Taylor, K. (2012). Semantics for the Internet of Things: Early progress and back to the future. *International Journal on Semantic Web and Information Systems*, *8*(1), 1–21. doi:10.4018/jswis.2012010101

Barwise, J., & Perry, J. (1980). The Situation Underground. In J. Barwise & I. Sag (Eds.), Stanford working papers in semantics (Vol. 1, pp. 1-55). Stanford Cognitive Science Group.

Béguin, P. (2007). In search of a unit of analysis for designing instruments. *Artifact*, *1*(1), 12–16. doi:10.1080/17493460600610830

Bodker, S., & Klokmose, C. N. (2011). The human–artifact model: An activity theoretical approach to artifact ecologies. *Human–Computer Interaction, 26*(4), 315-371.

Borgia, E. (2014). The Internet of Things vision: Key features, applications and open issues. *Computer Communications*, *54*, 1–31. doi:10.1016/j.comcom.2014.09.008

Bottazzi, E., & Ferrario, R. (2009). Preliminaries to a DOLCE ontology of organisations. *International Journal of Business Process Integration and Management*, *4*(4), 225–238. doi:10.1504/IJBPIM.2009.032280

Carmichael, A. (2013). *How to power the internet of things*. Professional Engineer.

Codegate, L. (2001). *Unauthorised Access Alert System*. Retrieved 27 February 2017 from http://www.codegate.co.uk/Unauthorised-Access-Alert-System

Compton, M., Neuhaus, H., Taylor, K., & Tran, K. N. (2009, October). Reasoning about sensors and compositions. In *Proceedings of the 2nd International Conference on Semantic Sensor Networks-Volume 522* (pp. 33-48). CEUR-WS.org.

Crilly, N. (2010). The roles that artefacts play: Technical, social and aesthetic functions. *Design Studies*, *31*(4), 311–344. doi:10.1016/j.destud.2010.04.002

Fan, X., White, I. M., Shopova, S. I., Zhu, H., Suter, J. D., & Sun, Y. (2008). Sensitive optical biosensors for unlabeled targets: A review. *Analytica Chimica Acta, 620*(1), 8-26.

Fleisch, E. (2010). What is the Internet of Things? an economic perspective. *Economics, Management, and Financial Markets*, (2), 125-157.

Frederix, I. (2009, May). Internet of things and radio frequency identification in care taking, facts and privacy challenges. In *Wireless Communication, Vehicular Technology, Information Theory and Aerospace & Electronic Systems Technology, 2009. Wireless VITAE 2009. 1st International Conference on* (pp. 319-323). IEEE. doi:10.1109/WIRELESSVITAE.2009.5172467

Fuhrer, P., & Guinard, D. (2006). *Building a smart hospital using RFID technologies: use cases and implementation*. Department of Informatics-University of Fribourg.

Gangemi, A., Guarino, N., Masolo, C., & Oltramari, A. (2003). Sweetening wordnet with dolce. *AI Magazine*, *24*(3), 13.

Greeno, J. G. (1994). *Gibson's affordances*. Academic Press.

Hachem, S., Teixeira, T., & Issarny, V. (2011, December). Ontologies for the internet of things. In *Proceedings of the 8th Middleware Doctoral Symposium* (p. 3). ACM.

Heartlands. (n.d.). Retrieved from https://www.zebra.com/content/dam/zebra/success-stories/en-gb/pdfs/heartlands-hospital-en-gb.pdf

Jambhulkar, P. W., & Baporikar, V. (2015). Wireless sensor network for heart disease detection using data mining technique. *International Journal of Innovative Research in Computer and Communication Engineering*, *3*(6), 5947–5953.

Khan, R., Khan, S. U., Zaheer, R., & Khan, S. (2012, December). Future internet: the internet of things architecture, possible applications and key challenges. In *Frontiers of Information Technology (FIT), 2012 10th International Conference on* (pp. 257-260). IEEE. doi:10.1109/FIT.2012.53

Kortuem, G., Kawsar, F., Sundramoorthy, V., & Fitton, D. (2010). Smart objects as building blocks for the internet of things. *IEEE Internet Computing*, *14*(1), 44–51. doi:10.1109/MIC.2009.143

Lampe, M., & Flörkemeier, C. (2004). *The smart box application model*. Academic Press.

Lenarcic, A. (2011). *Formalizing Affordances in Situation Theory* (Doctoral dissertation). Brock University.

Lenarčič, A., & Winter, M. (2013). Affordances in Situation Theory. *Ecological Psychology*, *25*(2), 155–181. doi:10.1080/10407413.2013.780495

López, T. S., Ranasinghe, D. C., Harrison, M., & McFarlane, D. (2012). Adding sense to the Internet of Things. *Personal and Ubiquitous Computing*, *16*(3), 291–308. doi:10.1007/s00779-011-0399-8

Michell, V. (2011). A focussed approach to business capability. *Proceedings of the First International Symposium on Business Modelling and Design*, 105-113.

Michell, V. (2014). The Internet of Things and Opportunities for Pervasive Safety Monitored Health Environments. In *Handbook of Research on Patient Safety and Quality Care through Health Informatics* (pp. 344–362). IGI Global. doi:10.4018/978-1-4666-4546-2.ch020

Michell, V., Tehrani, G., & Liu, K. (2012). Are clinical documents optimised for patient safety? A critical analysis of patient safety outcomes using the EDA error model. *Journal of Health Policy and Technology*, *1*(4), 214–227. doi:10.1016/j.hlpt.2012.10.003

Michell, V., & Tehrani, J. (2017). Clinical Pathways and the Human Factor: Approaches to Control and Reduction of Human Error Risk. In *Impact of Medical Errors and Malpractice on Health Economics, Quality, and Patient Safety*. IGI Global. doi:10.4018/978-1-5225-2337-6.ch001

Miorandi, D., Sicari, S., De Pellegrini, F., & Chlamtac, I. (2012). Internet of things: Vision, applications and research challenges. *Ad Hoc Networks*, *10*(7), 1497–1516. doi:10.1016/j.adhoc.2012.02.016

Nambi, S. A. U., Sarkar, C., Prasad, R. V., & Rahim, A. (2014, March). A unified semantic knowledge base for IoT. In *Internet of Things (WF-IoT), 2014 IEEE World Forum on* (pp. 575-580). IEEE. doi:10.1109/WF-IoT.2014.6803232

NIBIB. (2017). *What are sensor?* National Institute of Bioimage and Bioengineering. Retrieved 27February 2017 https://www.nibib.nih.gov/science-education/science-topics/sensors

Nitti, M., Pilloni, V., Colistra, G., & Atzori, L. (2016). The virtual object as a major element of the internet of things: A survey. *IEEE Communications Surveys and Tutorials*, *18*(2), 1228–1240. doi:10.1109/COMST.2015.2498304

Patel, P., Pathak, A., Teixeira, T., & Issarny, V. (2011, December). Towards application development for the internet of things. In *Proceedings of the 8th Middleware Doctoral Symposium* (p. 5). ACM. doi:10.1145/2093190.2093195

Perera, C., Zaslavsky, A., Christen, P., & Georgakopoulos, D. (2014). Context aware computing for the internet of things: A survey. *IEEE Communications Surveys and Tutorials*, *16*(1), 414–454. doi:10.1109/SURV.2013.042313.00197

Privat, G. (2012). Extending the Internet of Things. *Communications & Stratégies*, (87): 101.

Roubtsova, E., & Michell, V. (2013). A method for modeling of KPIs enabling validation of their properties. In *Proceedings of the 5th ACM SIGCHI Annual International Workshop on Behaviour Modelling-Foundations and Applications* (p. 3). ACM. doi:10.1145/2492437.2492440

Santos, A., Macedo, J., Costa, A., & Nicolau, M. J. (2014). Internet of things and smart objects for M-health monitoring and control. *Procedia Technology*, *16*, 1351–1360. doi:10.1016/j.protcy.2014.10.152

Sundmaeker, H., Guillemin, P., Friess, P., & Woelfflé, S. (2010). *Vision and challenges for realising the Internet of Things. In Cluster of European Research Projects on the Internet of Things*. European Commision.

Swan, M. (2012). Sensor mania! The Internet of Things, wearable computing, objective metrics, and the Quantified Self 2.0. *Journal of Sensor and Actuator Networks*, *1*(3), 217–253. doi:10.3390/jsan1030217

Tsiatsis, V., Gluhak, A., Bauge, T., Montagut, F., Bernat, J., Bauer, M., . . . Krco, S. (2010). *The SENSEI Real World Internet Architecture.* Paper presented at the Future Internet Assembly.

Van Harmelen, F., Lifschitz, V., & Porter, B. (Eds.). (2008). *Handbook of knowledge representation* (Vol. 1). Elsevier.

Vyas, D., & Dix, A. (2007). Artefact ecologies: Supporting embodied meeting practices with distance access. *Proceedings of UbiComp*, *2007*, 117–122.

Warell, A. V. (1999, September). Introducing a use perspective in product design theory and methodology. *Proceedings of the 1999 ASME Design Engineering Technical Conferences, DETC99/DTM-8782*.

## KEY TERMS AND DEFINITIONS

**Context:** Information about the state of an environment and the animals and objects in it at a particular instance of time that supports decision making.

**Ecosystem:** A collection of living organisms and passive objects that interact, such that the living organisms adjust their behaviour over time due to mutual influences and learning.

**Human-IoT Ecosystem:** A collection of human and intelligent devices and passive objects that interact such that the human and intelligent devices adjust their behaviour over time due to mutual influences and learning.

**Internet of Things:** Any system of physical devices that can measure the state of, or make a physical change in, the real world based on its application logic and its own captured data to communicate via the internet real time state information, alone and/or in concert with similar devices.

**Situation:** The state the state of an environment and the animals and objects in it at a particular instance of time.

**Situation Theory:** A logic based theory that models situations as 'sets of information' or infons and relationships between them.

# Chapter 13
# Computational Business Intelligence, Big Data, and Their Role in Business Decisions in the Age of the Internet of Things

**Javier Vidal-García**
*University of Valladolid, Spain*

**Marta Vidal**
*Complutense University of Madrid, Spain*

**Rafael Hernandez Barros**
*Complutense University of Madrid, Spain*

## ABSTRACT

*The evolution of the big data and new techniques related to the processing and analysis of large databases is revolutionizing the management of companies in the age of the Internet of Things (IoT). In this chapter, we examine the possibilities of big data to improve the services offered by companies and the customer experience and increase the efficiency of these companies. Companies must accept the challenge of self-assessment and measure the barriers that threaten to prevent them from reaching to get the maximum potential derived from big data and analytics. The combination of big data and computational business intelligence will change completely processes, logistics and distribution strategies, the choice of marketing channels and any aspect of the production and marketing of products and services. A case of GE is presented to showcase the use of the IoT and big data. All companies, regardless of size or sector, will improve their business operations due to big data generated from the social media and IoT applications and its use in computational business intelligence.*

DOI: 10.4018/978-1-5225-2104-4.ch013

## INTRODUCTION

The terms computational business intelligence and big data make reference to the trend of the advancement of technology that have opened the doors to a new approach to understanding and describing huge quantities of data that would take too long to load into a relational database for later analysis

There is hardly any area of economic activity in which the use of big data is not generating business opportunities and adding value. Exploiting the potential of big data is not just a technological achievement, but actually represents an organizational challenge since companies must change the way they make decisions regarding their business processes. Companies must put aside making decisions based on intuition, and learn to analyze information reliably and create structures and new roles that may affect the current balance of power.

While best performing companies are in an advanced position in their learning curve, with regard to the development of analytical competition, a lot of companies are still at the beginning of this process and must cope with various difficulties.

In this chapter we will refer briefly to the main challenges associated with the use of big data and computational business intelligence for business purposes. We will then discuss the implications of big data to the Internet of Things (IoT). We will present the case of GE, which has managed to develop a successful strategy based on big data and the IoT. We will use this example to illustrate the characteristics of the organization that favor the development of its analytical capacity, the ability of the organization to generate and use big data, computational business intelligence, and the IoT to improve performance. Finally, we will discuss how the development of analytical capacity in the age of the IoT is not limited to few companies, but instead can be taken in traditional companies and relatively small, with benefits for their performance.

## BACKGROUND

Regardless of the fascination that arise the incredible figures of data that are constantly produced, big does not mean the same thing in a large organization, which can manage multiple petabytes, or in a small, where some terabytes can represent a problem of management.

Obviously the complexity and the needs change for the different sizes, but the opportunities for improvement are real in all companies. One of the most common examples to explain the advantages that the medium-sized companies can obtain from big data is a sales company online that is dedicated to a particular product (Barney, 1991). The navigation study that follows consumers and the activity carried out in social networks can give very useful information about the consumption habits of customers (actual and potential) and the brand image that has built between them, and layout, product range and marketing strategy which will be more successful.

But the information obtained through the analysis of big data is not only useful to understand customers; the internal functioning of organizations can also be optimized. Continuing the example of the small e-commerce company, the study of the data obtained from supplier relationships, from internal processes, etc. can highlight the problems of communication between departments, reduce the cost of purchasing department and optimize the distribution process (Purcell, 2013).

Actually the secret behind the Big data and computational business intelligence is not new. To find the causes of the weak and strong aspects of any business has always been an objective for companies and institutions, and organization of information has been one of the most accurate tools for that. The importance of big data lies in the enormous amount of information that we face nowadays. Although there is a higher difficulty of the analysis, there are also more opportunities to do so.

Internet and new technologies have created a technological revolution that is affecting our private and professional life, and big data and computational business intelligence is the trigger for the next stage, as far as industry and consumption refers (Mayer-Schönberger & Cukier, 2014). The recent rise of the IoT is accelerrating the creation of big data and the use of computational business intelligence.

Similar to the impact of serial production at the end of the second industrial revolution, the combination of big data, computational business intelligence, and the IoT will change completely processes, logistics and distribution strategies, the choice of marketing channels and any aspect of the production and marketing of products and services. All companies, regardless of size or sector will improve due to big data and its use in computational business intelligence.

Nowadays companies discuss whether or not to adopt big data tools, however in the near future the question will be how instead of yes or no. The impact of big data, computational business intelligence, and the IoT will be even greater than the mass production because it will affect all businesses, not just the factories, as well as governmental organizations and non-profit.

## MAIN FOCUS OF THE CHAPTER

The use of computational business intelligence and big data to the field of economics are increasingly abundant although the application of these techniques in the economy is recent. It is increasingly common that companies use methodologies that make estimates in real time of the evolution of the prices or the cost of goods (Varian, 2014). The Billion Prices Project of MIT uses millions of prices of online shops in many countries to get a price index online that is updated in real time. This technology employs the stability or variations of the components between tags of language HTML used to create web pages to determine the variations in the prices of products in time (Butler, 2008). A program can, employing this methodology, identify the relevant information on a product and its price. The URL of the website where these products are indexed can be used to classify the products by category. For instance, Cavallo (2012) employs hundreds of thousands of prices of products on the Internet to examine the evolution of the official rate of inflation and the one obtained from catches of price information from online shops. He explains that while in Brazil, Chile, Colombia and Venezuela the variation of the official inflation and the one obtained from online prices follow similar patterns, in Argentina the difference is quite relevant. Inflation in Argentina, from 2007 to 2011, as shown by the online price index was 20.14% in comparison to the official inflation that was only 8.38%. This means a significant difference of 65% by March 2011.

Choi and Varian (2012) employed Google Trends to improve the forecasting ability of models on economic indicators obtained with very high frequency. The idea is to complement the information of past series with the searches present in some categories. For instance, the Department of Labor of the United States communicates each Thursday the number of people who is demanding unemployment benefits. Using a model AR(1) (autoregressive model of order 1) of historical data and the information on searches for words in categories such as jobs, welfare, unemployment, improves a 6% the forecasting capacity on average, and the changes of cycle in particular. Using the same methodology for the index of consumer confidence, they obtain an improvement of 9.3% in the forecasting power.

The use of aggregate information on credit cards and TPV is another relevant pattern of economic research at present. In a series of influential papers, Mian and Sufi (2009) use the information about credit cards to examine the economic causes of the real estate bubble and the financial crisis. Mian, Rao and Sufi (2013) examine the elasticity of consumption with respect to the housing wealth. The examination of consumption at country level is performed employing the purchases made through credit or debit card intermediaries. An important advantage of the data for their study is that consuming goods is classified with the NAICS codes that provide each trade where spending is performed. Mian and Sufi (2009) used all the mortgages obtained between 1990 and 2007 (available for any citizen in the Home Mortgage Disclosure Act) and the data on credit between 1991 and 2007 by type of credit provided by Analytical Services, a data provider from Equifax. Adding the information on debt counties, defaults and mortgage loans (granting or denial among other variables), Mian and Sufi (2009) show that in the counties with the greatest credit restrictions before the start of the real estate bubble is where the credit increased with the start of the expansion of real estate and where housing prices present the larger appreciation. They also show that at the beginning of the crisis in those same counties is where prices fell more intensively and foreclosures increased more. The number and quality of studies on this area has been increasing, an example is Jimenez et al. (2014), who use information about 24 million individual loans to examine the impact of monetary policy in the assumption of risk from financial institutions (Barker, D'Amato & Sheridon, 2008).

Currently, billions of IoT devices are generating tremendous amount of streaming data in real time. The relationship between big data and the Internet of Things (IoT) is becoming inseparable. While not all data generated from the IoT devices are useful, organizations should invest in a proper big data and computational business intelligence technologies to maximize the benefit from data generated from the IoT devices.

## Benefit of Computational Business Intelligence and Big Data for Business Decision Process

More companies are increasingly using big data and information technology as the basis of an efficient operation, compliance and a growing profitability. This dependence of big data for business decisions implies both risks and opportunities (Lazer, Kennedy, King, & Vespignani, 2014).

Beyond an opportunity to increase profitability, the role of big data and information is now integral to the whole business from the back office operations to marketing and sales, and from risk management to the expectations of the managers and the regulators. The use of big data and computational business intelligence implementation presents many opportunities for business:

- **Efficiency:** It is clear that the balance sheets of the companies are being completely refurbished by ongoing regulatory initiatives, especially after the wake of the financial crisis. In the case of financial companies, they are pushing return on the assets below the cost of capital. As a result, and with the intention of obtaining sustainable benefits and acceptable levels of organic capital, financial institutions have no alternative but to be more agile, simple and profitable in their operations. As an important element of the processes and efficient workflows, technology has a relevant role to play (Lambrecht & Tucker, 2013).
- **Knowledge:** The appropriate use of the increasing volume of data and to extract more value from this data is fundamental to the health of the organization and its success. The consequences are

extended through the model of business operation. In customer service and sales, companies are facing real challenges in the management and give meaning to the great amount of information available about the preferences, behavior and the needs of the customers, their perspectives and objectives (Edelman, 2015). Technologies for the analysis of data in real time are becoming more important as a tool for effective marketing and cross-selling.

- **Customer Experience:** The computational business intelligence technologies and data management are fundamental, in order to maintain the relations established with customers who are increasingly demanding more continuous access to company's products and services through mobile platforms. The integration of the different technologies that offer high quality data are essential elements in creating agile and satisfactory communications with customers. Consumers do not want complex processes, delays or inconsistencies. Companies that cannot have the necessary technology systems with their appropriate speed will be overtaken by the innovative, new players that take advantage of new technologies.
- **Risk Management:** The financial crisis and ongoing new regulations have put to greater emphasis on the need for an efficient management of risks in all contexts: the reputational risk, operational and regulatory frameworks. Companies face the dual challenge of managing risk and the reporting of evidence of its efficiency to interested parties such as regulators, customers, and shareholders. Collection, examination and presentation of the relevant data is essential for the creation and maintenance of strong relations with the different interest groups.
- **Operational Improvement:** The optimization of the daily operations means maximizing the employment of scarce resources and the guarantee that people have the proper information to make optimal decisions on time. This needs precise and consistent data, which can be used to both support the operational health of the company and meet internal and external requirements.

The combination of computational business intelligence and big data will achieve relevant improvements in the internal efficiency, external competitiveness and, possibly most important, stronger relations with the customers. Companies that do not adopt these models and technologies will probably have problems to survive in the business due to a competitive disadvantage (McGuire, Manyika, & Chui, 2012). In times of an ongoing technology revolution, to miss the train that will change the rules of the game could be equivalent to a company bankruptcy. We have seen this with organizations that have neglected with the emergence of the Internet and is likely to happen again with the emergence of a society based on data.

The increasing importance of an adequate management of data and information through the business places a huge importance to the capacity to capture, aggregate and examine the data to create a simple view of the business: a single complete information resource and with internal coherence that is able to meet all needs. Company winner will be the ones that can collect data in a consistent manner to meet these multiple needs with greater efficiency, this data will be used in operations which are customer-facing, systems and internal procedures or external reports. The sources of data should be accurate, complete, traceable and transparent, so that companies and its stakeholders can rely in the source data, and managers can be confident to take the right decisions.

The access and management of the data, which includes the examination of the value and relevance of the data, is an important step to obtain optimal results. It is significantly important the ability to synthesize data through the operational and financial information, and customers (Chen, Chiang, & Storey, 2012). It is important to be aware that many companies are not experienced using their own data even if the data that is already available.

Most companies are only starting to get familiar with the benefits of computational business intelligence and big data for business decision process and the data management process is getting more complex by the amount of new data types (Kruschwitz, 2011). Companies must first define what are their needs and the metric leaders of these measures to manage the business and define its strategy. Companies should then understand their own information and portfolio of data to align the application of new methods and technologies for a coordinated global strategy (McAfee, Brynjolfsson, Davenport, Patil, & Barton, 2012). This technique allows companies to address cross-cutting initiatives, avoiding the problems of information and facilitating the inclusion of new data types in a deliberately and organized manner that will align and will be compatible with a wider strategy.

Computational business intelligence and big data are also having an effect on the skills required for the resources of the department of finance, since the financial skill set is always evolving. It is expected that the new employees have not only needs to be fluent with data and the experience with the tools needed to manage and examine this data, but also computer programs to accurately manage this data with the objective to contribute to streamline the organization. This includes a deeper understanding of the operational areas of the company. The future leaders of innovative organizations must have data-oriented skills, at both levels strategic and operational. Although most of the initiatives that are being pursued with big data currently require a skill set that is not only concentrated in managing computers. The company management must be able to identify new opportunities in a more comprehensive manner within the organization and possess the skills to create consensus between the functions of the data unified collectively in support of strategic opportunities (Vidal, Vidal-García & Hernández-Barros, 2016).

The challenge of big data and analytics is not about collecting data but rather of the translation of data into knowledge and ideas that will contribute to increase profit and define a competitive advantage for companies. The value of big data and computational business intelligence for business is at the same time something without precedent.

Computational business intelligence and big data is going to organize companies in such a way that it is still barely conceivable. If companies are able to properly deal with this evolution, such dealing with issues such as privacy, big data and analytics will not be perceived as a big brother, but as a big value (Heffetz & Ligett, 2014).

The role of the CFO and the CIO will be essential to help define the best strategy for a company in this context of rapid development and guide investment decisions on the basis of a clear vision of the risks and benefits.

## Steps in the Implementation of Computational Business Intelligence Systems Using Big Data

Regarding the level of activities of big data and computational business intelligence in the currently existing companies (Shroeck & Shockley, 2012), results suggest four main phases in the process of adoption and evolution of big data and the implementation of computational business intelligence systems, these phases are called Educate, Explore, Interact and Run:

- **Educate:** Create a knowledge base. In the phase of education the focus is on awareness and the development of knowledge. Almost 25% of the companies surveyed indicated that they do not use used big data or computational business intelligence systems within their companies. While some still have relatively little information about the concept of big data, respondents suggest that most companies found at this stage that they are studying the potential benefits of technology and big data analytics and trying to understand how this can help them address significant business opportunities in their own sectors or markets. Within these companies, employees are the main responsible for collecting information, unlike formal working groups, and knowledge that is not yet are used by the company. As a result, business managers have not yet fully understood or embraced the potential of big data and computational business intelligence systems applied to business decisions.

- **Explore:** Define the business case and the business roadmap. In this phase, the focus is on developing the roadmap of the company for the development of big data and its application to the computational business intelligence system. Almost half of the companies recognized that are having formal talks underway within their organizations about how to use big data and company intelligence to address business challenges. The main objectives of these companies include developing quantifiable business cases and create a project of big data. The strategy and the roadmap take into account the data, the technology and existing skills and then establish where to start and how to develop a plan in line with the business strategy of the company.
- **Interact:** Adopt big data. In the phase of interacting companies begin to check the business value of big data and its computational business intelligence system, as well as to carry out an assessment of their technologies and skills. More than one out of five companies surveyed are currently developing big data proof of concept (POCs) to validate requirements associated with the implementation of big data initiatives and to articulate the expected results. Companies that are in this group are working (within a defined and limited scope) to understand and test the technologies and skills needed to exploit new sources of data.
- **Run:** Implement big data to scale. In the implementation phase, the level of operability and implementation of analytic functions and big data business intelligence is greater within the company. However, only the 6% of the companies surveyed have implemented two or more big data and computational business intelligence system solutions. This low number of organizations in the implementation phase is consistent with implementations we see in the market. And, more importantly, these leading companies are leveraging big data and business intelligence to transform their business, so they are getting the maximum value from their information assets. With the adoption rate of big data increasing rapidly (as shown by 22% of respondents in the phase of interaction, either with proof of concept (POC) or pilot projects under way), it is expected that the percentage of companies in this phase will increase in the future.

## Benefits of the Implementation of Computational Business Intelligence Systems and Big Data in Organizations

Once the importance of big data is known mainly thanks to the improvement that meant about relational models, it is worth pointing the most common benefits of big data and computational business intelligence for organizations:

- **Change Management:** Search new business opportunities through improved cross-selling and targeting (improved strategy). By applying analytical and predictive modeling data to customer accounts and transaction history, this allows companies to carry out a segmentation based on the likelihood that the customer buys services or complementary products of higher value (improved segmentation). See Lambrecht & Skiera (2006). By analyzing consumption of services and products by customers, the company can optimize cross-selling strategies, refine marketing campaigns and provide specific offers. It is possible to predict more accurately which products are most appropriate for each customer (improved strategy). To provide the right mix of services and products improve the effectiveness and efficiency of the sales force of the company, while more personalized strategy helps agents to forge closer ties with customers, which improves loyalty for each customer (improving the strategy). Using operational improvements the capacity of business visibility increase through more detailed reports (Nickerson & Rogers, 2014).

- **Analysis of Web Browsing and Online Habits of Consumption:** Social Network Analysis determines the social circles of customers from telephone interactions and online social networks generates a complete view of customers, identifying their role in their circles and their degree of influence. Viral Marketing (marketing that exploits social networks) detects the most influential clients, social roles to maximize the dissemination of products and services (better knowledge of customers and the market in social networks). Navigation data analysis examines web browsing and online habits of consumption: extract valuable new customer prospects. It identifies the user (location, terminal status, access services), sites and word searches, visited websites, browsing time, etc. are monitored (better knowledge of the customer). With dashboard in real time, the information is always available without waiting for updating the data (real time information).
- **Anticipating Problems:** A predictive analysis system and data matching allows us to anticipate possible problems that may arise in the future, such as a prediction of disaster risk that would adjust the pricing and provisioning funds for possible payments (it is useful for viewing the accuracy of the data to inaccurate data).
- **Process Improvement:** Allows simplifying current processes and business control (cost reduction). Security Analysis is a proactive analytics allows reducing risks and losses against fraud (cost reduction). See Hoffmann & Birnbrich (2012). It can detect complex patterns of fraud in real time analyzing historical data, the pattern of use of geolocation information, analysis of transactions and suspicious transactions (cost reduction).
- **Support Decision-Making Through Automatic Algorithms:** A sophisticated analytics to analyze all reports and data, helps in decision-making, reducing risks and discover information that previously could be hidden, yet important (helps to decision-making).

Other benefits for organizations include the reduction in costs, reduction in times, development of new products, optimized and customized offers, smarter decision making than with previous Business Intelligence systems, and security smart filters in e-business.

All these advantages can be grouped into a main one that derives from all the other advantages: To obtain more information/knowledge of customers of the company, including the company itself and the competition to gain a competitive advantage over competitors offering customers what they want or even to create a need that customers do not yet have.

Where big data and computational business intelligence really comes into play is in the process of finding information which can be transformed into knowledge among these large amounts of data collected by organizations and not on how the data are collected (Grossman & Siegel, 2014). The optimistic vision of a perfect combination of big data and computational business intelligence is one in which companies would be able to obtain data from any source, leverage that data and get the information that would become useful knowledge for the organization allowing incorporating all the previously mentioned advantages.

## Disadvantages of Big Data and Computational Business Intelligence

However big data presents some disadvantages. The main one being the adoption process of big data: The required software and hardware and cost. But there are also many other disadvantages such as the rejection by staff, training expenditure, necessary collaboration required by all departments, cost, privacy issues, problems of outdated information, filtering (not all data is information), and the so-called "taking passive decision". This last issue refers to the fact that before installation of Big Data, companies first wait for competitors to install it first and then see if they commit errors with the belief that they may adopt much faster.

Besides these problems, companies should consider a major drawback before considering a big data project and its application in computational business intelligence and it is as simple as knowing itself: Is it really useful to the organization? Does the company have need for big data and computational business intelligence project? Do you have the necessary resources to tackle a project of Big Data? What will it cost? Does my business really need big data or computational business intelligence? Despite all the benefits that a company could obtain. If the answer is yes, then the inconvenience should not matter since the advantages obtained will be much greater.

## Big Data Management for the Internet of Things and Business Applications

The rapid rise of the IoT has opened doors dramatically about the possibility that our everyday devices exceed their traditional functions to end up becoming business and payment platforms. Billions of IoT devices are generating tremendous amount of data every second. Managing and interpreting the data generated from these devices became a significant challenge to decision makers. The massive arrival of this class of devices to our everyday life could be just the first step towards development of connected households, with a wide range of devices coordinated and equipped with sensors that allow them detect our daily activity and provide our needs according to this information. With the growing popularity of the IoT and the increased complexity of big data management, it is urgently to put on the table a number of issues relevant to big data:

- **The Opportunity of New Business Models:** It opens the possibility of offering new products and services, especially around data stored as a result of monitoring our daily activities. We may link benefits or economic penalties to the monitoring of user activity. For example through smart scales that allow medical insurance providers reward their customers that meet a monthly target weight loss (See Hernandez Barros et al., 2016).
- **Reflection on Changes in User Experience:** Obviously, our user experience will not be the same if our refrigerator depends on an external device (such as our smartphone) to make payments if it hosts the data of our credit card or our Paypal account, allowing automatic payments. The key is that the user does not have to think about the day-to-day payment processes or the type of technology that makes them possible. In the IoT, payments must be invisible and transparent.
- **The Need for New Security Systems for Financial Information:** One of the big problems that payments will have to face in the Internet of the Things is that we do not use those things in the same way we use the rest of devices connected to the Internet (PC, tablet, smartphone, etc.): They are bought, installed and start operating indefinitely without requiring our attention, thus making difficult to receive a strange operation.

However, they are many studies that have detected large percentages of smart appliances operating and connected to the Internet without its users bothering to change their default settings (without password or with an insecure password). In some cases this was discovered under investigations of avalanches of spam from these devices. If there comes a time when payments are a key element of the Internet of Things, there will be a problem if manufacturers, developers and users do not put greater emphasis on security. And the problem complicates when we take into account aspects such as devices used by multiple users, in many cases not share family (case of vehicles).

So, in this context of serious risk to our financial data, banks could have a relevant role in their protection, thanks to its position as entities of confidence that already have their own technological infrastructure.

The IoT and big data has spent years sounding like one of the great trends and developments. However, although we already know what they offer, they have big challenges ahead. We explain the sectors which will serve as the engine for growth and expansion.

The IoT is a concept that goes back to late last century, linking Internet connection with daily objects. This connection of object to object or multiobject with different communication protocols, opens an immense field of applications in everyday life and business operations and a new approach to action-reaction in events when not all cases have to intervene humans.

The concept is simple, if we take any object and we link this with the network, with its utilities and the multiple uses that this object can have in the interconnection with communication with third parties, big data increases the potential of the IoT in the process of decision making. We can find the intelligent sneakers that monitor our running, or biomedical applications controlling how a pacemaker works correctly and provides critical situations in patients according to data extracted. The following are the key areas of the IoT applications:

- **Home Automation:** This is key in the Internet of Things. Questions like: Did I turned off the light when I left? Did I turn off the water? Could I turn on the heating depending on the outside temperature and environment? All these questions that we have done countless times will have their resolution in very short-term with the explosion of home automation and interconnection elements of our own living place. These tasks will be key niche of innovation and business models.
- **Biotechnology and Health Monitoring of Our Life:** The implementation of biometric control systems with our body, the control of vital signs, food, sleep, physical activity and other vital signs are the best sanitary way to prevent and apply corrective methods on our health.

This IoT combines with the overall processing of information and big data technology and with making subsequent decisions as simple as having interconnected clothes systems, exercise control systems in the shoes or the use of multiple clothes that get all the information we can provide. The field of health and personal care is an emerging sector in the development of new business models.

- **The Microtargeting:** Is a key business niche for the IoT and big data technology. Microtargeting is the advanced market segmentation at the individual level. Its expansion may be key in fashion and accessories from the moment we are able to monitor and identify trends in consumer use. For example, for a runner who does not have the right shoes for journeys or for the use of thermally more suitable clothes to standard environments, the IoT opens a new horizon of products and services with a much higher segmentation than usual marketing techniques segmentation.

Computational business intelligence will be used to process big data generated from the monitoring devices.

- **The Motor Industry and the Future of Intelligent Cars or Smart Cars:** Can we imagine a vehicle that is able to detect the best route in real time in a city to avoid traffic jams or traffic lights? This is possible as long as we interconnect our own car or auxiliary device with real-time traffic data. The IoT and big data will drive innovation in the auto industry.

Users recognize having devices for the Internet of Things for the saving money involved, others choose them for comfort while some users for its safety. There are mainly four reasons for the existence of IoT as value added applications.

- **Saving:** If we talk about the IoT is inevitable to talk of a home or office connected: with a smart electrical system in which from the lighting and temperature to appliances as the washing machine or refrigerator are connected to the network and scheduled to improve not only the welfare in the house, but also a reduction in invoices.

In the current market, with the connected energy system, consumers can save on around 20% per month; this might mean up to 250 dollars a year. Many users want to have thermostats connected and lighting connected; and many also the vacuuming, lawn mower, oven or the refrigerator, as well as other devices we have at home.

- **Safety and Protection:** The demand on security systems connected at home or office is increasing and the main reason is the protection they offer. The main benefit of this connection is to be able to alert the head of the household or the boss when there is any danger or there is something different from the usual routine. Therefore, most households recognize that want to have a safety system connected.

These systems use sensors to control when doors or windows are open and when there is movement within a property, whether the home or the business. Furthermore, it allows controlling this remotely using a smartphone. For example, when someone is traveling and wants to give the feeling that the there are people in the house, this person can activate the lights on an hour or even turn on the radio occasionally.

Thus, savings and security are two of the more valued benefits by consumers of Internet of Things, as it gives priority to energy and the connected safety.

In fact, after computers, game consoles, smartphones and tablets, intelligent connected systems are the devices more adopted at home.

- **Comfort and Convenience:** To control remote objects in a home or a business is no longer something of science fiction. The IoT devices have the ability of being able to check remotely a device, its operation, the turn on, and its turning off. This is to live in a world where someone no longer has to go back to the company to check that has closed the door, or whether has left a machine opened. The IoT applications relieve the anxiety that occurs when someone can not verify something.

- **Information:** The exchange of information that may be relevant to a particular activity is another of the reasons why users are interested in having different connected devices. For example, a connected car can detect its owner and through a mobile device automatically turn off the light or heat and turn on the security system. Most users find it interesting that all domestic devices can communicate and exchange information constantly in their connected home.

However, the IoT is also growing considerably interest in other connected devices, such as health monitors, the activity monitors, and elderly monitors. It is important to connect IoT devices seamlessly for data sharing. These shared data can be used to perform diagnostic checks, determine the probability of a defect or malfunction, detect the fault more precisely, and provide the manufacturer with options to improve future devices.

## Generic Electric: Big Data and the IoT

General Electric announced in 2014 a group of partnerships with leading technology companies to support his platform Predix, which is software designed to add intelligence to the various points of IoT.

For GE, the IoT, which the company calls Industrial Internet and the creation of a networking of machinery and equipment is an engine of growth. GE wants to position its turbines, motors and other equipment such as intelligent devices that connect through its software. In many ways, GE is a software and a technology company similar to IBM. GE is leading the movement to combine the IoT and the big data and computational business intelligence.

In the partnerships signed with Intel and Cisco, the companies will work with GE to create "Predix Ready" devices, which include metadata and open communication frameworks of sensors and devices based on robust networks of industrial routers in the cloud.

Intel aims to include the integration of GE in its processors and Cisco is including compatibility with Predix in its robust networks such as industrial routers. Predix architecture ties together cloud and data with Hadoop resources. GE opened the Predix platform to users and developers in 2015. The platform allows for customized industry applications, asset tracking and management and firewalls to protect the infrastructure.

Verizon's role in GE's initiative will be to connect its M2M cloud platforms to Predix. Under the alliance, Verizon and GE have launched services such as remote monitoring, diagnostics and maintenance solutions in the Predix platform. GE and Verizon are also they collaborating on a global identity module subscriber (SIM) for global use. Telecommunication companies have been working in the M2M connections as a way to strengthen their entrepreneurial efforts and put together the most profitable accounts. GE also reached agreements with Softbank and Vodafone to cover their wireless platforms abroad.

The focal point for the digital transformation is to have a strategy of the IoT, not so much connectivity, according to the CEO of GE Digital, Bill Ruh. The idea is simple: to imagine the world in the coming years and from there face an IoT strategy. The challenge, of course, is huge. The responsibility corresponds to Bill Ruh, CEO and Chief Digital Officer of GE Digital.

The focal point of IoT is not so much connectivity, but the digital transformation strategy. Bill Ruh explained that the creation of value is not in the connectivity of an asset, but on how to set up sustainable income. Hence it follows that in the world of digital transformation a company that manufactures or constructs assumes think that the greatest value is not necessarily found in its products but, from an IoT strategy and analytics, thus the company should think about how to get the best results. The Industrial Internet world is very different from the IoT for customers. He gave three examples of how the software and analytics impact in each industry:

- **Airbnb:** The largest provider of temporary locations that does not have a single a room.
- **Apple:** The largest hardware company with just a handful of applications.
- **Uber:** The largest taxi company, which does not have a single vehicle.

The GE executive explains that they do not think of the IoT as a technology, but consider the results they want to achieve and from there they rethink the way forward to obtain these results. For this purpose, GE has a more analytical architecture of software to exploit big data generated from the IoT devices. From the review of the previous technological architectures and the leading companies, GE states that they are in the early stages of the IoT, but the company needs to establish a strategy for the future. In this sense, Bill Ruh explains that the value is in the big data collected, analyze them and transform these into information for which architecture is required. He points out that otherwise others will do it with GE assets.

GE thinks that being a leader today does not mean that the company will remain as a leader in the future. Technology costs fall rapidly and that gives opportunities for new businesses. In 2000, the cost of entry for a startup was about US $5 million and in 2011 was around $5,000. This is the biggest challenge for GE. The company is in the biggest transformation since it was founded by Thomas Alva Edison in 1890. Competitors start thinking about GE as a new digital industrial conglomerate. To compete GE must be able to generate new results with new value propositions around the company assets. GE management believes that the value is in the big data collected, in the analysis and the transformation into information, for which the appropriate architecture is required.

GE summarizes in three steps the digital metamorphosis:

- New business models from the greatest opportunities offered by the software and analytics, while the information should be a revenue generator.
- Speed of change moving from months to days, and scalable architectures such as cloud-based platforms.
- Construct from the existing IT assets.

*Figure 1. The digital transformation*

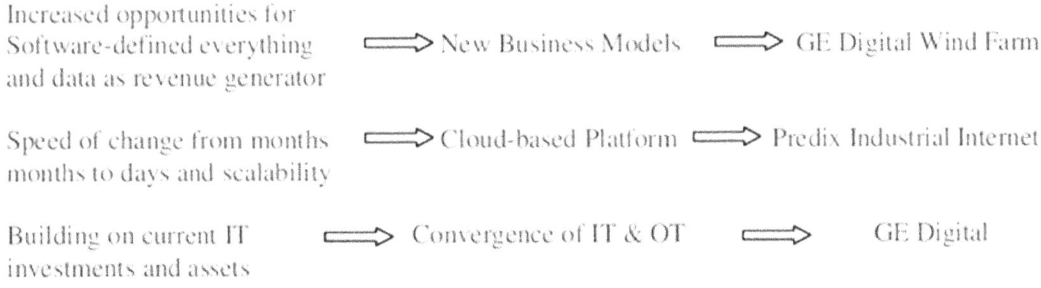

GE concludes that the digital transformation should not be done for customers: first it should think about the company and then in their users or customers. According to GE, business opportunities exist in productivity and efficiency for all industries and for that digitization is very important. GE understands that the digital transformation must be led from top to bottom. And there, the relationships between business and IT teams will be the key.

GE plans to connect Predix to machines from other companies to enable these companies to create their own software applications on Predix. This initiative includes employing the software from GE which allow them to predict whether developing this software is worthwhile by knowing cost savings in advance.

If the initiative is successful, it will affect millions of applications worldwide. In this sense, Cisco has already decided to install Predix inside its networking products; its first initiative has been to include a specialized computer router for harsh environments like oil fields. Intel has created a platform that includes Intel processors with the GE software.

Digital platforms are essential for industrial companies. Companies in business like transportation, aviation, oil and gas, mining, healthcare, and power generation account for more than 30% of the global GDP and influence the daily activities of almost every person. These business have long-term assets like aircrafts, locomotives, and turbines that are essential for their operations and need assistance throughout their lives. Thus, a new big data platform is needed that brings value to the data from these assets and will contribute to maximize productivity.

GE has a unique position to collaborate with software and hardware companies to create this platform. GE clients represent the whole industrial world and they understand their needs and their software requirements. Although the new era of industrial big data comprises an ecosystem bigger than GE if it is to change the industrial world and the global economy. Some of the innovative projects developed by GE include the following:

- **The Optimized Wind Farm:** It is a hardware and software services based on GM 2MW and 3MW wind turbine products, and a group of applications based on Predix, which creates a value added to the wind farm. This includes GE hardware of rotor diameters, turbine ratings, and tower heights. The modular turbine application allows modifying turbine parameters to adjust to pad-specific economic conditions.
- **The Optimized Mining Operation:** Mining operations has developed another relevant application of industrial big data. These kinds of operations include three steps: a) extracting ore, b) reducing it to powder for additional processing, c) separating the usable parts. Having appropriate assets is essential to the quality of the final product. Mining operations depend on a supply chain that transport and transforms raw materials at slower speed than wind farms.
- **The Optimized Transportation Company:** The transportation industry has also developed an industrial big data platform. Assets in the transportation industry include aircrafts and locomotives, which are thought to be employed for most of their operational lives. Data is obtained in different measures depending on the source, whether it comes from the machine or the company. Unlike the other big data platforms, in the case the transmission from these mobile assets and the company can only be done when the asset is at the final destination. This affects the way the data and its analytics are used.

Finally, GE considers the key requirements to optimize industrial data management and its operations:

1. **Data Gathering and Integration:** The platform should facilitate the gathering of big data from all industrial software systems and company devices. It should include and incorporate different types of data, varying response times, and business needs.
2. **Advanced Analytics:** The needs of industrial companies in terms of analytics to optimize their operations are in continuous improvement as the economic environment changes. For this purpose, GE has created a software-defined machine, where analytics adjust to the need of devices and company operations.
3. **Cloud Independence:** Cloud and mobility models support the technology changes that are transforming the business models. Industrial companies require a flexible architecture to meet technology requirement as their technological options vary.
4. **Customizability:** Industrial companies need to adjust to varying client requirements and changing competitive economy. This requires big data platforms that can adjust quickly to the new environment, including new devices, data types, and resources.
5. **Integration:** Company big data platform have to coordinate the data gathering, machine operations, analytics, and staff to make sure that the different parts of the big data platform operate in an effective way. This requires the management of all the parts involved in the process and synchronizing them together.
6. **User Involvement:** Industrial big data platforms have to provide user experiences based on the consumer technologies that clients are using. This means that platforms have to be relevant and adjusted for the specific client needs, which involves support for a group of diverse mobile devices and user interaction models.

## A Business Model Incorporating Big Data

Hartmann et al. (2014) propose a comprehensive theoretical framework to analyze and classify business models of startups which base their core business in some innovative ways of monetizing different offers, products or services, and they rely primarily on data mining. Their framework considers different characteristics and modular components that together allow to set a specific application of business model. They use as inspiration the components of Canvas Business Model of Osterwalder (2013) and as such is composed of six main dimensions: i) the value proposition, ii) processes, iii) resources and key partnerships, iv) how customer relationships are established, v) the channels through which customers are contacted, and vi) how all this generates income given a cost structure associated. The following discusses how big data can be incorporated in the business model.

1. **Key Resources:** By definition a business model based on big data considers these as the main key resource. This does not mean it is the only recourse, but most of the other resources will support the collection, management and analysis of them. From a standpoint of the type of data that can be considered literature classifies them in structured and unstructured. In addition, they can be classified according to whether their source is internal or external. Internal sources include sources that

already exist or are being developed in ICT systems company (CRM, ERP, SCM, etc. systems), and specific data generated for monitoring purposes, whether Web activities, such as web tracking, or acquired through physical sensors or through outsourcing tasks crowds through the Internet (Crowdsourcing). External data includes data that are purchased from third parties or provided by strategic partners which are private nature, as well as data that are freely available on the Internet. The latter can both be sub-categorized into open data (data freely available in electronic format and easily usable databases), social media data (from social networking sites like Facebook), and web-crawled data (data that can be collected through specialized software to filter, select and download data available online).

2. **Key Activities:** These include the "Collection", "Acquisition", "Processing", "Inclusion", "Analytics", "Display" and "Distribution" of big data. To collect and acquire data companies can generate their own data internally or can obtain them from an external source. The generation can be done in several ways, either manually by internal staff, automatically through the use of sensors and monitoring tools, or through outsourcing through crowdsourcing. Processing and aggregation include traditional tasks in the community of databases, such as extracting data from different databases, processing, cleaning, synthesis tables or summary reports.
3. **Value Propositions:** Following one of the definitions most commonly used by communities of data mining, the proposed models based on data business value can be categorized into three types: a) data which constitute a set of facts or measurements reality without an added interpretation, b) information and knowledge that comes from data processing giving context and meaning c) offers of additional value to products and industrial and commercial services, based on the data that is collected and analyzed. Examples of these may be companies that suggest a particular product or service, according to patterns of consumption or geolocation of a client, or as mentioned above, companies that offer preventive maintenance according to the behavior of the machinery that is possible deduced from the data captured by automatic sensors included in it (think of the case of a smart car or plane).
4. **Customer Segments:** According to the authors, there are various ways to segment customers, which typically include their psychological, demographic, geographic, purchase channels, behavioral, among others. However, they use the generic classification, dividing customers in business and individual consumers, it being possible to engage in addressing each segment separately or together.
5. **Income Generation Model:** To make a profitable business each company must have at least a sustainable source of income. Typically these are classified into seven categories, which are not mutually exclusive. A company can have one or more sources of revenue: direct or traditional sale of assets (tangible or intangible such as digital); lease or temporary loan asset - momentarily giving exclusive rights to use an asset in a defined time period; licensing - delivering the license of an asset in exchange for a payment; charging for use according to the measured in units per unit time consumption; subscription charged for the use of the asset; a commission for the intermediary between two parties that a product and service are transferred; and advertising.
6. **Cost Structure:** By offering a value proposition a company incurs costs and the use of resources which are limited (time, capital, labor, technology, etc.). On this point, the authors emphasize whether there are some relative advantage over the cost of using, collecting and analyzing data.

Typically, a company will have a specific cost advantage if the data used in their products or services are created independently (as a sub-product) of other goods and services. For example, a company that manufactures cars have that advantage by capturing and using big data that is automatically generated by the IoT-based systems and electronic sensors included in the car. However, other companies wishing to offer data services related to traffic will not have these cost advantages relative to the data, as not being directly generating them they should buy to third parties, for example, manufacturers of cars. Other classic examples of companies with competitive advantages over the cost of producing data are Internet companies such as Amazon, Google, Facebook, Twitter, among others, already have vast amounts of data of various types, whose marginal cost of generation is close to zero.

## CONCLUSION

Big data and the IoT applications generate ample opportunities to develop new models in business and improve the performance of companies, but also require the redesign and update of various aspects within the organization.

At least creating an analytical capacity requires organizations to develop analytical skills to create new models based on big data as well as skills to use these models in the execution of their daily operations. Obviously, this requires not only an advanced IT infrastructure, but also an organizational and government culture to support different initiatives. However, to start exploiting the benefits of big data is not strictly necessary for such profound changes immediately. Organizations can develop their analytical capacity incrementally involving key staff in processes that support their effectiveness and analytical intelligence. These efforts can produce market results quickly, starting the company transition to the goal of successfully implementing a strategy based on big data.

Big data technology not only applies to obtain large amounts of data, but also serves to analyze those huge volumes of data and thus get information and knowledge. It is a technology that is emerging gradually and although not all companies use it, it is designed to stay and mark a new stage in the world of technology. There are a large number of organizations that collect big data related to our privacy (e.g., data generated from sensor-based medical devices). Data security and privacy need be further strengthened in the age of the IoT.

Companies that use big data technology and computational business intelligence will be able to create more complex images of preferences and customer demands, along with its weaknesses and its competitors with which they will get a competitive advantage. However, these companies will have to have a very complete infrastructure not to suffer from data theft and corresponding compensation to their clients.

The big data technology and computational business intelligence should and can continue to evolve and thus take advantage of the great flood of data (e.g., data generated from the IoT devices and social media), although not all data of them is useful, as there is a lot of noise between them. It is worth pointing out the importance of capturing only those that may be subsequently transformed into information and knowledge.

## REFERENCES

Barker, K. J., DAmato, J., & Sheridon, P. (2008). Credit card fraud: Awareness and prevention. *Journal of Financial Crime, 15*(4), 398–410. doi:10.1108/13590790810907236

Barney, J. (1991). Firm resources and sustained competitive advantage. *Journal of Management, 17*(1), 99–120. doi:10.1177/014920639101700108

Cavallo, A. (2012). Online and official price indexes: Measuring Argentinas inflation. *Journal of Monetary Economics, 60*(2), 152–165. doi:10.1016/j.jmoneco.2012.10.002

Chen, H., Chiang, R. H., & Storey, V. C. (2012). Business intelligence and analytics: From big data to big impact. *Management Information Systems Quarterly, 36*(4), 1165–1188.

Choi, H., & Varian, H. (2012). Predicting the present with Google Trends. *Economic Inquiry, 88*(1), 2–9.

Edelman, B. (2015, April). How to launch your digital platform. *Harvard Business Review*.

Hartmann, P. M., Zaki, M., & Feldmann, N. (2014). *Big data for big business? A taxonomy of data-driven business models used by start-up firms.* University of Cambridge Working Paper.

Heffetz, O., & Ligett, K. (2014). Privacy and data-based research. *The Journal of Economic Perspectives, 28*(2), 75–98. doi:10.1257/jep.28.2.75

Hernandez Barros, R., Vidal-García, J., Vidal, M., & Martínez Torre-Enciso, M. I. (2016). New evidence in the definition of strategy for global insurers. *Economic Bulletin, 36*(3), 1829–1843.

Hoffmann, A., & Birnbrich, C. (2012). The impact of fraud prevention on bank-customer relationships. *International Journal of Bank Marketing, 30*(5), 390–407. doi:10.1108/02652321211247435

Jiménez, G. S., Ongena, S., Peydro, J. L., & Saurina, J. (2014). Hazardous times for monetary policy: What do 23 million loans say about the impact of monetary policy on credit risk-taking. *Econometrica, 82*(2), 463–505. doi:10.3982/ECTA10104

Kruschwitz, N. (2011). First look: The second annual new intelligent enterprise survey. *MIT Sloan Management Review, 52*(4), 87–89.

Lambrecht, A., & Skiera, B. (2006). Paying too much and being happy about it: Existence, causes, and consequences of tariff-choice biases. *JMR, Journal of Marketing Research, 43*(2), 212–223. doi:10.1509/jmkr.43.2.212

Lambrecht, A., & Tucker, C. (2013). When does retargeting work? Information specificity in online advertising. *JMR, Journal of Marketing Research, 50*(5), 561–576. doi:10.1509/jmr.11.0503

Lazer, D., Kennedy, R., King, G., & Vespignani, A. (2014). The parable of Google Flu: Traps in Big Data. *Analytical Sciences, 343*(6176), 1203–1205. doi:10.1126/science.1248506 PMID:24626916

Mayer-Schonberger, V., & Cukier, K. (2014). *Big data: A revolution that will transform how we live, work, and think*. Boston, MA: Houghton Mifflin Harcourt Print.

McAfee, A., Brynjolfsson, E., Davenport, T. H., Patil, D., & Barton, D. (2012). Big Data. The management revolution. *Harvard Business Review*, *90*(10), 61–67. PMID:23074865

McGuire, T., Manyika, J., & Chui, M. (2012). Why big data is the new competitive advantage. *Ivey Business Journal*, *76*(4), 1–4.

Mian, A., Rao, K., & Sufi, A. (2013). Household balance sheets, consumption and economic slump. *The Quarterly Journal of Economics*, *128*(4), 1687–1726. doi:10.1093/qje/qjt020

Mian, A., & Sufi, A. (2009). The consequences of mortgage credit expansion: Evidence from the U.S. mortgage default crisis. *The Quarterly Journal of Economics*, *124*(4), 1449–1496. doi:10.1162/qjec.2009.124.4.1449

Nickerson, D., & Rogers, T. (2014). Political campaigns and big data. *The Journal of Economic Perspectives*, *28*(2), 51–74. doi:10.1257/jep.28.2.51

Osterwalder, A., & Pigneur, Y. (2010). *Business model generation: A handbook for visionaries, game changers, and challengers*. Wiley.

Purcell, B. M. (2013). *Big data using cloud computing*. Holy Family University Working Paper.

Varian, H. (2014). Big Data: New tricks for econometrics. *The Journal of Economic Perspectives*, *28*(2), 3–28. doi:10.1257/jep.28.2.3

Vidal, M., Vidal-García, J., & Hernandez Barros, R. (2016). Big data and business decision-making. In M. K. Singh & K. G. Dileep (Eds.), *Effective big data management and opportunities for implementation* (pp. 140–157). Hershey, PA: IGI Global.

## ADDITIONAL READING

Atzori, L., Iera, A., & Morabito, G. (2010). The Internet of Things: A survey. *Computer Networks*, *54*(15), 2787–2805. doi:10.1016/j.comnet.2010.05.010

Butler, D. (2008). Web data predict flu. *NATNews*, *456*, 287–288. PMID:19020578

Dong, M.X., Ota, K., Yang, L.T., Chang, S., Zhu, H., & Zhou, Z.Y. (2014). Mobile agent-based energy-aware and user-centric data collection in wireless sensor networks. *Computer Networks, 74*(part B), 58-70.

Fox, G. C., Kamburugamuve, S., & Hartman, R. D. (2012). Architecture and measured characteristics of a cloud based Internet of Things. *Proceedings of International Conference Collaboration Technologies and Systems* (pp. 6-12.). Denver, CO. doi:10.1109/CTS.2012.6261020

Goransson, P., & Black, C. (2014). *In software defined networking: A comprehensive approach*. Netherlands: Elsevier.

Gubbi, J., Buyya, R., Marusic, S., & Palaniswami, M. (2013). Internet of Things (IoT): A vision architectural elements and future directions. *Future Generation Computer Systems*, *29*(1), 1645–1660. doi:10.1016/j.future.2013.01.010

He, J., Zhang, Y., Huang, G., & Cao, J. (2012). A smart web service based on the Context of Things. *ACM Transactions on Internet Technology*, *11*(4), 13–22.

Lee, I., & Lee, K. (2015). The Internet of things (IoT): Applications, investments and challenges for enterprises. *Business Horizons*, *58*(4), 431–440. doi:10.1016/j.bushor.2015.03.008

Ma, H. D. (2011). Internet of Things: Objectives and scientific challenges. *Journal of Computer Science and Technology*, *26*(6), 919–924. doi:10.1007/s11390-011-1189-5

Raggett, D. (2015). The web of things: Challenges and opportunities. *IEEE Computer*, *48*(5), 26–32. doi:10.1109/MC.2015.149

Shen, Q., Liu, Y., Zhao, Z., Ci, S., & Tang, H. (2010). Distributed hash table based ID management optimization for Internet of Things. *Proceedings of 6th International Wireless Communications and Mobile Computer Conference* (pp. 686-690). Caen, France. doi:10.1145/1815396.1815554

Shroeck, M., & Shockley, R. (2012). Analytics: The real-world use of Big Data. IBM Institute of Business Value in collaboration with Said Business School, University of Oxford.

Stankovic, J. A. (2014). Research directions for the Internet of Things. *IEEE Internet of Things Journal*, *1*(1), 3–9. doi:10.1109/JIOT.2014.2312291

## KEY TERMS AND DEFINITIONS

**Amazon Web Services:** Subsidiary of Amazon offering cloud computing services that form a computing platform.

**Business Analytics:** Skills, technologies, practices for ongoing exploration and investigation of previous company performance to gain insight and drive business planning.

**Business Intelligence:** The methodology for the acquisition and transformation of raw data into useful information for business analysis.

**Business Model Canvas:** A strategic management and entrepreneurial tool. It allows describing, designing and pivoting a business model.

**Computational Intelligence:** The ability of a computer to learn a specific task from data or experimental observation.

**Electronic Commerce:** A business model that enables to conduct business over the Internet.

**Hadoop:** An open-source software framework of very large data sets on computer clusters.

**Information Technology:** It is the use of any computers, storage, networking and other processes to create, store and exchange electronic data.

# Chapter 14
# IoT for Hospitality Industry:
## Paperless Buffet Management

**Asim Sinan Yuksel**
*Suleyman Demirel University, Turkey*

**Ibrahim Arda Cankaya**
*Suleyman Demirel University, Turkey*

**Sadi Fuat Cankaya**
*Suleyman Demirel University, Turkey*

## ABSTRACT

*Creating and updating meal tags, printing them on small-sized papers raise the costs, cause workload and affect the service quality negatively at the hotels with all-you-can-eat buffet system. Over the last few years, we have seen that many hotels started to make use of tablets to improve the service quality, decrease the costs, provide customers ability to order foods, make reservations, manage their rooms, etc. Going paperless and including more features by adopting new technologies increase the quality of service, help customer's and staff's decision-making processes more effective, improve customer and service personnel experience. In this chapter, authors designed and developed a flexible, cost effective, easy-to-use, customer-friendly and staff oriented paperless buffet management system for the restaurants that have all-you-can-eat buffet. Through this system, they aimed to achieve enhanced customer service, increased efficiency and customer satisfaction; save time, paper and printing costs; provide environmental benefits and efficient buffet management.*

## INTRODUCTION

A buffet is a system of serving meals by placing them on separate serving tables at restaurants and cafés. Guests are given plates and can approach the serving table to take as much food as they wish. A buffet table often consists of desserts, savory foods, soups, sea food, white and red meat. Many five-star hotels utilize this system for efficiency and simplicity of serving. Currently, most business with buffet systems use written, paper-based solutions to prepare menus, fulfill orders, and present them to their customers.

DOI: 10.4018/978-1-5225-2104-4.ch014

Prepared meals are placed on buffet tables according to their categories, and the service staff informs the customers about the meals (calorie, allergens, explanations in different languages) by placing paper-based labels next to the them. Guests choose their meals by visually seeing the dishes and reading the labels, selecting the foods that appeal to them. Buffet menus are determined according to the number of guests and the cost, variety and amount of the dishes. These issues are decided in advance and preparations are made accordingly. During peak hours, the meals can be consumed quickly, often resulting in a change of menu items, and requiring the serving staff to update the paper-based labels on the buffet. Current buffet management systems have not adapted to the digital era and still rely on the paper-based methods. These methods are inefficient, and often unreliable as labels are often forgotten, not changed, or mistaken and food items are being rotated in and out of the buffet while serving staff are dealing with a high volume of customers. This information is not reportable, classifiable, and filterable since they are in hand-written text form, reducing the efficacy of the service provided to the customer.

As technology becomes more important and strategic, the pressure on the hospitality industry to remain competitive is increasing. New services and products are being developed to help maintain the competitive edge. These improvements should be monitored (Nyheim, McFadden & Connolly, 2005; Wang & Qualls, 2007).

Serving with a buffet is a method that allows reducing staff and speeding up the service, making it a good commercial instrument for the business. Guests have the opportunity to choose freely from large prepared selections, easing the workload of the kitchen. There are also some notable disadvantages of the buffet system. During the peak hours, there may be a rush of people in front of the buffet, causing confusion. Since the buffet tables are prepared in advance and serving size is not limited, the guests may overeat and the meals may need to be changed frequently. The workload of the kitchen staff may increase during the preparation phase due to the quantities involved. For these reasons, updating, writing and placing the meal information on the buffets becomes even more difficult, burdening the service staff. Since the current system is completely paper-based, problems may arise surrounding the cost of papers, printing and staffing. In the event that people from different nationalities arrive at the facility, the service staff often struggle to prepare text in the languages of these customers.

The impact of the technology on the restaurants is not only about how the food products are prepared, but also about how they are presented on the menus (Bitner, 2001). The font, colors, display and design of the menu also affect the behavior of the customers (Reynolds, Merritt, & Pinckney, 2005). Electronic, Wi-Fi enabled tablet-based menus can be more useful than the conventional paper based menus, due to the ease of updating the information. Use of electronic menus improves the quality of the service, as well as the customer's experience. As a result, integration of the technology into the hospitality industry is indispensable. Most notably, many problems that arise in the buffet system can be eliminated by these new technological solutions.

In this study, researchers developed an Internet of Things (IoT) integrated, context aware, paperless, mobile buffet-management system and instructed the hotel service staff and business administrators in its use. By adopting this new technology, hotels and restaurants can manage buffets wirelessly, and present the meal information in an efficient way that is not possible with the paper-based tags. In the current buffet systems offered by hotels, the only communication between the chef and the hotel customers is via these tags. By using the IoT-enabled digital meal tags, the chef can present allergen information, calories, the quality of his cuisine, ingredients, and receipts more effectively. Additionally, the authors expect that the restaurants that introduce the IoT-enabled digital meal tags and the paperless buffet management system will achieve a high press visibility that will lead to increased sales. Therefore, the hardware and software investments will pay off quickly.

## BACKGROUND

Technological systems can be good methods for restaurant owners to increase their sales. If the appropriate technology is implemented with proper income management principles, it may increase the profit margin of all types of restaurants. This system also contributes to the sense of control of the customer; assigning staff members will be more efficient, and it will have a positive impact on the food experience of the customers (Dixon, Kimes, & Verma, 2009; Oronsky & Chathoth, 2007). In addition, the technology usage will decrease the workload per person, as well as the employment costs, and it will leave a positive impression on the restaurant staff.

Meeting with the technology is not a result but a process. Businesses may keep their customers, create new employment opportunities and increase their market share by following the technological developments and implementing the new technologies (Oronsky & Chathoth, 2007). According to the research that has been conducted in the United States of America, the yearly income of the businesses that serve fixed menu is approximately 180 billion dollars in the USA (Kimes, 2008). In the businesses that serve fixed menu, the income may be increased at the rate of 2% to 5% by using the typical income management (Hanks, 2002). This means that the average income increases from 3, 6 to 9 billion dollars. This income can be increased by adopting the right technology.

Income management is categorized in two groups; time management and pricing (Kimes, 1998). Time management requires control and knowledge. If the preparation time can be decreased when there are a high number of customers, the service can be provided for more customers in a shorter amount of time, potentially leading to an increase in income.

Service facilitation is related to the will of customers to protect their time and effort. The increase in the facilitation is related to the increase in the satisfaction (Berry, Seiders, & Grewal, 2002). Restaurants may use the Internet technology for the accessibility. In order to do that, they may facilitate the order of the food or eliminate the confusions about the food choice by the right explanation. It is likely that the customer satisfaction will increase when they feel that they have the control (Averill, 1973; Hui & Bateson, 1991). Therefore, the developed system will increase the sense of control of the customer that leads to their satisfaction about the hotel.

Hsu and Wu (2013) have examined the relationship between customer satisfaction about restaurant services in the hospitality industry and the use of the technology; namely the tablet-based menu. In their study, they received assistance from a fully-equipped restaurant that uses the iPad as a tablet-based menu. They have obtained data for their study from a questionnaire that they asked 219 customers to respond to. They used a conceptual model for determining the customer satisfaction. They allege that customer satisfaction depends on three different factors. Those factors are technological innovations, briefing and the services that are expected from the staff. According to the obtained results, the use of electronic tablet based menus have a positive impact on the customer satisfaction.

Wang & Qualls (2007) have suggested a Technology Acceptance Model (TAM) to identify the adaptation process of the hotel businesses to the technology. They stated in their study that the strategic importance of the technology for the hotel business should be carefully analyzed. The suggested model has a great importance in understanding the adoption process of the hotel businesses to the technology.

In a study by Yepes (2014), the impacts of the food choice through the electronic tablet-based menu by students born after 2000 has been examined. Attraction of the tablet-based menu on the students and the general and emotional impacts of these menus on the students have been examined. Each participant has been asked to choose a menu display. Attractive graphical displays were effective on the food choice of the participants. Furthermore, all participants stated that these graphical displays should definitely be on the menus.

Brewer and Druin (2010) developed iMenu, which is an interactive menu for restaurants, providing customers more control over the food during the ordering process. The customers can customize and order meals using the device, leading to higher customer satisfaction. The study targeted children since they are not as experienced as adults, and the satisfaction of the children directly influences the satisfaction and mood of their parents. The study showed that digital menus can also be used to satisfy children when they are designed appropriately. Tan et al. (2010) developed an automated ordering system that uses touch screens to order food, and then uses wireless robots to serve meals. Researchers aimed to serve a large number of guests in short time frames with high population, reduce staff costs by receiving orders and serving meals digitally. The developed system proved that restaurants can save time as well as staffing costs through automated systems.

In the study by Chen, Lin, and Yen (2011), researchers designed and developed an interactive tabletop system for a restaurant in Taiwan. They showed that interactive devices enhance the dining experience when they are applied to restaurants by offering features such as customizable interfaces and games.

Igelmund, Kutscher, and Wambach (2011) designed Good Choice Table for Group Decision Support Systems (GDSS) in a restaurant. They aimed to transfer the knowledge of face-to-face GDSS to non-business environments. They designed a tabletop to display a main user interface for two users seated face-to-face at the table. According to the results, most of the participants preferred the system over traditional paper menus. The authors stated that digital menus that are combined with a recommender system increase the satisfaction of the guests.

## APPLICATION OF IOT IN HOSPITALY INDUSTRY

When developing the system, authors adopted an agile software development method which is widely used and considered as appropriate to the project's needs. In complicated projects, the development process is unlikely to complete the previous step precisely before passing to the next phase. For example, despite identifying the needs of the customer in the start-up phase of the project, some needs can become clearer only in the progressive phases. Since the agile software development methodology is completely based on customer satisfaction, it is also the most appropriate method to develop the buffet management system. Researchers interviewed the managers and the service staff and defined the following 4 phases to develop the system.

1. **Determining the Requirements:**
    a. **Determining the Context:** It is determined which information will be on the part that will be presented to the customer. That information will be recipe, ingredients (vegetables, meat, spices, oil and sauces), cooking style, allergens and calorie information.
    b. **Supported Languages:** English has been identified as the native language due to being a world language. Besides that, Turkish, German and Russian have also been included by taking

into consideration the conditions of Turkey and tourist profiles of the hotels. The number of languages can be easily increased, if required.

c. **User Interface Requirements:** Decisions regarding how the screens will be presented, which colors and fonts will be used have been taken.
d. **Tablet Requirements:** Optimum requirements for tablets such as memory, Wi-Fi, CPU and screen size of the tablets are determined.
e. **IoT Requirements:** Since the communication of the system will be provided through a wireless network (IoT Infrastructure), the requirements for creating the appropriate infrastructure are identified.
f. **Context Server Requirements:** Requirements regarding the server in which the data about the meal will be held are identified.

2. **Design:** In this phase, relation of the system modules with each other is designed by considering the requirements that are identified in the first phase.
3. **Implementation:** The designed system is developed and put into service.
4. **Test:** The developed system is tested; the bugs are eliminated.

## Software Architecture

The system is composed of three basic modules. Those are Context, Staff and Customer modules. The Context module works as the meal server. It contains the database that stores all the information regarding the meals; the services that allow communication with staff module; the interfaces that allow entering the meal and the context information.

Staff module contains the mobile application which allows service staff to update the meals that are on the buffet. The staff gets the meal information from the meal server through the developed IoT infrastructure and the mobile administrator application; chooses the meal tablet that he wishes to update from the screen. Then he chooses the meal that he wishes to be on the tablet and that meal information is sent to the tablet in seconds.

The customer module contains the digital meal tag which is associated with any meal that is on the buffet. This is the part where the customer can see all of the relevant information about the meal and the context. Additionally, the module contains the sub module that will connect to the Bluetooth bracelet that is given to the customer. This module checks whether a customer approaches or not by scanning each second. When the distance between the customer is less than 50 cm, it detects the language of the customer and changes its interface language accordingly. Personal information of the customer is taken during the check-in, so the alerts and suggestions that are specific to the customer can be displayed on the screen. Those are customer's allergen information and alerts or suggestions regarding her/his diet, if the customer is on a diet. Figure 1 shows the architectural diagram of the system which explains this interaction. The administrator interface is shown in Figure 2.

## Digital Meal Tag Design

In the menu presentation process, Mills and Thomas (2008) have emphasized that displaying the picture of the meal on the menu, information about nutritional value of the meal, and the ingredients of the meal have a great impact on the food experiences of the customers. Despite the fact that the requirements regarding the process of meal representation on the menu are expensive (Almanza, Nelson, &

Figure 1. Architectural diagram of the system

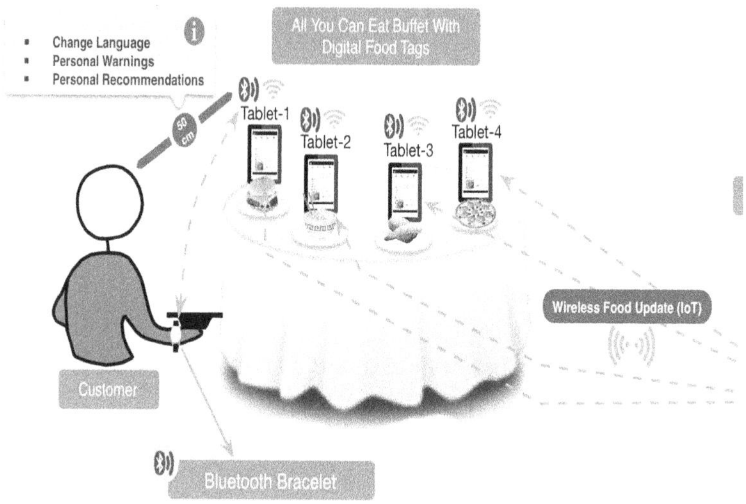


Figure 2. Administrator interface

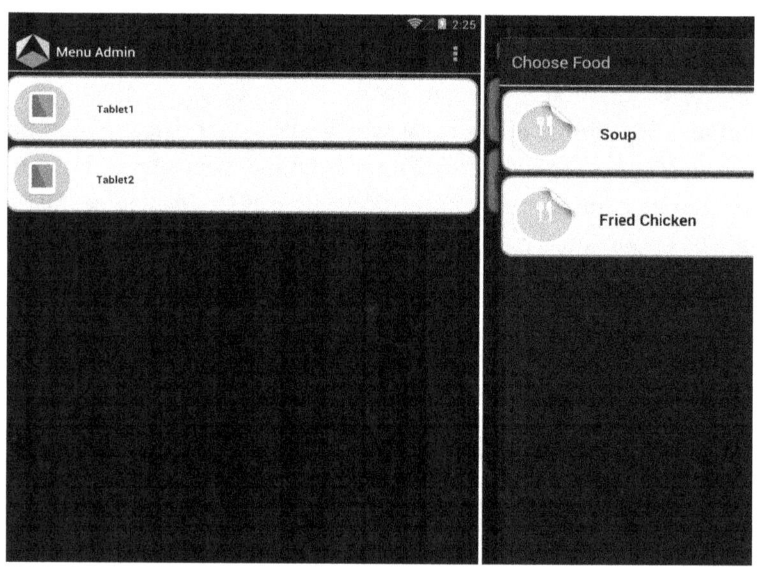


Chai, 1997), the impact of the meal representation on the customers' meal choice caused them to do so (Swartz, Braxton, & Viera, 2011). According to the recent legal arrangements, a new purpose of the restaurant businesses is to decrease the obesity rate and increase the healthy meal choices (U.S. Food and Drug Administration, 2014). Therefore, the authors designed and implemented a digital meal tag interface, which will inform the customer ideally, ensure customers to choose their meal properly and be placed on the buffet. Figure 3 shows this design.

*Figure 3. Digital meal tag*

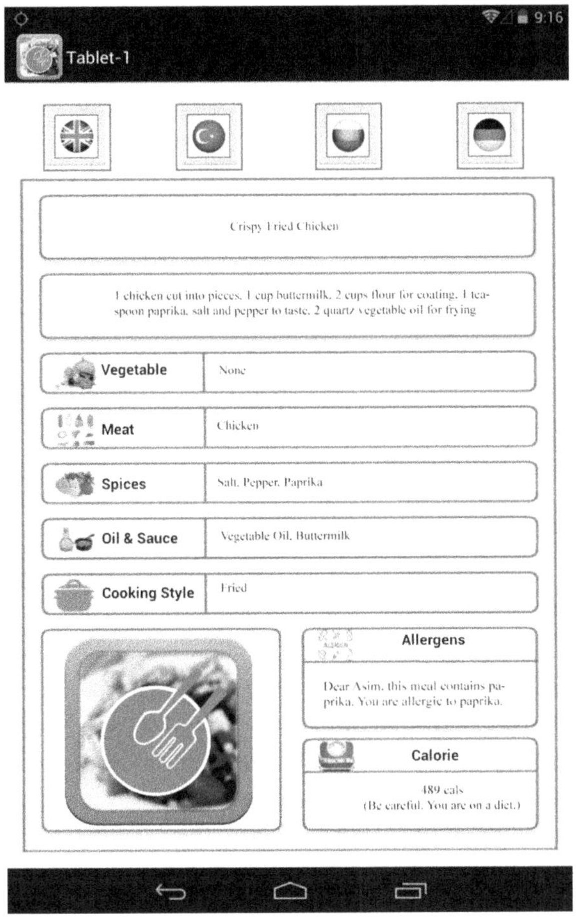


Country flags which can be switched by the customer through touching are on the top of the interface. The customer can switch the language of the meal by touching these buttons. If a bluetooth bracelet has been given to the customer, the language is automatically recognized and the language of the meal is changed. The meal name and the recipe are displayed under the language section. The other sections contain vegetables, meats, spices, sauces and oils and the cooking style. Visuals and allergen information that are specific to the customer and calories of the meal are on the bottom section.

## IoT Integration

IoT technology has its own characteristics and concepts. It combines different technologies such as sensors, semantic web, and cloud computing (Whitmore, Agarwal, & Xu, 2014). In this section, we introduce the IoT concept as it applies to the project. We present necessary information to understand it and explain how we integrated IoT into our system.

IoT Concept: The Internet is continuously evolving. In the early days, it was a network of linked static documents called hypertext and characterized by the World Wide Web. Now, it has become dynamic (Web 2.0) and it provides two-way communication that enables users to collaborate, participate and interact with each other. Social networks such as Facebook, Twitter, blogs, and wikis are modern examples of this dynamic structure. Although Web 2.0 dominates the Internet, the current research focuses on another goal that is known as Web 3.0 or Semantic Web. This technology makes the web understandable by machines and allows them to behave intelligently. Consequently, it allows machines to process and share their own data without needing human intervention.

In parallel to the developments in the Internet, technologies such as Sensor Networks, Near Field Communication, and Bluetooth Low Energy have also been evolving. The union of these technologies opens new possibilities that allow direct communication between machines, connecting more machines and letting them interact with each other, and providing self-organization capabilities over the Internet. These developments and visions have created the concept that is called the Internet of Things (IoT).

Over the past decade, IoT concept has begun gaining popularity both in academia and in industry. It has begun to involve in many technological developments in the fields of mobile technologies, new Internet systems, inter-device communication, and wearable technologies. The capabilities of the IoT and what it offers are the main reason for this interest. It builds a world where all surrounding objects are connected to the Internet and communicate with each other with minimum human intervention (Kortuem, Kawsar, Fitton & Sundramoorthy, 2010). This connection produces many applications in many different domains such as supply chain management, automotive, aerospace, transportation, logistics, healthcare, telecommunication, entertainment, smart buildings and smart cities, hotels, agriculture, and many others. Smart devices with home automation and the devices which can automatically adjust themselves according to whether the house is empty or not, habits of the household (at what time they decrease or increase the temperature) and other similar criteria (Paradiso, 2010); sports balls which can store information by using sensors such as the speed of the ball (km/h), how many of the shoots qualify as a goal or which foot (left or right) was used for kicking the ball (Knaus, 2015); devices that are developed for monitoring the items used in daily life can be given as the examples for the usage areas of the IoT.

In this study, researchers used an open-source framework, Alljoyn Alliance (2016), that is extremely flexible and helps developers to develop applications that have abilities to discover nearby devices, and communicate with each other directly. Different OS's, as well as different devices with different brands can make use of this framework that leads to removing boundaries.

With the Alljoyn framework, authors enabled tablet-to-tablet communication by developing an information exchange protocol and created wireless communication between the tablets that present meal information and the administrative tablets that are used by the service staff to manage the meal contexts. Service staff can update the meal context anywhere and anytime with the administrative application. Thus, authors developed a solution which derives profit from paper and time, is free from the distance, and eliminates the traffic of the service staff between the kitchen and the meal.

## Context Awareness

We humans interact with our environment and other people, becoming aware of the information surrounding us and interpreting the implications of that information. We can show our reactions according to the context of situations and make a logical deduction. For instance, by observing the mimics, gestures and voice tone of a person, one can react in an appropriate manner. However, computers do not have the same ability to make a deduction from their environments as the people do. They can only take advantage if such information is explicitly provided; this becomes a research challenge. Context information becomes important in mobile environments, since the needs, interactions and environments change rapidly. In the research areas such as human computer interaction, adaptable user interfaces, augmented reality, ubiquitous computing, and wearable computing, usage and interpretation of context information can add great value. In this section we discuss the concepts of context and context-awareness, explain how we achieved context-awareness in our system, how it adds value to the hospitality industry.

The definition of context-awareness was first introduced by Schilit and Theimer (1994) followed by Ryan, Pascoe, and Morse (1990). However, Abowd et al. (1999) stated that these definitions were too specific and cannot be applied to identify the context and context-awareness concepts. Therefore, they defined the context as "Context is any information that can be used to characterize the situation of an entity. An entity is a person, place, or object that is considered relevant to the interaction between a user and an application, including the user and applications themselves." and the context-awareness as "A system is context-aware if it uses context to provide relevant information and/or services to the user, where relevancy depends on the user's task."

In this study, researchers accepted the above definitions, since a customer interacts with digital meal tag (the context) and the system provides relevant allergen, diet information to the user; changes the language upon approach to the meals (context awareness). In context-aware applications, capturing the context requires additional sensors/programs. The applications also should be intelligent to process the provided information and make a deduction. In their system, applications capture the customer's information (given during check-in process) via Bluetooth Low Energy devices according to the proximity of customer. Furthermore, the meal ingredients and allergen information, calorie of the meal and diet information are compared to make deduction about the customer. Finally, the customer is warned accordingly.

Tablets displaying meal information need to be close enough to the customers in order to sense them and give them specific information. This operation should not be difficult for the customers or limit them. The cost requirements of this personal solution should be examined and the lowest rate should be chosen. Providing a wireless communication in terms of use offers a solution for this problem. The communication between the tablet and the customer will have reasonable costs through the use of Bluetooth devices. The beacon devices that can make Bluetooth communication have been used for this communication method and they have reasonable costs. Beacons are small Bluetooth devices that broadcast signals that work with Bluetooth Low Energy (BLE) communication protocol. Energy consumption of these devices is lower than that of the other wireless communication devices. Therefore, low energy consumption of the Bluetooth devices would be cost-effective, while establishing a quality connection between the user and tablets. Figure 4 shows the BLE bracelet.

The bracelets are given to the customers by the hotels and they act as devices that broadcast Bluetooth signals. They provide the communication between the customer and the tablets that display meal context. This bracelet uses the RadBeacon Dot, a brand of Beacon devices, that is developed by the Radius Networks. The device is very light and has a long battery life. When the battery is empty, it can be replaced with a new one. The device can recognize customers at a distance of maximum 50 meters (RadBeacon Dot, 2015). It is a sufficient distance when considering that the customers stand very close (approximately 50 cm) to the meals in order to choose. The bracelet also has a button which shuts down the signal sending feature. That prevents the battery level to decrease when the device is not being used. The battery life information which changes according to the signal sending frequency of the device is shown in the Table 1.

Those rates can be changed any time according to the use. This bracelet is given to the customers when they check in and taken back when they check out. As a result, the same bracelet can be used by multiple customers just by changing the information. That saves the bracelet costs. Before giving the

*Figure 4. Bluetooth low energy bracelet*

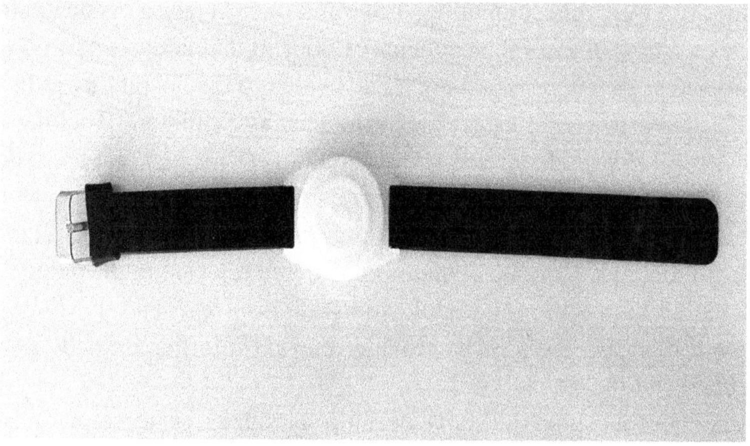

*Table 1. Battery life information of BLE bracelets*

| Advertising Rate | Battery Life |
|---|---|
| High – 100ms | 30 days |
| Medium – 500ms | 145 days |
| Low – 1000ms | 285 days |

bracelet to a customer, private information and alerts that the customer should see on the meal tablet are stored by entering the customer information during check-in process.

When the customers approach to the meal they intend to choose (and therefore to the tablet that shows information about the meal), meal information is displayed in the customer's language by automatically detecting the customer's language. Besides that, the digital meal tags show the allergen information that are specific to the approaching customer and information regarding his diet, if the customer is on a diet. When the customer is walking away from the tablet at a distance and keep glancing at other meals, the tablet detects it and sets menu's language in default language which is English. The language can also be changed by touching the flags of countries that are on the digital meal tag. Thus, authors achieved context-aware, interactive and satisfying service with higher quality.

## DISCUSSION AND RESULTS

There are many benefits for hotels with all-you-can-eat buffet systems who want to adopt an IoT based system to manage their buffets. One of the benefits is potential decrease in costs and time. The other benefits are increased efficiency and becoming green/environment-friendly. All of these lead to the most important benefit that is customer satisfaction. Hotels and restaurants will continue to keep their customers happy and new customers will become long-standing loyal ones. Additionally, the system supports the idea of becoming more civilized (Krebs, 2008).

## Cost Benefits

One of the important benefits is cost savings. Replacing paper based meal tags with digital meal tags eliminates the printing related costs. The hotels who will go paperless will see an important decrease in their printing supply costs as it was seen in the study by Thompson (2008). According to the authors, an urgent care clinic was able to save approximately $6,000 to $7,500 per year on reduced paper related costs. Ryan (2008) showed that a firm that sells and installs equipment for DISH Network reduced printing costs (such as printer toner) and saved during the process around $3,400 per year. Finally, there will be a decrease in the printing hardware. The hotels will reduce the number of printers and replace them less which will lead to a real cost savings.

Another cost saving is related to the office space. By using the new system, service personnel can manage the buffets remotely from anywhere, translators can translate the food information to any languages remotely, and administrators can add new food information on the go. Consequently, hotels will drastically reduce the need for office space, leading to direct savings by reducing building overhead.

In hotels, cost management of meals start with menu management. Menus are not only a management instrument, but also advertisement and sale instrument (Ninemeier & Kasavana, 1986). Authors analyzed the personnel related costs and the cost of replacing paper based meal tags with digital meal tags. Their results indicate that hotels save costs if they adopt our system. They observed that there are differences in terms of management instruments and the number of service personnel. Cost related differences can be listed as follows:

1. In traditional system, papers are used to provide meal information. On the contrary, in IoT based system, no paper is used.
2. In traditional system, meal information is prepared and printed for breakfast, lunch and dinner. Average of 50 paper tags are prepared and printed for each meal time that cause need for additional personnel.
3. Although the initial cost of buying software and hardware is high in our system, this cost is one time only and there will be no need for additional service personnel for extra tasks such as printing and coating.

Table 2 shows the cost comparison of traditional paper based system and IoT based system for two-year time period for 50 meals and 3 meal times. Authors assumed that the lifetime of a tablet is its warranty period that is 2 years. Furthermore, they assumed that paper based meal tags need to be replaced every 3 months because of stain or damage and the cost of bulk purchasing A4 size papers (500 piece) that is $2.3, the cost of coating per paper that is $0.08. Another assumption they make is cartridges need to be replaced after 1000 prints and the cost is approximately $23.9. The cost of buying an average quality printer is $136.5 and buying a coating machine is $273.5.

The tablets, that are used as digital meal tags need to support Wi-Fi and Bluetooth connections, should be large enough to provide better customer experience (8 inch). The cost of such a tablet is approximately $136.9. Since there are 50 different meals, hotels need to buy 50 tablets and additional stands (costs $22.2 per tablet) for protecting them from oil and heat. The cost of an average server that will be used as meal server is approximately $342. Furthermore, in traditional system, authors assumed that average of 3 service employees will be working for printing and coating related tasks, arranging the meals and the buffet, and providing meal related information to customers. In IoT based system, maximum 2 service employees will be enough to manage the buffet. They assumed that minimum employee wage (determined according to the economic conditions in Turkey) is $787.

As it is seen from Table 2, hotels will be saving $15,537 in two years. Furthermore, customer satisfaction will be instantly fulfilled when the system is adopted. Figure 5 shows the Cost-Time graphic and Figure 6 shows Cost-Meal graphic. It is shown that even if the initial costs of the new system is high, the overall cost and cost per meal is always lower than the traditional system.

## Time Benefits

Paperless buffet management affects the performance of service personnel. By using the developed mobile buffet management application, service personnel were able to easily and rapidly manage the

*Table 2. Cost comparison of paper based system and IoT based system*

| | **Supply Amounts** | | **Costs** | | **Savings** |
|---|---|---|---|---|---|
| | **Traditional System** | **IoT Based System** | **Traditional System** | **IoT Based System** | **Total** |
| Paper Usage (For Each Meal) | 36000 | 0 | $172 | 0 | $172 |
| Plastic Coating (For Each Meal) | 36000 | 0 | $3082 | 0 | $3082 |
| Printer Cartridge | 36 | 0 | $863 | 0 | $863 |
| Printer | 2 | 0 | $273 | 0 | $273 |
| Coating Machine | 2 | 0 | $547 | 0 | $547 |
| Tablet | 0 | 50 | 0 | $6849 | -$6849 |
| Tablet Stand | 0 | 50 | 0 | $1113 | -$1113 |
| Server | 0 | 1 | 0 | $342 | -$342 |
| Personnel | 3 | 2 | $56712 | $37808 | $18904 |
| Total | $72043 | $103 | $61649 | $46112 | $15537 |

*Figure 5. Cost-time graphic*

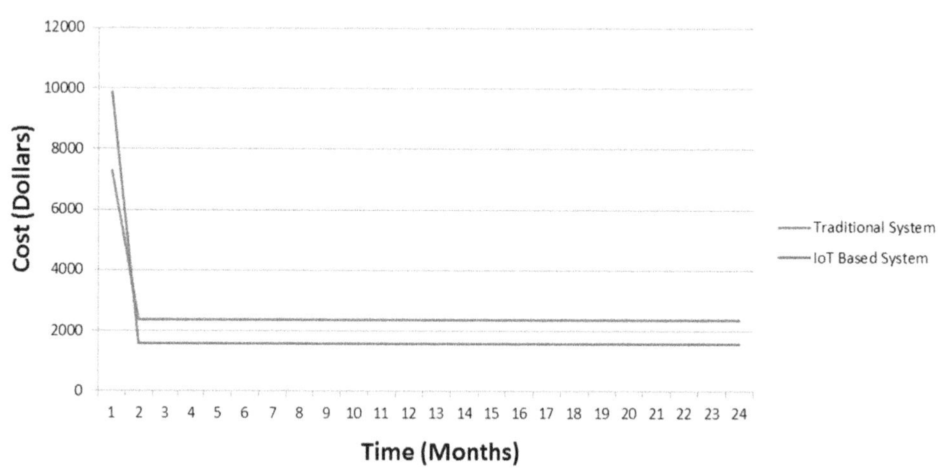

*Figure 6. Cost-meal graphic*

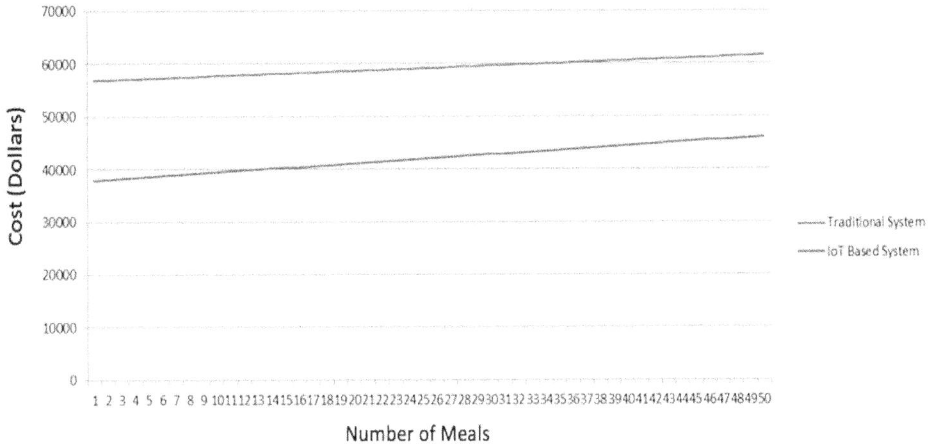


buffets. In traditional buffet management systems, the buffet management process that includes preparing the meal information, printing them on papers, coating them with plastic and instantly translating meals when a meal is added is time consuming. Authors analyzed the time to manage the buffets in the IoT-based system and in the traditional system, and compared with each other.

In the traditional paper based system, a service employee takes the meal list that will be served during the day (breakfast, lunch, dinner) and prints them on papers. Additional plastic coating is applied to protect the paper based meal tags from damage. On the contrary, in IoT based system a service employee only selects the meals from a meal server without needing any information or hardware and sends the meal information to the tablet with just one click of a button. In case there is a need for instant meal updates because of over-consumption, the usual process of managing the meals repeats itself, causes overhead, and increases customer waiting times in the traditional system. On contrary, in the IoT-based system, there is no overhead. Another problem in the traditional system is the inaccurate translation of meals and time to translate them. Translation is done by the same employee who also manages the buffet. However, in the IoT-based system, there is no need for translation task. The meal information is already translated or additional translation can be done remotely by professional translators. Table 3 shows the time (in seconds) savings per meal.

*Table 3. Time comparison of traditional system and IoT based system*

| | Traditional System (Seconds) | IoT Based System (Seconds) | Time Savings (Seconds) |
|---|---|---|---|
| Retrieving Meal Information | 4 | 1 | 3 |
| Entering Meal Information | 20 | 3 | 17 |
| Coating | 60 | 0 | 60 |
| Placing Meal Tags on Buffets | 5 | 0 | 5 |
| Instant Meal Updates | 189 | 4 | 185 |
| Total | 278 | 8 | 270 |

Authors assumed that 50 different meals will be served during the day which means that the buffet will need 50 meal tags. They also created a physical test environment and recorded the time to manage the buffets. In the traditional system, printing the meal information on paper, coating it with plastic and placing it on buffet approximately take 89 seconds. In the IoT-based system, it only took 4 seconds. In case of need for instant update, translation of the meal with a new meal, additional 100 seconds is added. In the IoT-based system, instant update only takes 4 seconds and the other steps are not included that leads to direct time savings. As it is seen from the Table 3, the whole process (for one meal) takes 4.63 minutes in the traditional system while it takes 4 seconds in the IoT-based system. Therefore, approximately 11 hours can be saved in one day for three different meal times by adopting this technology. Figure 7 shows the time analysis that shows the comparison of the traditional system with the digital system by considering the number of meals and the time to manage them.

## Environmental Benefits

In today's world, we have concerns about the environment. Supporting green products and going paperless will save the trees and the environment. Ryan (2008) mentioned that offices consume 350 pounds of paper per employee every year. Shapley (2007) emphasized the 15 facts about the paper industry, global warming and environment. He mentioned that the United States would prevent the emission of 1.6 million tons of greenhouse gases (the equivalent of taking 280,000 cars off the road) by cutting of the office paper by only 10% and paper accounts for 25% of landfill waste (and one third of municipal landfill waste). In addition to these benefits, the hotels will earn the reputation of being green/environmentally-friendly that will lead to customer satisfaction and win new customers who pay attention to green environments.

## Improved Efficiency

In current buffet management systems, the hotels apply the following inefficient steps to manage the buffet:

*Figure 7. Time analysis of paper based system vs. digital system*

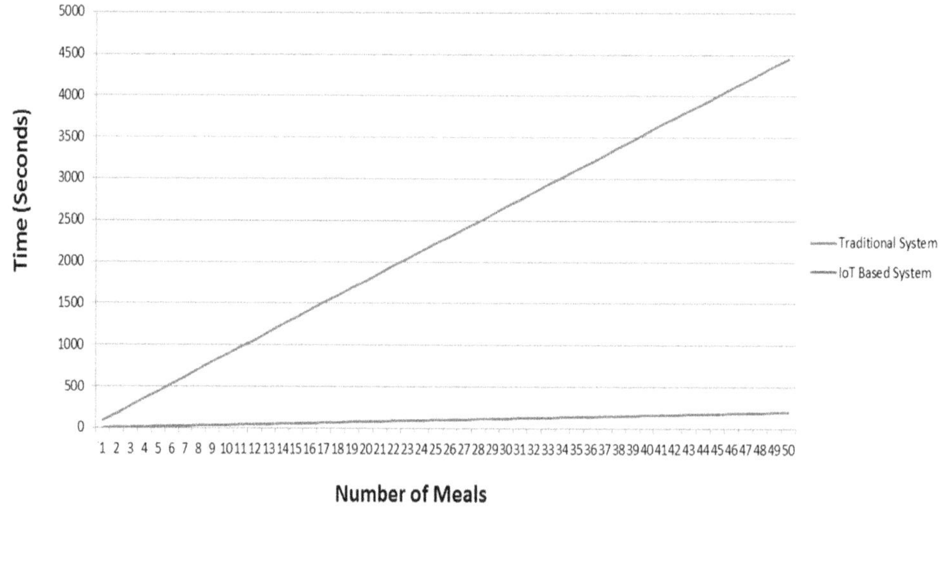

1. One of the service employees either creates the meal tags on computer (meal names and their translation in limited number of languages), prints them, cuts them accordingly or writes the information by hand.
2. Another service employee places the paper based meal tags in front of the meals before the customers arrive.
3. If a meal is consumed and needs to be changed, previous steps are followed. A traffic of replacing and printing the new meals is generated.
4. In the traditional system, meal information is prepared and printed for breakfast, lunch and dinner. Average of 50 paper tags are prepared and printed for each meal time that cause need for additional personnel.
5. A service employee waits near the buffet and explains if a customer needs additional information about the meal.

In this process, employees spent hours chasing and printing paper based meal tags. There are several benefits of the IoT-based system that improves the efficiency of the current buffet management systems. These are improved documentation, remote management (anytime, anywhere), faster access to meals and faster meal updates, professional meal translation, and decreased personnel costs. By using the new IoT based system, the personnel can electronically (wirelessly) send the meal information to the digital meal tags with a single touch of a button that eliminates paper-related costs and saves time. Additionally, the system stores the meal information in a database that provides digital access. This efficiency and time savings affect the customers and staff directly. The customers will not wait longer while deciding which meal to take and the staff will perform their jobs more quickly and effectively than before.

### Customer Benefits

Customers will have instant access to meals and meal updates, and will see their diet or allergen related information when they approach to the buffet. Therefore, they will choose their meals easily without the intervention of the service personnel. This will make the customers feel special and think that the hotel cares about themselves. Becoming green/going paperless will also have a positive impact on customers who care about environment. The idea of going paperless will not only affect cost savings but also hotel customers. Furthermore, when the hotels start reducing their operating costs, they will be able to reduce rates and offer more incentives for the customers. Hotels that are well organized and more efficient will better serve their customers. Consequently, in today's competitive hospitality industry, hotels that better serve their customers will stand and create loyal customers who will give out referrals.

## FUTURE RESEARCH DIRECTIONS

IoT technology is already gaining popularity and being adopted by traditional industries. The hospitality industry is not different. With the decrease in costs related to wireless technologies and the rise of mobile phones, tablets, hotels of tomorrow must embrace the IoT technology to remain competitive. In this chapter, authors developed a system for hospitality industry and it can be integrated to any existing system that requires information to be updated and the context to be changed transiently. Although the proposed system provides an IoT and sensor based solution that is already a emerging trend, there are still numerous future directions to explore. One of these possible future directions is context-aware music streaming in hotel animations. Same concept that is applied for language awareness can also be applied for music choices in animations. By storing and analyzing information related to customers' music preferences during the check-in process and with the help of BLE bracelets, the animation staff can stream music by tracking the customers who are currently attending the animation through bracelets and retreiving their information throught IoT infrastructure. One another possible research oppurtunity is indoor navigation and location identification. Since GPS signals are very weak in indoor places, a smart Bluetooth beacon based indoor location positioning system can be developed to provide the abilitiy to understand when a customer is moving and which direction he is moving. Combining current smartphone sensors like the compass and gyroscope with BLE technology, customers' locations can be determined and the customers can be guided to the places where they want to navigate inside the hotel without using GPS.

## CONCLUSION

The hospitality industry is developing day by day. The number of newly-opened hotels are increasing in parallel to that development. Hotel administrators should follow the right strategies, innovations, and trends that are becoming more prevalent throughout the world. In the hospitality field, digital solutions are already being used to save time and money when it comes to filling rooms, arranging staffing needs, and many other things. Innovation has been an important process in all sectors during recent years. Hotel businesses need to catch up with this movement and implement the innovation practices for products and services. The developed IoT-based system offers innovations and contributes the profit and customer satisfaction by presenting the meals digitally. The system eliminates problems and deficiencies of hotels with a buffet system, provides a unique and innovative solution with its features such as integration of the IoT to the buffet system; manages contexts wirelessly by going paperless, offers context awareness and an interactive experience to the customer with its BLE technology. It decreases the burden of the service staff and saves time for them that leads to decrease the operating costs and increase the customer satisfaction. It can be integrated to any existing system that requires information to be updated and the context to be changed transiently by the staff.

## REFERENCES

Abowd, G. D., Dey, A. K., Brown, P. J., Davies, N., Smith, M., & Steggles, P. (1999). Towards a Better Understanding of Context and Context-Awareness. Handheld and Ubiquitous Computing Lecture Notes in Computer Science, 304-307. doi:10.1007/3-540-48157-5_29

Alliance, A. (2016). *AllJoyn Documentation*. Retrieved June 17, 2016, from https://allseenalliance.org/framework/documentation/learn

Almanza, B. A., Nelson, D., & Chai, S. (1997). Obstacles to Nutrition Labeling in Restaurants. *Journal of the American Dietetic Association*, *97*(2), 157–161. doi:10.1016/S0002-8223(97)00041-2 PMID:9020243

Averill, J. R. (1973). Personal control over aversive stimuli and its relationship to stress. *Psychological Bulletin, 80*(4), 286–303. doi:10.1037/h0034845

Berry, L. L., Seiders, K., & Grewal, D. (2002). Understanding Service Convenience. *Journal of Marketing, 66*(3), 1–17. doi:10.1509/jmkg.66.3.1.18505

Bitner, M. J. (2001). Service and technology: Opportunities and paradoxes. *Managing Service Quality Managing Service Quality: An International Journal, 11*(6), 375–379. doi:10.1108/09604520110410584

Brewer, R., & Druin, A. (2010, May). iMenu: Designing an Interactive Restaurant Menu for Children. *LSAMP Undergraduate Research Symposium.*

Chen, T., Lin, H., & Yen, Y. (2011). Mojo iCuisine: The Design and Implementation of an Interactive Restaurant Tabletop Menu. Human-Computer Interaction. Towards Mobile and Intelligent Interaction Environments Lecture Notes in Computer Science, 185-194. doi:10.1007/978-3-642-21616-9_21

Dixon, M., Kimes, S. E., & Verma, R. (2009). Customer preferences for restaurant technology innovations. *Cornell Hospitality Report., 9*(7), 4–16.

Food and Drug Administration, HHS. (2014). Food labeling; nutrition labeling of standard menu items in restaurants and similar retail food establishments. Final rule. *Federal Register, 79*(230), 71155.

Hanks, R. (2002). Discounting in the hotel industry: A new approach. *The Cornell Hotel and Restaurant Administration Quarterly, 43*(4), 94–103. doi:10.1016/S0010-8804(02)80046-5

Hsu, L., & Wu, P. (2013). Electronic-tablet-based menu in a full service restaurant and customer satisfaction-a structural equation model. *International Journal of Business. Human Technology, 3*(2), 62–71.

Hui, M. K., & Bateson, J. E. (1991). Perceived Control and the Effects of Crowding and Consumer Choice on the Service Experience. *J CONSUM RES Journal of Consumer Research, 18*(2), 174. doi:10.1086/209250

Igelmund, G., Kutscher, M., & Wambach, M. (2011). Development and evaluation of group support systems in non-business environments on tabletop interfaces. *World Usability Conference.*

Kimes, S. E. (2008). The Role of Technology in Restaurant Revenue Management. *Cornell Hospitality Quarterly, 49*(3), 297–309. doi:10.1177/1938965508322768

Kimes, S. E., & Chase, R. B. (1998). The Strategic Levers of Yield Management. *Journal of Service Research, 1*(2), 156–166. doi:10.1177/109467059800100205

Knaus, M. (2015). Persuasive Technologies and Applications in Health and Fitness. *Persuasive Technologies and Applications, 3*(2), 5–11.

Kortuem, G., Kawsar, F., Fitton, D., & Sundramoorthy, V. (2010). Smart objects as building blocks for the Internet of things. *IEEE Internet Computing IEEE Internet Comput., 14*(1), 44–51. doi:10.1109/MIC.2009.143

Krebs, J. M. (2008). Paper, Paper Everywhere? *The ASHA Leader, 13*(12), 20–22. doi:10.1044/leader.FTR3.13122008.20

Mills, J. E., & Thomas, L. (2008). Assessing Customer Expectations of Information Provided On Restaurant Menus: A Confirmatory Factor Analysis Approach. *Journal of Hospitality & Tourism Research (Washington, D.C.)*, *32*(1), 62–88. doi:10.1177/1096348007309569

Networks, R. (2016). *RadBeacon Dot*. Retrieved June 17, 2016, from http://www.radiusnetworks.com/radbeacon/specs/dot/

Ninemeier, J. D., & Kasavana, M. L. (1986). *Planning and control for food and beverage operations*. Educational Institute of the American Hotel & Motel Association.

Nyheim, P. D., McFadden, F. M., & Connolly, D. J. (2005). *Technology strategies for the hospitality industry*. Upper Saddle River, NJ: Prentice Hall.

Oronsky, C. R., & Chathoth, P. K. (2007). An exploratory study examining information technology adoption and implementation in full-service restaurant firms. *International Journal of Hospitality Management*, *26*(4), 941–956. doi:10.1016/j.ijhm.2006.04.001

Paradiso, M. (2010). Google and the Internet: A Mega-Project Nesting Within Another Mega-Project. *Engineering Earth,* 49-65. doi:10.1007/978-90-481-9920-4_4

Reynolds, D., Merritt, E. A., & Pinckney, S. (2005). Understanding Menu Psychology. *International Journal of Hospitality & Tourism Administration*, *6*(1), 1–9. doi:10.1300/J149v06n01_01

Ryan, J. T. (2008). *Document-management systems offer efficiency, save paper*. Central Penn Business Journal.

Ryan, N., Pascoe, J., & Morse, D. (1999). Enhanced reality fieldwork: The context aware archaeological assistant. *Bar International Series*, *750*, 269–274.

Schilit, B., & Theimer, M. (1994). Disseminating active map information to mobile hosts. *IEEE Network*, *8*(5), 22–32. doi:10.1109/65.313011

Shapley, D. (2012). *15 Facts About the Paper Industry, Global Warming and the Environment and What You Can Do About It*. The Daily Green.

Swartz, J. J., Braxton, D., & Viera, A. J. (2011). Calorie menu labeling on quick-service restaurant menus: An updated systematic review of the literature. *Int J Behav Nutr Phys Act International Journal of Behavioral Nutrition and Physical Activity*, *8*(1), 135. doi:10.1186/1479-5868-8-135 PMID:22152038

Tan, Y., Lee, K., Khor, Z., Goh, K., Tan, K., & Lew, B. (2010). Automated Food Ordering System with Interactive User Interface approach. *2010 IEEE Conference on Robotics, Automation and Mechatronics*. doi:10.1109/ramech.2010.5513147

Thompson, T. (2008). Less Paper. *Trumps Paperless. Health Management Technology*, 42–43. PMID:18524167

Wang, Y., & Qualls, W. (2007). Towards a theoretical model of technology adoption in hospitality organizations. *International Journal of Hospitality Management*, *26*(3), 560–573. doi:10.1016/j.ijhm.2006.03.008

Whitmore, A., Agarwal, A., & Xu, L. D. (2014). The Internet of Things-A survey of topics and trends. *Information Systems Frontiers Inf Syst Front*, *17*(2), 261–274. doi:10.1007/s10796-014-9489-2

Yepes, M. F. (2014). Mobile Tablet Menus: Attractiveness and Impact of Nutrition Labeling Formats on Millennials Food Choices. *Cornell Hospitality Quarterly*, *56*(1), 58–67. doi:10.1177/1938965514546371

## ADDITIONAL READING

Adukaite, A., Reimann, A. M., Marchiori, E., & Cantoni, L. (2013). Hotel mobile apps. The case of 4 and 5 star hotels in European German-speaking countries. In Z. Xiang (Ed.), *Information and Communication Technologies in Tourism 2014* (pp. 45–57). Switzerland: Springer International Publishing. doi:10.1007/978-3-319-03973-2_4

Barnaghi, P., Wang, W., Henson, C., & Taylor, K. (2012). Semantics for the Internet of Things: Early progress and back to the future. *International Journal on Semantic Web and Information Systems*, *8*(1), 1–21. doi:10.4018/jswis.2012010101

Chen, K. Y., Hsu, Y. L., & Wu, C. C. (2012). Mobile phone applications as innovative marketing tools for hotels. *International Journal of Organizational Innovation (Online)*, *5*(2), 116.

Chianese, A., & Piccialli, F. (2014). Designing a smart museum: When cultural heritage joins IoT. In *2014 Eighth International Conference on Next Generation Mobile Apps, Services and Technologies* (pp. 300-306). IEEE. doi:10.1109/NGMAST.2014.21

DeMicco, F., Seferis, J., Bao, Y., & Scholz, M. E. (2014). The Eco-Restaurant of the Future: A Case Study. *Journal of Foodservice Business Research*, *17*(4), 363–368. doi:10.1080/15378020.2014.945893

Deugo, D. (2016, January). Using Beacons for Attendance Tracking. In *Proceedings of the International Conference on Frontiers in Education: Computer Science and Computer Engineering (FECS).*

Guo, Y., Liu, H., & Chai, Y. (2014). The embedding convergence of smart cities and tourism internet of things in China: An advance perspective. *Advances in Hospitality and Tourism Research*, *2*(1), 54–69.

Hui, T. L. T., Au, N., & Law, R. (2016). Customer Experiences with Hotel Smartphone: A Case Study of Hong Kong Hotels. In A. Inversini (Ed.), *Information and Communication Technologies in Tourism 2016* (pp. 455–466). Switzerland: Springer International Publishing. doi:10.1007/978-3-319-28231-2_33

Jara, A. J. (2014, October). Wearable Internet: Powering Personal Devices with the Internet of Things Capabilities. In *Identification, Information and Knowledge in the Internet of Things (IIKI), 2014 International Conference on* (pp. 7-7). IEEE.

Lee, H. E., & Choi, H. S. (2016). Improvements of the Korean Tourism Application, Visit Korea, for Foreigners-Based on Beacon Functions. *International Journal of Software Engineering and Its Applications*, *10*(4), 103–116. doi:10.14257/ijseia.2016.10.4.11

Li, S., Da Xu, L., & Zhao, S. (2015). The internet of things: A survey. *Information Systems Frontiers*, *17*(2), 243–259. doi:10.1007/s10796-014-9492-7

Lin, K. P., Lai, C. Y., Chen, P. C., & Hwang, S. Y. (2015, October). Personalized Hotel Recommendation Using Text Mining and Mobile Browsing Tracking. In *Systems, Man, and Cybernetics (SMC), 2015 IEEE International Conference on* (pp. 191-196). IEEE. doi:10.1109/SMC.2015.46

Mbasera, M., Du Plessis, E., Saayman, M., & Kruger, M. (2016). Environmentally-friendly practices in hotels. [-pages.]. *Acta Commercii*, *16*(1), 8. doi:10.4102/ac.v16i1.362

Mo Kwon, J., Bae, J. I., & Blum, S. C. (2013). Mobile applications in the hospitality industry. *Journal of Hospitality and Tourism Technology*, *4*(1), 81–92. doi:10.1108/17579881311302365

Navarro, D. A., Boaz, M., Krause, I., Elis, A., Chernov, K., Giabra, M., & Singer, P. (2015). Improved meal presentation increases food intake and decreases readmission rate in hospitalized patients. *Clinical Nutrition*. Lai, I. K. (2013). Traveler acceptance of an app-based mobile tour guide. *Journal of Hospitality & Tourism Research (Washington, D.C.)*.

Pan, B., & Yang, Y. (2015). *Book Chapter for: Management Science in Hospitality and Tourism: Theory*. Practice and Applications.

Posdorfer, W., & Maalej, W. (2016). Towards Context-aware Surveys Using Bluetooth Beacons. *Procedia Computer Science*, *83*, 42–49. doi:10.1016/j.procs.2016.04.097

Prasad, K., Wirtz, P. W., & Yu, L. (2014). Measuring hotel guest satisfaction by using an online quality management system. *Journal of Hospitality Marketing & Management*, *23*(4), 445–463. doi:10.1080/19368623.2013.805313

Sen, K., & Kaushik, T. (2016). Recent innovative measures across different functions in the Indian hospitality industry–a case study from Accor Hotels. *Worldwide Hospitality and Tourism Themes, 8*(4).

Yan, M., & Shi, H. (2013). Smart Living Using Bluetooth-Based Android Smartphone. *International Journal of Wireless & Mobile Networks*, *5*(1), 65–72. doi:10.5121/ijwmn.2013.5105

## KEY TERMS AND DEFINITIONS

**All-You-Can-Eat Buffet:** A system of serving meals by placing them separately on tables at restaurants and cafés.

**Beacon:** Devices that broadcast their identifier to nearby devices. An action is performed when devices are in close proximity to a beacon.

**Bluetooth Low Energy:** Power friendly version of Bluetooth technology that was built for Internet of Thing.

**Context Awareness:** Providing relevant information and/or services to the user depending on a user's task.

**Internet of Things:** A network of objects, devices, buildings, embedded devices that enables these objects to communicate, interact with each other and exchange data.

**Tablet:** A mobile computer that has touch screen display, circuitry, battery, sensors and a mobile operating system in a single device.

**Wi-Fi:** Wireless networking technology that allows devices to connect to the network over a wireless signal.

# Compilation of References


Abdullah, L., & Najib, L. (2014). A new type-2 fuzzy set of linguistic variables for the fuzzy analytic hierarchy process. *Expert Systems with Applications*, *41*(7), 3297–3305. doi:10.1016/j.eswa.2013.11.028

Aboelmaged, M., & Gebba, T. R. (2013). Mobile banking adoption: An examination of Technology Acceptance Model and Theory of Planned Behavior. *International Journal of Business Research and Development*, *2*(1), 35–50. doi:10.24102/ijbrd.v2i1.263

Abowd, G. D., Dey, A. K., Brown, P. J., Davies, N., Smith, M., & Steggles, P. (1999). Towards a Better Understanding of Context and Context-Awareness. Handheld and Ubiquitous Computing Lecture Notes in Computer Science, 304-307. doi:10.1007/3-540-48157-5_29

Abraham, J., & Pane, M. M. (2014). The mediating role of social competition identity management strategy in the predictive relationship between susceptibility to social influence, Internet privacy concern, and online political efficacy. In Lecture notes in computer science: Vol. 8407. Information and communication technology (pp. 492-499). Berlin: Springer. doi:10.1007/978-3-642-55032-4_50

Abraham, J., & Sharron. (2015). Perceived risk of anti-corruption e-learning, email phishing literacy, and anomia. In J. J. J. H. Park, Y. Pan, H.-C. Chao, & G. Yi (Eds.), *Lecture notes in electrical engineering: Vol. 331. Ubiquitous computing application and wireless sensor* (pp. 577-584). Springer. 10.1007/978-94-017-9618-7_59

Abraham, J., & Falah, A. (2016). Is virtual marriage acceptable? A psychological study investigating the role of ambiguity tolerance and intimacy illusion in online dating among adolescents and early adults. *Journal of Psychological and Educational Research*, *24*(2), 117–143.

Aggarwal, C. C., Ashish, N., & Sheth, A. (2013). The internet of things: A survey from the data-centric perspective. In Managing and mining sensor data (pp. 383-428). Springer US. doi:10.1007/978-1-4614-6309-2_12

Ahmed, E., Yaqoob, I., Gani, A., Imran, M., & Guizani, M. (2016). Internet-of-things-based smart environments: State of the art, taxonomy, and open research challenges. *IEEE Wireless Communications*, *23*(5), 10–16. doi:10.1109/MWC.2016.7721736

Ajzen, I. (1985). From intention to actions: a theory of planned behavior. In J. Kuhl & J. Beckmann (Eds.), *Action-control: From cognition to behavior*. Heidelberg, Germany: Springer. doi:10.1007/978-3-642-69746-3_2

Ajzen, I. (1991). The Theory of Planned Behavior. *Organizational Behavior and Human Decision Processes*, *50*(2), 179–211. doi:10.1016/0749-5978(91)90020-T

Ajzen, I., & Fishbein, M. (1980). *Understanding and predicting social behavior*. Englewood Cliffs, NJ: Prentice Hall.

Akçayır, M., Akçayır, G., Pektaş, H. M., & Ocak, M. A. (2016). Augmented reality in science laboratories: The effects of augmented reality on university students laboratory skills and attitudes toward science laboratories. *Computers in Human Behavior*, *57*, 334–342. doi:10.1016/j.chb.2015.12.054

Akhbar, F., Chang, V., Yao, Y., & Muñoz, V. M. (2016). Outlook on moving of computing services towards the data sources. *International Journal of Information Management*, *36*(4), 645–652. doi:10.1016/j.ijinfomgt.2016.03.014

Akyildiz, I. F., Su, W., Sankarasubramaniam, Y., & Cayirci, E. (2002). A survey on sensor networks. *IEEE Communications Magazine*, *40*(8), 102–114. doi:10.1109/MCOM.2002.1024422

Al-Azawei, A., Parslow, P., & Lundqvist, K. (2016). Investigating the effect of learning styles in a blended e-learning system: An extension of the Technology Acceptance Model (TAM). *Australasian Journal of Educational Technology*, *33*(2), 1–23. doi:10.14742/ajet.2741

Albrecht, K., & Michael, K. (2013). Connected: To everyone and everything [Guest Editorial: Special Section on Sensors]. *IEEE Technology and Society Magazine*, *32*(4), 31–34. doi:10.1109/MTS.2013.2291170

Alcaide, A., Palomar, E., Montero-Castillo, J., & Ribagorda, A. (2013). Anonymous authentication for privacy-preserving IoT target driven applications. *Computers & Security*, *37*, 111–123. doi:10.1016/j.cose.2013.05.007

Alliance, A. (2016). *AllJoyn Documentation*. Retrieved June 17, 2016, from https://allseenalliance.org/framework/documentation/learn

Allied Market Research. (2015). *3D Printing Market by Technology and Material-Global Opportunity Analysis and Industry Forecast 2014-2020*. Electronic Systems and Devices.

Almanza, B. A., Nelson, D., & Chai, S. (1997). Obstacles to Nutrition Labeling in Restaurants. *Journal of the American Dietetic Association*, *97*(2), 157–161. doi:10.1016/S0002-8223(97)00041-2 PMID:9020243

Al-Mawee, W. (2012). *Privacy and Security Issues in IoT Healthcare Applications for the Disabled Users* (Master Thesis). Computer Science., Western Michigan University.

Al-Turjman, F. M., Al-Fagih, A. E., Alsalih, W. M., & Hassanein, H. S. (2013). A delay-tolerant framework for integrated RSNs in IoT. *Computer Communications*, *36*(9), 998–1010. doi:10.1016/j.comcom.2012.07.001

Ambasna-Jones, M. (2015). *Will automation and the internet of things lead to mass unemployment?* Retrieved March 5, 2016 from https://www.theguardian.com/media-network/2015/may/27/internet-of-things-automation-unemployment

Amendola, S., Lodato, R., Manzari, S., Occhiuzzi, C., & Marrocco, G. (2014). RFID technology for IoT-based personal healthcare in smart spaces. *IEEE Internet of Things Journal, 1*(2), 144-152.

Andrews, C., El-Attrash, F., Jarvis, E., Johnson, N., & Moss, H. (n.d.). *The Internet of Things: What IoT means for the public sector*. Retrieved from GovLoop: http://www.isaca.org/Groups/Professional-English/cybersecurity/GroupDocuments/IoT%20in%20the%20Public%20Sector.pdf

Antoncic, B., & Hisrich, R. D. (2004). Corporate entrepreneurship contingencies and organizational wealth creation. *Journal of Management Development*, *23*(6), 518–550. doi:10.1108/02621710410541114

APICS. (2016). *SCOR*. Retrieved August 26, 2015, from http://www.apics.org/sites/apics-supply-chain-council/frameworks/scor

Arlbjørn, J. S., de Haas, H., & Munksgaard, K. B. (2011). Exploring supply chain innovation. *Logistics Research*, *3*(1), 3–18. doi:10.1007/s12159-010-0044-3

Armenteros, M., Liaw, S.-S., Fernández, M., Díaz, R. F., & Sánchez, R. A. (2013). Surveying FIFA instructors behavioral intention toward the multimedia teaching materials. *Computers & Education*, *61*, 91–104. doi:10.1016/j.compedu.2012.09.010

Arora, V., & Ravi, V. (2013). Data mining using advanced ant colony optimization algorithm and application to bankruptcy prediction. *International Journal of Information Systems and Social Change*, *4*(3), 33–56. doi:10.4018/jissc.2013070103

Ashton, K. (2009). That 'internet of things' thing. *RFiD Journal*, *22*(7), 97–114.

Ashton, K. (2009). That internet of things' thing. *RFID Journal*, *22*(7), 97–114.

ASTM International. (2015). *Standard Terminology for Additive Manufacturing*. Retrieved Sep 09.2013 from http://web.mit.edu/2.810/www/files/readings/AdditiveManufacturingTerminology.pdf

Atzori, L., Iera, A., & Morabito, G. (2010). The Internet of Things : A survey. *Computer Networks*, *54*(15), 2787–2805. doi:10.1016/j.comnet.2010.05.010

Atzori, L., Iera, A., & Morabito, G. (2014). From" smart objects" to" social objects": The next evolutionary step of the internet of things. *IEEE Communications Magazine*, *52*(1), 97–105. doi:10.1109/MCOM.2014.6710070

Atzori, L., Iera, A., Morabito, G., & Nitti, M. (2012). The social Internet of Things (SIoT) - when social networks meet the Internet of Things: Concept, architecture and network characterization. *Computer Networks*, *56*(16), 3594–3608. doi:10.1016/j.comnet.2012.07.010

Au, A. U., Huynh, W., Horowitz, L. F., Folch, A., & Angew. (2016). 3D-Printed Microfluidics. Angewandte Chemie International Edition, 55(12), 3862-3881. doi:10.1016/j.wneu.2013.07.009

Austin, J., Stevenson, H., & Wei-Skillern, J. (2006). Social and commercial entrepreneurship: same, different, or both?. *Entrepreneurship Theory and Practice, 30*(1), 1-22.

Averill, J. R. (1973). Personal control over aversive stimuli and its relationship to stress. *Psychological Bulletin*, *80*(4), 286–303. doi:10.1037/h0034845

Badkas, C.K., Shahade, M.R., & Ramteke, U.S. (2015). Review of Internet of Things (IoT): A vision and future directions. *International Journal of Research in Science & Engineering, 1*(1), 129-134.

Bailey, C. (2012). Design, simulation and modelling for nanopackaging applications: current capabilities and future requirements. *12th IEEE Conference on Nanotechnology*. doi:10.1109/NANO.2012.6322238

Balakrishnan, A. (2016, December 5). *There's no need to check out at the Amazon Go store*. Retrieved January 4, 2017, from NBC News: http://www.nbcnews.com/tech/tech-news/there-s-no-need-check-out-amazon-go-store-n692201

Banderker, N., & Van Belle, J.-P. (2009). Adoption of mobile technology by public healthcare doctors. *International Journal of Healthcare Delivery Reform Initiatives*, *1*(3), 38–54. doi:10.4018/jhdri.2009070103

Bandyopadhyay, D., & Sen, J. (2011). Internet of Things: Applications and challenges in technology and standardization. *Wireless Personal Communications*, *58*(1), 49–69. doi:10.1007/s11277-011-0288-5

Banks, J. (2008). *Understanding RFID Part 9: RFID Privacy and Security*. Retrieved May 5, 2016 from http://www.secureidnews.com/news-item/understanding-rfid-part-9-rfid-privacy-and-security

Bao, Y., Bao, Y., & Sheng, S. (2011). Motivating purchase of private brands: Effects of store image, product signatureness, and quality variation. *Journal of Business Research*, *64*(2), 220–226. doi:10.1016/j.jbusres.2010.02.007

Baptista, G., & Oliveira, T. (2015). Understanding mobile banking: The unified theory of acceptance and use of technology combined with cultural moderators. *Computers in Human Behavior*, *50*, 418–430. doi:10.1016/j.chb.2015.04.024

Bardaki, C., Kourouthanassis, P., & Pramatari, K. (2012). Deploying RFID-enabled services in the retail supply chain: Lessons learned toward the internet of things. *Information Systems Management*, *29*(3), 233–245. doi:10.1080/10580530.2012.687317

Barker, K. J., DAmato, J., & Sheridon, P. (2008). Credit card fraud: Awareness and prevention. *Journal of Financial Crime*, *15*(4), 398–410. doi:10.1108/13590790810907236

Barnaghi, P., Wang, W., Henson, C., & Taylor, K. (2012). Semantics for the Internet of Things: Early Progress and Back to the Future. *International Journal on Semantic Web and Information Systems*, *8*(1), 1–21. doi:10.4018/jswis.2012010101

Barney, J. (1991). Firm resources and sustained competitive advantage. *Journal of Management*, *17*(1), 99–120. doi:10.1177/014920639101700108

Barricelli, B. R., Fischer, G., Mørch, A., Piccinno, A., & Valtolina, S. (2015). Cultures of participation in the digital age: Coping with information, participation, and collaboration overload. In P. Díaz, V. Pipek, C. Ardito, C. Jensen, I. Aedo, & A. Boden (Eds.), Lecture notes in computer science: Vol. 9083. *End-user development* (pp. 271–275). Springer International Publishing. doi:10.1007/978-3-319-18425-8_28

Barwise, J., & Perry, J. (1980). The Situation Underground. In J. Barwise & I. Sag (Eds.), Stanford working papers in semantics (Vol. 1, pp. 1-55). Stanford Cognitive Science Group.

Battisti, G., Canepa, A., & Stoneman, P. (2009). E-Business usage across and within firms the UK: Profitability, externalities and policy. *Research Policy*, *38*(1), 133–143. doi:10.1016/j.respol.2008.10.021

Bechtel, C., & Jayaram, J. (1997). Supply chain management: a strategic perspective. *The International Journal of Logistics Management, 8*(1), 15-34.

Becker, C., Gonzalez-Ba, H. H., Latombe, J. C., & Tomasi, C. (1995). An Intelligent Observer. *Fourth International Symposium on Experimental Robotics, ISER'95.*

Beck, S., & Kenning, P. (2015). The influence of retailers family firm image on new product acceptance: An empirical investigation in the German FMCG market. *International Journal of Retail & Distribution Management*, *43*(12), 1126–1143. doi:10.1108/IJRDM-06-2014-0079

Béguin, P. (2007). In search of a unit of analysis for designing instruments. *Artifact*, *1*(1), 12–16. doi:10.1080/17493460600610830

Beldad, A., van der Geest, T., de Jong, M., & Steehouder, M. (2012). A cue or two and Ill trust you: Determinants of trust in government organizations in terms of their processing and usage of citizens personal information disclosed online. *Government Information Quarterly*, *29*(1), 41–49. doi:10.1016/j.giq.2011.05.003

Beldona, S., Morrison, A. M., & OLeary, J. (2005). Online shopping motivations and pleasure travel products: A correspondence analysis. *Tourism Management*, *26*(4), 561–570. doi:10.1016/j.tourman.2004.03.008

Bélissent, J. (2010). *Getting clever about smart cities: new opportunities require new business models*. Academic Press.

Bensaou, M. (1997). Interorganizational cooperation and the use IT: An empirical comparison of U.S. and Japanese supplier relations. *Information Systems Research*, *8*(2), 107–124. doi:10.1287/isre.8.2.107

Berry, L. L., Seiders, K., & Grewal, D. (2002). Understanding Service Convenience. *Journal of Marketing*, *66*(3), 1–17. doi:10.1509/jmkg.66.3.1.18505

Bertino, E. (2016). Data Security and Privacy in the IoT Paper. *9th International Conference on Extending Database Technology (EDBT)*, 1-3.

Bhasin, H. (2016). *New Product Development*. Retrieved July 3, 2016 from http://www.marketing91.com/new-product-development/

Bhattacharya, M. (2015). A conceptual framework of RFID adoption in retail using Rogers stage model. *Business Process Management Journal*, *21*(3), 517–540. doi:10.1108/BPMJ-06-2014-0047

Bhide, V. (2014). A Survey on the Smart Homes using Internet of Things (IoT). *International Journal of Advance Research in Computer Science and Management Studies*, *2*(12), 243–246.

Bhuiyan, N. (2011). A framework for successful new product development. *Journal of Industrial Engineering and Management*, *4*(4), 746–770. doi:10.3926/jiem.334

Biniari, M. G. (2012). The emotional embeddedness of corporate entrepreneurship: The case of envy. *Entrepreneurship Theory and Practice*, *36*(1), 141–170. doi:10.1111/j.1540-6520.2010.00437.x

Bin, S., Yuan, L., & Xiaoyi, W. (2010). Research on data mining models for the internet of things. *Proc. International Conference on Image Analysis and Signal Processing*, 127-132.

Bitner, M. J. (2001). Service and technology: Opportunities and paradoxes. *Managing Service Quality Managing Service Quality: An International Journal*, *11*(6), 375–379. doi:10.1108/09604520110410584

Bi, Z., Xu, L. D., & Wang, C. (2014). Internet of things for enterprise systems of modern manufacturing. *IEEE Transactions on Industrial Informatics*, *10*(2), 1537–1546. doi:10.1109/TII.2014.2300338

Björck, F., Henkel, M., Stirna, J., & Zdravkovic, J. (2015). Cyber resilience – fundamentals for a definition. In A. Rocha, A. M. Correia, S. Costanzo, & L. P. Reis (Eds.), *Advances in intelligent systems and computing: New contributions in information systems and technologies* (Vol. 353, pp. 311–316). doi:10.1007/978-3-319-16486-1_31

Blanter, A., & Holman, M. (2014). *Internet of Things 2020: A Glimpse into the Future*. Last Access at https://www.atkearney.com/documents/4634214/6398631/A.T.+Kearney_Internet+of+Things+2020+Presentation_Online.pdf/af7e6a55-cde2-4490-8066-a95664efd35a

Bleecker, J. (2006). A Manifesto for Networked Objects - Cohabiting with Pigeons, Arphids and Aibos in the Internet of Things - Why Things Matter What' s a Blogject? What about Spimes? *Proc. of the 13th International Conference on Human-Computer Interaction with Mobile Devices and Services, MobileHCI*.

Bodker, S., & Klokmose, C. N. (2011). The human–artifact model: An activity theoretical approach to artifact ecologies. *Human–Computer Interaction, 26*(4), 315-371.

Bonsor, K., & Keener, C. (2010). *How Stuff Works "How RFID Works"*. Retrieved from http://electronics.howstuffworks.com/gadgets/high-tech-gadgets/rfid.htm

Boos, D., Guenter, H., Grote, G., & Kinder, K. (2013). Controllable accountabilities: The Internet of Things and its challenges for organisations. *Behaviour & Information Technology*, *32*(5), 449–467. doi:10.1080/0144929X.2012.674157

Borgia, E. (2014). The internet of things vision: Key features, applications and open issues. *Computer Communications*, *54*, 1–31. doi:10.1016/j.comcom.2014.09.008

Borgohain, T., Kumar, U., & Sanyal, S. (2015). Survey of Security and Privacy Issues of Internet of Things. *Int. J. Advanced Networking and Applications*, *6*(4), 2372–2378.

Böse, F., & Windt, K. (2007). Catalogue of Criteria for Autonomous Control in Logistics. In M. Hülsmann & K. Windt (Eds.), *Understanding Autonomous Cooperation and Control in Logistics - The Impact on Management, Information and Communication and Material Flow*. Berlin: Springer. doi:10.1007/978-3-540-47450-0_5

Bose, R. (2008). Competitive intelligence process and tools for intelligence analysis. *Industrial Management & Data Systems*, *108*(4), 510–528. doi:10.1108/02635570810868362

Bottani, E., & Rizzi, A. (2008). Economical assessment of the impact of RFID technology and EPC system on the fast-moving consumer goods supply chain. *International Journal of Production Economics*, *112*(2), 548–569. doi:10.1016/j.ijpe.2007.05.007

Bottazzi, E., & Ferrario, R. (2009). Preliminaries to a DOLCE ontology of organisations. *International Journal of Business Process Integration and Management*, *4*(4), 225–238. doi:10.1504/IJBPIM.2009.032280

Brandpipe. (2015). *How augmented reality is shaping the retail industry*. Retrieved from http://www.brandpipe.co.uk/how-augmented-reality-is-shaping-the-retail-industry/

Brewer, R., & Druin, A. (2010, May). iMenu: Designing an Interactive Restaurant Menu for Children. *LSAMP Undergraduate Research Symposium.*

Brock, D. L. (2001). *The Electronic Product Code (EPC) A Naming Scheme for Physical Objects*. Retrieved from http://cocoa.ethz.ch/downloads/2014/06/None_MIT-AUTOID-WH-002.pdf

Brody, P., & Pureswaran, V. (2015). The next digital gold rush: How the internet of things will create liquid, transparent markets. *Strategy and Leadership*, *43*(1), 41–36. doi:10.1108/SL-11-2014-0094

Broman Toft, M., Schuitema, G., & Thøgersen, J. (2014). Responsible technology acceptance: Model development and application to consumer acceptance of smart grid technology. *Applied Energy*, *134*, 392–400. doi:10.1016/j.apenergy.2014.08.048

Brown, I. (2015). *Regulation and the Internet of Things. GSR discussion paper*. ITU.

Brown, M., Coughlan, T., Lawson, G., Goulden, M., Houghton, R. J., & Mortier, R. (2013). Exploring interpretations of data from the Internet of Things in the home. *Interacting with Computers*, *25*(3), 204–217. doi:10.1093/iwc/iws024

Brun, E. & Steinar, A. (2009), Managing ambiguity in New Product Developments. *Creativity and Innovation Management, 18*(1), 24-34. 10.1111/j.1467-8691.2009.00509.x

Brusey, J., Floerkemeier, C., Harrison, M., & Fletcher, M. (2003). Reasoning about Uncertainty in Location Identification with RFID. *Workshop on Reasoning with Uncertainty in Robotics at IJCAI-2003*, Acapulco Mexico.

Brynjolfsson, E., Hitt, L. M., & Kim, H. H. (2011). *Strength in numbers: How does data-driven decisionmaking affect firm performance?* Available at SSRN 1819486

Bucherer, E., & Uckelmann, D. (2011). Business models for the internet of things. In *Architecting the internet of things* (pp. 253–277). Springer Berlin Heidelberg. doi:10.1007/978-3-642-19157-2_10

Bughin, J. (2010). The power laws of enterprise 2.0. In Encyclopedia of e-business development and management in the global economy. IGI Global. doi:10.4018/978-1-61520-611-7.ch003

Bughin, J. (2016). Reaping the benefits of big data in telecom. *Journal of Big Data*, *3*(2), 3–14.

Bughin, J., Chui, M., & Manyika, J. (2013). Ten IT-enabled business trends for the decade ahead. *The McKinsey Quarterly*, *13*(May).

Bughin, J., Chui, M., & Manyika, J. (2015). An executive guide to the Internet of Things. *The McKinsey Quarterly*, *3*.

Butler, B. S., Bateman, P. J., Gray, P. H., & Diamant, E. I. (2014). An attraction-selection-attrition theory of online community size and resilience. *Management Information Systems Quarterly*, *38*(3), 699–728.

Butner, K. (2010). The smarter supply chain of the future. *Strategy and Leadership*, *38*(1), 22–31. doi:10.1108/10878571011009859

Buyya, R., Yeo, C. S., Venugopal, S., Broberg, J., & Brandic, I. (2009). Cloud computing and emerging IT platforms: Vision, hype, and reality for delivering computing as the 5th utility. *Future Generation Computer Systems*, *25*(6), 599–616. doi:10.1016/j.future.2008.12.001

Capon, N., John, U. F., & Scott, H. (1990). Determinants of Financial Performance: A Meta-Analysis. *Management Science*, *36*(10), 1143–1159. doi:10.1287/mnsc.36.10.1143

Cardon, P., & Marshall, B. A. (2008). National culture and technology acceptance: The impact of uncertainty avoidance. *Issues in Information Systems*, *9*(2), 103–110.

Carmichael, A. (2013). *How to power the internet of things*. Professional Engineer.

Carson, B. (2016, September 24). *REVEALED: Secret video shows Snapchat's new glasses*. Retrieved January 4, 2017, from Business Insider: http://www.businessinsider.com/snapchat-glasses-2016-9

Carter, L., & Weerakkody, V. (2008). E-government adoption: A cultural comparison. *Information Systems Frontiers*, *10*(4), 473–482. doi:10.1007/s10796-008-9103-6

Castells, M. (2002). *The Internet galaxy: Reflections on the Internet, business, and society*. Oxford University Press.

Castrogiovanni, G. J., Urbano, D., & Loras, J. (2011). Linking corporate entrepreneurship and human resource management in SMEs. *International Journal of Manpower*, *32*(1), 34–47. doi:10.1108/01437721111121215

Cavallo, A. (2012). Online and official price indexes: Measuring Argentinas inflation. *Journal of Monetary Economics*, *60*(2), 152–165. doi:10.1016/j.jmoneco.2012.10.002

Cay, T., & Uyan, M. (2013). Evaluation of reallocation criteria in land consolidation studies using the Analytic Hierarchy Process (AHP). *Land Use Policy*, *30*(1), 541–548. doi:10.1016/j.landusepol.2012.04.023

CBR. (2016). *Re-inventing retail with Internet of Things: Engaging with connected consumers to earn their loyalty*. Retrieved from http://www.cbronline.com/blogs/cbr-rolling-blog/re--inventing-retail-with-internet-of-things-engaging-with-connected-consumers-to-earn-their-loyalty

CENELEC. Smart Grids. (n.d.). Online at http://www.cenelec.eu/aboutcenelec/whatwedo/technologysectors/smartgrids.html

Cha, I., Shah, Y., Schmidt, A. U., Leicher, A., & Meyerstein, M. V. (2009). Trust in M2M communication. *IEEE Vehicular Technology Magazine*, *4*(3), 69–75. doi:10.1109/MVT.2009.933478

Chang, H. H. (2010). Task-technology fit and user acceptance of online auction. *International Journal of Human-Computer Studies*, *68*(1), 69–89. doi:10.1016/j.ijhcs.2009.09.010

Chang, H. H., Tsai, Y. C., Wong, K. H., Wang, J. W., & Cho, F. J. (2015). The effects of response strategies and severity of failure on consumer attribution with regard to negative word-of-mouth. *Decision Support Systems*, *71*, 48–61. doi:10.1016/j.dss.2015.01.007

Chan, S. L., & Ip, W. H. (2011). A dynamic decision support system to predict the value of customer for new product development. *Elsevier Science Direct*, *52*(1), 178–188.

Chapman, S., & Carter, P. (1990). Supplier/customer inventory relationships under just-in-time. *Decision Sciences*, *21*(1), 35–51. doi:10.1111/j.1540-5915.1990.tb00315.x

Chaudhuri, A. (2015). *Address Security and Privacy Concerns to Fully Tap into IoT's Potential*. White paper. Retrieved May 5, 2016 from http://www.tcs.com/resources/white_papers/Pages/Security-Privacy-IoT-Potential.aspx

Chen, T., Lin, H., & Yen, Y. (2011). Mojo iCuisine: The Design and Implementation of an Interactive Restaurant Table-top Menu. Human-Computer Interaction. Towards Mobile and Intelligent Interaction Environments Lecture Notes in Computer Science, 185-194. doi:10.1007/978-3-642-21616-9_21

Chen, H., Chiang, R. H., & Storey, V. C. (2012). Business intelligence and analytics: From big data to big impact. *Management Information Systems Quarterly*, *36*(4), 1165–1188.

Chen, J. C., Cheng, C. H., Huang, P. B., Wang, K. J., Huang, C. J., & Ting, T. C. (2013). Warehouse management with lean and RFID application: A case study. *International Journal of Advanced Manufacturing Technology*, *69*(1–4), 531–542. doi:10.1007/s00170-013-5016-8

Chen, M., Mao, S., & Liu, Y. (2014). Big data: A survey. *Mobile Networks and Applications*, *19*(2), 171–209. doi:10.1007/s11036-013-0489-0

Chen, Y. H., & Barnes, S. (2007). Initial trust and online buyer behaviour. *Industrial Management & Data Systems*, *107*(1), 21–36. doi:10.1108/02635570710719034

Chen, Y. K. (2012, January). Challenges and opportunities of internet of things. In *17th Asia and South Pacific Design Automation Conference* (pp. 383-388). IEEE. doi:10.1109/ASPDAC.2012.6164978

Chen, Y. S., & Huang, S. Y. (2016). The effect of task-technology fit on purchase intention: The moderating role of perceived risks. *Journal of Risk Research*, 1–21. doi:10.1080/13669877.2016.1165281

Chen, Y., Guo, J., & Hu, X. (2010). The research of Internet of things' supporting technologies which face the logistics industry. *International Conference on Computational Intelligence and Security (CIS)*, 59-63.

Chesbrough, H., & Crowther, A. K. (2006). Beyond high tech: Early adopters of open innovation in other industries. *R & D Management*, *36*(3), 229–236. doi:10.1111/j.1467-9310.2006.00428.x

Cheung, R., & Vogel, D. (2013). Predicting user acceptance of collaborative technologies: An extension of the Technology Acceptance Model for e-learning. *Computers & Education*, *63*, 160–175. doi:10.1016/j.compedu.2012.12.003

Choi, H., & Varian, H. (2012). Predicting the present with Google Trends. *Economic Inquiry*, *88*(1), 2–9.

Choi, S. H., Yang, Y. X., Yang, B., & Cheung, H. H. (2015). Item-level RFID for enhancement of customer shopping experience in apparel retail. *Computers in Industry*, *71*, 10–23. doi:10.1016/j.compind.2015.03.003

Chong, A. Y.-L., Ooi, K. B., Lin, B., & Tan, B. I. (2010). Online banking adoption: An empirical analysis. *International Journal of Bank Marketing*, *28*(4), 267–287. doi:10.1108/02652321011054963

Chui, M., Löffler, M., & Roberts, R. (2010). The internet of things. *The McKinsey Quarterly*, *2*, 1–9.

Chuu, S. J. (2014). An investment evaluation of supply chain RFID technologies: A group decision-making model with multiple information sources. *Knowledge-Based Systems*, *66*, 210–220. doi:10.1016/j.knosys.2014.05.012

Ciriani, V., Vimercati, C.D., Foresti, S., & Samarati, P. (2007). k-Anonymity. In *Secure Data Management in Decentralized Systems* (pp. 323-353). Springer US.

Cisco. (2012). *The Internet of Everything How More Relevant and Valuable Connections Will Change the World.* Retrieved February 1, 2016 from http://www.cisco.com/c/dam/en_us/about/ac79/docs/innov/IoE.pdf

Clark, S. (2008). *Casagras takes a step towards defining the 'Internet of Things'.* Retrieved from http://www.nfcworld.com/2008/12/12/3387/casagras-takes-a-step-towards-defining-the-internet-of-things/

CMI. (2015, January). Things on the Internet to 'The Internet of Things - Market Overview. *Competitive Market Intelligence.*

Codegate, L. (2001). *Unauthorised Access Alert System.* Retrieved 27 February 2017 from http://www.codegate.co.uk/Unauthorised-Access-Alert-System

Coetzee, L., & Eksteen, J. (2011, May). The Internet of Things-promise for the future? An introduction. In *IST-Africa Conference Proceedings, 2011* (pp. 1-9). IEEE.

Colmenar, E., Al-Turjman, F., & Biglarbegian, M. (2014). Data delivery and gathering in IoT applications: An overview. *Local Computer Networks Workshops (LCN Workshops), IEEE 39th Conference*, 790-795.

Compton, M., Neuhaus, H., Taylor, K., & Tran, K. N. (2009, October). Reasoning about sensors and compositions. In *Proceedings of the 2nd International Conference on Semantic Sensor Networks-Volume 522* (pp. 33-48). CEUR-WS.org.

Cosseboom, L. (2014, September 26). *This startup is building smartphone-powered "fishtech" for Indonesia's commercial aqualife.* Retrieved January 4, 2017, from *Tech in Asia*, https://www.techinasia.com/this-startup-is-building-smartphone-powered-fishtech-for-indonesias-commercial-aqualife

Craig, B., González-Baños, H., Latombe, J. C., & Tomasi, C. (2005). An Intelligent Observer Human Augmentation. *Lecture Notes in Control and Information Sciences*, *223*(4), 151–160.

Criel, J., Vanderhulst, G., Kawsar, F., & Trappeniers, L. (2011). *A co-creation platform for creative engagement of end-users in a connected object space. In Proceedings of the 2011 International Workshop on Networking and Object Memories for the Internet of Things - NoME-IoT'11* (pp. 9–14). New York, NY: Association for Computing Machinery. doi:10.1145/2029932.2029936

Crilly, N. (2010). The roles that artefacts play: Technical, social and aesthetic functions. *Design Studies*, *31*(4), 311–344. doi:10.1016/j.destud.2010.04.002

CSCMP. (2016). *Supply chain management.* Retrieved August 26, 2016, from https://cscmp.org/supply-chain-management-definitions

Cuervo-Cazurra, A., & Ramos, M. (2005). Explaining the process of internationalization by building bridges among existing models. In S. W. Floyd, J. Roos, C. D. Jacobs, & F. W. Kellermanns (Eds.), *Innovating strategy processes.* Wiley & Sons.

da Silva Junior, D. P., de Souza, P. C., & Maciel, C. (2016). Establishing guidelines for user quality of experience in ubiquitous systems. In N. Streitz & P. Markopoulos (Eds.), Lecture notes in computer science: Vol. 9749. *Distributed, ambient and pervasive interactions* (pp. 46–57). Springer International Publishing. doi:10.1007/978-3-319-39862-4_5

Da Xu, L., He, W., & Li, S. (2014). Internet of things in industries: A survey. *IEEE Transactions on Industrial Informatics, 10*(4), 2233-2243.

Da Xu, L. (2011). Information architecture for supply chain quality management. *International Journal of Production Research*, *49*(1), 183–198. doi:10.1080/00207543.2010.508944

Dai, H., & Tseng, M. M. (2012). The impacts of RFID implementation on reducing inventory inaccuracy in a multi-stage supply chain. *International Journal of Production Economics*, *139*(2), 634–641. doi:10.1016/j.ijpe.2012.06.005

Daim, T., & Suntharasaj, P. (2009). Technology diffusion: Forecasting with bibliometric analysis and Bass model. *Foresight*, *11*(3), 45–55. doi:10.1108/14636680910963936

Danado, J., Dias, E., Romão, T., Correia, N., Trabuco, A., Santos, C., . . . Serpa, J. (2003, January). *Mobile augmented reality for environmental management (MARE)*. In Eurographics 2003 Conference, Granada, Spain.

Daubert, J., Wiesmaier, A., & Kikiras, P. (2015). A view on privacy & trust in IoT. IoT/CPS-Security Workshop. *IEEE International Conference on Communications, ICC*. doi:10.1109/ICCW.2015.7247581

Dave, B., Kubler, S., Främling, K., & Koskela, L. (2016). Opportunities for enhanced lean construction management using Internet of Things standards. *Automation in Construction*, *61*, 86–97. doi:10.1016/j.autcon.2015.10.009

Davis, F. D. (1989). Perceived usefulness, perceived ease of use, and user acceptance of information technology. *Management Information Systems Quarterly*, *13*(3), 319–340. doi:10.2307/249008

De Ruyter, K., Wetzels, M., & Kleijnen, M. (2001). Customer adoption of e-service: An experimental study. *International Journal of Service Industry Management*, *12*(2), 184–207. doi:10.1108/09564230110387542

Deb, M., & Chaudhuri, H. R. (2014). Impact of firms reputation and ethnocentrism on attitude towards foreign products. *Marketing Intelligence & Planning*, *32*(5), 646–664. doi:10.1108/MIP-04-2013-0070

Decker, C., Berchtold, M., Chaves, L. W. F., Beigl, M., Roehr, D., Riedel, T., ... Herzig, D. (2008). Cost-benefit model for smart items in the supply chain. Lecture Notes in Computer Science (Including Subseries Lecture Notes in Artificial Intelligence and Lecture Notes in Bioinformatics), 4952, 155–172. doi:<ALIGNMENT.qj></ALIGNMENT>10.1007/978-3-540-78731-0_10

Delaney, J. (2013). Belkin WeMo Light Switch. *PC Magazine*. Retrieved September 10, 2016 from http://www.pcmag.com/article2/0,2817,2426758,00.asp

Demiralp, G., Guven, G., & Ergen, E. (2012). Analyzing the benefits of RFID technology for cost sharing in construction supply chains: A case study on prefabricated precast components. *Automation in Construction*, *24*, 120–129. doi:10.1016/j.autcon.2012.02.005

Devaraj, S., & Kohli, R. (2000). Information technology payoff in the health-care industry: A longitudinal study. *Journal of Management Information Systems*, *16*(4), 41–67. doi:10.1080/07421222.2000.11518265

Dewan, S., Ganley, D., & Kraemer, K. (2010). Complementarities in the diffusion of personal computers and the Internet: Implications for the global digital divide. *Information Systems Research*, *21*(5), 924–940.

Dey, S., Joshi, S. D., Patil, S., Kumar, K., & Kagi, V. K. (2016). A Survey of the Internet of Things. *IOSR Journal of Computer Engineering*, *18*(1), 80–85. doi:10.9790/0661-18138085

Dimakopoulou, A. G., Pramatari, K. C., & Tsekrekos, A. E. (2014). Applying real options to IT investment evaluation: The case of radio frequency identification (RFID) technology in the supply chain. *International Journal of Production Economics*, *156*, 191–207. doi:10.1016/j.ijpe.2014.06.005

Ding, D., Cooper, R. A., Pasquina, P. F., & Fici-Pasquina, L. (2011). Sensor technology for smart homes. *Maturitas*, *69*(2), 131–136. doi:10.1016/j.maturitas.2011.03.016 PMID:21531517

Dishaw, M. T., & Strong, D. M. (1999). Extending the technology acceptance model with task–technology fit constructs. *Information & Management*, *36*(1), 9–21. doi:10.1016/S0378-7206(98)00101-3

Dixon, M., Kimes, S. E., & Verma, R. (2009). Customer preferences for restaurant technology innovations. *Cornell Hospitality Report.*, *9*(7), 4–16.

Domingo, M. C. (2012). An overview of the Internet of Things for people with disabilities. *Journal of Network and Computer Applications*, *35*(2), 584–596. doi:10.1016/j.jnca.2011.10.015

Dominici, G., Roblek, V., Abbate, T., & Tani, M. (2016). Click and drive: Consumer attitude to product development: Towards future transformations of the driving experience. *Business Process Management Journal*, *22*(2), 420–434. doi:10.1108/BPMJ-05-2015-0076

Dorsemaine, B., Gaulier, J., Wary, J., Kheir, N., & Urien, P. (2016). Internet of Things: A definition and taxonomy. *Proceedings of The 9th International Conference on Next Generation Mobile Applications, Services and Technologies*, 72-77. doi:10.1109/NGMAST.2015.71

Dull, T. (2014, December 10). *Big data and the Internet of things: Two sides of the same coin?* Retrieved January 4, 2017, from http://www.smartdatacollective.com/tamaradull/286381/big-data-and-internet-things-two-sides-same-coin

Dull, T. (2015a). *Is privacy dead? And the survey says …* Retrieved January 4, 2017, from http://www.sas.com/en_id/insights/articles/marketing/is-privacy-dead.html

Dull, T. (2015b, July 27). *It's your life, starring your data*. Retrieved January 4, 2017, from http://www.socialmediatoday.com/technology-data/tamaradull/2015-07-24/its-your-life-starring-your-data

Durbach, I., Lahdelma, R., & Salminen, P. (2014). The analytic hierarchy process with stochastic judgements. *European Journal of Operational Research*, *238*(2), 552–559. doi:10.1016/j.ejor.2014.03.045

Dutot, V. (2015). Factors influencing Near Field Communication (NFC) adoption: An extended TAM approach. *The Journal of High Technology Management Research*, *26*(1), 45–57. doi:10.1016/j.hitech.2015.04.005

Dutton, W. H. (2014). Putting things to work: Social and policy challenges for the Internet of things. *Info*, *16*(3), 1–21. doi:10.1108/info-09-2013-0047

Economides, N., & Katsamakas, E. (2006). Two-sided competition of proprietary vs. open source technology platforms and the implications for the software industry. *Management Science*, *52*(7), 1057–1071. doi:10.1287/mnsc.1060.0549

Edelman, B. (2015, April). How to launch your digital platform. *Harvard Business Review*.

Eltayeb, M., & Dawson, M. (2016). Understanding user's acceptance of personal cloud computing: Using the Technology Acceptance Model. In S. Latifi (Ed.), *Information technology: New generations* (Vol. 448, pp. 3–12). Springer International Publishing. doi:10.1007/978-3-319-32467-8_1

Erumban, A. A., & de Jong, S. B. (2006). Cross-country differences in ICT adoption: A consequence of culture? *Journal of World Business*, *41*(4), 302–314. doi:10.1016/j.jwb.2006.08.005

Escribano, B. (2013). *Privacy and security in the Internet of Things: challenge or opportunity*. Retrieved May 10, 2016 from http://www.olswang.com/media/48315339/privacy_and_security_in_the_iot.pdf

Estes, A. C. (2015, July 16). *Apple might start showing people ads based on their bank balances*. Retrieved January 4, 2017, from http://gizmodo.com/apples-thinking-about-showing-people-ads-based-on-their-1718218638

Etemad, H. (1999). Globalization and the small and medium-sized enterprises: Search for potent strategies. *Global Focus*, *11*(3), 85–104.

European Union. (2015). *Digital agenda for Europe: Monitoring and control*. Retrieved from http://ec.europa.eu/digital-agenda/en/monitoring-and-control

Evans, D. (2011). *The Internet of Things How the Next Evolution of the Internet Is Changing Everything*. Cisco White Paper.

Evans, D., & Eyers, D. (2012). Efficient data tagging for managing privacy in the Internet of Things. *GREENCOM '12 Proceedings of the 2012 IEEE International Conference on Green Computing and Communications*, 244-248. doi:10.1109/GreenCom.2012.45

Evanschitzky, H., Iyer, G. R., Pillai, K. G., Kenning, P., & Schütte, R. (2015). Consumer trial, continuous use, and economic benefits of a retail service innovation: The case of the personal shopping assistant. *Journal of Product Innovation Management*, *32*(3), 459–475. doi:10.1111/jpim.12241

Fan, X., White, I. M., Shopova, S. I., Zhu, H., Suter, J. D., & Sun, Y. (2008). Sensitive optical biosensors for unlabeled targets: A review. *Analytica Chimica Acta, 620*(1), 8-26.

Fan, T. J., Chang, X. Y., Gu, C. H., Yi, J. J., & Deng, S. (2014). Benefits of RFID technology for reducing inventory shrinkage. *International Journal of Production Economics*, *147*(PART C), 659–665. doi:10.1016/j.ijpe.2013.05.007

Fan, T., Tao, F., Deng, S., & Li, S. (2015). Impact of RFID technology on supply chain decisions with inventory inaccuracies. *International Journal of Production Economics*, *159*, 117–125. doi:10.1016/j.ijpe.2014.10.004

Farooq, M. U., Waseem, M., Khairi, A., & Mazhar, S. (2015). A Critical Analysis on the Security Concerns of Internet of Things (IoT*). International Journal of Computers and Applications*, *111*(7), 1–5. doi:10.5120/19547-1280

Ferber, S. (2013). How the internet of things changes everything? *Harvard Business Review*. Retrieved from https://hbr.org/2013/05/how-the-internet-of-things-cha/

Fernández Robin, C., McCoy, S., Yáñez Sandivari, L., & Yáñez Martínez, D. (2014). Technology acceptance model: Worried about the cultural influence? In F. F.-H. Nah (Ed.), Lecture notes in computer science: Vol. 8527. *HCI in business* (pp. 609–619). Springer International Publishing. doi:10.1007/978-3-319-07293-7_59

Ferreira, J. (2001). Corporate entrepreneurship: A strategic and structural perspective. *New England Journal of Entrepreneurship*, *4*(2), 59.

Figueroa, N., Dong, H., & Saddik, A. H. (2013, Nov 24). *From Sense to Print: Towards Automatic 3D Printing from 3D Sensing Devices*. Paper presented at IEEE International Conference on Systems, Man, and Cybernetics(SMC). doi:10.1109/SMC.2013.833

Fisher, D., DeLine, R., Czerwinski, M., & Drucker, S. (2012). Interactions with big data analytics. *Interaction*, *19*(3), 50–59. doi:10.1145/2168931.2168943

Fleisch, E. (2010). What is the internet of things? An economic perspective. *Economics, Management, and Financial Markets,* (2), 125-157.

Fleisch, E. (2010). What is the Internet of Things? an economic perspective. *Economics, Management, and Financial Markets*, (2), 125-157.

Floerkemeier, C., Roduner, C., & Lampe, M. (2007). RFID application development with the Accada middleware platform. *IEEE Systems Journal*, *1*(2), 82–94. doi:10.1109/JSYST.2007.909778

Food and Drug Administration, HHS. (2014). Food labeling; nutrition labeling of standard menu items in restaurants and similar retail food establishments. Final rule. *Federal Register*, *79*(230), 71155.

Fornell, C., & Larcker, D. F. (1981). Structural equation models with unobservable variables and measurement error: Algebra and statistics. *JMR, Journal of Marketing Research*, *18*(3), 382–388. doi:10.2307/3150980

Fowler, T. (2014). AliveCor Heart Monitor Now Available Over the Counter: Interview with CEO Euan Thomson. *medGadget*. Retrieved September 10, 2016 from http://www.medgadget.com/2014/02/ fda-over-the-counter-approval-for-alivecor-heart-monitor-interview-with-ceo-euan-thomson.html

Franceschi-Bicchierai, L. (2016, October 21). *Blame the Internet of Things for destroying the Internet today*. Retrieved December 11, 2016, from http://motherboard.vice.com/read/blame-the-internet-of-things-for-destroying-the-internet-today

Franses, P. H. (2015). The life cycle of social media. *Applied Economics Letters*, *22*(10), 796–800. doi:10.1080/13504851.2014.978069

Frederix, I. (2009, May). Internet of things and radio frequency identification in care taking, facts and privacy challenges. In *Wireless Communication, Vehicular Technology, Information Theory and Aerospace & Electronic Systems Technology, 2009. Wireless VITAE 2009. 1st International Conference on* (pp. 319-323). IEEE. doi:10.1109/WIRELESSVITAE.2009.5172467

Fuchs, C. (2014). *Social media: A critical introduction*. London: Sage Publications. doi:10.4135/9781446270066.n2

Fuhrer, P., & Guinard, D. (2006). *Building a smart hospital using RFID technologies: use cases and implementation*. Department of Informatics-University of Fribourg.

Furdik, K., Pramudianto, F., Ahlsén, M., & Rosengren, P. (2014). *Food traceability chain supported by the ebbits IoT middleware*. Academic Press.

Gandomi, A., & Haider, M. (2015). Beyond the hype: Big data concepts, methods, and analytics. *International Journal of Information Management*, *35*(2), 137–144. doi:10.1016/j.ijinfomgt.2014.10.007

Gangemi, A., Guarino, N., Masolo, C., & Oltramari, A. (2003). Sweetening wordnet with dolce. *AI Magazine*, *24*(3), 13.

Gantait, A., Patra, J., & Mukherjee, A. (2016). Securing IoT devices and gateways: From authentication, including certificate-based authentication, to authorization, to application ID validation. *IBM DeveloperWorks*. Retrieved September 12, 2016 from http://www.ibm.com/developerworks/library/iot-trs-secure-iot-solutions1/index.html

Ganti, R. K., Ye, F., & Lei, H. (2011). Mobile Crowdsensing: Current State and Future Challenges. *IEEE Communications Magazine*, *49*(11), 32–39. doi:10.1109/MCOM.2011.6069707

Gao, L., & Bai, X. (2014). A unified perspective on the factors influencing consumer acceptance of internet of things technology. *Asia Pacific Journal of Marketing and Logistics*, *26*(2), 211–231. doi:10.1108/APJML-06-2013-0061

Gao, L., & Waechter, K. A. (2015). Examining the role of initial trust in user adoption of mobile payment services: An empirical investigation. *Information Systems Frontiers*, 1–24.

Garrett, R. (2016, December 5). *Taming big data in the IoT | supply & demand chain executive*. Retrieved January 4, 2017, from http://www.sdcexec.com/article/12271216/taming-big-data-in-the-iot

Gartner Press Release. (2014). *Gartner's 2014 Hype Cycle for Emerging Technologies Maps the Journey to Digital Business*. Retrieved May 22, 2015 http://www.gartner.com/newsroom/id/2819918

Gartner. (2014). *Gartner says 4.9 billion connected 'things' will be in use in 2015*. Press release, November 11, 2014.

Gartner. (2014). *Gartner says the internet of things will transform the data center*. Retrieved September 23, 2016 from http://www.gartner.com/newsroom/id/2684616

Gartner. (2015). *Gartner says the Internet of things installed base will grow to 26 billion units by 2010*. Retrieved from http://www.gartner.com/newsroom/id/2636073

Gartner. (2015, November 10). *Gartner says 6.4 Billion connected "things" will be in use in 2016, up 30 percent from 2015*. Retrieved January 4, 2017, from http://www.gartner.com/newsroom/id/3165317

Gavras, A., Karila, A., Fdida, S., May, M., & Potts, M. (2007). Future internet research and experimentation: The FIRE initiative. *Computer Communication Review*, *37*(3), 89–92. doi:10.1145/1273445.1273460

Geerts, G. L., & OLeary, D. E. (2014). A supply chain of things: The EAGLET ontology for highly visible supply chains. *Decision Support Systems*, *63*(1), 3–22. doi:10.1016/j.dss.2013.09.007

Gefen, D., Karahanna, E., & Straub, D. W. (2003). Trust and TAM in online shopping: An integrated model. *Management Information Systems Quarterly*, *27*(1), 51–90.

Geller, J. (2014). Why home automation is being disrupted? *SmartThings*. Retrieved 29 Sept 2016 from https://blog.smartthings.com/editorial/why-home-automation-is-being-disrupted/

Geroski, P., Steve, M., & Reenen, J. C. (1993). The Profitability of Innovating Firms. *The Rand Journal of Economics*, *24*(2), 198–211. doi:10.2307/2555757

Gerpott, T. J., & May, S. (2016). Integration of Internet of Things components into a firms offering portfolio - a business development framework. *Info*, *18*(2), 53–63. doi:10.1108/info-11-2015-0051

Girish, D. (2016). *4 Innovative Internet of things examples in retail*. Retrieved from http://blog.beaconstac.com/2015/10/4-innovative-internet-of-things-examples-in-retail/

Glaser, B. G., & Strauss, A. L. (1967). *The discovery of grounded theory*. London: Weidenfeld and Nicholson.

Gluhak, A., Krco, S., Nati, M., Pfisterer, D., Mitton, N., & Razafindralambo, T. (2011). A survey on facilities for experimental internet of things research. *IEEE Communications Magazine*, *49*(11), 58–67. doi:10.1109/MCOM.2011.6069710

Gnimpieba, D. R., Nait-Sidi-Moh, A., Durand, D., & Fortin, J. (2015). ScienceDirect Using Internet of Things technologies for a collaborative supply chain: Application to tracking of pallets and containers. *Procedia - Procedia Computer Science, 56*, 550–557. <ALIGNMENT.qj></ALIGNMENT>10.1016/j.procs.2015.07.251

Goodhue, D. L., & Thompson, R. L. (1995). Task-technology fit and individual performance. *Management Information Systems Quarterly*, *19*(2), 213–236. doi:10.2307/249689

Gosling, S. D., & Mason, W. (2015). Internet research in psychology. *Annual Review of Psychology*, *66*(1), 877–902. doi:10.1146/annurev-psych-010814-015321 PMID:25251483

Grand View Research. (2016). *IoT Market Analysis By Component (Devices, Connectivity, IT Services, Platforms), By Application (Consumer Electronics, Retail, Manufacturing, Transportation, Healthcare) And Segment Forecasts To 2022*. Last access at http://www.grandviewresearch.com/industry-analysis/iot-market

Greeno, J. G. (1994). *Gibson's affordances*. Academic Press.

Gregory, J. (2015). The Internet of things: Revolutionizing the retail industry. *Accenture Strategy*. Retrieved from https://www.accenture.com/_acnmedia/Accenture/Conversion-Assets/DotCom/Documents/Global/PDF/Dualpub_14/Accenture-The-Internet-Of-Things.pdf

Grunow, M., & Piramuthu, S. (2013). RFID in highly perishable food supply chains - Remaining shelf life to supplant expiry date? *International Journal of Production Economics*, *146*(2), 717–727. doi:10.1016/j.ijpe.2013.08.028

GS1. (2010). *EPC Tag Data Standard 3 Version 1.5*. Available from http://www.gs1.org/gsmp/kc/epcglobal/tds/tds_1_5-standard20100818.pdf

Gu, Y., & Qingqi, L. (2014). Research on the application of the internet of things in Reverse Logistics Information Management. *Energy Development, 860–863*(4), 3017–3020. http://doi.org/<ALIGNMENT.qj></ALIGNMENT>10.4028/www.scientific.net/AMR.860-863.3017

Gubbi, J., Buyya, R., Marusic, S., & Palaniswami, M. (2013). Internet of Things (IoT): A vision, architectural elements, and future directions. *Future Generation Computer Systems, 29*(7), 1645–1660. doi:10.1016/j.future.2013.01.010

Guimaraes, T., Cook, D., & Natarajan, N. (2002). Exploring the importance of business clockspeed as a moderator for determinants of supplier network performance. *Decision Sciences, 33*(4), 629–644. doi:10.1111/j.1540-5915.2002.tb01659.x

Guinard, D., Trifa, V., Karnouskos, S., Spiess, P., & Savio, D. (2010). Interacting with the soa-based internet of things: Discovery, query, selection, and on-demand provisioning of web services. *IEEE Transactions on Services Computing, 3*(3), 223-235.

Guo, B., Zhang, D., Wang, Z., Zhiwen, Y., & Xingshe, Z. (2013). Opportunistic IoT: Exploring The Harmonious Interaction between Human and the Internet of Things. *Journal of Network and Computer Applications*. 10.1016/j.jnca.2012.12.028

Hachem, S., Teixeira, T., & Issarny, V. (2011, December). Ontologies for the internet of things. In *Proceedings of the 8th Middleware Doctoral Symposium* (p. 3). ACM.

Haghighy, T. K. (2009). *Internet banking Technology Acceptance Model: A focus on Hofstede cultural dimensions* (Unpublished doctoral dissertation.). Graduate School of Business Faculty of Business and Accountancy, University of Malaya, Malaysia.

Hajduk, S. (2016). The concept of a smart city in urban management. *Business. Management in Education, 14*(1), 34–49.

Hakima, C. (2010). *The Internet of Things – Connecting Objects to the Web*. London, UK: Wiley.

Hakima, C. (2013). *The Internet of Things – Connecting Objects*. London, UK: Wiley.

Haller, S., Karnouskos, S., & Schroth, C. (2008, September). The internet of things in an enterprise context. In *Future Internet Symposium* (pp. 14-28). Springer Berlin Heidelberg.

Hanks, R. (2002). Discounting in the hotel industry: A new approach. *The Cornell Hotel and Restaurant Administration Quarterly, 43*(4), 94–103. doi:10.1016/S0010-8804(02)80046-5

Ha, O. K., Song, Y. S., Chung, K. Y., Lee, K. D., & Park, D. (2014). Relation model describing the effects of introducing RFID in the supply chain: Evidence from the food and beverage industry in South Korea. *Personal and Ubiquitous Computing, 18*(3), 553–561. doi:10.1007/s00779-013-0675-x

Harbor Research. (2013). *IoT Market Opps*. Paper 2013.

Hargreaves, I. (2011). *Digital opportunity: a review of intellectual property and growth: an independent report*. Academic Press.

Harrington, T. S., & Srai, J. S. (2016). Designing a 'concept of operations' architecture for next-generation multi-organisational service networks. *AI & Society*, 1–13. doi:10.1007/s00146-016-0664-5

Hartmann, P. M., Zaki, M., & Feldmann, N. (2014). *Big data for big business? A taxonomy of data- driven business models used by start-up firms*. University of Cambridge Working Paper.

Ha, S., & Stoel, L. (2009). Consumer e-shopping acceptance: Antecedents in a technology acceptance model. *Journal of Business Research, 62*(5), 565–571. doi:10.1016/j.jbusres.2008.06.016

Hausman, K. K., & Horne, R. (2014). *3D Printing for dummies*. Hoboken, NJ: John Wiley & Sons, Incorporation.

Heartlands. (n.d.). Retrieved from https://www.zebra.com/content/dam/zebra/success-stories/en-gb/pdfs/heartlands-hospital-en-gb.pdf

Heckathorn, D. D. (2002). Respondent-driven sampling II: Deriving valid population estimates from chain-referral samples of hidden populations. *Social Problems*, *49*(1), 11–34. doi:10.1525/sp.2002.49.1.11

Heffetz, O., & Ligett, K. (2014). Privacy and data-based research. *The Journal of Economic Perspectives*, *28*(2), 75–98. doi:10.1257/jep.28.2.75

Henderson, R. M., & Clark, K. B. (1990). Architectural innovation: The reconfiguration of existing product technologies and the failure of established firms. *Administrative Science Quarterly*, *35*(1), 9–30. doi:10.2307/2393549

Henke, N. (2016). *The age of analytics: Competing in a data-driven world.* McKinsey Global Institute.

Hermans, P. (2014). *How could the Electronics Industry use 3D Printing?* Retrieved Jan 17,2014 from http://www.3dprintingelectronicsconference.com/3d-printing-electronics-conference/how-could-the-electronics-industry-use-3d-printing/

Hernandez Barros, R., Vidal-García, J., Vidal, M., & Martínez Torre-Enciso, M. I. (2016). New evidence in the definition of strategy for global insurers. *Economic Bulletin*, *36*(3), 1829–1843.

Hernández-Muñoz, J. M., Vercher, J. B., Muñoz, L., Galache, J. A., Presser, M., Gómez, L. A. H., & Pettersson, J. (2011, May). Smart cities at the forefront of the future internet. In The Future Internet Assembly (pp. 447-462). Springer Berlin Heidelberg. doi:10.1007/978-3-642-20898-0_32

He, W., Yan, G., & Xu, L. D. (2014). Developing vehicular data cloud services in the IoT environment. *IEEE Transactions on Industrial Informatics*, *10*(2), 1587–1595. doi:10.1109/TII.2014.2299233

Hillman, A. J., Withers, M. C., & Collins, B. J. (2009). Resource dependence theory: A review. *Journal of Management*, *35*(6), 1404–1427. doi:10.1177/0149206309343469

Hoffman, D. L., & Novak, T. P. (2015). *Emergent experience and the connected consumer in the smart home assemblage and the Internet of things.* Available at SSRN 2648786

Hoffmann, A., & Birnbrich, C. (2012). The impact of fraud prevention on bank-customer relationships. *International Journal of Bank Marketing*, *30*(5), 390–407. doi:10.1108/02652321211247435

Hofman, W., Punter, M., Bastiaansen, H., Cornelisse, E., Dalmolen, S., Palaskas, Z., & Gonzalez-Rodriguez, M. et al. (2016). An interorganizational IT infrastructure for self-organization in logistics: Situation awareness and real-time chain composition. *International Journal of Advanced Logistics*, *5*(2), 101–115.

Hofstede, G. (2001). *Culture's consequences: Comparing values, behaviors, institutions, and organizations across nations* (2nd ed.). Thousand Oaks, CA: Sage Publications.

Holmes, R. (2014, June 5). *Fitness trackers: A narcissist's dream, but what else is behind the boom?* Retrieved January 4, 2017, from http://fortune.com/2014/06/03/fitness-trackers-a-narcissists-dream-but-what-else-is-behind-the-boom/

Hongming, C., & Xu, L. D. (2014). IoT based Configurable Information Service Platform for Product Life cycle management. *IEEE Transactions on Industrial Informatics, 10*(2), 1558-1567. doi: 10.1109/TII.2014.2306391

Horvath, L. (2001). Collaboration: The key to value creation in supply chain management. *Supply Chain Management: An International Journal*, *6*(5), 205–207. doi:10.1108/EUM0000000006039

HP. (2014). *HP Study Reveals 70 Percent of Internet of Things Devices Vulnerable to Attack.* Retrieved January 12, 2015 from http://www8.hp.com/us/en/hp-news/press-release.html?id=1744676#.VNKPaRE5A2w

Hsueh, C.-F., & Chang, M.-S. (2010). A model for intelligent transportation of perishable products. *International Journal of Intelligent Transportation Systems Research*, *8*(1), 36–41. doi:10.1007/s13177-009-0004-y

Hsu, L., & Wu, P. (2013). Electronic-tablet-based menu in a full service restaurant and customer satisfaction-a structural equation model. *International Journal of Business. Human Technology*, *3*(2), 62–71.

Huang, X., Fu, R., Chen, B., Zhang, T., & Roscoe, A. (2012). User interactive Internet of Things Privacy Preserved access control. *Seventh International conference for Internet Technology and secured transaction ICITST United Kingdom*, 597-602.

Huijts, N. M. A., Molin, E. J. E., & Steg, L. (2012). Psychological factors influencing sustainable energy technology acceptance: A review-based comprehensive framework. *Renewable & Sustainable Energy Reviews*, *16*(1), 525–531. doi:10.1016/j.rser.2011.08.018

Hui, M. K., & Bateson, J. E. (1991). Perceived Control and the Effects of Crowding and Consumer Choice on the Service Experience. *J CONSUM RES Journal of Consumer Research*, *18*(2), 174. doi:10.1086/209250

Hülsmann, M., & Grapp, J. (2006). Monitoring of Autonomous Cooperating Logistic Processes in International Supply Networks. *Proceedings of 11th International Symposium on Logistics (11th ISL)*, 113-120.

Iansiti, M., & Lakhani, K. R. (2014). Digital Ubiquity: How Connections, Sensors, and Data Are Revolutionizing Business (Digest Summary). *Harvard Business Review*, *92*(11), 91–99.

IBM. (2010). *The Smarter Supply Chain of the Future*. Retrieved January 21, 2015 from http://www-935.ibm.com/services/us/gbs/bus/html/gbs-csco-study.html

IDC. (2014). *Worldwide and regional internet of things (IoT) 2014–2020 forecast: A virtuous circle of proven value and demand*. Retrieved May 28, 2015, http://www.idc.com/downloads/idc_market_in_a_minute_iot_infographic.pdf

IDC. (2014). *Worldwide and Regional Internet of Things (IoT) 2014–2020 Forecast: A Virtuous Circle of Proven Value and Demand*. Retrieved May 28, 2015, http://www.idc.com/downloads/idc_market_in_a_minute_iot_infographic.pdf

Identity Theft Resource Center (2015). *Identity Theft, Resource Center breach report hits record high in 2014*. Author.

Igelmund, G., Kutscher, M., & Wambach, M. (2011). Development and evaluation of group support systems in non-business environments on tabletop interfaces. *World Usability Conference*.

Ilkinson, L. W., & Riendly, M. F. (2009). *History Corner: The History of the Cluster Heat-Map*, *60622*. doi:10.1198/tas.2009.0033

International Telecommunication Union. (2012). *ITU-T Y.2060 — (06/2012) — Next Generation Networks — Frameworks and functional architecture models — Overview of the Internet of things*. ITU.

Internet of Things Privacy & Security in a Connected World. (2015). FTC Staff Report January. Retrieved March 25, 2016 from https://www.ftc.gov/news-events/press releases/2015/01

IoT Case Studies. (2016). *Heidelberg Pioneers the Smart, Connected Printing Press*. Retrieved Jan 1,2016 from http://www.ptc.com/internet-of-things/use-cases

iRythm Technologies. (2016). Retrieved on Aug 10,2016 from http://www.irhythmtech.com/patients-heart-arrhythmias-afib.php

Isenberg, M. A., Werthmann, D., Morales-Kluge, E., & Scholz-Reiter, B. (2011). The Role of the Internet of Things for Increased Autonomy and Agility in Collaborative Production Environments. In D. Uckelmann, M. Harrison, & F. Michahelles (Eds.), *Architecting the Internet of Things*. Springer-Verlag Berlin Heidelberg. doi:10.1007/978-3-642-19157-2_8

ISTAG. (2008). *Working Group Report on "Web-based Service Industry"*. Retrieved from ftp://ftp.cordis.europa.eu/pub/ist/docs/web-based-service-industry-istag_en.pdf

ITU Internet Reports. (2005). *The Internet of Things, November 2005*. ITU.

ITU. (2012). *New ITU standards define the internet of things and provide the blueprints for its development.* Retrieved from http://www.itu.int/ITU-T/newslog/New_ITU_Standards_Define_The_Internet_Of_Things_And_Provide_The_Blueprints_For_Its_Development.aspx

Jackson, T. (2016, June 15). *IoT.Nxt plots Internet of things "revolution" from SA*. Retrieved January 4, 2017, from Features: http://disrupt-africa.com/2016/06/iot-nxt-plots-onternet-of-things-revolution-from-sa/

Jaffe, M. (2014). IoT Won't Work without Artificial Intelligence. *Wired.* Retrieved from https://www.wired.com/insights/2014/11/iot-wont-work-without-artificial-intelligence/

Jambhulkar, P. W., & Baporikar, V. (2015). Wireless sensor network for heart disease detection using data mining technique. *International Journal of Innovative Research in Computer and Communication Engineering*, *3*(6), 5947–5953.

James, T. (2016). *The Future of Fashion Is 3D Printing Clothes at Home.* Retrieved April 15, 2016 from http://www.bloomberg.com/news/articles/2016-04-15/3D-printing-is-poised-to-bring-haute-couture-into-the-home

Janssen, C. (2015). *Platform.* Retrieved from http://www.techopedia.com/ definition/3411/platform

Jara, A. J., Zamora, M. A., & Skarmeta, A. F. (2011). An internet of things–based personal device for diabetes therapy management in ambient assisted living (AAL). *Personal and Ubiquitous Computing*, *15*(4), 431–440. doi:10.1007/s00779-010-0353-1

Jian, Y., Chen, S., Zhang, Z., & Zhang, L. (2007). Protecting Recevier-Location Privacy in Wireless Sensor Networks. *IEEE 26th International Conference on Computer Communications,* 955-1963. doi:10.1109/INFCOM.2007.227

Jiménez, G. S., Ongena, S., Peydro, J. L., & Saurina, J. (2014). Hazardous times for monetary policy: What do 23 million loans say about the impact of monetary policy on credit risk-taking. *Econometrica*, *82*(2), 463–505. doi:10.3982/ECTA10104

Jing, Q., Vasilakos, A. V., Wan, J., Lu, J., & Qiu, D. (2014). Security of the Internet of Things: Perspectives and challenges. *Wireless Networks*, *20*(8), 2481–2501. doi:10.1007/s11276-014-0761-7

Jing, T., Dancheng, L., & Ye, Z. (2016). *Study of Impact on Undergraduates' Entrepreneurial Failure based on the Model of Psychological Resilience-Knowledge Acquisition. English Language Teaching, 9(8).* doi:10.5539/elt.v9n8p224

Jo, H. J., Paik, J. H., & Lee, D. H. (2014). Efficient privacy-preserving authentication in wireless mobile networks. *IEEE Transactions on Mobile Computing*, *13*(7), 1469–1481. doi:10.1109/TMC.2013.134

Johnson, D. S., Bardhi, F., & Dunn, D. T. (2008). Understanding how technology paradoxes affect customer satisfaction with self-service technology: The role of performance ambiguity and trust in technology. *Psychology and Marketing*, *25*(5), 416–443. doi:10.1002/mar.20218

Johnson, K. D. (2015). *Machine-to-Machine: Reinventing Embedded Devices for Smart Services*. Academic Press.

Jones, G. R., & Butler, J. E. (1992). Managing internal corporate entrepreneurship: An agency theory perspective. *Journal of Management*, *18*(4), 733–749. doi:10.1177/014920639201800408

Jones, M. V., Coviello, N., & Tang, Y. K. (2011). International entrepreneurship research (1989–2009): A domain ontology and thematic analysis. *Journal of Business Venturing*, *26*(6), 632–659. doi:10.1016/j.jbusvent.2011.04.001

Kaloxylos, A., Wolfert, J., Verwaart, T., Terol, C. M., Brewster, C., Robbemond, R., & Sundmaker, H. (2013). The Use of Future Internet Technologies in the Agriculture and Food Sectors: Integrating the Supply Chain. *Procedia Technology, 8*, 51–60. <ALIGNMENT.qj></ALIGNMENT>10.1016/j.protcy.2013.11.009

Kambies, T., Raynor, M. E., Pankratz, D. M., & Wadekar, G. (2016). *Closing the digital divide: IoT in retail's transformative potential*. Retrieved from http://dupress.com/articles/internet-of-things-iot-retail-strategies/

Karakostas, B. (2013). A DNS architecture for the internet of things: A case study in transport logistics. *Procedia Computer Science, 19*, 594–601. <ALIGNMENT.qj></ALIGNMENT>10.1016/j.procs.2013.06.079

Karakostas, B. (2013). A DNS architecture for the internet of things: A case study in transport logistics. *Procedia of Computational Science, 19*, 594–601. doi:10.1016/j.procs.2013.06.079

Karimi, K., & Atkinson, G. (2013). *What the Internet of Things (IoT) needs to become a reality*. White Paper, FreeScale and ARM.

Karkouch, A., Mousannif, H., Al Moatassime, H., & Noel, T. (2016). Data quality in internet of things: A state-of-the-art survey. *Journal of Network and Computer Applications, 73*, 57–81. doi:10.1016/j.jnca.2016.08.002

Karnouskos, S. (2011, July). Cyber-physical systems in the smartgrid. In *2011 9th IEEE International Conference on Industrial Informatics* (pp. 20-23). IEEE. doi:10.1109/INDIN.2011.6034829

Karnouskos, S., Baecker, O., De Souza, L. M. S., & Spiess, P. (2007, September). Integration of soa-ready networked embedded devices in enterprise systems via a cross-layered web service infrastructure. In *2007 IEEE Conference on Emerging Technologies and Factory Automation (EFTA 2007)* (pp. 293-300). IEEE. doi:10.1109/EFTA.2007.4416781

Karshenas, M., & Stoneman, P. L. (1993). Rank, stock, order, and epidemic effects in the diffusion of new process technologies: An empirical model. *The Rand Journal of Economics, 24*(4), 503–528. doi:10.2307/2555742

Kashyap, S. (2016, August 26). *10 real world applications of Internet of things (IoT) – explained in videos*. Retrieved January 4, 2017, from https://www.analyticsvidhya.com/blog/2016/08/10-youtube-videos-explaining-the-real-world-applications-of-internet-of-things-iot/

Kaur, N., & Sood, S. K. (2015). Cognitive decision making in smart industry. *Computers in Industry, 74*, 151–161. doi:10.1016/j.compind.2015.06.006

Keh, H. T., & Xie, Y. (2009). Corporate reputation and customer behavioral intentions: The roles of trust, identification and commitment. *Industrial Marketing Management, 38*(7), 732–742. doi:10.1016/j.indmarman.2008.02.005

Kelley, D., Bosma, N. S., & Amorós, J. E. (2011). *Global Entrepreneurship Monitor 2010 Executive Report*. Last access at http:// www.gemconsortium.org

Kennedy, J. (2016, February 1). *Internet of Things to raise stakes in cyber security*. Retrieved January 4, 2017, from https://www.siliconrepublic.com/machines/internet-of-things-cyber-attacks-pwc

Khan, R., Khan, S. U., Zaheer, R., & Khan, S. (2012). Future Internet: The Internet of Things Architecture, Possible Applications and Key Challenges. In *2012 10th International Conference on Frontiers of Information Technology (FIT): Proceedings* (pp. 257-260). Institute of Electrical and Electronics Engineers Inc.

Khan, R., Khan, S. U., Zaheer, R., & Khan, S. (2012, December). Future internet: the internet of things architecture, possible applications and key challenges. In *Frontiers of Information Technology (FIT), 2012 10th International Conference on* (pp. 257-260). IEEE. doi:10.1109/FIT.2012.53

Khan, J. S., Aulakh, V., & Bosworth, A. (2009). What It Takes. *Characteristics of the Ideal Personal Health Record Health Aff (Millwood), 28*(2), 369–376. doi:10.1377/hlthaff.28.2.369 PMID:19275992

Khanna, A., & Misra, P. (2014). *The Internet of Things for Medical Devices - Prospects, Challenges and the Way Forward.* Retrieved May 10, 2016 from http://www.tcs.com/resources/white_papers/Pages/Internet-of-Things-Medical-Devices.aspx

Kim, H. Y., Lee, J. Y., Mun, J. M., & Johnson, K. K. (2016). Consumer adoption of smart in-store technology: assessing the predictive value of attitude versus beliefs in the technology acceptance model. *International Journal of Fashion Design, Technology and Education*, 1-11.

Kim, K. K., & Prabhakar, B. (2004). Initial trust and the adoption of B2C e-commerce: The case of internet banking. *ACM SIGMIS Database, 35*(2), 50-64.

Kimberly-Clark. (2014). *Kimberly-Clark Connecting With Startup Innovation at CES 2015.* Retrieved January 22, 2015 from http://investor.kimberly-clark.com/releasedetail.cfm?ReleaseID=886180

Kim, D. H., Cho, J. Y., Kim, S., & Lim, J. (2015). *A Study of Developing Security Requirements for Internet of Things (IoT). In Advanced Science and Technology Letters* (Vol. 87, pp. 94–99). Art, Culture, Game, Graphics, Broadcasting and Digital Contents.

Kime, M. B. (2016). *Trane At IoT World.* Retrieved May 4,2016 from http://www.trane.com/commercial/north-america/us/en/about-us/newsroom/press-releases/trane-at-iot-world.html

Kimes, S. E. (2008). The Role of Technology in Restaurant Revenue Management. *Cornell Hospitality Quarterly, 49*(3), 297–309. doi:10.1177/1938965508322768

Kimes, S. E., & Chase, R. B. (1998). The Strategic Levers of Yield Management. *Journal of Service Research, 1*(2), 156–166. doi:10.1177/109467059800100205

Kim, S. K., Park, M. J., Ahn, E. J., & Rho, J. J. (2015). Investigating the role of task-technology fit along with attractiveness of alternative technology to utilize RFID system in the organization. *Information Development, 31*(5), 405–420. doi:10.1177/0266666913513277

Kim, S., Gajos, K. Z., Muller, M., & Grosz, B. J. (2016). *Acceptance of mobile technology by older adults: A preliminary study. In Proceedings of the 18th International Conference on Human-Computer Interaction with Mobile Devices and Services - MobileHCI '16* (pp. 147–157). New York, NY: Association for Computing Machinery. doi:10.1145/2935334.2935380

King, W. R., & He, J. (2006). A meta-analysis of the technology acceptance model. *Information & Management, 43*(6), 740–755. doi:10.1016/j.im.2006.05.003

Kiritsis, D. (2011). Closed-loop PLM for intelligent products in the era of the Internet of things. *CAD Computer Aided Design, 43*(5), 479–501. doi:10.1016/j.cad.2010.03.002

Kirzner, I. M. (1985). *Discovery and the capitalist process.* University of Chicago Press.

Klein, G. T., Lu, Y., & Wang, M. Y. (2013). *3D printing and neurosurgery--ready for prime time?* Retrieved Jul 16, 2013 from https://www.ncbi.nlm.nih.gov/pubmed/23871811

Klopping, I. M., & McKinney, E. (2004). Extending the technology acceptance model and the task-technology fit model to consumer e-commerce. *Information Technology, Learning and Performance Journal, 22*(1), 35.

Knaus, M. (2015). Persuasive Technologies and Applications in Health and Fitness. *Persuasive Technologies and Applications, 3*(2), 5–11.

Konomi, S. I., & Roussos, G. (2007). Ubiquitous computing in the real world: Lessons learnt from large scale RFID deployments. *Personal and Ubiquitous Computing*, *11*(7), 507–521. doi:10.1007/s00779-006-0116-1

Kortuem, G., Kawsar, F., Sundramoorthy, V., & Fitton, D. (2010). Smart objects as building blocks for the internet of things. *IEEE Internet Computing*, *14*(1), 44–51. doi:10.1109/MIC.2009.143

Koster, M. (2013). *Data models for the Internet of Things*. Available from iot-datamodels.blogspot.co.uk

Kotis, K., & Vouros, G. (2016). Trust Semantics in IoT Entities' Deployment. *Workshop on Artificial Intelligence and Internet of Things(AI-IoT)*, Athens, Greece.

Krause, D. R., Handfield, R. B., & Tyler, B. B. (2007). The relationships between supplier development, commitment, social capital accumulation and performance improvement. *Journal of Operations Management*, *25*(2), 528–545. doi:10.1016/j.jom.2006.05.007

Krebs, J. M. (2008). Paper, Paper Everywhere? *The ASHA Leader*, *13*(12), 20–22. doi:10.1044/leader.FTR3.13122008.20

Krishnan, V., & Karl, T. U. (2001). Product Development Decisions: A Review of the Literature. *Journal of Management Science*, *47*(1), 1–21. doi:10.1287/mnsc.47.1.1.10668

Kruschwitz, N. (2011). First look: The second annual new intelligent enterprise survey. *MIT Sloan Management Review*, *52*(4), 87–89.

Kubler, S., Min-Jung, Y., Cassagnes, C., Främling, K. D., & Skilton, M. (2015). *Opportunity to Leverage Information-as-an-Asset in the IoT -- The Road Ahead*. Paper published in Future Internet of Things and Cloud (FiCloud), 3rd International Conference. doi:10.1109/FiCloud.2015.63

Kumar, J., & Patel, D. (2014). A Survey on Internet of Things: Security and Privacy Issues. *International Journal of Computer Applications*, *90*. doi: 10.5120/15764-4454

Kumar, A., Niu, F., & Ré, C. (2013). Hazy: Making it easier to build and maintain big-data analytics. *Communications of the ACM*, *56*(3), 40–49. doi:10.1145/2428556.2428570

Kuratko, D. F., Hornsby, J. S., Naffziger, D. W., & Montagno, R. V. (1993). Implementing entrepreneurial thinking in established organizations. *SAM Advanced Management Journal*, *58*(1), 28.

Kurzgesagt – In a Nutshell. (2016, December 7). *A new history for humanity – the human era*. Retrieved January 4, 2017, from https://www.youtube.com/watch?v=czgOWmtGVGs

Kushmaro, P. (2016, September 23). The IoT and big data: Making the connection. *Huffington Post*. Retrieved from http://www.huffingtonpost.com/philip-kushmaro/the-iot-and-big-data-maki_b_12116608.html

Lambrecht, A., & Skiera, B. (2006). Paying too much and being happy about it: Existence, causes, and consequences of tariff-choice biases. *JMR, Journal of Marketing Research*, *43*(2), 212–223. doi:10.1509/jmkr.43.2.212

Lambrecht, A., & Tucker, C. (2013). When does retargeting work? Information specificity in online advertising. *JMR, Journal of Marketing Research*, *50*(5), 561–576. doi:10.1509/jmr.11.0503

Lampe, M., & Flörkemeier, C. (2004). *The smart box application model*. Academic Press.

Laplante, P. A., & Laplante, N. (2016). The Internet of Things in healthcare: Potential applications and challenges. *IT Professional Magazine*, *18*(3), 2–4. doi:10.1109/MITP.2016.42

Larson, Q. (2016, December 5). *Connecting Asia's startup ecosystem*. Retrieved January 4, 2017, from Tech in Asia: https://www.techinasia.com/talk/learn-code

Lasch, F. (2011). Beyond the concept of human and social capital: The impact of the regional environment on high-tech venturing. *International Journal of Entrepreneurship and Small Business*, *14*(1), 56–76. doi:10.1504/IJESB.2011.042163

Lazarescu, M. T. (2013). Design of a WSN platform for long-term environmental monitoring for IoT applications. *IEEE Journal on Emerging and Selected Topics in Circuits and Systems*, *3*(1), 45–54. doi:10.1109/JETCAS.2013.2243032

Lazer, D., Kennedy, R., King, G., & Vespignani, A. (2014). The parable of Google Flu: Traps in Big Data. *Analytical Sciences*, *343*(6176), 1203–1205. doi:10.1126/science.1248506 PMID:24626916

Lee, I. (2015). The Internet of Things (IoT) for Supply Chain Innovation: A Conceptual Framework and Analysis of Fortune 200 Companies. *Asia Pacific Journal of Innovation and Entrepreneurship*, *9*(1), 81-103. Accessible at http://apjie.org/wp/?page_id=4808&uid=32&mod=document

Lee, H. J., & Yang, K. (2013). Interpersonal service quality, self-service technology (SST) service quality, and retail patronage. *Journal of Retailing and Consumer Services*, *20*(1), 51–57. doi:10.1016/j.jretconser.2012.10.005

Lee, I., & Lee, K. (2015). The Internet of things (IoT): Applications, investments and challenges for enterprises. *Business Horizons*, *58*(4), 431–440. doi:10.1016/j.bushor.2015.03.008

Lee, J., & Kim, Y. (1999). Effect of partnership quality on IS outsourcing success: Conceptual framework and empirical validation. *Journal of Management Information Systems*, *15*(4), 29–61. doi:10.1080/07421222.1999.11518221

Lee, Y., Kozar, K. A., & Larsen, K. R. T. (2003). The technology acceptance model: Past, present, and future. *Communications of the Association for Information Systems*, *12*, 752–780.

Legris, P., Ingham, J., & Collerette, P. (2003). Why do people use information technology? A critical review of the technology acceptance model. *Information & Management*, *40*(3), 191–204. doi:10.1016/S0378-7206(01)00143-4

Lehtonen, M., Oertel, N., & Vogt, H. (2007, June). Features, identity, tracing, and cryptography in product authentication. In *2007 IEEE International Technology Management Conference (ICE)* (pp. 1-8). IEEE.

Lenarcic, A. (2011). *Formalizing Affordances in Situation Theory* (Doctoral dissertation). Brock University.

Lenarčič, A., & Winter, M. (2013). Affordances in Situation Theory. *Ecological Psychology*, *25*(2), 155–181. doi:10.1080/10407413.2013.780495

Leung, J., Cheung, W., & Chu, S. C. (2014). Aligning RFID applications with supply chain strategies. *Information & Management*, *51*(2), 260–269. doi:10.1016/j.im.2013.11.010

Li, C., Raghunathan, A., & Jha, N. K. (2011). Hijacking an Insulin Pump: Security Attacks and Defenses for a Diabetes Therapy System. *IEEE 13th International Conference on e-health Networking, Applications and Services.* doi:10.1109/HEALTH.2011.6026732

Lidan, T., Chunxiao, F., Zou, J., & Zhang, X. (2011). Analysis and Research for Fourth Party Logistics Based on Internet of Things. *International Conference Instrumentation, Measurement, Computer, Communication and Control*, Beijing, China.

Li, F., & Xiong, P. (2013). Practical secure communication for integrating wireless sensor networks into the Internet of Things. *IEEE Sensors Journal*, *13*(10), 3677–3684. doi:10.1109/JSEN.2013.2262271

Li, H., Jiang, J., & Wu, M. (2014). The effects of trust assurances on consumers initial online trust: A two-stage decision-making process perspective. *International Journal of Information Management*, *34*(3), 395–405. doi:10.1016/j.ijinfomgt.2014.02.004

Li, M., Yu, S., Zhen, Y., Ren, K., & Lou, W. (2012). Scalable and Secure Sharing of Personal Health Records in Cloud Computing using Attribute-based Encryption. *IEEE Transactions on Parallel and Distributed Systems*, *24*(1), 131–143. doi:10.1109/TPDS.2012.97

Liñán, F., & Chen, Y. W. (2009). Development and Cross-Cultural application of a specific instrument to measure entrepreneurial intentions. *Entrepreneurship Theory and Practice, 33*(3), 593-617.

Liñán, F. (2008). Skill and value perceptions: How do they affect entrepreneurial intentions? *The International Entrepreneurship and Management Journal*, *4*(3), 257–272. doi:10.1007/s11365-008-0093-0

Lin, B. W., Li, P. C., & Chen, J. S. (2006). Social capital, capabilities, and entrepreneurial strategies: A study of Taiwanese high-tech new ventures. *Technological Forecasting and Social Change*, *73*(2), 168–181. doi:10.1016/j.techfore.2004.12.001

Lin, C. (1998). Success factors of small-and medium-sized enterprises in Taiwan: An analysis of cases. *Journal of Small Business Management*, *36*(4), 43–56.

Lin, W. S. (2012). Perceived fit and satisfaction on web learning performance: IS continuance intention and task-technology fit perspectives. *International Journal of Human-Computer Studies*, *70*(7), 498–507. doi:10.1016/j.ijhcs.2012.01.006

Li, Q., Wang, Z. Y., Li, W. H., Li, J., Wang, C., & Du, R. Y. (2013). Applications integration in a hybrid cloud computing environment: Modelling and platform. *Enterprise Information Systems*, *7*(3), 237–271. doi:10.1080/17517575.2012.677479

Li, S., Da Xu, L., & Zhao, S. (2015). The internet of things: A survey. *Information Systems Frontiers*, *17*(2), 243–259. doi:10.1007/s10796-014-9492-7

Li, S., Oikonomou, G., Tryfonas, T., Chen, T. M., & Xu, L. (2014). A Distributed Consensus Algorithm for Decision Making in Service-Oriented Internet of Things. *IEEE Transactions on Industrial Informatics*, *10*(2), 1461–1468. doi:10.1109/TII.2014.2306331

Li, S., Xu, L., Wang, X., & Wang, J. (2012). Integration of hybrid wireless networks in cloud services oriented enterprise information systems. *Enterprise Information Systems*, *6*(2), 165–187. doi:10.1080/17517575.2011.654266

Liu, E., Liu, Z., & Shao, F. (2014). Digital Rights Management and Access Control in Multimedia Social Networks. *Genetic and Evolutionary Computing*, *238*, 257–266. doi:10.1007/978-3-319-01796-9_27

Liu, W., & Gao, Z. (2014). Study on IOT based Architecture of Logistics Service Supply Chain. *International Journal of Grid and Distributed Computing*, *7*(1), 169–178. doi:10.14257/ijgdc.2014.7.1.15

Li, X., Hess, T. J., & Valacich, J. S. (2008). Why do we trust new technology? A study of initial trust formation with organizational information systems. *The Journal of Strategic Information Systems*, *17*(1), 39–71. doi:10.1016/j.jsis.2008.01.001

Li, Y., Hou, M., Liu, H., & Liu, Y. (2012). Towards a theoretical framework of strategic decision, supporting capability and information sharing under the context of Internet of Things. *Information Technology Management*, *13*(4), 205–216. doi:10.1007/s10799-012-0121-1

Lonergan, K. (2016). The autonomous Internet of Things: how the IoT will become context-aware and self-sufficient. *Information Age*. Retrieved from http://www.information-age.com/autonomous-internet-things-how-iot-will-become-context-aware-and-self-sufficient-123460740/

Lopez Research. (2013a). *An Introduction to the Internet of Things*. White Paper published by Cisco.

Lopez Research. (2013b). *Things Your Business Should Know About Internet of Things*. Retrieved February 15, 2016, from: http://www.lopezresearch.com/2013/12/10/4-things-your-business-should-know-about-internet-of-things/

López, T. S., Ranasinghe, D. C., Harrison, M., & McFarlane, D. (2012). Adding sense to the Internet of Things. *Personal and Ubiquitous Computing*, *16*(3), 291–308. doi:10.1007/s00779-011-0399-8

Lu, H. P., & Yang, Y. W. (2014). Toward an understanding of the behavioral intention to use a social networking site: An extension of task-technology fit to social-technology fit. *Computers in Human Behavior*, *34*, 323–332. doi:10.1016/j.chb.2013.10.020

Lumb, D. (2015, March 11). How the Internet of Things is changing work. *The Future of Work*. Retrieved January 4, 2017, from https://www.fastcompany.com/3052936/the-future-of-work/how-the-internet-of-things-is-changing-work

Lumpkin, G. T., & Dess, G. G. (1996). Clarifying the entrepreneurial orientation construct and linking it to performance. *Academy of Management Review*, *21*(1), 135–172.

Lunden, I. (2016, November 18). *French IoT startup Sigfox nabs €150M series E, reportedly at €600M valuation*. Retrieved January 4, 2017, from https://techcrunch.com/2016/11/18/french-iot-startup-sigfox-confirms-e150m-series-e-at-a-valuation-of-around-e600m/

Lu, X., Qu, Z., Li, Q., & Hui, P. (2015). Privacy Information Security Classification for Internet of Things Based on Internet Data. *International Journal of Distributed Sensor Networks*, *11*(8), 932941. doi:10.1155/2015/932941

Macdonald, E., Salas, R., Espalin, D., Perez, M., Aguilera, E., Muse, D. & Wicker. (2014). 3D Printing for the Rapid Prototyping of Structural Electronics. *IEEE Access, 2*, 234-242. doi: 10.1109/ACCESS.2014.2311810

MacManus. (2010). Chinese Premier Talks Up Internet of Things. Journal of Democracy, 22(2), 32-46.

Madhura, P.M., Bilurkar, N., Jain, P., & Ranjith, J. (2015). A Survey on Internet of Things: Security and Privacy Issues. *International Journal of Innovative Technology and Research*, *3*(3), 2069 – 2074.

Madlmayr, G., Ecker, J., Langer, J., & Scharinger, J. (2008). Near field communication: State of standardization. *Internet of Things*, *177*, 10.

Magruk, A. (2012). *The internet of things as the future technological trend of the innovative development of logistics*. Academic Press.

Mainetti, L., Patrono, L., & Vilei, A. (2011). Evolution of wireless sensor networks towards the Internet of Things: A survey. *2011 19th International Conference on Software, Telecommunications and Computer Networks (SoftCOM)*, 1-6.

Manyika, J. (2015). *Unlocking the potential of the Internet of Things*. McKinsey Global Institute.

Manyika, J., & Chui, M. (2015). *By 2025, Internet of things applications could have $11trillion impact*. Retrieved from http://www.mckinsey.com/insights/mgi/in_the_news/by_2025_Internet_of_things_applications_could_have_11_trillion_impact

Mariani, J., Quasney, E., & Raynor, M. E. (2015). Forging links into loops: The Internet of Things' potential to recast supply chain management. *Deloitte Review*, (17). Retrieved from https://dupress.deloitte.com/content/dam/dup-us-en/articles/internet-of-things-supply-chain-management/DUP1159_DR17_ForgingLinksIntoLoops.pdf

Marti, S., Ganesan, P., & Garcia-Molina, H. (2004, March). SPROUT: P2P routing with social networks. In *International Conference on Extending Database Technology* (pp. 425-435). Springer Berlin Heidelberg.

Martinez-Sala, A. S., Egea-Lopez, E., Garcia-Sanchez, F., & Garcia-Haro, J. (2009). Tracking of Returnable Packaging and Transport Units with active RFID in the grocery supply chain. *Computers in Industry*, *60*(3), 161–171. doi:10.1016/j.compind.2008.12.003

Martin, J. (2015). Data, data, everywhere. *Mechanical Engineering (New York, N.Y.)*, *137*(7), 46–51.

Maslakovic, M. (2016, November 22). *Top fitness trackers and health gadgets you can buy right now - health & fitness gadgets & wearables*. Retrieved January 4, 2017, from http://gadgetsandwearables.com/2016/11/22/best-fitness-trackers/

Mattern, F. (2013). Die technische Basis für M2M und das Internet der Dinge. M2M und das Internet der Dinge. *Münchner Kreis*, 46-69.

Mavrogiannopoulos, N. (2013). *Secure communications protocols and the protection of cryptographic keys* (Dissertation). Arenberg Doctoral School of Science, Engineering & Technology. Available at: https://securewww.esat.kuleuven.be/cosic/publications/thesis-225.pdf

Mayer, C. P. (2009). Security and privacy challenges in the internet of things. *Electronic Communications of the EASST*, *17*, 1–12.

Mayer-Schonberger, V., & Cukier, K. (2014). *Big data: A revolution that will transform how we live, work, and think*. Boston, MA: Houghton Mifflin Harcourt Print.

Mazanai, M., & Fatoki, O. (2012). Access to finance in the SME sector: A South African perspective. *Asian Journal of Business Management*, *4*(1), 58–67.

McAfee, A., Brynjolfsson, E., Davenport, T. H., Patil, D., & Barton, D. (2012). Big Data. The management revolution. *Harvard Business Review*, *90*(10), 61–67. PMID:23074865

McCaskill, S. (2015). *Coca-Cola Is Using The IoT To Create New Coke Flavors*. Retrieved from http://www.techweek-europe.co.uk/networks/m2m/coca-cola-using-iot-create-new-coke-flavours-180916#wBezSPZAQXStZszf.99

McDougall, P. P. (1989). International versus domestic entrepreneurship: New venture strategic behavior and industry structure. *Journal of Business Venturing*, *4*(6), 387–400. doi:10.1016/0883-9026(89)90009-8

McFarlance, D., & Sheffi, Y. (2006). The impact of automatic identification on Supply Chain Operations. *International Journal of Retail & Distribution Management*, *34*(1), 6–24. doi:10.1108/02656710210415703

McGuire, T., Manyika, J., & Chui, M. (2012). Why big data is the new competitive advantage. *Ivey Business Journal*, *76*(4), 1–4.

McIntyre, K. (2016a, December 2). *What does housewives' porn consumption have to do with your startup? It's in the data*. Retrieved January 4, 2017, from https://www.techinasia.com/how-to-big-data-insights-tiajkt2016

McIntyre, K. (2016b, November 23). *GE partners with Indonesian big data startup to make unforeseen blackouts history*. Retrieved January 4, 2017, from https://www.techinasia.com/dattabot-ge-digital-partnership-iot-tiajkt2016

McKendrick, J. (2016, November 13). With Internet of Things and big data, 92% of everything we do will be in the cloud. *Forbes*. Retrieved from http://www.forbes.com/sites/joemckendrick/2016/11/13/with-internet-of-things-and-big-data-92-of-everything-we-do-will-be-in-the-cloud/#66823f49593f

McKinsey Global Institute (2011). *Big data: The next frontier for innovation, competition, and productivity*. Author.

McKinsey Global Institute. (2015). *The internet of things: Mapping the value beyond the hype*. Retrieved September 18, 2016 from https://www.mckinsey.de/sites/mck_files/files/unlocking_the_potential_of_the_internet_of_things_full_report.pdf

McKinsey. (2013). *The Internet of Things and the Future of Manufacturing*. McKinsey & Company. Retrieved February 15, 2016, from: http://www.mckinsey.com/insights/business_technology/the_internet_of_things_and_the_future_of_manufacturing

McLellan, C. (2015, March 2). *The Internet of Things and big data: Unlocking the power*. Retrieved January 4, 2017, from http://www.zdnet.com/article/the-internet-of-things-and-big-data-unlocking-the-power/

Medaglia, C., & Serbanati, A. (2010). Internet of things: An overview of privacy and security issues in the Internet of things. *20th Tyrrhenian Workshop on Digital Communications Springer*, 389-395. doi:10.1007/978-1-4419-1674-7_38

Meister, M., Pias, M., Töpfer, E., & Coulouris, G. (2008). Application Scenarios for Cooperating Objects and their Social. *Legal and Ethical Challenges. In Adjunct Proceedings First International Conference on The Internet of Things.*

Mellis, D. A., Buechley, L., Resnick, M., & Hartmann, B. (2016). *Engaging amateurs in the design, fabrication, and assembly of electronic devices. In Proceedings of the 2016 ACM Conference on Designing Interactive Systems - DIS'16* (pp. 1270–1281). New York, NY: Association for Computing Machinery. https://doi.org/10.1145/2901790.2901833

Mendelson, H., & Pillai, R. (1998). Clockspeed and information response: Evidence from the information technology sector. *Information Systems Research*, *9*(4), 415–433. doi:10.1287/isre.9.4.415

Mennicken, S., Zihler, O., Juldaschewa, F., Molnar, V., Aggeler, D., & Huang, E. M. (2016). "It's like living with a friendly stranger": Perceptions of personality traits in a smart home. *Proceedings of the 2016 ACM International Joint Conference on Pervasive and Ubiquitous Computing - UbiComp '16* (pp. 120-131). New York, NY: Association for Computing Machinery. doi:10.1145/2971648.2971757

Mentzer, J. T., Min, S., & Zacharia, Z. G. (2000). The nature of interfirm partnering in supply chain management. *Journal of Retailing*, *76*(4), 549–568. doi:10.1016/S0022-4359(00)00040-3

Mian, A., Rao, K., & Sufi, A. (2013). Household balance sheets, consumption and economic slump. *The Quarterly Journal of Economics*, *128*(4), 1687–1726. doi:10.1093/qje/qjt020

Mian, A., & Sufi, A. (2009). The consequences of mortgage credit expansion: Evidence from the U.S. mortgage default crisis. *The Quarterly Journal of Economics*, *124*(4), 1449–1496. doi:10.1162/qjec.2009.124.4.1449

Miaou, S. G., Hsu, C. M., Tsai, Y. S., & Chao, H. M. (2000). A Secure Data Hiding Technique with Heterogeneous Data-Combining Capability or Electronic Patient Records. *22nd Annual EMBS International Conference*, 280-283. doi:10.1109/IEMBS.2000.900730

Michell, V. (2011). A focussed approach to business capability. *Proceedings of the First International Symposium on Business Modelling and Design*, 105-113.

Michell, V. (2014). The Internet of Things and Opportunities for Pervasive Safety Monitored Health Environments. In *Handbook of Research on Patient Safety and Quality Care through Health Informatics* (pp. 344–362). IGI Global. doi:10.4018/978-1-4666-4546-2.ch020

Michell, V., Tehrani, G., & Liu, K. (2012). Are clinical documents optimised for patient safety? A critical analysis of patient safety outcomes using the EDA error model. *Journal of Health Policy and Technology*, *1*(4), 214–227. doi:10.1016/j.hlpt.2012.10.003

Michell, V., & Tehrani, J. (2017). Clinical Pathways and the Human Factor: Approaches to Control and Reduction of Human Error Risk. In *Impact of Medical Errors and Malpractice on Health Economics, Quality, and Patient Safety*. IGI Global. doi:10.4018/978-1-5225-2337-6.ch001

Miles, M. P., Paul, C. W., & Wilhite, A. (2003). Modeling corporate entrepreneurship as rent-seeking competition. *Technovation*, *23*(5), 393–400. doi:10.1016/S0166-4972(02)00156-6

Miles, R. E., & Snow, C. C. (2007). Organization theory and supply chain management: An evolving research perspective. *Journal of Operations Management*, *25*(2), 459–463. doi:10.1016/j.jom.2006.05.002

Mills, J. E., & Thomas, L. (2008). Assessing Customer Expectations of Information Provided On Restaurant Menus: A Confirmatory Factor Analysis Approach. *Journal of Hospitality & Tourism Research (Washington, D.C.)*, *32*(1), 62–88. doi:10.1177/1096348007309569

Mineraud, J., Mazhelis, O., Su, X., & Tarkoma, S. (2016). A gap analysis of Internet-of-Things platforms. *Computer Communications*, *89-90*, 5–16. doi:10.1016/j.comcom.2016.03.015

Mingxiu, Z., Chunchang, F., & Minggen, Y. (2012). The Application used RFID in Third Party Logistics. *Physics Procedia*, *25*, 2045–2049. doi:10.1016/j.phpro.2012.03.348

Miorandi, D., Sicari, S., De Pellegrini, F., & Chlamtac, I. (2012). Internet of things: Vision, applications and research challenges. *Ad Hoc Networks*, *10*(7), 1497–1516. doi:10.1016/j.adhoc.2012.02.016

Mirsa, S. (2013). Physician review of the iPhone AliveCor ECG heart monitor, the clinical reality of the device. *iMedicalApps + MedPage Today*. Retrieved October 2, 2016 from http://www.imedicalapps.com/2013/03/physician-review-iphone-alivecor-ecg-heart-monitor/

Mishra, D., Gunasekaran, A., Childe, S. J., Papadopoulos, T., Dubey, R., & Wamba, S. (2016). Vision, applications and future challenges of Internet of Things: A bibliometric study of the recent literature. *Industrial Management & Data Systems*, *116*(7), 1331–1355. doi:10.1108/IMDS-11-2015-0478

Montag, C., Duke, É., & Markowetz, A. (2016). Toward Psychoinformatics: Computer science meets psychology. *Computational and Mathematical Methods in Medicine*, *2016*, 1–10. doi:10.1155/2016/2983685 PMID:27403204

Montgomery, B. (2016). *The 10 most terrifying IoT security breaches you aren't aware of (so far)*. Retrieved January 4, 2017, from http://www.iotone.com/guide/the-10-most-terrifying-iot-security-breaches-you-aren-t-aware-of-so-far/g456

Montoya-Weiss, M. M., & Calantone, R. (1994). Determinants of New Product Performance: A Review and Meta-Analysis. *Journal of Product Innovation Management*, *11*(5), 397–417. doi:10.1016/0737-6782(94)90029-9

Moore, J. F. (1993). Predators and prey: A new ecology of competition. *Harvard Business Review*, *71*(3), 75–83. PMID:10126156

Moosavi, R., Gia, N., Nigussie, E., Rahmani, M., Virtanen, S., Tenhunen, H., & Isoaho, J. (2016). End-to-end security scheme for mobility enabled healthcare Internet of Things. *Future Generation Computer Systems*, *64*(C), 108–124. doi:10.1016/j.future.2016.02.020

Morgan-Thomas, A., & Veloutsou, C. (2013). Beyond technology acceptance: Brand relationships and online brand experience. *Journal of Business Research*, *66*(1), 21–27. doi:10.1016/j.jbusres.2011.07.019

Morra, J. (2016). Artificial Intelligence Gets its Head out of the Cloud. *Electronic Design*. Available from http://electronicsofthings.com/expert-opinion/internet-of-artificial-intelligence

Moses, A. (2012). *LG smart fridge tells you what to buy*. Retrieved January 10, 2012 from http://www.smh.com.au/digital-life/hometech/lg-smart-fridge-tells-youwhat-to-buy-cook-and-eat-20120110-1ps9z.html

Moura, J., & Hutchison, D. (2016). Review and analysis of networking challenges in cloud computing. *Journal of Network and Computer Applications*, *60*, 113–129. doi:10.1016/j.jnca.2015.11.015

Mu-Hyun, C. (2016, December 11). *Korean startup prevents fire with the power of IoT*. Retrieved January 4, 2017, from http://www.zdnet.com/article/korean-startup-prevents-fire-with-the-power-of-iot/

Myler, T. (2015, October 22). *How the Internet of Things will impact our productivity*. Retrieved January 4, 2017, from https://www.infoq.com/articles/iot-impact-productivity

Nalepa, G., & Zi, P. (2006). Integrated embedded Prolog platform for rule-based control systems. *Proceedings of the International Conference Mixed Design of Integrated Circuits and System. MIXDES 2006*. doi:10.1109/MIXDES.2006.1706678

Nambi, S. A. U., Sarkar, C., Prasad, R. V., & Rahim, A. (2014, March). A unified semantic knowledge base for IoT. In *Internet of Things (WF-IoT), 2014 IEEE World Forum on* (pp. 575-580). IEEE. doi:10.1109/WF-IoT.2014.6803232

Nashiya, S. (2015). *3D Printing + IoT= Future*. Retrieved Sep 01, 2015 from https://www.fingent.com/blog/3d-printing-iot-the-future

Nativi, J. J., & Lee, S. (2012). Impact of RFID information-sharing strategies on a decentralized supply chain with reverse logistics operations. *International Journal of Production Economics*, *136*(2), 366–377. doi:10.1016/j.ijpe.2011.12.024

Networks, R. (2016). *RadBeacon Dot*. Retrieved June 17, 2016, from http://www.radiusnetworks.com/radbeacon/specs/dot/

Ngai, E. W. T., Cheung, B. K. S., Lam, S. S., & Ng, C. T. (2014). RFID value in aircraft parts supply chains: A case study. *International Journal of Production Economics, 147*(Part B), 330–339. 10.1016/j.ijpe.2012.09.017

Ng, I. C. (2010). The future of pricing and revenue models. *Journal of Revenue and Pricing Management*, *9*(3), 276–281. doi:10.1057/rpm.2010.11

NIBIB. (2017). *What are sensor?* National Institute of Bioimage and Bioengineering. Retrieved 27February 2017 https://www.nibib.nih.gov/science-education/science-topics/sensors

Nickerson, D., & Rogers, T. (2014). Political campaigns and big data. *The Journal of Economic Perspectives*, *28*(2), 51–74. doi:10.1257/jep.28.2.51

Ninemeier, J. D., & Kasavana, M. L. (1986). *Planning and control for food and beverage operations*. Educational Institute of the American Hotel & Motel Association.

Ning, H., & Liu, H. (2015). Cyber-physical-social-thinking space based science and technology framework for the Internet of Things. *Science China Information Sciences*, *58*(3), 1–19. doi:10.1007/s11432-014-5209-2

Ning, H., Liu, H., & Yang, L. T. (2013). Cyberentity security in the Internet of Things. *Computer*, *46*(4), 46–53. doi:10.1109/MC.2013.74

Nistor, N., Gögüs, A., & Lerche, T. (2013). Educational technology acceptance across national and professional cultures: A European study. *Educational Technology Research and Development*, *61*(4), 733–749. doi:10.1007/s11423-013-9292-7

Nitti, M., Pilloni, V., Colistra, G., & Atzori, L. (2016). The virtual object as a major element of the internet of things: A survey. *IEEE Communications Surveys and Tutorials*, *18*(2), 1228–1240. doi:10.1109/COMST.2015.2498304

Nyheim, P. D., McFadden, F. M., & Connolly, D. J. (2005). *Technology strategies for the hospitality industry*. Upper Saddle River, NJ: Prentice Hall.

Odenwald, T. (2007). Putting M2M into Business Context. *M2M Pioneer Magazine, 5*(2).

Ondemir, O., & Gupta, S. M. (2014). Quality management in product recovery using the Internet of Things: An optimization approach. *Computers in Industry*, *65*(3), 491–504. doi:10.1016/j.compind.2013.11.006

Oppliger, R. (2011). Security and privacy in an online world. *Computer*, *44*(9), 21–22. doi:10.1109/MC.2011.292

OPTOMEC. (2016). *Technology*. Retrieved August 03, 2016, from Optomec.com: http://www.optomec.com/Additive-ManufacturingTechnology/Overview

Oronsky, C. R., & Chathoth, P. K. (2007). An exploratory study examining information technology adoption and implementation in full-service restaurant firms. *International Journal of Hospitality Management, 26*(4), 941–956. doi:10.1016/j.ijhm.2006.04.001

Osterwalder, A., & Pigneur, Y. (2010). *Business model generation: A handbook for visionaries, game changers, and challengers*. Wiley.

Osweiler, K. (2013). *IRhythm drives innovation with the internet of things*. Retrieved Dec 4,2013 from https://gigaom.com/2013/12/04/irhythm-drives-innovation-with-the-internet-of-things-2/

Ou, W. M., Abratt, R., & Dion, P. (2006). The influence of retailer reputation on store patronage. *Journal of Retailing and Consumer Services, 13*(3), 221–230. doi:10.1016/j.jretconser.2005.08.014

Ozturk, A. B., & Hancer, M. (2015). The effects of demographics and past experience on RFID technology acceptance in the hospitality industry. *International Journal of Hospitality & Tourism Administration, 16*(3), 275–289. doi:10.1080/15256480.2015.1054756

Pace, P., Aloi, G., Caliciuri, G., & Fortino, G. (2016). A Mission-oriented coordination framework for teams of mobile aerial and terrestrial smart objects. *Mobile Networks and Applications, 21*(4), 708–725. doi:10.1007/s11036-016-0726-4

Pal, S. (2015). How IoT is helping to address chronic disease management. *Electronic Health Reporter*. Retrieved September 20, 2016 from http://electronichealthreporter.com/iot-helping-address-chronic-disease management/#more-11473

Pal, A. (2015). Internet of Things: Making the hype a reality. *IT Professional, 17*(3), 2–4. doi:10.1109/MITP.2015.36

Pang, Z. (2013). *Technologies and architectures of the Internet-of-things (IoT) for health and well-being*. Royal Institute of Technology Stockholm.

Pantano, E., & Timmermans, H. (2014). What is smart for retailing? *Procedia Environmental Sciences, 22*, 101–107. doi:10.1016/j.proenv.2014.11.010

Papagiannidis, S., Pantano, E., See-To, E. W., & Bourlakis, M. (2013). Modelling the determinants of a simulated experience in a virtual retail store and users product purchasing intentions. *Journal of Marketing Management, 29*(13-14), 1462–1492. doi:10.1080/0267257X.2013.821150

Paradiso, M. (2010). Google and the Internet: A Mega-Project Nesting Within Another Mega-Project. *Engineering Earth*, 49-65. doi:10.1007/978-90-481-9920-4_4

Park, J., Gunn, F., Lee, Y., & Shim, S. (2015). Consumer acceptance of a revolutionary technology-driven product: The role of adoption in the industrial design development. *Journal of Retailing and Consumer Services, 26*, 115–124. doi:10.1016/j.jretconser.2015.05.003

Patel, P., Pathak, A., Teixeira, T., & Issarny, V. (2011, December). Towards application development for the internet of things. In *Proceedings of the 8th Middleware Doctoral Symposium* (p. 5). ACM. doi:10.1145/2093190.2093195

Patnayakuni, R., Rai, A., & Seth, N. (2006). Relational antecedents of information flow integration for supply chain coordination. *Journal of Management Information Systems, 23*(1), 13–49. doi:10.2753/MIS0742-1222230101

Pavlou, P. A. (2003). Consumer acceptance of electronic commerce: Integrating trust and risk with the technology acceptance model. *International Journal of Electronic Commerce, 7*(3), 101–134.

Pavlou, P. A. (2003). Consumer acceptance of electronic commerce: Integrating trust and risk with the Technology Acceptance Model. *International Journal of Electronic Commerce, 7*(3), 101–134.

Peppet, S. (2014). Regulating the Internet of things: First steps toward managing discrimination, privacy, security, and consent. *Texas Law Review*, *93*(1), 85–176.

Perera, C., Ranjan, R., Wang, L., Khan, S. U., & Zomaya, A. Y. (2015). Big data privacy in the Internet of Things era. *IEEE IT Professional Magazine*, *17*(3), 32–39. doi:10.1109/MITP.2015.34

Perera, C., Zaslavsky, A., Christen, P., & Georgakopoulos, D. (2014). Context aware computing for the internet of things: A survey. *IEEE Communications Surveys and Tutorials*, *16*(1), 414–454. doi:10.1109/SURV.2013.042313.00197

Perera, C., Zaslavsky, A., Christen, P., & Georgakopoulos, D. (2014). Sensing as a Service Model for Smart Cities Supported by Internet of Things. *Transactions on Emerging Telecommunications Technologies*, *25*(1), 81–93. doi:10.1002/ett.2704

Pering, T., Agarwal, Y., Gupta, R., & Want, R. (2006, June). Coolspots: reducing the power consumption of wireless mobile devices with multiple radio interfaces. In *Proceedings of the 4th international conference on Mobile systems, applications and services* (pp. 220-232). ACM. doi:10.1145/1134680.1134704

Petersen, K. J., Ragatz, G. L., & Monczka, R. M. (2005). An examination of collaborative planning effectiveness and supply chain performance. *Journal of Supply Chain Management*, *41*(2), 14–25. doi:10.1111/j.1055-6001.2005.04102002.x

Pfeiffer, D. U., & Stevens, K. B. (2015). Spatial and temporal epidemiological analysis in the big data era. *Preventive Veterinary Medicine*, *122*(1-2), 213–220. doi:10.1016/j.prevetmed.2015.05.012 PMID:26092722

Pfitzmann, A., & Kohntopp, M. (2000). Anonymity, unobservability, and pseudonymity - A proposal for terminology. *International Workshop on Design Issues in Anonymity and Unobservability*, 1-9. doi:10.1007/3-540-44702-4_1

Ping, L., Liu, Q., Zhou, Z., & Wang, H. (2011). Agile supply chain management over the Internet of Things. *2011 International Conference on Management and Service Science (MASS)*, 1-4. doi:10.1109/ICMSS.2011.5998440

Podsakoff, P. M., MacKenzie, S. B., Lee, J. Y., & Podsakoff, N. P. (2003). Common method biases in behavioral research: A critical review of the literature and recommended remedies. *The Journal of Applied Psychology*, *88*(5), 879–903. doi:10.1037/0021-9010.88.5.879 PMID:14516251

Polonetsky, J., & Wolf, C. (2014). *RE – Spring Privacy Series: Mobile Device Tracking, PROJECT NO. P145401*. Retrieved from https://fpf.org/wp-content/uploads/Comments-of-the-Future-of-Privacy-Forum-on-Mobile-Device-Tracking.pdf

Poniszewska-Maranda, A., & Kaczmare, D. (2015). Selected methods of artificial intelligence for Internet of Things conception. *Proceedings of the Federated Conference on Computer Science and Information Systems*, 1343–1348. doi:10.15439/2015F161

Pookulangara, S., & Koesler, K. (2011). Cultural influence on consumers usage of social networks and its impact on online purchase intentions. *Journal of Retailing and Consumer Services*, *18*(4), 348–354. doi:10.1016/j.jretconser.2011.03.003

Popescul, D., & Radu, D. (2016). Data security in smart cities: challenges and solutions. *Informatica Economica, 20*(1). Retrieved September 15, 2016 http://dx.doi.org.libproxy.uml.edu/10.12948/issn14531305/20.1.2016.03

Porter, M. E., & Heppelmann, J. E. (2014). *How Smart, Connected Products Are Transforming Companies*. Retrieved August 24, 2016, from https://hbr.org/2014/11/how-smart-connected-products-are-transforming-competition

Porter, C. E., & Donthu, N. (2006). Using the Technology Acceptance Model to explain how attitudes determine Internet usage: The role of perceived access barriers and demographics. *Journal of Business Research*, *59*(9), 999–1007. doi:10.1016/j.jbusres.2006.06.003

Porter, M. E., & Heppelmann, J. E. (2014). How smart, connected products are transforming competition. *Harvard Business Review*, *92*(11), 64–88.

Pramatari, K. (2007). Collaborative supply chain practices and evolving technological approaches. *Supply Chain Management: An International Journal*, *12*(3), 210–220. doi:10.1108/13598540710742527

Prayoga, T., & Abraham, J. (2016). Behavioral intention to use IoT health device: The role of perceived usefulness, facilitated appropriation, Big Five personality traits, and cultural value orientations. [IJECE]. *Iranian Journal of Electrical and Computer Engineering*, *6*(4), 1751–1765. doi:10.11591/ijece.v6i4.10546

Privat, G. (2012). Extending the Internet of Things. *Communications & Stratégies*, (87): 101.

Priya, R. V., Vadivel, A., & Thakur, S. (2012). Maximal pattern mining using fast CP-Tree for knowledge discovery. *International Journal of Information Systems and Social Change*, *3*(1), 56–74. doi:10.4018/jissc.2012010106

Purcell, B. M. (2013). *Big data using cloud computing*. Holy Family University Working Paper.

Purwaningsih, A. (2015). Analysis of customer mindset change and accounting practice of garbage bank as medium of edupreneurship. *International Journal of Monetary Economics and Finance*, *8*(4), 332–344. doi:10.1504/IJMEF.2015.073228

Qazi, A., Raj, R. G., Tahir, M., Waheed, M., Khan, S. U. R., & Abraham, A. (2015). Corrigendum to "A preliminary investigation of user perception and behavioral intention for different review types: Customers and designers Perspective". *The Scientific World Journal*, *1–2*. doi:10.1155/2015/258150 PMID:25945359

Quek, C. (2016, May 16). *5 innovative made-in-Singapore IoT solutions to improve labour productivity*. Retrieved January 4, 2017, from https://www.techinasia.com/talk/madeinsingapore-iot-solutions-improve-labour-productivity

Rainie, L., & Wellman, B. (2012). *Networked: the new social operating system*. Cambridge, MA: The MIT Press.

Ramakrishnan, R., Gaur, L., & Singh, G. (2016). Feasibility and Efficacy of BLE Beacon IoT Devices in Inventory Management at the Shop Floor. *International Journal of Electrical and Computer Engineering, 6*(6). Retrieved from http://iaesjournal.com/online/index.php/IJECE/article/view/10807

Ramakrishnan, R., & Gaur, L. (2016, Jan 21). Smart electricity distribution in residential areas: Internet of Things (IoT) based advanced metering infrastructure and cloud analytics. *International Conference on Internet of Things and Applications (IOTA)*. doi:10.1109/IOTA.2016.7562693

Reaidy, P. J., Gunasekaran, A., & Spalanzani, A. (2015). Bottom-up approach based on Internet of Things for order fulfillment in a collaborative warehousing environment. *International Journal of Production Economics*, *159*, 29–40. doi:10.1016/j.ijpe.2014.02.017

Rehiman, R. K., & Veni, S. (2015). Security, Privacy and Trust for Smart Mobile devices in Internet of Things. *International Journal of Advanced Research in Computer Engineering & Technology*, *4*(5), 1775-1779.

Reinartz, W., Dellaert, B., Krafft, M., Kumar, V., & Varadarajan, R. (2011). Retailing innovations in a globalizing retail market environment. *Journal of Retailing*, *87*, S53–S66. doi:10.1016/j.jretai.2011.04.009

Rcn, J., Li, Y., & Li, T. (2009). Routing-Based Source-Location Privacy in Wireless Sensor Networks. *IEEE International Conference on Communications*, 1-5. Doi:10.1109/ICC.2009.5199430

Ren, L., Zhang, L., Tao, F., Zhang, X., Luo, Y., & Zhang, Y. (2012). A methodology towards virtualisation-based high performance simulation platform supporting multidisciplinary design of complex products. *Enterprise Information Systems*, *6*(3), 267–290. doi:10.1080/17517575.2011.592598

Research and Markets. (2015). *Retail IoT Market Growth & Forecast 2015 to 2020*. Retrieved from http://www.marketsandmarketsblog.com/retail-iot-market.html

Research and Markets. (2016). *Business Report 2016-2022: Intelligent, Digitized & Automated Smart Factories to Transform the Manufacturing Industry - Research and Markets*. Retrieved September 15, 2016 from http://www.researchandmarkets.com/research/s2dt9h/smart_factory

Rex, D., & Stoli, S. (2014). *Application of 3D laser scanning in a Production Environment*. Retrieved Jan 21, 2014 from http://publications.lib.chalmers.se/records/fulltext/202372/202372.pdf

Rey-Martí, A., Ribeiro-Soriano, D., & Sánchez-García, J. L. (2016). Giving back to society: Job creation through social entrepreneurship. *Journal of Business Research*, *69*(6), 2067–2072. doi:10.1016/j.jbusres.2015.12.010

Reynolds, D., Merritt, E. A., & Pinckney, S. (2005). Understanding Menu Psychology. *International Journal of Hospitality & Tourism Administration*, *6*(1), 1–9. doi:10.1300/J149v06n01_01

Ricardo, B. (2013). *Coca-Cola shows off the untapped potential for 3D printing in advertising*. Retrieved August 20,2013 from http://venturebeat.com/2013/08/20/coca-cola-3d-printing/

Riemer, K., & Johnston, R. B. (2012). Place-making: A phenomenological theory of technology appropriation. *Proceedings of the 33rd International Conference on Information Systems - ICIS 2012* (pp. 1-19). Orlando, FL: Association for Information Systems. Retrieved January 4, 2017, from http://aisel.aisnet.org/icis2012/proceedings/SocialImpacts/5/

Riemer, K., Overfeld, P., Scifleet, P., & Richter, A. (2012). Eliciting the anatomy of technology appropriation processes: A case study in enterprise social media. *Proceedings of the 20th European Conference on Information Systems – ECIS 2012*. Barcelona, Spain: Association for Information Systems. Retrieved January 4, 2017, from http://aisel.aisnet.org/ecis2012/134/

Rishikesha, T. K., & Ganesh, N. P. (1999). *Creating Successful New Products: Challenges for Indian Industry*. Retrieved July 31, 1999 from http://www.iimb.ernet.in/~rishi/epwcsnp.pdf

Rogers, E. M. (1995). *Diffusion of innovations* (4th ed.). New York: The Free Press.

Roman, R., Najera, P., & Lopez, J. (2011). Securing the Internet of Things. *Computer*, *44*(9), 51–58. doi:10.1109/MC.2011.291

Roman, R., Zhou, J., & Lopez, J. (2013). On the features and challenges of security and privacy in distributed internet of things. *Computer Networks*, *57*(10), 2266–2279. doi:10.1016/j.comnet.2012.12.018

Rose, K., Eldridge, S., & Chapin, L. (2015). *The Internet of Things: An Overview Understanding the Issues and Challenges of a More Connected World*. ISOC.

Rosenthal, D. M. (2011, July). Forthcoming in. *New York*, 1–22.

Roubtsova, E., & Michell, V. (2013). A method for modeling of KPIs enabling validation of their properties. In *Proceedings of the 5th ACM SIGCHI Annual International Workshop on Behaviour Modelling-Foundations and Applications* (p. 3). ACM. doi:10.1145/2492437.2492440

Rowley, M. J. (2016). How the Internet of Things is aiding the garbage crisis. *The network Cisco's Technology News Site*. Retrieved October 5, 2016 from https://newsroom.cisco.com/feature-content?articleId=1757267

Ruta, M., Scioscia, F., Loseto, G., Gramegna, F., Pinto, A., Ieva, S., & Di Sciascio, E. (2012). A logic-based CoAP extension for resource discovery in semantic sensor networks. *SSN'12 Proceedings of the 5th International Conference on Semantic Sensor Networks, 904,* 17-32.

Ryan, T. (2016). *Would 'driveless' carts enhance shopping in stores?* Retrieved from http://www.retailwire.com/discussion/would-driverless-carts-enhance-shopping-in-stores/

Ryan, J. T. (2008). *Document-management systems offer efficiency, save paper*. Central Penn Business Journal.

Ryan, N., Pascoe, J., & Morse, D. (1999). Enhanced reality fieldwork: The context aware archaeological assistant. *Bar International Series*, *750*, 269–274.

Ryu, C. (2015). IoT-based intelligent for fire emergency response systems. *International Journal of Smart Home*, *9*(3), 161–168. doi:10.14257/ijsh.2015.9.3.15

Saaty, T. L. (1990). How to make a decision: The analytic hierarchy process. *European Journal of Operational Research*, *48*(1), 9–26. doi:10.1016/0377-2217(90)90057-I

Santos, A., Macedo, J., Costa, A., & Nicolau, M. J. (2014). Internet of things and smart objects for M-health monitoring and control. *Procedia Technology*, *16*, 1351–1360. doi:10.1016/j.protcy.2014.10.152

SAP SE. (2014). *CEO Perspective: The Internet of Things for Utilities, Top Priorities to Build a Successful Strategy*. Retrieved from https://www.sap.com/bin/sapcom/ko_kr/downloadasset.2014-10-oct-28-03.ceo-perspective-the-internet-of-things-for-utilities-pdf.html

SAP SE. (2014). *SAP Solutions for the Internet of Things – Built for Your Business*. Author.

Sarma, S., Brock, D. L., & Ashton, K. (2000). *The networked physical world*. Auto-ID Center White Paper MIT-AUTOID-WH-001.

Sartori, M., (2016). *Integration of an IEEE802.15.4g compliant transceiver into the Linux-based AMBER platform*. Universit`a degli studi di Padova.

Schepers, J., & Wetzels, M. (2007). A meta-analysis of the technology acceptance model: Investigating subjective norm and moderation effects. *Information & Management*, *44*(1), 90–103. doi:10.1016/j.im.2006.10.007

Schilit, B., & Theimer, M. (1994). Disseminating active map information to mobile hosts. *IEEE Network*, *8*(5), 22–32. doi:10.1109/65.313011

Schumacher, A., Erol, S., & Sihn, W. (2016). A maturity model for assessing industry 4.0 readiness and maturity of manufacturing enterprises. *Procedia CIRP*, *52*, 161–166. doi:10.1016/j.procir.2016.07.040

Shapley, D. (2012). *15 Facts About the Paper Industry, Global Warming and the Environment and What You Can Do About It*. The Daily Green.

Sheldon, P. (2016). Facebook friend request: Applying the theory of reasoned action to student-teacher relationships on Facebook. *Journal of Broadcasting & Electronic Media*, *60*(2), 269–285. doi:10.1080/08838151.2016.1164167

Shepherd, D. A., Covin, J. G., & Kuratko, D. F. (2009). Project failure from corporate entrepreneurship: Managing the grief process. *Journal of Business Venturing*, *24*(6), 588–600. doi:10.1016/j.jbusvent.2008.01.009

Shin, S., & Eksioglu, B. (2015). An empirical study of RFID productivity in the U.S. retail supply chain. *International Journal of Production Economics*, *163*, 89–96. doi:10.1016/j.ijpe.2015.02.016

Shin, T. H., Chin, S., Yoon, S. W., & Kwon, S. W. (2011). A service-oriented integrated information framework for RFID/WSN-based intelligent construction supply chain management. *Automation in Construction*, *20*(6), 706–715. doi:10.1016/j.autcon.2010.12.002

Shirey, R. (2000). *RFC 2828 Internet Security Glossary*. Retrieved May 10, 2016 from https:// www. ietf. Org /rfc/rfc2828.txt

Siau, K., Sheng, H., Nah, F., & Davis, S. (2004). A qualitative investigation on consumer trust in mobile commerce. *International Journal of Electronic Business*, *2*(3), 283–300. doi:10.1504/IJEB.2004.005143

Singh, D., Tripathi, G., & Jara, A. J. (2014). A survey of Internet-of-Things: Future vision, architecture, challenges and services. *2014 IEEE World Forum on Internet of Things (WF-IoT).*

Slade, E. L., Dwivedi, Y. K., Piercy, N. C., & Williams, M. D. (2015). Modeling consumers adoption intentions of remote mobile payments in the United Kingdom: Extending UTAUT with innovativeness, risk, and trust. *Psychology and Marketing*, *32*(8), 860–873. doi:10.1002/mar.20823

Soni, P. K., Gary, L. L., & David, T. W. (1993). Industrial Innovation and Firm Performance: A Re-conceptualization and Exploratory Structural Equation Analysis. *International Journal of Research in Marketing*, *10*(1), 365–380. doi:10.1016/0167-8116(93)90019-U

Soper, D. S. (2014). *A-priori sample size calculator for structural equation models* [software]. Available from http://www.danielsoper.com/statcalc

Sousa Nunes, D. S., Zhang, P., & Sa Silva, J. (2015). A survey on human-in-the-loop applications towards an Internet of all. *IEEE Communications Surveys and Tutorials*, *17*(2), 944–965. doi:10.1109/COMST.2015.2398816

Spanjol, J., Tam, L., & Tam, V. (2015). Employer-employee congruence in environmental values: An exploration of effects on job satisfaction and creativity. *Journal of Business Ethics*, *130*(1), 117–130. doi:10.1007/s10551-014-2208-6

Spiess, P., & Karnouskos, S. (2007, July). Maximizing the business value of networked embedded systems through process-level integration into enterprise software. In *Pervasive Computing and Applications, 2007. ICPCA 2007. 2nd International Conference on* (pp. 536-541). IEEE.

Staff, J. (2014). *Transforming 3D Printing Using Recycled Plastic Bottles.* Retrieved Jun 17, 2014 from http://www.coca-colacompany.com/stories/ekocycle-transforming-3d-printing-using-recycled-plastic-bottles

Stankovic, J.A., (2008). When Sensor and Actuator Networks Cover the World. *ETRI Journal, 30*(5), 627-633.

Starner, T. (2015, November 4). *How the Internet of Things will affect the workplace.* Retrieved January 4, 2017, from http://www.hrdive.com/news/how-the-internet-of-things-will-affect-the-workplace/408593/

Statista. (2016). *Revenue of the Internet of Things in Japan from 2013 to 2020 (in billion U.S. dollars).* Last access at http://www.statista.com/statistics/512254/iot-revenue-japan

Steers, R. M., Meyer, A. D., & Sanchez-Runde, C. J. (2008). National culture and the adoption of new technologies. *Journal of World Business*, *43*(3), 255–260. doi:10.1016/j.jwb.2008.03.007

Streetline Inc. (2013). Retrieved Jan 10, 2013 from http://www.prnewswire.com/news-releases/streetline-closes-25m-financing-to-enable-internet-of-things-for-smart-cities-186319301.html

Stringer, J. (2011). *Protecting personally identifiable information: What data is at risk and what you can do about it.* A Sophos White Paper.

Sue, P. (2016). The Atj Report. *American Journal of Transplantation.* Retrieved Sep 10, 2016 from http://onlinelibrary.wiley.com/doi/10.1111/ajt.2016.16.issue-5/issuetoc

Suki, N. M., & Suki, N. M. (2011). Exploring the relationship between perceived usefulness, perceived ease of use, perceived enjoyment, attitude and subscribers' intention towards using 3G mobile services. *Journal of Information Technology Management*, *22*(1), 1–7. Retrieved from http://jitm.ubalt.edu/XXII-1/article1.pdf

Sullivan, B., & Thompson, H. (2013). Brain, interrupted. *New York Times, 3.*

Sun, C. (2012). Application of RFID Technology for Logistics on Internet of Things. *AASRI Procedia*, *1*, 106–111. doi:10.1016/j.aasri.2012.06.019

Sundmaeker, H., Guillemin, P., Friess, P., & Woelfflé, S. (2010). *Vision and challenges for realising the Internet of Things, CERP-IoT – Cluster of European Research Projects on the Internet of Things*. Retrieved August 16, 2014 from http://www.researchgate.net/publication/228664767_Vision_and_challenges_for_realising_the_Internet_of_Things

Sundmaeker, H., Guillemin, P., Friess, P., & Woelfflé, S. (2010). *Vision and challenges for realising the Internet of Things. In Cluster of European Research Projects on the Internet of Things*. European Commision.

Sundmaeker, H., Guillemin, P., Friess, P., & Woelfflé, S. (2010). *Vision and challenges for realizing the Internet of Things. Cluster of European Research Projects on the Internet of Things*. European Commision.

Sundmaeker, H., Guillemin, P., Friess, P., & Woelffle, S. (Eds.). (2010). *Vision and challenges for realizing the Internet of things*. European Commission Information Society and Media.

Swan, M. (2012). Sensor mania! the internet of things, wearable computing, objective metrics, and the quantified self 2.0. *Journal of Sensor and Actuator Networks, 1*(3), 217–253. doi:10.3390/jsan1030217

Swartz, J. J., Braxton, D., & Viera, A. J. (2011). Calorie menu labeling on quick-service restaurant menus: An updated systematic review of the literature. *Int J Behav Nutr Phys Act International Journal of Behavioral Nutrition and Physical Activity, 8*(1), 135. doi:10.1186/1479-5868-8-135 PMID:22152038

Swedberg, C. (2013). Trane Restocks Supplies at Assembly Plant Via RFID. *RFID Journal*. Retrieved online Jul 23, 2013 from http://www.rfidjournal.com/articles/view?10851

Szczerba, R. J. (2015). *No Donor Required: 5 Body Parts You Can Make With 3-D Printers*. Retrieved Jun 17, 2015 from http://www.forbes.com/sites/robertszczerba/2015/06/17/no-donor-required-5-body-parts-you-can-make-with-3-d-printers-2/#7f2b96094a3b

Tajer, S., Poor, H. V., & Cui, S. (2011). Distributed Joint Cyber Attack Detection and State Recovery in Smart Grids. *IEEE International Conference on Smart Grid Communications*, 202-207. doi:10.1109/SmartGridComm.2011.6102319

Tan, L., & Wang, N. (2010, August). Future internet: The internet of things. In *2010 3rd International Conference on Advanced Computer Theory and Engineering (ICACTE)* (Vol. 5, pp. V5-376). IEEE.

Tanwar, S., & Prema, K.V. (2012). Solution to PKI Inter- Domain Interoperability Issue. *International Journal of Scientific and Engineering Research.*

Tan, Y., Lee, K., Khor, Z., Goh, K., Tan, K., & Lew, B. (2010). Automated Food Ordering System with Interactive User Interface approach. *2010 IEEE Conference on Robotics, Automation and Mechatronics*. doi:10.1109/ramech.2010.5513147

Tao, F., LaiLi, Y., Xu, L., & Zhang, L. (2013). FC-PACO-RM: a parallel method for service composition optimal-selection in cloud manufacturing system. *IEEE Transactions on Industrial Informatics, 9*(4), 2023-2033.

Tao, F., Zuo, Y., Xu, L. D., & Zhang, L. (2014). IoT based intelligent perception and access of manufacturing resource towards cloud manufacturing. *IEEE Transactions on Industrial Informatics, 10*(2), 1547–1557. doi:10.1109/TII.2014.2306397

Tao, F., Zuo, Y., Xu, L., & Lv, L. (2014). Internet of Things and BOM based life cycle assessment of energy-saving and emission-reduction of product. *IEEE Transactions on Industrial Informatics, 10*(2), 1252–1261. doi:10.1109/TII.2014.2306771

TCS. (2016). *Enterprise Insights*. Last access at http://sites.tcs.com/blogs/enterpriseinsights/establishing-iot-strategy

The Networked Economy. (2014). *Revolution in Progress: in MIT Technology Review*. Retrieved February 1, 2016, from: https://s3.amazonaws.com/files.technologyreview.com/p/pub/campaign/sap/2014/SAP_Networked_Economy.pdf

Thiesse, F., Al-Kassab, J., & Fleisch, E. (2009). Understanding the value of integrated RFID systems: A case study from apparel retail. *European Journal of Information Systems*, *18*(6), 592–614. doi:10.1057/ejis.2009.33

Thiesse, F., & Buckel, T. (2015). A comparison of RFID-based shelf replenishment policies in retail stores under suboptimal read rates. *International Journal of Production Economics*, *159*, 126–136. doi:10.1016/j.ijpe.2014.09.002

Thiesse, F., & Köhler, M. (2008). An Analysis of Usage-Based Pricing Policies for Smart Products. *Electronic Markets*, *18*(3), 232–241. doi:10.1080/10196780802265751

Thompson, T. (2008). Less Paper. *Trumps Paperless. Health Management Technology*, 42–43. PMID:18524167

Thramboulidis, K. (2015). A cyber-physical system-based approach for industrial automation systems. *Computers in Industry*, *72*(C), 92–102. doi:10.1016/j.compind.2015.04.006

Tischler, L. (2011). *Intel's virtual footwear wall for Adidas turns boutiques into shoe-topias*. Retrieved from http://www.fastcompany.com/1715933/intels-virtual-footwear-wall-adidas-turns-boutiques-shoe-topias-video

Toma, I., Simperl, E., & Hench, G. (2009, June). A joint roadmap for semantic technologies and the internet of things. *Proceedings of the Third STI Roadmapping Workshop*, 1.

Townsend, K. (2016, December 6). *Examine data collection problems with big data, IoT in mind*. Retrieved January 4, 2017, from http://searchdatacenter.techtarget.com/feature/Examine-data-collection-problems-with-big-data-IoT-in-mind

Tsai, C.-W., Lai, C.-F., Chiang, M.-C., & Yang, L. T. (2014). Data mining for Internet of Things: A survey. *IEEE Communications Surveys and Tutorials*, *16*(1), 77–97. doi:10.1109/SURV.2013.103013.00206

Tsiatsis, V., Gluhak, A., Bauge, T., Montagut, F., Bernat, J., Bauer, M., . . . Krco, S. (2010). *The SENSEI Real World Internet Architecture*. Paper presented at the Future Internet Assembly.

Turk, T., & Trkman, P. (2012). Bass model estimates for broadband diffusion in European countries. *Technological Forecasting and Social Change*, *79*(1), 85–96. doi:10.1016/j.techfore.2011.06.010

Uckelmann, D., Harrison, M., & Michahelles, F. (2011). *An Architectural Approach Towards the Future Internet of Things*. <ALIGNMENT.qj></ALIGNMENT>10.1007/978-3-642-19157-2

Uckelmann, D., Harrison, M., & Michahelles, F. (2011). An architectural approach towards the future internet of things. In *Architecting the internet of things* (pp. 1–24). Springer Berlin Heidelberg. doi:10.1007/978-3-642-19157-2_1

Uckelmann, D., Harrison, M., & Michahelles, F. (Eds.). (2011). *Architecting the Internet of Things*. Springer-Verlag Berlin Heidelberg. doi:10.1007/978-3-642-19157-2

Umar, A. (2005). IT infrastructure to enable next generation enterprises. *Information Systems Frontiers*, *7*(3), 217–256. doi:10.1007/s10796-005-2768-1

Upadhyay, P., & Jahanyan, S. (2016). Analyzing user perspective on the factors affecting use intention of mobile based transfer payment. *Internet Research*, *26*(1), 38–56. doi:10.1108/IntR-05-2014-0143

Ustundag, A., & Tanyas, M. (2009). The impacts of Radio Frequency Identification (RFID) technology on supply chain costs. *Transportation Research Part E, Logistics and Transportation Review*, *45*(1), 29–38. doi:10.1016/j.tre.2008.09.001

Vaidya, O. S., & Kumar, S. (2006). Analytic hierarchy process: An overview of applications. *European Journal of Operational Research*, *169*(1), 1–29. doi:10.1016/j.ejor.2004.04.028

Van Harmelen, F., Lifschitz, V., & Porter, B. (Eds.). (2008). *Handbook of knowledge representation* (Vol. 1). Elsevier.

van Kranenburg, R., Anzelmo, E., Bassi, A., Caprio, D., Dodson, S., & Ratto, M. (2011). The internet of things. A critique of ambient technology and the all-seeing network of RFID. *Network Notebooks, 2*.

van Kranenburg, R. (2007). *The Internet of Things: A Critique of Ambient Technology and the All-Seeing Network of RFID*. Amsterdam, The Netherlands: Institute of Network Cultures.

Vandoninck, S., dHaenens, L., & Roe, K. (2013). Online risks. *Journal of Children and Media*, *7*(1), 60–78. doi:10.1080/17482798.2012.739780

Vanian, J. (2015). Cisco's CEO: The Internet of things is real (and confusing). *Fortune*. Retrieved September 15, 2016 from http://fortune.com/2015/10/05/cisco-chuck-robbins-Internet/

Varian, H. (2007, February 8). Kaizen, that continuous improvement strategy, finds its ideal environment. *New York Times*.

Varian, H. (2014). Big Data: New tricks for econometrics. *The Journal of Economic Perspectives*, *28*(2), 3–28. doi:10.1257/jep.28.2.3

Vasilomanolakis, E., Daubert, J., Luthra, M., Gazis, V., Wiesmaier, A., & Kikiras, P. (2015). On the Security and Privacy of Internet of Things: Architectures and Systems. *International Workshop on Secure Internet of Things (SLOT)*, 49-57. doi:10.1109/SIOT.2015.9

Vasseur, J. P., & Dunkels, A. (2008). *Ip for smart objects*. IPSO Alliance, White paper, 1.

Venkatesh, V., & Davis, F. D. (2000). A theoretical extension of the technology acceptance model: Four longitudinal field studies. *Management Science*, *46*(2), 186–204. doi:10.1287/mnsc.46.2.186.11926

Venkatesh, V., Morris, M. G., Davis, G. B., & Davis, F. D. (2003). User acceptance of information technology: Toward a unified view. *Management Information Systems Quarterly*, *27*(3), 425–478.

Venkatesh, V., Thong, J. Y. L., & Xu, X. (2012). Consumer acceptance and use of information technology: Extending the unified theory of acceptance and use of technology. *Management Information Systems Quarterly*, *36*(1), 157–178.

Ventola, C. L. (2014). *Medical Applications for 3D Printing: Current and Projected Uses*. Retrieved Oct 2014 from https://www.ncbi.nlm.nih.gov/pmc/articles/PMC4189697/

Verdouw, C. N., Beulens, A. J. M., & van der Vorst, J. G. A. J. (2013). Virtualisation of floricultural supply chains: A review from an internet of things perspective. *Computers and Electronics in Agriculture*, *99*, 160–175. doi:10.1016/j.compag.2013.09.006

Verdouw, C. N., Wolfert, J., Beulens, A. J. M., & Rialland, A. (2015). Virtualization of food supply chains with the internet of things. *Journal of Food Engineering*, *176*, 128–136. doi:10.1016/j.jfoodeng.2015.11.009

Vermesan, O., & Friess, P. (2013). *Internet of Things: From Research and Innovation to Market Deployment*. River Publishers.

Vermesan, O., & Friess, P. (Eds.). (2014). *Internet of Things- from research and innovation to market deployment*. River Publishers.

Vermesan, O., Friess, P., Guillemin, P., Gusmeroli, S., Sundmaeker, H., Bassi, A., & Doody, P. et al. (2011). Internet of Things Strategic Research Roadmap. In O. Vermesan & P. Friess (Eds.), *Internet of Things - Global Technological and Societal Trends*. River Publishers.

Vermesan, O., Friess, P., Guillemin, P., Gusmeroli, S., Sundmaeker, H., Bassi, A., & Doody, P. (2011). Internet of things strategic research roadmap. Internet of Things: *Global Technological and Societal Trends*, *1*, 9-52.

Vermesan, O., Friess, P., Guillemin, P., Gusmeroli, S., Sundmaker, H., Bassi, A., & Doody, P. et al. (2011). *Internet of Things Strategic Research Roadmap*. Aalborg, Denmark: River Publishers.

Versel, N. (2011). *Bosch Healthcare chief is bullish on Telehealth-enabled care management.* Retrieved September 15, 2011 from http://www.mobihealthnews.com/13245/bosch-healthcare-chief-is-bullish-on-telehealth-enabled-care-management

Vidal, M., Vidal-García, J., & Hernandez Barros, R. (2016). Big data and business decision-making. In M. K. Singh & K. G. Dileep (Eds.), *Effective big data management and opportunities for implementation* (pp. 140–157). Hershey, PA: IGI Global.

Virkki, J., & Chen, L. (2013). Personal Perspectives: Individual Privacy in the IOT. *Advances in Internet of Things*. doi:10.4236/ait.2013.32003

*Vision and Challenges for Realising the Internet of Things*. (2010). European Union.

Vlachos, I. P. (2014). A hierarchical model of the impact of RFID practices on retail supply chain performance. *Expert Systems with Applications*, *41*(1), 5–15. doi:10.1016/j.eswa.2013.07.006

Volpe, J. (2011). *SK Telecom's Smart Cart syncs to phones, reminds you to buy milk.* Retrieved from https://www.engadget.com/2011/07/27/sk-telecoms-smart-cart-syncs-to-phones-reminds-you-to-buy-milk/

VoucherCloud News. (2015, April 5). *Every day big data statistics – 2.5 quintillion bytes of data created daily.* Retrieved January 4, 2017, from http://www.vcloudnews.com/every-day-big-data-statistics-2-5-quintillion-bytes-of-data-created-daily/

Vyas, D. A., Bhatt, D., & Jha, D. (2016). IoT: Trends, Challenges and Future Scope. *International Journal of Computer Science & Communication*, *7*(1), 186–197. doi:10.090592/IJCSC.2016.028

Vyas, D., & Dix, A. (2007). Artefact ecologies: Supporting embodied meeting practices with distance access. *Proceedings of UbiComp*, *2007*, 117–122.

Wang, X., & Liu, N. (2014). The application of internet of things in agricultural means of production supply chain management. *Advanced Materials Research, 926–930*(7), 4118–4121. http://doi.org/<ALIGNMENT.qj></ALIGNMENT>10.4028/www.scientific.net/AMR.926-930.4118

Wang, D., Li, X. R., & Li, Y. (2013). Chinas smart tourism destination initiative: A taste of the service-dominant logic. *Journal of Destination Marketing & Management*, *2*(2), 59–61. doi:10.1016/j.jdmm.2013.05.004

Wang, H., Zhang, T., Quan, Y., & Dong, R. (2013). Research on the framework of the Environmental Internet of Things. *International Journal of Sustainable Development and World Ecology*, *20*(3), 199–204. doi:10.1080/13504509.2013.783517

Wang, L., Da Xu, L., Bi, Z., & Xu, Y. (2014). Data cleaning for RFID and WSN integration. *IEEE Transactions on Industrial Informatics*, *10*(1), 408–418. doi:10.1109/TII.2013.2250510

Wang, S. J., Wang, W. L., Huang, C. T., & Chen, S. C. (2011). Improving inventory effectiveness in RFID-enabled global supply chain with Grey forecasting model. *The Journal of Strategic Information Systems*, *20*(3), 307–322. doi:10.1016/j.jsis.2011.03.003

Wang, W. T., & Li, H. M. (2012). Factors influencing mobile services adoption: A brand-equity perspective. *Internet Research*, *22*(2), 142–179. doi:10.1108/10662241211214548

Wang, Y., & Qualls, W. (2007). Towards a theoretical model of technology adoption in hospitality organizations. *International Journal of Hospitality Management*, *26*(3), 560–573. doi:10.1016/j.ijhm.2006.03.008

Wang, Y., & Wen, Q. (2011). A privacy enhanced dns scheme for the internet of things. *International Conference on Communication Technology and Application, ICCTA 2011*, 699-702. doi:10.1049/cp.2011.0758

Wan, J., & Jones, J. (2013). Managing IT service management implementation complexity: From the perspective of the Warfield version of systems science. *Enterprise Information Systems*, *7*(4), 490–522. doi:10.1080/17517575.2011.625572

Want, R., Schilit, B. N., & Jenson, S. (2015). Enabling the Internet of things. *Computer*, *48*(1), 28–35. doi:10.1109/MC.2015.12

Warell, A. V. (1999, September). Introducing a use perspective in product design theory and methodology. *Proceedings of the 1999 ASME Design Engineering Technical Conferences, DETC99/DTM-8782.*

Weber, J. (2016). *3D Printing is poised to bring haute couture into the home*. Retrieved April 15, 2016 from http://www.bloomberg.com/news/articles/2016-04-15/3d-printing-is-poised-to-bring-haute-couture-into-the-home

Weber, R. H. (2009). Internet of things–Need for a new legal environment?. *Computer Law & Security Review, 25*(6), 522-527.

Weber, R. H. (2009). Internet of things–Need for a new legal environment? *Computer Law & Security Report*, *25*(6), 522–527. doi:10.1016/j.clsr.2009.09.002

Weber, R. H. (2010). Internet of Things – New security and privacy Challenges. *Computer Law & Security Report*, *2010*(January). Retrieved from https://www.researchgate.net/profile/Rolf_Weber3/publication/222708179_Internet_of_Things_-_New_security_and_privacy_challenges/links/0c96053cab03fee371000000.pdf

Weijters, B., Rangarajan, D., Falk, T., & Schillewaert, N. (2007). Determinants and outcomes of customers use of self-service technology in a retail setting. *Journal of Service Research*, *10*(1), 3–21. doi:10.1177/1094670507302990

Wei, Q., Zhu, S., & Du, C. (2011). Study onkey technologies of internet of things perceiving mine. *Procedia Eng.*, *26*, 2326–2333. doi:10.1016/j.proeng.2011.11.2442

Westerlund, M., Leminen, S., & Rajahonka, M. (2014). Designing Business Models for the Internet of Things. *Technology Innovation Management Review*, *4*(7), 5–14.

Westin, A. F. (1968). Privacy and freedom. *Washington and Lee Law Review*. Retrieved May 10, 2016 from http://scholarlycommons.law.wlu.edu/wlulr/vol25/iss1/20

White, C. C. III, & Cheong, T. (2012). In-transit perishable product inspection. *Transportation Research Part E, Logistics and Transportation Review*, *48*(1), 310–330. doi:10.1016/j.tre.2011.08.006

Whitmore, A., Agarwal, A., & Xu, L. (2015). The Internet of things—A survey of topics and trends. *Information Systems Frontiers*, *17*(2), 261–274. doi:10.1007/s10796-014-9489-2

Whitney, H. (2015). *The 'World's First' 3D Printed Air Conditioner Sells in China for $6395*. Retrieved Mar 13, 2015 from https://3dprint.com/50805/3d-printed-air-conditioner

Wikipedia. (2016). *Radio Frequency Identification*. Retrieved August 19, 2016, from https://en.wikipedia.org/wiki/Radio-frequency_identification

Wilson, C. E., & Rosenbaum, S. (2005). Categories of return on investment and their practical implications. Cost-Justifying Usability. *An Update for the Internet Age*, *2*, 215–263.

Wohlsen, M. (2013, May 2). *Guys like this could kill Google Glass before it ever gets off the ground*. Retrieved January 4, 2017, from Business: https://www.wired.com/2013/05/inherent-dorkiness-of-google-glass/

Wong, D.H., & all. (2011). Predicting the diffusion pattern of Internet-based communication applications using Bass model parameter estimates for e-mail. *Journal of Internet Business*, *9*, 26–50.

Woollaston, V. (2015). *The end of fitting room queues? Smart mirrors lets you virtually try on clothes and order drinks.* Retrieved from http://www.dailymail.co.uk/sciencetech/article-2906563/The-end-fitting-room-queues-Smart-mirrors-lets-virtually-try-clothes-order-drinks.html#ixzz4D2FoDyhs

Wu, M.-Y., Chou, H.-P., Weng, Y.-C., & Huang, Y.-H. (2011). TAM-2 based study of website user behavior-using web 2.0 websites as an example. *WSEAS Transactions on Business and Economics, 4*(8), 133-151. Retrieved January 4, 2017, from http://www.wseas.us/e-library/transactions/economics/2011/53-665.pdf

Wu, Q., Ding, G., Xu, Y., Feng, S., Du, Z., Wang, J., & Long, K. (2014). Cognitive internet of things: A new paradigm beyond connection. *IEEE Internet of Things Journal*, *1*(2), 129–143. doi:10.1109/JIOT.2014.2311513

Xiao, G., Guo, J., Xu, L., & Gong, Z. (2014). User interoperability with heterogeneous IoT devices through transformation. *IEEE Transactions on Industrial Informatics*, *10*(2), 1486–1496. doi:10.1109/TII.2014.2306772

Xie, Y., & Allen, C. (2013). Information technologies in retail supply chains: A comparison of Tesco and Asda. *International Journal of Business Performance and Supply Chain Modelling*, *5*(1), 46–62. doi:10.1504/IJBPSCM.2013.051648

Xu, B., Xu, L. D., Cai, H., Xie, C., Hu, J., & Bu, F. (2014). Ubiquitous data accessing method in IoT-based information system for emergency medical services. *IEEE Transactions on Industrial Informatics*, *10*(2), 1578–1586. doi:10.1109/TII.2014.2306382

Xu, B., Xu, L., Cai, H., Xie, C., Hu, J., & Bu, F. (2014). Ubiquitous Data Accessing Method in IoT-Based Information System for Emergency Medical Services. *IEEE Transactions on Industrial Informatics.*, *10*, 2233–2243. doi:10.1109/TII.2014.2300753

Yaghoubi, N.-M., & Bahmani, E. (2010). Factors affecting the adoption of online banking: An integration of Technology Acceptance Model and Theory of Planned Behavior. *Pakistan Journal of Social Sciences*, *7*(3), 231–236. doi:10.3923/pjssci.2010.231.236

Yang, L., Qiu, X., & Zhang, L. (2011). Design of urban public rental bicycle system based on the Internet of Things. *Proceedings of the Third International Conference on Transportation Engineering - ICTE 2011* (pp. 2784-2789). Reston, VA: American Society of Civil Engineers. doi:10.1061/41184(419)460

Yang, H. D., Kang, S., Oh, W., & Kim, M. S. (2013). Are all fits created equal? A nonlinear perspective on task-technology fit. *Journal of the Association for Information Systems*, *14*(12), 694.

Yang, L., Yang, S. H., & Plotnick, L. (2013). How the internet of things technology enhances emergency response operations? *Technological Forecasting and Social Change*, *80*(9), 1854–1867. doi:10.1016/j.techfore.2012.07.011

Yang, S. U. (2007). An integrated model for organization—public relational outcomes, organizational reputation, and their antecedents. *Journal of Public Relations Research*, *19*(2), 91–121. doi:10.1080/10627260701290612

Yan, L., Zhang, Y., Yang, L. T., & Ning, H. (2008). *The Internet of Things: From RFID to the Next-Generation Pervasive Networked Systems (Wireless Networks and Mobile Communications)*. Auerbach Publications. doi:10.1201/9781420052824

Yan, Z., Zhang, P., & Vasilakos, A. V. (2014). A survey on trust management for Internet of Things. *Journal of Network and Computer Applications*, *42*, 120–134. doi:10.1016/j.jnca.2014.01.014

Yavuz, M., Iphar, M., & Once, G. (2008). The optimum support design selection by using AHP method for the main haulage road in WLC Tuncbilek colliery. *Tunnelling and Underground Space Technology*, *23*(2), 111–119. doi:10.1016/j.tust.2007.02.001

Yee-Loong Chong, A., Liu, M. J., Luo, J., & Keng-Boon, O. (2015). Predicting RFID adoption in healthcare supply chain from the perspectives of users. *International Journal of Production Economics*, *159*, 66–75. doi:10.1016/j.ijpe.2014.09.034

Yen, D. C., Wu, C. S., Cheng, F. F., & Huang, Y. W. (2010). Determinants of users intention to adopt wireless technology: An empirical study by integrating TTF with TAM. *Computers in Human Behavior*, *26*(5), 906–915. doi:10.1016/j.chb.2010.02.005

Yepes, M. F. (2014). Mobile Tablet Menus: Attractiveness and Impact of Nutrition Labeling Formats on Millennials Food Choices. *Cornell Hospitality Quarterly*, *56*(1), 58–67. doi:10.1177/1938965514546371

Yon, H. T. (2016, December 2). *AIRmaker unveils 5 new IoT startups that will tackle critical problems, from maternal care to clean water*. Retrieved January 4, 2017, from https://e27.co/airmaker-unveils-5-new-iot-startups-that-will-tackle-critical-problems-20161202/

Yoon, C. (2009). The effects of national culture values on consumer acceptance of e-commerce: Online shoppers in China. *Information & Management*, *46*(5), 294–301. doi:10.1016/j.im.2009.06.001

Yoo, Y., Henfridsson, O., & Lyytinen, K. (2010). Research commentary-The new organizing logic of digital innovation: An agenda for information systems research. *Information Systems Research*, *21*(4), 724–735. doi:10.1287/isre.1100.0322

Yu, H., Kaminsky, M., Gibbons, P. B., & Flaxman, A. (2006, September). Sybilguard: Defending against sybil attacks via social networks. *Computer Communication Review*, *36*(4), 267–278. doi:10.1145/1151659.1159945

Yu, T. F.-L. (2001). Towards a theory of the entrepreneurial state. *International Journal of Social Economics*, *28*(9), 752–766. doi:10.1108/EUM0000000005692

Yu, X. Y., Chen, Y., & Nguyen, B. (2014). Knowledge management, learning behavior from failure and new product development of new technology ventures. *Systems Research and Behavioral Science*, *31*(3), 405–423. doi:10.1002/sres.2273

Yuxi, L., & Zhou, G. (2012). Key Technologies and Applications of Internet of Things. *Fifth International Conference on Intelligent Computation Technology and Automation Key Technologies and Applications of Internet of Things*, Zhangjiajie, Hunan, China.

Zahra, S. A. (1991). Predictors and financial outcomes of corporate entrepreneurship: An exploratory study. *Journal of Business Venturing*, *6*(4), 259–285. doi:10.1016/0883-9026(91)90019-A

Zanella, A., Bui, N., Castellani, A., Vangelista, L., & Zorzi, M. (2014). Internet of things for smart cities. *IEEE Internet of Things Journal, 1*(1), 22-32.

Zanella, A., Bui, N., Castellani, A. P., Vangelista, L., & Zorzi, M. (2014). Internet of things for smart cities. *IEEE Internet of Things*, *1*(1), 22–32. doi:10.1109/JIOT.2014.2306328

Zarei, M., Mohammadian, A., & Ghasemi, R. (2016). Internet of Things in Industries: A Survey for Sustainable Development. *International Journal of Innovation and Sustainable Development*, *10*(4), 419–442. doi:10.1504/IJISD.2016.079586

Zeleny, M. (2013). Integrated knowledge management. *International Journal of Information Systems and Social Change*, *4*(4), 62–78. doi:10.4018/jissc.2013100104

Zhang, L., Atkins, A., & Hongnian, Y. U. (2012). Knowledge Management Application of Internet of Things in Construction Waste Logistics with RFID Technology. *International Journal of Computing Science and Communication Technologies*, *5*(1), 760–767.

Zheng, J., Simplot-Ryl, D., Bisdikian, C., & Mouftah, H. T. (2011). The internet of. *IEEE Communications Magazine*, *49*(11), 30–31. doi:10.1109/MCOM.2011.6069706

Zhong, Y., Jin, L., & Chen, X. (2012). Relationship between decision styles and decision types for innovative opportunities: Empirical study on Chinese Internet of Things industry and the cognitive decision support approach. *Journal of Computers*, *7*(7), 1574–1582. doi:10.4304/jcp.7.7.1574-1582

Zhou, J., Leppänen, T., Harjula, E., Ylianttila, M., Ojala, T., Yu, C., & Jin, H. (2013, June). Cloudthings: A common architecture for integrating the internet of things with cloud computing. In *Computer Supported Cooperative Work in Design (CSCWD), 2013 IEEE 17th International Conference on* (pp. 651-657). IEEE. doi:10.1109/CSCWD.2013.6581037

Zhou, C., & Peng, X. M. (2008). The entrepreneurial university in China: Nonlinear paths. *Science & Public Policy*, *35*(9), 637–646. doi:10.3152/030234208X363187

Zhou, H., Liu, B., & Wang, D. (2012). Design and research of urban intelligent transportation system based on the internet of things. In *Internet of Things* (pp. 572–580). Springer Berlin Heidelberg. doi:10.1007/978-3-642-32427-7_82

Zhou, L., Chong, A. Y. L., & Ngai, E. W. T. (2015). Supply chain management in the era of the internet of things. *International Journal of Production Economics*, *159*, 1–3. doi:10.1016/j.ijpe.2014.11.014

Zhou, T. (2014). An empirical examination of initial trust in mobile payment. *Wireless Personal Communications*, *77*(2), 1519–1531. doi:10.1007/s11277-013-1596-8

Zhou, T., Lu, Y., & Wang, B. (2010). Integrating TTF and UTAUT to explain mobile banking user adoption. *Computers in Human Behavior*, *26*(4), 760–767. doi:10.1016/j.chb.2010.01.013

Zhou, Z., Tsang, K. F., Zhao, Z., & Gaaloul, W. (2016). Data intelligence on the Internet of Things. *Personal and Ubiquitous Computing*, *20*(3), 277–281. doi:10.1007/s00779-016-0912-1

Zhou, Z., & Zhou, Z. (2012). Application of Internet of things in agriculture products supply chain management. *International Conference on Control Engineering and Communication Technology (ICCECT)*. doi:10.1109/ICCECT.2012.262

Ziegeldorf, J. H., Morchon, O. G., & Wehrle, K. (2014). Privacy in the Internet of Things: Threats and Challenges. *Security and Communication Networks*, *7*(12), 2728–2742. doi:10.1002/sec.795

Zorzi, M., Gluhak, A., Lange, S., & Bassi, A. (2010). From todays intranet of things to a future internet of things: A wireless-and mobility-related view. *IEEE Wireless Communications*, *17*(6), 44–51. doi:10.1109/MWC.2010.5675777

# About the Contributors

**In Lee** is a professor in the School of Computer Sciences in the College of Business and Technology at Western Illinois University. He received his MBA from the University of Texas at Austin and Ph.D. from University of Illinois at Urbana-Champaign. He is a founding editor-in-chief of the International Journal of E-Business Research. He has published his research in such journals as Communications of the ACM, IEEE Transactions on Systems, Man, and Cybernetics, IEEE Transactions on Engineering Management, International Journal of Production Research, International Journal of Production Economics, Computers and Education, Computers in Human Behavior, Computers and Operations Research, Computers and Industrial Engineering, Business Process Management Journal, Journal of E-Commerce in Organizations, International Journal of Simulation and Process Modeling, and others. His current research interests include technologies for SMEs, e-commerce technology development and management, investment strategies for computing technologies, and intelligent simulation systems.

* * *

**Juneman Abraham** is a Senior Faculty Member-Subject Content Coordinator of Community Psychology Studies at Bina Nusantara University, Jakarta, Indonesia; Member of Asian Association of Social Psychology (AASP) and World Association of Personality Psychology (WAPP); President of Association of Behavioural Researchers on Asians, Indonesia Chapter (ABRAindonesia); Past Secretary-General of Asian Psychological Association (APsyA); and Head of Organizational Compartment, National Office of Indonesian Psychological Association (HIMPSI). Site: http://branded.me/juneman.

**M. S. Balaji** is an Assistant Professor in Marketing at Nottingham University Business School China, University of Nottingham Ningbo China. He received his Doctoral Degree in Business Administration with a major in Marketing at The ICFAI University Dehradun, India. His research has appeared in many academic journals including European Journal of Marketing, Information & Management, Journal of Business Research, International Journal of Hospitality Management, Journal of Services Marketing, Service Industries Journal, Journal of Strategic Marketing, Service Business Journal, International Journal of Bank Marketing, Asia Pacific Journal of Marketing and Logistics and among others. His current research work focuses on social media, service failure, vicarious experiences and customer experience.

**Preetam Basu** is an Associate Professor in the Operations Management Group of IIM Calcutta. He has a doctorate degree in Operations Management from University of Connecticut, USA. Earlier, he did his MS in Applied Mathematics from University of Minnesota, USA. His doctoral thesis focused on business problems at the interface of operations and finance. He has published articles on project management, risk management and supply chain management in various international journals such as European Journal Operational Research, Decision Support Systems, Journal of Operational Research Society and presented his work at numerous prestigious international conferences. His research interests include project management, supply chain management, risk management and revenue management.

**Jacques Bughin** is a senior partner at McKinsey & Company, based in Brussels, with client focus on high-tech, telecom and media industries. He is also a Director of the McKinsey Global Institute and has published multiple reports on Internet of Ihings as well big data. He is a Fellow of ECARES and of the University of Leuven. He is the co-author of "Managing Media Companies" (Wiley & Sons) and has written about 50 academic articles for top peer-reviewed journals, such as the European Economic Review, Management Science, Journal of Economic Behavior and Organization and Journal of Big Data.

**Ibrahim A. Cankaya** received his B.S. degree in 2012 from Suleyman Demirel University Computer Engineering Department, Isparta, Turkey. He continues his Ph.D. education at Suleyman Demirel University Computer Engineering Department, Isparta, Turkey. He has been working as a Research Assistant in Suleyman Demirel University Computer Engineering Department since 2012. His research interest includes algorithm and programming, database management, mobile programming, IoT.

**Sadi F. Cankaya** received his B.S. degree in 2013 from Suleyman Demirel University Faculty of Technology, Isparta, Turkey. He continues his Master's at Suleyman Demirel University Computer Engineering Department, Isparta, Turkey. He has been working as a Research Assistant in Suleyman Demirel University Computer Engineering Department since 2014. His research interest includes signal processing, artificial intelligence, mobile programming.

**Edward T. Chen** is a professor of Management Information Systems of Operations and Information Systems Department in the Manning School of Business at University of Massachusetts Lowell. Dr. Chen has published numerous refereed research articles in scholarly journals and refereed chapters in reference books. Dr. Chen has served as vice-president, board director, track chair, and session chair of many IS/IT professional associations and conferences. Professor Chen has also served as journal editor, editorial reviewer, and ad hoc reviewer for various academic journals. Dr. Chen has received the Irwin Distinguished Paper Award at the Southwestern Federation of Administrative Disciplines conference and the Best Paper Award at the International Conference on Accounting and Information Technology. His main research interests are in the areas of Telemedicine, Project Management, Internet of Things, and Software Development.

**Alain Yee-Loong Chong** is currently the Director of Research and Associate Professor in Information Systems at Nottingham University Business School China, University of Nottingham (China campus). Prior to that, he was a postdoctoral research fellow at Hong Kong Polytechnic University. Dr. Chong is also a visiting fellow at University of Greenwich, U.K. and Hong Kong Polytechnic University. His papers have been published in Decision Support Systems, International Journal of Production Research, International Journal of Production Economics, Production Planning and Control, Expert Systems with Applications and Journal of Computer Information Systems. Dr. Chong is the co-editor in chief of Industrial Management & Data Systems. He is also serving as senior editor of Decision Support Systems, and editorial advisory board member of Online Information Review.

**Michael Chui** is a Partner at the McKinsey Global Institute and based in San Francisco, where he directs research on the impact of long-term disruptive technology trends, such as artificial intelligence, data & analytics, social technologies, and the Internet of Things, on business, the economy and society. Michael 's research has been cited in publications such as the Wall Street Journal, New York Times, Financial Times, Fast Company, Forbes, The Economist, WIRED, and Les Échos. Michael holds a B.S. in Symbolic Systems from Stanford University and earned a Ph.D. in Computer Science and Cognitive Science, and a M.S. in Computer Science, from Indiana University.

**Loveleen Gaur** is Faculty in Amity International Business School. She is a PhD and M.Phil in Computer Applications and has done her M.C.A. She has more than 12 years of experience teaching, consulting, research and mentoring activities. She has honoured with Senior Women Educator & Scholar Award by National Foundation for Entrepreneurship Development on Women's Day, "Sri Ram Award" by Delhi Management Association (DMA) and Distinguished Research Award: Allied Academies presented this award in Jacksonville, Florida and outstanding research contributor award by Amity International Business School. She has written numerous books with renowned publishers and has presented many research papers in international and national conferences. She is also serving as paper reviewer for many National and International Journals.

**Rohollah Ghasemi** has a Ph.D. in production and operations management. He has been a visiting lecturer in University of Tehran since 2013. He published several academic papers in international journals such as Journal of Cleaner Production, Total Quality Management and Business Excellence, and International Journal of Innovation and Sustainable Development. He has more than 6 years of experience in operations management especially in supply chain operations improvement, business process improvement, strategic and operational planning, market research, and new technology transfer. His research interests include supply chain management, sustainable development, corporate entrepreneurship, and technology management.

**Rafael Hernández Barros**, PhD, Universidad Autonoma de Madrid; MBA, IESE Business School. For more than 20 years, Rafael has been working as Senior Manager in front and back office (consulting, operations and finance) management roles in the financial services industry, and is currently Financial Support Director at Aon Spain, business support area on financial strategic planning and corporate compliance. As a Professor, He undertakes regular lecturer assignments about Financial Management and Corporate Finance at master's and bachelor's levels at Universidad Complutense de Madrid and Universidad Carlos III de Madrid, and his academic activity includes research in finance and risk management, done in institutions such as IESE Universidad de Navarra, Cass Business School (City University London), Universidad Autónoma de Madrid and Universidad Complutense de Madrid. His recent research work has been published in The Journal of Business Economics and Management, The Geneva Papers on Risk and Insurance or The Operational Risk Journal, among others; and He also serves as board member and editor-in-chief in some other international journals. Rafael is author of the book "Gestión del Riesgo y Fundamentos Prácticos de Solvencia", published by Editorial Complutense. He is also founding partner, adviser and consultant to several organizations and start-ups.

**Ahmad Jamalian** has a master of Industrial Management and published a number of academic papers in international journals such as European Journal of Social Science. He also participated in several international conferences such as International Conference on Management, Economics and Humanities.

**K. Jayashree** is an Engineer by qualification, having done her Doctorate in the area of Web services Fault Management from Anna University, Chennai and Masters in Embedded System Technologies from Anna University and Bachelors in Computer Science and Engineering from Madras University. She is presently Associate Professor in the Department of Computer Science and Engineering at Rajalakshmi Engineering College, affiliated to Anna University Chennai. Her areas of interest include Web services, Cloud Computing, Data Mining and distributed computing. She is a member of ACM, CSI.

**Bill Karakostas** is the VLTN Cloud Services Director. He holds an MSc in Computer Engineering and Informatics, from Patras University and an MSc and PhD in Software Engineering, both from UMIST, UK. Previously senior lecturer in the School of Informatics, City University. He has a fifteen plus year research track in areas such as business engineering (process simulation, modelling, redesign and workflow management), reuse and component-based development, application of cloud technologies in transport. He has led research in the e-Freight project in the virtualisation of e-Freight applications and he is leading the iCargo Ecosystem and CORE Ecosystem Architecture.

**Vaughan Michell** is a graduate of Oxford University (D.Phil, Robotics -Engineering Science), UCL (BSc Mechanical Engineering) and Warwick University (MBA). He has spent many years in industry in process/systems design and reengineering in defence, banking and software organisations. Vaughan lectures in Informatics. He is Programme Director for the MSc in Business Technology Consulting and MA Digital Technology Leadership at Henley Business School. He is also an honorary Senior Lecturer at the Simulation Unit at the Royal Berkshire Hospital. His research focuses on people- digital technology interaction covering digital product and process design, invention and architecture, knowledge management and human factors in technology interaction. His specialist research areas include technology affordance and capability, and knowledge intensive processes (invention/design and innovation). He has produced a number of papers on health informatics and patient safety and digital technology such as Internet of things and 3D printing.

**Suvendu Naskar** holds bachelor degree in Electronics & Telecommunication Engineering from Jadavpur University. He has 11+ years of experience in Information Technology Industry with small stint in Education sector as a lecturer. He completed Post Graduate Diploma in Business Administration from Indian Institute of Management Kozhikode with major in Finance, Operations and Information Systems. He has worked in different capacity which includes responsibilities of Business Analysis, Business Development, Managing Strategic Alliances, Program Manager and Operations Manager. He has experience of working with Global clients in Banking & Financial Services, Manufacturing and Engineering. Currently, Suvendu is pursuing his fellowship from Indian Institute Management with specific interest of exploring applications of analytics in Supply Chain and advanced information management thinking like Internet of Things, Big Data Analytics.

**Thomas Ochs** is the CIO of the Villeroy & Boch Group. Within Villeroy & Boch he introduced the complete supply chain management support for all shops, subsidiaries, and production locations within the Tableware Division. Furthermore, he introduced a fully integrated CRM software while integrating marketing, call center, and sales as well as a corporate-wide portal solution using the latest technical features with a high degree of usability. This has been accompanied with the harmonization of the business lines and organizational change from country-specifically organized IT departments to one globally acting corporate IT with a harmonized SAP system landscape available for the entire company. This IT effort serves as a basis for the optimization of the IT cost, further standardization, and the enablement of an outsourcing of the entire IT infrastructure as well as the coordination of digitalization projects at Villeroy & Boch. Mr. Ochs is also lecturer for computer science teaching e-business at the Saarland University of Applied Sciences, Germany. In his private life he enjoys golf with his friends and family.

**James Edward Olweny** is a first year Ph.D. student at the University of Reading studying under Dr Vaughan Michell. His research interests are centered around the interaction between Humans and Internet of Things (IoT), with specific emphasis on human interaction with ambient Intelligent ecologies and the opportunities and challenges. Broadly, James' methodological research focuses on designing conceptual models of affordances for IoT ecologies against relevant theory and practical use within healthcare. He holds a Master's of Arts in Management Studies from the University of Westminster and Masters of Science in Health Informatics from the University of Bath.

**Tommy Prayoga** is an alumnus of Psychology Department, Bina Nusantara University, Jakarta, Indonesia; Full-time staff writer and editor at Content Collision, a media agency and technology firm in Southeast Asia. Site: https://tommyyoung.c2live.com/.

**Babu Rajendiran** is a Research Scholar in Anna University. He has completed his Masters in Software Engineering with a merit of 2nd rank in the University and Bachelors in Computer Science and Engineering from Rajalakshmi Engineering College affiliated to Anna University. His areas of interest include Web Services, Service Oriented Architecture, Cloud Computing, Big Data Analytics and Internet Of Things. He is a life member of CSI and served as a Management Committee Member for two years. He has received Active Participation Award – Youth from CSI. He also received Faculty Excellence Award from Infosys in Faculty Enablement Program for two successive years.

**Ravi Ramakrishnan** is an MBA from Faculty of Management Studies Delhi University and has further done a Post Graduate Diploma from AIMA in IT systems, DOEACC A level certified and a Post Graduate Diploma in Operations Management from IGNOU after a Bachelors in Science. He is a Prince 2 certified professional, Microsoft Certified Professional and a Oracle Certified professional and has 19 years of global experience and is an award winning Global CIO with a strong technical and managerial background and has done numerous global rollouts of Enterprise Information Systems –ERP/CRM/BI and M2M/Mobility and IoT solutions which have been widely acknowledged and awarded in different forums. He is currently pursuing his Doctorate in Information Technology Management with focus on IoT strategies and technologies and has published papers on IoT in Springer, IJECE and IEEEXplore.

**Ute Riemann** was born and grew up in Dortmund, gained a Master in Computer Science and an MBA from the University of Cologne. Additionally, she participated at a management training at the University of St. Gallen. She started her career as a consultant for IT systems. Before she joined SAP she worked for companies such as T-Systems, Kurt Salmon Associates and Giesecke & Devrient where she led the organization and business transformation focused on the process optimization and implementation. Within SAP she is in the department of business transformation focusing on large transition projects supporting the company's strategy and the achievement of the defined targets. Ute Riemann published various articles in the area of business process, change management and process controlling. With her expertise in business transformation and process development, she teaches change management at the University of Applied Science in Villingen-Schwenningen and the University of Applied Science in Mannheim.

**Sanjit Kumar Roy** is Assistant Professor of Marketing, The University of Western Australia, Australia. He was awarded UWA's Vice-Chancellor's Early Career Investigators Award 2015. His research interests include Services Marketing, Marketing in Emerging Economies and Consumer-Brand Relationships. He has Guest Edited a special issue on India for International Journal of Bank Marketing. He also co-edited Marketing Cases for Emerging Markets. He has published in journals including European Journal of Marketing, Journal of Business Research, Journal of Marketing Management, Internet Research, Studies in Higher Education, Journal of Services Marketing, Journal of Strategic Marketing, Journal of Service Theory & Practice, Journal of Brand Management, and Computers in Human Behaviour. He was Visiting Research Fellow at Middlesex University, UK and Visiting Research Scholar at Bentley University, USA.

**Aditi Sarkar Sengupta** is an Assistant Professor in Department of Marketing and Strategy at IBS Hyderabad. She has published research articles in reputed International journals like Journal of Business Research, International Journal of Bank Marketing and International Journal of Emerging Markets. She spent about a year at University of Memphis, USA as a Visiting Scholar. She published book chapter with Springer International Publishing. She has presented papers in international conferences such as, Winter Educator's Conference of American Marketing Association and Annual Conference of Academy of Marketing Science. Her paper was awarded as the most commendable paper in International Journal of Emerging Markets in the year 2013. Her research interests are in the area of Services Marketing, Consumer Behavior, User Generated Online Contents and Experimental Designs. She teaches Services Marketing, Marketing Management and Principles of Management at post graduate and undergraduate level.

**Javier Vidal** is an Assistant Professor of Finance, University of Valladolid. Spain. He graduated with a BSc in Management from Queen´s University Belfast, MSc in Finance from Aston Business School, MA in Economics from Autonomous University of Madrid, Phd in Financial Economics from Complutense University of Madrid and has been postdoctoral fellow at the Harvard Business School.

**Marta Vidal-García** is a BSc and MBA from ESADE Business School, PhD student in Management at Complutense University, Assistant Professor of Management at European University of Madrid.

**Asim S. Yuksel** obtained his B.S. degree in computer engineering from Ege University, Izmir, Turkey in 2006. He completed his Masters degree in Computer Science from Indiana University School of Informatics and Computing, Indiana, USA in 2010. He obtained his Ph.D. degree in Istanbul University Department of Computer Engineering. He worked as a research assistant in Suleyman Demirel University Department of Computer Engineering between 2012-2015. He is currently working as an Assistant Professor in Suleyman Demirel University Department of Computer Engineering. His research interests include mobile application development, social networks, software engineering, IoT.

**Mohammad Zarei** has a master of corporate entrepreneurship and published several academic papers in international journals such as International Journal of Management and Enterprise Development and International Journal of Innovation and Sustainable Development. He has experienced third, governmental, as well as private sectors for organisational development for the last five years. He has also participated in a number of the national projects and achieved several letters of appreciation from the Iran Telecommunication Research Center (ITRC) and Ministry of ICT, Information Technology Organization of Iran. His research interests include strategies of corporate entrepreneurship and new emerging technologies.

# Index

## T



## W

# Encyclopedia of Information Science and Technology, Third Edition (10 Vols.)

**Mehdi Khosrow-Pour, D.B.A.** (Information Resources Management Association, USA)
**ISBN:** 978-1-4666-5888-2; **EISBN:** 978-1-4666-5889-9; © 2015; 10,384 pages.

The **Encyclopedia of Information Science and Technology, Third Edition** is a 10-volume compilation of authoritative, previously unpublished research-based articles contributed by thousands of researchers and experts from all over the world. This discipline-defining encyclopedia will serve research needs in numerous fields that are affected by the rapid pace and substantial impact of technological change. With an emphasis on modern issues and the presentation of potential opportunities, prospective solutions, and future directions in the field, it is a relevant and essential addition to any academic library's reference collection.

[1] 30% discount offer cannot be combined with any other discount and is only valid on purchases made directly through IGI Global's Online Bookstore (www.igi-global.com/books), not intended for use by distributors or wholesalers. Offer expires December 31, 2016.

## Free Lifetime E-Access with Print Purchase

### Take 30% Off Retail Price:

**Hardcover with Free E-Access:**[2] **$2,765**
~~List Price: $3,950~~

**E-Access with Free Hardcover:**[2] **$2,765**
~~List Price: $3,950~~

**Recommend this Title to Your Institution's Library:** www.igi-global.com/books

[2] IGI Global now offers the exclusive opportunity to receive free lifetime e-access with the purchase of the publication in print, or purchase any e-access publication and receive a free print copy of the publication. You choose the format that best suits your needs. This offer is only valid on purchases made directly through IGI Global's Online Bookstore and not intended for use by book distributors or wholesalers. Shipping fees will be applied for hardcover purchases during checkout if this option is selected.

The lifetime of a publication refers to its status as the current edition. Should a new edition of any given publication become available, access will not be extended on the new edition and will only be available for the purchased publication. If a new edition becomes available, you will not lose access, but you would no longer receive new content for that publication (i.e. updates). Free Lifetime E-Access is only available to single institutions that purchase printed publications through IGI Global. Sharing the Free Lifetime E-Access is prohibited and will result in the termination of e-access.

www.ingramcontent.com/pod-product-compliance
Lightning Source LLC
LaVergne TN
LVHW082052011026
849162LV00019B/1439